The Notorious Life of Gyp

The Notorious Life of Gyp

Right-Wing Anarchist in Fin-de-Siècle France

WILLA Z. SILVERMAN

New York   *Oxford*

OXFORD UNIVERSITY PRESS

1995

OXFORD UNIVERSITY PRESS

Oxford   New York
Athens   Auckland   Bangkok   Bombay
Calcutta   Cape Town   Dar es Salaam   Delhi
Florence   Hong Kong   Istanbul   Karachi
Kuala Lumpur   Madras   Madrid   Melbourne
Mexico City   Nairobi   Paris   Singapore
Taipei   Tokyo   Toronto

and associated companies in
Berlin   Ibadan

Published by Oxford University Press, Inc.,
200 Madison Avenue, New York, New York 10016

Oxford is a registered trademark of Oxford University Press

Library of Congress Cataloging-in-Publication Data
Silverman, Willa Z., 1959–
The notorious life of Gyp : right-wing anarchist
in fin-de-siècle France / Willa Z. Silverman.
p. cm.   Includes bibliographical references and index.
ISBN 0-19-508754-2
1. Gyp, 1849–1932—Biography.
2. Women novelists, French—19th century—Biography.
3. Women novelists, French—20th century—Biography.
4. France—Politics and government—1870–1940.
5. Politics and literature—France—History.
6. Women anarchists—France—Biography.
7. Right and left (Political science).
8. Authoritarianism—France—History.
I. Title.   PQ2347.M6Z87   1995
843'.8—dc20   [B]   94-18605

Friedrich Nietzsche, *On the Genealogy of Morals*,
trans. Walter Kaufmann. © Copyright 1967.
Reprinted by permission of Random House, Inc.

1 3 5 7 9 8 6 4 2

Printed in the United States of America
on acid-free paper

For My Parents

Acknowledgments

I find it both fulfilling and somewhat saddening in its finality to thank some of the many people who have helped me with this project and without whom it surely could not have been completed. My greatest intellectual debt is to two far-sighted mentors, Richard Sieburth and Michel Winock, who encouraged me to transform what was originally intended to be a rather dry case study of right-wing nationalism in fin-de-siècle France into an intellectual biography. Although Gyp was as unfamiliar to them as she was to me when I began my research, Richard and Michel, on both sides of the Atlantic, shared my intuition that Gyp was indeed a fascinating, troubling personality. I am immensely grateful to them for believing in my capability as I undertook what became an ever more formidable project, and for their judicious guidance as I persevered.

This project could never have taken shape without the exceptional generosity of numerous private collectors in France. Many of them were descendants of Gyp's circle of acquaintances. A few had even known Gyp before her death, in 1932, and thus provided me with an important physical and emotional link to her. I am especially indebted to Sibylle Gaudry, Gyp's heir, who lent me family correspondence and photographs, and whose interest in my project over the past decade has been unflagging. The hours we spent together puzzling over Gyp have undoubtedly found their way into this biography. Jean-Etienne Cohen-Séat and Elisabeth Laye at Calmann-Lévy facilitated my work in the archives of Gyp's primary publisher. Mme. Paul Bazin hospitably received me in Paris and in Mirabeau, as did Henri de Sancy de Rolland in Janville. The following descendants also graciously lent me documents or assisted me in other ways: Yves Barbet-Massin, François Benjamin, Eugénie de Brancovan, Mme. Jean Chagnaud-Forain, General Jean Le Harivel de Gonneville, M. d'Isoard de Chenerilles, Foulques de Jouvenel, Dr. Charles Lucas, Mme. Louis de Maigret, Jacques Maurras, Edith Silve, Mme. Soulier-Cappiello, Mme. Charles-Arnaud de Vaugelas. Many other individuals in France shared materials, provided tips, or helped elucidate some of the numerous topics my research led me to explore. Among them, I would like to thank Antoine Bertrand, Laurence Bertrand-Dorléac, Thierry Bodin, M. de Boisguilbert, Michel Dixmier, Patricia Ferlin, Dominique Franciosi, Gilles Picq, Dr. Isabelle Mahéo-de la Tocnaye, Jean-Yves Mollier, Pierre Michel, Jean-François Nivet, Anne-Marie Thiesse, and Jean-Claude Wartelle.

The staffs of all the libraries, archives, and museums I had contact with in

France, England, and the United States were uniformly knowledgeable and helpful, and to them I owe a collective debt. A few individuals went well beyond the call of duty, often because of their personal interest in Gyp. Florence Callu (Manuscripts Division, Bibliothèque Nationale) permitted me to consult the correspondence between Gyp and Maurice Barrès before it was catalogued. M. Guillot (Archives Nationales) personally led me into the depths of the archives to locate several dust-covered cartons containing scores of letters from Gyp to Paul Déroulède. Others who provided similar exceptional assistance were Jean-Claude Garretta (Bibliothèque de l'Arsenal), François Macé de Lépinay (Musée Carnavalet), Jacques Perrot (Musée de l'Armée), Florence Roth (Société des Auteurs et Compositeurs Dramatiques), Francine Roze and Claire Aptel (Musée Historique Lorrain), Paul Sadoul (Société Archéologique Lorraine), and Jean-Yves Veillard (Musée de Bretagne).

For their inspiration, advice, and insightful criticism of my work, I thank Michel Beaujour, Tony Judt, Nicholas Wahl and Jindrich Zezula of New York University. While a doctoral student at NYU, I was awarded a Bourse Chateaubriand by the French government, which allowed me to conduct preliminary research for my project. Penn State University provided additional generous financial assistance in the form of a Research Initiation Grant and an Alumni Faculty Fellowship, which helped support the extensive travel to collections that the research for this biography entailed; I would like to thank Dean David Palermo and Baiba Briedis in this connection. Others at Penn State to whom I am grateful include the staff of Pattee Library's interlibrary loan division for its expertise in tracking down obscure French works; Sanford Thatcher, director of Penn State Press, for helping me sort out the intricacies of international copyright law; Stanley Weintraub for information about Gyp's British connection; and Dominique Laurent, for his help with translations.

I owe many thanks, as well, to several editors and staff members at Oxford University Press. Liz Maguire guided me through the editing process with patience, professionalism and great good humor. She never wavered in her energetic support of this biography of "countess bitch." I was lucky enough to find in Henry Krawitz both a meticulous copy editor and a fellow devotee of the belle époque. My thanks also go to Liz Maguire's assistant, Elda Rotor, to Eleonora Bertacchi for compiling the index, and to Oxford's marketing and design staffs. Finally, I wish to thank those who read the entire manuscript, including James Smith Allen, Antoinette Blum, and at least one anonymous reviewer for their most helpful suggestions, which certainly have enhanced the quality of the final product.

My friends offered humor, relief, encouragement, praise, criticism—and sometimes references. My gratitude goes to Michael Bernhard and Paula Golombek, the Badessi family, Eric Cahm, Randall Cherry, Venita Datta, Elisabeth Fouquoire-Brillet and Georges Brillet, Isabelle Genest, Mitchel Lenrow, and Shanny Peer. My family provided a different form of sustenance—profound, collective, and unconditional. I offer my loving thanks to the Berkmans, Julie Eagle-Cardo, Marlene and Gerald Green, Bessie Silverman, and Ethan Silverman. My husband,

Acknowledgments

Michael Berkman, knew just how and when—and always patiently, lovingly—to humor, nurture, encourage, and push me. But my greatest debt is to my parents: to my father, Ken, who taught me, among much else, the value of a simple declarative sentence, and to my mother, Sharon, who showed me why women should strive to succeed. This book is dedicated to them.

State College, Pa.   W.Z.S.
Fall 1994

Contents

Contents

The Notorious Life of Gyp

The slave revolt in morality begins when *ressentiment* itself becomes creative and gives birth to values; the *ressentiment* of natures that are denied the true reaction, that of deeds, and compensate themselves with an imaginary revenge. While every noble morality develops from a triumphant affirmation of itself, slave morality from the outset says No to what is "outside," what is "different," what is "not itself"; and *this* No is its creative deed.

Nietzsche, *On the Genealogy of Morals,* trans. Walter Kaufmann

Introduction

In late June and July 1940, the few French newspapers that managed to be printed in the panic of exodus and occupation reported some shocking news: on the eve of the German army's entry into Paris, Dr. Thierry de Martel, "star of French surgery,"[1] had killed himself. Immaculately dressed, this aloof and charismatic "d'Artagnan of surgery" was found at home, an empty vial of phenobarbital and a copy of Hugo's *Hernani* at his side.

By his death, de Martel showed his refusal to witness another amputation of France, as his parents had been obliged to do seventy years earlier. His suicide left ambiguous, however, whether he despaired more over the military might of France's external enemy or over the impotence of the political class that for him represented the nation's internal one. He had often blasted the "idiot Jacobins,"[2] those leaders of the Third Republic who, he felt, had led the country to the brink of the abyss, and whose incompetence had impelled him, by virtue of his "mystical, absolute nationalism,"[3] to adhere, between the two world wars, to the tenets of Action française, Le Faisceau, and the newspaper *Candide*.

All the obituaries of de Martel recalled his memorable lineage. For the great Revolutionary orator Mirabeau was de Martel's ancestor, as was an equally impassioned counter-Revolutionary, the notorious Mirabeau-Tonneau. And eclipsing the influence of this legendary pair of brothers, the press noted, was that of a woman, de Martel's mother, "the brilliant woman of letters who was famous as Gyp."[4] A brilliant woman, then, and a celebrity. Yet, as the press reminded

3

the public, Gyp had also been a "fanatically French"[5] woman and a "partisan soul, without justice and without charity."[6]

A "brilliant woman of letters." Writing indeed brought fame to Sibylle-Gabrielle Marie-Antoinette de Riquetti de Mirabeau, comtesse de Martel de Janville, or rather to her male literary persona known as Gyp, "man of letters." Her literary production, spanning the two decades preceding and the three following 1900, was enormous and ended when she was in her eighties. She wrote over one hundred novels, twenty plays, hundreds of articles, four volumes of recollections, and kept up a voluminous correspondence. Her works, translated into a dozen languages, were read in Paris, the provinces, and at royal courts. They were praised by Anatole France and Friedrich Nietzsche—and damned by Octave Mirbeau as "filth"[7] and by Ezra Pound as "unreadable."[8] Yet this second-generation bluestocking insisted throughout her life that she hated writing.

Gyp was a versatile writer, practicing a panoply of styles and genres particular to the turn of the century, as well as a malicious satirist of French politics and society under the Third Republic. "[M]istress . . . of one of the happiest of forms,"[9] according to Henry James, Gyp excelled at the *roman dialogué*, or dialogue–novel. Many of her novels in dialogue form are society novels (*romans mondains*), satires of Parisian and provincial aristocratic and bourgeois society. Set against a backdrop of the premieres, horse races, and salons she frequented, these novels were one of her many poisoned arrows aimed at a crew of snobs, parvenus, and courtesans—the "chic people" she so detested. Dialogue novelist and *romancière mondaine*, she was also known as a children's writer, and was a particular favorite of adolescent girls. Her child-protagonist and male pendant, Petit Bob, appeared in numerous novels and "illustrated" others. Spoiled, precocious, irreverent, this "innocent" enfant terrible, simultaneously anarchistic and reactionary, became the mouthpiece for many of Gyp's satires (while also marking her as a fin-de-siècle comtesse de Ségur). And her athletic, slang-enamoured heroines (who were also her doubles) presented, in this era of "the new woman," an unconventional model of feminine beauty and argued for marriages based on love and not reason. No wonder some women lauded Gyp as a feminist—a characterization she violently repudiated.

Gyp the novelist was also a talented, highly successful polemicist. Her novels constitute a right-wing nationalist's account, lying somewhere between chronicle and fable, of the major political upheavals of the Third Republic: Boulangism and the Panama Scandal; the Dreyfus Affair and the 1905 separation of church and state; World War I and the interwar activities of Action française. It was Gyp who created the "powerful images"[10] so admired by Charles Maurras, that helped give an ideology shape in the popular mind. With her literary creation of Schlemmerei, Sinaï, Wildes-Swein, Judasfrüss, Ubel de Saint-Sabbas, and other beastly Jews, Gyp helped "perfect" the anti-Semitic novel.

"Anti-Semite." It was thus, and not as "writer," that Gyp chose to identify her "profession" when testifying at the 1899 trial of purported nationalist conspirators. The repulsiveness of her anti-Semitism may help account for her total neglect as a "fitting" subject for a biography. But so, too, may a willful desire to erase, by omission, the lasting contribution of an aristocratic woman in Republican France to the development of an arsenal of destructive images, and to the cultivation of hatred as a way of life, both of which endure a century after the Dreyfus Affair. The 1994 centenary of this cataclysmic event—Gyp's personal "belle époque"—as well as the anxieties and political turbulence marking both Gyp's fin de siècle and ours now necessitate a study of her life and career. Such a study might illustrate and explain, as I hope this first one will, the unanticipated explosion on the Right of a violent, defensive nationalism during the period between the Franco-Prussian War and World War I.

For Gyp, who claimed to prefer politics to literature, was a major figure of the nationalist Right, indeed, the "feminine center of nationalism."[11] In the last two decades of the nineteenth century, she coupled her other literary activities with those of a political propagandist and caricaturist. She campaigned for Boulangist deputies and against Dreyfusard ones. She joined right-wing leagues, scoured the streets of Paris for professional rabble-rousers, and turned her salon into a nationalist bastion. She became the friend and confidante of Maurice Barrès and Paul Déroulède, and was considered a go-between for nationalist factions. She used her rebellious personality as a weapon, too, exhibiting in public the same "unheard-of indecency"[12] that had made her great-grandfather Mirabeau-Tonneau one of the most shocking and despised figures of the Revolution. In so doing, she left no one unmoved. While to her employer and friend Edouard Drumont she was "the good *Gauloise* Gyp,"[13] anarchist writer Laurent Tailhade depicted her as a bloodsucker.[14] Gyp "claws, she bites," the novelist Abel Hermant concluded. "[She] wages war."[15]

Irrespective of family tradition, Gyp's political activism is even more remarkable given her gender. Her example highlights the nature and limits of the involvement in politics, at the century's end, of those traditionally excluded from it. The ballot box and the Chamber of Deputies were closed to women; how, then, were these marginals, both singly and collectively, able to effect political change? What means *were* available to them? And did their gender in any way shape the variety of their political orientations and beliefs?

In Gyp's case, gender and ideology meshed. Her identification with an authoritarian Right was part of a potent fiction she relied on throughout her life, that of her "maleness." She had cause to regret her gender, as her family constantly reminded her, for she was "the last of the Mirabeau" and a woman; with her marriage this august ancestral name would become extinct. The political expression of Gyp's personal myth of maleness was her own brand of sentimental Bonapartism. Indeed, in the opening pages of her *Souvenirs* she would claim—falsely—to share Napoleon's birthday (15 August). Throughout her life she attached herself to male idols whom she considered incarnations of Napoleon: her grandfather (a veteran of the Napoleonic wars), Bazaine, Boulanger, Morès, Guérin, Déroulède, Barrès. The general and emperor exemplified Gyp's ideal type of authority: militaristic, charismatic, and "masculine," yet also demagogic and vaguely populist. In this sense she typified the aspirations of the "revolutionary Right"[16] at the end of the nineteenth century: to combine right-wing authoritarianism with extreme left-wing Radicalism. Yet her example also helps explain the failure of this same Right. Forced to choose between ideological rigor and class loyalty, she most often renounced the former, spurning "the people'''she claimed to adore in the name of bourgeois–aristocratic traditionalism. Thus would the "revolutionary Right" of 1870–1900 lose its revolutionary cast and make way for the more militant program of Action française.

"Revolution" and "reaction" characterized Gyp as a woman as well and made her feminism problematic. Yes, the woman to whom feminists "owed a great deal,"[17] in the words of Gyp's colleague Gérard d'Houville (née Marie-Antoinette de Heredia), vigorously denounced the corset and legally attempted to add her family name to her sons'. She was one of a small number of fin-de-siècle women writers whose novels featured superficially unconventional female characters. And she provided women with a rare model of female financial independence and professional success. Gyp's story is, to some extent, simply that of a woman furiously and publicly trying to obtain what has been denied women—power and autonomy. But no desire to improve the status of women motivated Gyp. She blasted the suffragist movement, befriended recognized misogynists such as Degas, and proclaimed her preference for bearing sons rather than daughters. And she treated her own daughter with the same cruelty and contempt her mother had shown her. Her unorthodox remarks and behavior indeed reflect not an appreciation of her gender but rather her repudiation of it. And yet for many of her contemporaries Gyp was a feminist.

While trying to establish Gyp's importance as a literary and political figure in her own right, this biography also serves, to use Barbara Tuchman's phrase, as a "prism of history."[18] It provides a kaleidoscopic (if selective) view of French culture, society, and politics between 1850 and 1930. Yet Gyp's life merits telling simply on the basis of the eccentricities and scandals with which she became identified. She was an often infamous public figure whose quirks were grist for the gossip-mongering Parisian press. As Parisian high society knew, Gyp went to bed at 5 A.M after writing all night with a goose quill dipped in violet ink. And who had not heard about the outlandish sleeveless gowns that exposed her muscular arms, or about her strange custom of burying dogs in her backyard? After all, this was the writer who, as a notorious object of outrage, was once doused with sulfuric acid by a "veiled woman," and who at the age of fifty fell victim to a bizarre kidnapping.

Felicitously for her biographer, the intensely public, even exhibitionistic, Gyp has left traces everywhere. A corpus of published works provided a starting point for my research: Michel Missoffe's largely anecdotal monograph *Gyp et ses amis* (1932); Gyp's novels and articles; and her four volumes of recollections. Yet I have also pieced together her life and personality from a trove of previously unpublished written and visual documents from dozens of public and private archives in France, Great Britain, and the United States. Three collections, containing several hundred letters by Gyp, were particularly valuable for this biography: the papers of Maurice Barrès and of Paul Déroulède, and the archives of Gyp's publisher, Calmann-Lévy. The latter, representing half a century's worth of correspondence, contracts, and payment records, reveals in fascinating detail the strange mixture of cowardice and calculation that sometimes bound, and at other times separated the anti-Semitic author and her Jewish publisher.

During the several weeks I spent reading this material in the Calmann-Lévy offices, housed in the same elegant nineteenth-century townhouse facing the Opéra where Gyp frequently turned up, I was struck by how the past she embodied seemed to linger in the present. The feeling remained with me when visiting the châteaux of Janville in Normandy and of Mirabeau in Provence (now owned by the heirs of Barrès, to whom Gyp sold the property in 1907). It occurred again when spotting copies of Gyp's novels in a Parisian bookstore that specializes in the works of extreme right-wing authors past and present, and yet again when an elderly woman I visited in a rest home referred to Louis XVI as "our king." This constant impression of déjà vu, this bridge between present and past, convinced me even more of the relevance of Gyp's life to contemporary readers.

Of course, Gyp would have flatly rejected any suggestion of her "modernity." She damned electricity, automobiles, fountain pens, and other symbols of what she deemed "the age of fake," just as she spurned the female gender and the Jewish "race." Yet, paradoxically, she depended on these malevolent "others" in order to create her own identity. She defined herself by what she was *not*. Contradiction is indeed what characterizes this descendant of both Mirabeau and Mirabeau-Tonneau. Gyp was both a realist and a symbolist, a feminist and a misogynist, youthful and antiquated, a right-wing anarchist who mirrored a turn of the century in which the modern and the traditional coexisted in often startling ways.

Gyp was undoubtedly a disturbed and angry person. Yet she was also—and still is—important. She remains, as Edmond de Goncourt found her in 1895, "unhealthily seductive."[19] How would she have reacted to the prospect of this first biography of her? Perhaps she would have spat out the title of her own novel damning psychological portraiture in the works of Stendhal: "Ohé! les psychologues!" Or would she have have issued a provocation in the form of the motto that, impressed in wax, adorned all her correspondence: "Et puis après? . . . " "So what? . . . "

So what? . . .

I

Sibylle de Mirabeau

1849–1860

One always fights for what one does not have.

Attributed to André Boniface de Riquetti,
vicomte de Mirabeau, known as Mirabeau-Tonneau

Arundel-Joseph and Marie

Ancient hatreds and the fervor of religious pilgrims have inspired travelers on the road from Vannes to Sainte-Anne-d'Auray in the Morbihan, a route replacing one constructed by Romans two millennia ago. This road snakes over a somber and desolate wooded height—Coëtsal in Breton—dotted with craggy rock formations, vestiges of the megalithic epoch. Both the Bretons and the Romans realized the strategic importance of this foreboding height. Shielding them from their enemies, it allowed them to swoop down and suddenly attack without mercy.

On one side of this road looms the château of Coëtsal, once the property of feudal seigneurs bearing the same name. This château represented part of their fief, which encompassed dozens of neighboring hamlets and parishes. After belonging to one family for over two hundred years, in the late seventeenth century Coëtsal passed to a new owner, Jean de Robien. He and his two successors, André-Joseph and Pierre-Dymas de Robien, were members of Brittany's *noblesse de robe* and powerful landowners in the Morbihan.

With the marriage in 1788 of Pierre-Dymas' daughter, Jacquette, to André Boniface de Riquetti, vicomte de Mirabeau, the younger brother of the Orator, Coëtsal once again changed hands. Although born in Provence, Jacquette's husband Mirabeau-Tonneau—nicknamed "the Barrel" because of his corpulence as well as his intemperance—had by the time of his marriage become a zealous

9

crusader for Brittany's traditional privileges, which exempted the province from royal control. Tonneau repaired the crumbling château before bequeathing it to his son, Victor-Claude-Dymas, who in turn left Coëtsal to the eldest of his three sons, Gabriel. In 1843 Gabriel sold the château to his younger brother, Arundel-Joseph. Five years later, on 30 October 1848, Arundel married a woman from Nancy, Marie le Harivel de Gonneville. The two had met when Arundel came to Nancy to discuss the publication of correspondence between the Revolutionary orator Mirabeau and Prince d'Arenberg with Marie's uncle Adolphe de Bacourt, who was responsible for the project. Arundel's family also owned several farms in Lorraine. The new master of Coëtsal then brought his twenty-one-year-old bride back from the animated, refined urban center of Lorraine to the mysterious primeval forest that enshrouded his feudal château. Nine and a half months later, on 16 August 1849, Marie gave birth to the couple's first and only child, a girl.

The next morning the *châtelain* Arundel appeared with his daughter before a sleepy tribunal in the commune of Plumergat to register the birth. For the legal record,

> in the year One thousand eight hundred forty-nine, the seventeenth of August at nine o'clock in the Morning . . . arroudel joseph Requitie Comt de Mirabeau, proprietor, twenty-eight years old, residing in the Chathaux of Coëtsal in this commune, came before us and presented a child of the female sex, born yesterday at eleven o'clock in the Morning in said Chathaux of Coëtsal, born of him, he declared, and of Marie Le Harivel de Gonneville, his wife, . . . twenty-two years old, and to whom he wished to give the first names Sibille émée marie antoinette . . . . [1]

In 1853 the said "Arroudel" again came before a Breton tribunal to signal both spelling errors and an important omission in the original birth certificate. He requested that "the name Gabrielle, which had been omitted, be added, that Arroudel be written 'Arundel' and Requitie 'Riquetti,' that Comt be spelled 'Comte' and émée 'Aimée.' "[2]

With the patronymic "Gabrielle" added, the name Sibille Aimée Marie Antoinette Gabrielle[3] evoked two maternal and two paternal ancestors. Sibille was derived from Sibylle de Fos, Sibylle's maternal grandmother. Marie was taken from Marie Le Harivel de Gonneville, her mother. Antoinette referred to Jean-Antoine de Riquetti de Mirabeau, Mirabeau-Tonneau's grandfather. Trampled and mutilated while doing battle for Louis XIV, this warrior could keep his head up only with the help of a metal neck brace; hence his nickname Cou d'Argent (Silver Neck). Finally, Gabrielle recalled the illustrious orator Honoré Gabriel de Riquetti, comte de Mirabeau, Sibylle's great-grand-uncle. The past resonated in Sibylle's name, symbol of her parents' pride in their heritage, which they wished to transmit to their daughter. To this couple, their ancestral past was more than dusty portraits and oft-repeated anecdotes. It was a timeless legend.

Sibylle's father, Arundel-Joseph de Riquetti de Mirabeau, may have been descended from a family of Florentine patricians originally named Arrigheti, or perhaps from a family of merchants from Digne. The Riquettis, who acquired the fief of Mirabeau in the late sixteenth century, had served the monarchy for centuries. Born in Vannes on 9 December 1820,[4] Arundel was the third of four children of Victor-Claude-Dymas de Riquetti de Mirabeau, a retired cavalry officer, and of Louise-Eléonore Danthon, who was from a Breton Legitimist family.[5] Little is known about the father Sibylle herself barely knew yet to whose memory she remained profoundly attached. No portrait exists, no physical description except for Sibylle's dim and idealized recollection, written more than a half-century after her father's death. As she remembered him in her *Souvenirs*, Arundel had "a charming face, light eyes, chestnut-colored hair and an attractive and slight blond mustache."[6] His physique was "heavy and muscular."[7] Raised with scant parental supervision (his own father had died when Arundel was eleven), he had been left alone with his two brothers and his sister to hunt and fish and ride horses in the backwoods of Brittany: "[They] grew up recklessly . . . with no supervision nor education."[8]

This rough-hewn *rentier*-sportsman could not have held a more than superficial appeal for his wife, Marie, habitué of Nancy's elegant drawing rooms. Coëtsal's eerie atmosphere depressed her. Miserable, she entreated her father to come from Nancy to mediate her disputes with Arundel. Despite Gonneville's efforts to preserve the barely two-year-old marriage (and his daughter's reputation), the couple separated in 1850. Gonneville accompanied his estranged daughter back to Nancy, leaving the infant Sibylle to stay with her father's elderly aunt in Brittany. Shortly thereafter, Marie and her parents traveled again from Lorraine to Brittany, where Marie retrieved her daughter. That same year Arundel, to his brother's dismay, sold Coëtsal to a Monsieur Graux, realtor. Gabriel tried to buy back the château but was unsuccessful. Coëtsal had definitively passed out of the Mirabeaus' possession.

Arundel remained in Brittany after the couple's separation. He saw his daughter only twice annually: in Lorraine for two weeks during the hunting season (provoking Marie's departure to Normandy) and, after 1855, in Brittany. During his visits to Brittany, Sibylle's father became a kind of local hero, going hunting or fishing while peasants escorted his daughter to the basilica at Sainte-Anne-d'Auray, or to her Coëtsal birthplace. They amused themselves by dressing the girl as a Breton boy in a white vest and a jacket with gold buttons decorated with fleurs-de-lys. Although she spent little time there, Sibylle would vividly remember her birthplace, recalling "the desolate and charming moor, and the green sea of the Morbihan, which have remained clearly etched in my mind."[9] Despite the Mirabeau family's roots in Provence, she would always consider herself a Breton.[10]

These twice yearly reunions between Sibylle and her father did not always take place in Lorraine or Brittany. In 1859 Arundel again costumed his ten-year-old daughter as a Breton peasant boy, and the two journeyed to Frohsdorf, Austria, at the invitation of a man whom many of Emperor Napoleon III's subjects considered a living anachronism: Henri, comte de Chambord, the last Bourbon pretender to the French throne. The 1830 ascension to the throne of the younger, rival royal branch, the Orléans, had forced the count and his entourage into exile.

Since 1840 the court had been entertaining a fiction of royal pomp in Frohsdorf. Surrounded by such precious mementos as Louis XVI's bloodstained vest and Marie-Antoinette's slipper, which she had lost on her way to the guillotine, the pretender spent his days in this isolated outpost of Legitimism, hunting, reading, and praying. He also hosted Legitimists who had trekked from France to inform their sovereign of the prospects for a Legitimist restoration.

Arundel de Mirabeau was one such impassioned servitor. As a boy he had often saluted the count. To prove his continued fidelity, he wished to present the count with his living legacy to Legitimism—his daughter. True, owing to the "tragedy" of her gender, Sibylle would be "the last of the Mirabeau." Yet standing before the count (himself childless) in boy's clothing, she created the illusion that the Mirabeau name and mystique would be perpetuated, a comforting illusion for a man incarnating a class and political tradition whose future in 1859 seemed precarious.

The Frohsdorf expedition created a bond between father and daughter that was shattered the following year with Arundel's sudden death. Ever the comte de Chambord's devoted knight, in 1860 Arundel enlisted in an elite corps of twenty-five thousand international volunteers, the papal Zouaves. Général Christophe Juchault de Lamoricière, an imperial proscript notorious for his merciless raids during the Algerian conquest, commanded this corps. His goal was to protect the pope's temporal powers in Rome against armies of nationalists sweeping up from Sardinia, who were tacitly supported by Napoleon III. To the comte de Chambord, this was no mere military confrontation but the potential victory of "Christian civilization over revolutionary barbarism." He hailed Lamoricière as a "Christian hero."[11] Yet the ardor of these latter-day crusaders did not ensure victory. On 18 September 1860 Cialdini's Piedmontese troops routed Lamoricière's Zouaves at Castelfidardo.

It was not a nationalist's gun but that of a careless comrade that killed Sibylle's father twelve days after the defeat. According to his death certificate, "on 30 September 1860, at six-thirty in the morning, the infantrymen de Mirabeau and de Bessey were on guard duty together at the artillery depot, and wishing to inspect their arms (these two soldiers bearing Pistols called revolvers), de Bessey's gun inadvertently fired, and the shot mortally wounded de Mirabeau, who died instantly, having been struck in the head."[12] To allay the tragic "banality" of "this frightful and stupid death,"[13] Sibylle would later rewrite it as a heroic event, relying on clichés about the nobility of military life, some of them received from Arundel himself: "[T]o be killed in war seemed to me normal and expected," she reflected, "and it was, in my eyes, the most beautiful of all deaths."[14] In fact, she would dedicate much of her life and works to recreating this absent, adored father, this fervent yet distant soldier, this leader.

Unlike her brief, idealized contacts with her father, Sibylle's relationship with her mother was unrelentingly complicated, antagonistic, and bitter. Born in her grandfather's house in Nancy on 28 April 1827, Marie was descended from two of the oldest aristocratic families from Normandy and Lorraine. Her father's ancestors, with possible roots in Denmark (Harwel), had participated in the Norman

Conquest, while one of her mother's forebears, Saint-Pierre Fourier de Matain-court, had preached against Protestantism in Lorraine during the Reformation and had founded a religious order for the education of poor girls.

Marie's upbringing in many ways prefigured her daughter's. She was an only child, brought up largely by a father old enough to be her grandfather—Gonne-ville was forty-three at his daughter's birth. The colonel raised both his daughter and then his granddaughter as a tomboy. Both girls heard the same bawdy military stories and straddled the same retired officers' knees. After her precocious sep-aration from her husband, Marie returned to Nancy to resume a full round of teas, balls, and receptions with military personnel. She often traveled to visit friends in Paris or Normandy, leaving her daughter with her parents. A single mother conscious of her social marginality, Marie tried to compensate for this "defect" by becoming a recognized socialite in Nancy and by pursuing a writing career, one of the few options acceptable for women under the Second Empire.

Sibylle's reaction to the mother who showed her so little affection was a com-bination of jealousy and animosity. She grudgingly conceded her mother's at-tractiveness, admiring her "beautiful, light chestnut-colored hair, thick and silky, that she wears coiled around her head; her shoulders are broad, her waist exag-geratedly narrow. Her hands are large, but superb, quite like those of a statue. Her physique is rather ordinary, but her air is distinguished."[15] Yet Sibylle also insisted on Marie's haughtiness, frivolity, and critical nature. She recalled her mother's dismay at her daughter's eccentricities and inability to "be like everyone else," and noted her mother's displeasure concerning her daughter's looks, her name, and her "stupidity." Sibylle also recounted an incident revealing both her hatred and her terror of her mother. Marie's decision to have her daughter's ears pierced precipitated a fistfight between the two. It also made Sibylle realize her impotence and prompted her resolution to cultivate her strength, to defend herself against "oppressors." "This time," she told herself, "there's nothing to do about it, but later, when they want to do things like that to me, I'll defend myself . . . I want to become strong . . . very strong . . . "[16] In her writings she would gener-alize Marie's unappealing traits, presenting them as emblematic of innate female character. If, to the young Sibylle, Arundel appeared as the white knight, Marie was the epitome of female deceitfulness, Eve incarnate.

The Family Circle: Gonneville

Two other relatives, Sibylle's maternal grandfather and maternal great-uncle, served as her mentors. Surrogate father, teacher, and friend, colonel Aymard Olivier Le Harivel de Gonneville was the single most important figure in his granddaughter's life. So decisive was his influence that in her will Sibylle re-quested that his portrait be placed beside her in her coffin. She described him in glowing, unequivocally adoring terms: "My grandfather held in my life the first and best place. He is what I have loved most completely and best. His influence on me was profound. I owe him any goodness that is in me. His memory is

13

luminous and pure, unblemished.''[17] A portrait and a photograph depict Gonneville as a young officer in the Napoleonic army—Sibylle's fantasy lover—and as an elderly man, her benevolent father figure. In the former, Gonneville sports his high-necked uniform, with its gold buttons and epaulets, from which hang three large medals, including the Légion d'honneur. Heavy-lidded eyes stare intensely out of a perfectly oval face fringed with sparse blond curls. He has extremely thick lips and a small, well-groomed mustache. In the photograph, presumably taken in Nancy in the 1850s or 1860s, Gonneville sits erect in a chair placed at an angle to the camera, holding a top hat and cane. His long black frock coat contrasts with his white shirt and light-colored trousers. Age has accentuated the thickness of his lips and the puffiness of his eyes, yet his height and posture give him a dignified bearing.

To Sibylle, her grandfather's participation in the Napoleonic military epic endowed him with a quasi-mythical status. Portraits of Napoleon and Murat had stared down imperiously at the three-year-old Sibylle as she awoke for the first time in her Nancy bedroom. ''It's between this Napoleon and these battles that I lived until I was sixteen.''[18] Incarnations of the emperor would dominate her adult life, as they had framed her childhood.

Yet Gonneville's affiliation with the Napoleonic legend seems anomalous given his background. He was born in 1783 in Caen, where his father served as the king's riding master and police lieutenant and his grandfather as the king's secretary. The specter of the guillotine abruptly ended this royalist idyll. The Revolutionary crowd dragged an aristocratic friend of Gonneville's father from his house and killed him, after which a woman reputedly tore out his heart and roasted and devoured it ''with the rage of a tiger.''[19] Needing no further warning of things to come, Gonneville's family dispersed in panic. His father barely escaped, emigrating to Prussia to join the prince de Condé's counter-Revolutionary armies, while his mother and the children took refuge in a fisherman's hut near Rouen. In their absence from Caen, all the family goods and property were stolen or sold.

Undaunted by the excesses of the Terror, Legitimists were keeping their hopes alive in Normandy, and Gonneville's mother wished to devote her eleven-year-old son to the cause. She sent Aymard to run messages to général Frotté, one of the chiefs of the *chouannerie*. But général Hoche quelled this rebellion in 1795, and Gonneville's family again found itself without money, without property, and without a cause.

But a new star was rising just as Gonneville reached adulthood. Determined to save the family honor by pursuing an acceptably aristocratic vocation, Gonneville was willing to strike a compromise with the empire. In 1804 he enlisted in the twentieth cavalry regiment, in which displaced Legitimists like himself rubbed elbows with tough Republican veterans. For the next eleven years Gonneville's fate paralleled that of the Napoleonic armies. He fought in Italy, Prussia, Spain, Austria, and Poland, emerging eleven campaigns, several medals, and one wound later with the rank of sergeant.[20] According to reports from his commanding officers, he had distinguished himself by his zeal and bravery, yet also by his modesty. He was "one of our finest cavalry officers . . . an officer of the utmost distinction."[21]

Gonneville obeyed Napoleon as long as he remained the legitimate ruler and military commander. The emperor's abdication and the epilogue of the Hundred Days, however, signaled Gonneville's own defection from the Napoleonic camp. On Napoleon's landing in France in March 1815, Gonneville fled Corsica, where he was stationed. The emperor's return had stirred up pro-Bonapartist sentiment in Corsica, pitting "the near-savage breed"[22] of peasants and some military officers against Legitimists like Gonneville. Once on the mainland, Gonneville tried to merge with the counter-Revolutionary émigré armies of the duc d'Angoulême, eager to hasten a Bourbon restoration. When this failed, he retreated to Normandy. Unwilling to serve during the "usurpation," he submitted his resignation from the army one month before Waterloo.[23] In Normandy Gonneville continued to whip up ultraroyalist sentiments in former strongholds of the *chouannerie*. Between Louis XVIII's ascension to power in April 1815 and the proclamation of the Royal Charter in June, he crusaded in the duc d'Aumont's Rassemblement Royaliste. For these activities he was placed under surveillance, alarming his family, who remembered the Gonnevilles' fate during the Terror.[24]

Gonneville survived the transition to the Restoration, and was incorporated into Charles X's personal guard. Fifteen years later, the revolution of 1830 once again terminated the Legitimists' idyll. Passing uproarious crowds as he traveled by coach from Normandy to Poitiers in 1830, Gonneville felt "an intense repulsion"[25] in the face of this uncontrolled manifestation of popular Orleanist sentiment. Reflecting back on his hostility towards this mob, Gonneville would write: "Nothing ever seemed to me as hideous as a popular riot."[26] This unruly crowd could find no place in his chivalric mental universe. Although he denounced the new government and expressed hopes for a third Bourbon restoration, by 1836 Gonneville was ready for a quiet retirement.

Yet now there was no Napoleon offering "redemption" in the form of a brilliant military career to interior political exiles like Gonneville. The colonel was fifty-three and had known nothing except military life for the past thirty-two years. Finding himself idle, he devoted himself to his friends, his *Souvenirs*, and to the upbringing first of his daughter and then of his granddaughter. In the absence of Sibylle's father—and often her mother—it was Gonneville who looked after and disciplined the child, who became the companion of his old age. Contemporary residents of Nancy recalled seeing a lively, curly haired girl, hoop in hand, trotting beside a dignified elderly gentlemen. On these daily walks, Gonneville would meet other retired Napoleonic officers, whose memories would mix with talk of the Crimean War in progress or of the cholera epidemic decimating the army.

Gonneville was also largely responsible for Sibylle's early education. In a seeming effort to simulate a type of paramilitary training, Gonneville rigorously divided up his granddaughter's day. Periods were allotted for intellectual and leisure activities, such as playing with her toy soldiers (gifts from Gonneville) or leafing through a picture book of famous generals. Gonneville also reserved several hours a day for physical activity: horseback riding, dancing, long walks, and even more strenuous sports. Astounded by his granddaughter's force, the result of her broad shoulders and muscular legs, he made her practice gymnastics daily, hoping both to satisfy her physical energy and increase her strength. By encouraging such "masculine" activities, Gonneville was perhaps both vicariously reliving his own experiences and creating a fiction surrounding his granddaughter's gender in order to offset the family calamity resulting from it.

Gonneville cultivated not only Sibylle's physical prowess but also her intellect. Whenever she exercised, he would recite verses from Racine's *Phèdre*. Eventually he taught her to read. She insisted on this when she learned that the comtesse Dash, "the lady who wrote the books with red covers that are in Little Mother's library,"[27] was moving to Nancy. Sibylle's first readings from an enormous bible were followed by Madame de Genlis, Perrault, and La Fontaine (gifts from Gonneville), and ancient Greek and Roman history and mythology (from her great-uncle, the ambassadeur Bacourt). A few years later she read novels by Walter Scott, George Sand, and Alexandre Dumas *père*. But what interested her most were the red covers adorning the works of the comtesse Dash, with titles such as *Les Bals masqués* and *Les Fruits défendus* (*Forbidden Fruits*), which were kept out of reach in her mother's library.

Gonneville's mixture of "paternal goodness and . . . proud reserve"[28] had a charismatic effect on Sibylle. Her earliest memories, dating from her awakening in "the bedroom of battles"[29] in Gonneville's house, were of him. She would recall that "the pretty hands, that's Grandma; the thick mustache, that's Grandpa . . . Besides, it's him I already knew the best."[30] Sibylle's affection for her grandfather surpassed mere filial devotion. Hers could also be interpreted as an erotic attachment. She described her memories of Gonneville's apotheosis in this way: "Grandfather seems to me just magnificent. I see only his impressive stature, his elegant style, his blue eyes, his extreme distinction. I don't notice that his thick lips mar his handsome face. I find him admirable, I devour him with my eyes, and it is he who, from that moment on, dominates and will dominate my entire life."[31]

Yet Sibylle's combination of reverence for and physical attraction to Gonneville was not unmixed with fear. Their great age and physical difference in part explains this. Despite the intimacy of their relationship, the seven decades separating Sibylle from her grandfather conspired to keep her in a state of perpetual subordination—another self-revelation of her weakness. This incongruity made Gonneville's power over his granddaughter seem even more impressive to her and slightly frightening. "I adored my grandfather savagely and tenderly," Sibylle would write, "yet he was the only one I feared among my relatives."[32] To Sibylle Gonneville was more than a father figure, teacher, or friend. He represented the ideal leader, either military or civilian, a charismatic chief eliciting "savage and tender" devotion, yet also a disciplinarian commanding respect and assuring order, the solid foundation of a family, an army, a country.

The Family Circle: Bacourt

If "Gonneville's way" would lead Sibylle to a political militancy colored by sentimental Bonapartism, that of her godfather Adolphe de Bacourt—"l'ambassadeur"—would take her into the rarefied atmosphere of both international aristocratic and Parisian literary circles. Bacourt, younger brother of Gonneville's wife Sophie, was born in 1801 in Nancy. After holding diplomatic posts in Sweden and Holland, he was sent to London in 1830, where he became Ambassador Talleyrand's secretary and later his executor. The ambassador appreciated his devoted aide, as he revealed in a letter to King Louis-Philippe: "I know few people whose mind can be compared to that of Monsieur de Bacourt, and I have *never* encountered any who were more honest."[33] Talleyrand's patronage helped Bacourt gain admittance to aristocratic London salons and also procured him a mistress in the person of the ambassador's niece, the duchesse de Dino, eight years Bacourt's senior. The cachet of this slightly scandalous liaison only enhanced his reputation.

Bacourt's next stay, at the court of the Grand Duke of Baden, ended in 1839 and was followed by an unhappy term as plenipotentiary in Washington. The egalitarianism of American society repelled him, and he returned to France in 1842. The year 1847 found him serving as ambassador to Sardinia. Yet one year after his appointment, in the midst of revolutionary upheaval, Alphonse de Lamartine's provisional government revoked him. Rather than serve a regime he despised—revolutionary "vulgarity" horrified him—he resigned in 1848. Thus the prestigious career begun under the July Monarchy ended in bitterness and anger. Like his brother-in-law, Bacourt became another political casualty—but of the Orleanist stripe.

By the time Sibylle became acquainted with her godfather, his diplomatic career—Talleyrand, *la liaison*, royal courts, the United States, friendship with Stendhal[34]—had become the stuff of local legend in Nancy. Retired, Bacourt devoted himself to writing and visiting friends in Europe. He made a point, however, of keeping his stays in Nancy brief. His family's hatred of Orleanism made him uncomfortable, despite their respect for him. During dinners at the Gonnevilles, Bacourt sat silently, scarcely participating in the conversation, eating only an egg poached in bouillon and some apple marmalade.[35] He turned down scores of social invitations awaiting him on his arrival, shunning potentially boring and pretentious company for that of Nancy's clique of Orleanists.

Bacourt served not only as a social mentor for his goddaughter but also as a literary one. His Parisian salon attracted the unexiled elite of the anti-imperial literati. Lamartine, Lucien Prévost-Paradol, François Buloz (editor of the liberal and Orleanist *Revue des deux mondes*), and Marceline Desbordes-Valmore all attended Bacourt's biweekly luncheons. Sibylle's first visit to her uncle's salon in 1859 (where she was warned not to step on Lamartine's toes) exposed her to a type of literary milieu—cultivated, Parisian, and politically opposed to the ruling regime—which she would continue to frequent, and to a certain extent replicate, under the Third Republic. Bacourt also commissioned his goddaughter's first "writing job." From 1861 to 1865 Sibylle was paid ten sous a letter to painstakingly copy Talleyrand's memoirs, which Bacourt had been charged with setting in order after his mentor's death. Although this tedious activity classed her as no more than an intellectual underling, it was nevertheless an important introduction into the world of letters.

Finally, Bacourt embodied a personal style—elegant yet also eccentric and anachronistic—that Sibylle would later appreciate and tailor to her own use. She recalled having been "bewitched"(médusée)[36] by this svelte, melancholic, and infinitely refined man, who arrived in Nancy from Baden with his faithful Hanoverian servant, Frederick, mustached and seven feet tall. She adored his ravishing (albeit odd) clothing and admired his snubbing of Nancy society. Bacourt was a magnificent dandy.

The Legacy

The family portraits hanging in Gonneville's house served not only a decorative but also a didactic purpose. Cou d'Argent, Tonneau, Mirabeau, and Saint-Pierre Fourier were all visual reminders of a past which, while remote, nevertheless guided both present and future. This past also legitimized the social position of the nineteenth-century aristocracy, whose prestige, it felt, rested not on wealth or talent but on birth and ancestry. Genealogy was the aristocracy's favorite fetish.

Genealogy was also a program, a set of moral imperatives. From her ancestors Sibylle inherited values and attitudes that she would assimilate. The resulting ethos was a composite amalgam of ideas, reflecting her ancestors' varied political backgrounds. While Legitimism and sentimental Bonapartism furnished the raw material of Sibylle's political consciousness, the Revolutionary and Orleanist traditions were also present, bequests of Mirabeau and Bacourt. More than mere political doctrines, each of these four tendencies encompassed a broad sensibility and worldview. This legacy, which proffered occasionally conflicting conceptions of history, social and political organization, and gender roles, was thus an eclectic inheritance.

That the past had been a better time than either the present or the future seemed a truism to Sibylle's family. The question, though, was which past? Legitimists (the majority of Sibylle's family members), Bonapartists, Orleanists, and Revolutionaries had all attempted to rewrite history, glorifying specific periods and damning—or even editing out—others. As a child Sibylle was thus confronted with several allegedly official histories. To Legitimists, the golden age was situated in France's distant past, the time of cathedral-building and the Crusades. This past was premodern, preindustrial, Christian, and monarchic. The ideal monarchy, however, was not the rationalized, centralized one of Louis XIV but the medieval one of Saint Louis, founded on a mystical devotion to the person of the king and France's past. The monarch would preside over a corporatist and antiegalitarian society, the embodiment of a "natural order." The latter was exploded by the Revolution. The events of 1789 to 1799, unspeakably nefarious for Legitimists, had not only killed the monarch but also challenged the monarchy's social hegemony. While the restoration of the Bourbon kings Louis XVIII and Charles X had temporarily put France's history back on the right course, the revolution of 1830 had once again derailed it by bringing France's "regicide" branch to the throne.[37] So went the story.

How could these historical "aberrations" be explained? As no "rational" reason could be imagined by Legitimists, they found their answer in the "devil theory of history."[38] The revolution of 1789, Legitimists advanced, could only have been the work of occult forces, a plot concocted by any number or combination of non-Legitimist groups: Freemasons, Orleanists, or the English, for example. The *complot* thus became a fundamental component of the Manichaean historical vision of the Legitimists and one of their standard tools of exegesis. Sibylle was nourished on such myths. For example, she had often been told the story of the prince de Condé, who, according to the Legitimist fiction, was assassinated by Orleanist agents. Even as an adult she would continue to insist on the veracity and historicity of "her story." Her refusal to consider alternate explanations both engendered and was symptomatic of a disturbing historical amnesia.

The family of Sibylle's father and of her future husband represented a particular style of intransigent Legitimism. Once these Legitimists had rationalized history's disastrous (for them) evolution, how did they respond when forced into the opposition? Defense against future catastrophes was the answer, yet this could take either a passive or active form. The first option entailed retreat, first abroad (as occurred during the Terror) and then into *la France profonde*. After 1830 many Legitimists retired to their châteaux, emigrating "to the interior of their country and their times."[39] They preferred to become living anachronisms rather than suffer another disappointment. Totally isolated from non-Legitimists, they were left to pray for the return of their prince in exile, the comte de Chambord.

While this first group of Legitimists favored a quiet retrenchment, the other faction declared trench warfare. The extremism of these vigilante reactionaries, who swelled the ranks of the *chouannerie* and the White Terror brigades after Napoleon's Waterloo defeat, is perhaps best embodied by Sibylle's great-grandfather, Mirabeau-Tonneau. Like a demonic alter-ego of the Orator, his younger brother André Boniface was a zealous spokesman for the equally impassioned counter-Revolutionary Right. With several notorious military adventures and participation in the battle of Yorktown behind him, in 1788 he was elected to represent the nobility of Limoges in the Estates General. Meanwhile, the commoners of Aix-en-Provence were hailing his older brother as their tribune. With hysterical zeal the obese Tonneau defended aristocratic privilege against both king and commoners. Often seen menacingly brandishing his sword and shaking his fists at opponents, he was also known for his dueling and drinking. He frequently arrived drunk at sessions of the Estates General. A pamphlet soon began circulating, denouncing his "unheard-of indecency."[40]

The Orator soon fell victim to Tonneau's outrageousness when, unwilling to let his brilliant brother upstage him, Tonneau decided to use his girth as a weapon.

During the Constituent Assembly session of 3 May 1790, Tonneau's obstinacy verged on the farcical: "[H]e climbs up to the rostrum at the same time as [Mirabeau] and crushes him with his corpulence. Only after a lengthy discussion does he cede the space to [his brother]."[41] Yet Tonneau's crusade to save the absolute monarchy failed. On the day Louis XVI swore fidelity to the Revolutionary constitution, Tonneau dramatically broke his sword in two before the Constituent Assembly, declaring: "Since the king is renouncing his kingdom, a gentleman no longer needs a sword to defend him."[42] *Persona non grata* in France, he emigrated to Prussia, where he raised three thousand troops, nicknamed the "hussars of death," to march against the Revolutionary armies. He stormed France in August 1792 and raided a Jacobin club. But his jealousy of other émigrés and his chronic inebriation foiled him. He died in 1792 in Prussia, officially of apoplexy but perhaps of wounds from a duel.[43]

As illustrated by Tonneau, whom Sibylle would hail as "an adorable and witty bad boy,"[44] Legitimism prescribed a vision of history, its exegesis, and its means of defense. History was largely past history, that of "old France," expurgated of all allusions to democracy, creation (after all) of a vile conspiracy. The defense of the Legitimist view of history necessitated nothing less than a holy war in which heavy ammunition was needed, as well as a style both vigilant and violent, paranoid and *frondeur*.

Aside from explaining historical evolution and prescribing a model of social organization, Legitimism also encompassed a conception of authority, which was transmitted to Sibylle. Post-Revolutionary Legitimists inherited from their ancestors an intense faith in the symbolic power of the monarch and the monarchy. The king was, like Charlemagne, *rex et sacerdos*, a temporal and religious leader consecrated by God alone. Coupled with these powers, the monarch was endowed with those of a warrior; the king, like Saint Louis, was France's foremost warlord, ready to lead battalions into the fray to defend France against "barbarism." Love, respect, and awe were emotions worthy of these kings, who exerted unquestioned authority over family, army, and kingdom. In some ways the Bonapartist model of authority, known to Sibylle through the stories of Gonneville, replicated the Legitimist one. Napoleon Bonaparte's 1804 coronation at Notre-Dame rivaled that of any Bourbon king in terms of its pomp and mystery, and instantly endowed the emperor with near-divine status. His authority as a military leader reinforced his temporal power. And Napoleon cultivated the same charismatic image as the absolute monarchs, combining remoteness with benevolence. Authority, Sibylle learned at a young age, was both absolute and charismatic, and was comprised of religious, secular, and military powers. No society or polity could exist without this stabilizing authority.

One dissident voice from Sibylle's past, however, belied this conception—that of the family's notorious renegade, Mirabeau. Throughout his life he adopted the cause of those abused by an oppressive royal authority: the press, the Third Estate, the Jews. Far from wishing to destroy the monarchy, however, he prayed for its reform. A more humane, less arbitrary monarchy was his ideal. His tirades against the absolute monarchy seem anomalous, given his Legitimist antecedents, and perhaps reflect his hatred of tyranny as symbolized by his father. The Physiocrat Victor Riquetti, marquis de Mirabeau, was horrified by his son's pockmarked face and scandalous existence; as a young man Mirabeau had engaged in an incestuous relationship with his sister, squandered his money, and penned an abundant quantity of pornographic literature in his Vincennes prison cell, which adjoined that of the marquis de Sade. But the marquis de Mirabeau also envied his son's eloquence and powers of seduction. "L'Ami des Hommes" set out to debase his defenseless son. He forced him into the army, had him imprisoned repeatedly, and even robbed him of his name, designating him as the innocuous "Monsieur Honoré." To the marquis his son was "a consummate scoundrel who needed to be erased from human memory."[45]

The same coincidence of ideological, political, and psychological factors that perhaps explain Mirabeau's vindication of the rights of the Third Estate also figured importantly in the formulation of Sibylle's attitude toward authority. The void left by her father's death led her to seek strong paternal authority not only within her family but also on the national level, a venture perfectly in line with her Legitimist and Bonapartist heritage. While searching for this authority, however, Sibylle chafed at her oppressed state, the result of her upbringing as an only child—and a female one—by both a domineering mother and a patriarchal grandfather. With few peers or playmates, she developed an acute sense of powerlessness when faced with an abstract yet menacing authority that she came to despise, as had her renegade ancestor Mirabeau. Yet, unlike the Orator, she tried not to modify or reform this authority but rather, like Tonneau, to destroy it. The paradoxical meeting in Sibylle of a profound need for strong authority and a revulsion toward it produced the makings of a hybrid: an authoritarian anarchist.

An accretion of diverse historical epochs and political ideologies, this legacy was Sibylle's birthright. Though largely symbolic, it was nevertheless manifold. Family portraits and mementos as well as Gonneville's anecdotes all served a historiographic function, revealing the past and tacitly dictating the future. In the eventuality of another historical "aberration" like the Revolution, appropriate weapons of defense were available; Tonneau's menacing sword and fists, virulent pamphlets, and scathing speeches had shown the way. The legacy also encompassed an unwritten set of values. Christian piety and devotion to family, for example, were sacrosanct. Also prized were chivalric and martial virtues associated with the Legitimist and Bonapartist models of authority: physical and moral strength, courage, and stamina.

These were all attributes traditionally identified with the male. The legacy indeed depended on a male-centered conception of authority and ultimately of social and political organization. Not only did it condone masculinity as a superior, exemplary state; it also depended on the male to perpetuate these values. For although a woman could serve as a "conductor" for the legacy as easily as her husband, she could not pass on the one crucial feature which, like a chromosome, symbolically "carried" hereditary material: the family name. To the nineteenth-century French aristocracy a name, like a talisman, bore almost mythical powers.

It symbolized the family's ethos. And there were names that spoke a thousand words. Mirabeau was one.

But both of Arundel's brothers died childless. With Sibylle's marriage the name Mirabeau would disappear: she was "the last of the Mirabeaus." The declining power of both the aristocracy and organized Legitimism during the second half of the nineteenth century only magnified the "tragedy" of Sibylle's gender, for the family name was another potential form of ammunition in this battle to preserve a certain image of France.

The irony of this tragic situation lay in Sibylle's seeming masculinity. Family acquaintances often mistook her for a boy. At Frohsdorf she stunned guests by riding in a man's saddle. A friend of her father's whispered to him: "[Y]our daughter . . . seems so little like a girl to me . . . "[46] Gonneville was also astounded by his granddaughter's masculine personality. In her *Souvenirs* Sibylle recalled his sighing to a fellow retired colonel: "That little girl has all the tastes of a boy! . . . She plays only with soldiers, only likes violent things . . . "[47] And she recreated her reaction to a conversation between Gonneville and maréchal Canrobert, in which the colonel expressed his regret about his granddaughter's gender to the hero of the Crimean War: "I understood that, on the way, Grandfather and he had spoken about the fact that I was not a boy! . . . I'm often reproached for not being a boy! . . . And no one, of course, regrets it as much as me! . . . "[48]

Given Sibylle's seeming "predisposition" to masculine behavior, encouraged by those arround her, it was not difficult for her family to impose a male identity on the child in the hope of creating a fiction to offset the imminent disappearance of the name Mirabeau. Sibylle's acceptance of this imposed identity would be ambiguous. Reared to regret her gender, and already conscious of "innate" female viciousness as embodied by her mother, she may have wanted to cultivate a male identity at all costs. Yet the infliction of this sexual identity—yet another revelation to her of her complete powerlessness—made her bridle. Sibylle would be left to design a new identity.

I I

Gabrielle
1861–1869

Never did a chaste girl read novels.
> Rousseau, preface to *Julie, ou la Nouvelle Héloïse*

Scenes from Provincial Life

The graceful eighteenth-century town house at 8, place Carrière had once housed the pages of duc Stanislas. A century later, Gonneville and his family occupied half this residence, while the other half quartered top-ranking military officers garrisoned in Nancy. The former *hôtel des pages* fronted the place Carrière, which was linked by a triumphal arch to Nancy's central place Royale, framed by gilded iron gates. A tree-lined mews separated the back of Gonneville's home from another eighteenth-century legacy, the place de la Pépinière. As Gonneville and his family could observe from their drawing-room windows, here smartly uniformed officers and fashionable ladies went strolling every afternoon.

The Nancy of Sibylle's adolescence in many ways resembled other small French provincial capitals. Artisans and farmers provided the basis of a traditional economy barely penetrated by industrialization; vineyards still flourished within the city itself. The nobility, a minority of Nancy's forty-seven thousand residents,[1] lived off their *rentes* or served as diplomats, magistrates, or officers. Some of these aristocrats had only recently settled in Lorraine, hoping to maintain a rank higher than any they could possibly occupy in Paris. Nancy's bourgeoisie, including a sizable number of Jews,[2] had always included notaries, lawyers, and doctors. Under the Second Empire, industrialists, bankers, and engineers also rose to prominence. Finally, an important military colony added a distinctive accent to the society of Nancy, a garrison city since the eighteenth century.

Superficially Sibylle's adolescence in Nancy, framed by her father's death in 1860 and her marriage in 1869, was happy, filled with such frivolous mischief as dropping small water bombs on passersby from Gonneville's roof. During this decade, her attachment to her grandfather grew (''[H]e is absolutely everything for me''[3]), as did her feeling of estrangement from her mother and grandmother. Only a shared hatred of physical ugliness, so intense it actually provoked ''genuine suffering''[4] in both Sibylle and her pious, conservative grandmother, united the two. On every other issue Sibylle and Sophie were at odds. As for Marie, her frequent absences, her ''obsession with crowned heads,''[5] and her difficult personality alienated her from her daughter. Yet despite Sibylle's antipathy toward her mother and grandmother, it was these two women who introduced her to Nancy high society. As a child and adolescent, she spent countless hours in Nancy's musty drawing rooms or at nearby châteaux, attending parties, teas, picnics, and later balls frequented by a joint aristocratic–military elite, pale imitations of the Parisian imperial fête. Marie coveted these invitations, yet they were sometimes withheld from her. For the aggressive comtesse de Mirabeau, her daughter later recalled, ''[was] on bad terms with half the city . . . .''[6]

Often the only young person at these gatherings, Sibylle would sit in a corner playing chess with herself. She also eavesdropped on conversations, which were inevitably risqué; Nancy's elite tolerated indiscretions as long as they adhered to rules of etiquette. Hence her mystification about the meanings of ''mistress'' and ''to cheat,'' words often repeated in the salons. Could these words perhaps explain why her mother once recoiled in horror when her fingers touched those of an oddly beautiful woman also reaching for an eclair in a pastry shop? Did they have anything to do with the ''slightly painted ladies''[7] Sybille sometimes spied gracing a theater loge?

Occasionally something spectacular interrupted Sibylle's routine, as occurred in 1866, when Nancy hosted Empress Eugénie and the prince imperial during festivities commemorating the centennial of Lorraine's annexation to France. The imperial visit prompted a flurry of social events. Sibylle, accompanied by forty-year-old vicomte de Borrelli, was allowed to attend horse races. And the next night, she arrived at a château in Baccarat for her first ball, where actors from the Théâtre des Français performed a play by Musset. Sibylle found the production ridiculous but appreciated the exquisite women who continued dancing until early morning.

Like many of her friends, Sibylle yearned to offer the empress flowers during her procession through the city. But her family refused, uttering contemptuous references to ''Badinguet.''[8] Sibylle's ''Bonapartism,'' a concoction inspired by Gonneville's war stories, the portraits and memorabilia adorning his house, and her cherished ''book of generals,'' seemed a disturbing anomaly to the resolutely Legitimist family. In fact, she remembered Gonneville confiding to a friend: ''She sprouted like a strange and bizarre mushroom in a family devoted solely to the Bourbons . . .''[9] Despite her unequivocal, emotional Bonapartism, however, she had been disappointed by the emperor's appearance when he had visited Nancy several years before Eugénie. She had not immediately recognized him, a small man in a frock coat, with thick hair matted by the rain. How little did he resemble *her* Napoleon, leading Gonneville and his troops to victory! The divergence between appearance and reality disconcerted her and created an uncomfortable void in her life. Her fantastic imagination would soon compensate for what was lacking in her hero's nephew, as it would create antidotes for other notable "lacks" in her own life.

Scenes from Parisian Life

At least three times between 1860 and her marriage in December 1869, Sibylle left the provinces for the capital. Paris enchanted her. Her early contacts with the city baron Haussmann was transforming into the "jewel of Europe" contributed to her lifelong impression of the Second Empire as a golden age, a time of ravishing women, refined gentlemen, and endless gaiety. During visits in 1860 and 1861, she, Gonneville, and Marie lodged in a hotel in the rue des Mathurins, near both the Madeleine and Bacourt's pied-à-terre. Marie and Sibylle remained in this neighborhood in 1867, staying in an apartment in the rue de Marignan, a street in one of Paris' newly fashionable districts, close to the boulevards. Old and new mingled in this rapidly metamorphosing neighborhood. Bacourt's strolls with his great-grand-niece brought the pair past goats and donkeys grazing on a terrain soon cleared to build the church of Saint Augustine.

As many of Gonneville and Marie's friends lived near the Madeleine, Sibylle was once again brought along for endless visits to the innumerable dowagers, countesses, and clerics who would later people her novels. She would later recall one of her hostesses, the comtesse de Boigne, as "a little shapeless lump,"[10] a faded, heavy face peering out of a jumble of lace and ribbons. When her mother and grandfather could not look after Sibylle, they entrusted her to cousins, aunts, uncles, and other relatives. These included two whom she scarcely knew: her father's brothers Edouard and Gabriel de Mirabeau.

While Gabriel, "le marquis," was a *mondain*, his younger brother Edouard was a denizen of bohemia and the demimonde. Sibylle had first met Edouard in 1859 in Nantes, on her way home from Frohsdorf. She had been astounded by her uncle's physical appearance. Small yet wiry and broad-shouldered, Edouard had a long, "baroque" nose, a huge mouth, and sported bushy side-whiskers. His ugliness, to Sibylle, was "droll . . . and nightmarish at the same time."[11] Her father had confided to her that although Edouard was "the most decent fellow one could ever meet,"[12] he was also completely mad. Attending the theater one night (an activity scorned by Nantes society), Sibylle and her father had seen the crowd shout and throw apples at one of the actresses, who happened to be Edouard's mistress. Suddenly, in a gesture worthy of his grandfather Tonneau, the indignant Edouard, poorly dressed in checkered pants and a cocked hat, leapt into the crowd while screaming and brandishing his fists, and then hurled an umbrella into the midst of the spectators. In Paris Edouard, who was fond of calling his niece "little toad," took her to *cafés-concerts*. There, aristocrats and demimondaines alike greeted the infamous Edouard ("legendary in certain milieus"[13]) on his entrance. Sibylle relished her uncle's irreverence but would have few contacts with him, as he married and died mysteriously in Karloff, Russia, in 1873 or 1875.

Unlike the endearing extremist Edouard, Sibylle's other paternal uncle, Gabriel, was a retiring, eccentric gentleman whom Sibylle considered "crotchety, unjust, surly, and very goodhearted."[14] Perhaps she saw him as a cruder version of Bacourt, emblem of elegance and good taste. She renewed acquaintance with her father's older brother on her 1861 trip to Paris. Earlier that year, Gabriel, out of a sense of obligation to his recently deceased brother, had traveled to meet his niece at the Normandy beach resort where she was vacationing with her mother. Estranged from his sister-in-law's family since 1849, when they quarreled, Gabriel had also come to Normandy to make amends. But he found himself snubbed again; Gonneville and Marie detested him.

A childless widower with a spartan lifestyle, Gabriel shared his younger brother's odd physique: "very short, but solid, strongly built, with small eyes, dark and sparkling, a huge nose and a mocking mouth."[15] Physical resemblance, however, was all that linked the two brothers. Of the four Mirabeau children, only Gabriel—who was, according to Sibylle, "nearly civilized,"[16]—had attempted to provide himself with a rudimentary education. Nevertheless, he wrote poorly and often dictated letters to his niece. After serving in the cavalry in Algeria, where he somehow disgracefully compromised himself—the family's lips were tightly sealed on this matter—Gabriel returned to Paris. Here he divided his time between his "historical research" and his social club, the Cercle de l'Union, a life of leisure befitting a dandy—even a destitute one like Gabriel. He occasionally interrupted his routine to take his niece to the Louvre or the Luxembourg gardens, where the two sometimes ran into one of Gabriel's fellow clubmen, such as colonel Gaston de Galliffet, just back from the Mexican campaign.

Gabriel and Edouard, representatives of a patriarchy that continued to condition their brother's daughter throughout her adolescence, introduced her to yet another determining influence on her works and thought: the theater. Sibylle adored the theater. In Nancy Gonneville and Marie, the latter a regular theater goer herself, allowed Sibylle to attend performances of dramas and comic operas. Marie was, in fact, a minor dramatist who also liked to stage informal productions, as she did during an 1861 vacation in Normandy. The troupe of family friends rehearsing Musset's *On ne badine pas avec l'amour* included an actress from the Comédie–Française and the "official" imperial author Octave Feuillet. Sibylle, who attended premieres of Feuillet's *Belle au bois dormant* and *Julie* would speak of the playwright and family friend as "very kind, very charming, and infinitely seductive."[17] Relegated to an adjoining room with instructions to play billiards with herself, she looked on as her mother and the others rehearsed. Dressed, as always, in her "little Breton boy" costume (thus confusing Feuillet about her gender),[18] the girl comprised a critical audience of one.

Sybille's discovery of the theater in the provinces readied her to appreciate the vitality of Parisian theater under the Second Empire. In Paris she was chaperoned by her uncles or by Gonneville, who prescribed weekly theater outings as part of his granddaughter's regimen. It was toward the boulevards that a carriage would drive them, arriving at the Gymnase Dramatique, the Théâtre des Français, or the Théâtre de l'Odéon to enjoy plays by Sardou and Pailleron, or vaudevilles by Meilhac and Labiche.

Theater going was only one of the activities Sibylle enjoyed in Paris during this period. For her, imperial Paris was surely not the "ant-seething city"[19] haunting Baudelaire in his *Tableaux parisiens*. Rather, the capital was the modern Babylon exalted in Offenbach's 1866 operetta *La Vie parisienne*, promising "breathtaking pleasure."[20] Afternoon outings often led Sibylle to the Bois de Boulogne, where at three o'clock in winter and five in summer the aristocratic elite and the demimonde emerged, on horseback or in splendid carriages, for its daily promenade. Sibylle would remember that "[t]his parade was ravishing. The carriages [were] pulled by strong horses, the dresses [were] partly hidden by cascading furs that covered the knees and fell in huge waves in the victorias and calèches. In summer the dresses spilled over, light as clouds."[21] Elegance was also de rigueur at the Longchamp racetrack, where Sibylle mingled with "what was most attractive and most completely chic."[22] Jockey Club swells sporting canes, kid gloves, and top hats chatted with parasol-touting ladies whose skirts billowed over immense cages and layers of crinoline. The emperor, accompanied by Eugénie, often looked on from his stand. Also in attendance were members of the imperial court: the emperor's illegitimate brother, the natty duc de Morny; his illegitimate cousin, the comte Walewski (son of the first Napoleon), and princesse Metternich, wife of the Austrian ambassador to France and another of Sibylle's future bêtes noires.

As an adolescent, Sibylle's fascination with the Second Empire stemmed from her limited participation in a glittering and somewhat unreal spectacle of opulence and pomp. "Unconsciously I loved a government that made life easy and gay," she would write, "and that for twenty years gave France a good deal of glory and much happiness."[23] And this admiration of a social phenomenon, the imperial fête, would evolve into political support for the regime. Her imperialism would remain, in large part, instinctive and emotional, a measure of her happiness under the empire.

Against the Grain

While the adolescent Sibylle appeared to uphold and reshape myths and conventions respected by her family and class, she also challenged them. Her rebellion took several forms, among them undisciplined behavior at school. Before entering the Catholic Sacré-Coeur school, Sibylle had been taught by private tutors and Gonneville. In October 1860 her family forced her to renounce these sympathetic teachers for the severe nuns running the convent school. As a day student, Sibylle would leave Gonneville's house at six–thirty in the morning, not to return until early evening. The intervening hours consisted of a rigorous routine. Classes in geography or French grammar were comprised largely of recitation, and one forgotten word could warrant punishment. Periods were allotted for mathematics and religious instruction, for piano and needlework, punctuated by an unappetizing lunch and outdoor recreation time.

Sibylle proved an indifferent student. Obviously precocious, she was advanced one grade on arrival. Yet she seemed lazy and undisciplined, attentive only to the few subjects that interested her. One of her report cards bore the following evaluation, foreboding for a future writer: "Religious instruction: Good; Handwriting: Messy; Math: Doesn't understand it; French Grammar: Doesn't learn it; Style: Careless; Geography: Never knows it."[24] Her lack of intellectual rigor reflected her resistance to an authority she considered domineering and oppressive, and attempts at discipline only provoked her further. In class she sat drawing caricatures and responded to questions in slang or with a shocking answer. She also refused confession, a seeming sacrilege that reflected not a lack of religious faith but rather her hatred of the Jesuit priests affiliated with the school, whom she viewed as members of a "foreign" order, wedded to Rome. The Jesuits' services, moreover, seemed to attract Nancy's most ostentatious social climbers. Her faith, on the other hand, was instinctively and profoundly "French," an early measure of her chauvinism. "I was religious without being pious," she would explain. "But I had an unshakable faith, the absolute conviction that my religion was the best one, and the formal resolution never to criticize it. I was Catholic as I was French, passionately and unalterably."[25]

Sibylle's teachers, then, embodied for her the same brutal, absolute authority as did her family. At school or at home, it was female authority that she viewed as particularly despotic. Despite Gonneville's gentle insistence that his granddaughter obey (buttressed by comparisons of school and the army), she only halfheartedly conformed to the discipline imposed on her.

The girl's "unladylike" behavior at school convinced Gonneville, Sophie, and Marie that the aristocratic and feminine name Sibylle was now inappropriate. The 1862 publication of Octave Feuillet's novel of the same name only made her appear more ridiculous. Feuillet's languid heroine, Sibylle de Férias, with her "graceful body" and her "ardent and melancholic soul,"[26] epitomized contemporary feminine sensibility. Quite the opposite was Sibylle de Mirabeau, once a cute little girl with curly hair and an upturned nose, now an awkward adolescent regularly insulted by her family, most cruelly by her mother. In her *Souvenirs* she would have Marie pronounce: "We must take away her name Sibylle for good . . . She's becoming too ugly to be called that any longer! . . . "[27] The family council decided on Gabrielle, the second of Sibylle's four first names and an evocation of the Orator, Honoré Gabriel. Sibylle disliked this name, deeming it ugly for a woman, and preferred Antoinette. But the family's authority again proved unflinching. Suddenly, with the feminine first name yielding to the patronymic, Sibylle had become Gabrielle.

Aside from her misbehavior at school, Gabrielle was guilty of another, potentially more serious indiscretion: reading. The tempting red-covered books by the comtesse Dash were kept out of Gabrielle's reach for good reason: her family feared the girl might sin by imitation, heedless of Rousseau's warning that the girl who dared read a page of his *Julie* would instantly become "une fille perdue."[28] Gabrielle's readings of Molière, Racine, Marivaux, and Hugo (replacing Scott and La Fontaine) had already made her family uneasy. But it was her penchant for Mürger— son of a Parisian concierge and glorifier, in his *Scènes de la vie de bohème*, of the "dangerous classes"—that seemed most scandalous. Marie soon relegated Mürger's works to the same locked cabinet as those of the comtesse Dash. Another taboo author was Pascal, whose *Provinciales* Gabrielle bought secretly from her family's book dealer, hoping to strengthen her case against the Jesuits. She would recount her elderly servant's reluctance to accompany her to the bookstore, the book dealer's amazement at her selection, and Gonneville's angry insistence that she give him the book, through whose uncut pages she had seen that "Pascal and I [were] in complete agreement . . ."[29] Reading such forbidden books allowed Gabrielle to assert her independence from her family, even if this meant straying from an acceptable model of behavior for young aristocratic girls.

Péchés mignons: Marie Turns to Writing

While Gabrielle was being emancipated through reading, her mother was also earning her autonomy through writing. Her husband's death in 1860 had left Marie in straitened circumstances. Neither Gonneville's pension nor whatever sum (most likely negligible) Arundel may have bequeathed her,[30] could sustain her free-spending lifestyle. To support herself she requested a position as lady-in-waiting to Empress Eugénie, hoping to rely on the empress' indulgence toward papal defenders like Arundel. But Marie's bid proved unsuccessful, a humiliation for the aggressive social climber. After this rejection, she realized that to buy new ball gowns, travel, and keep up with the "seasons" in Paris and on the Normandy coast, she would have to finance these luxuries herself.

It was above all this financial need that decided Gabrielle's mother on writing for a living. Yet a sense of vocation may have figured in her decision too. As a young woman, Marie, like her daughter, had helped her uncle Bacourt edit Talleyrand's memoirs, an experience, she later asserted, that had given her "the liking and habit of work."[31] Her desire to write may also have reflected a basic need for independence, for freedom from the constraints represented by the parents and daughter with whom she lived into her thirties. In the early 1860s she launched a literary career that would span a quarter of a century and encompass the writing of novels, plays, and pamphlets. Through this endeavor, she would become her daughter's mentor—and later her rival—in a profession already difficult for women to penetrate. For if a career as a writer may have seemed natural to Marie, it nevertheless presaged obstacles, especially given her gender and class. The ideology of "separate spheres," supported by the Church, prescribed the dominant model for aristocratic and bourgeois families in nineteenth-century France. While the husband's realm was the public space, the wife was supposed to guard and provide nurture in the home. Any deviation from this model was tantamount to lowering oneself in the social hierarchy, especially for aristocratic women, whose gender and class both committed (or condemned) them to a life of idleness.[32]

Despite the stigma attached to pursuing a remunerative profession, writing did represent one of the very few professional options available to women in mid-nineteenth-century France. Aristocratic women in particular possessed both the leisure time and education conducive to writing. Madame de Staël and George Sand had proved that women could achieve recognition by means of their pen. Yet the overall percentage of women writers at midcentury probably remained small,[33] and those who did persevere had to endure the sting of misogynous critics inspired by the early nineteenth-century Catholic philosopher Joseph de Maistre, for whom any woman wishing to "emulate" men by pursuing a "masculine" profession "is nothing but a monkey."[34] Unfortunately, de Maistre's assertion, although extreme, just amplified existing public opinion.

To succeed as a writer, as Gabrielle would learn, women had to make concessions. For the Second Empire literary establishment, reproducing the values of French society, also ascribed to the doctrine of separate spheres. The first of these was the adoption of a pseudonym, usually male. Many women would not publish under their own names for fear of scandalizing their families. The first of Marie's several male pseudonyms, comte Honoré Gabriel, of course alluded to the Orator. The cachet of this name, so familiar to the French, was undeniable, and perhaps Marie hoped to capitalize on it. Yet the use of a male pen name must not be considered an exclusively antifemale act, as Gabrielle's example will more clearly illustrate. Rather, it also symbolized these women writers' desire to fashion their own identity in a society in which "woman" was largely a construct shaped by others—parents and husband, church and state. Hence the ambiguity of the male pseudonym: conformity to or rebellion against a male-dominated literary establishment and society?

The second concession tacitly required of women authors under the Second Empire was limitation of their writing to specific genres. Among these often overlapping categories were literature for children and for adolescent girls, memoirs, and Catholic or "moral" literature—all viewed as outgrowths of a woman's "natural" role as mother and educator of young children. Compared with drama or the novel, these genres and themes were deemed subordinate by both the public and colleagues. Yet many women authors, including the comtesse de Mirabeau, were willing to degrade themselves in the literary field in order to maintain or upgrade their social status. Especially for unprosperous aristocratic authors, this type of literary "prostitution" was an evil necessary to perpetuate the illusion of a leisured lifestyle,[35] as Gabrielle would later discover.

Of the six works written by the comtesse de Mirabeau between 1860 and 1869, four were coauthored by the vicomte de Grenville,[36] one was a collection of stories first appearing in two women's publications, *La Mode Nouvelle* and *La Revue à la mode*,[37] and one was a "Christian work" published under the patronage of a powerful prelate, Monsignor Félix Dupanloup, bishop of Orléans. The publication of this last work reveals a mixture of obsequiousness and shrewd business acumen typical of Gabrielle's mother. In late March 1869, Marie, who was in Paris for several weeks, wrote to père Lagrange, vicar of Orléans. Relying on Lagrange as intermediary, Marie hoped to solicit Dupanloup's help in publishing her untitled manuscript. Well known for actively defending both Legitimism and Gallicanism, Dupanloup had belonged to the commission voting in favor of the 1850 Falloux Law, which significantly strengthened Church control of education. Indeed, Marie felt that the aid of the renowned prelate would consecrate her career.

After presenting herself to père Lagrange, Marie proceeded to remind him that, given the brevity of her stay in Paris, she needed word of Dupanloup's decision quickly so she could make publication arrangements with her editor.[38] She then reiterated her desire to dedicate herself to "the Holy Cause" and, utilizing her most flowery style, reminded the prelate of her relation to Bacourt, whom Dupanloup knew: "[I]f Your Excellency does not find me unworthy to write for the Holy Cause, my pen will be devoted to it. Please tell His Highness that I am the niece . . . of Monsieur de Bacourt to whom he granted his friendship. I invoke this dear memory in the hope that Your Excellency will receive my humble prayer with greater indulgence."[39] Two and a half weeks later Marie again wrote to Lagrange, uneasy about not yet having received a response. The next week the coveted letter arrived. Dupanloup agreed to sponsor Marie's manuscript and proposed the title *Prières et pensées chrétiennes (Christian Prayers and Thoughts)*. Overjoyed, Marie announced her imminent trip to Orléans. She wished to thank Dupanloup personally and to solicit "his Holy Blessing, which will bring my daughter happiness."[40] After the visit, she wrote to express her "fervent gratitude"[41] for Dupanloup's "indulgence," attributing this kindness, in part, to the influence of Bacourt, "[who] protected my work as he protected me. . . ."[42] And she repeated her intent to devote herself to writing for the Holy Cause. In 1870 the Parisian publishing house of Vaton frères brought out the comtesse de Mirabeau's *Prières et pensées chrétiennes*, preceded by letters from the author to Bishop Dupanloup.

Marie's reputation as a writer of Catholic and women's literature, albeit a minor one, was now established. In fact, this publication confirmed the first act of legitimization of her status, which had taken place seven years earlier: admission into the Société des gens de lettres, an institution founded in 1838, at Balzac's urging, to protect writers' economic and legal rights in a rapidly expanding literary market. At that time Marie had been recommended to the Société with the following optimistic evaluation: "Madame de Mirabeau writes with ease, even elegance, and . . . she will be able to establish a favorable place for herself in the world of letters when she acquires a bit more experience."[43] Despite these auspicious beginnings, a decade after Dupanloup's endorsement Marie would no longer be serving the "Holy Cause" but rather an eminently profane one: Marcelin's titillating weekly *La Vie Parisienne*. And her "Christian prayers and thoughts" would fall prey to sweet temptation. In 1881 Calmann-Lévy would publish Marie's *Péchés mignons*, penned under a rather unholy pseudonym: "Chut!"

"The First Female Wickedness"

While her mother furthered her literary career, Gabrielle was turning into a young woman—and soon to become a wife. When she was ten or eleven, an incident occurred that affected her profoundly. Her accidental witnessing of a confrontation between an adulterous couple made explicit to her the discrepancy between her milieu's virtuous appearance and its sordid reality. It also destroyed her idealistic conception of love. She would later alleviate (or relive?) the trauma of the voyeuristic scene in her novels, in which a child or adolescent unwittingly observes a couple's sexual intimacy.

Gabrielle had surmised from conversations overheard at home that many Nancy society women had liaisons with either unmarried officers or several notable bachelors, "almost the only chic young people in Nancy."[44] She had often surprised a "respectable" married woman darting into one of Nancy's back alleys. And she knew that capitaine Lostanges, Nancy's most desirable military man, kept a pied-à-terre in town, as did many other officers. While sensing that adultery was fairly common among her family's friends (although kept hushed so as not to jeopardize the sacrosanct family), Gabrielle did not realize that a married woman could ever be adulterous with anyone else but an unmarried man. The thought of a liaison between two married people seemed inconceivable to her.

It was this unwelcome truth that emerged during a picnic at Liverdun, on the banks of the Moselle. As usual, Gabrielle was the only child present. She cast herself in the accustomed role of silent observer registering the day's occurrences. Reflecting, in a letter to Maurice Barrès, on her situation as an introspective only child, she would muse: "Children raised alone amidst adults generally have a sharp eye. I don't think I was an exception. Children see many things they never talk about, and they reflect—unconsciously—a lot."[45] While the ladies were dressing in a cabana after a swim, Gabrielle had been sent to do the same in the woods. It was from this vantage point, "hidden in a thicket yet as close up as I could be,"[46] that she observed the confrontation between a married officer and his married mistress, whom the officer had just seen leave the cabana with another man. Planted several feet in front of the camouflaged Gabrielle, the officer rebuked his mistress for betraying him and for ruining his own marriage. With no sign of remorse, his mistress proceeded to verbally humiliate him. Suddenly the officer began to sob.

Stunned, Gabrielle watched this emotional scene. The sight of the usually dignified soldier crying had an "abominable" effect on her. As the picnickers called her to lunch, she remained in her hiding place, paralyzed: "I was so upset that my legs felt like cotton."[47] Yet her shock quickly degenerated into disgust: "[I] was frightfully revolted, and disgusted, and almost sick. I, who ordinarily had a remarkable appetite, was unable to eat lunch . . . ."[48]

This primal scene shattered all Gabrielle's illusions about upper-class respectability, a value championed by those surrounding her. The fiction of bourgeois–aristocratic "virtue" exploded before her eyes. Watching the couple debasing each other before her, Gabrielle began questioning the very meaning of love and fidelity. She would later recall her cynical reflection that "*love*, which my older cousins and their friends spoke about in my presence, lifting their eyes to the heavens with dreamy and pretentious airs, made people do really wicked things."[49] The Liverdun incident also represented for her an allegory, a story with universal value. For everyone she knew, as she would later assert, "it has almost always and invariably been the Liverdun story repeating itself."[50] This tale was, for Gabrielle, simply the struggle of good against evil, virtue against vice, personified by Man and Woman. In Gabrielle's later analysis of this incident, Man, even when adulterous, still remains noble and sincerely contrite, "regretting the wrong he does—when he does it—and worrying when he's cheated on, because he simply feels grief, and in all cases seeking to show off, to exalt and glorify to others the woman he loves."[51] Woman, on the other hand, is "reserved, calculating, tricky, always cunning . . . and tormenting herself, when she is cheated on, not because of grief but *because of vanity*."[52]

In revealing to Gabrielle female "original sin," or, in her words, "the first female wickedness,"[53] the Liverdun incident was a watershed in her childhood. What she witnessed legitimized and intensified the rage she felt toward her mother. It also made her a de facto apologist for the opposite sex. She would sum up the effect of this experience on her: "[I]t was *horrible* for me. I suspected neither the cynicism nor the impudence nor anything else that was revealed to me that day, leaving me with an impression of bitterness and disgust."[54]

The result of her naïve transgression at Liverdun—the substitution of a personal myth of female vice and male virtue for the bourgeois–aristocratic fictions she had been raised to accept—perhaps revealed a certain logic. For she seemed to need these myths to help her fashion her own identity. Yet the development of a female identity proved extremely difficult for her, given both her view of the women exerting control over her as a tribe of harpies and her own shame over her seeming lack of "feminine graces." How could she avoid internalizing her mother's unrelenting attacks on her appearance, projections perhaps of Marie's doubts about her own gender identity? As she would later assert, this brainwashing had succeeded in convincing Gabrielle of her "freakishness" as a woman: "When, from morning until night, people repeatedly tell a sixteen-year-old girl, who's disinclined to be full of herself, that she's ugly, graceless, clumsy, and irritating to look at, it is impossible for her not to admit that it's almost the truth."[55] Furthermore, Gabrielle's realization of her "aberration" as a woman paralleled her recognition of a seemingly "masculine" predisposition. Her physical strength and agility, she would note, destined her for the circus, not the salon.[56] Again, she may have been attempting to fulfill her family's wish for a male heir. In any case, as an adolescent she viewed herself as a type of transsexual, a man trapped inside a woman's body.

Despite her selective misogyny, Gabrielle did not reject all models of femininity. She admired the beauties gracing the salons and balls in Nancy and Paris. She also found engaging several spunky dowagers, including the baronne de Soubeyran, wife of a Nancy official, a corpulent, mustached, snuff-taking old woman "with jarring, mannish features, eyes sparkling with mischief, who does her hair like a concierge and who dresses no one knows how and with no one knows what . . . ."[57] Perhaps it was the baronne's "mannish" features that endeared her to Gabrielle, or perhaps merely her unconventionality. This eccentric woman was, in fact, an early example of what Gabrielle herself would become in old age.

The more Gabrielle matured, moreover, the more she indeed began to cultivate a "feminine" appearance. She wore flattering new dresses and accessories befitting a young lady of fifteen or twenty during her strolls around Nancy. On one such walk she caught the eye of an officer, who invited her to dinner at Beaudot, Nancy's chic restaurant. This news prompted Gonneville to allow his granddaughter to walk unescorted, no longer shadowed closely by her dutiful servant Nicolas. And while not beautiful or glamorous, by age twenty Gabrielle had developed into an attractive young woman, far from being the hideous creature depicted by her mother. A photo shows her standing behind a chair, wearing a white dress with a lacy ruffled skirt. She wears neither jewelry nor hair ornaments. Her frizzy, dirty-blond hair is casually piled atop her head, with curly bangs unevenly fringing her small, heart-shaped face. Her light eyes are deep-set, she has a snub nose and her lips are narrow, yet her expression is lively and pleasant.

Not unattractive, spirited, intelligent, and from an esteemed family, Gabrielle thus appeared, at least by Nancy standards, an appealing candidate for marriage. But her dowry, consisting of one hundred thousand francs bestowed by her grandparents, was modest. Nevertheless, at least one suitor professed interest. At fifteen she received her first marriage proposal from a family friend, an obese, wealthy cavalry commander named Adalbert, aged forty-three. Both Marie and the Mirabeaus urged the girl to marry, perhaps worrying that she would never receive another offer. Uncle Gabriel even hurried from Paris in the hope of persuading his niece. Yet Gabrielle, supported by Gonneville, declined. Age was not the problem. In fact, she claimed she was interested only in men over thirty-five. Rather, sentiment (or lack thereof) stood in the way. She could not foresee marrying a man for whom she felt no more than a sincere platonic affection.

However, due to an unexpected circumstance, the spurned Adalbert was not to be the last of Gabrielle's suitors. Bacourt's death in April 1865 made Marie the beneficiary of three hundred thousand francs, one third of which she turned over to her daughter. Gabrielle's dowry, which also included several hundred railroad bonds, as well as "clothing, linens, . . . jewelry, and other objects,"[58] had thus doubled. And her renown increased exponentially. She now possessed, for a small provincial capital, a large fortune. "Overnight," she would state, "I became a celebrity."[59] Marriage proposals—five in three months—began pouring in. Yet Gabrielle persisted in refusing them, mystifying everyone except her grandfather.

Her hesitation reflected her ambivalence about marriage, which she considered solely a financial arrangement. An only child accustomed to solitude, she viewed marriage as the end of the freedom she reveled in and regarded prospective husbands as unwelcome intruders unfortunately sanctioned by law. Her later recollections of her adolescent feelings about marriage—which inspired in her "a type of instinctive horror"[60]—could be read as an eloquent feminist statement: "The thought that a man would have the right to enter my quarters at any hour, to walk around as if it were his place, to speak to me, and that I was supposed to tolerate him, answer him, and appear delighted to see him there, gave me shivers."[61] To Gabrielle marriage equaled slavery. Yet most women accepted this servitude, she reasoned, in exchange for both the respectable title "Madame" and the "right" to give birth. Gabrielle herself longed to have children. And assessing her particular situation, she anticipated another, more odious form of enslavement if she did not marry. Gonneville's death, she feared, would leave her the defenseless prisoner of her mother and grandmother. Given the alternative, Gabrielle deemed marriage the lesser of two evils, a chance to free herself from the matriarchy she so despised.

In the spring of 1867 eighteen-year-old Gabrielle met her future husband. She was in Paris with her mother as guests of Henry de Riancey, press magnate and director of the monarchist newspaper *L'Union*. Marie had met Riancey through the publisher of *La Mode*, a women's magazine in which her stories appeared. Riancey's son Adrien, who was also a journalist, had stayed at Gonneville's home while covering the empress' visit to Nancy. At the publisher's home in Passy, Gabrielle was introduced to the entire Riancey clan. She met Riancey's sister, her husband, comte Alfred René de Martel de Janville, and his three children from a first marriage, which had ended in 1852 with his wife's death. The contrast between husband and wife shocked Gabrielle. While Riancey's sister, "a veritable monster of ugliness,"[62] needed to be transported on a chair due to a mysterious illness, her fifty-seven-year-old husband exuded an air of robust good health. Gabrielle would affectionately remember her future father-in-law as "superb. Very tall, strongly built, with magnificent eyes and very long lashes. He had a distinguished and kind air. He was, in all its purity, the handsome model of a Frenchman from the West."[63] This handsome "westerner" was in fact a Norman who could trace his ancestry back to the thirteenth century. Like the Gonnevilles, the ancestors of Alfred René de Martel de Janville—Legitimists all—had served the monarchy in the royal bureaucracy and armies in Normandy. In 1837 Alfred married sixteen-year-old Clementine de Cavelier de Montgeon. Official documents refer to the count as *propriétaire*, living comfortably off the *rentes* from his land in Paris and Normandy.[64]

Of Alfred's three children, all of whom were present at the Riancey soirée, it was the youngest and only girl who immediately captivated Gabrielle. Despite her large mouth, "incorrect" nose, and thick eyebrows, sixteen-year-old Marie de Martel de Janville seemed to Gabrielle "ravishing."[65] Her gorgeous skin, dark, wavy hair, and healthy appearance attracted Gabrielle, as did her sense of humor. But what enchanted her most was the girl's admission that she was "a kind of savage, raised as a boy ... "[66] Of Marie de Martel de Janville's two brothers, only the elder appealed to Gabrielle. Marie François Roger de Martel de Janville was born on 9 March 1848 in Paris, one year earlier than his future wife. Educated by a private tutor, an abbé, he enjoyed the same leisured sportsman's life as had Gabrielle's father. It is likely that Gabrielle felt strongly about the Norman *rentier*, although she would later claim she loved him because he resembled his sister

Marie.[67] Roger was not unattractive, but an 1869 photograph presents a terribly vacuous-looking young man. He sits in a chair wearing a double-breasted suit with one elbow resting on a railing behind him and his fingers supporting his tilted head. Despite this romantic pose, his gaze is stupid rather than intense. A small, finely groomed mustache rests above a slightly open mouth, while slick, wavy hair, parted in the middle, hangs ungracefully over a protruding ear.

After meeting in the spring of 1867, Roger, his brother and sister, and the Rianceys visited Gabrielle and Marie in Nancy that summer. Roger impressed his future bride with his equestrian abilities, and the group enjoyed racetrack outings. In the two years between the couple's first encounter and their marriage, Roger decided to make himself useful. Given his lack of professional training and his family background, the army seemed a likely choice. In 1869 he made plans to enlist in his village's National Guard unit. A letter to a superior officer contained Roger's request to be named company captain, a request, he asserted, solely motivated by patriotism: "My desire to be useful to my country, and the respectability of my family, make me hope that you will receive my request favorably."[68] Despite Roger's confident tone, a postscript indicates his hesitation about asking for this rank. If the unit would not name him captain, he would accept the rank of lieutenant.

Roger—who is now nothing more than an archival blip—would be Gabrielle's husband for more than half a century. Yet he was far from the charismatic older officer of her fantasies. Rather, he was a young man the same age as Gabrielle, from a similar milieu and sharing similar tastes for horses, the Norman countryside, and society balls. Little, really, seemed to unite the headstrong, opinionated Gabrielle and her conventional future husband. Again the chasm between dream and reality opened even wider for her.

If Gabrielle's marriage to Roger was to be almost banal, irrelevant—she devotes only one line to it in the four volumes of her recollections—her wedding date had great symbolic importance for her. Surely it was her conscious choice to wed in Nancy on 2 December 1869, the anniversary of Napoleon's coronation at Notre-Dame, of his legendary victory at Austerlitz the next year, and of Napoleon III's coup d'état. Like her birth, Gabrielle's marriage transpired under the sign of Napoleon.

III

La Comtesse de Martel

1870–1879

Woe to that man through whom scandal comes.

Matt. 18:7

The Terrible Year

For the "victim of December second," as Gabrielle jokingly referred to herself, the imperial fête continued unabated after her marriage. She did not imagine that before the end of 1870 France would be militarily bludgeoned and then occupied by the Prussian army, losing Alsace and part of Lorraine. For Gabrielle the violins played on and the couples waltzed, though perhaps more frenetically than before. These were the empire's last strains.

After their wedding in Nancy, Gabrielle and Roger spent a few months in Paris. They stayed in a town house owned by comte de Martel père in the aristocratic enclave of the faubourg Saint-Germain. In Paris Gabrielle strolled, visited art exhibits, went riding in the Bois de Boulogne, and relaxed in pâtisseries with her sister-in-law Marie, also a newlywed. When neither with Marie (seldom) nor with Roger (often), Gabrielle sought out such new acquaintances as the sculptor Carpeaux (for whom she posed as a nymph) or the promising lawyer Edgar Demange. Married to one of Gabrielle's childhood friends from Nancy, Demange was also the son of a regiment comrade of Gonneville's. At the moment he was involved in the defense of the emperor's cousin, prince Pierre Bonaparte, who was accused of shooting the journalist Victor Noir. Nearly three decades later, Gabrielle would again encounter Demange, this time defending a new client, Alfred Dreyfus.

The couple's return to Nancy in early 1870 did not interrupt their life of leisure. While Roger indulged his two passions, hunting and horseback riding, Gabrielle paid social calls or spent time with her grandfather. The couple's placid routine might have gone on indefinitely. Instead it was suddenly halted. Disembarking at the Nancy train station on 19 July 1870, after riding in the nearby countryside, Gabrielle and Roger were stunned to see people scattering in all directions, panic-stricken. A friend told them the news: France had declared war on Prussia.

The war's outbreak found Gabrielle in the same state as most of the French: aghast and unprepared. She had known "very vaguely"[1] that the French government had opposed the offer of the Spanish throne to a Hohenzollern relative of the Prussian king, an offer that was eventually declined. But she never suspected that what seemed merely a diplomatic blunder—precipitated by the French envoy's request to Prussia for guarantees against future aggression and worsened by William I's response, the insulting "Ems telegram"—would result in war. The French had not even completed their disorganized mobilization when the Prussian armies, almost twice their size, crossed the border. Prussia's military strength, already evident during its 1866 victory over Austria at Sadowa, surpassed that of the French, whose copper cannons rattled feebly against the new Krupp artillery. French political and military leadership also seemed incompetent beside the disciplined Prussian staff. Although France's war minister had assured the parliament of the army's preparedness, patriotism was insufficient ammunition against the invader. After only six weeks of combat, France was defeated, the emperor captured, the empire crushed.

Like many French, especially those from Alsace and northern Lorraine (annexed to Germany in May 1871),[2] Gabrielle was uprooted by the war and occupation. At the start of hostilities, Roger, now a captain, was mobilized in Normandy. Gabrielle was obliged to accompany her husband despite her reluctance to leave her grandparents, who were encircled by Prussian troops stationed outside Nancy. Yet the patriarchal Gonneville, regarded as a de facto intermediary between local residents and the occupier, could not abandon his sinking ship of Nancy. And as he sternly advised his granddaughter once again, duty dictated that she obey her husband. "It is in Normandy that your husband will be mobilized and will probably remain . . . It is thus to Normandy that you must go . . . "[3]

For most of the period between the onset of the war, in July 1870, and the ending of the Commune, in May 1871, Gabrielle stayed in her father-in-law's château in Normandy, periodically venturing to Nancy and Paris. Receiving little news from the front, she continued to believe in an eventual French victory, even after Napoleon III's capture at Sedan and maréchal Bazaine's surrender at Metz in the fall of 1870 sealed the French defeat. Her months at Janville consisted of a dull routine. As Prussian troops continued their march on Paris, she went riding with her father-in-law (a captain in the National Guard), wrote letters, and drew caricatures, evoking the vicissitudes of life at Janville, for a satirical "review" edited by her new in-laws. Marie arrived from Nancy at the outset of a cold, difficult winter. Worshipers attending Christmas midnight mass in Janville's chapel saw rats gnawing the candles. From Janville Gabrielle traveled frequently to visit Roger, who was garrisoned in Rouen and Le Havre. One of her husband's companions, an elegant-looking soldier who was "very tall, very blond, very slender,"[4] impressed her. Félix Faure would become a friend, and eventually a president of the Third Republic. In Roger's absence, the dutiful daughter-in-law accompanied René on a hunting jaunt to Caen. Here they learned about the Commune, whose effects Gabrielle would witness firsthand the next May.

For Gabrielle, as for most French who survived the trauma that Hugo branded as "the terrible year," 1870 marked a profound rupture in the nation's history. While the material consequences of the defeat—annexation of Alsace-Lorraine, partial occupation of French territory, and an indemnity totaling five billion francs—were damaging enough, the psychological and spiritual effects were disastrous. The military debacle and the empire's ensuing collapse, compounded by the birth of a dynamic new empire across the Rhine, called into question for many French such notions as progress, patriotism, and civilization—cornerstones of French national identity.[5]

Without question, 1870 represented a turning point in Gabrielle's personal history as well. Her twentieth year coincided with the defeat. Yet, unlike many members of this war generation, she was not obsessed with revenge against Germany. While chagrined by the French loss, she felt that France's real enemy lay not without but within. Indeed, France's military defeat seemed to her a less ominous fate than the empire's demise. The proclamation of the Republic on 4 September 1870 would have an important double effect on her. First, it would fuel her personal imperial mythology, which rested on both the period's charm and the regime's prestige, incarnated for her in its authoritarian father figure, the emperor. Second, the change of regime would also lead Gabrielle to align herself with a new, hybrid group of "patriots," born of discontent. Opposed to the messianic patriotism stemming from the Revolution, this nationalism would define itself in terms of exclusivity and ethnocentrism. It would focus on French "decadence" and on rooting out the country's "internal enemies." Although Gabrielle's nationalism would not erupt until the late 1880s, with the Boulangist episode, its roots lay both in the French defeat and in the passage from empire to republic.

So blatant was Gabrielle's fraternization with Prussian soldiers during the occupation that many acquaintances soon shunned her. By coincidence, the Prussian officers quartered at Janville had known Bacourt during his diplomatic tenure in Baden. This connection provided a starting point for polite exchanges, in French and German, between the Martel de Janvilles and the enemy soldiers, although Gabrielle would later admit to having felt "constrained"[6] by the situation. Her petite frame, short skirts, and mane of blond curls convinced the officers she was a girl. The Prussians' parting gift to the twenty-one-year-old newlywed was a doll. In Nancy, which was overrun by German troops when Gabrielle returned there in April 1871, residents considered her cordial behavior toward the occupier almost criminal. Most Nancy civilians, intensely Germanophobic, purposely crossed the street on sighting an approaching Prussian. Gabrielle and Roger, by contrast, cheerily saluted the passing victors. Gabrielle even made neighborly calls on Prussian military governor baron von Manteuffel. Uneasily observing his granddaughter's actions, Gonneville rebuked Gabrielle for her tactless manner, which was already provoking suspicion among the local populace.

The behavior many Nancy residents perceived as blatant collaboration with the enemy was, in Gabrielle's view, wholly in keeping with her personal and familial values. As a girl she had made annual summer trips to the residence of Bacourt's former patron, Queen Augusta, in Coblenz. These stays perpetuated a tradition of friendship between her family and Prussian military and aristocratic elites. If France did have a hereditary enemy, Gabrielle reasoned, it was not the military might of Germany but the dynastic diplomacy of Austria. Personified by the Metternichs, Austria had been "conspiring" since the 1815 Congress of Vienna to keep European thrones Bonaparte-free.

To the ethnocentric Gabrielle, the supreme menace to France lay not across the Vosges but within the country's own borders. As she later recalled, the emperor's capture at Sedan and the Republic's simultaneous proclamation in Paris stunned her: "I was stupefied. I hadn't thought of that! . . . It had never occurred to me for an instant that because the Emperor had been beaten he would be driven away."[7] On her arrival in Paris in late September 1870, she was shocked by the aggressive behavior of the mob in the place de la Concorde, which was determined to beat up former imperial ministers and dump them in the Seine in a symbolic brutalization of the empire. The moment the Republic was declared, Gabrielle would assert, she became "passionately Imperialist,"[8] as if to supplant the undeniable political reality of the present with a personal myth of the past.

A new political configuration indeed confronted Gabrielle when she again returned to Paris in May 1871 to check on the condition of her father-in-law's house after the fall of the Commune. With the Bonapartists discredited, the National Assembly elected on 8 February 1871 was dominated by a monarchist majority opposed to continuing the war against Prussia. The Republic's first president was Adolphe Thiers, the man notorious for one of his initial acts in office: repression of the Commune. He incarnated everything Gabrielle detested. The Legitimist in her hated the Orleanist. The aristocrat despised the bourgeois parvenu. Observing Louis-Philippe's former minister at a public mass for victims of the Commune, she felt convinced that Thiers was secretly engineering the return of the Orleanist pretender, the comte de Paris.[9] Given this prospect—"a return of this lame monarchy"[10]—even the Republic seemed preferable to her.

Gabrielle's antipathy toward Thiers may have made her sympathetic to the Parisian Communards, who were battling both the Prussian invader and Thiers' Government of National Defense. Although she remained in Normandy during the Commune's brief existence, Gabrielle most likely reacted to news about it with the same mixture of admiration and suspicion she would later express toward other popular movements. She nourished a secret affinity for the Communards' violent energy and their stand against capitalism (in the case of the extreme left-wing faction of the Communards). Yet she also feared their penchant for democracy as well as, perhaps, their less-than-aristocratic social origins. With the impetus of Boulangism, a portion of this extreme Left would fuse with part of the Right to form a front united against the bourgeoisie, a virulent nationalist Right.

Above all, Gabrielle persisted in feeling that France was infected from within. What she sensed in 1870 was a profound national void that needed filling. The most obvious loss for her was material. The Paris she returned to in May 1871 barely resembled the sumptuous imperial playground of her adolescence. Cadavers littered the square in front of the Hôtel de Ville, the Cour des Comptes smoldered, and the Tuileries lay in ruins. Yet to her delight some traces of the fantasy world of Napoleon III's court did outlive the Commune. Once the capital was cleared of the last reminders of the hecatomb, nothing stopped her from dining at the trendy Café Anglais on the boulevard des Italiens, riding in the Bois, or catching the latest production at the Gymnase Dramatique. And a military review she attended in June 1871, given added luster by the participation of such imperial stars as maréchal Mac-Mahon and général Galliffet, convinced her, as a latter-day imperialist, that the empire's martial allure had not been tarnished by the defeat: "True, we had been beaten by the Prussians. But this army created an intense impression of power and life, and the vanquished country displayed vigor, wealth, elegance, and joy."[11]

Gabrielle was not completely deluded in sensing the empire's persistence during the period she would memorialize as "the joyous childhood of the Third Republic." Despite the Republic's almost pro forma proclamation, the mere existence of both the emperor and the prince imperial left open the possibility of a Bonapartist comeback. In 1871 many French citizens also believed another monarchist restoration was imminent. The country's ruling elites, moreover, had changed little since the empire. The "monarchist republic" constituted a transitional period when Bonapartists could reasonably, albeit temporarily, work up fantasies of an imperial revival.

The ambiance of the imperial fête could be approximated. But Gabrielle could not immediately compensate for a much more tragic loss: Gonneville's death on 28 September 1872, followed less than four months later by that of Napoleon III. To Gabrielle the sudden death of her grandfather, "this friend of every instant, whom I worshiped,"[12] was, as she later remarked, "my first great sorrow."[13] Although Gonneville still seemed fit at nearly ninety, he had been "terribly shaken"[14] by the defeat. With his death, Gabrielle lost a friend, a fantasy lover, and a father, replacing the one already deceased and grieved: "It was my happy childhood that was vanishing. Only he had had any influence over me, and I had, with him, absolute confidence and abandon that I well knew I would never find with anyone else."[15]

But the simultaneous passing of these two symbolic fathers—one personal, the other national—meant more to Gabrielle than the closing of her childhood. The two deaths, coming in the wake of the empire's own murder/suicide, made explicit to her the destruction of her ideal type of authority: charismatic, authoritarian, military, and "male." A political as well as a gender model was gone. And these absences provided a starting point for her own quest. Most of her later life and works would involve the pursuit, internalization, and reconstruction of specific models of authority and masculinity, personified by her father and grandfather and epitomized politically by Napoleon. Gabrielle would project these personal fantasies onto the national plane. Conversely, she would internalize various periods of national history. Striving to combat a perceived "feminization" of France, she would campaign actively to restore to her country the type of "male" authority she felt was lacking in her own life.

Bazaine: A Soldier's Honor

Gabrielle's newfound vocation as an apologist for the empire and the type of male authority it exemplified for her received a new impetus three years after the defeat with the court-martial of maréchal François Achille Bazaine. Gabrielle had met Bazaine in 1864 when he came to Nancy as army commander. He was already an imperial celebrity, but his record of fidelity to the empire was far from spotless. He had won his heroic reputation for his part in two legendary imperial battles, Sébastopol and Solferino. Promoted to commander-in-chief, he next found himself in Mexico in 1862, a member of the utopian debt-collecting mission that served as a pretext for Napoleon III's attempted replacement of the existing regime with a French puppet government. Yet Bazaine worked surreptitiously to depose the very ruler Napoleon III himself had placed on the Mexican throne. Austrian Archduke Maximilian faced a firing squad once French troops departed. Disgraced, Bazaine returned to France, but the emperor quickly forgave him. In 1864 Bazaine even received the coveted marshal's baton, as well as responsibility for all eventual military operations in Lorraine. He thus took up temporary quarters in Nancy.

As usual, Gonneville and his family befriended the new military officer-in-residence on his arrival in the capital. And Bazaine tried to encourage a friendship between Gabrielle and his Mexican wife. At fifty-four, Bazaine, a short, corpulent, goateed man, had married seventeen-year-old Pepita de la Peña. Gabrielle, thrilled to improve her connections with the imperial family, became the maréchale's unofficial escort and interpreter. For Gonneville's granddaughter, Bazaine's tenure in the capital of Lorraine brought to the provinces a bit of imperial éclat.

But the events of August 1870 quickly destroyed Bazaine's reputation for bravery and sangfroid. The Prussian offensive of late July devastated Lorraine, persuading the emperor and maréchal Bazaine, who was stationed in Metz, to each lead their troops west to Verdun to counter the next assault. When the two armies separated at Gravelotte, however, Bazaine did not try to join the other French armies in the region. Instead, he quickly retreated to Metz and stayed there as the enemy army slowly encircled his troops. Informed of Bazaine's plight, maréchal Mac-Mahon's army set off from Châlons to reach Metz. But the Prussians beat him back at Sedan, where they captured Napoleon III. For the next two months, despite one desultory attempt to break the Prussian siege, Bazaine sat passively in Metz. Then, on 27 October, he capitulated.

Victim or traitor? It was this question that the military tribunal addressed in October 1873, with the opening of the unprecedented trial for treason of an imperial marshal. Gabrielle attended the trial, the first of many she would enliven.

She temporarily pitched camp in the Paris apartment of her grandmother, who had left Nancy after Gonneville's death. With her mother, who also kept lodgings in the capital now, Gabrielle traveled daily by coach to Versailles, where proceedings had been shifted for fear of a possible riot in Paris. On arriving, they saw that the colonnade separating the two Trianon palaces had been converted into a makeshift courtroom. One of the palaces served as Bazaine's temporary prison.

As Gabrielle would learn from testimony read during the trial, the committee investigating the circumstances of Metz's fall accused Bazaine of a capitulation unparalleled in French history. The marshal, the committee charged, had fraternized with the enemy while neglecting the conditions of his own wounded. He had surrendered French flags, ammunition, and weapons instead of destroying his matériel. What had motivated Bazaine's suicidal strategy, his detractors argued, enraging Gabrielle, was not the impending strangulation of his army by the Prussians. Instead, Bazaine was reacting to political developments in France itself, specifically to the Republic's proclamation on 4 September. Rather than associate himself with an eventual "republican" victory over Prussia, the sometimes faithful imperial knight preferred to sabotage his army to protest the change of regime. To many Bazaine's "schizophrenia"—his "patriotic" betrayal of the empire he had already once betrayed—was incomprehensible.

But to unequivocal advocates of Bazaine like Gabrielle and Marie, the marshal was not a criminal but a victim of circumstance. His retreat to Metz? A tactical error, a case of unsound judgment. Once encircled by the Prussians, according to this version, he had no choice but to surrender to avert a slaughter. Thus to Marie, defending the hapless marshal in an 1874 pamphlet, "Bazaine . . . was unfortunate and not guilty!"[16] Gabrielle would later rephrase the same opinion: "The marshal was not incapable; he just wasn't up to it, that's all. Superbly brave, he lacked clairvoyance and tact."[17] For Gabrielle could not dissociate Bazaine from the empire. And the empire of her youth—and her imagination—was beyond reproach. Once again, Gabrielle and her mother protested, the new republic, not the empire, represented the potentially most heinous criminal in this affair. Those sharing this opinion—"Better Bismarck than Blanqui"—could find an advocate in Marie, who publicly damned the government of 4 September as "a far greater disgrace than the invasion by foreigners."[18] And if, to Gabrielle and Marie, Bazaine's association with the "virtuous" empire established his innocence, so did his very profession. The Soldier, given his keen sense of duty and devotion to country, was to these women necessarily, almost organically, infallible.

Upholding this credo, Gabrielle's mother sought out and procured for Bazaine the testimony of Prussian officers involved in the capture of Metz. A presumed international code of military ethics, Marie thought, would work to help exonerate the marshal. Her success in eliciting this enemy testimony reveals her subtle, ever-scheming persistence. But it also reflects her blindness to the troubled state of Franco-German relations in the early 1870s. As with her initial publications, Marie first sought an intermediary who, like père Lagrange of Orléans, could help her reach the top echelons, in this case not of the ecclesiastical hierarchy but rather of both the German military and the imperial court. In February 1873, eight months before the trial, she wrote to Field Marshal von Manteuffel, the amiable occupier of Nancy, who had directed two battles against Bazaine before his retreat to Metz. She asked Manteuffel to forward a letter to the German emperor, William I, asking the emperor's permission to allow his nephew, Prince Frederick-Charles, a former army commander during the siege of Metz, to testify in Bazaine's defense. Her plan succeeded, and the prince himself sent word from Berlin that he had just expedited to Bazaine's lawyer "a declaration that will undoubtedly quash the unjust accusations against the marshal."[19]

The German prince's testimony would not change Bazaine's fate. Yet the warm, often coquettish, correspondence between Marie and the two German officers outlasted the trial. In a long letter to "Madame la comtesse," Manteuffel reaffirmed that Bazaine had actually "saved" the French army by capitulating. He praised the marshal's conduct as "that of a patriot and a chevalier."[20] Quoting Napoleon, he justified his surprising defense of Bazaine simply by citing the cessation of hostilities between the two countries. Later that year Frederick-Charles echoed Manteuffel, declaring his "great esteem" for Bazaine and thanking Marie for the opportunity to express it publicly.[21]

But the most revealing—and prophetic—letter in this exchange concerned Marie's own behavior throughout the trial. It came later in 1874 from Manteuffel, who teased the comtesse de Mirabeau for her combativeness: "Everything you tell me about maréchal Bazaine interested me, and I'd like to know how many duels Madame la comtesse would have fought, with her noble frankness, if she had indeed been a Lieutenant. The fact is amusing and characteristic."[22] Manteuffel's whimsical image of Marie as a dueling lieutenant was indeed "characteristic." For this was not the last time either Marie or Gabrielle would be compared to, or even mistaken for officers. As the bemused Manteuffel implied, Marie's (and later her daughter's) partisanship and aggressiveness seemed to him more befitting a lieutenant than a lady. Once again Marie's "masculinity" was being evoked, as Gabrielle's would be. And both women would sometimes aspire to and at other times reject the characterization.

If the performance of mother and daughter during Bazaine's trial established for observers their "virility," their hero Bazaine's own "maleness" was not much in evidence. He was tired and pale from imprisonment in the Trianon palace, unrelieved by the ministrations of his faithful Pepita, hurrying every day from the convent to which she had retired. Gabrielle, observing Bazaine from her post at the back of the overcrowded courtroom when the marshal first entered it on 6 October 1873, thought he looked "disastrous."[23] She knew immediately he would be found guilty. Over the next two months, the nine generals judging the marshal, in addition to spectators and the press, heard testimony from 272 prosecution and 60 defense witnesses, including officers, government ministers, and of course Prince Frederick-Charles. Despite Marie's avowed patriotic motives in procuring the prince's testimony, much of the press mocked his deposition and considered it proof of Bazaine's overt collaboration with Prussia.

On 10 December Bazaine, convinced of his innocence, heard a guilty verdict.

His crime—capitulation without exhausting all possible means of defense—called for military demotion and death. Given his previous record, however, President Mac-Mahon commuted his fellow marshal's punishment to a fine and a twenty-year prison sentence. Bazaine was exiled to the island of Sainte-Marguerite. Yet he soon engineered a nocturnal escape by rowboat and reached Spain, where he died in 1888, abandoned by the imperial family, destitute.

For Gabrielle Bazaine's trial gave form to many previously nebulous issues: the integrity of the French army; the record of the collapsed regime; the relation between domestic and foreign politics; as well as the broader meanings of masculinity and femininity, guilt and innocence. These issues would resurface for her a quarter century later during the Dreyfus Affair. But then her sympathies would no longer lie with the purported traitor, again accused of complicity with Germany. For a new constellation of symbols would surround the person of capitaine Dreyfus, all of them odious to Gabrielle. She would see in the Affair a sinister antithesis of the Bazaine trial.

Marie: A Lady's Virtue

To many French citizens, Bazaine's court-martial seemed a morality play, dramatizing the fall from grace and punishment of a figurehead endowed with a supreme national responsibility. Yet the trial was also a drama about sexuality, presenting the country with the marshal's progressive emasculation. Stripped of his traditional male attributes—money, power, strength, and such symbolic accoutrements as the eagle-studded marshal's baton—Bazaine in 1874 seemed only a frail reminder of the imperial icon of a decade earlier.

Bazaine's "betrayal" of certain accepted gender roles parallels that of his archsupporter, Marie de Mirabeau. In the years following Bazaine's condemnation, Gabrielle's mother diversified her literary production, abandoning the Christian anthology and the moralizing tracts with which she began her career in favor of other genres still theoretically out-of-bounds for women: political propaganda, drama, humorous sketches, and journalism. This literary eclecticism, explained by Marie's mercenary and worldly rather than aesthetic considerations, earned her a reputation as an "unfeminine" author. Field Marshal Manteuffel's would-be lieutenant alternately hid this label and exploited it to scandalous advantage. Through these incursions into obscure regions of the literary and publishing worlds, Marie would again break ground for her daughter. She would become both a model for Gabrielle in her thinking about herself, and later a rival.

In the 1870s Marie produced pamphlets and novels that identified her as a minor political propagandist, antidemocratic and Legitimist. Whereas her daughter admired the Communards, Marie felt nothing but revulsion toward this rabble. The martyr-hero of *Henri de l'Espée*, "this perfect model of a gentleman of yore"[24] according to Marie, volunteered for combat in 1870. Appointed prefect of Saint-Etienne in March 1871, his desire to help local workers was rewarded only with brutality. For in a show of characteristic ingratitude, the Saint-Etienne

Communards murdered the patriotic Frenchman, revealing, in Marie's words, "the personal hatred that the people almost always feels toward the one who governs them."[25] Other pamphlets focused on the tragic destinies of Norman Legitimists during the 1793 Terror. In *Le Baron d'Aché* Marie traces the life of this exemplary young Norman, "[who] had no other cult on earth than that of the royal family."[26] Yet his heroism earns only betrayal and assassination, like that of *Elisabeth de Faudoas*, a fifteen-year-old guillotined before the bloodthirsty crowd, and in sight of her mother, who dies instantly of shock. Gonneville's turbulent childhood is the inspiration for *Le Comte de Belzunce*, a pamphlet detailing the stabbing and mutilation of a Caen lieutenant by a bloodthirsty crowd that cooks and devours Belzunce's heart. The retelling of these Gothic horror stories in the context of post-1870 France underscores Marie's affirmation of a bridge between the immense "collective sins" of 1793 and 1870. In both cases "un-French" (revolutionary and democratic) elements had tormented the "real," Legitimist France. The most recent civil war, the Commune, was only the most serious reverberation from that irreparable geological fault of the Revolution. Thus was historical evolution envisioned by Marie, self-appointed denunciator of "crimes" against the Bourbon monarchy and fabulist of a Legitimist paradise regained.

Mercifully, 1876 marked both the beginning and end of Marie's short career as a dramatist. A front-page review by the renowned drama critic of *Le Temps*, Francisque Sarcey, chronicled the disastrous opening night, at the Gymnase Dramatique, of Marie's *Châteaufort*. The play might never have been staged but for the playwright's dogged persistence. "The author," Sarcey revealed, "has moved heaven and earth to bring this play to the stage."[27] Although accepted for production, the play's text was modified by censors, for Marie had the poor judgment to give her unscrupulous gigolo-hero a title. Sarcey commented that such "immorality" seemed unfitting for a woman. But he attributed Marie's crudeness to her lack of experience in "softening" reality for bourgeois audiences: "[T]his woman is a novice [who] innocently, naïvely brought to the stage what she had seen in the world."[28] The critic urged the aspiring playwright to respect the conventions of the stage by injecting a dose of "dramatic verisimilitude"[29] into her *own* reality. Nevertheless, the reality of July 1876 looked bleak for Marie, as *Châteaufort* did not survive past opening night. "The play by Madame la comtesse de Mirabeau," Sarcey announced, "thus failed its first evening; and it does not seem that it will ever recover from this deplorable fall."[30]

Having thus transgressed the boundaries of virtue and vice delineated by bourgeois drama, the comtesse de Mirabeau next set out to find a new home for her unethical aristocrats. She succeeded in this the following year, when she joined the team of talented literary and artistic contributors to *La Vie Parisienne*. Founded in 1863, the popular weekly for which Marie now regularly wrote prolonged the mood of pleasure-seeking and frivolity often associated with the Second Empire. The creator of this mildly licentious concoction was Marcelin Planat, illegitimate son of Nestor Roqueplan, a famous Second Empire wit and dandy. Marcelin himself had known the imperial court, having organized theater parties and masked balls for the emperor and empress. The newspaper's lavishly illustrated pages advised readers on the appropriate outfit for a stroll down the Champs-Elysées or pointed out what distinguished "real chic" from "fake chic." Dialogues, reviews, fashion notes, and gossip were offered by regular contributors dressed in such pseudonyms as "Nitchevo," "Sahib," "Lone-Lone," "Robin Goodfellow," and "Kamoushka." Part tattler, part etiquette manual, *La Vie Parisienne* gave readers a glimpse of both high society and demimonde.

An ambitious socialite, Marie seemed well chosen to write the naughty fluff provided by *La Vie Parisienne*. Baptized by Marcelin as "Zut," "ZZZ," "ZX," "Chut," "Tom," and "Robert," she drew on her own experience in serving up sketches and dialogues featuring aristocratic and military characters and set against such backdrops as the racetrack or the Opéra. In "Mon Régiment," "Poisson d'avril," and similar pieces, her fanciful neuter or male pen name served as a protective device. Writing of any sort—and especially what Marie described as the *"slightly risqué* style"[31] found in Marcelin's pages—was not considered a respectable and appropriate activity for an aristocratic woman "of virtue." The pious readers of Marie's *Prières et pensées chrétiennes* (not to mention Archbishop Dupanloup) would have been scandalized to discover the true identity of Zut.

Aware of the tone of her articles, Marie deliberated before choosing a publisher for a proposed collection of her *Vie Parisienne* pieces. Marcelin had suggested the possibility of an anthology to his protégée, believing it potentially profitable to both author and patron. Yet Marie suspected that the firm of Pierre-Paul Didier, publisher of several of her more "serious" novels, would never risk its reputation as the founder of the "Bibliothèque d'éducation morale" by sponsoring the works of Chut and Zut. She was thus obliged to find a less prudish publisher. Overestimating her talents as usual (and acting on a tip from Marcelin), she decided to sound out the innovative firm of Pierre-Jules Hetzel, erstwhile imperial proscript and publisher most notably of Hugo, Sand, and Verne. Marie knew that a decade earlier Hetzel had published *Entre nous*, a collection of titillating stories by Gustave Droz, one of Chut's *Vie Parisienne* colleagues. Hetzel's prestige did not daunt her. In January 1878 she initiated contact with the publisher, boldly scheduling an interview which, she stressed, she would have great difficulty changing, for "my time [is] so much *taken up* that I am annoyed when I make a trip for nothing."[32]

Once granted an appointment (although not at her suggested time), Marie wrote again, explaining that her purpose was to procure the promise of a contract for her collection. After chronicling her relations with Marcelin, she implicitly acknowledged the popularity of her articles and, with a coyness natural to her, intimated to Hetzel the degree of her prestige: "I do not dare tell you that my articles are successful," wrote Marie. "I would seem a *very vain* person."[33] If not precisely critical successes, as Marie claimed, Zut's contributions to *La Vie Parisienne* had at least piqued its readers' curiosity by their mysterious "paternity." According to Marie, their racy contents and military characters had convinced Marcelin's customers that the author camouflaged by the enigmatic pen name was in fact a military man. "They have been attributed to an officer," Marie let it be known, referring to her articles, "and *the officer is being sought.*"[34] But a careful reading of *La Vie Parisienne* from 1877 and 1878 reveals no trace of the legendary notice to the officer requesting him to collect his paycheck chez Marcelin. Marie's explanation of the "procreation" of her articles by a mythical officer was thus pure fiction, a fiction that would be adapted and exploited by her daughter.

Preoccupied with her career in 1878, Marie felt it prudent to downplay that aspect of her writing readers might perceive as unfeminine. She urged Hetzel to conceal "the officer's" identity in the interest of the author's future. Marcelin had in fact suggested she publish under the pseudonym she had used for several articles in *Le Figaro* and *Paris-Journal*: Aymar de Flagy. Half-begging, half-commanding, Marie requested: "I beg you to keep *this secret.* . . . The articles I write are *scarcely feminine*, and if I were found out, my pen would be paralyzed."[35] But Marie had no cause to worry. Hetzel did not reveal Chut's secret, nor did he offer her/him a contract. The collections proposed to Hetzel would nevertheless eventually find a publisher, to whom Gabrielle would also owe her own success: Calmann-Lévy.[36]

"Scamp" at *La Vie Parisienne*

Following her mother's lead, Gabrielle launched her own literary career—by accident, she would claim—shortly before leaving Nancy in late 1879.[37] A dinner party at a château in Maxéville, yet another in this "very elegant . . . very boring"[38] milieu she frequented, inspired her first piece of fiction. Gathered around the table was a slice of Nancy's high society: the prefect and his wife, an imperialist general, the *mondain* Charles Haas, as well as others. As the evening wore on, the conversation became less refined, degenerating into an exchange of politely racy stories. Bored, Gabrielle reverted to her childhood habit of observing and mentally recording the scene while coloring it with malice. She then translated her observations, for the first time in her life, into a fictionalized exchange among the dinner guests. Her next decision, coming several days later, was also spontaneous and without thought of remuneration. Why not send her dialogue (omitting her real name and her address) to a familiar publication most likely receptive to the tone of her piece, *La Vie Parisienne*.

The details of Gabrielle's 1879 debut in Marcelin's pages are unclear. No contemporary accounts of it exist, only Gabrielle's contradictory and perhaps deliberately confused reminiscences from a half century later. In one interview she stated that she had signed the dialogue with the enigmatic pen name "Gyp." Yet "Gyp" is absent from *La Vie Parisienne* until the early 1880s. More plausibly, her dialogue was "authored" by "Scamp," a pseudonym perhaps chosen by Gabrielle but more likely by Marcelin himself.[39] Encouraged by her initial success, she sent Marcelin a dozen or so dialogues in the same vein. In these she shifted the settings to include hunting scenes and teas but relied on the same character types: provincial administrators, military personnel, imperialists, aristocrats, assorted dandies and snobs. These dialogues, too, appeared in *La Vie Parisienne* shortly after Marcelin received them. Because of their Nancy settings, the articles' authorship aroused intense curiosity among local residents, who attributed them to Charles Haas or Ferri de Ludre, minor Nancy celebrities known for their trenchant wit. Marcelin was equally mystified by the author's identity. The combination of the articles' garrison-town backdrop and characters and the bold yet elegant handwriting filling up the pile of oversized sheets consumed for each dialogue determined Marcelin's conclusion: as in the case of Marie, he presumed the author was in fact an aristocratic officer afraid of compromising himself.[40]

Gabrielle would give conflicting accounts of what happened next. According to one version of her story, Marcelin sent her a written summons, inviting "the person who signs Gyp . . . to stop by our office."[41] In another the frustrated publisher inserted a notice in his own publication at the end of 1879, calling on "the officer with the large handwriting who sent dialogues from Nancy to collect his pay at the newspaper's office."[42] But no such announcement can be found in *La Vie Parisienne* for 1879. Did Marcelin invent the "officer," or did Gabrielle?

Gabrielle's presumed invention of, or at least insistence on, a fictitious officer-author, like Marie's, is a revealing indicator of her ambivalence toward both her literary profession and her gender. Clearly, her transfer of the responsibility for these fictions to the chimeric soldier reflected her desire, as an aristocratic woman from a traditional background, to dissociate herself from the scandal of pursuing a lucrative profession, especially one as questionable as contributor to *La Vie Parisienne*. She would never profess any particular aptitude for the literary profession, asserting instead that the few options available to her as an aristocratic woman determined her career. "I could only do that [writing] or the circus,"[43] she would say, alluding to her prodigious acrobatic and equestrian abilities as a child. Given these two rather incongruous options, she chose what her family would most easily accept if ever it discovered her identity. And she never ceased to emphasize her "horror" of writing (far less interesting to her than politics, she claimed) or the tedium of "putting black on white": "Writing bores me to tears."[44] Furthermore, she would insist on clearly distinguishing her literary persona, who turned out at least two novels a year for the next half century, from the aristocratic countess who entertained lavishly every Sunday and summered on the Normandy coast.

Yet through the creation of this "other," Gabrielle also realized many of her most profound fantasies about aspiring to a male identity. And given her family's military cult, her choice of an officer as alter-ego was certainly not gratuitous. By "becoming" the soldier, she could symbolically effect the gender switch so desired by her father and grandfather. By emulating the officer, she could fortify the myth of her maleness.

If the fledgling writer was emulating anyone in late 1879, it was, of course, her mother. It was Marcelin's own "Chut!" who had revealed to her daughter the risks and strategies involved in becoming a woman writer. And Marie's 1878 correspondence with Hetzel suggests that the real creator of the officer was in fact the comtesse de Mirabeau. It is quite possible that Gabrielle, in narrating her own literary beginnings, merely retold the legend fabricated and handed down by her mother. The apocryphal soldier's story, finally, conveys something else about Gabrielle besides her ambivalence regarding gender, class, and profession. In 1879 she was thirty, had never written a line, and claimed to be incapable of describing anything but the "real." Yet despite this professed fidelity to pure reality, Gabrielle, the eternal subordinate, had proved herself a potent creator of fictions, both as the author of imaginative prose writings and as a fabulist—for the first time—of her own identity.

As Gabrielle was establishing her literary identity, she was also directing her energies toward fulfilling the responsibilities of a young wife and mother, while still endlessly traveling and socializing. If, as Gabrielle would often assert, she had married for no other reason than to have children, she could by 1877 deem her marriage a success. On 8 September 1873, four years after her wedding, twenty-three-year-old Gabrielle gave birth in Nancy to Aymar-Marie-Roger-Amédée de Martel de Janville, namesake of both Gonneville and Roger. Eighteen months later, in nearby Maxéville, another son was born, whom she named Thierry-Jean-Marie-François. The third child, born in Maxéville two and a half years later, was a girl, Nicole-Renée-Marie-Alice. The birth of her three children was proof to Gabrielle of her "femaleness," at least in the biological sense. As she would write to Maurice Barrès, "I wasn't very womanly? . . . In the 'feminine' sense of the word, perhaps. In the 'animal' sense, I was. The proof is that, instinctively detesting being forced to live as part of a couple, I married because I was determined to have children."[45] Given her growing animosity toward women, however, it is perhaps not surprising that she would later publicize her preference for "raising six sons rather than one daughter."[46]

During the children's infancy, their father was probably often absent, a shadowy presence in the lives of his wife and children. Roger and Gabrielle, ill suited for each other from the outset, tacitly agreed to lead separate lives, a practice not uncommon among the aristocracy. While Gabrielle spent her winters in Nancy attending the theater and her summers at the Normandy beach resort of Tréport, Roger stayed in the Maxéville château pursuing one of his few interests: hunting. Even on vacation, husband and wife stayed apart. At Ems in 1877, they dined at different hours. And while Gabrielle practiced her German, Roger galloped through the woods with Russian noblemen, drunk on champagne, practicing his hunting skills by shooting matchboxes off the tops of his companions' hats.

Gabrielle felt indifferent to her husband's activities. She was equally unimpressed by his extramarital affairs, which he made no effort to conceal. Shortly after her marriage, as she would recall, "Roger was already cheating on me as much as he could, and rather showily."[47] She enjoyed her independence and felt little sentimental attachment to her husband: "It was all the same to me."[48] Furthermore, Roger's infidelities, she thought, sanctioned her own, provided they were with unmarried men: "I considered myself entirely authorized to use my body as I saw fit."[49]

In late June 1879 Gabrielle decided to leave Nancy permanently. The war and occupation had sapped some of the vitality from the city of her childhood and adolescence. Her grandmother and her mother had already moved to the capital. Moreover, as Marie had realized earlier, literary fortunes were made in Paris, not the provinces. Gabrielle would again follow her mother's example in order to support the ever-increasing costs of her household.

A conflicting account reveals a scandalous version of Gabrielle and Roger's departure from Nancy. The narrator of this tale of banishment is Gisèle d'Estoc, née Marie-Elise Courbe. The woman who signed her works Gyz-El was herself a shocking, androgynous writer and painter, as well as the mistress of Maupassant. Born in Nancy in 1863, the flamboyant cross-dresser d'Estoc could comment knowingly and indignantly in her *Récits lorrains* on the cruelty of Nancy's bourgeoisie, especially toward individualistic writers. "The provinces are not kindly toward literary types!" d'Estoc wrote in "De l'inconvénient d'être noix sur le chemin des corneilles" ("On the Disadvantage of Being a Nut Along the Path of Crows"), making a mysterious reference to the "scandal" of Gabrielle.[50] "Provincial society sees only [writers'] singularity, which offends it. The best that they can hope for is indifference, which saves them from persecution."[51]

But Gabrielle was not destined to be ignored. As d'Estoc told her readers,

> this young woman . . . had to flee the fury of an entire city, pursuing her with its sarcasm, its cruel mockery, and its pitiless curiosity. No one thought to look beneath the eccentric appearance that was being branded to discover the profound originality of a budding talent that would soon reveal itself on a much larger stage. In the meantime, people treated this supremely intelligent woman like a nobody.[52]

Brash, smart, and unconventional, friend of the hated Prussians, and daughter of one of the most despised women in Nancy (doubly damned as a single mother and a writer), the young woman some Nancy residents now suspected of being a second-generation *amazone* was virtually being chased from her home. And this was not the last time Gabrielle would be scornfully told to take her leave.

Years after this humiliation, Gabrielle would look back with bitterness at her childhood and realize that she had left unchallenged many of the fictions ruling her life. These included notions of infallibility, both of the military and of a civilized elite, as the Liverdun picnic had already made clear to her. Only after leaving Nancy would she echo d'Estoc's criticism of its repressive and hypocritical society. She would remember Nancy as "a scarcely welcoming province, where several communities formed little groups that were hostile to one another, and where the receptions always seemed ostentatious."[53] In her 1891 novel *Un raté* she would evoke the capital's intolerance of those who strayed from social norms: "For original or eccentric newcomers, the provinces are . . . ferocious. They do not pardon those who attract or seek to attract attention. . . ."[54] And this closed society exhibited no particular mercy toward its own. Gabrielle would describe the daily promenade of Nancy *élégants* on the Pépinière as a brutal competition: "There, people gossip, they scrutinize, they judge, they bad-mouth, and above all, above all, they slander!"[55]

The Third Republic was also entering a new phase the year of Gabrielle's flight to the capital. January 1879 marked the end of the seven-year term of President Mac-Mahon, a "republican monarch" who owed to the empire his reputation as a military hero. His successor was a man of a very different political style: Jules Grévy, a moderate bourgeois republican. Arriving in Paris on 20 June, Gabrielle found another piece of disturbing news: the twenty-three-year-old prince imperial, whom many Bonapartists considered the most likely agent of that dynasty's return, had died in South Africa. Clearly, the Republic's "joyous childhood" was over, Gabrielle mused, and its disturbed adolescence had just begun.

IV

Gyp, "Man of Letters"
1880–1887

Neuilly

Although considered part of Paris when Gabrielle, Roger, and their three children settled there in late 1879, Neuilly-sur-Seine more closely resembled the country than it did the capital. Separated from the neighboring districts of Ternes in 1859 and Levallois-Perret in 1866, Neuilly in 1881 quartered a population of 25,235, roughly half that of Nancy.[1] Cows grazing in vacant pastures heightened the community's rural appearance. "I'm in *the provinces* in Neuilly,"[2] Gyp would often tell friends. Yet its deserted and ill-lit streets, often bordered by hedges concealing splendid mansions, and its nearness to the Bois de Boulogne and the Ile de la Grande Jatte, renowned sites of duels made vivid in Aristide Bruant's cabaret songs, had given Neuilly a sinister reputation. The only public transportation linking it to Paris was a small horse-drawn tram making hourly runs until 10 P.M. Even in 1900 residents of Neuilly rarely saw cars. Nevertheless the town seemed to thrive on its elegant isolation.

Despite its seclusion, Neuilly was affected by the westward shift of the Parisian centers of power during the second half of the nineteenth century. For with the rise of new political and economic elites under the Second Empire and Third Republic, the monolithic aristocratic fortress of the faubourg Saint-Germain was losing some prestige as both a social power center and supreme arbiter of chic. Now rivaling *the* faubourg were other neighborhoods, such as the faubourg Saint-Honoré and the Chaussée d'Antin, fiefs of the political and financial barons. The opulent mansions of these elites, which were signs of their recently acquired wealth, soon gentrified other districts in western Paris: the Champs-Elysées, the Plaine-Monceau, Passy. Neuilly's nearness to western Paris, combined with its quaintness, made it a natural extension of these latest *beaux quartiers*. By the century's end, Neuilly's annual three-week fair, initiated under the Second Empire, had become a society event. All types of carriages drove curious Parisians up the avenue de Neuilly from the Porte Maillot, perhaps stopping to watch Miarka the fighting bear or to glimpse the aging Moulin Rouge can-can dancer La Goulue tame a neurasthenic lion.

Neuilly attracted many nineteenth-century writers, artists, and journalists. Baudelaire had rented an apartment there in 1860. Gautier had lived there, too. It was in Neuilly that Dumas fils had written *La Dame aux camélias*. More recent arrivals included the well-known salon painter Pascal Dagnan-Bouveret and Ernest Judet, editor-in-chief of *Le Petit Journal* and soon of *L'Eclair*, both of whom lived on Gabrielle's street. Toward the century's end, increasing numbers of politicians, press magnates, and socialites—many to become Gabrielle's future friends—settled in Neuilly, attracted by its beauty, tranquility, and proximity to Paris. But for many the choice of residence was also a type of mimesis that reflected both their social and literary ambitions. This was particularly true in the case of certain categories of institutionally marginal writers, such as the popular novelists, especially those from the provinces. For these writers social success, either real or simulated, was a crucial step in legitimizing their literary accomplishments. Yet, as Gabrielle's example will illustrate, few of these writers could actually afford to maintain the ostentatious lifestyle necessitated by their profession. Consequently they were often condemned, to quote one such writer, to a ''gilded misery,'' sometimes resulting in eviction or seizure of property.[3]

When the Martel de Janvilles arrived in 1879, Neuilly in many ways resembled both a remote, charming village and a country club for the wealthy, whose cultural life intersected with—in fact, depended on—that of Paris. Gabrielle's house sat at the corner of the rue de Chézy and the boulevard Bineau, an extension of the elegant avenue de Villiers of Paris' XVIIième arrondissement. The house was square, three stories high, and was covered with ivy and trellises of jasmine and roses. A veranda off the salon opened onto a spacious lawn and garden, where large trees shaded the property. Entering through the main gate, visitors could follow one of two wide paths, ending up either at the house or the stables. Another small pavilion on the grounds soon stored Gabrielle's vast library. The house's interior served as a repository for Gabrielle and Roger's heirlooms. Downstairs, a foyer led to the salon and the dining room, on whose walls hung Aubusson tapestries and faïence dishes. The upper two floors consisted of the living quarters: the children's bedrooms, those of Roger and of Gabrielle, and less comfortable accommodations for the children's governess, tutor, and other servants.

Gabrielle's bedroom and bathroom, which doubled as her study and studio, were always in disarray. A chaise, an armchair, a wardrobe, a dressing table littered with perfume bottles, and a bed with no pillows (Gabrielle insisted on sleeping perfectly horizontally)—these were the only furnishings indicating the suite's function as a bedroom. Otherwise, dozens of bibelots, as well as vases of flowers, ornate fans and screens, and later paintings and caricatures by Forain, Willette, and Gabrielle herself transformed the room into an unwitting gallery of kitsch. In one corner of the room, warmed by the fireplace and facing an open window, was a desk, perpetually cluttered with reams of paper, bottles of ink, and sticks of sealing wax. Here, while the rest of the household slept, was where Gabrielle wrote. Between midnight and five or six in the morning, she covered countless large sheets of paper with her enormous handwriting, forceful strokes penned with a quill or matchstick dipped in violet ink—the writing implements she would never abandon for more modern ones.[4]

La Vie Parisienne and Calmann-Lévy

In Neuilly Gabrielle resumed the literary career she had begun a year earlier at *La Vie Parisienne*. Not until the year after her migration to the capital did Gabrielle-"Scamp" remember to collect her pay from Marcelin. On a Wednesday in 1880, bringing a handwriting sample as identification, she climbed the stairs to Marcelin's first floor office, located on the Champs-Elysées. Here the concierge showed her to one of several individual waiting rooms, dubbed *isoloirs* by Marcelin, where the journal's contributors awaited their employer. Marcelin insisted on this temporary solitary confinement. Former impresario of the imperial court, he respected the aristocratic prejudice against gainful employment as well as the one in favor of a "right to laziness."[5] The *isoloirs*, like his writers' pseudonyms, helped hide their identities from both one another and from the public. They permitted aristocratic authors to maintain an illusion of complete idleness.

Before slipping into her *isoloir*, Gabrielle was sighted by one of Marcelin's newest and youngest recruits, the illustrator and caricaturist Ferdinand Bac, recently arrived in the capital from Austria. Sitting haplessly on a low stool in a room usually reserved for delivery boys, Bac spotted "a small, elegant lady with a pleasing expression on her face, which was pale and thin, shaded by one of those pointed bonnets with ribbons that prolonged awkwardly the charms of the Second Empire."[6] In her gloved hand was a tightly rolled paper tied with a ribbon. Mouselike, she scurried to her hiding place "with the visible desire not to attract attention."[7] But before disappearing, she smiled and let slip a sarcastic comment to her bewildered-looking colleague, one of several younger men she would "adopt." To Gabrielle Bac would always be "my dear collabo" and would share with her, on the day of the Grand Prix, the privilege of watching the procession of carriages along the Champs-Elysées from Marcelin's balcony.[8] At five o'clock Marcelin emerged from his living quarters. Acute dropsy condemned him to long naps and an all-milk diet. He ushered his visitor into his office, where Gabrielle unrolled the paper covered with her handwriting. Marcelin was astonished to realize that this spritely caller was, in fact, the infamous "officer" from Nancy! Without hesitation Marcelin urged his newest staff member to continue writing her attention-getting dialogues.

Despite Marcelin's enthusiasm, for the next two years Gabrielle decreased her production of the dialogues that had amused her so much in 1879. The care of three children and adjustment to Parisian life left little time for writing. In addition, the family could comfortably live off Roger and Gabrielle's income, which consisted of his *rentes* and her dowry. But this financial self-sufficiency did not last long. By 1882 the couple could no longer afford to live like *rentiers*. Within three years of moving to the capital, Roger had succeeded in squandering most of the income generated by his wife's dowry, which was legally his according to the couple's marriage contract.[9] And he showed no inclination for forfeiting the unproductive lifestyle he considered his birthright. Meanwhile, the costs of maintaining the house in Neuilly and its staff, raising the children, and hosting an expanding group of friends were constantly increasing. And Gabrielle's protector Gonneville was dead now, and Marie, supporting herself for over a decade, could not help her daughter financially.

Like her mother a decade earlier, Gabrielle suddenly found herself forced to work, and she returned to Marcelin. Beginning in 1881, each issue of *La Vie Parisienne* featured at least one dialogue by "Scamp." The first dialogue series, illustrated by "Sahib" and sometimes by Gabrielle herself, introduced "Petit Bob," a cocky, slang-speaking eight-year-old who delighted in mocking the pretentious bourgeois–aristocratic society surrounding him. Every week Marcelin's readers opened their paper to read about "Bob au Salon," "Bob au Jardin d'Acclimatation" ("Bob at the Zoo"), "Bob à l'Hippique"("Bob at the Races"), or "Bob très admirateur des femmes" ("Bob Very Admiring of Women").[10] By late 1882 Bob had ceded to Paulette, the equally impertinent, superficially unconventional heroine of *Autour du mariage*, whose marital tribulations kept readers engrossed through mid-1883. Episodes of *Autour du mariage* alternated with those of another series, *Les Chasseurs*, in which visits to the kennel and dinners at the hunting lodge provided the excuse for elaborate flirting and gossiping among aristocratic characters.

Despite her initial literary success, Gabrielle had managed to conceal her real identity from everyone except her equally discreet editors. But in October 1883 "the bomb exploded,"[11] in her own estimation, with the opening of the dramatic adaptation of *Autour du mariage* at the Gymnase Dramatique. In reviewing the play, several critics signaled that the author parading behind various pseudonyms in *La Vie Parisienne* was actually "a woman from the highest society,"[12] a certain madame de Martel. Predictably, the revelation horrified most of Gabrielle's relatives. They knew of *La Vie Parisienne*'s reputation as "corruptor" of young girls and apologist for *le flirt* and other vices. As Gabrielle would later put it: "*La Vie Parisienne* caused great harm and considerable damage in the provinces. It 'tarnished' some young girls. It made too many young women believe that licentiousness, when it is elegant and refined, is perfectly acceptable; that it is necessary—in order to be chic—to admit certain liberties, certain ways of behaving, speaking, and dressing."[13] Gabrielle thus understood—even condoned— her family's anger at her: "The entire 'Faubourg' side of the family shunned me. . . . I thoroughly understood their disapproval, which seemed to me perfectly normal. *I did not like myself very much.*''[14] Unlike Gabrielle's conservative family, Marcelin's public was delighted to have the mystery of the "officer's" identity solved at last. Readers finally realized that this "woman from the best circles of society" was identical with the person masked by the pen name now making regular and eagerly anticipated appearances in Marcelin's pages: Gyp.

Why "Gyp?" The origins of this pseudonym-sobriquet are enigmatic. Was Gyp, as Gabrielle vaguely suggested, a contraction of her first two names, Sibylle and Gabrielle? Did the animal lover Gabrielle, as she also hinted, choose Gyp because it resembled the name of a little dog she remembered from her reading of *David Copperfield*?[15] Or did she have in mind a character from *Uncle Tom's Cabin*, a work she presumably read and enjoyed?[16] A play by Victorien Sardou, which Gabrielle may have seen or read as a child, also includes a character called Jyp. Little evidence, however, supports these attempted explanations. Nor did Gabrielle stress any intentional connection between "Gyp" and "gypsy." In fact, she would certainly have repudiated such an overt reference to bohemia.

A more convincing explanation of the pseudonym lies in its onomatopoetic qualities. Some compared the sound of Gyp to the crack of a whip, others to the powerful release of a slingshot.[17] They found in Gyp a metaphor for Gabrielle's cutting, potentially violent personality. Nor is it possible to overlook the similarity—and the difference—between Gyp and the female prefix "gyno–", although neither Gabrielle nor Marcelin may have been conscious of this linguistic link. Gyp is "gyno" gone wrong, abruptly stunted and redirected by its final consonant. Gyp also seems an oxymoron, distilling the contradictions between the feminine and the masculine aspects of her personality, as defined by the standards of her times, into a neat three letters. Pseudonym as destiny? Whatever the source of its conception, Gyp soon acquired a personality and a male gender. As Marie had shown, this type of gender transgression was often necessary for women writers intent on being taken seriously and disinclined to limit themselves to "lesser" genres. Yet in choosing a male pseudonym, Gabrielle was doing much more than obeying socioliterary convention. She was creating not only a public and literary persona but also a fantasy identity. For the first time, she was choosing a name for herself.[18]

"Gyp" was the signature that adorned the cover of Gabrielle's first book-length work, *Petit Bob*. The 1882 publication of these successful *Vie Parisienne* dialogues marked the first of over sixty collaborative efforts between Gyp and the publishing house of Calmann-Lévy. Between 1882 and 1884 Calmann-Lévy published all but three of the sixteen Gyp titles that appeared in Paris and the provinces, often after serialization in *La Vie Parisienne*.

The firm was, along with that of Gervais Charpentier, the giant of nineteenth-century French literary publishing. Michel and Calmann Lévy were sons of a Jewish ragpicker and book peddler from Alsace-Lorraine, who in the mid-1820s migrated to Paris with his wife and six children. Here he opened a small reading room near Les Halles which served as a training ground for his sons. From these modest beginnings, Michel and his older brother Calmann created a publishing empire, revolutionizing the publishing world in 1856 by slashing the prices of acknowledged classics. Their action forced major competitors to follow suit, making literature accessible to a readership whose numbers increased constantly during the nineteenth century due to improved education and growing literacy. Not only did this innovative approach to publishing prove the Lévy brothers' acumen. It also symbolized their belief that reading might facilitate social progress while affording pleasure. And pleasure came in the form of small, yellow-jacketed volumes bearing the names of Stendhal, Balzac, Michelet, Sand, Flaubert, Dumas fils, Loti, Baudelaire, and Meilhac and Halévy—to name just a few.

The commercial and financial success of Gyp's publishers Michel and Calmann Lévy—they were among the richest Frenchmen of their century[19]—parallelled their spectacular social ascension. Whereas his father spoke a heavily accented French, Michel Lévy, at his death in 1875, could boast all the outward signs of a *grand bourgeois*: friendship with the Orleanist elite; the rosette of the Légion d'honneur; a table at the Café Riche; a luxurious town house on the Champs-Elysées; and a loge at the Opéra, across the street from his rue Auber headquarters.

To some observers, the meteoric ascension of the Lévy brothers seemed a bit too visible, given their religion. The July Monarchy and the Second Empire had witnessed the rise of numerous Jewish families, especially but not exclusively in banking and finance. They would not suffer systematic attack by anti-Semites until the late 1880s. Yet hints of what was to come appeared earlier in the decade. In July 1880 an anonymous front-page article in *Le Voltaire* warned of the dangers of "Calmannization." It accused the Lévy brothers of having created "in the midst of a democracy, a commercial aristocracy."[20] The same year the minister of justice approved Paul and Georges Lévy's request to legally change their surname to Calmann-Lévy in deference to their father—a bourgeois practice not without aristocratic pretensions. Yet the minister's legal brief ended with an unpleasant judgment that found its way into the papers: "[W]hen a family . . . can take, without relenting, 40% on all books of an era . . . and create, in the midst of the nineteenth century, that feudal and Shakespearian tradition (see Shylock), I consider . . . that that family has indisputable rights to nobility."[21]

Unlike these enemies, in the early 1880s Gyp seems to have maintained cordial relations with the entire Calmann-Lévy family. Author and publishers shared roots in Lorraine, and thus an almost instinctive *revanchisme*. The Lévy brothers' contacts with the Mirabeaus stretched back to their 1864 publication of Marie's *Histoire des deux héritières*, first of a half dozen or so of her works to bear the prestigious Calmann-Lévy imprint on their covers.[22] Most likely the professional relationship begun two decades earlier had, over the years, mellowed into a friendship. In her memoirs Gyp later sketched a sympathetic portrait of Calmann: "Monsieur Calmann-Lévy was an odd and amusing fellow. Short and stout, lively, authoritarian and witty, he said and did unexpectedly funny . . . things that delighted me."[23]

Gyp felt particularly drawn to Calmann's son Paul, who with his father assumed the firm's direction at Michel's death in 1875. Four years younger than Gyp, Paul was a suave man-about-town, the kind of "chic type" she found seductive. Calmann's son loved horses, pistols, swords, all violent sports, as well as music and the theater. But he also shared his father's remarkable business acumen. Warm and apparently flirtatious relations linked Gyp and Paul Calmann-Lévy, antedating her professional contacts with the publishing house. Her *Vie Parisienne* chronicle of 27 September 1879[24] concerns the predicament of a young reserve officer named Paul, who is invited to the Normandy summer home of a countess friend. She presumably represents Gabrielle, playing madam to the younger Paul. Confronted by a band of seductive châtelaines, Paul ends up spending the night with local prostitutes, as he is unable to satisfy all the countess' demanding female guests. This type of lightly veiled *fait divers*, based perhaps on Paul's boasting of his own exploits, was destined to amuse a public accustomed to reading semifictionalized accounts of personalities and situations familiar to *La Vie Parisienne*'s gossip-mongers.

A letter from Paul to his friend, the vicomte Spoelberch de Lovenjoul, confirms the encounter between himself and Gabrielle. "Nothing leads to slothfulness like the sloth's profession I'm pursuing,"[25] he wrote, describing his desultory efforts to become an officer by effecting twenty-eight days of military service in Normandy. Luckily Gabrielle was there, eager to help her protégé. Thanks to her efforts, wrote Paul, he is the most fortunate of all his fellow reservists, for "there's not one of my officers to whom she hasn't written, when she hasn't herself gone to see them to request leaves for me."[26]

Like her personal ties with the Calmann-Lévy family, Gyp's business dealings with her publisher in the early and mid-1880s seem solid. In May 1884 she and Calmann drew up a four-page contract, valid until 1890, stipulating the conditions under which the firm would publish Gyp's work. Penned in an elegant script, it gave Calmann-Lévy the "exclusive right"[27] to publish not only Gyp's most recent novel, *Le Monde à côté*, but all works written in the following six years. Gyp could publish each work in one magazine or review before ceding it to Calmann-Lévy for publication as a book. To protect the firm, the contract made clear that if any of Gyp's works appeared "of a nature unsuitable to the clientele,"[28] Calmann-Lévy could refuse it, freeing her to seek another publisher. Similarly, if Calmann-Lévy did not issue a second printing of a book within a year, Gyp could solicit another publisher, but only after securing Calmann-Lévy's written assurance that the firm had scheduled no further reprintings.[29]

The 1884 contract, binding Gyp and Calmann-Lévy for the next six years, benefited the publisher more than the author. Calmann-Lévy procured exclusive rights to the works of an author who, in two years, had proven herself not only prolific but also a popular success. A week after its publication, *Autour du mariage* had already reached a fifth printing and would eventually go through a hundred of them. In fact, the rue Auber firm was buying into a string of bestsellers, assuring Calmann-Lévy both increased renown and profits. Gyp, for her part, received the assurance of a much-needed steady income, provided her literary output remained steady. And she, too, could now share the prestige conferred on all authors published by the illustrious firm. A calling card in the Parisian literary world, the name Calmann-Lévy would facilitate her attempts to succeed in journalism and theater. To a certain extent, then, Calmann-Lévy's strict control accommodated Gyp: her publisher became her agent. But, at the same time, it obliged her to obey her publisher's terms, especially regarding her works' "acceptableness" to audiences. Actually, the Calmann-Lévy family would prove surprisingly open-minded on this point—that is, until it could no longer ignore the personally offensive contents of Gyp's works.

The Dialogue–Novel: Genesis of a Style

The novels comprising Gyp's initial spurt of publication, and largely responsible for her success, contained the germ of much of her later work. What stands out, indeed what characterizes her earliest novels is a style: the *roman dialogué*, or dialogue-novel. Serialized mostly in *La Vie Parisienne* and then collected into one volume, these novels consist of a series of chapters in dialogue form, primarily linked by a common character (Bob, Paulette) or theme (virtue, marriage, adultery). The reappearance in each novel of a group of worldly secondary characters, settings, and situations provides additional structural coherence. Descriptions of these characters and settings often take the form of cryptic notations: "On the Champs-Elysées, in a very elegant dining room. MONSIEUR JOHN O'STER, Irish nobleman; fifty-eight years old, white hair, crimson complexion, fatter than he is tall, stately limbs, dull intelligence."[30] The novels offer no explicit psychological analysis of characters. "[T]heir entire psychology," one critic remarked, "resides in the knot of their tie and the shade of their vest."[31] The novels consist only of rapid-fire, breathy dialogue hurtled along by exaggerated punctuation (!!!, . . .) that often conveys irony, as do such other traditional theatrical devices as asides and visual puns (characters hiding in closets, surprise entrances). In fact, the dialogue-novel's close resemblance to drama, evidencing the influence of Gyp's theatergoing under the Second Empire, allowed her to stage several of her novels, with only slight modifications of the original text. What differentiates Gyp's dialogue-novels from much drama is their extremely loose plot structure, discontinuous narrative, and one-dimensional characters.[32] As the example of *Autour du mariage* will show, these features may explain why several of Gyp's dramatic adaptations were fiascos.

Several literary critics cited Gyp as the inventor of the dialogue-novel. Albert Thibaudet singled her out as the "initiator" of the style subsequently adopted by Henri Lavedan, Maurice Donnay, Abel Hermant, and Pierre Veber.[33] And Henry James referred with respectful irony to Gyp—"mistress . . . of one of the happiest of forms," "muse of general looseness"—as the inspiration for his own 1899 dialogue-novel *The Awkward Age*.[34] As "queen" of the dialogue-novel, one critic declared categorically, "Gyp reigned."[35] Others, however, identified more distant precursors of the dialogue-novel, with Gyp merely its most prolific and adept exponent. As early as the second century A.D., the Greek satirist Lucian was offering up piquant dialogues. Even some Egyptian precedents have been cited. The dialogue triumphed in the mid nineteenth century with novels by Gustave

Droz and Ludovic Halévy, before reaching its apogee at the end of the century. Gyp claimed as her own literary forebear the writer and caricaturist Henri Monnier, whose dialogues, vaudevilles, and comedies ridiculed his prototypical solemn and smug bourgeois, Joseph Prudhomme.[36] The dialogist Gyp may also belong to the tradition of the French *moralistes*, whose aim was to observe man, often satirically or maliciously, as a social being. No specific genre unites the *moralistes*; La Rochefoucauld's maxims or Montesquieu's *Lettres persanes* both achieve the desired effect. To the critic Georges Pellissier the *moraliste* most akin to the late nineteenth-century dialogists is La Bruyère, whose *Caractères* "are composed of unrelated chapters that, taken separately, have as little unity as our collections of dialogues."[37]

This very narrative discontinuity, and Gyp's bare, stripped-down style, formed the focal point for a critical debate concerning her "realism." To some, Gyp's stark, almost evanescent prose stamped her as a realist whose talent consisted in presenting a pure, objective distillation of reality, devoid of psychological or symbolic resonances. According to Georges Pellissier, the dialogue-novel's fidelity to nature proved its superiority to both theater, burdened by rules and traditions, and the novel, often overloaded with psychological description. The dialogue-novel, on the other hand, had liberated itself from these stylistic impediments, offering instead "no conventions, just pure reality."[38] While some critics hailed Gyp's realism, however, others saw in her writing something quite different. So bare was Gyp's narrative exposition, they argued, that its details would have to be filled in by the reader's imagination. One critic compared her style to "those blouses whose soft silk offers a loose outline to the eye and leaves a pleasing liberty to the imagination."[39] And several critics compared Gyp's characters to silhouettes or puppets: oversimplified, even childish, yet carefully controlled and articulated by the puppeteer. This second group of critics placed Gyp's style at the other extreme, in the realm of fantasy and symbolism.

Why did Gyp show such a preference for the dialogue-novel in the 1880s? With characteristic unconcern for literary craft, she pointed out that the genre's "facility" allowed her to maximize her production with minimum effort. She adopted the dialogue form, she confided to a friend, "because it's revoltingly easy, whereas narrative requires a semblance of effort. I have no illusions about the intellectual value of a series of scenes written slapdash and hurriedly, like everything I do."[40] At least one critic agreed with Gyp's evaluation of the dialogue-novel as easily produced literature, calling for neither imagination nor talent: "It requires neither inventiveness, because dialogue has no real 'subject,' nor composition, because the characters speak in fits and starts, nor style, because the language of 'the upper crust,' is, it seems, frightful gibberish."[41] An effortless genre, then, and lucrative as well. For not only would the author be paid by the publication in which the dialogue appeared, but he or she would most likely also receive royalties from several editions of the book version.

If Gyp appeared self-serving in her choice of writing dialogue-novels, she also sensed the demands of the market. This market was comprised largely of Parisian and provincial bourgeois readers, especially members of the *nouvelles couches sociales*, the new social strata that emerged during the early years of the Third Republic. "In my region," remembered one journalist, "notary, doctor, magistrates got together to delight in reading *Petit Bob*. . . ."[42] This readership did not have abundant leisure time. It preferred literature that could be read in snatches and with little effort—"between two railroad stations, in the bathtub, in bed, while riding a bicycle."[43] Busy readers of reviews like *La Vie Parisienne* demanded "fragmentary books"[44] devoid of annoyingly lengthy passages, books they could begin at any point in the text and pick up or place aside as their schedule permitted.

Like other forms of contemporary entertainment (the circus and the music-hall, for example),[45] Gyp's dialogue-novels seemed synchronized with the rhythms of modern readers. Typographically the novels contained much white space when laid out on the newspaper or book page, allowing a reader's eyes to skim the dialogue rapidly, without excessive concentration. To Pellissier this visual feature of the dialogue, as well as Gyp's constant recourse to ellipses in the text, captured, through absence itself, the vacuousness of both the characters and the readers, their "premature decay."[46] Gyp's many references to contemporary political events, moreover, and her incorporation in the dialogues of real-life characters, combined elements of both short story and news chronicle, fiction and journalism. That Gyp had in mind the mechanisms of supply and demand when producing her dialogues seems clear from the following rather cynical admission: "I have neither self-respect nor esteem for the readers since I see what they like."[47] But might her contention—that the dialogue-novel was an exclusively commercial venture for her—have been a bluff? Both the critical success of her work and the drive and self-discipline she brought to her profession make one suppose that for Gyp writing meant more than just "putting black on white."

Gyp's Enfant Terrible and "Pretty Little Poison": Petit Bob and Paulette

The first phase of Gyp's literary career encompassed not only the stylistic innovations of the dialogue-novel but also two trademark characters, Petit Bob and Paulette, both modeled on Gyp herself and serving as prototypes for many of her later characters. From Gyp's early novels also emerged a core group of themes, many of which were to resurface in her later novels, and which fall roughly into two categories. The first, inscribed in the social and political context of the early Third Republic, targeted a group of "decadent" aristocrats and bourgeois parvenus whom Gyp considered a social menace. A second thematic category concerned women and encompassed girlhood and adolescence, women's position at home and in society, marriage, adultery, and divorce. Gyp's preoccupation with issues relating to women seemed so significant to her early readers that the press and literary critics were soon hailing the biological woman Gyp as a feminist, a label her literary male persona violently repudiated.

The widely read dialogue-novel *Petit Bob* was the first of a series spotlighting

Gyp's irreverent little boy protagonist. *Bob au salon* (1888), *Bob au salon de 1889* (1889), *Bob à l'exposition* (1889), and *Une élection à Tigre-sur-Mer, racontée par Bob* (1896) further acquainted readers with the naughty gamin, whose childlike drawings (signed "Bob" and in fact penned by Gyp) now illustrated the text. *Les Gens chics* (*The Chic People*) (1895), *Ohé! les dirigeants!* (*Hey! The Leaders!*) (1896), and *En Balade* (*Out for a Stroll*) (1897) also boasted "colored images" by Petit Bob, who now became Gyp's artistic persona as well. The combination in a series of books of innocuous social satire in dialogue form and simplistic, brightly colored illustrations identifies Gyp's first works as early examples of the comic strip.[48] The Bob series also belongs to the wealth of literature both for and about children published in France at the end of the nineteenth century. Jules Vallès' *L'Enfant* (1879), Anatole France's *Livre de mon ami* (1885), Franc-Nohain's *Jaboune*, Paul and Victor Marguerite's *Poum*, and Jules Renard's *Poil de carotte* (1894) are a few of the better-known examples of this literary category. These works reflect, in part, the growing concern in France with the country's declining birthrate, especially in light of the 1870 defeat and Germany's population boom. An insecure France, intent on revenge, was now more than ever concerned with education and child-rearing.[49]

The hero of Gyp's children's stories for adults is an eight-year-old, the eldest of four children, from a traditional Parisian aristocratic family. Like all Gyp's protagonists, Petit Bob is blond and is always impeccably and stylishly dressed in the latest fashion. His fastidious appearance, however, contrasts with his brash character. He is an enfant terrible, reminiscent of his later American comic-strip counterpart, Buster Brown. In a series of tableaux unfolding both in the privacy of his home and in public places (the circus, an art gallery, the Jardin des Plantes), Bob explodes the ethical code proffered by his parents, grandfather, and tutor, a well-meaning priest. Gyp's satire in the Bob series, as elsewhere in her work, functions primarily through oppositions, in this case, as Maurice Barrès noted, the opposition between the "gamin and any stiff personality."[50]

Readers became accustomed to Bob's ungrammatical, slangy French. They witnessed his indifference to his studies and his delight in practical jokes. They observed his shockingly bad manners. Bob talks incessantly, with observations, jokes, and questions mixing in a slangy babble. He eavesdrops on the adults' dinner conversation and, at eight, is already a shameless womanizer. What redeem him from being a hopeless brat are his generosity and sentimentality. After offering his mother his favorite bibelot for her birthday, "Bob stretches out like a calf on the carpet, almost crying with satisfaction."[51]

Bob's indiscriminate attacks on authority and convention reveal an anarchistic streak. One critic labeled him a "great-grandson of the Revolution."[52] Yet his taste for subversion paradoxically accompanies reactionary attitudes and respect for certain types of authority. A fervent admirer of both the French army and the Bonapartes, Bob revels in reenacting Crimean War battles. His attachment to the past, in this case Bonapartist, is one component of his antimodernism. Visiting the various world's fairs, he sneers at the innovative machines and constructions, including the Eiffel Tower, which herald changes in traditional French lifestyles.

Like Gyp, Petit Bob is an authoritarian anarchist, combining features of both Mirabeau-Tonneau and Mirabeau.

Author and character share much else besides temperament. Petit Bob, like the girl Gyp, loves nature and animals, as well as his grandfather. He is a male precursor of Colette's Claudine. Like Gyp again, he is a poor student with a prodigious memory, whose literary tastes run to Corneille and Hugo. Specific autobiographical details provide a further link. Bob repeats Gyp's girlhood prank of dropping water bombs on innocent pedestrians. Even the traumatic Liverdun incident, involving the voyeuristic revelation of adultery to Gyp, is transposed here, with Little Bob spying on an intimate encounter between his rakish uncle and an unfamiliar woman. Gyp's relation to Petit Bob is nostalgic. He is the little boy she wished she could have been, and perhaps strove to become through her writing. To her this autobiographical connection was patent. In creating Bob, Gyp wrote, "I incorporated . . . much of the child I once was."[53] Because of her perceived affinity with Bob, Gyp was mystified by critics who considered her character perverse, the corrupt product of an equally degenerate aristocracy. "Sinister kid,"[54] warned one critic. "Decadent flower; fin-de-siècle type,"[55] pronounced another. For an American critic—*Petit Bob* was published in an English translation in 1900[56]—Gyp's character was "the depraved child of rich and degenerate parents . . . the conscious little sinner, surrounded on all sides by bad examples. . . ."[57] Bob's worldiness earned him the titles "child of the boulevards"[58] and "Gavroche of the upper crust."[59] Some compared him to the city of Paris, others to Candide.[60] Still others read Gyp's novel as a condemnation of religion (represented by the buffoonish abbot) or of domestic education.[61]

Gyp dismissed all these arguments as gross misrepresentations of her literary persona. She insisted on Bob's purity: "I didn't want to create a little cad but a little boy, instinctive, teasing, undisciplined, curious, a bit rough, but very kind, and above all very naïve. People wanted to see in Bob a type of mean and vicious kid. He's not that at all."[62] In fact, Gyp argued, Bob's innocence and virtue brought into sharper contrast the vices of a social group whose "immorality" threatened the stability of French society. Gyp referred to a new bourgeois–aristocratic elite—cosmopolitan, moneyed, snobbish—whose existence seemed exclusively to revolve around the salon and the clubhouse. Confronted with such a specter of degeneration, she launched a counterattack with "ferocious gaiety."[63] The parasitic swarm of snobs roving through her early novels like so many caricatures of Proustian characters—the adulterous Madame Seyrieux and baronne de Flirt; Joyeuse with the obligatory gardenia in his buttonhole; Lemondyn, Sangène, and Xaintrailles—became targets for Gyp's poisoned arrows. For Gyp, declared fellow society novelist Abel Hermant, was the "enemy of ridiculousness."

For Gyp, the cardinal sin of these socialites is hypocrisy. Bob's elders preach honesty, piety, and marital fidelity. Yet the boy's married uncle and grandfather constantly ogle women. Virtue is again the theme of *La Vertu de la baronne* (1882), a novel whose "respectable" protagonist cannot resist the temptations offered by two young suitors. In *Sans voiles!* (*Without Veils!*) (1885) the veils concealing female vice are ripped away, revealing that the "charitable" women directors of a philanthropic organization, the "Repentir Momentané" ("Momentary Repentance") have sold sexual favors in exchange for donations, violating both sexual and business ethics. Finally, *Elles et lui* (1885) illustrates that in Gyp's early novels vice and hypocrisy are not exclusive birthrights of the female sex. The elegant and narcissistic vicomte Gérard de Galb despises women but courts them in the hope of manipulating them. Successive chapters pair this nihilistic Bel-Ami with generic women—"Celle qui l'aime" ("The one who loves him"), "Celle qu'il ménage" ("The one he spares"), "Celle qui voudrait bien" ("The one who'd like to")—each helping de Galb advance to his dual goals of being "free . . . free . . . free . . . "[64] and experiencing "heedless pleasure,"[65] desires most likely not alien to Gyp as well.

In Gyp's literary world, social decay is portrayed as both cause and consequence of a corrupt political system. Democracy, she asserted, was ruining France. As a stalwart imperialist, she was increasingly repelled by the governing "Opportunist" republic, presided over by the moderate Jules Grévy and so named because of its tenuous and shifting alliances among its republican factions. For Gyp, apologist of order, hierarchy, and authority, the Republic was a gigantic mess. And nowhere was this mess more evident than in the Chamber of Deputies, which Gyp's spokesman Bob was eager to visit, for, as he said, "I always wanted to see people fighting each other . . . "[66]

Not only did the Republic threaten social order, as Gyp's novels illustrated, but it also risked subverting morality. Gyp insisted that, contrary to its virtuous pretentions, the Third Republic was profoundly corrupt. Social and political satire converge in a chapter of *La Vertu de la baronne*. A peaceful village in the Indre department has just greeted its sixteenth prefect since the Republic's inception. This intruder into the French heartland is the thirty-five-year-old bachelor Brutus Nadébat, a black-eyed, brown-bearded, thick-lipped man from the Midi. Brutus' republican convictions are unflinching. He will restore the republic of virtue in a France "rotted by twenty years of corruption."[67] Just as fervent in his beliefs is the marquis d'Esprycour, a royalist adored by local peasants. On behalf of the villagers, d'Esprycour calls on Brutus, hoping to obtain financing for badly needed repairs to the church. The dignified marquis is, to his horror, greeted by a nude woman with a "brutally snub nose, lips coated with an intense red . . . black, wavy hair . . . wild eyes . . . thick lashes . . . savage appearance . . . large, unevenly rimmed ears, flared fingers and toes, and heavy joints."[68] Recovering from this lewd, grotesque vision of Woman, d'Esprycour finds Brutus. The prefect agrees to repair the church, but not without exacting a steep price: the marquis must hand over to the prefect his most precious possession, a ring kissed by the pope.

Gyp's clearly delineated oppositions—republic versus empire and monarchy, southern versus northern France, bourgeoisie versus feudal aristocracy and peasants, rootlessness versus rootedness, republican "faith" versus Catholicism, cupidity versus generosity—leave no doubt as to where real virtue resides. But if further evidence of this Manichaean dichotomy is needed, the "savage" physiognomies of both the traitor Brutus and his mistress hint at another, more sinister agent of corruption, soon to be identified by Gyp: the Jew.

While Petit Bob is Gyp's demystifier of bourgeois virtue, his spiritual sister Paulette incarnates the author's views on women. Twenty-year-old Paulette is another of Gyp's essential character types: *la jeune fille*. The adult Gyp's recurrent portrayal of herself as a female (and sometimes male) child or adolescent hints at her nostalgia for her girlhood—and also reflects her inability to become an adult. Like Bob and Paulette, Gyp would always be a cocky brat, chafing against maternal apron strings.

Paulette d'Hautretan is the heroine of two of Gyp's novels, both serialized in *La Vie Parisienne* and then published as books by Calmann-Lévy. The wildly successful *Autour du mariage* (1883) went through over ninety editions and established Gyp's reputation as a novelist. Paulette, an alluring, headstrong young woman resembling Gyp in many ways, unwillingly submits to an arranged marriage with the older, ineffectual marquis d'Alaly. When the marquis tries to subjugate his wife, the willful Paulette swears to separate from him. But d'Alaly manages to redeem himself by writing Paulette love poems. The couple happily reunite.

Paulette appeared three years later in the equally popular companion piece *Autour du divorce*, which reached a forty-eighth printing shortly after publication. This novel was one of several ridiculing the 1884 Naquet Law, which reinstated divorce after nearly a century. Paulette d'Alaly has married to "be free." Yet she now finds herself pestered by her jealous but faithful husband. She resolves on divorce to find "true" freedom. But, according to the Naquet Law's provisions, to obtain her divorce she must first prove herself the victim of "grave insult or injury" before witnesses. Against a backdrop of chic Parisian theaters, salons, and racetracks, Paulette seeks the best opportunity to provoke her husband. A ball provides the occasion. As the marquis takes his wife's arm, Paulette begins shaking it vigorously. Her "wounded" arm then becomes the pretext for initiating divorce proceedings. An elaborate legal battle ensues, featuring magistrates portrayed as either senile or lecherous. Once divorced, the flirtatious Paulette rejoins the Parisian social whirl, but her attempts to enjoy herself are half-hearted. For the only man attracting her is her ex-husband, now a debonair bachelor. The theme of rupture and reconciliation, which Gyp's readers remembered from *Autour du mariage*, closes the novel: Paulette and her ex reconcile and remarry.

Many readers and critics of *Autour du mariage* and *Autour du divorce* saw Paulette as the new, modern woman, no longer content to remain the demure guardian of the household. As one of the novel's characters reflects, Paulette is "a funny little modern product."[69] Like Bob, she is independent, frank, and slangy, seemingly blasé and unsentimental while still speaking as an apologist for marriages based on love. She is also seductive, but in a strange way. Fresh and girlish, she wears no jewelry and, like Gyp, energetically refuses the corset. Her little upturned nose, large mouth, blond curls in disarray, and lithe, athletic body seemed to herald a new, less "womanly" ideal of female beauty.[70] Dressed for a ball in the sexually ambiguous costume of the ace of clubs, Paulette has every man's gaze riveted on her.

Several critics of the period commented on Paulette's androgynous quality. Jules Lemaître, one of the most influential critics of his day, regarded Paulette as the emblem of

> the most modern feminine type, the one which perhaps best belongs to these last ten years, that of a slightly androgynous being, very feminine in its capriciousness, nervousness and lack of logic, but masculine in its behavior, disdain of feeling, and also a bit in its dress. A provocative contrast, in which the boyish element brings out the other, makes the woman more tempting and savory.[71]

And, indeed, several critics noted that Paulette might become the woman of the future. Echoing Lemaître, Lucien Muhlfeld, a literary critic for *La Revue Blanche*, confidently declared that "women of the last third of this century were, are, will be Paulettes. . . ."[72]

The discovery by critics and readers of a "feminist" Gyp again astounded the author, unaware that she had created a role model for some French women. "[A]round 1883," remembered Gyp, "I realized with astonishment that Paulette, who was only, in my eyes, 'a pretty little poison,' was liked, admired, and taken as a model by young women of that time."[73] According to Gyp, public opinion had fabricated a character totally divergent from the author's intentions. A feminist Paulette seemed to her as strange as a corrupt Petit Bob. Indeed, in an article entitled "La Femme de 1885" Gyp made explicit her ambivalence about changes in French women's status and behavior. This "little creature, independent and strange," Gyp wrote of the "new woman," "studies, crams, passes her exams, obtains her bachelor's degree, speaks several languages"[74]—all laudable accomplishments to the author. Yet she cautioned women not to forget one of their crucial duties, namely, to please men. "She is wrong to be too good-natured and to lack bearing completely."[75] And although she energetically denounced the corset—"I am against the corset with all my might," she informed a male correspondant—her opposition was based not on the corset's oppression of the female body but rather on its abolition of distinctions among waist sizes: "[I]t makes waists '*commonplace*' . . . it mars those that are attractive without embellishing those that are ugly."[76] Despite the generally warm reception given Gyp's female characters in the 1880s, at least one critic detected that her tone toward women was not necessarily sympathetic. Reviewing *Autour du mariage*, Henri de Bornier charged that "these pages written by a woman constitute the cruelest indictment ever leveled against women, and what emerges from the work is that woman is the guilty party, the principal agent of social disorganization."[77]

In the end, for all Paulette's seeming unconventionality—Lemaître called her "a revolutionary . . . almost a nihilist"[78]—she remains fundamentally conventional. Her aggressive flirtations while married never lead to adultery, although extramarital affairs are common for those in her milieu. Paulette remains virtuous—and, in fact, naïve. Despite her cocky pose, she would never consider marrying outside aristocratic circles. And her antirepublican jibes reveal her conservative political outlook. Paulette is part femme fatale, part convent girl, a mixture of "the little savage and . . . the girl from the best circles of society."[79] If Paulette is a revolutionary, she is also a reactionary.

Gyp's own case combined revolt and reaction to an extreme degree. For as a woman she had many accounts to settle. Not only was she rebelling against the lack of power which, like an affliction, seemed the birthright of all women. She was also battling the very fact of being female, a condition upheld by her family as enviable in the abstract but most unfortunate in her case, given the Mirabeaus' lack of a male heir. As for Gyp's female role models, Marie de Mirabeau certainly did not encourage her daughter's respect for women. Gyp's father and grandfather, by contrast, seemed to her paragons of male virility, honor, and virtue. Gonneville's granddaughter wished not to improve her status as a female but to flee it. Ironically, the superficially unconventional behavior and ideas that to some proved Gyp's feminism were really the marks of her misogyny.

Although known primarily as a dialogist who had earned her spurs at *La Vie Parisienne*, Gyp in the 1880s was also trying to promote herself as a dramatist. The popularity of *Autour du mariage* convinced her to adapt the novel for the stage. With the collaboration of Hector Crémieux (librettist, with Ludovic Halévy, of Offenbach's *Orphée aux enfers*), several scenes from the novel were dropped and the ending changed. The play opened on 19 October 1883 at the Gymnase Dramatique, where Gyp herself had attended countless productions during the Second Empire. *Autour du mariage* was a failure, recalling the fate of her mother's 1876 fiasco *Châteaufort*. Once again Francisque Sarcey was on hand to record the embarrassment. So readable in *La Vie Parisienne* and in book form, Sarcey commented, Gyp's piquant dialogues, when transferred to the stage, could not compensate for the lack of both plot and psychologically complex characters. The play, he declared flatly, "does not exist."[80] Apparently the audience agreed. Its response to *Autour du mariage* was "very cold . . . glacial."[81]

In what was to become a typical pattern, the opening weeks of *Autour du mariage* found Gyp preparing a lawsuit. She was furious that *La Vie Moderne* had accompanied a rather unfavorable review of her play with an unretouched drawing of her based on a photograph she found unflattering. Had this contributed to her play's failure, she wondered? In a preliminary hearing, Gyp demanded both the removal from circulation of the injurious issue and damage payments. But the judge refused, obliging Gyp to present her case before a civil tribunal. *La Vie Moderne*'s lengthy apology to Gyp apparently placated her into abandoning the case. Expressing surprise at Gyp's legal maneuvers, the publisher of *La Vie Moderne*, "a newspaper where the respect of propriety [is] a tradition," made clear that "in publishing a portrait of Madame de Martel, dramatist and journalist, that was produced as carefully as possible, we believed that we were neither exceeding our right nor, more importantly, causing this author the slightest harm . . . . Let us hope that Madame de Martel will see things our way and that she will not harbor toward *La Vie Moderne* more rancor than we harbor toward her."[82]

Recovered from the failure of both her play and her lawsuit, Gyp was thinking about a second production three years after the Gymnase debacle. This time she had a script for a play called *Le suis-je?* but no backer, perhaps because of her inglorious 1883 debut. Dreyfus, director of the Théâtre du Palais-Royal, tacitly consented to produce the play but demanded substantial changes in the script. A determined Gyp tracked down Ludovic Halévy, one of her sponsors for admission into the Société des gens de lettres, and asked him to read and then praise the script in a letter that she could then show Dreyfus: "Thus, dear monsieur, could you read *Le suis-je?* and tell me quite frankly if it's bad? If, on the contrary, you find that it's *playable*, you would be ever so kind to tell me this in writing *'with an air of conviction'*; I would show them *your opinion*, and that would remove all difficulties."[83] In fact, Gyp's problems with Dreyfus were not over. The theater director at first hedged and then reneged on his agreement. Gyp suspected the Palais-Royal's financial troubles made Dreyfus reluctant to back a play whose box-office success seemed doubtful.[84]

Snubbed by Dreyfus, Gyp next propositioned the codirectors of the Théâtre des Variétés, Eugène Bertrand and Louis Baron. She had mentally cast the Variétés' vedette, Milly Meyer, in the role of Velléda, "the maid who becomes a prostitute,"[85] and Halévy's recommendation, she reasoned, would guarantee her a production. So she pressured him again, coyly: "I see full well that they *are going to consult you* to find out if the role suits Milly. I beg of you, tell them it's *charming*!!! (Even if you don't believe a word of it.)"[86] Halévy's cachet and Gyp's machinations, however, did not entice Bertrand and Baron. Twice rejected, *Le suis-je?* was never staged.

Sibylle de Mirabeau at age six; frontispiece to Gyp's *Souvenirs d'une petite fille (Sibylle Gaudry collection, Paris)*

". . . an admirable and exquisite being." Colonel Aymard Olivier Le Harivel de Gonneville in 1831 *(Copyright, Photo Musée de l'Armée, Paris)*

Gonneville in Nancy in the 1850s or 1860s *(Sibylle Gaudry collection, Paris)*

The future "women of letters" Marie de Mirabeau and her daughter, Sibylle, reading in Nancy *(Musée historique Lorrain, Nancy, Cliché Mignot)*

Gabrielle de Mirabeau at about age twenty in Nancy *(Sibylle Gaudry collection, Paris)*

Gabrielle and Roger de Martel de Janville around the time of their marriage, in Ems
(Photo von Huck & Cie, Sibylle Gaudry collection, Paris)

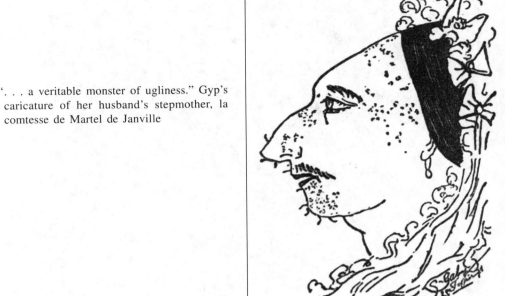

"... a veritable monster of ugliness." Gyp's caricature of her husband's stepmother, la comtesse de Martel de Janville

Marcelin, impresario of *La Vie Parisienne*

Gyp dans les rues de Nancy, par le vicomte d'IRISSON (1871).

"[T]his young woman . . . had to flee the fury of an entire city." Drawing of Gyp in Nancy in 1871 by vicomte d'Irisson

Janville in Normandy, Gyp's home during the Franco-Prussian war

68, rue Chézy, Gyp's home in Neuilly *(Sibylle Gaudry collection, Paris)*

Gyp's rendering of Petit Bob and "m'sieu l'abbé," his tutor, from the 3 November 1889 issue of *Le Triboulet*

1884 poster for one of Gyp's first novels published by Calmann-Lévy

Michel *(left)* and Calmann Lévy *(below)*

V

The "Appalling Hussy"
1880–1887

As a man, would have been an influential orator or a
preacher specialized in conversions.

Psychic dictating to Gyp, 12 January 1882

From the Boulevards to Bohemia

Gyp's employment in the 1880s by both Marcelin and Calmann-Lévy not only
provided her with solid professional relationships but also facilitated her literary
socialization. It introduced her to the personalities and coteries shaping Parisian
literary, artistic, and journalistic life during this period. At the beginning of her
career, she met scores of writers, journalists, painters, actors, and boulevardiers,
many of whom would become her personal and political allies—or enemies.

Gyp's association with Calmann-Lévy won her a privileged place in the firm's
famous bookstore, La Librairie Nouvelle. Founded during the Second Empire,
the bookstore, situated at the intersection of the boulevard des Italiens and the
rue de Gramont, had become an unofficial landmark by the time of Gyp's arrival
on the scene. It was also Calmann-Lévy's most ingenious form of publicity for
the publishing house. Between 5 and 7 P.M. writers, journalists, politicians, actors,
aristocrats, as well as those eager to gape at this unique society crammed into the
bookstore to exchange impressions and gossip before setting off for the Café
Riche or the Opéra Comique, located just two doors away. A favorite haunt of
Paris' social, literary, and political elite, the Librairie Nouvelle was to Gyp ''one
of the most amusing spots in Paris.''[1]

But patrons also came to the Librairie Nouvelle to read and buy books, for its
reputation as an arbiter of literary taste was impeccable. Much of the credit was
due to the talents of the bookstore's manager, Achille, a prodigious salesman and

adviser. Gyp would remember Achille as a "disreputable, intelligent, lively" sort of person. "[H]aving seen, read, and retained everything, he was never mistaken. One could ask him the most unexpected questions; ask him dates, publishing figures, anything one wanted; he advised clients instantly, and without the slightest hesitation."[2] Gyp was amazed hearing Achille recommend to customers books published not only by Calmann-Lévy but also by the firm's competitors, which the bookstore sold as well. This unorthodox practice, she concluded, was just another measure of her publisher's great commercial acumen.

When Calmann was not pushing chairs aside to prevent his bookstore from becoming a salon, Gyp could find herself elbow to elbow with a pantheon of renowned literary and artistic celebrities past, present, and future. Such Second Empire luminaries as Sainte-Beuve, Alexandre Dumas fils, Octave Feuillet, Henri Meilhac and Ludovic Halévy, and Hortense Schneider often made appearances at the bookstore, usually before or after a performance. At their side was a new generation of writers, many of whom—including Jean Lorrain and Henri de Régnier—were drawn to the symbolists. There were also humorists (Aurélien Scholl and Charles Haas), journalists (Arthur Meyer and Henri Rochefort), painters (Edouard Manet, Edouard Detaille), actors (Coquelin aîné), playwrights (Hector Crémieux, Edouard Pailleron, and Emile Augier), and a smattering of nobility and even royalty. Gyp also spotted a small boy, accompanied by his maid, who asked Achille for works by Molière and Lamartine. He was "very pale, with magnificent brown eyes, velvety and deep, infinitely gentle and intelligent."[3] Gyp had seen the boy playing on the Champs-Elysées with Antoinette Faure, holding two hot potatoes to warm his hands. About a decade later, Gyp would again meet Marcel Proust, now a young man, at Robert de Montesquiou's.

Among the Librairie Nouvelle's celebrated patrons, Gyp found two literary mentors whose reputations dated from the Second Empire: Ludovic Halévy and Alexandre Dumas fils, both of whose works were published by Calmann-Lévy. Her rapport with Halévy was particularly cordial. As an adolescent visiting imperial Paris, Gabrielle had enjoyed Halévy's operatic collaborations with Meilhac and Offenbach. As an adult she appreciated his novels and admired him as a stylish reminder of the empire and habitué of Parisian salons. To Gyp, a newcomer to Paris, Halévy, who was ten years her elder, epitomized *parisianisme*, a subtle mixture of philosophy, wit, and malicious observation. And perhaps Halévy saw in his caustic protégée a literary heir.

Halévy acted as a benevolent mentor to his enthusiastic yet respectful and flattered younger colleague. In 1882 Gyp thanked him for commenting favorably on *La Vertu de la baronne*: "It really does not deserve the honor you have bestowed on it,"[4] she demurred, adding that she would incorporate the suggestions Halévy had conveyed to her at the Librairie Nouvelle. She again expressed her gratitude to Halévy the next year and thanked him for reading her latest work: "I cannot tell you just how much Gyp is stupefied and flattered to learn that you have *read Ce que femme veut . . . ?*"[5] Halévy reciprocated by sending Gyp copies of his own books. Gyp delighted in *Criquette*, *Les Deux Mariages*, and *La Famille Cardinal*, which Halévy sent her in 1883 when she was sick.[6] The next year she let Halévy know she was in the midst of her third reading of *Mon camarade Muffard*. She also praised *Princesse* and was impressed by Halévy's approximation of a "feminine" sensibility: "Your *Princesse* is charming and *real*; one would think you were a *young girl*!"[7] Along with this coquettish literary banter, Gyp's letters to Halévy communicated a wealth of practical information, such as the address of the Oller swimming pool and the fact that Friday was indeed the day reserved for women.[8]

Gyp's other mentor, Alexandre Dumas fils, proved less accessible than Halévy, probably owing to his greater renown. When the author of *Petit Bob* met the author of *La Dame aux camélias*, his reputation as the creator of one of the nineteenth century's greatest dramatic successes had placed him atop the literary Olympus. The 1880s found him writing moralizing plays which, like many of Gyp's works, concerned marriage, divorce, illegitimate children, and adultery. While illegitimate males were often the unsung heros of Dumas fils' plays, adulterous women were always cast as villains. And despite his support of the 1884 divorce law, Dumas fils remained an adamant lobbyist against women's rights. That he attracted so many women—including Gyp, who was twenty-five years his junior—may seem odd. Yet he was only the first in a line of outspoken male misogynists with whom Gyp would cultivate friendships.

Something of the intimacy Gyp felt with Dumas fils is reflected in her solicitous request for help in obtaining seats for premieres of his plays. Aware of Gyp's passion for the theater, in November 1884 Dumas fils complied with her request for a loge at the opening of *Denise* at the Théâtre Français.[9] Gyp adored the play, and in a note she imparted to its author what she had wished to tell him in person: "It is *superb*, and I would have liked to convey to you all my admiration, but you are never to be found in the avenue de Villiers, are you?"[10] When some theater contacts failed to procure a loge for the premiere of *Francillon* in 1887, Gyp asked for Dumas fils' permission to watch one of the dress rehearsals.[11]

Relying on her own success and on her connections with Halévy and Dumas fils, in 1888 Gyp asked the two writers to support her candidacy for admission to the Société des gens de lettres. As had her mother twenty years earlier, she felt that membership in what some considered a minor version of the Académie française would not only conspicuously confirm her achievements but also protect her against the vagaries of the market. In 1883 she had questioned Halévy about the possible usefulness of membership in the Société. She had also humbly requested him to be her sponsor—or "godfather," to use the society's term—"since you are so kind as to consider me your colleague,"[12] after the Société itself asked her to join.

Given Halévy and Dumas fils' assurances of sponsorship, Gyp set out to collect the items and documents required by the Société: several volumes of her works; an entry fee; a copy of her birth certificate, which was slow in reaching Paris from a sluggish village "deep in the heart of the Morbihan";[13] her husband's written authorization allowing her to join;[14] her own written request for admission, signed "Gyp";[15] and a note from Halévy and Dumas fils, testifying to Madame de Martel's "great talent, which can only honor our society."[16] With such a prestigious endorsement, her acceptance by the Société was a matter of form. In May 1888, after learning of her admission, she sent an effusive message to Halévy—"my dear Sponsor"—thanking him and transmitting "very affectionate regards from your 'godson,' Gyp."[17]

If Gyp's contract with Calmann-Lévy, friendships with Halévy and Dumas fils, and membership in the Société des gens de lettres all marked her as a member of the French literary establishment, her visits to the Montmartre cabaret Le Chat Noir provided her with a different type of literary socialization. She first ventured to the unorthodox cultural laboratory of Emile Goudeau and Rodolphe Salis around 1882, about a year after its opening on the boulevard Rochechouart. Here, in a smoky room hung with drawings by Willette, Steinlen, and Caran d'Ache, she enjoyed Henri Rivière's ingenious shadow theater renditions of *La Tentation de Saint-Antoine*, plus pantomime, songs, poetry readings, political declarations—whatever unusual brew the regulars could concoct. Among those contributing their talents to the Chat Noir enterprise was one of her *Vie Parisienne* colleagues, the humorist Maurice Donnay, and two future friends and collaborators, François Coppée and Willy.[18]

Despite the images associated with fin-de-siècle Montmartre—cocottes, pimps, absinthe dens, the murky beer halls frequented by Mürger's bohemians—it was not unusual to find aristocratic patrons like the comtesse de Martel. Baron Haussmann's feats of urban planning under the Second Empire, which created major east–west and north–south axes, had made outlying districts like the village of Montmartre more accessible to all Parisians. Many were also drawn there by nostalgia for the serpentine, cobblestoned streets and mix of social classes once found in the old neighborhoods destroyed during Haussmann's renovations. While bourgeois and aristocratic patrons were now penetrating the inner confines of bohemia, the artists and writers of the Montmartre cabarets were similarly making an equally energetic appeal to the bourgeoisie. Emile Goudeau, founder (1878) of the café-theater known as the Hydropathes, had painted a rather grim portrait of the material hardships of bohemian life in two volumes of memoirs, *La Vache enragée* and *Dix ans de bohème*. His lean years in bohemia had made him an apologist for a return to bourgeois life. Intent on attracting a broader public, he began to turn the Chat Noir into a commercial venture. Posters, the *Chat Noir* newspaper, the entertainment offered—all helped provide publicity for the cabaret, its artists, and avant-garde movements like symbolism and impressionism. This "commercialized Bohemia"[19] succeeded in drawing to the Chat Noir such *mondains* as Edmond de Goncourt, Joris-Karl Huysmans, Guy de Maupassant, Robert de Montesquiou, the duchesse d'Uzès, and the Prince of Wales.

The marketing of the Chat Noir held a special appeal for Gyp. While the cabaret's efforts to draw bourgeois patronage were quite serious, they were never without criticism, indicating bohemia's distance from the same bourgeoisie it sought to cultivate. On entering the cabaret, patrons were greeted with noble titles and exaggerated politeness, while at Le Mirliton, Aristide Bruant's later incarnation of the Chat Noir, the owner hurled insults at arriving guests. Chat Noir waiters dressed as members of the venerable Académie française. This *zutisme*, or railing at revered individuals and institutions, could not but please Gyp. To the escapee from Nancy's stifling drawing rooms, a rebel rejecting her mother, her teachers, and other "oppressors," the Chat Noir's outrageousness offered a form of catharsis. It was a perpetual saturnalia, where, for once, the "masters" were relegated to the role of "slaves."

The Chat Noir's equivocal damning of social and cultural elites was paralleled by its similarly equivocal "populism," which was also attractive to Gyp. Bruant's slangy songs about the desperate and destitute of Montmartre made him a hero to certain socialist and anarchist groups. Yet his interest in the laboring classes seems to have been purely romantic, even reactionary. His 1898 campaign for a National Assembly seat, laced with anti-Semitism and a defense of order and authority, unmasked him as a man of the Right. He ended his days relaxing in his château, attended by his servants. Gyp also espoused this Chat Noir populism. Her idealization of peasants and workers never reflected any sincere interest in seeing their condition improve. And many of her friends, like Laurent Tailhade and Edouard Drumont, would also retrace Bruant's itinerary, veering from extreme left-wing anarchism or socialism to right-wing nationalism. The Chat Noir thus presented Gyp with two postures, one *zutiste*, the other "populist," which she incorporated into her own life and works.

Aside from the Librairie Nouvelle and the bohemian Montmartre cabarets, Gyp could avail herself of a third network of literary contacts in Neuilly. Her fellow Neuilly resident Maurice Barrès, for one, informed his neighbor about the world of the "little reviews," often associated with symbolism, for which he was writing in the 1880s. It was most likely Barrès who proposed Paul Verlaine as a tutor for Gyp's children. Gyp rejected the choice, judging the needy Verlaine's poetry excellent yet offended by his dirty clothes and reputedly unsavory habits.[20] Instead, she settled on Jules Tellier, a neoclassical poet much admired by Barrès, who died of typhus in 1889 at the age of twenty-six. Gyp replaced Tellier with his friend, the young poet Paul Guigou, who in turn succumbed to tuberculosis after he left Gyp's service.

Another poet Gyp encountered in Neuilly was Stéphane Mallarmé, the ex-Parnassian who was soon to become the acknowledged *maître* of the young generation of symbolists. The chance meeting took place, as Gyp recalled many years later, shortly after her move to Neuilly. Very early one morning she was awakened by the sounds of a gruff voice, wheels screeching, and a whip cracking. Opening the veranda blinds, she saw a driver whipping and cursing his horse, which had fallen in the ice-covered street in front of her house. Wearing only a light robe, she ran into the street and began berating the mean-spirited coachman, threatening him with legal action by the Société protectrice des animaux, of which she was the president. The driver, in turn, menaced Gyp with his whip handle, whereupon she fainted.

Regaining consciousness on a sofa in an unfamiliar room, Gyp perceived beside her "a man in his thirties, very distinguished, with very gentle eyes and a curly beard, who offered me a flask of smelling salts while fanning me with his other hand."[21] The polite gentleman—he was actually closer to forty—explained that he was spending Christmas in Neuilly with friends. The screams, he said, had drawn him to the window. Seeing a young woman lying immobile in the street, he did not hesitate to carry her to his friends' house, where she would not risk catching a cold. Anxious about the countess' condition, Mallarmé called on her at home the next day. He gallantly proffered a bouquet of roses and a small book of poetry, tied up with ribbons of black and pink silk. The volume's beige cover had its title stamped in gold: *L'Après-midi d'un faune*. Seduced by Mallarmé's charm and polite manners, Gyp nevertheless found his poetry "unreadable," "bizarre, incomprehensible,"[22] too hermetic, too unrealistic for the author of *Petit Bob*. After this incident, the two met rarely, perhaps only at the home of Villiers de l'Isle-Adam, shortly before that author's death in 1889.

Most of the dozens of literary acquaintances Gyp made between 1879 and 1888 proved superficial. Yet her contacts with Anatole France, by contrast, bloomed into a particularly intimate if ill-fated friendship. France was living in Neuilly when Gyp moved there in 1879. He had just begun publishing with Calmann-Lévy and was a regular at the Librairie Nouvelle. Given these common networks, a Gyp–France meeting seemed inevitable.

At the time of their first encounter in 1882, France, five years Gyp's senior, was still relatively unknown. As Gyp remembered, France was "completely ignored, except by a few well-read people. . . . His awkwardness, his timidity, his total ignorance of the practices of high society, everything destined him to remain *out of it*, regardless of his talent."[23] Son of a Parisian bookstore owner, he inherited his father's veneration for books, as well as his republicanism and anticlericalism. Like most writers during the Second Empire, France sided with the literary opposition to Napoleon III. In the late 1860s, under Leconte de Lisle's patronage, he drifted into the Parnassian orbit. After the Commune (which he abhorred), he began submitting articles and reviews to *Le Temps*, whose prestigious literary column, "La Vie littéraire," he would oversee from 1887 on. A job at the Senate library and his marriage to Valérie Guérin de Sauville saved him from financial obscurity. His fortunes further improved with Calmann-Lévy's 1878 publication of *Jocaste*, followed in 1881 by *Le Crime de Sylvestre Bonnard*. By the mid-1880s, he had already been decorated Chevalier de la Légion d'honneur, and he frequented many of the most exclusive Parisian literary salons. It was at Madame Aubernon's in 1876 or 1877 that he met the intelligent, authoritative, and rich Léontine Arman de Caillavet, who a decade later would become his counselor and ultimately his mistress.

Despite France's initial awkwardness, later smoothed over by Madame de Caillavet—"[she] educated him from head to toe,"[24] Gyp would later write—he had many qualities that appealed to his colleague. In fact, Gyp found his unconventionality refreshing. France, like Gyp, was a rationalistic, often skeptical observer of human nature. His hatred of "mediocrity" and support of an intellectual elite made him hostile to the early Third Republic. Indeed, these attitudes of the 1880s, as well as his passionate defense of the French language, Greek antiquity, and the army, seemed to brand him as a traditionalist. Yet the following two decades would reveal that France was not the intransigent reactionary Gyp had imagined. The skeptic France was equally wary of all "isms," including the nascent nationalism and anti-Semitism of the 1880s and 1890s. He remained a staunch partisan of intellectual pluralism. While the personal ties between Gyp and France (and their respective families) would grow even stronger during the 1890s, ideological differences created an ever-widening rift between them.

"Jewish France"

Gyp's increasingly frequent, violent written and verbal attacks against Jews in the 1880s were alienating her from friends such as France. And they were now publicly marking her as an anti-Semite. To a certain extent, her behavior was symptomatic of an anti-Semitic explosion—directed against less than 1 percent of the French population[25]—that was beginning to inflame France in the 1880s. This anti-Jewish crusade drew its strength from two essential sources, one Christian and the other protosocialist. Ever since the Revolution—and even before—conservative Catholics had drawn on a rich arsenal of anti-Semitic myths to combat Jews. They insisted that the fall of the Old Regime—which signaled both a weakening of the Church's power and the granting of citizenship to Jews—was the most nefarious manifestation of a Jewish–Masonic plot that heralded the reign of the Antichrist. Such dogma found believers throughout the nineteenth century. After 1870 new circumstances combined to again put the Church on the defensive. Like the Revolution a century earlier, the establishment of the Third Republic promised a new era of laïcism, shading off toward sometimes rabid anticlericalism. The historic Ferry Laws greatly diminished the Church's stronghold over primary education, while the equally important Naquet Law reestablished divorce for the first time since 1816. The Third Republic, inspired by the scientific dogma of positivism and served by a counterclergy of Freemasons, was intent on completing its mission of secularization begun during the Revolution.

Conservative Catholics again found it convenient to blame the Jews for France's "dechristianization," thus combining religious and nationalistic arguments. A growing Catholic press spewed its venom at the Jews. *La Croix*, for example, was published by the Assumptionist Fathers, an order that gained prominence after the 1870 defeat. The Assumptionists interpreted 1870 as a near-apocalyptic event heralded by a century of sin. To expiate this catastrophe, they proposed pilgrimages to Lourdes, intense prayer, and donations to build the Sacré-Coeur basilica. Their fanatical mysticism reflected the mood of anxiety gripping many in post–1870 France, especially the petite bourgeoisie. To such Catholic extremists, contemporary events seemed to sanction—even invite—anti-Jewish persecution. They viewed the pogroms decimating Jewish communities in Russia, Rumania, and Germany in the 1880s as a just punishment of the Jewish "will to power." When Eugène Bontoux's Catholic-based bank, the Union Générale, went bankrupt in 1882 due to mismanagement, his supporters—many of them small investors ruined by the bank's collapse—quickly found a scapegoat in the Rothschilds.

The Union Générale crash highlighted another source of anti-Semitism in France which was left-wing and anticapitalist in inspiration. "Jewish finance," supported by a sinister, all-powerful institution, "la Haute Banque" ("the Big Bank"), was the parasite endangering France. The recession of the 1880s, the influx of foreign immigrants and products into France, the development of banking and finance, and worker discontent all seemed to fuel these arguments. Grafted onto these two types of anti-Semitism—one Catholic and the other economic— were various racialist theories. The word "race," in the nineteenth-century sense, did not necessarily imply ethnicity. In fact, it was often used as a synonym for "community." Only with the publication in 1855 of such works as Ernest Renan's *Histoire générale et systématique comparée des langues sémitiques* did the idea of a racial struggle between "superior" Aryans and "inferior" Semites become commonplace in France. Distortions of both Darwinism and positivism multiplied with the publication of "research" by pseudoanthropologist Vacher de Lapouge. Assisted by his eager student, Paul Valéry, Vacher de Lapouge measured six hundred skulls dug up from a cemetery. His results, he claimed, constituted scientific "proof" of Aryan preeminence and of Jewish racial "defects."

In 1886 a literary explosion that rocked France transformed anti-Semitism from a current of thought into an ideology. This best-seller of the latter half of the nineteenth century in France was Edouard Drumont's book *La France juive: Essai d'histoire contemporaine*. Within forty-eight hours the first edition had sold out; 114 editions were published within a year. Drumont's anti-Semitic breviary underwent 201 printings in all, the last in 1941. A fat man with steel-rimmed glasses, long black hair, and a billowing black beard and mustache, Drumont more closely resembled the semiticized horrors he depicted in *La France juive* than the Aryan heroes he extolled. Whether a prophet, as many claimed, or a first-rate demagogue, the so-called Pope of Anti-Semitism began his career as a petty bureaucrat but soon became a journalist. His "talent" lay in turning anti-Semitism into "a global system of explanation,"[26] in which the Jew was made responsible for *all* France's problems. "Everything is caused by the Jew; everything benefits the Jew,"[27] Drumont declared flatly in the book's opening pages. Grotesque, racist descriptions of Jews were Drumont's stock-in-trade. He constantly contrasted a heroic, chivalric Aryan race with the greedy, sly Jewish race, all punctuated by nostalgic evocations of an idyllic, precapitalist "old France" threatened with extinction by Jewish agents of "modernity." In *La France juive* Drumont gave every reader a reason to hate something about the Jews. His "discovery" of anti-Semitism as a coherent and malleable ideology catalyzed the development of anti-Semitic institutions, attracting both left- and right-wing enemies of the Jews. The success of *La France juive* also accelerated the publication of thousands of other anti-Semitic books, pamphlets, and articles, spewed out largely by a sizable journalistic proletariat and sanctioned by the Third Republic's easing of censorship laws.

Gyp's wrath toward the Jewish "race" emanated from some of the myriad sources of anxiety tapped (and also created) by Edouard Drumont, her future friend and collaborator, whom she hailed as "a visionary."[28] To the aristocrat Gyp, descendant of Mirabeau-Tonneau and Cou d'Argent, the Jew represented the bourgeois. This "parvenu" threatened to replace a social hierarchy based on land ownership and privilege with one founded on financial capital, while still aping the distinctive signs of aristocratic life. Such distortions, of course, usually have some grounding, however tenuous. Gyp's resentment resulted, in part, from the spectacular, highly visible success of a small number of middle-class French Jews.[29] To the sentimental Bonapartist of Legitimist descent, the Jew became synonymous with the hated democratic Republic, which brought to power a new, largely bourgeois political class and dethroned the aristocracy in the civil service, magistrature, and elsewhere. The Catholic traditionalist, whose father died while fighting to preserve "Christian civilization," had little trouble identifying the Jew with Satan. Finally, the apologist of "old France"—"the France of old, the pretty France, bubbly like champagne, always light and always victorious,"[30] to which Gyp would soon be compared—spurned the Jew as a representative of anti-France. The advent of Jewish "domination" at a time when French national identity was in flux marked for Gyp, as one of Drumont's titles mournfully predicted, "the end of a world."[31]

Gyp's unleashing of a torrent of anger and anxiety at the Jews betrayed her socioeconomic and political background. Yet her prejudice differed markedly from that of many contemporaries in its degree of extremism. For her anti-Semitism also stemmed from her simultaneous embrace and condemnation of power, which was rooted in her ambivalence toward gender. The Jewish scapegoat of her invention was a dual symbol of her impotence as a woman. On the one hand, he was the archetypal oppressor, crushing the world with his sacks of gold coins; Gyp's novels and caricatures abound with such clichés. In lambasting the Jews, she was battling the sense of helplessness she had felt since childhood and the shame inherent in being a female and "the last of the Mirabeaus." Her anti-Semitism was the most violent manifestation of her hatred of all "oppressors," beginning with her mother. It was a measure of her acute sense of marginality as a woman, an aristocrat, and a writer trying to eke out a living in a competitive market. Frustrations with the many prominent Jewish middlemen on whom her professional life depended—most notably her publisher, Calmann-Lévy, but also Hector Crémieux and the theater directors Dreyfus, Bertrand, and Baron, among others—only aggravated her hostility. Indeed, the vicissitudes of her literary career would, to a certain extent, determine the tenor of her anti-Semitism.

Although Gyp intended to eliminate these cumbersome Jewish enemies and indeed wished to supplant them, she also felt attracted to, and even identified with them. She would later admit that she was, like her repulsive, money-grubbing Jews, "dazzled by the money question."[32] She clearly saw in "the Jew" the ambition, the will to power she could not always admit in herself but felt safe to fictionalize. "I want to become strong . . . very strong . . ."[33]

An almighty tyrant, both detested and admired, the Jew was also, paradoxically,

Gyp's symbol of impotence and decay. In codemning the Jew, she denounced not only strength but its opposite, namely, the weakness, the "feminine" she tried to obliterate in herself. She had insisted, after all, that her literary persona Gyp was male, as was her artistic persona Bob. Her attitudes and behavior support the contention that "the Jews were sometimes identified with femininity, and hostility to Jews may have been an expression of women's rejection of their gender and its disabilities."[34] Gyp damned in the Jew what revolted and frightened her in others and in herself. Her antithesis and her double, the "other" enabling her to define herself through opposition, the Jew cast back at her "a troubling image, which is her own . . . ."[35]

Four years before the publication of *La France juive*, Gyp was already beginning to popularize the anti-Jewish clichés associated with Drumont. She derided the Jewish conspiracy for socioeconomic dominance in *La Vertu de la baronne*, which was published in 1882, the same year as the Union Générale crash. In one sketch the comte de Provence, unwilling to believe his mistress avaricious, disguises himself and spies on a run-down house near the Bourse, site par excellence of Jewish conspiracy. Here the financier Singemann (translatable as "monkeyman") entertains a clan of Jews, all cursing, eating vulgarly, and plotting the Union Générale's collapse. Witnessing this, the count concludes: "They are the Creator's masterpiece; below them is the entire human race, above them, no one!"[36] It was Jewish social pretensions that Gyp satirized in *Autour du divorce* (1886). At the Théâtre des Français the marquis d'Alaly is dismayed by the presence of numerous Jews, including baron Ephraïm, "[who] hardly knows how to read, but [who] counts marvelously well and throws splendid parties at which he has not yet been able to ensure the presence of the upper crust."[37] The parvenu Ephraïm is an uncivilized intruder in this exclusive setting. Despite his efforts to ape an aristocratic lifestyle, he is incapable of being assimilated. He belongs to a different race.

Gyp's conception of the "Jewish question" as one of race, not religion, is explicit in her 1886 pamphlet *Une gauche célèbre* (*A Famous Left*). The title alludes to a much-publicized news item concerning Drumont and Arthur Meyer, a converted Jew and publisher of the faubourg's gossipy social monitor *Le Gaulois*. The foppish Meyer, whose hair was attentively curled each morning by his coiffeur, had been slandered by Drumont in *La France juive*. Like an honorable gentleman, Meyer challenged the polemicist to a duel. During their armed confrontation, the frightened Meyer grasped Drumont's well-aimed sword in his left hand while with his own sword he pierced Drumont's thigh. Humiliated by his cowardly conduct, Meyer remarked afterward: "It would take a major war to make people forget this."[38] In Gyp's booklet à clef, Drumont becomes Lacroizade, author of the best-selling *Le Monde nègre*. The Jewish Meyer is here the black Anatole Bamboula, "editor of the newspaper *The Panache of High Life* (which criticizes worldliness), the socialite par excellence (in spite of his color)."[39] Bamboula is tagged by certain racial "particularities," such as his offensive body odor. Lacroizade and Bamboula duel. The publisher is tried and acquitted, proving again the power of the black/Jewish "race," antithesis of the virtuous French "race".

From her earliest novels, then, Gyp vilified Jews, exploiting socioeconomic and racial arguments that were beginning to be disseminated in the popular press and elsewhere. Even the "pure" Petit Bob of 1882 recounts a meeting with "an old [Jew], all dirty, who once came to buy ol'books from the Rev . . . "[40] Bob's anti-Semitism was to become more vicious, and so was Gyp's.

"A Nasty Business"

With her career blossoming in the 1880s—Paul Valéry, on vacation in Italy in 1887, reported to a friend that Gyp's works were among those which "sold the most"[41] in that country—and her circle of friends and acquaintances expanding, Gyp's life was growing more hectic. But it was also turning macabre, bizarre, even violent, the result of her blunt personality and controversial views. She was becoming famous—and notorious—as a public personality and adventurer.

Police reports and newspaper articles recounted that on 27 October 1884, at 6 P.M., Madame de X, "a young woman with an old name, notorious for several scandalous books,"[42] was leaving Marcelin's Champs-Elysées office. Suddenly she was accosted by "a respectably dressed woman of medium height, her face veiled in thick gauze wrapped around a plumed toque."[43] The veiled woman lunged at Gyp, showering her with "a *burning and freezing* liquid."[44] Just as quickly, the *vitrioleuse* disappeared into carriage 2827, which sped off toward l'Etoile. By the next day Parisian newspapers had already sensationalized the story. The sulfuric acid, it was reported, had eaten into Gyp's neck and shoulders. In fact, she received only superficial burns on her hands and chest. Shortly after the attack, she attended a performance of *Hernani* in a provocative décolleté.

Grisly, sometimes graphically illustrated accounts of attacks by *vitrioleuses* added an eerie note to the news items in late nineteenth-century French newspapers. Many conservatives and police officials deemed these *vitrioleuses* a disturbing new social danger and proof of innate female instability. Police Chief Gustave Macé lashed out at these social pariahs in his memoir cum didactic tract, *Les Femmes criminelles*. Tracing the history of this weapon of female passion, Macé evoked Jeanne de la Cour, who scorched out her lover's eyes so he would not see her age, and described women pouring acid into the holy water founts of Parisian churches at Christmas. Abandoning the macabre for the moral, Macé blamed certain mothers both for raising their daughters "à l'américaine," that is, as boys, and for neglecting their religious education. Without the proper psychological corseting by the Church and the family, he warned, all women might become hysterical, acid-wielding androgynes.

But here Gyp was the attacked, not the attacker. And she intended to solve the mystery of this "Corsican-style vendetta."[45] The police opened an administrative and then a judicial inquiry. The coachman of carriage 2827 was questioned, confronted with several demimondaines "over whom hung vague suspicions,"[46] and then released. Two weeks after her dousing Gyp received anonymous letters threatening new aggressions. In response she requested armed protection from the police prefect and was obviously delighted to be sent a husky personal bodyguard.[47] The police paired him up with a second agent after Gyp saw a woman questioning her coachman outside Marcelin's building: "[I]t is *decidedly* at the exit to Monsieur Marcelin's that someone is waiting for me,"[48] Gyp informed the prefect.

After several weeks of investigation, the police announced a suspect, a former Bouffes-Parisiennes actress and cocotte named Alice Regnault.[49] She was the mistress of the novelist and polemical journalist Octave Mirbeau,[50] whose taste for social justice was matched only by his desire to succeed in the Parisian literary world. A search of Regnault's apartment turned up nothing, not even the suspect, and the motives for her "crime" were unclear. Was Gyp her literary rival? A romantic one? If the anecdote recounted by the writer J.-H. Rosny aîné can be believed, this was indeed the case. In Rosny's account, a certain "Madame de K . . . ," easily identifiable as Gyp, "had, for Mirbeau, a liking that he peremptorily refused to satisfy" because the aristocratic paramour in question had scrofula![51] At the height of the exasperating investigation, Mirbeau himself corroborated this image of Gyp as physically and morally repellent in a letter to the writer Robert de Bonnières: "I realize she puts the impotent, obscene, elderly judges in heat," snarled the mercurial Mirbeau. "But I won't invite her to play the courtesan with them because I noticed yesterday, when she leaned over, that her neck is badly scarred with scrofula. There's a good story to spread around: *Gyp's Scrofula*, a legal novel."[52] Perhaps wishing to punish Gyp for embroiling him and his mistress in a notorious and now very public legal proceeding, he publicly flayed the scrofulous countess as a practictioner of "obscene" literature: "When on a road I come across a puddle of excrement" (Gyp makes her appearance here), "I avoid it; when I see certain names on the covers of certain books, I pass by quickly, holding my nose. . . . I know of nothing stupider than these adventure stories written with dirty bidet water. . . ."[53] With a disgusted Mirbeau and a furious and determined Gyp continuing to trade swipes, the investigation dragged on, eventually being dismissed for lack of evidence. The case, as Macé noted, remained mysterious, "with the exception of a few initiates."[54]

But the affair had not ended. Nine months after her assault, Gyp was again targeted for violence. According to *Le Temps*' "*faits divers*" column, at 2 A.M. on 28 July 1885 Gyp, as usual, was at her writing table beside an open window. Roger was absent and the children and servants were asleep. Hearing the bell ring at the outside gate, Gyp approached the window, expecting to see the children's tutor returning from a late-night outing. Instead she heard gunfire and then realized that a large bullet, shot from "a luxury weapon," as it was later determined, had just grazed her window shutters and had missed her head by only several inches.[55] Hours after the presumed attempt on her life, Gyp convoked police officers and magistrates and began to orchestrate the investigation herself. This time there was a possible motive. A month before the shooting, Havard had published Gyp's novel *Le Druide, roman parisien* (*The Druid, A Parisian Novel*), a roman à clef in which she recreated her now infamous acid bath and slung verbal acid back at her suspected *vitrioleuse*, Alice Regnault. Apparently, two days after the work's publication, Havard received an unexpected call from one of the novel's subjects and, after a talk, agreed to recall the book. Furious, Gyp accused Havard of breaching their contract. With some legal help, she forcibly restored her novel to the display windows of Parisian bookstores. This resumption of sales, the police inferred, may have provoked Gyp's would-be murderer.

In Gyp's view, she was the victim of a cabal. This belief may have been legitimized for her by the broader fin-de-siècle craze for the occult and spiritism, which had actually begun under the Second Empire. This preoccupation with the occult—which in France manifested itself in art, literature, and in a proliferation of spiritist groups and publications—was one thrust of a protean revolt against the late nineteenth century's dominant secular dogma: scientific materialism. There were more things in heaven and earth, it was realized, than could be explained by positivist philosophy. Nevertheless, magnetists, mesmerists, and other conversants with the afterworld often claimed a pseudoscientific authority shared by, for example, racialist "ethnologists" like Vacher de Lapouge.

If occultism represented a counterpositivism, it also assuaged the fears of many for whom the transition to modernity was cause for anguish. The 1870 defeat and the Commune, the French loss of European hegemony, the advent of both a new republican political class and an organized proletariat, technological and scientific progress—to many, the world founded on these changes seemed senseless, alien, mysterious. "The truth is that we are shrouded in mystery, that we live in mystery,"[56] moaned Edouard Drumont, a particularly anxiety-ridden Frenchman. The "mystery" of France's brusque transformation, argued Drumont and others, could not be explained rationally. Rather, it was engineered by occult powers, inevitably sinister.

Gyp's friend Drumont indeed established an equivalence between Jews and the occult. Despite the polemicist's efforts to pierce the "mystery," he concluded that the gates to the afterworld were closed to him by the "real" initiates, the Jews, who were permanent residents of this shadowy place. The imagery Drumont and Gyp associated with the "Jewish plot"—night and shade, clandestineness, initiation rites, passwords, codes—further linked the Jews to an occult space. But if such anti-Semites as Drumont, his collaborator Gaston Méry, Gyp, and others felt victimized by an occult plot, they could also manipulate occultism to their advantage. Gathered around the séance table, connected to their neighbors by their fingertips, these initiates could claim to form a counterfraternity, united not to unleash evil but to reveal divine truth. Their embrace of occultism became the basis for a type of "counterplot" to subvert Jewish domination.[57] Occultism at the fin de siècle thus served as a double-edged sword, allowing some of its adepts to wage war as both victims and aggressors.[58]

Gyp's novel *Le Druide*, the presumed cause of the two mysterious attacks against her, crudely reveals the author's paranoia about being the victim of a cabal. Like the discourse of many fin-de-siècle spiritists, her novel relies on contrasting images of light and obscurity, truth and secrecy. Even the novel's epigraph encapsulates her obsession with these Manichaean dualities. Quoting Mirbeau, she introduces the novel's thesis: "If, instead of striving to hide shameful acts, as is the custom, we unveiled them dramatically, I imagine that all would work out for the best."[59] Those guilty of "veiling" shameful truths, in Gyp's novel, are all employees of *Le Druide*, a thinly disguised *Le Gaulois*. She again caricatures *Le Gaulois'* editor, Arthur Meyer, a Jew too assimilated for her tastes, as Anatole Solo, whose motto is "I shall succeed."[60] He mysteriously finagles his way into the press "thanks to the unexplained patronage of a financier."[61] Solo has hired a Mr. Müller—Germanic in name at least—as his personal spy. Among Solo's henchmen is the caustic journalist Daton (Mirbeau), member of a secret society "that only works 'openly' in certain corners where you will never go."[62] Also on the staff is Geneviève Roland, who signs the gossipy "Paris-Bloc" column of *Le Gaulois* with various pseudonyms: "Gant de Velours" ("Velvet Glove"), "Spy," "Tout le Monde" ("Everyone"). (Alice Regnault wrote for *Le Gaulois* under the pseudonym "Mitaine de Soie" ["Silk Mitten"]). Roland, the narrator concedes, has a certain beauty. Yet her "semiticized" features—"thick . . . skin, coarse ears, heavy haunches, swollen joints . . . "[63]—almost ideographically tip off the reader: "Gant de Velours" cannot be trusted.

In fact, Roland has a vendetta against "Meg" de Garde. The motive? Meg/Gyp is the protector and friend of her sister-in-law, Suzanne, who is in love with Pierre, Roland's former flame. Meg's story now parallels Gyp's: she receives anonymous threatening letters, gets splashed with vitriol, and parades around Paris with police guards. The novel's ending anticipated that of Gyp's investigation: neither an official police inquiry nor another search of Regnault's apartment turned up conclusive evidence proving her complicity in Gyp's assaults. Nor did they establish the guilt of Mirbeau, whom Gyp accused of the actual shooting. The journalist would subsequently be drawn into another legal quagmire, this time involving a confrontation with the attorney general, Camille Bouchez, leaving him to fume against the "appalling hussy"[64] who had crossed him, and his friend Claude Monet to wonder: "I do not know what has happened in his life, it must be quite extraordinary for he finds himself somehow indicted in a nasty business initiated by this Madame de Martel who signs [her works] Gyp and who has written about him the book called *Le Druide*. I believe him to be on the eve of great troubles."[65]

Repeatedly confounded by the esoteric—and "very inclined to believe in the supernatural"[66]—Gyp was still determined to become an initiate. If she could not yet unravel the mysterious workings of the universe, she reasoned, perhaps she could fathom some of her personal mysteries. In January 1882, her face veiled, she called on "Desbarolles," a society psychic and graphologist whose clients included Sarah Bernhardt and Ludovic Halévy. Holding his visitor's left hand, the paralyzed Desbarolles dictated to Gyp, who with her free hand transcribed his dictation. The resulting document, entitled "Nature physique et morale," contains the seer's insights into Gyp's character and his predictions for her future.[67]

After examining the lines in Gyp's palm, Desbarolles commented on his client's family, tastes, and character. On Gyp's father's side, Desbarolles saw "frequent accidents and violent deaths."[68] Gyp, he noted, had three children, "two much more profoundly traced."[69] One of them, he said, must be a girl. Among Gyp's passions, Desbarolles listed children, animals, theater, and "violent exercise."[70] Describing Gyp's character, Desbarolles contrasted the writer's *"very great simplicity"*[71] with her equally "great energy,"[72] energy that often gave way to "violent outbursts."[73] Gyp, the psychic concluded, "[w]ould not hesitate to give or receive blows. Great confidence in her physical force, which is real and uncommon for a woman. . . ."[74] Finally, the old man sketched his client's future. She would live a long life, maybe close to eighty years; her health was excellent. She would earn a certain celebrity at thirty, but real fame would not come until forty, lasting for fifteen years. At sixty, Desbarolles predicted, "I see another aura that this time comes not directly from you but rather from a child."[75] Gyp's success, then, seemed certain. "I would be very surprised if *you yourself* do not one day become famous,"[76] asserted Desbarolles. And he asked his interlocutor to underline this sentence. Gyp could thus feel relieved. She had succeeded in unveiling her future—and it augured well, it seemed.

VI

La Comtesse de Martel-Mirabeau
1888–1894

He will return . . .   Boulangist anthem

The "Brav'Général": Boulanger

In late 1887 a funeral procession snaked through Paris, led by Alexandre Dumas fils, Hippolyte Taine, Ferdinand Bac, and Gyp. Marcelin, founder of *La Vie Parisienne,* was dead. His "grateful student" Gyp—*Petit Bob* bore this dedication to her mentor—shared Bac's wistful musing: "It was a bit of the Second Empire that was being buried, with its elegant frivolity and delightful recklessness."[1] Gyp observed that with Marcelin's death, imperial frivolity was indeed now gone, buried under Republican corruption and chaos. Despite repeated Republican electoral victories since 1870 (excluding the 1885 monarchist resurgence), the regime's stability often seemed precarious. Cabinets coalesced and collapsed in rapid succession as the main Republican factions, Opportunists and Radicals, split over revenge against Germany, colonial policy, the separation of church and state, and revision of the "monarchist" constitution of 1875. Troubling social and economic conditions further discredited the Republic. The phylloxera epidemic of 1882–83 stifled agricultural production, while expansion of department stores marginalized small-business owners. Artisans and industrial workers were also threatened. A worldwide depression, foreign competition, the financial crisis provoked by the Union Générale crash, and the state's inability to invest while shackled by reparation payments contributed to France's distressing unemployment. But the regime ignored workers' demands for social legislation. The mid-1880s thus witnessed strikes that were often violently repressed by government troops.

To Gyp and others, the Republican regime had failed to resolve two questions crucial to France's future, one national *(la Revanche)*, the other social (integration of the working class into French society and politics). Instead, the concerns of Opportunist Republicans corresponded quite literally to their title. Shortly before Marcelin's death, Daniel Wilson, a deputy and son-in-law of President Jules Grévy, was caught trafficking in military decorations out of an Elysée office and using the profits to fatten his stock portfolio. "L'affaire Wilson" prompted Grévy's resignation, leaving the ex-president to contemplate, in the words of a popular song, "the misfortune of having a son-in-law." Grévy's successor, the colorless Sadi Carnot, boasted an impeccable republican pedigree, yet to many Marianne had become a slut.

Who would clean out the Republic's Augean stables, Gyp wondered? Was it général Georges Boulanger, the former servant of the Republic turned symbol of anti-Republican discontent? Boulanger entered the government in 1886 as war minister (with the help of a lycée friend, the Radical deputy Georges Clemenceau). Boulanger's mission was to "republicanize" an army with a marked Catholic and reactionary bent. *Act 1* (March 1886): The general wins the favor of both government and workers by preventing troops from shooting at miners striking in Decazeville, and by proposing instead an alliance between labor and the military. *Act 2* (Bastille Day, 1886): Conscious of his growing popularity, Boulanger casts himself as hero in the military review at Longchamp, parading past the presidential tribunal on his black horse while the adoring crowd shouts "Vive Boulanger!" *Act 3* (April 1887): The German police arrest a French border official for trespassing on German territory. Boulanger's swift intervention procures Schnaebelé's release and demonstrates the war minister's willingness to act firmly toward Bismarck while averting an armed confrontation. From now on Boulanger would be "le général Revanche." Some observers, however, among them the painter Jacques-Emile Blanche, remained baffled by this "unbelievable fit of exaltation surrounding a kepi, a goatee, and a black horse."[2]

Yet the apogee of the general's popular success marked the beginning of his demise as war minister. Suspicious of his overnight celebrity, the Opportunists excluded him from a cabinet formed in late May 1887. As a further security measure, the government named him commander of a division in Clermont-Ferrand, a virtual deportation to the provinces. The day Boulanger departed, more than fifteen thousand people swarmed into the Gare de Lyon. Some lay across the tracks to prevent their hero's impending martyrdom, while others sang Boulangist anthems. A week later, Boulangist demonstrations, led by Paul Déroulède's Ligue des patriotes, the new shock troops of Boulangism, again interrupted Parisian Bastille Day celebrations. The previous year the crowd had acclaimed Boulanger as a Republican deity. But in 1887 it hailed the absent general as an opponent of Republican incompetence and impotence. Once synonymous with Jacobin principles, Boulangism had become "the revolt of the *excluded* against the parliamentary Republic."[3]

Disavowed by many of his former Republican supporters, including Clemenceau, Boulanger was now a pawn disputed by various anti-Republican factions eager for a return. November 1887 found him negotiating with prominent Orleanists, whose purses amply filled Boulangist coffers. In January 1888 he crossed the Swiss border to meet Prince Jérôme Napoléon. Alarmed at the prospect of another 2 December, the government relieved Boulanger of his military duties, thus enabling him to run for election as deputy. A National Committee composed of Déroulède, the journalist Henri Rochefort, and the Radical senator Alfred Naquet was formed to draw up a Boulangist platform. Its cornerstone was a revision of the 1875 constitution, with provisions for a president elected by universal suffrage and frequent recourse to plebiscites. Boulanger thus proposed a republic both more democratic and more authoritarian, one reminiscent of Louis-Napoléon's republican interlude of 1848–51.

Yet Boulanger's status as a popular idol could not compensate for his unpopularity in the French parliament. Denunciation by the Paris municipal council, and by most socialists and republicans, forced him to resign as deputy from the Nord, where he had been elected in April 1888. But he was the master of the surprise comeback. Luckily for him, the first rumors that Republican deputies had received hush money following the bankruptcy of Ferdinand de Lesseps' Panama Company seemed to justify Boulanger's new vocation as the Republic's "purifier." On 27 January 1889 a huge majority elected him deputy in the Seine, a republican bastion. Once again pro-Boulangist cliques in the army, police, and work forces, excited by the Ligue des patriotes, invaded the streets around the place de la Concorde. Boulanger's aides urged him to stage a coup, but he refused any illegal scenario. The minutes ticked by with no sign of Boulanger. By 12:10 A.M. Boulangism was already waning.

The collapse of the movement proceeded swiftly, after Prime Minister Ernest Constans vowed to punish the refractory general. He dissolved the Ligue des Patriotes and ordered Boulanger to appear before a special Senate court formed to judge crimes against state security. Signing the court order was Attorney General Jules Quesnay de Beaurepaire, a fake noble and former imperialist who sometimes wrote for *La Vie Parisienne* under the name Lucie Herpin. Boulangist leaders would nurture a vendetta against "the Herpin girl," yet Quesnay de Beaurepaire would resurface at their sides during the Dreyfus Affair.

Once again Boulanger fled, shocking his fans and leaving his henchmen to stand trial for an attempted coup and embezzlement. He met with the comte de Paris in London to discuss strategies for the upcoming legislative elections of September–October 1889. Once a powerful propaganda machine, Boulangism could now survive only through an electoral victory. Yet even the National Committee's frantic efforts and the duchesse d'Uzès' subsidies could not prevent Boulangism's electoral Waterloo. Republican discipline triumphed over Boulangist confusion; the April 1890 Parisian municipal elections confirmed the Boulangist debacle. Pessimistic and also disgusted by Boulanger's unwillingness to return to France à la Bonaparte, the National Committee disbanded. The Boulangist drama, rich in surprise entrances, crowd scenes, and false endings, now lacked only a memorable denouement. Boulanger complied in September 1891 by shooting himself in a Belgian cemetery at the tomb of Marguerite de Bonnemains, his recently deceased mistress. The journalist Séverine, a disenchanted ex-supporter of the general, saw this ending as appropriate. For Boulanger, she wrote, "arrived like Caesar, lived like Catalina . . . succumbed like Romeo!"[4]

Although receiving some support from the extreme Left, Boulangism died on the Right, leaving the Republic to emerge shaken but strengthened by this ordeal. The worldly abbé Mugnier correctly noted in his diary that "this gunshot in the Ixelles cemetery is a new triumph for the Republic."[5] Yet the Boulangist cadres outlived Boulanger, and they planned to avenge their "révolution manquée."[6] The anti-Republican ripples created by Boulanger in 1889 would swell into a forceful current after his death. A new breed of patriots had emerged, which claimed to love its nation as much as any republican. But, it insisted, France's greatness could only be restored after some vigorous housecleaning. Boulangism thus gave birth to nationalism, marking a crucial step in Gyp's own political and ideological evolution. The Dreyfus Affair would, in turn, baptize this nascent ideology.[7]

Into the Boulangist maelstrom "Gyp threw herself frantically."[8] She had first seen the general in Paris on 20 April 1888, shortly after his election as deputy from the Nord. This was his first public appearance in the capital since being exiled to Auvergne the year before. On display in an open carriage, which was followed by others containing his cronies, Boulanger, ever the lackey of public opinion, drove from the Louvre to the Chamber of Deputies, stopping to slowly ride once around the obelisk on the place de la Concorde. Gyp, enjoying a drink in the Tuileries with her two brothers-in-law, reported that "when the carriage emerged from the rue de Rivoli, which had to be closed off to ensure free passage of the carriages, the enormous, densely packed crowd in the square let out a howl that was really breathtaking. That, indeed, was truly a popular movement."[9]

Only Boulanger, Gyp realized, could give France a badly needed housecleaning, like the street sweeper in a contemporary cartoon, shown whisking Republican "debris"—a hook-nosed Jew, a Freemason, the Senate, and Chamber of Deputies—toward the sewer.[10] He would protect French workers against foreign competition, concentrate on revenge against Germany instead of wasting French money on colonial expeditions, and replace parliamentary incoherence with a strong authority resting on popular support. He would return "France to the French."

Aside from promising a specific political agenda, for Gyp Boulanger was a symbol. Like her father and grandfather, he was an officer, epitomizing her preferred "masculine" virtues of physical force, bravery, and charisma. And like her childhood idol Napoleon, Boulanger was a "savior," single-handedly rescuing France from chaos.[11] Indeed, Boulanger's "Caesarism," plus the similarity of the Bonapartist and Boulangist electoral maps, their common antiparliamentarianism, reliance on a charismatic military leader, and left-wing origins followed by right-wing endings, all marked Boulangism as a type of neo-Bonapartism.[12] Although many saw through Boulanger, Gyp endowed the general with the mystical qualities once conferred on France's absolute monarchs and on the first Napoleon. A friend noted Gyp's naïveté: "She readily endowed him with the qualities of conquerors which, unfortunately, he lacked: audacity, steadfastness, bravery, intelligence, and guts, that magic virtue she valued above all else.''[13] Gyp's Boulanger, then, though a substitute father, remained a two-dimensional figure, a cartoon image—like the portraits of Napoleon in her bedroom in Nancy, or Petit Bob's childish drawings.

Gyp also saw in Boulangism the opportunity to throw herself—with all the violence, daring, and crusading fervor of a Mirabeau—into an anti-Republican and antibourgeois mass movement. Politics, along with writing, now became the arena in which she unleashed her hatreds and resentment. But as a woman, of course, she was barred from the ballot box and the Chamber of Deputies. She compensated for this institutional exclusion by using other means, which were extrapolitical and sometimes illegal—fiction writing, journalism, caricature, appalling behavior—to influence public opinion. Her marginality obliged her to diversify the forms of her protest and to cultivate verbal, visual, and even physical extremism. Paradoxically, her gender would become essential to her notoriety and effectiveness as a Boulangist—and eventually anti-Semitic and anti-Dreyfusard—demagogue.

The height of Gyp's Boulangist activity coincided with the lively campaign for the September–October 1889 legislative elections. Boulangism had by then overtaken Boulanger, who was absent from France. The movement had become the voice of a coalition of malcontents united by a demand for constitutional revision. Gyp electioneered zealously in Lion-sur-Mer, the Norman seaside resort where she summered, during an election pitting the Opportunist Gravier against the marquis de Cornulier, a reactionary and revisionist. Abetted by a former mayor of Lion, Monsieur de Blagny, Gyp stunned the peaceful coastal community with her impassioned style. Her political activity was recounted in *Le Temps:*

> Gyp resolved to devote her leisure time during her country holiday to helping the revisionist candidate. Never did an electoral agent use more comic verve, nor more tireless ardor, in the service of a cause. You had to hear Gyp . . . celebrating Monsieur Boulanger, haranguing the peasants and fishermen, stuffing their children with candy and [smothering them with] hugs,—trotting along muddy roads from morning until night, with her oversized, reddish-brown coat, the green ribbons of her bonnet flapping in the wind.[14]

With all Lion worked up by her one-woman show, Gyp delivered a final pre-election blow to the opposition by distributing signed posters insulting the government. Her propaganda tactics worked and Cornulier was elected deputy. The victory celebration, orchestrated by Gyp, proved as emotional as the campaign. ''Twenty-one cannon shots were fired, people rejoiced, the village was lit up, champagne flowed.''[15] The villagers enjoyed a display of fireworks, which was paid for by Gyp. Later that night, she led a procession of rabble-rousers through the village; they carried flags and Chinese lanterns and sang in front of the homes of republicans. A judge later rebuked Gyp for instigating the free-for-all, fining her five francs for a ''nocturnal disturbance''; ex-mayor de Blagny escaped with a three-franc fine. *Le Temps* reported that Gyp planned an appeal.

Gyp recorded her participation in the 1889 campaign in two works, *Une élection à Tigre-sur-mer* and *C'est nous qui sont l'histoire!!!* (It's Us Who's History!!!). In the first, Bob, acting as narrator and illustrator, describes the campaign as a gigantic prank, an attitude that Gyp shared. The contest between "Hubert de Fontaine" (Cornulier) and "Alfred Caillou" (Gravier) was in fact eclipsed by a third person, "a beautiful, very chic lady who tore down the official posters when they were plastered to her house . . . she had the knack for that like no one else . . ."[16] When not removing republican posters, the eager campaigner distributed revisionist propaganda: "That was a lady who walked around with her dogs . . . distributing little brochures and supplements to *Le Gaulois* . . . at night she scattered them everywhere . . . so that people would find them in the morning on their way to the market . . ."[17] Bob's slangy, childlike narration matches the naïveté of "his" drawings. In one a group of imbecilic-looking sailors—"the people" Gyp claimed to adore—gapes at a life-size portrait, hanging in "Tigre's" town hall, of Boulanger on his black horse. But "Boulanger" is merely Napoleon III repainted, as Bob notes: "And then the portrait o' the general! . . . 'Twas the emperor that ha' been repainted . . . they gave him a blond beard 'stead of a black mustache, a black horse 'stead of a white horse . . . but it was still beautiful . . ."[18] And Gyp, in fact, was as credulous as the barefoot sailors in Bob's drawing, for she too willingly confounded Boulanger with Napoleon.

"L'affaire Caillou" is also evoked in the epilogue to *C'est nous qui sont l'histoire!!!* in the form of a farcical play in verse dramatizing Gyp's judicial appeal. A court official briefs lawyers and judges about the case:

> A demonstration of hatred
> Held the day after the elections
> Of the month of September; here's what brings
> These appeal seekers.
> They have, gentlemen, sad to say
> Offered a real charivari
> To a man who all admire
> Who is adored in the country!
> They paraded around with lanterns
> Shouted seditious cries
> And labeled old fogeys
> Those who did not do like them.[19]

Despite the plea of Caillou's lawyer to press charges against the "marquis, bourgeois, sailors"[20] responsible for the election-night melee, the judge yields to the more influential defense lawyers and pardons the accused. The attention now shifts from the guilt or innocence of "these revolutionaries / These aristos who want to fight"[21] to what the author considers a far more serious problem, namely, the corruption of the judicial system.

While not specifically treating the 1889 elections, several of Gyp's other works dramatize her Boulangist and anti-Republican sentiments. Boulanger is often their absent hero, as in an 1888 dialogue entitled "Feu Longchamps" ("The Late Longchamps"), published in *La Revue bleue.* While the nameless older characters assembled at the Longchamp track—"an Empire-era tart," "a lady who was very pretty in 1841,"[22]—reminisce about carriages, clothing, entertainment, the weather, even ways of "carrying" the female bust, a "little modern woman"[23] eagerly waits for Boulanger to pass by on his black horse as he did in 1886, but the general never appears.[24] Boulanger is also an absent presence in two illustrated book-length dialogues, *Bob au Salon de 1888* and *Bob à l'Exposition.* Relying on Petit Bob as her spokesman, Gyp sounds off against her bêtes noires: President Carnot (visually depicted as a stiff wax figure); the Eiffel Tower ("Ain't it a stupid thing, that Eiffel Tower!");[25] France's colonial policy; the 1875 constitution; and the Opportunists ("even their name . . . makes me sick!")[26] In contrast, President Mac-Mahon, the former imperial marshal, receives Bob's praise: "He was superb, in his pretty, simple Victoria, with a beautiful horse."[27] France needs a soldier-president, Bob asserts, for "a government that doesn't ride horseback ain't a government! . . ."[28] The ominous silhouette of Boulanger often lurks in the corners of Bob's drawings. At the 1889 World's Fair, celebrating the centennial of the French Revolution, Bob is disappointed not to see Boulanger's cardboard figure in a diorama beside those of Sarah Bernhardt, Rochefort, and Mac-Mahon. Although Bob's tutor reminds him of the general's departure from France, the boy continues to fantasize about the general-Messiah's return.

At least one reviewer felt dismayed by "Bob's" politics. In an open letter to *Le Temps* addressed to "Monsieur Bob," the anonymous "T" declared himself "surprised and afflicted"[29] by both Bob's adoration of Boulanger and antipathy to Carnot, "an 'honest man' who doesn't seem to you sufficiently 'decorative.'"[30] Was Bob really such an easy dupe, wondered "T"? "For if you are so enamored of tough guys and men with a gutsy allure, how do you manage, my dear Monsieur Bob, to have such admiration for the man . . . who took flight to London. . . . Does the black horse sufficiently compensate for so many unfortunate traits?"[31] Evidently Gyp's partisanship, as incarnated in Bob, was now obscuring critical evaluation of her literary merit. "T" announced that if Bob continued to like Boulanger, he would stop liking Bob.

Finally, Gyp's marionette play, commissioned by the editor Monnier, also featured the shadow of Boulanger. The resulting *Tout à l'égout! (Everything to the Sewer!)* (which was also published by Calmann-Lévy in book form) opened on 10 January 1889 at the Café du Helder, a smoky, overcrowded room on the boulevards that was a favorite haunt of military officers. There patrons in evening clothes packed in to watch what Jules Lemaître considered "[the] most original soirée of the season."[32] *Tout à l'égout!*—"exquisite, very elegantly incoherent,"[33] to Lemaître—represents the summation of all Gyp's sympathies and aversions during the height of Boulangism, each personified by a marionette. The heroes include a worker, Henri Rochefort, and Edouard Drumont. Among the numerous villains are the anti-Boulangist prime minister, Charles Floquet, a decadent poet, Stendhal (whom Gyp ridicules),[34] and a Moses with horns.

This motley group meets to tour Paris. Here, Drumont chases Moses, who is lugging the inevitable sack of gold coins, and finally catches up with him at the Bourse, where Moses has hurried—inevitably again—to worship the golden calf. This sacrilegious tableau allows Drumont to launch into a song, unusually violent for the period, attacking the Republic and capitalism through the Jew:

> For the bankers, it's over
> Down with the Bourse
> Hit them, go ahead!
> Speculators! It's war!
> Let's offer to the flames and to the sword
> Their hellish temples!
> Ah! hit them, hit them, hit them!
> Piff, paff, pouff, hit them!
> Let them pay,
> Let them pay,
> But mercy never, no never![35]

By means of marionettes, childish songs, nonsense syllables, and a relaxed café setting, Gyp succeeded through satire in rendering acceptable to her audiences an incitement to a pogrom. Jules Lemaître reported that "it was a lot of fun."[36]

At the end of the revue, all the characters wind up in the Parisian sewers. The *tout-à-l'égout* of the title refers to an innovative Parisian sewage system, dating from 1886, which rapidly directed underground wash water and human waste. This image of filth, murk, and poison serves as Gyp's metaphor for the current state of French politics. "To the sewers! . . . Let's go to the sewers!" the marionettes sing, "For that's where History is made! . . ."[37] Overhead is the Chamber of Deputies, from which filters down into the sewer the roar of a brawl. Above the fray, the voice of revisionist deputy and newspaper publisher Paul de Cassagnac menaces the Chamber: "You are nothing more than a cadaver . . . and the gravedigger awaits. . . ."[38] Again Boulanger's silhouette seems to float across this page in the text. It is Gyp's visual hint of impending apocalypse.

Boulangist Friends

Aside from the political, literary, and symbolic significance of Boulangism for Gyp, her participation in the movement resulted in several important friendships. Boulangism brought together people from highly diverse political and social backgrounds: an aristocratic, sentimental imperialist like Gyp; a chauvinistic Republican like Déroulède; an ex-Communard like Rochefort; and a young aesthete like Barrès. To each of these individuals Boulangism promised something different. In certain cases, as with Anatole France, common Boulangist sympathies merely solidified an existing relationship. Although France, like most Parisian literati, distrusted Boulanger and ultimately disavowed him, he also despised parliamentary "mediocrity." He thus briefly let himself be wooed by the general, and to prove his support he sported on his lapel Boulanger's favorite flower, a red carnation.

Other Boulanger devotees proved less fickle than France. Gyp certainly felt great admiration, if not more, for Paul Déroulède, the man who provided Boulanger with a badly needed political organization. Like Boulanger, Déroulède's political origins were republican. Born in 1846, nephew of the Second Empire playwright Emile Augier, Déroulède had opted for a career as a dramatist. The war of 1870, however, interrupted his plans. Déroulède volunteered for combat, was captured, escaped, saved his brother's life, and rejoined the army, emerging as an apostle of *la Revanche* as preached by Léon Gambetta. He expressed his despair over France's humiliation and his hope for her regeneration in his 1872 best-seller, *Les Chants du soldat*, an anthology of patriotic poems that, under Jules Ferry's presidency, became required primary school reading. With Gambetta as patron, Déroulède joined the Commission d'éducation militaire, formed to cultivate ''patriotic spirit and physical aptitude'' among French youth in preparation for the next war against Germany. The same wish to revitalize the nation led to Déroulède's founding, in May 1882, of the Ligue des patriotes.

With its hierarchical organization and dynamic membership, the league lacked only a forceful leader. This problem was resolved in 1883 when Déroulède met Boulanger. The general's charisma was matched by that of Gambetta's heir, Déroulède, a tall, lanky, bearded man who some claimed resembled Don Quixote. In 1888 Déroulède offered Boulanger the institutional support of the league and its newspaper, *Le Drapeau,* whether it be in distributing electoral propaganda or in staging Boulangist rallies—all this for a cause initially identified with a left-wing, Jacobin patriotism. But with the growing anti-Republican sentiment fostered by the economic depression of the 1880s and the temporary failure of Radical politics, due to Gambetta's death and the Opportunist ascension, Boulangism shifted to the Right and Déroulède moved along with it. By 1889, after his election as deputy from Angoulême and the league's dissolution, he was firmly in the nationalist camp.[39]

After Boulanger's suicide, Déroulède would replace him as Gyp's idol. And through Déroulède Gyp would meet Marcel Habert, another Boulangist impresario and Déroulède's second-in-command. The itineraries of Déroulède and Habert—indeed, of Gyp herself—unlike those of such fellow Boulangist aides as the Radicals Alfred Naquet and Georges Laguerre, would lead them from militant Boulangism to equally energetic anti-Dreyfusism. The progression from Boulangism to anti-Dreyfusism would also be traced by another of Gyp's comrades, who had come to Boulangism from extreme left-wing Radicalism: the notorious polemicist Henri Rochefort.

Rochefort, nearly two decades Gyp's senior, had a fiery nature. Ferdinand Bac remembered ''his deep-set, elusive eyes, his handsome mask . . . bearing traces of smallpox, his black mane of frizzy flames, flames of revolt and exaltation.''[40] Rochefort had begun his journalistic career under the Second Empire. His weekly attacks against the regime in *La Lanterne,* the newspaper he founded in 1868, led to his prosecution and flight to Brussels, where he continued to publish his views.

Returning to France in 1869, he was arrested, released, and then elected deputy from Paris. The journalist Victor Noir's assassination by Prince Pierre Bonaparte the same year infuriated Rochefort. His calls for insurrection won him a six-month stay in prison. Liberated, he briefly entered the Republican government, then switched his allegiance to the Commune. His "incitements to civil war" (so the Republican government judged his activities) were again punished. In 1873 a ship carried this unusual Communard to New Caledonia and life in exile. But even the confines of a penal colony could not retain him. With five other outlaws he escaped and made off for Australia. For the next six years he wandered across the United States, Ireland, England, Belgium, and Switzerland before the 1880 amnesty law allowed him to return to France. No sooner home but he began lashing Opportunist Republicans in his newly founded *L'Intransigeant*. In 1885 his power as a talented and fearless editorialist helped him win a seat as deputy from Paris by running on a Guesdist-Blanquist platform. He resigned the next year fully to devote himself to Boulangism. In keeping with a personal tradition, he was again condemned for conspiracy and slapped with a sentence of deportation for life. Of course, Rochefort would return.[41]

In many ways Rochefort offended Gyp. He was fiercely anticlerical, antimilitarist, and, worst of all, anti-imperialist. Yet for Gyp membership in the Boulangist militia redeemed him of all sins. Besides, Rochefort was an aristocrat, born the marquis de Rochefort-Luçay. Despite his origins, though, he cultivated a "popular" persona, as did Gyp, punctuating his speech with slangy interjections and running for elections on a vaguely socialist platform. His sympathies for the downtrodden, however, were highly dubious; this "[a]ristocrat [became] nauseous on contact with the people."[42] Rochefort's pseudopopulism, anti-Opportunism, and anti-Semitism obviously pleased Gyp. Yet what drew her even closer to Rochefort were his anarchistic leanings. For Rochefort, wrote one observer, "was above all a destroyer,"[43] like Gyp, blaster of oppressive authority, whether maternal, conjugal, or political. As Boulangism made way for the Dreyfus Affair, Rochefort's partisanship and violence, like Gyp's, became more pronounced. "The blows he was delivering," Léon Daudet wrote, "began by causing black and blue marks, then scratches, then burns, then serious wounds."[44] Gyp, too, was "in a permanent state of insurrection."[45] She shared Rochefort's apocalyptic view of politics, as is evident from an 1894 letter to him, written after a wave of anarchist bombings had rocked Paris: "When on earth is the government going to blow up, with or without a bomb?"[46]

Rochefort's bluntness contrasted with the refinement of Maurice Barrès, another Boulangist and thirty years his junior, who would become Gyp's lifelong friend. Among much else, Gyp and Barrès shared roots in Lorraine, and thus an acute sense of humiliation over the 1870 defeat. Barrès was born in 1862 to a bourgeois family from Charmes-sur-Moselle. Like Gyp, he was the grandson of an imperial officer. As a boarder at the Collège de la Malgrange, near Nancy, he had often spotted a distinguished-looking young woman—the comtesse de Martel, he was told—riding through the Lorraine countryside. Later, in Nancy, the sight of Gyp again fascinated the young student, "when she was a brilliant young woman and he still a boy, at circus performances, in the central loge where equestriennes who knew of her love for horses came to salute her."[47] While the "brilliant young woman" Gyp was taking mental notes during dinners at local châteaux, the student Barrès was intoxicating himself on larges doses of Flaubert, Gautier, and Baudelaire, administered by his classmate Stanislas de Guaïta. Both Gyp and Barrès yearned to leave their *province* and, like literary Rastignacs, to conquer the capital with their talent and ambition.

The two transplanted natives of Nancy (Barrès made it to Paris in 1883, four years after Gyp) finally met in the capital sometime between 1886 and 1890. They were introduced by the painter Henri Rondel, who had done his military service in Nancy and with whom Barrès rented the house of the salon painter Jules Bastien-Lepage in the rue Legendre. By the time of their first encounter, Gyp-Bob was a famous, widely read writer and one of Calmann-Lévy's latest successes. If she represented the spirit of the boulevards, Barrès, thirteen years Gyp's junior, identified himself with a younger, more avant-garde literary generation. He extolled the symbolists in various reviews, including his own, short-lived *Taches d'encre*, and frequented the bohemian Café Vachette. Yet literary respectability was conferred on Barrès through his friendship with Anatole France, who had initially insulted his younger colleague's work but still ushered him into the salon of the venerable Parnassian Charles Leconte de Lisle. Here Barrès met other literary patriarchs such as José Maria de Heredia, Sully Prudhomme, and even Victor Hugo.

It is difficult to understand Barrès' initial appeal for Gyp. Where she was extroverted, aggressive, and instinctual (traits she sometimes hid under a polite veneer), Barrès was often cold, cerebral, yet also sensual. Champion and analyst of the self in his trilogy *Le Culte du moi (The Cult of the Ego)*, he adored Stendhal, whom Gyp despised. Yet his physical appearance was initially more attractive to Gyp than his literary tastes. According to his friend and portraitist Jacques-Emile Blanche, Barrès resembled Gyp's childhood idol, the young Napoleon I: "Many women thought of a Bonaparte when seeing him as I painted him at twenty-five, his hair scanty and flat, his skin olive-colored, thin, wearing a gray vest, a yellow carnation in his buttonhole, his arms crossed over his chest."[48] Despite Barrès' affectations, Gyp was not indifferent to the aloof seductiveness of this "prince of youth."[49] The gossipy abbé Mugnier records in his *Journal* that the novelist and literary critic Rachilde revealed to him that Barrès was Gyp's lover.[50] Yet there is absoutely nothing in either the tone or the content of the many letters Gyp and Barrès exchanged over the course of three decades that hints of this.

Even better, as far as Gyp was concerned, was that Barrès worshiped Boulanger. For both Gyp and Barrès Boulangism was a form of anti-Opportunism. But whereas Gyp's attraction to Boulanger was above all a symptom of her particular emotional and psychological needs, Barrès conceived of Boulangism as a type of aesthetic revolt. For Barrès Boulanger was the "prince of men" apostrophized at the end of *Sous l'oeil des barbares (Under the Eye of the Barbarians)*, a harmonizing force selected by the national instinct to repel the unidentified "barbarians." Only Boulanger, Barrès argued, could tap the unchecked energies of "the masses," allowing each person, in turn, to discover his or her own individuality through participation in a popular movement. Barrès had mapped out the same progression from alienation to engagement to self-realization in his hugely successful trilogy *Le Culte du moi*. Art and politics, to Barrès, were one.

Led to Boulangism through "a mixture of dilettantism, ambition, and disgust for the regime,"[51] Barrès decided to translate his aesthetic into action. He joined forces with members of the National Committee, founded a revisionist newspaper, *Le Courrier de l'est*, and returned to Nancy in the fall of 1889, this time as a revisionist Republican candidate running for the seat of deputy in a working-class district. Many were surprised to find the privileged, ivory-tower denizen wooing his constituents with promises of social reform. These accusations of bad faith were perhaps not unfounded as far as Barrès' working-class sympathies were concerned. However, the intensity of the twenty-six-year-old deputy's committment to Boulanger, a secular deity "through whom great hopes are born,"[52] could not be disputed. But like Déroulède and Rochefort, Barrès was drifting toward the Right. The aesthete with pseudosocialist convictions would soon become both theorist and practitioner of right-wing nationalism.

Gyp and Barrès admired one another as nationalist partisans and as writers. Despite their contrasting personalities, the two former Nancy residents shared an ironic sense of humor and a taste for action which would draw them and their families even closer, as both friends and accomplices.

VII

La Comtesse de Mirabeau-Martel

1888–1894

~~~➤⭐◀~~~

Gyp and Bob Request the Pleasure of Your Company . . .

One day in early March 1892, Stéphane Mallarmé opened his mail to find an invitation: "Gyp and Bob beg you to do them the honor of looking at their pictures and pastels, exhibited at the Bodinière Galleries."[1] The card bore a drawing of a haughty-looking woman holding a lorgnette in her left hand and sporting a sash printed with the words "La Critique." Lying on the train of her dress, his hands lifted in supplication, is a little boy wearing black knickers. In the bottom left corner can be discerned the "artist's" unmistakable signature, surrounded by a cloud of curlicues: "Bob."

The Bodinière exhibit was Gyp's first solo show. It legitimized the writer's complementary vocation as painter and caricaturist. She had taken up drawing as a hobby while confined to Janville during the Franco-Prussian War, and began publishing her work in the early 1880s to accompany the "Bob" series. Her gallery debut occurred in 1891, when she participated in a group show, "Poil et Plume" ("Bristle and Pen"), featuring works by nineteenth-century writers dabbling in painting. This "Salon des Littérateurs-Peintres" also took place in the gallery at 18, rue Saint-Lazare run by Charles Bodinier, the secretary-general of the Comédie–Française. This gallery—where artists such as Jules Chéret, Bac, and Steinlen had had their first one-man shows—doubled as a foyer to Bodinier's Théâtre d'Application, where Gyp's one-act play *Sauvetage* had opened the year before to mediocre reviews.[2] Curious visitors to "Poil et Plume" could see dis-

99

played the artistic endeavors of Charles Baudelaire, the Goncourt brothers, Octave Mirbeau, and Anatole France. Gyp contributed painted fans whose "charming coloring"[3] pleased one reviewer; they were clearly reflections of the current fad for *japonisme*. One fan opened to reveal a watercolor of another of her bêtes noires, the psychological and sentimental novelist Georges Ohnet, proclaiming his love to an allegorical figure of the French language.

Gyp included the fan in her one-woman show at the "La Bodinière" the next year, alongside numerous other items, signed either "Gyp" (for "serious" paintings and pastels) or "Bob" (for "infantile" caricatures and drawings). She displayed her caricatures from the satirical newspaper *Le Rire*; a drawing of Barrès emerging from the Boulangist emblem, a red carnation; pastels; and many paintings, mostly realistic portraits of conventional subjects (for example, a man in evening clothes, a boy with his governess, a gentleman-farmer toting a gun on his shoulder, dogs, and babies). The official salons overflowed with this uninspiring art, which nevertheless impressed at least one critic. Firmin Javel of *Gil Blas*, expressing his "joy" over Gyp's "immense progress," reserved special praise for her "series of surprisingly lively and sincere portraits."[4] He even compared Gyp to Whistler. Although a modest critical success, the Bodinière exhibit did not reap the financial profits Gyp desired. Money generated by entrance fees, she complained in a letter, amounted to no more than "a ridiculous sum."[5]

Now acknowledged by the artistic establishment, Gyp sent entries to the Salon du Champ de Mars in 1893, 1894, 1896, and 1897. Her portraits (of the actress Réjane in *Madame Sans-Gêne*, of Madame Barrès, and of her daughter Nicole) and an *Annonciation* blended well with the landscapes and genre scenes displayed by such academic painters as Carolus-Duran and by fellow Neuilly residents Pierre Puvis de Chavannes, Albert Aublet, Léon Courtois, and Pascal Dagnan-Bouveret.[6] These benign visions clashed with the provocative fantasies on view during the same years at the Salon de la Rose+Croix and the Salon des Cent, suggesting that despite her literary image as an enfant terrible, Gyp the artist remained visibly conservative.

Sometimes the artist turned critic. The dialogue-novels *Bob au Salon* and *Bob au Salon de 1889*, in fact, are organized around a stroll through these official exhibits. Echoing Gyp, Bob acts as tour guide, offering an unexpurgated, illustrated commentary on the latest paintings by Jean-Léon Gérôme or Jean Béraud. Similarly, a dialogue in *La Revue illustrée* allows Gyp, speaking through a group of five characters, to publicize her enthusiasm for the 1889 exhibit of her future portraitist, Albert Aublet.[7] Harsher words were reserved for portrait photographers, whom Gyp accused of promoting a "rage of imitation."[8] She would remain hostile to photography, as she would to all forms of mechanical reproduction. Her suspicion of the new blending of art and technology revealed not only her antimodernism but perhaps also her vanity. She chastised the photographer Paul Nadar for selling his unauthorized photo-portrait of her, which she found unflattering. And she ordered him to "*immediately* remove the photos that are in the different shops where you had them placed."[9]

Like her personal or political sympathies, Gyp's evaluations of art were never neutral. She regularly attended gallery openings and offical salons, the ne plus ultra of society events. Here women in Pre-Raphaelite gowns and gentlemen sporting canes and top hats admired each other rather than the paintings. And celebrities like Sarah Bernhardt, surrounded by admirers, often breezed through the show. Spurning these fads, Gyp, "dressed very simply. . . slid discreetly through the crowd, where she was recognized only by a few friends. Under her moss green bonnet adorned with a velvet mouse, her mischievous eyes, from behind her lorgnette, systematically reviewed the paintings and people whose slightest quirk did not escape her."[10] Only a fortunate few escaped being relegated to purgatory by Gyp. She would announce the tally of the blessed and the damned in the next "Bob," or perhaps to friends. Writing to the aesthete and dandy (and her Neuilly neighbor) Robert de Montesquiou, she blasted one portrait by Dagnan-Bouveret, which she likened to a puree of peas, deeming it "purely hideous and ridiculous, too, and fantastically pretentious."[11]

Scurrying through the galleries, Gyp often crossed two artist friends, who, like her, were likely expressing their disdain for both the crowd and some of the paintings displayed. Edgar Degas was fifteen years older than Gyp. His unidealized paintings and pastels, like many of Gyp's novels, reflected an interest in contemporary subjects and settings such as the track or the opera. Both were keen observers of modern life, although Degas' work lacked Gyp's raw, satirical bite. In his personal life Degas was a gruff and misanthropic bachelor known for scorning women. Politically conservative, his nationalism and anti-Semitism had not yet erupted into frenzy, as they would during the Dreyfus Affair. He lived alone as an ascetic in a three-story house in Montmartre, attended by his servant, Zoé. Because of Degas' poor vision, Zoé would lull him to sleep with readings from his favorite works: the feuilleton from *Le Petit Journal*, *The Thousand and One Nights*, and *Petit Bob*. On learning that Degas was one of her fans, Gyp sent the artist her mushrooming number of dialogue-novels, which even a robust delivery man had trouble hauling up the stairs.[12] The painter, in an uncharacteristic act of gratitude, thanked Gyp and was soon dining regularly in Neuilly, expanding the circle of zealots, cynics, and misogynists who seemed to gravitate toward her.

Another initiate to Gyp's group was Degas' disciple and friend, the painter and caricaturist Jean-Louis Forain. Born three years after Gyp to a petit bourgeois family, Forain began his career roughing it in bohemia. He briefly shared a hovel with Rimbaud, who nicknamed him "Gavroche," and exchanged paintings for clothing. His penury made him hate the bourgeoisie and sympathize with the poor. Yet his situation improved in the mid-1880s with the publication of his drawings in *Le Courrier français* and *Le Figaro* and the launching of his short-lived *Le Fifre*. He was also excelling as a political caricaturist, an activity he shared with Gyp. In 1890 he enjoyed his first one-man show. Suddenly Forain, the former anarchistic bohemian, had become a man-about-town, both coveted and feared by Parisian high society. His personality had much to do with this. Like Degas and Gyp, Forain was a "Grand Inquisitor" capable of destroying an enemy's reputation with a word or a brushstroke. He hated the Jews, he hated the army, he hated everyone, it seemed, except the poor. But his benevolence toward the oppressed could not mask his universal contempt. "[I]n Forain's magnificent gaze," Ferdinand Bac sensed, "lived a dreadful hatred."[13]

"Madame Gavroche in a Ball Gown"

Gyp's appearances at social gatherings always drew attention.[14] Returning home from one of Alphonse Daudet's "jeudis" in March 1894, where guests had exchanged news of the latest anarchist bomb tossing, Edmond de Goncourt recorded in his journal the interest and excitement he had felt at the arrival of a newcomer:

> This evening, coming for the first time to Daudet's was Madame Martel, or rather Gyp. A large nose, a slightly faded blondness, but a bent elegance of the body in a white dress of a thoroughly distinguished taste, and voluptuous, exciting. She speaks lovingly about animals, about her horse, who tramples her feet and to whom she cannot resist bringing lumps of sugar daily, about cats she adores, about dogs for whom her house is a refuge; and as the conversation revolves around food, she says she likes only chops and boiled eggs and that sometimes she eats only that for lunch and dinner.[15]

Goncourt was not the only habitué at Daudet's who was impressed by forty-five-year-old Gyp. The fledgling literary and art critic Albert Flament, who was not yet twenty and for whom a coveted invitation to Daudet's rue de Bellechasse apartment promised initiation into the hermetic world of Parisian literati, was overwhelmed by Gyp's girlish appearance:

> Gyp . . . was holding with both arms a spray of flowers from her garden in Neuilly. She wore a white dress whose shape I would not know how to describe, except that it was long, tight, and bore no resemblance to those we were accustomed to seeing. To enter a meeting of thirty men of letters, the most famous of their time . . . to enter this study where Loti and Jules Lemaître, the habitués of the "Grenier Goncourt," might be found that evening, with these flowers, that white dress (at that time only girls or very young women would have allowed themselves that *boldness*) revealed a behavior, an education, acquired traits, and a simplicity that were certain and particular.
>
> Her hair was light brown, parted in the middle; her eyes and her teeth were bright. And the newcomer offered her flowers with exquisite grace to that elderly man . . . who was holding out his hands to her.[16]

Provocative yet immature, quirky yet refined, poised, smart, Gyp had arrived. The same year as her appearance at Daudet's, the society portraitist Giovanni Boldini captured in paint what Goncourt described in his journal as Gyp's "unhealthy seduction." Head slightly tilted, thick eyebrows arched, mouth curled into something between a smile and a sneer, Gyp in her low-cut dress stares directly—almost brazenly—at the viewer.

By 1894, of course, she was already famous. She had authored over forty books, including the wildly successful *Petit Bob* (which would reach a sixty-ninth edition) and *Autour du mariage* (107 printings). She was well known as the "leader" of a school of *dialoguistes* and as an artist. But her debut at Daudet's marked a new step in her literary and social ascent. For in prestigious salons such as Daudet's contacts were made, reputations solidified, and candidacies to the Académie française often determined. The salons linked *le monde* and the literary and political worlds, giving each coherence and enhancing the status of their respective members.

Moribund after the 1870 defeat, by the 1880s the salons again enlivened Parisian literary and social life. The anima of each salon was usually a woman, the *salonnière*. Tutelar deity, mistress of ceremonies, liaison, arbiter of taste, and divining rod for talent, the *salonnière* exercised considerable power over her flock. A celebrity-studded salon, like an address in one of Paris' most chic neighborhoods, could in turn bring both increased prestige and influence to women. And many *salonnières* relied on these newly acquired advantages to compensate for a too visible social "flaw," whether illegitimate birth and petit bourgeois background (in the case of Madame de Loynes), divorce or separation (Madame de Loynes, Madame de Pierrebourg, Madame Aubernon), or Jewish origin (Madame de Caillavet, Madame Cahen-d'Anvers, Madame de Fitz-James).[17]

Gyp frequented many of the exclusive salons to which her young colleague Marcel Proust anxiously sought entry. In the 1880s and early 1890s she moved easily among the homes of *salonnières* with varying political orientations, a privilege that ended with the Dreyfus Affair. At the hôtel of Napoleon I's niece, princesse Mathilde, where Gyp frequently turned up, Bonapartist obedience was de rigueur. A devoted lover of the arts, princesse Mathilde often gathered together Georges Bizet, Ludovic Halévy, Ernest Renan, Edmond de Goncourt, and younger writers like Pierre Loti, Maurice Barrès, and Paul Bourget. At the home of Madame Aubernon de Nerville, niece of the July Monarchy banker Laffitte, the hostess' political sympathies tended toward Radical republicanism. Wednesday dinners for twelve often brought to the same table Ferdinand Brunetière, editor of *La Revue des deux mondes*, Ernest Renan, Dumas fils, Bourget, the playwright Henri Becque, and the poet Heredia. Women were rarely present. The food, according to some guests, was execrable, the conversation excellent. Yet many resented the overbearing style of "la précieuse radicale," who often dictated discussion topics and interrupted speakers with a ring of her porcelain bell. Several of her faithful seceded, including Léontine Arman de Caillavet, a lively and erudite woman five years older than Gyp. Madame de Caillavet's own gatherings soon rivaled those of her former patron. Playwrights, actors, and poets such as Edouard Pailleron, Victorien Sardou, Henri Lavedan, Coquelin aîné, Sarah Bernhardt, Réjane, and Leconte de Lisle, in addition to such young friends of her son Gaston as Proust and Reynaldo Hahn, all passed through the hôtel on the avenue Hoche, as did Gyp. But the salon's undisputed oracle, of course, was Anatole France. Nearby, on the Champs-Elysées, another Egeria held court. The comtesse de Loynes, née Jeanne Detourbet and an illegitimate daughter of a Reims textile merchant, had succeeded in attracting an impressive crowd by relying on her intelligence and the help of a few well-placed lovers, including

Sainte-Beuve. Renan, Taine, Dumas fils, and Guy de Maupassant attended Friday-night dinners, often staged to show off the talents of the countess' protégé, Jules Lemaître.

For those adventurous enough to leave Paris for "the country," Gyp's salon awaited. Beginning in the mid-1880s, she entertained every Sunday, from noon until midnight, in a large, square room suffused with light filtering through four floor-to-ceiling windows that opened onto the lawn and garden. The eclectic profusion of bibelots, portraits, memorabilia, and furniture crammed into the room, a reflection of Gyp's individualism and eccentricity, jarred some visitors but intrigued others. "Never have I seen," Philippe Barrès asserted, "intimacy with history cultivated to such a degree of naturalness. . . ."[18]

History was indeed on view in the dozens of ancestral portraits dominating the salon's tapestry-covered walls. A bust of Mirabeau rested on a column in a corner. These visual fragments of Gyp's genealogy alternated with images of the hostess herself: Louise Abbéma's portrait; Louise-Catherine Breslau's pastel of her in a green plush gown; Albert Aublet's full-length rendering of Gyp standing on the beach wearing a snug brown dress, lorgnette in one hand and, in the other, a parasol. The rococo display on the walls matched that in the rest of the room. A large circular divan in the center, upholstered in striped maize-colored velvet and divided into four armchairs, was topped by a faïence swan overflowing with plants and flowers. Couches and armchairs in matching fabric lined the walls, and divans, stools, rocking chairs, and assorted other seats cluttered the remaining space. The pièce de résistance, as far as seating was concerned, was found to the left of the fireplace: "a majestic and deep armchair"[19] on wheels that had once belonged to Talleyrand now awaited guests of honor. Across from it and to the right of the fireplace was a low armchair and small footstool reserved for Gyp.

Screens and fans painted by "Bob," potted palms, a Louis XV cupboard full of porcelain, tables, Oriental vases containing roses and tulips, porcelain cats, a tall clock in the form of a wasp-waisted lady, a faïence monkey, books, a phonograph playing melodies by Reynaldo Hahn, a photo of Napoleon III with the prince imperial on his knees—this bric-a-brac gave a feeling of studied casualness to Gyp's salon, which to Philippe Barrès seemed "neglected, eroded by the sun and by time."[20] Oil lamps and candles illuminated the room in the evening, never ceding to electricity.

On a given Sunday Gyp's circle might include the Barrès family, Anatole France, the poet François Coppée, Paul Déroulède, Henry Becque, and Degas. Also present, inevitably, was Monsieur Genest. Little is known about Gyp's lawyer friend—and possibly her lover—except that he was the son of a teacher at the prestigious Lycée Saint-Louis and a grandson of the lawyer for the city of Paris. A discreet yet constant presence in Gyp's life, Genest was a habitual guest at her homes in Neuilly and, in the summer, in Lion-sur-Mer.

The day began with lunch. "The fare was delicious and carefully selected," commented one visitor, and meals ended with "exquisite pastries made from precious recipes."[21] The hostess' dress was, as ever, unconventional. She often appeared corsetless, in a caftanlike "papal" robe, black or white and trimmed with fur or lace, whose elbow-length sleeves exposed her muscular arms.[22] She amused her friends with anecdotes about the theater, track, or clubhouse. Sometimes her husband, Roger, joined her guests for lunch. Polite and congenial, if unrefined, he engaged visitors with his "slightly coarse sense of humor."[23] After the meal he retreated to his garden with a few friends for informal shooting practice. (Bullets invariably spattered the lawn of neighbor Ernest Judet, publisher of the nationalist newspaper *L'Eclair*.) Even the boldest guest proved no match for the experienced shot Roger. One humbled challenger remembered that the comte de Martel "massacred us one by one."[24]

Between lunch and dinner Gyp's guests gathered in the salon. Until the Dreyfus Affair erupted, the salon was not yet defined by nationalism. The reigning mood nevertheless remained one of conservatism, whether literary, artistic, or political. Writers like Coppée, Heredia, and Becque represented the French literary establishment, with links to such powerful politico-literary institutions as the Institut de France and the Académie française. Other writers present included Julia Daudet and Gérard d'Houville, whose pseudonym masked the fact that she was Heredia's daughter and wife of the poet Henri de Régnier. Many neighbors from Neuilly strolled over, including Barrès and his family, the publisher Judet, Robert de Montesquiou, the painter Léon Courtois, and the sculptor Jean-Joseph Carriès. Degas came often but rarely spoke.

Unlike many *salonnières* who purposely allowed their protégés to outshine them, Gyp was the star here. Making her entrance dressed in one of her trademark billowing dresses (velvet in winter, crêpe in summer)—"a strange little person,"[25] as one visitor remarked—she settled into her armchair by the fireplace. Then, leaning forward with her feet tucked under the chair, "her eyes sparkling with mischievousness,"[26] she began, in her faint Lorraine accent, to do what she did best, namely, to tell stories, slangy stories about the theater, the track, or politics, stories others had told her or ones of her own invention. She spoke excitedly, stumbling over her words, punctuating her narratives with "a little laugh, crystal-clear and nervous."[27] Julia Daudet also recalled this remarkable patter: "[S]he chats, this Gyp, about everything and everyone, about literature, which she knows thoroughly, about Edouard Drumont . . . to whom she is dedicating her new book, about her rides on horseback, about painting, which she adores; she's really an individual, an original."[28] As she continued her monologue, the obstinate line of her mouth periodically softening into an ironic smile, she stared intently, almost hypnotically, into the eyes of her interlocutors. One member of Gyp's audience could not forget "her clear eyes, lively and jeering, sparkling with intelligence, where the most fleeting impressions of life were reflected; they became fired up with such intensity during conversation that one forgot their form and their color."[29]

Gyp's salon served as a form of publicity for its hostess, whose gender denied her access to other official institutional networks of recognition, such as those provided by the university or the Académie française. Her salon allowed her to develop ties with members of the Paris elite, to conspicuously display the wealth and luxury expected of someone of her social and literary status, and to sustain a dramatic and eccentric persona. And finally, the many anecdotes interiorized and recounted every Sunday were providing new grist for her literary mill. As one guest noted, "all the Parisian gossip winds up in her salon, from which it pours out into her books."[30]

Lion-sur-Mer

When the Parisian "season" ended early each summer, self-respecting aristocrats and society figures headed for the Normandy coast, preferably Deauville or Trouville, the beach resorts made fashionable under the Second Empire by Napoleon III's illegitimate half-brother, the duc de Morny. Following suit, for several months each summer from 1885 to 1896, Gyp rented a châlet with an ocean view in Lion-sur-Mer which had once belonged to the painter Horace Vernet. She painted its walls with flowers, vines, and monkeys and housed her numerous guests there; she and her family occupied a more modest coach house overlooking a garden. Summers in Lion, one of the smaller seaside resorts, provided relief from the hay fever that plagued her in Neuilly. But they did not eliminate her obligation, as both aristocrat and widely read society novelist, to entertain and socialize. "I saw as many people there as I did in Paris, *if not more*," Gyp retorted in a hostile letter meant to counter her mother's assertion that the months in Lion saved her daughter both energy and money.[31]

It was enough of a financial strain just to support her extended family, not to mention her myriad guests. First there were her three children. Aymar was fourteen years old when his mother wrote the following description of him in *Un trio turbulent*: "stockier than his brother . . . a pleasant, gay face . . . unkempt . . . ease and laziness . . . distinguishing characteristic: extraordinarily strong."[32] Exceptional physical strength, a hallmark of the Mirabeaus, also characterized thirteen-year-old Thierry, whose passion for sports—especially cycling, boxing, and fencing—was detracting from his studies at the Lycée Condorcet and then at the Lycée Janson de Sailly. Although the family destined him for a diplomatic career worthy of Bacourt, Thierry was fascinated by science and in 1893 obtained a high school degree in this field. He already hoped to become a surgeon, despite his grandmother's condemnation of this career as unworthy of "a scion of his race."[33] "Tall, thin, nervous, distinguished, a mocking expression, very well groomed,"[34] Gyp wrote of her distant, slightly mysterious son. Something of Aymar's carefreeness and Thierry's tense insolence is conveyed in Louise-Catherine Breslau's pastel of the two brothers in loose-fitting blue and white striped flannels. Aymar wears his jaunty straw hat and rests his arm on his brother's shoulder, while Thierry, ramrod straight, hand on hip, stares pointedly at the viewer.

Finally, nine-year-old Nicole, "all blond and pink . . . nose in the air, mischievous eyes . . . tiny and strong at the same time,"[35] shared her mother's impishness. The novelist Roger Martin du Gard, who spent his childhood in Neuilly and visited Gyp's family in Lion, fondly remembered Nicole's "lively eyes . . .

her retorts . . . her blond hair ruffled by the sea breeze.''[36] Years later, in 1917, Martin du Gard would write to one of Nicole's relatives by marriage, asking her to present to Nicole ''the respectful homage of her companion in seaside games, himself the father of a little girl of ten.''[37] Gyp, whom Aymar, Thierry, and Nicole called ''Mam'' or ''Gros'Mam,'' treated them more like younger comrades-in-arms than like her own children. In the interest of inner strength and self-reliance, she imposed on them the same paramilitary discipline to which Gonneville had accustomed her. She greeted them with firm handshakes and, as one guest noticed, rarely hugged them.

Accompanying the children each summer were their tutors, the poet Jules Tellier and, after his premature death from typhus, Paul Guigou. Completing the entourage was the children's governess, Madame de Montégut, eminently well qualified, according to Gyp, if only because of having accompanied Empress Eugénie to the opening of the Suez Canal. Madame de Montégut, jovial and portly, struggled to keep the children out of mischief. Emulating yet also inspiring Petit Bob, the trio upset villagers by stealing Louis-Philippe's bust from the town hall and sticking it in the butcher's window, thereby replacing a cow's head. Of course, their mother's own pranks provided a model. Gyp's 1889 election-night shenanigans, plus her literary barbs at local aristocracy and bourgeoisie, had stirred up fear and suspicion in Lion. Yet she was also a hero among the poorer villagers. On her solitary nocturnal strolls along the beach, surrounded by her dogs, she often crossed paths with fishermen, to whom she readily dispensed money for needed repairs on their boats and sails. During one of his stays in Lion, Anatole France commented on his hostess' generosity: ''Yesterday I met her in the village street, holding by the hand two little beggars for whom she was going to buy trousers. She feeds all the lost dogs. She's an excellent creature.''[38]

Aside from the children, their tutor, their governess, and the inevitable Genest, house guests often swelled Gyp's ménage. During the day they were free to swim, fish for shrimp, or float in a canoe christened ''Bob.'' Gyp, perpetually dressed in a bathing suit, spent most of the day writing or in the water. After dinner the guests, joined by a local *châtelain,* chatted about art or literature or entertained themselves by singing songs by MacNab and Bruant.[39]

Gyp's most consistent guest was Anatole France, who spent at least one month in Lion each summer between 1891 and 1894. Although Gyp had met France around 1884, it was the deterioration of his marriage in the early 1890s that sanctioned closer relations between Gyp and both France and his future ex-wife. One evening Madame France showed up at Gyp's home in Neuilly after the couple had argued. France, it seemed, had been having his study walls covered with velvet cloth given him by his mistress, Madame de Caillavet. While Madame France had ordered the upholsterer to stop working, her husband urged him to continue. The scene ended with Madame France locking her husband and the workman in the study and escaping to Gyp's. But no sooner had she arrived than Gyp insisted that she return. A comic scene awaited Madame France at home: a large crowd, drawn by the upholsterer's cries for help, had gathered in the street and was trying to break down the door. France, meanwhile, was peacefully writing at his desk. Angered when his wife interrupted his work, France purportedly cursed her and, dressed in a nightgown and nightcap and clutching his inkwell and his article, calmly took his leave for good.[40]

Gyp became the divorcé's confidante, the position of lover already being occupied. France came to Neuilly for lunch every Sunday with his daughter, Suzon, while Madame France collected her after dinner. The writer expressed his gratitude to Gyp with gifts. "What a superb fan you sent me!"[41] "Thank you so much for the eau de cologne!,"[42] Gyp wrote, indicating her appreciation for this homage, which bore all the trappings of a courtship.

But in Lion Gyp and France actually saw little of each other, and often only at mealtimes. Both spent most of the day writing, and frequently commuted to Paris for meetings at Calmann-Lévy's offices. Independence was the rule in Lion, as Gyp informed France before his arrival in August 1893:

> Here's your setup: Suzon at the *Châlet Vernet*, in Nicole's room, a large room with two beds that until this year was used by Aymar and Thierry. You at the *the Farandole*(!) facing it; you will be *alone* as much as you like. . . . You will have a bedroom on the first floor, and the salon with a desk . . . at which to work, *all alone;* . . . the salon and dining room for *meeting* are in the Châlet Vernet. . . . We have lunch at noon. We dine at seven-thirty. Everyone has breakfast whenever he wishes, and there's the life! There it is! . . . Not very amusing, but very, very *independent*.[43]

France appreciated Gyp's discretion, as he confided to Madame de Caillavet: "Madame de Martel is an excellent creature. I only see her at meals, and the rest of the time she makes her presence known only through her care and consideration."[44] Yet he objected to even the minimal etiquette Gyp imposed. He often showed up late for dinner, hands unwashed, wearing a flannel shirt, mismatched socks, and yellow boots or espadrilles. At dinner he ignored most of Gyp's guests, "insignificant Norman country squires, who bore me."[45] An apparently unobservant Gyp found France's unconventionality charming: "France was delightful, always content with everything, in a good mood, even-tempered and pleasant."[46] She recalled that "often, around six o'clock, he used to go for a walk. The children followed him, gathering other children, who also followed. . . . We used to dine at eight, but almost all the other swimmers dined at seven-thirty or even seven. At eight-thirty France had not returned, and the panic-stricken parents mobilized all their servants and sent them rushing to the house. Around nine France would arrive, smiling and satisfied, followed by his flock."[47]

But for both Gyp and France such whimsical moments were rare. During the summers in Lion Gyp was preoccupied by a series of novels—including *Monsieur le Duc*, *Le Journal d'un philosophe*, and *Le Mariage de Chiffon*—and by a continuous output of articles. In August 1893, France, encouraged by Madame de Caillavet, began a roman à clef entitled *Le Lys rouge*. During his stays in Lion he also worked on *Jeanne d'Arc*, *Le Jardin d'Epicure*, and *Les Opinions de M. Jérôme Coignard*. As Gyp and France's friendship developed, so did their mutual appreciation of each other's literary talent. "The latest Bergeret are exquisite!"

Gyp gushed.[48] France was equally complimentary, if considerably less effusive: "Last night I read the continuation of the *Philosophe*. It's very good and interests me greatly. And, moreover, it's a way of being with you again."[49]

While in Lion, France felt his writing was suffering from the absence of his counselor, who in August 1893 was sailing off the northern coast of France on her husband's yacht. "I have learned that you are drinking to the dregs the pleasures of the inimitable life to which your husband has dragged you,"[50] France informed his mistress. Recovering from his desperation, he added that he needed thirty pages to finish *Jérôme Coignard*. Would Madame de Caillavet kindly oblige? As the summer neared its end, France continued to languish for his lover and frequent ghostwriter. "My room is very nice, but it is not as good as the study on the avenue Hoche."[51] Impatient to join Madame de Caillavet and her family at their château in the Gironde at the end of September, France sighed, "I'm becoming stupid far from you."[52]

Finally, France was briefly involved in an ill-fated literary collaboration with Gyp, Barrès, and Genest. In 1892 the four decided to write an epistolary novel modeled on Georges Sand's *La Croix de Berny*. France agreed to participate only if no one revealed his identity. Gyp, hoping to turn the project to profit as usual, proposed it to the editor of *Le Figaro,* Francis Magnard, at the rather exorbitant rate of three francs per line. Magnard accepted, believing the secret fourth writer was Renan, but offered a mere one franc per line. Problem followed problem. France produced nothing after the first letter, causing Gyp to complain to Barrès: "I hope you don't think it is I who am negligent and dishonest and who do not pass on the copy when I receive it. But I haven't received *anything* from France(!)"[53] The project soon collapsed, leaving Gyp to fret even more about her finances.

Money was not Gyp's only worry in Lion. She was also vexed by her daughter. Nicole was four years older than France's daughter, Suzon, whom Gyp described as "slender, fragile" with "magnificent eyes and a mass of rich blond hair. A very intelligent air."[54] Suzon reciprocated Gyp's affection. "She does not stop speaking of you with the tone of a respectful attachment," France wrote of Suzon. "You have given her, Madame, long, golden hours whose memory will charm her again."[55] No such idyll existed between Gyp and her own daughter. In an 1895 letter an irate Gyp informed France that eighteen-year-old Nicole "was seen smoking . . . and that made people *gossip* about me. She knows perfectly well that I forbid her to smoke *even in the house*. I cannot trust her at all when it comes to tact or moderation. She lacks them completely and needs *direct* surveillance. She's not at all like Suzon, who is infinitely tactful."[56] Luckily, Gyp recalled, Madame de Montégut was available to restrain her rebellious daughter, "whose nature I *vaguely* suspected."[57] The antagonism between the two women would intensify, with Gyp hysterically reenacting her own mother's tyranny. Nicole would become one victim of Gyp's hatred of her own mother and, to a large extent, of all women.

It was, in fact, against her mother that Gyp would lash out years later, in a particularly heated ten-page letter written in 1915, in which she explained to a seemingly dubious comtesse de Mirabeau the financial strains which in 1896 forced her to end her costly summers in Lion:

> I'm responding right away to what you say to me about *"the 2 or three months spent at the seashore, and which, fortunately, were not detrimental to my earnings" (!!!)* that, first of all, . . . you . . . you were not surprised that I was able to raise three children, to care for their teeth, their clothing, their education, their health, to take them to the seashore—for it was *because of Thierry* that we went there *from 1885 to 1896*—to have—because of the same Thierry, who was not studying at the lycée—a tutor, with the 9,000 francs of income that I had, and when the house—that is, the lodging—cost 5,000!!!. . . . I had *taken* the house, I had to *pay for it*. . . . So *in 1895,* to be able to pay for the house in Lion . . . I stayed *alone in Neuilly* (which proves to you that *I was finding that the stay at the seashore "was detrimental to my earnings!!"*")[58]

Even twenty years after she was forced to end her stays in Lion, Gyp was furious. A paradox enraged her: the more she made, the more she had to spend to maintain a fiction of an elegant and leisured life, one commensurate with her market value as a writer. Given the shaky status of the aristocracy, moreover, compounded by the marginal space to which her gender condemned her, this constant and compulsory expenditure perhaps seemed to her a type of expiation. And paradoxically again, her mother infuriated her for believing in this illusion which Gyp had struggled to create. For Gyp had expected her fellow writer Marie to realize when fiction ended and reality began. And Gyp's reality, financially at least, was distressing.

"Semitic Troubles"

Gyp's worries over the châlet Vernet combined with other problems during the late 1880s and early 1890s, especially those with Calmann-Lévy. Why would the firm not advance her money when she needed it? Why was the firm so reluctant to let her do business with other publishers? And why did it sometimes object to her "innocent" Jewish characters and at other times not? Gyp's increasingly marked anti-Semitism irritated the Calmann-Lévy family. In fact, according to Gyp, her publisher had expressed dissatisfaction with some of her novels as early as 1886.[59] As prominent Jews, the publishers were becoming targets for attack in the wake of Drumont's best-seller *La France juive.* Gyp's anti-Semitic mania, on the other hand, eventually led her to dissociate herself from these members of the accursed "race" and to seek new takers for her slanderous prose. However, other considerations—literary, economic, social, and personal—mitigated not only the firm's desire to censure but also that of the author to libel. The result of these tensions was, on the part of Calmann-Lévy, an intermittently repressive editorial policy and, for Gyp, a type of sporadic self-censure. And these peculiar forms of repression and expression in turn reveal the complex aspirations and antipathies sometimes bonding and sometimes separating the Jewish publisher and the anti-Semitic author.

The issue of anti-Semitism was by the late 1880s beginning to dictate that Calmann-Lévy censure Gyp's novels, and that she express her hatred freely, two seemingly incompatible objectives. Spectacularly successful members of the French Jewish bourgeoisie and publishing "barons" with links to financial institutions and the press (both mythical centers of Jewish "dominance"), the Calmann-Lévy family came under assault in the last decades of the century. In 1880 they had already been branded as Shylocks and as perpetrators of "Calmannization." Twelve years later, anticipating by two months the first issue of Drumont's anti-Semitic daily *La Libre Parole,* Edmond de Goncourt's February 1892 journal entry described "these Michel-Lévy" as "the greatest cutthroats, the most ferocious usurers of literature."[60]

Such comparisons undoubtedly pained Gyp's publisher. Highly assimilated Jews by the mid-nineteenth century, the Calmann-Lévy family nevertheless had roots in a community whose shared religion and suffering helped foster a sense of Jewish identity among its members.[61] Given both the demonization of the Calmann-Lévys, and their own identification, however minimal, with the less than 1 percent of the French population who were Jews, they were reluctant to publish, market, and profit from polemics that victimized them. They wanted neither to invite further attacks against themselves and other Jews nor to appear to collaborate in their own destruction. Yet vulnerable ideologically, they could invert this relationship of dominated to dominator in the publishing field by pursuing new editorial strategies. For instance, they published the letters of the prominent Jewish actress Rachel. And they requested that Gyp edit her novels. For, as both her 1884 and 1889 contracts specified, she had presented material that was clearly "not of a nature suitable to the clientele [of Calmann-Lévy]."[62]

So the firm required that Gyp remove characters with such telling names as "Sinaï" and "Schlemmerai." Citing precedent, an indignant Gyp reminded her publisher that in 1889 the firm had published *Tout à l'égout!,* "in which Drumont was hounding Moses . . . in which there were *couplets* and *entire pages on the two of them,* in which Moses was much more unpleasant than my Baron Sinaï. . . ."[63] No response followed, simply orders for Gyp to expunge, in *Monsieur le Duc* (1892) and *Madame la Duchesse* (1893), references to Drumont and to anything else that, in Gyp's words, "might shock"[64] the publisher. Her 1894 *Journal d'un philosophe*, a diary à clef recording events surrounding the Panama Scandal, contained such a "multitude of unpleasant things"[65] for both the Jews and the Orléans princes (intimate friends of the Calmann-Lévy family whose politics the Bonapartist Gyp found "deplorable"[66]) that Paul Calmann-Lévy ceded the manuscript to his competitor Charpentier rather than publish it himself. While nineteenth-century French authors were used to accepting cuts in their work in order not to offend their bourgeois readership, the impetus for this censure in Gyp's case was clearly her publisher's religion.

If, for Calmann-Lévy, sensitivity to anti-Semitism guided a policy of censorship, for Gyp an almost physical need to express the biases that were essential to her identity compelled her to proclaim them at all costs. Her publisher's directive to remove offensive passages from *Monsieur le Duc*, she contended, was "unpleasant and even *painful*."[67] Self-censure, she insisted, would "wound [her] infinitely";[68] it was, indeed, "impossible." The firm's attempts to clamp down on the woman who chafed at any form of oppression only fueled her anti-Semitism. And these "Semitic troubles"[69] with "les Calmann," as she dubbed her problems in a letter to Anatole France, spurred her to convince her publisher either to drop the rights to her works or to publish them as they were—two strategies enabling her to express herself in print without restrictions.

Occasionally Gyp's strategies worked. While "regretting greatly"[70] her refusal of suggested corrections, Paul Calmann-Lévy agreed to publish *Monsieur le Duc*. Why did he consent to print this work, whose ingratiating, selfish, foreign-born baron Sinaï is scorned by all the other characters? After all, just a few months earlier in 1892, the marquis de Morès, a notorious hater of Jews, had in a headline-making duel pierced the lung of a Jewish army officer, killing him. Calmann-Lévy's seeming indifference to fictional anti-Semitism when anti-Jewish sentiment was, in fact, about to reach a paroxysm in France can be explained, at least in part, by the conditions—specifically economic and financial—under which Gyp's novels were produced. From this perspective, it was not ideology that dictated editorial and literary strategies but money. Gyp was one of Calmann-Lévy's best-selling authors. Profits from the sale of her works brought the firm prestige, enhancing its already glorious reputation. And prestige brought more profits; by 1900 the business would be worth about seventeen million francs. For publishing by the fin de siècle was a capitalistic venture, closely linked to banking and international finance; Calmann-Lévy strategically married three of his children to members of affluent Czech, Dutch, and French banking families. And publishers, many of whom founded their businesses under the July Monarchy and shared its liberal economic ethos, had become businessmen.[71]

Yet Calmann-Lévy's position as a literary publisher was paradoxically as fragile as it was dominant due to the risky and speculative nature of the firm's activities. And the publisher's status was further jeopardized by a severe crisis, beginning in the late 1880s, that endangered certain sectors of the book trade and prompted changes in editorial strategies. An 1892 letter from Paul Calmann-Lévy to Gyp reveals the firm's financial difficulties, which prevented it from giving the chronically indebted author further advances: "[O]ur situation as administrators . . . is extremely difficult, and is even becoming worse. . . . Under these conditions, you must understand what extreme caution is imposed on us."[72]

The "krach de la librairie" was to a certain extent part of a broader economic downturn following the boom years of the Second Empire and preceding those of the belle époque. Between 1885 and 1896 poor agricultural productivity hampered industrial development. Unemployment increased, profits decreased, and investments were placed not in the shaky French market but abroad. Consumers were also uneasy. Extra money tended to be saved rather than spent—certainly not on luxury items such as books. Yet the decline in book consumption and production was not exclusively a symptom of sluggish economic growth. It also mirrored the phenomenal expansion of the popular press, "liberated" by the July 1881 laws reinstating freedom of the press after almost a century. Less expensive and longer than their antecedents, many fin-de-siècle newspapers boasted literary supplements and front-page feuilletons, which could be cut out and "bound" to resemble costlier book versions. The press had clearly captured part of the shrinking market of literary publishers. Calmann-Lévy faced competition not only from the press and from the nascent "culture industry" but from other publishers as well. The 1881 press laws (which also applied to publishing) abolished the required certificate authorizing individuals to publish. With these legal restraints eliminated, the number of new publishers predictably soared, and fierce competition for authors and readers ensued. In this Darwinian environment, the weak floundered—many publishers went bankrupt during the 1880s and 1890s—and only the fittest survived.

The vagaries of the late nineteenth-century French publishing market compelled Calmann-Lévy to pursue new editorial strategies to ensure profits. One such strategy involved attempts to buy out competitors, with the aim of controlling a larger part of the contracting market. Yet Calmann-Lévy's 1883 bid to purchase the financially troubled firm of Charpentier, publisher of the immensely successful works of Zola and the naturalists, failed. The memory of what would have been a publishing coup perhaps made Calmann-Lévy regret even more than usual its 1893 decision to cede to Charpentier and Fasquelle Gyp's *Du Haut en Bas*, despite Gyp's warning, upon submitting the manuscript, that "there are things *of the same nature*"[73] as in *Monsieur le Duc*.

Paradoxically, the publishing crisis dictated not only the firm's policy of rigor toward Gyp but also one of lenience. For, given the extreme fragility of publishers in times of economic hardship, they were more than ever inclined to print works by authors with proven commercial success, such as Gyp's. And the firm's desire to publish "the greatest possible number of volumes by Gyp"[74] also reflected its need to retain, at all costs, a group of house authors and to protect them against the lures of competitors; it was with difficulty that Calmann-Lévy convinced Gyp not to accept a contract offer from Marpon in 1889. For this reason, the firm chose to disregard the content of some of her offensive works and to publish them in order not to lose a sure source of profit. And surely both author and publisher realized the potential commercial value of anti-Jewish literature. Calmann-Lévy's proprietary attitude toward Gyp is apparent in an 1888 letter refusing her permission to offer her novel *Petit bleu* to another publisher:

> How . . . could we resign ourselves to seeing one of your books published by one of our colleagues with our consent? . . . If *Petit bleu* is published elsewhere, the name "Gyp" is still listed in another catalog; you thus stop . . . belonging to our firm, and that is what we absolutely insist on avoiding. For you as for us, dear Madame, it is preferable and more advantageous in all respects . . . to protect yourself from this scattering of your works, from this dispersion of your name. . . . The best thing would be . . . for us wholeheartedly to direct . . . our goodwill toward our common interests.[75]

To prevent Gyp's defection to a rival, Calmann-Lévy sometimes categorically refused to let her propose manuscripts to other publishers. In exchange, the firm tolerated the author's anti-Semitic expression more than it might have in a period of economic expansion, when financial solvency, and its ancillary professional and social benefits, were not at stake. So Calmann-Lévy published *Petit bleu.*[76]

Similarly for Gyp, the necessity of a cash flow enabling her to maintain her aristocratic social status prompted the occasional toning down of her works. For just as the firm could not risk losing one of its star authors, Gyp could not afford severance from her creditor. As the sole source of income in her household, she depended on checks from Calmann-Lévy for survival. "I don't do literature," she reminded her publisher, "simply for my pleasure."[77] Her need became particularly urgent with her husband's 1895 announcement that "he had *nothing* left, not 5 francs worth of revenue."[78] So she demanded advances relentlessly. In 1887 she entreated Paul Calmann-Lévy to help allay her financial embarrassment by publishing a collection of her *Vie Parisienne* dialogues. "The farmers pay less and less, the apartments are not renting well and, in addition, the *very generous* presents my grandmother used to give me have been eliminated since she no longer disposes of her revenue."[79] Sometimes she supplied not even this vaguest justification. In June 1894 she brazenly demanded an advance of ten thousand francs "because I absolutely need this sum."[80]

The financial need evident in Gyp's letters intensified in the last decades of the century, as did competition in the literary field. So she was obliged to be "by *reason* greedier than I would be by *temperament*."[81] The crowding of the literary field by a new generation of graduates made it harder for writers to eke out a decent living. If this was the era of failed publishers, it was also that of literary failures. Indeed, the prominence in publishing and the press of men named Meyer, Natanson, Ollendorff, Alcan, and Calmann-Lévy may have helped turn certain literary underlings into anti-Semites.

Gyp's desperate need for cash, aggravated by the economic crisis, influenced several of her literary strategies. She continued to specialize in little esteemed yet highly remunerative literary styles, such as the dialogue-novel (published first as a feuilleton, at a generous rate of one franc per line, and then bound and sold as books). Like the majority of her colleagues, she was obliged to supplement her novelist's income—in her case with those of a playwright, journalist, caricaturist, and painter. She willingly practiced a type of literary prostitution to maintain her financial status. For the same reason, she accepted some of Calmann-Lévy's suggestions for removing anti-Semitic material from her novels, and probably imposed similar restraints on herself. She simply could not afford to antagonize her publisher.

Moreover, Gyp knew that at Calmann-Lévy every aspect of the production and distribution of her works received attention, with the aim of increasing sales: "[I]n your firm," Gyp concluded during her 1909 reconciliation with her publisher, "[everything] runs so much better than elsewhere."[82] The firm included her works in a few of the moderately priced, extremely lucrative collections for which it was famous. Prepublication of some of her novels was assured in the prestigious *Revue de Paris*, a bimonthly launched by Calmann-Lévy in 1894 in an attempt to end the hegemony of the conservative *Revue des deux mondes*. A serial in the *Revue de Paris* earned Gyp additional profits while allowing her publisher to test the commercial success of the future book. An excerpt from Gyp's *Mariage de Chiffon* appeared in the first issue (February 1894) of the *Revue de Paris*, as did texts by Balzac, Renan, Loti, and d'Annunzio. Once a Gyp novel appeared, it was reviewed—usually favorably—in one of a number of Calmann-Lévy–owned publications, advertised in these publications and in catalogs, displayed at the Librairie Nouvelle, and sold both in Paris and at the many provincial bookstores with which Calmann-Lévy cultivated close business relations.

What Gyp appreciated so much and what, in part, inspired her promise to purge some of her works of anti-Semitism was this highly developed commercialization of her books, which generated substantial income. So, like her publisher, she sometimes practiced self-control in the interest of profit. At the same time, though, this aristocratic Catholic traditionalist hated speculation, the decline of artisanal production, and the extreme division of labor symbolized by the mass production of the book. Yet, like her repulsive, money-grubbing Jewish characters, she was, as she would later admit, "dazzled by the money question."[83] From this perspective, might not some of her fictional anti-Semitic episodes be read as *mises en abîme* of her own story and powerful revelations of her own self-hatred?

So both Gyp and her publisher willingly degraded themselves ethically or ideologically to upgrade their economic status. What motivated this strategy of voluntary self-repression, however, was not solely a desire for money as an end in itself. The social value of money was also coveted by both. For the Calmann-Lévys capital signified their successful social ascension, allowing them, in turn, to retain and transmit their *grand bourgeois* status. And the family's hard-earned professional and financial successes had special significance for the Calmann-Lévys as Jews: they were for them symbols of their perfect assimilation and full equality with other French citizens. The nineteenth century was a type of golden age for French Jewry. Calmann's sons enjoyed friendship with the sons of Louis-Philippe, frequented aristocratic salons, and felt totally French. The family's drive toward assimilation provides yet another explanation for its occasional tolerance of Gyp's literary anti-Semitism. It may well have viewed acceptance of her racist prose as the ultimate proof of its assimilation, its "Frenchness." On the other hand, when the firm refused to print her unflattering depictions of Jews, was it not tacitly acknowledging its vulnerability and, indeed, signaling its "difference," which it had labored to efface?

For Gyp's publisher, then, economic capital could be converted into social capital (and vice versa), both being crucial to the firm's professional legitimacy. The same was true for Gyp, who, like her publisher, tacitly agreed to accept censure or impose it on herself in order to maintain or improve her social status. Money enabled her to entertain the luxurious fiction of an aristocratic lifestyle necessitated by both her social background and her status as a well-known writer and public personality. She invested much of her royalties in the distinctive signs of aristocratic life to which the Parisian nobility attached almost fetishistic power during the fin de siècle: her Neuilly home and weekly salon; servants; and summers spent at the Normandy coast. This social success (either real or simulated) was, in turn, for Gyp a crucial step in legitimizing her professional accomplishments to both public and publishers, who would "reward" her financially. It was precisely this equivalence among her perceived social, economic, and literary values to which she referred when describing, in a letter to her mother, the financial strains that ended her costly summers in Normandy: "I couldn't *diminish* (*outwardly,* anyway) the *lifestyle* and *upkeep* in Neuilly," she asserted, "given that, if people had seen a dilapidated house, dirty servants, or no servants at all, I would immediately have been offered 3 sous per line when I was being paid 10."[84]

For both author and publisher a yearning to accrue economic and social capital was especially intense, given their relative social marginality. Although they were clearly bourgeois dynasts by the end of the century, the Calmann-Lévys were nevertheless Jews. Although she was a member of an aristocratic caste that had furnished France's elites for centuries, this caste was on the wane—and Gyp was a woman. Representative of the country's new and old elites, yet at the same time atypical of them, Gyp and her publisher were, to a certain extent, social analogues. And because money could help "correct'" their social "defects," perhaps both author and publisher wanted even more urgently to pursue ultimately profitable editorial and literary strategies even if that meant compromising moral or ethical principles.

In 1894, what Gyp referred to as the "hitch"[85] represented by baron Sinaï worsened the conflict between herself and her increasingly irritated publisher. The manuscript in question was *Le Journal d'un philosophe,* bearing a dedication to Edouard Drumont from "an admirer of his gutsiness and his talent—Gyp."[86] In this diary of a fictitious politician and man of letters reporting on France's "decline" from mid-1892 to mid-1893, the pessimistic "philosophe" sounds off against Zola and the republic of Wilson and Panama while championing Déroulède. The philosopher's wife, Sybille, envies her husband's political career and his manhood: "[S]he regrets—I'm sure of it— not being the man."[87] For Maurice Barrès, *Le Journal d'un philosophe* identified Gyp as a literary anarchist, epitome of "the spirit of revolt in literature."[88] In contrast to the theories of Goethe, Gyp represented a group of writers "too limited but so interesting [Barrès includes Byron and Drumont] who by temperament are little disposed to accept men and things only becauses the latter are legal and the former powerful."[89] In a letter to Dumas fils concerning her latest—and favorite—work, Gyp corroborated Barrès' evaluation of her as demolisher of legitimate authority: "I have a wretched temper that prevents me from keeping quiet when I feel like crying out, and I can't stand seeing despicable people showered with consideration without having, to the utmost, this desire! And that explains the Philosophe."[90]

Despite Gyp's reluctant substitution in the manuscript of the word "foreigner" for "Jew," she refused to alter the comments of her bigoted hero for reasons both aesthetic and personal. She notified Georges Calmann-Lévy of her decision:-

"I've really thought it over. Not only is it impossible for me to distort a character who will be the *hero* of a *book*, but in addition, I cannot make changes without them being interpreted in a manner that would wound me infinitely."[91] On his side, the publisher jotted down a list of passages of the *Journal* compromising Jews and members of the Orléans dynasty. A note appended to the list indicated the publisher's verdict on Gyp's manuscript: "[I]f we remove the attraction of some well-known personalities and the powerful fascination of the *clefs,* little of interest remains. . . . Certainly, I shall not publish [the book], although I very much like the talent of Madame de Martel when she expresses herself spontaneously."[92] This time Gyp had gone too far in testing Calmann-Lévy's indulgence. The Jewish publisher found it increasingly difficult to diffuse anti-Semitic slander, despite its profitability. Three years after the *Philosophe,* Gyp would be persona non grata in Calmann-Lévy's rue Auber headquarters.[93]

Mirabeau-Martel

In the late 1880s and early 1890s, Gyp felt threatened. Her two sources of power—money and literature—were being denied her. Roger was gobbling up the first and Calmann-Lévy was censuring the second. But she still possessed one last inalienable trump: her Mirabeau name. To most French, the name conjured up exemplary might, leadership, fervor, and eloquence, with a dash of notoriety. It was a name linked with both France's feudal past and with the Revolution, a name both aristocratic and popular, anachronistic and modern—to many the quintessence of France. Calmann-Lévy (albeit self-servingly) had warned Gyp against "the dispersion of your name." The Orator's great-grand-niece would fight against this admonition.

Professionally, of course, she remained "Gyp." And "Gyp" was still a man, as she/he reminded her publisher in 1894: "Would you be so kind, when there are advertisements like those in *Le Gaulois* or *L'Echo,* to have Gyp spoken of in the *masculine,* 'the most charming *he* has published' instead of '*that she* has published?'"[94] Similarly, on learning that *L'Eclair* was thinking of including Gyp in its "Men of the Day" column, she requested that "in speaking about *him*, one *simply* say 'Gyp,' not Madame."[95] But in her personal life she could perhaps retain her maiden name and even transmit it to her children, at least to her sons. She began signing her correspondence "Mirabeau-Martel." And in October 1888 she asked Roger to appear before the minister of justice on behalf of Aymar and Thierry. She proposed that her name be added to theirs, to become "de Martel de Janville Riquetti de Mirabeau."[96]

Gyp's unconsciously feminist act interested the press.[97] Among the intrigued was the ether-drinking writer Jean Lorrain—"always adorned with gardenias," as the abbé Mugnier noted, "covered with rings and stinking of perfume, with [his] painted nails."[98] In an article published in *L'Evénement* Lorrain acknowledged the modernity of this "true Parisienne of tomorrow"[99] in asking Monsieur de Martel, "since there is a Monsieur de Martel,"[100] to lobby for the name change.

He cited Gyp's motive as "the religion of memory"[101] and shared her respect for certain names, "the tragic and pompous names of the dear great men whose memory we preserve fiercely. . . ."[102] Finally, however, Lorrain advised Gyp to let the name Mirabeau "sleep in the dust of history,"[103] warning that "it is too perilous to think of meddling with certain glories."[104] Besides, he added, the brilliant aura of the ancestral name seemed at odds with the bizarre persona Gyp had created for herself. Lorrain concluded that, "given the wittily perverse talent of Madame de Martel, her quips by Loulou and her exaggerated 'bobism,' . . . her mad dog hairstyles spilling out of her ample velvet *Kate Greenaway* hoods, I would like *Mirabelle* just as much: it would be more savory, more like her, more original."[105]

As Lorrain wished, the minister of justice quashed Gyp's initiative, leaving her desperate for new means of asserting her independence and self-fashioned identity. In June 1895 she finally succeeded in legally separating her property and assets from Roger's.[106] According to the dotal system under which the couple married, any income derived from Gyp's assets had, until now, belonged to Roger. The count's extravagance, however, had nearly bankrupted his wife. Now she would control her own finances. Yet this arrangement did not seem to improve the couple's security. In November 1895 Roger had to sell the house in the rue Barouillière, which he had inherited from his father.[107] The next month Gyp sold a family farm in Normandy to pay for costly repairs on her Neuilly home.[108]

Gyp was barely solvent. And financially, ideologically, and sexually she felt condemned to a perpetual, unbearable tutelage. Forbidden to create an identity based on her own attributes, she would increasingly be forced to seek revenge on her "masters" and to identify herself exclusively as their antithesis. The Dreyfus Affair would make this possible.

VIII

"Bel-Ami as a Woman"
1895–1897

What [the anti-Semite] flees even more than Reason is the intimate consciousness he has of himself.

Sartre, *Réflexions sur la question juive*

Are you satisfied to be a woman?
Oh! No!

Gyp, interview

History of the Third Republic

"God knows that I did not seek out this magistracy and that I did nothing to [help] obtain it," President-elect Félix Faure confided to Gyp in January 1895. "I wish to do my duty, and I need the help of my friends—you are, Madame, among the best—thus I [wish] from you the constancy of this kindness that you have shown me for such a long time."[1] Gyp would have liked to offer Faure her continued friendship. After all, she had known him since 1870, when he and Roger were stationed in Le Havre. Through Faure, Gyp had met high-ranking republican politicians, diplomats, and foreign royalty.

But by late 1895 Gyp's relations with Faure were becoming increasingly strained. Until then she had seen no contradiction between ideology and friendship. She obliged German friends while proclaiming her Germanophobia and entertained enemies of Boulanger at the height of Boulangism. Yet during the years separating the "failed revolution" of Boulangism from the Dreyfus Affair, politics and ideology, for Gyp, had superseded personal ties. And despite his "monarchist spirit,"[2] love of military pageantry, and expensive clothes, Faure was a moderate republican and a Freemason—in short, for Gyp, the enemy. She revealed her dilemma to Ludovic Halévy: "I continue to adore the Faure family— who deserve it, I assure you—just as if they weren't the first family, but that doesn't make me like the government, oh! no . . . only, Bob can't touch it, that annoys him, and me too. . . . I don't have much manners for the Elysée! . . . and

I hardly know how to restrain myself.''[3] New battle lines had been drawn, with Gyp and Faure entrenched in opposing camps.

Indeed, everything in Gyp's life—her relationships, writing, behavior, her entire worldview—was now being shaped by nationalism and anti-Semitism. In this she joined a small but growing army of anti-Semites who had been reinvigorated in 1892 by the disclosure of the Panama Scandal, in which two Jewish financiers acted as middlemen between Ferdinand de Lesseps and Republican deputies. Profiting from the indignation caused by the scandal, and also reacting against the continued successes of a small number of upper-bourgeois Jews, Drumont launched his anti-Semitic daily *La Libre Parole* and signed Gyp on as a regular collaborator. As fellow journalist Jean Drault remembered, she appeared at the paper's office every afternoon at two, ''her head snugly covered by her legendary little bonnet, and laughing behind her lorgnette.''[4] Soon she was joined by the journalist Séverine (Caroline Rémy), who had come to anti-Semitism from left-wing Radicalism, having first been a supporter of the Commune and later a Boulangist. The odd ''cohabitation'' of ''the good Gallic woman''[5] Gyp and Séverine, Drault wrote, ''gave us a witty and caustic aristocrat and a revolutionary from the school of Vallès. This contrast was the ultimate touch for a newspaper that was already read 'by curés and Communards.'''[6]

But it was only in late 1894 that Gyp's anti-Semitism, as well as that of many others in France, began to reach its climax. In October of that year, the Havas News Agency announced that a French army officer had been arrested, accused of handing over classified military documents to the Germans. Shortly thereafter—signaling the crucial role the popular press would play in reporting, marketing, indeed, in creating the scandal—*La Libre Parole* identified the culprit: capitaine Alfred Dreyfus, a Jew of Alsatian origin. The war ministry, in whose offices Dreyfus worked, ordered a court-martial, which took place in closed session in December. In the first of many instances of the systematic corruption of justice that would punctuate the Affair, Dreyfus' lawyers were barred from examining the one piece of purportedly incriminating evidence against Dreyfus: the infamous *bordereau,* or memorandum, whose handwriting allegedly resembled Dreyfus'. Not surprisingly, Dreyfus was unanimously convicted of treason. He endured a humiliating degradation ceremony in the courtyard of the Ecole Militaire, during which his decorations were stripped off and his sword broken as he screamed his innocence before a jeering crowd. Sentenced to permanent exile, he was shipped to Devil's Island, the gruesome penal colony off the coast of French Guiana, to begin a life in solitary confinement.

The first ''act'' of the Affair was over—but not for long. For the arrest, conviction, and deportation of Dreyfus exacerbated tensions that, since Boulangism, had been increasingly agitating and dividing the French. Much of the discord revolved around the Republic itself, whose reputation had been sullied by its scandals and by the brewing colonial conflict with Great Britain. Enemies of the Republic now looked to what they considered the potentially revolutionary situation presented by the presence of a Jewish spy in the French army to accomplish what their "failed revolution" of 1889 had not: the discrediting, if not the elimination, of the regime. These foes of the Republic arrived, as they had during Boulangism, from political horizons as diverse as anarchism, royalism, and imperialism. But it was anti-Semitism—a polyvalent, supple anti-Semitism, synthesizing all varieties of anti-Jewish arguments common in France since the mid-nineteenth century, if not earlier—that would provide their powerful common bond.

For Gyp the Dreyfus incident had almost allegorical meaning. To her Dreyfus was no Bazaine, a "patriotic" traitor surrendering to the Germans only in order to sabotage an eventual victory of his despised Republic. No, Dreyfus was a Jew, and consequently, because of a perverse axiom, he necessarily embodied many other evils as well. By his very Jewishness, he stood for Judas, Treason incarnate. Barrès stated that he did not need to be convinced of Dreyfus' guilt since his race made it inevitable.[7] The Alsatian origins of many French Jews such as Dreyfus, and their cultural and geographic proximity to Germany, also made the officer's collusion with the enemy seem, to Gyp and many others, self-evident. Indeed, Dreyfus' "foreign" origins seemed repugnant to apologists of "France for the French." Traditional associations linked Dreyfus as a Jew to capitalism, secularism, positivist philosophy, and the hated Opportunist Republic, with its scandals and parliamentary incoherence; it was the Republic, after all, which in 1791 had granted citizenship to French Jews and in 1871 to those in Algeria.

An 1895 drawing by Gyp published in *Le Rire*, a satirical weekly founded in 1894 and initially untinged by anti-Semitism, strikingly underscored many of the imagined connections among Jews, capitalism, and the Republic. It shows a golden-haired figure of France being nailed to a stake by smartly dressed "Jews," who hold sacks of gold and signs marked "Panama" while they trample the French flag, a priest, and a soldier.[8] The quiet, patriotic, and very French man Alfred Dreyfus mattered little in this crusade, despite his subjection to a torrent of ad hominem attacks. What did matter to his antagonists was what he represented: everything that was wrong with France.

In attacking Dreyfus, Gyp and fellow nationalists were also defending specific ideals and institutions: the Church; an authoritarian, undemocratic political system; a social hierarchy capped by the aristocracy; and, of course, the army. Nationalists valued the late nineteenth-century French army, with its largely Catholic and aristocratic makeup, as one of the last holdouts against republicanism. The army symbolized for them sacred "French" values: hierarchy, order, courage, virility. The army, instrument of an eventual revenge against Germany, was the "Holy Ark." To attack the institution that had consecrated the reputations of so many members of Gyp's family or, even worse, to betray it was to attack France herself.

Gyp was gearing up for this holy war, which would not fully begin until Esterhazy's court-martial in January 1898. She would fight, a friend wrote, "with the independence of a feudal warlord, the courage of a laid-off soldier, and the cockiness of a street urchin."[9] She would join the collectivity of hatred against the traitor as an aristocrat, a Catholic traditionalist, a Bonapartist—but also as a woman. For the Jew Dreyfus, like most Jews she knew or imagined, was for her a dual symbol of her lack of power as a woman. He represented the generic oppressor and nemesis (with whom she paradoxically identified), but he also stood for the victim with whom she identified.[10] More generally, Dreyfus as a Jew symbolized for Gyp and many others France's weakness and decadence, so apparent in 1870. France had been "emasculated" and needed to regain its "virility." A Jewish traitor in the army promised only further degeneration of the nation itself.

Gyp's simultaneous embrace and condemnation of power, which stemmed in part from her ambivalence about gender, was one source of the consuming anti-Semitism that would become her trademark during the Dreyfus Affair. Another source, also related to her unease with gender, was her sexuality. Many of her Jewish characters and images, female and male, are either sexually irresistible or repulsive or both. Some examples are found in a special color issue of *Le Rire* published 14 November 1896. In this issue, entitled "Histoire de la Troisième République," Gyp and Bob allegorized their vision of France's demise and the ascension of the infernal couple Jew–Republic. In one drawing from this revisionist history, a female figure representing the Republic opens her arms to recently naturalized Algerian Jews, depicted as a swarm of hideous insects with spindly tentacles, which lunge toward a plump, alluring Marianne. In another drawing a corpulent Marianne has left her sickbed and slumbers in a chair while "Jewish" rats, "her beloved little rats, which she adores,"[11] nibble away at bags of gold and tease her dress while a huge cat with Edouard Drumont's face superimposed waits to pounce. In a third drawing a now obese Marianne with enormous, flabby breasts "has become powerful. She only trembles before the friend to whom she can refuse nothing."[12] This, of course, is the Jew, here shown pouring coins from a sack labeled "Good French dough—Export product."[13] These tableaux, which portray Jews as insistent, oversexed lovers—even potential rapists—suggest an extremely unhealthy eroticism. Contact with Jewish sexuality, as rabid as Jewish avarice, transforms Marianne from a virgin into a whore. Both hypersexuality and greed, Gyp suggests, are equally dangerous since they produce nothing tangible.

A fairly literal interpretation of these ambiguous images of Jewish sexuality might point to Gyp's mixed feelings of erotic attachment and repugnance for certain Jewish men she knew, among them her publisher Paul Calmann-Lévy. The strong feelings of sexual attraction that she most likely felt toward some Jews might be interpreted as a fascination with evil, in essence a form of sadism.[14] But Gyp's insistence, in many of her novels and drawings, on rabid Jewish sexuality is also an angry and fearful distortion of her own repressed sexuality.[15] Her public persona was sensual, even lascivious, but her desire doubtfully expressed itself in more than a superficial way; she was a tease and a voyeur. Arms bare and sheathed in a tight white satin dress, she appeared to Edmond de Goncourt, at the time of the Affair, as "voluptuous, exciting" and "unhealthily seductive."[16] An article in *Le Siècle* was not alone in alluding to Gyp's "rather hot temperament.''[17] And one reviewer deemed novels featuring the prurient Petit Bob ''obscenities.''[18] The press linked Gyp amorously to Maurice Barrès, Anatole France, and Félix Faure. Yet the voluminous correspondence between these men and Gyp does not even hint at this claim. She did surround herself with a coterie of men with whom she flirted energetically and publicly, but they were nearly all elderly or quite young. And the liaisons she may have had were with men who, like Genest, appear to have been fairly docile, self-effacing bachelors.

It is likely that Gyp felt anxious about her sexuality. She had little contact with her unfaithful husband. What prevented Gyp from doing the same? Her convent-school upbringing? The harsh legal sanctions against female adultery? Perhaps it was her experience at the Liverdun picnic, a type of traumatic primal scene she recast in many of her novels. Or perhaps it was the result of confusion about her gender. For Gyp was, in her own words, ''a man of letters''; an occasional cross-dresser; and an outstanding athlete with muscular arms. But she was also the grande dame, with her ball gowns and her salon, a feminist to some, and the mother of three children. Did she see herself as a type of androgyne, a man trapped in a woman's body?

Gyp's sexual anxiety, finally, conflicted with the ideal of respectability on which fin-de-siècle nationalism rested. The ''aesthetics of nationalism and respectability''[19] dictated new definitions of normal and abnormal sexuality based on the notion of control. Any lack of sexual ''control''—whether manifested in masturbation, homosexuality, androgyny, or deviance from clearly delineated gender roles—was denounced in scientific and political discourse of the period as ultimately harmful to the nation.[20] Given this emphasis on sexual control and sexual dimorphism as analogies for national vigor, Gyp may have wanted to distance herself from her socially problematic sexuality. So this outsider ritually cast her contradictions and her violence onto other outsiders: women, blacks, city dwellers, foreigners. But mainly Jews. Effeminate or lustful (for love and gold), rootless and dispersed, these enemies both threatened and confirmed for Gyp her own identity and that of her nation.

Morès and Friends

During the Affair, Gyp's approval and rejection of strong authority channeled itself into support for a specific political agenda, of which anti-Semitism was always an integral part. She constantly called for a strong man—whether Morès, Guérin, or Déroulède—yet at the same time she often urged violence and the destruction of all social and political order. This modern blend of authoritarianism and nonconformism verging on anarchism, though it rarely went beyond a rhetoric of exceptional violence, characterized all her activities during the Dreyfus Affair. It affected her friendships with nationalist leaders and participation in their organizations, her literary and artistic production, and even her private life.

Following Boulanger's suicide, and awaiting Déroulède's reemergence as nationalist tribune, Gyp shifted her adoration to a new hero, the marquis de Morès. Morès continued the effort to institutionalize and ideologize the different strands of anti-Semitism, a task begun by Drumont and carried on by the short-lived Ligue Antisémitique de France. Whether he was considered a dashing cavalier, "handsome and brave, like a lion,"[21] or a "booted and helmeted mercenary knight, a fugitive from the obscurantism of the Middle Ages,"[22] Morès left no one unmoved. Antoine-Amédée Marie Vincent Manca de Vallembrosa, marquis de Morès et de Monte Maggiore, belonged to a distinguished Italian aristocratic family, ennobled in France during the eighteenth century. After depleting his mother's fortune, he set off for the United States, where new treasures awaited. Marriage with Medorah-Marie de Hoffmann, daughter of a wealthy banker, financed his extravagant cattle-ranching business in the Dakotas, but the venture proved a fiasco. Several years later, a still-furious Morès tried to avenge his failure by launching a press campaign in *La Libre Parole* against Jewish butchers he accused of selling contaminated meat to the army. Morès' cattle ranching in the Wild West preceded tiger hunting in Bengal and then railroad building in 1888 in Tonkin—another disaster, for which he blamed the Opportunist government of Ernest Constans, which had sold him the concession. With several hatreds festering in him, Morès returned to France in 1889, ready to become a politician.

The man Gyp now idolized frequented the Jockey Club, sported a stylish felt cowboy hat, and was constantly dueling. Yet despite his reputation as an "excessive reveler,"[23] he was not just a picturesque folk hero. The police feared him as "an adventurer whose qualities of taking action and initiative are very real."[24] Under the banner of "Morès and Friends," the marquis preached the same union of nationalism and socialism that made Boulangism so popular. But he added much heavier doses of anti-Semitism and violence than had the general. In presenting the Jew as enemy of both the patriot and the worker, he attracted broad political support, including both royalists and anarchists. The social backgrounds of Morès' followers were equally diverse. Aristocrats rubbed elbows with workers in an uneasy and sometimes comical alliance. An 1892 police report noted that Morès' working-class supporters were stupified by "this type of solicitude for the people, displayed by well-dressed, well-heeled gentlemen wearing patent leather boots and clean gloves. . . ."[25] Evidently Morès planned to exploit his aristocratic "cachet" to woo the workers. According to another police report, "[he] likes to let titles of nobility ring in the ears of workers only in order to excite them the more."[26]

Morès played up as essential features of his campaign not only aristocratic "refinement" but also working-class "coarseness." In public he was constantly flanked by his personal bodyguards, twelve butchers from the slaughterhouse district of La Villette, in northern Paris. These brawny thugs, "decent folk, whose anti-Semitism would make one shudder,"[27] were known to burst into the offices of *La Libre Parole* toting large hunting horns, with which they played a resounding "Tallyho for the Jew"[28] so loudly, it was said, that the building shook. Morès equipped his loyal henchmen with "anti-Semitic canes" in case of unexpected difficulties. Sheaths of bamboo concealing hefty shafts of metal, these unique weapons, which weighed at least five pounds, were, according to a police report, "veritable bludgeons, very well made, moreover. . . ."[29] In 1896 Morès embarked for Africa, vowing to break English colonial domination. He was killed there by tribesmen (and not, as Drumont claimed, by a Jewish agent of England). The nationalist cause had gained a new martyr. Morès' funeral in Paris attracted thousands. In subsequent years the faithful would gather on the anniversary of his death to hear speeches in his honor.

Gyp, who displayed a bust of Morès in her salon, attended all these rallies. She was an enthusiastic convert to the new nationalist formula Morès incarnated: a charismatic leader relying on both violence and propaganda to elaborate an ideology that was authoritarian, populist and, above all, anti-Semitic. Gyp, like Morès, represented a curious alliance of patrician and populist, of reactionary and revolutionary, of "archaic France and modern France," as Barrès wrote, "united in one soul."[30]

"Bijou Will Wind Up Wicked"

The same contradictions that characterized Gyp's nationalism and anti-Semitism at the beginning of the Dreyfus Affair also marked her attitudes toward women and her writings about them. Gender and ideology had indeed become inextricably linked for her. Of course, she continued to demolish gender stereotypes. She dressed outlandishly, acted brashly, and remained financially independent from her husband. Most important, she won acclaim as a professional novelist, playwright, journalist, and caricaturist, a feat virtually unheard of for a late nineteenth-century French woman. She proclaimed her opinions of women without hesitation. In an article entitled "Les Femmes," she praised the "solid little battalion of modern women" who were replacing "this gracious swarm of women, a little too blond, a little too mawkish, a little too delicate, a little too ideal perhaps. . . ."[31] Superficially Gyp seemed one of early French feminism's most likely recruits.

But, again, her eagerness to break with traditional models of femininity reflects not an appreciation of her gender but rather a denunciation of it. She blasted women writers in a letter to Ludovic Halévy, in which she also reaffirmed Gyp's "masculinity": "Women who write are unpleasant to almost everyone, and I would like to make people forget as much as possible that Gyp is a woman."[32] Her contempt for women was becoming evident in her literary depictions as well. For replacing her "charming" enfants terribles, spiritual descendants of Paulette, were two new types of heroines: the victim and the femme fatale. Each of these, in turn, incarnated Gyp's own feelings of helplessness and rage in the 1890s.

To be sure, Gyp's heroines physically resemble each other and their creator. These young aristocrats are blond, svelte, with voluptuous mouths, milky skin and teeth, and pert noses. Nearly all are nearsighted, like Gyp. All despise the corset. Like Colette's heroines, Gyp's illustrated for some observers a new, more realistic conception of female beauty:[33] that of seventeen-year-old Violette de Lizy, heroine of *Tante Joujou (Aunt Plaything)*, with her "unfinished and bizarrely haggard-looking . . . face, slim waist, awkward movements,"[34] or of Liane de Gueldre in *Une Passionnette (An Infatuation)*, who muses: "I know very well that I am—not pretty—but nice . . . that I am pleasing . . . that I am . . . attractive. . . ."[35] Yet all these young women refuse to acknowledge their femaleness. "[T]here is nothing womanly about me . . . I'm a savage . . . ," Chiffon asserts.[36] Another character remarks about Violette: "It ain't a woman, it's a plaything! . . ."[37] Despite their similar appearance, however, much separates these heroines. Fifteen-year-old Loulou is a female Petit Bob. Slangy, athletic, "devilishly boyish,"[38] Loulou goes from the salon to the Bois to the theater, commenting impertinently on all she sees. She is mischievous, not malevolent, an insolent gamine.

Gyp's later heroines are older and more complex than Paulette and Loulou. The author's experimentation with the psychological novel reflects this complexity, through description and interior monologue, in a way the dialogue-novel could not. Several of these women are tragic victims. Madame de Barroy, known as Totote, is the unhappily married wife of a diplomat. When her lover of six years abruptly ends their liaison, she kills herself by swallowing cyanide. Similarly, the heroine of *Une Passionnette* drinks morphine after learning that her lover—whom she sought out when her husband, "a big Breton guy . . . carefree and fickle,"[39] began flaunting his own affairs—plans to marry someone else. The plot parallels Gyp's later account to Barrès of Roger's infidelities during this period and of her reaction to them. In *Tante Joujou* a triangle is complicated by rivalry between two sisters. Joujou's sister, Alice, marries Bernard, whom Joujou loves, and then begins an affair with a Scottish aristocrat. Joujou witnesses the adulterous couple kissing (one of Gyp's numerous allusions to her experience at the Liverdun picnic) and feels "an awful shock, a painful revolt. She rubbed her little clenched fists into her eyes like a baby and ran away, not wanting to look any longer."[40] After Alice's liaison is disclosed, she and Bernard divorce. The jilted husband then disappears for a six-year voyage. When he returns, he proposes marriage to Joujou. She refuses a civil ceremony, the only one Bernard will accept, and dies of chagrin, causing one character to muse: "It had 'principles' all the same, that Plaything . . . that's why it broke! . . ."[41]

Gyp surely shared her heroines' sense of victimization, which is so intense that it results in death. Yet she reversed it in two other novels written in the 1890s, in which the oppressed become the oppressors. The heroine of *Le Mariage de Chiffon*, the best known and most frequently translated of Gyp's works,[42] has not led an easy life. She has been plagued by her overbearing, egomaniacal mother, who is "very much infatuated with herself,"[43] "very vulgar in her behavior and appearance,"[44] possessing "no finesse in either her sentiments or her perceptions. . . ."[45] The marquise de Bray has shown no warmth toward her daughter, Corysande, nicknamed Chiffon (Rag), insulting her appearance and embracing her only twice a year. Gyp never made a character based on Marie appear more diabolical than in this novel. Chiffon's own revenge takes the form of a diatribe against various "oppressors," including Freemasons, graduates of the Ecole Polytechnique, Protestants, and foreigners, or, in her words, "people who rally in order to fell solitary individuals . . ."[46] She also emotionally tortures "uncle Marc," a sensitive and adoring man eighteen years her senior. She brags to him incessantly about her other suitors but finally agrees to marry him.

The most destructive of Gyp's "charming" femmes fatales is Denyse de Courtaix, or Bijou (Jewel). Kind, intelligent, goodness incarnate, twenty-one-year-old Bijou is everyone's darling, "a marvelous little creature."[47] Yet her half-girlish, half-womanly beauty, "troubling and rare,"[48] is a dangerous weapon. By the end of the novel, she has spurned six potential lovers, wrecked several marriages, ruined friendships, and caused a suicide—smiling all the while. Serenely emerging from the carnage, she settles for a lonely, pathetic bachelor, nearly forty years her senior.

Bijou horrified critics. In the estimation of one of them, she was a "little monster with a guileless air, who causes catastrophe and suicide . . . with little-girl looks."[49] Emile Faguet was even less indulgent. "She's the most complete egotist who ever existed in the world," he wrote. "She loves absolutely nobody but herself."[50] For Faguet Bijou had only one wish: "To dominate, to dominate ceaselessly, to dominate always, to dominate without anybody escaping her control. . . ."[51] Referring to the manipulative hero of Maupassant's 1885 novel, Faguet continued: "Bijou is a bit like Bel-Ami as a woman; . . . You can be sure that this exploiter of women, this cold and ferocious actor of love, began by loving women."[52] In Bijou, then, readers could witness "goodness" and "obedience" degenerate into spite and destructiveness: "Bijou will wind up wicked."[53] In conclusion, Faguet correctly signaled the resemblance between the author and her diabolical protagonist: "There are already some hints of this in the story of her childhood, as Gyp has recounted it, and which are, . . . in the author's mind, the intuition of what her character would later become."[54] If Gyp, then, was akin to Loulou, the mischievous brat, she was also like Totote, whose sense of complete impotence could only be resolved by suicide, and like Bijou, the former slave turned master, the former victim turned murderer—resentment gone berserk.[55]

Regardless of the skepticism of many of her critics, it was Gyp's reputation as a feminist, creator of unconventional female heroines, as well as her talent as a caricaturist that resulted in an offer to join the staff of the fledgling daily newspaper *La Fronde*. Founded in December 1897 by Marguerite Durand, a journalist and former actress at the Comédie-Française, *La Fronde* was explicitly feminist in its aims. Durand had attended a feminist convention in 1896 and had realized that the embryonic women's movement in France badly needed its own press and institutions. *La Fronde* would thus devote itself, Durand wrote, to publicizing women's "approvals . . . criticisms . . . [and] rightful demands."[56] The entire staff, from typesetters to collaborators such as Séverine and Daniel Lesueur, would be female, and every female primary school teacher in France would receive a gratis copy of the pioneering newspaper.

Gyp initially seemed enthusiastic about contributing to *La Fronde*. She wrote to Durand during the summer of 1897, inquiring about the correct size for her drawings and the date for their submission. However, at the end of her letter she asked, as ingenuously as might Petit Bob himself, "Will Bob be able to address *everything?* What will be the color of the paper?"[57] As Gyp soon learned, the newpaper's "color" was militantly humanitarian and Dreyfusard. Durand would thus impose on her, she realized, the same intolerable restrictions as Calmann-Lévy. Ever the refined grande dame, and avoiding the question of anti-Semitism completely, Gyp explained to Durand: "You are a thousand times kind to insist on having Bob, but he would not feel *free enough*. . . . Decidedly, we are, Bob and I, creatures too independent to do journalism. We have to stick to our good little old books in which we caricature, in complete liberty, everything that suits us. I am very touched by your so gracious insistence, and I thank you for it. . . ."[58]

The tug-of-war between the two women continued. Durand begged Gyp to submit only drawings devoid of anti-Semitic references; Gyp insisted on total artistic freedom. Finally Gyp lost her patience when Durand characterized her anti-Semitism as sacrilegious. Imperiously Gyp asserted that "I would never have thought of dealing with religion. Being very religious myself, I respect the beliefs of others regardless of what they are. As for not being anti-Semitic, it is impossible for Bob. . . . The Jewish question . . . is absolutely *impossible* to ignore in caricatures of *current events*. . . . And moreover, Madame, if you have looked at the [drawings by] Bob, you must have seen that the Hebrew profiles play a role that I would not be able to eliminate."[59] Gyp was not attacking the Jews as a religious group, she argued, but "only" as an economic and racial one. Furthermore, she insisted, anti-Semitism was so central to her work that she could not abandon it. Without the "Hebrews" she could produce nothing, be nothing.

But Durand did not grasp this; it was time for Gyp to break definitively with *La Fronde*. With coy condescension she took her leave: "I greatly regret to be unable to collaborate with *La Fronde*—whose title is charming. . . ."[60] Soon after, Durand announced Gyp's decision to the paper's readers: "Gyp had promised us, once a week, a drawing by Bob, who would have been our 'Forain,' but she wanted to be able to express anti-Semitism. Upon my refusal, she withdrew. Our newspaper, indeed, shall be the newspaper of all French women."[61] Séverine, Gyp's former colleague at *La Libre Parole* and now a regular contributor to *La Fronde,* as well as a Dreyfusard, seconded Durand's decision. "If Gyp is not one of us, it is not because 'we did not want her,' for we offered her a place, and we regret her absence. . . . She turned down the invitation, not knowing what subject she might use, aside from the Synagogue and the Elysée, to demonstrate for us her brilliance, her verve, her incisive and delightful talent."[62] No lack of talent, then, caused *La Fronde* to shun Gyp. Rather, it was her affiliation with an extremist, prejudiced minority of French women that Durand and her colleagues found so distasteful. Gyp thus found herself brusquely excluded from this respectable sorority.

"The Liquidation . . . Is Going To Be Rather Painful . . . "

It is difficult to understand how Durand could initially have been oblivious to the venomous tone—Bijou's perverse spirit—that was increasingly pervading Gyp's novels. Of course, Gyp the society novelist was still ridiculing aristocratic and bourgeois foibles in numerous dialogue-novels that were relatively devoid of anti-Semitic references—in *Eux et elle (Them and Her)* and *Joies d'amour (Joys of Love)*, for example—and in such plays as *Mademoiselle Eve*, which received favorable reviews after opening in 1895 at the Comédie-Parisienne.[63] The young avant-garde director Aurélien Lugné-Poe, contemplating a new production in the early 1890s, resigned himself to the fact that Gyp was the obvious crowd pleaser. He was familiar with her style from having acted in and staged *Le Premier Sentiment de Loulou* in 1892 at the Cercle Volney. She, in turn, had praised the actor-director's talent and intelligence to Alexandre Dumas fils and Ludovic Halévy, who were to judge him in the upcoming competition held by the Conservatoire dramatique.[64] The founder of the Théâtre de l'Oeuvre, the veritable temple of symbolist drama, recalled that "the comtesse de Martel [represented] at that moment for our schoolboys Parisian wit at its most biting and satirical . . . but at that time I was preoccupied by something other than 'parisianism.' What could I do about it?—Gyp was . . . 'scintillating' and Ibsen was darned not!"[65] Despite Lugné-Poe's recollection of Gyp as "scintillating," however, her one-act comedy *Rencontre (Encounter)*, staged later in 1895 at the Institut dramatique et lyrique, did not fare well. *Le Temps'* Francisque Sarcey, traditionally hostile to Mirabeau mère and fille, snubbed the play as "vintage Gyp, second-rate, and even third."[66]

But to her literary activities as a prolific author of society novels, novels for adolescent girls, and dialogue-novels featuring her bratty protagonist Petit Bob, Gyp was now adding those of an anti-Semitic activist and propagandist. In so doing, she was helping give an ideology shape in the popular mind. As Léon Blum noted in his *Souvenirs sur l'Affaire,* to understand fin-de-siècle anti-Semitism "one ought to refer to the literary and artistic documents of the period, to the novels by Gyp. . . ."[67] Charles Maurras categorically asserted Gyp's importance, deeming her, after Edouard Drumont, "the writer who fixed in the minds of French people the most powerful anti-Semitic images."[68]

What made Gyp the "undisputed master"[69] of popular anti-Semitic prose? One element of her success lies in the reception of her writings. In some respects she was simply an extremely astute publicist attuned to the literary tastes of an expanding, increasingly politicized readership. She belonged to a constellation of writers around Drumont who understood anti-Semitism's mass appeal—and lucrativeness. She knew that what pleased her readers was not only the anti-Semitic content of her novels but also their unusual amalgam of genres and styles: dialogue-novel, society novel, boulevard drama, news chronicle. Easily produced, quickly consumed ephemera, Gyp's novels adapted well to the eclectic literary tastes of an equally diverse readership.

Gyp also benefited from the new respectability conferred on anti-Semitism, which made her writings even more attractive to a broad public. No longer confined to the works of doctrinaire ideologues like Drumont, by the fin de siècle anti-Semitism had become a diffuse, even banal discourse. It was palpable in medical and scientific literature, ethnographic texts, children's books, and even the Republican press. Thus even in October 1897 Camille Pissarro, who was Jewish, felt no qualms about sending his grandson Gyp's anti-Semitic picture books, with this description: "[T]hese are comic things, light literature."[70] And no clandestineness surrounded the publication of anti-Semitic polemics. On the contrary, prominent firms such as Charpentier and Marpon et Flammarion (publishers of *La France juive*) added anti-Semitic works to their lists. In 1883 Albert Savine founded anti-Semitism's first specialized press, La Bibliothèque Antisémitique. Advertising and serialization in mass-circulation dailies, protected by the 1881 law restoring freedom of the press, further legitimized popular anti-Semitism. So Gyp not only took advantage of but also catalyzed public receptiveness to this newly stylish theme.

But this sociological analysis offers only a partial explanation of Gyp's popularity. What of the texts themselves, specifically the cluster of polemical, highly topical works she published at the height of the Affair?[71] (These will be considered here, at the risk of blurring chronology, in order to better understand Gyp's appeal.) It was not her themes that were new; she combined and simplified all the arguments found in *La France juive*, the master intertext for much anti-Jewish literature of this period. Furthermore, several of her plot patterns resemble those of contemporary anti-Semitic novelists. Her characters were familiar, too. Her countless venal bankers and exotic Jewesses belong to the long-established, prolific source of stock characters—descendants of Fagin, Gobsec, Rebecca, Salomé, and others—who were familiar to Gyp as a prodigious reader and theatergoer.[72]

What Gyp did offer were commanding *romans à thèse*, novels with an ideological thesis drawing force from their obsessive redundancy, both internal and external.[73] But unlike the majority of anti-Semitic novels by Gyp's contemporaries, whose tone is often ponderous, hers are *comic*, even farcical in tone, an effect largely conveyed through her use of rapid-fire, emphatically punctuated dialogue and of verbal and visual caricature. Contemporary critics invariably characterized her anti-Semitic novels as "amusing" or "entertaining." "Face to face with the sinister scapegoat of a new society," the novelist and critic Rachilde wrote of Gyp's gleefully vicious attitude, "she simply stuck out her tongue."[74]

Consider, for example, *Israël,* published by Flammarion in February 1898. That same month Drumont's paper favorably reviewed and prominently advertised its collaborator's latest work. The timing was flawless; the novel appeared during the lull separating the bombshell of "J'Accuse" and Zola's first trial from his second one, both of which Gyp covered for *La Libre Parole*. *Israël* arrived just in time to fuel—and, for many, to justify—the outburst of anti-Semitism generated by the first Zola trial. The anti-Dreyfusard press hailed Gyp, reminding readers of her didactic intent. *"Israël,"* one critic wrote, "is a biting satire of the dirty, pretentious and parvenu 'Kikery,' [which] plays such a wretched role in our old modern society and [which] it is good to denounce."[75] And this from *La Nouvelle Revue:* "Gyp delights in running the red-hot iron of her scathing irony over the open wounds that are the humiliation of our society."[76] The reviewer called on Gyp, in the name of the army, to prove "the triumph of Good"[77] and to stigmatize evil. Predictably, *Israël* sold well to a public receptive to such images and was translated into German the next year.

Gyp's *Israël* hammers relentlessly on nationalist and anti-Semitic themes. The novel consists of thirteen loosely connected vignettes in dialogue form, most of them previously published in *La Libre Parole.* Its story unfolds in a present roughly contemporaneous with that of the 1898 reader, and there are many topical references to specific newspaper articles, politicians, and participants in the Dreyfus Affair. The skeletal plot revolves around a hunting weekend hosted by the comte MacChabé de Clairvaux. He incarnates all the sins of "Israël," as the novel makes clear in chapters ironically titled "Leur sens moral," "Leur tact," and so on. MacChabé has chartered a train so his guests, chic but destitute aristocrats, can visit his recently purchased château. Countless Manichaean oppositions highlight the Jews' culturally negative qualities: they are clumsy, falling off horses, bumping into furniture, flailing helplessly while swimming; they are urban, ridiculously out of place in the country; they are venal, having "ostensibly stolen in every country and every business venture . . . ,"[78] and are fond of hunting only because it entails getting something for nothing. Non-Jews here represent stability, Jews dislocation. The polarities could be enumerated ad nauseam: citizenship versus naturalization; morality versus immorality; landed wealth versus capital; agriculture versus industry; the man of honor versus the nouveau riche; tradition versus modernity; property versus expropriation; patriotism versus cosmopolitanism. While these dyads underscore the Jews' evil nature, it is up to the vicomte de Sangeyne, one of Gyp's spokesmen in the absence of a narrator, to offer the moral to this tale of ceaseless conflict. "When the parliamentary Republic cedes to a dictatorship, or to an empire, or to any other type of authoritarian regime," Sangeyne prophesies, "the liquidation . . . is going to be rather painful . . ."[79]

The moral offensiveness of Gyp's Jews has a physical equivalent. In a "delirium of metonymy"[80] Gyp stigmatizes Jews through looks, names, and language. The Jews in *Israël* are nearly all racially tagged by their flab, greasy black hair, fetid odor, and obligatory protruding nasal appendage. In a descriptive gloss that also functions as a type of interpretive commentary by a phantom narrator, a man identified simply as "Le Gros Monsieur" is introduced as "very fat, with yellow and flaccid flab. Puffy eyes, flattened nose, flabby lips. Black hair."[81] This type of cryptic, damning notation, typical of Gyp's style in the dialogue-novel, reduces characters to marionettelike caricatures. The "fat man's" greasy physique is consonant with his greasy occupation: marketing tablets of concentrated hippopotamus fat to make soup. This adulterated food contrasts with the natural aliments of the non-Jewish characters and links the Jews, through equally lubricious metaphors, to excess, decadence, instability, lewdness, and bribery.

The Jews' deformed bodies are linked to equally caricatured names. Fin-de-siècle novelists and dramatists often distinguished their Jewish characters by German, Alsatian, or "exotic" proper names. But only Gyp, whose personal and literary trademark was exaggeration, created a tribe of burlesque Jews whose links to purported Jewish internationalism, criminality, and profanity are forecast onomastically. They are named Sem and Salomon MacChabé de Mazas, les Cayenne de Rio, Tripoly, Madame de Kuraçao, le marquis de Rancio y Santander, le baron de Wildes Swein, Ubel de Saint Sabbas, Pickledpork, Schlemmerai, Nathan Silberschmidt, and Daniel, Ismaël, and Raphaël de Judasküss. Gyp's unleashing of a torrent of horrible names might perhaps be related to the crucial importance of names, and identity, in her own life. Hadn't her mother forcibly substituted her daughter's second name, Gabrielle, for her first name, Sibylle, deeming her too ugly to continue bearing the name of Octave Feuillet's heroine? And the extinction, with Gyp's marriage, of the Mirabeau name was viewed as a family tragedy for which Gyp was held responsible. So she projected onto the Jews the same cruelty her mother had shown her when she chose a name commensurate with her daughter's ugliness. Wildes Swein and Schlemmerai are Gyp's destructive weapons, part of her "polemic strategy in the poetics of anti-Semitism."[82]

Gyp's Jews, like those of some other fin-de-siècle polemicists, babble a guttural, near-incomprehensible language. Like their deformed bodies and exaggerated names, this linguistic debasement signals a cultural and genetic one. Their consonantal jibberish,[83] marking them not as exotic but as unassimilable, is a foil for both the measured language of classicism and the slangy folk speech of Gyp's working-class characters (and, very likely, readers). One Jew can hardly speak at all: "[She] speaks in the strangest manner, making a violent effort to articulate."[84] In *Israël* Gyp's play with language reduces Jews to hostile, garbled sound nearly devoid of meaning, to abstractions. This nonspeech perhaps most clearly designates the Jew as Other, not the man without a country but the "man without a language."[85]

Another of Gyp's strategies in her anti-Jewish crusade was to have her characters propose, for the first time in her novels, various "solutions" to the Jewish "question." In her 1895 dialogue-novel *Les Gens chics,* Gyp's spokesman, the *grinchu* ("grump"), hints at the possibility of internment. He reminisces about the good old days when Jews were confined to "neighborhoods where a cautious police incited them not to go out . . . [T]here were chains for shutting [them in] . . . that's more like it! . . . Give me that police anytime! . . ."[86] The same character also suggests deportation: "So that's what they're like, the chic people! . . . [H]ow I'd send them back where they came from . . . or elsewhere . . . God, what a cleaning up! . . ."[87] Gyp's suggestions for ridding France of Jews were, of course, reinforced by the larger ideological system of anti-Semitism, to which both she and her readers ascribed. Conversely, *Israël* and other novels by Gyp gave unforgettable shape to these formerly nebulous ideas. In fact, both the novel's ideological line and the imagery that conveys it—"I'd put them . . . in a morter and grind [them] up at random,"[88] Gyp wrote in *Les Gens chics* in 1895— seem to foreshadow the baroque imaginings in the hateful lists *La Libre Parole* published in late 1898, known as the Monument Henry.

Gyp's anti-Semitic texts are indeed stifling spaces. Yet they also contain some curious contradictions that prevent them from becoming irritatingly redundant. The vapid, aristocratic snobs and dandies in *Israël* are just slightly less reprehensible than the Jews they happily exploit. If the Jews have become the new aristocracy, Gyp suggests, the old one is partly to blame through its decadence.[89] And the slangy folk speech of her working-class characters is, in fact, nearly as grotesque and incoherent as that of her Jews. For Gyp's "populism" was always of the Chat Noir variety and barely concealed her distaste for real encounters with "the people." Equally surprising as Gyp's bleak portraits of aristocrats and workers is her rendering of an "atypical" Jew—who resembles the author. Perhaps the only sympathetic Jewish character in the novel, from Gyp's perspective, Odette de Cayenne de Rio despises Jews: "I'm horrified by those of my race! . . .")[90] Stranger still, she proclaims she will marry only if her assets are legally separated from those of her husband. Gyp's difficult struggle to accomplish this same act was one of the great personal dramas of her life, and she fictionalized it repeatedly. The traces of nihilism in Gyp's *Israël* and the clue about her bizarre identification with the Jews paradoxically ensure the novel's coherence, as they prevent it from becoming a hellish echo chamber.

Visual caricature, finally, is another penetrating weapon in Gyp's "polemic strategy." She belonged to a generation of talented satirical illustrators, among them Adolphe Willette and Forain, whose success was facilitated by advances in the photorelief printing process. She frequently contributed to the anti-Semitic illustrated press and supplied several of her novels with "colored images" signed "Bob." In the 1897 dialogue-novel *En Balade*, for example, visual caricature complements and reinforces its verbal counterpart. The crude, childlike style of the drawings seems almost a visual pendant to the dialogue-novel, with its trenchant notations and minimal narrative exposition. A troop of famous historical figures from all eras descends on Paris, hoping to see the tsar. But their stroll becomes a nightmarish journey through Jewish Paris. In a stylized, parklike landscape that hints at the belle époque fad for *japonisme*, the tourists encounter a group of Jewish children. The drawing's caption informs the reader that "they are the hope of France."[91] Like her novels—and arguably more effectively because of their concision and immediacy—drawings like this one distill and synthesize a range of anti-Jewish arguments and emphasize the visually centered nature of anti-Semitism. Here "racial" inferiority is signaled by the children's clawlike hands and kinky hair, which contrast sharply with the "Aryan" looks of the two nannies who frame this horrifying menagerie.[92] The large, flat planes of color, heavily outlined, share something with the decorative panels of Vuillard. They distort the Jewish figures, which appear almost abstract but, at the same time—because of Gyp's reliance on the traditional iconographic elements of anti-Semitism—shockingly recognizable.[93]

Gyp's verbal and visual sadism did not go unnoticed. The Dreyfusard press, which often equaled its opponents in its talent for polemic, began to ridicule and attack her. A month before *L'Aurore* changed the course of the Affair by publishing

Zola's "J'Accuse," the same newspaper castigated Gyp on its front page. In "Le Cas de Gyp" Abraham Dreyfus sarcastically linked Gyp's anti-Semitism to her snobbery and slavish attention to "fashions," whether vestmental, ideological, or other. Gyp was the woman, after all, whose originality was signaled by the baronne Staffe, a prominent fin-de-siècle etiquette writer. In a piece on "the important question of writing paper," the baronne praised the author's choice of square, sky-blue writing paper and ivory sealing wax, imprinted with her cynical, provocative "So what?"[94]

Abraham Dreyfus thus felt he had evidence to support his charge that Gyp was not only ridiculous but also dangerous. "This rabid rebel, who boasts of sparing no government,"[95] the author asserted, was an anti-Semite—as she had been Boulangist and anti-Wagnerian—because, in the words of Parisian couturières, "'that will still be very stylish this winter.'"[96] He reminded readers that "this Mademoiselle Loulou, Bijou, Voyou, etc.," while claiming to love "the people," actually belonged among "the real snobs"—*La Vie Parisienne*'s public, for example. Gyp's collaboration with Drumont, Dreyfus continued, had made her an "expert'" in sociology and ethnology. Hence her widely publicized view that the "Negro and Jew" represented two distinct, primitive races. In response, Dreyfus mocked Gyp by satirizing her stereotypes of Jews and blacks. Parroting the language of "the savage," he concluded his article: "Me good Negro Jew, me not bad, me still love Gyp, despite Boulangism and anti-Semitism. Me very mad to see her lose little by litte verve and gaiety as well as good taste, which she had so much of before. . . . Real loud today, good Gyp!, but not much talent left. . . . Oh! no, almost none at all. . . ."[97]

Mirabeau

Perhaps it was Gyp's sense of anxiety about a future that promised to be turbulent, perhaps a desire to further legitimize her status in the Parisian worlds of literature, society, and politics, or perhaps a Barrèsian belief in the importance of "rootedness" that, in August 1897, led her to purchase, sight unseen, the château of Mirabeau. The Orator had spent his youth in this château, a fortresslike, eleventh-century castle that hovers imposingly on a hill overlooking the Durance River, not far from Aix-en-Provence. At the foot of the hill lies the hamlet of Mirabeau, whose appearance has not changed greatly since Barrès described it in the early 1900s: "Little, Saracen-looking village in the hills of Provence, with its houses crowded together and scorched, its narrow streets, its square, its fountain and its main street shaded by plane trees."[98] Burned and pillaged during the Revolution, the château was subsequently confiscated and sold to a peasant. For five hundred francs the new owner ceded the charred remnants of the château (described in public records of 1838 as a "ruin") to Mirabeau's illegitimate adopted son. Lucas de Montigny determined that this vestige of his illustrious father's past would never again leave the family's possession. Faithful to his wish, Jean-Marie de Montigny and his son, Philippe-Joseph, restored the castle and bought several neighboring properties. In 1894 Charles-François-Gabriel Lucas de Montigny, an army commander living in Aix, acquired the estate. It was he who, for twenty-five thousand francs, sold the "old château, entirely restored," as well as woods and other terrain totaling twenty-two hectares, to the great-grand-niece of the Orator.[99]

In early September 1897, accompanied by her dog and an auto mechanic (a necessity when traveling in this expensive and unreliable novelty), the new *châtelaine* embarked on one of her infrequent trips from Paris. She had informed Anatole France of her departure in the hope that her regular summer guest in Lion might accept a change of scenery. "[I]t doesn't seem possible to me that I should have Mirabeau," she wrote, "and that you can't come inaugurate it—as ugly as it may be?"[100] Nearing the hamlet of Mirabeau, she may have looked up to see—as would Barrès' secretaries, the Tharaud brothers, ten years later—"a rugged fort, flanked by four towers with flat roofs, with tiles scorched by the sun. . . ."[101] This dramatic facade, however, masked a crumbling ruin that had become a refuge for owls. The despair Gyp must have felt when confronted with this relic—which, despite renovations, was uninhabitable—contrasts with the romanticized account of her arrival by Barrès, all of whose descriptions of Mirabeau would be equally idealized: "Your arrival was recounted to me: at the first houses, a little girl was waiting for you with a bouquet, and in the courtyard of the château the village band, three musicians led by old Camille, . . . regaled you with an aubade."[102]

During her stay in Mirabeau, Gyp sifted through the rubble of the château and fretted over the cost of renovations. Faithful to personal tradition, she was relying on advances from her publisher to finance the repairs. Yet the latter denied her requests for funds, claiming Gyp had breached her contract with them by giving the manuscript of *En Balade* to another publisher without Calmann-Lévy's permission. And the firm, although discreet on this point, was undoubtedly increasingly angry and apprehensive about the content of Gyp's novels. Irate, Gyp countered her publisher's arguments with the only one she had left: her commercial value. "I am, I believe, after France," she fumed, "the best-selling . . . of your authors. I must have earned your firm hefty sums."[103] "Annoyed and constrained,"[104] as she let her publisher know in an earlier letter, she spent much of her time in Mirabeau writing in order to force the much-needed advance from Paris. In Philippe Barrès' picturesque version of the experience Gyp most likely considered a distasteful waste of time, "the shepherds still remember her light, which shone all night through her open window . . . while she was finishing *Totote*, in that large study on the ground floor. . . ."[105] Despite Gyp's labors, no advance arrived. Agitated by the costs of her new property, and admittedly also "dazzled by the money question,"[106] Gyp informed her publisher that she would not renew her contract in 1897.[107] As a result, other publishers—Charpentier et Fasquelle, Juven, Flammarion, Mongrédien—became the beneficiaries of her anti-Semitic slander.

Gyp diverted herself from her latest "Semitic troubles" by taking long walks. On one of these she came upon the small Romanesque chapel of Sainte-Madeleine, atop a cliff perched above the Durance. An inscription marked the spot where peasants had seen a comet pass. She decided that this chapel, near the tempestuous Durance and watched over by Mirabeau's tutelar deities—her ancestors the Orator, le Bailli, and Cou d'Argent—would be an appropriate burial site for her.[108] Finally, she felt she had identified a spot where she might eventually find respite. In March 1898 she drew up her will. What had inspired her to write it at age forty-nine, as she asserted on the first of twenty-one handwritten pages, was her fear of being buried alive.[109] To avert this fate, she stipulated that once she had died, her heart was to be removed and sealed inside a metal casket that would rest beside her body in her coffin. "If I make this eccentric request," she noted, "it is to avoid embalming, which is lengthier and dirtier."[110] After the operation, she wanted her body resewn and displayed in a white or yellow dress, and her hair styled "as best as possible";[111] above all, her tiny waist should be preserved. She asked that three additional objects be placed in her coffin: a lapis cross, the corpse of her dog (chloroformed discreetly after his mistress' death "in order to avoid all troubles with the Church"),[112] and a portrait of her grandfather Gonneville, "an admirable and exquisite being."[113] Thus would the couple nestle lovingly in death, their union, so long desired by Gyp, at last consummated. "I don't want him to leave me."[114]

Gyp requested a simple funeral: "A second-to-last-class funeral will be arranged. The one immediately preceding that of the poor."[115] Only close friends, including the Faure family and Anatole France, would be invited. If by chance she had sold Mirabeau before her death, she would be buried in Neuilly in a crypt with room for her husband and children. A simple cross would suffice as a tombstone. Finally, naming Genest her executor, she indicated who would receive some of her possessions, mainly portraits. She entreated her husband and children to live together and care for one another. Above all, they should try to keep the château of Mirabeau in the family.

In its macabre details—the carefully extracted heart, chloroformed dog, and meticulous embalming—Gyp's will reveals its author's exaggerated preoccupation, at the century's end, with death. Although in good health, she asserted in her will that she would be "greatly surprised" if her mother died before her. And she foresaw an early, even imminent, death for herself. Her life was now becoming a struggle for survival, and this applied to her anti-Dreyfusard fight as well. Some sort of disaster, she felt, was approaching. Would she be trapped under the avalanche, left gasping for breath?

IX

"Countess Bitch"

1898

~~~~)x(~~~~

Be very careful about what you do, for you will be rewarded
or punished on the basis of your actions.

<div style="text-align:right">Inscription on Sainte-Madeleine chapel, near Mirabeau</div>

Allies and Enemies

Gyp needed all her energy in 1898. Two years earlier, in March 1896, lieutenant-colonel Georges Picquart, then head of the Statistical Section of the French army, had come across a document that appeared to exonerate capitaine Dreyfus. The so-called *petit bleu* indicated that another man—major Walsin Esterhazy, a far from upright officer—was indeed the German spy. When Picquart presented this new evidence to his superiors, however, he was promptly sent on a mission to Tunisia; the army simply did not want to reopen the Dreyfus case. Events of the following year, though, would require this. Informed of the details of the case, the vice-president of the Senate, Auguste Scheurer-Kestner (an Alsatian, like both Dreyfus and Picquart), became convinced of Dreyfus' innocence. So, too, did a group of young intellectuals surrounding Emile Zola, who now began to write eloquently in *Le Figaro* in defense of Dreyfus. And Dreyfus' family continued to work indefatigably for his release.

With pro- and anti-Dreyfus lobbies now taking shape, and with public opinion excited by the press, Esterhazy, the real traitor, was finally brought before a court-martial. Yet on 11 January 1898 he was unanimously acquitted. The army's honor seemed safe and anti-Dreyfusards exulted—but not for long. Two days later Zola exploded a journalistic bomb. In ''J'Accuse,'' an open letter to President Faure published in Clemenceau's *L'Aurore*, the celebrated author denounced top military commanders for deliberately corrupting justice. On the fourteenth the same newspaper printed a petition calling for a review of the 1894 trial; it was signed by several hundred "intellectuals," as Clemenceau baptized them. Zola was arrested, tried, and forced to flee to London, but his journalistic coup had achieved what he desired. The Dreyfus Affair now troubled the nation's conscience, making it difficult for well-informed Frenchmen and women to remain neutral. In February the prominent deputy Ludovic Trarieux founded the Ligue des droits de l'homme, which united the left in protest against both Zola's trial and the irregularities of the 1894 court-martial. The same month Forain launched his illustrated journal *Psst . . . !*, (which was immediately challenged by Gabriel Ibels' *Le Sifflet* [*The Whistle*]), thus marking the beginning of a campaign of image-slinging set in motion by the Affair. And as support for *la révision* grew, so did opposition to it, with each side demanding fierce devotion to its cause.

As a member of the anti-Dreyfusard avant-garde, Gyp embodied *la furia francese*, or French fury. Her exceptional ardor shocked those who knew her and were accustomed to her courteous, grande dame manner. "She was insatiable and very earnest, very solidly sincere,"[1] commented Eugénie Buffet, an Algerian-born cabaret singer won over to nationalism. Gyp now flaunted her anti-Semitism like a badge of honor. In an 1898 interview she declared herself a "ferocious anti-Semite."[2] Asked for her solution to the "Jewish question," she replied: "What I would like . . . is *to see them leave, so let's frighten them!* I'm not personally asking that they be killed. . . . But let's chase them out, let's not do like the Russians, who keep and pen them up. Let's chase them out!"[3] Confronted with such violent provocations, the Dreyfusard press began to treat Gyp in kind. An 1898 broadside entitled "Le Syndicat," for instance, shows a horde of nationalism's and anti-Semitism's "heralds" marching past downtrodden workers, most of whom bow before the passing procession. Led by Esterhazy, the sinister band includes Déroulède, Drumont, Judet, Arthur Meyer, and representatives of the Church and Army. And close to the front of the procession stands a by now familiar, bonneted figure: Gyp, "countess bitch."[4]

Gyp prepared herself for the upcoming combat by choosing her friends cautiously. She systematically and brutally broke off relations with anyone sympathetic to Dreyfus. At the same time, she shielded herself behind other anti-Dreyfusards. In doing so, she acted out a scenario repeated throughout France, but especially in Paris. For the Affair, "like a shell full of asphyxiating gas," divided most of the urban bourgeoisie into two clans, "[poisoning] and [destroying] the best and most faithful friendships."[5] Thus Paul Valéry, spotting a photo of colonel Picquart in the home of his friend the writer Marcel Schwob, stormed out, vowing never to return. Similar fierce hatreds prompted Edgar Degas to shun his close friends Camille Pissaro and the Halévy family (the former Jewish, the latter converted Jews). These ideological purges, amounting to "society pogroms,"[6] also occurred in the salons. Madame de Caillavet lost Charles Maurras to nationalism but gained a new recruit in the person of Jean Jaurès. In the opposing camp, her former friend Madame de Loynes excommunicated Clemenceau, *Le Temps'* Adrien Hébrard, and the novelist Paul Hervieu, Dreyfusards all, but welcomed such notable refugees from Dreyfusard salons as Forain.

Gyp proved just as categorical as her fellow *salonnières* in her refusal to associate with supporters of Dreyfus. She began with her servants. "I'm kicking out my warder from Mirabeau, who is a Dreyfusard,"[7] she told Paul Déroulède. Friends came next. The painter Louise-Catherine Breslau, who had vacationed in Lion, no longer received invitations to Gyp's seaside home once she learned of her Dreyfusism. Gyp allowed only one Dreyfusard to take part in her Sunday dinners, the American-born Madame Gautreau, a society figure who frequented political milieus and was known as the "Republican Venus." Gyp excused her longtime friend, reasoning that "being American, it is normal that she execrates us unconsciously, and that she instinctively turns toward those who wish to strike us down."[8] Otherwise, Gyp reported to Déroulède, she had "liquidated" all remaining Dreyfusards. "Aside from her, I no longer receive anyone from that camp."[9]

The Affair also complicated Gyp's relationships with Edgar Demange (husband of a childhood friend) and Fernand Labori, who happened to be Dreyfus' lawyers. While she continued to act with a modicum of civility toward her old family friend Demange, a widely respected lawyer, she rebuffed Labori. In 1897 Labori had paid Gyp ten thousand francs for *Le Baron Sinaï*, which appeared in three installments in his *Revue du Palais*. Shortly after, Gyp was listed on the cover of the review as a "regular contributor," along with Anatole France, Barrès, Léon Daudet, Catulle Mendès, Paul Bourget, Henry Becque, Quesnay de Beaurepaire, and others. But Labori's defense of Zola in February and July 1898 forced Gyp (who was covering the trials for *La Libre Parole*) to dissociate herself from the lawyer. She demanded that her name, as well as Barrès', be removed from the review's cover. Labori complied.[10]

Another casualty of the Affair was Gyp's fifteen-year friendship with Anatole France. France's skepticism made him hostile to the sanctity of the *res judicata*, the justification supplied by both the army and government for not reopening the 1894 court-martial. And the years spent in his father's rare-book shop had taught him the importance of authenticating documents. Dreyfus' conviction, after all, rested on a comparison of handwriting samples, and the military and political authorities repeatedly presented forged documents as "proof" of Dreyfus' guilt. The former Boulangist France became a preeminent Dreyfusard, the second intellectual after Zola to sign *L'Aurore*'s 1898 petition. His ensuing breakup with Gyp was understated. One Sunday, when Gyp expected him for lunch as usual, he wrote to his hostess, excusing himself because of "congestion." He never again made his Sunday trip to Neuilly, but Gyp would assert, too insistently perhaps, that no ill will existed between them.[11]

While damning many of her former friends, Gyp proved an adoring companion to her new anti-Dreyfusard fellow travelers. Some, like the nationalists Déroulède, Marcel Habert, and Rochefort, were veterans of Boulangism. Others had reached anti-Dreyfusism via anti-Semitism, monarchism, or anarchism. During the Affair, relations among these factions often resembled elaborate marriages of convenience, with each group hoping to gain a different reward from the post-Dreyfus debacle. Gyp had friends in each camp, as well as at the Elysée. She was the consummate insider—yet at the same time, because of her gender, an outsider. Since her own political vision combined features of nationalism, anti-Semitism, and anarchism, many regarded her as a valuable (or dangerous) intermediary among the anti-Dreyfusard factions, "the link," the Dreyfusard *Le Siècle* noted, "among these politicians who, with a variety of ulterior motives, are aiming to destroy the Republic."[12]

Ever since Boulangism, Gyp had nurtured her friendship with Paul Déroulède. The poet of *revanchisme* turned proponent of the coup d'état was Gyp's latest idol. His Ligue des patriotes had been dissolved in 1889 by frightened Republicans. By the end of 1898 it was reconstituted. Larger (boasting thirty thousand members), better organized, and more disposed to violence than during Boulangism, the Ligue, in Déroulède's view, would be the agent of an eventual putsch. His goal was the replacement of a weak parliamentary regime with one dominated by an authoritarian, perhaps military, leader and sanctioned through plebiscites.

Gyp seconded Déroulède's plan. An imperialist, she was nevertheless skeptical about the likelihood of a Bonapartist restoration. She would consent to rally around a republic—"the regime that divides us least," in Thiers' words—as long as it had a distinctly Caesarean cast. She explained her views in an interview:

> No, certainly, I like neither the Republic nor other parliamentary regimes, and I'm instinctively on the side of those who are against those people! I'm an imperialist, a Caesarist, to be more precise: My dream is of a leader whose neck could be severed if he betrayed the country . . . a man . . . personally and directly responsible. . . . [A]s I am at the same time authoritarian and democratic, I find myself very close to Déroulède, who is a plebiscitary republican, and there you have it.[13]

Like Boulanger before him, Déroulède was everyone's panacea, the heir to numerous, often rival, political fortunes. The suppleness of nationalist politics during the Dreyfus Affair (and perhaps also the opportunism of its leaders) proved both its strength and its weakness.

Gyp's relations with Déroulède were not only professional but also social. She cultivated him as the star of her weekly dinners, much as she had Anatole France. From early 1898 through his arrest in August 1899, Déroulède was in attendance most Sundays. Gyp surrounded the nationalist tribune with those close to him: his sister; Marcel Habert, his second-in-command; and Genest, Rochefort, and militant anti-Dreyfusard attorneys such as Georges Grosjean and Charles Chenu. The extravagant Boni de Castellane often turned up. Heir to one of the oldest aristocratic names in France and, through his wife Anna Gould, to one of the largest fortunes in America, Boni proceeded to jeopardize both by amassing huge debts. Châteaux, yachts, paintings, tapestries, carriages driven by lackeys in powdered wigs—Boni bought all these but saved some cash for donations to nationalist and anti-Semitic leagues. Déroulède was grateful to Gyp for creating a comfortable atmosphere for him. He conveyed his feelings with gifts, a gallant gesture Gyp appreciated—and expected. She thanked him for his patriotic anthology *Nouvelles feuilles de route* (which reminded her of "such sad memories"),[14] and also for red carnations and for candies. She assured him that "we devour them while speaking about you."[15]

Gyp moved easily between nationalist and anti-Semitic elites. In early 1898 the chief of the French anti-Semitic movement was Jules Guérin, Morès' former adjunct. The man Gyp admired as "an extraordinarily brave and intelligent fellow"[16] had more than one skeleton to hide. In 1888 he had set fire to his own nearly bankrupt business to collect the insurance money, ruining several partners in the process. A sly businessman, in 1897 he decided to try and generate new profits by reviving Morès' Ligue antisémitique. Guérin's gamble succeeded. The league's membership increased from eleven thousand to twenty thousand following Zola's trial, which had sparked a wave of anti-Semitic rioting in France and Algeria. Guérin targeted the same anarchistic working-class and petit bourgeois public as had Morès. The league denounced taxes, foreign competition, big business, and the Church. Its leader had uneasy alliances with the other anti-Dreyfusard groups. Guérin found Drumont too stodgy (the two eventually stopped speaking) and Déroulède both lacking in "clairvoyance"[17] (for having accepted Jews into the Ligue des patriotes) and averse to brutal and immediate action. Only the Orleanists were valuable allies, mainly because they had money. The duc d'Orléans funded Guérin's newspaper *L'Antijuif* and his Grand Occident de France in the rue de Chabrol. In return, the pretender hoped to rely on Guérin's working-class support and army of potential rioters to bring off an Orleanist coup.[18]

The principal go-between linking the duc d'Orléans to Guérin's Ligue antisémitique was Gyp's cousin, Jean de Sabran-Pontevès. Sabran, a cavalry commander, had reputedly led a raid across Persia, India, and the Crimea in the late 1880s. The 1890s found him back home as head of La Jeunesse Royaliste de France, campaigning in the slaughterhouse district of La Villette on a platform combining royalism and anti-Semitism. He hired ruffians, or *apaches,* living on the outskirts of Paris to tack up posters that commanded: "For the honor and salvation of France, don't buy anything from the Jews. Long live the King!"[19] Gyp felt affection for her Jew-hating cousin—"a great guy,"[20] "such a gentle nature, an exquisite being."[21] Yet obeying family tradition, she remained hostile to Orleanism. Besides, she added, "there are too many Jews surrounding the duc d'Orléans."[22] Gyp's anti-Orleanism earned her the disapproval, even the wrath, of prominent royalists, who remained baffled by the imperialist convictions of Tonneau's great-granddaughter. The royalist and anti-Semitic *Gazette de France* went so far as to label Gyp philosemitic and republican! "Gyp is very simply R.e.p.u.b.l.i.c.a.n.," the paper warned its readers. "Marianne's role appeals to her!"[23]

"Death to Zola!"

Aside from serving as "ambassador" among the various nationalist and anti-Semitic organizations, Gyp was personally making life extremely unpleasant for prominent Dreyfusards. Her first opportunity came in February 1898, with Zola's trial before the Assize Court in Paris. The trial ostensibly concerned Zola's defamation of top military personnel in "J'Accuse," but its real subject was that of the 1894 court-martial: the guilt or innocence of Alfred Dreyfus, and now also the prospects for a review of the first trial. Two hundred witnesses, including the staff of the war ministry and Esterhazy himself, took the stand. All of them categorically insisted on Dreyfus' guilt. Just as adamantly the defense witnesses, notably colonel Picquart and several handwriting experts, swore that Esterhazy was the culprit. Outside the Palais de Justice, huge, menacing crowds disrupted the proceedings at every occasion, screaming "Vive l'Armée! Mort à Zola!" Inside Déroulède and hundreds of army officers banged their sword handles on the floor, while curious society figures enjoyed this Parisian event. The hostility of the mob toward Zola reflected that of the judges. Zola received the maximum sentence of one year in prison and a fine of three thousand francs. Perrenx, managing editor of *L'Aurore*, got off with a lesser penalty.

Gyp was one of the scores of French and foreign journalists covering this sensational event. Armed with her press pass, *La Libre Parole*'s correspondent charged into the courtroom daily. The next day Drumont's readers could delight in Gyp's malicious observations. In keeping with the tone of the paper, these anti-Semitic diatribes constituted a campaign of "journalistic extermination."[24] In a 3 March 1898 article, for instance, Gyp seemed more preoccupied with Zola's supporters—"les Izolâtres"—than with the accused himself. The Jewish society figures she spied in the galleries reeked of "violent odors,"[25] while Zola's lawyers, Jewish in Gyp's estimation, were "dreadful to look at."[26] She characterized Picquart as "the pretty blond Jewess."[27] And so on.

Gyp coupled her journalistic activities during Zola's trial with other forms of agitation. Her notoriety as one of nationalism's most energetic cheerleaders during the Zola trial received impetus, of course, from the simultaneous publication of her dialogue-novel *Israël,* whose exaggerated yet forceful depictions of "innate" Jewish opportunism gave many readers ample reason to believe both Dreyfus and Zola guilty. And when Zola began to attract some public sympathy, Gyp immediately combed the dreariest neighborhoods of Paris, scouting out professional hooligans who for forty sous promised to cause trouble for the enemies of whoever paid them. She was indeed an expert rabble-rouser, as she admitted in this description of her technique:

> They could be found . . . inside the barricades made of planks that extended along the end of the rue Réamur, then under construction. The "forty sous" worked for us or for the Dreyfusards. Each time I was entrusted . . . with hiring them . . . for the exit of a hearing that promised to be tumultuous, I always chose those who seemed to me the worst, the most "hooligan." And I always received compliments on my "forty sous." They were the best, the gutsiest.[28]

Sometimes Gyp urged her friends to mobilize their own *apaches*. Informed of an upcoming Dreyfusard gathering, she asked Barrès: "Wouldn't your little nationalists do well *at the exit* of that [event]? . . . [The Dreyfusards] have often disturbed our functions and theirs have never been disturbed . . . and besides, we could do better than disturb things.''[29] Despite the genteel tone of her letter, Gyp championed violence as a political weapon. She was as fanatical as Anatole France's fictional *Trublions*, figures from an obscurantist past who wore themselves out with their "furious cries and quite insane speeches.''[30]

During the lull separating the first and second Zola trials, Gyp found new victims to crucify among the candidates in the May 1898 legislative elections. As in the Boulangist campaign of 1889, she conducted self-styled revival meetings, terrifying Norman sailors with visions of the damnation awaiting them if they voted for a Republican. Writing from the château of Cossesseville, the Gonneville family property in Normandy, she related her activities to Déroulède: "We have here Sunday a repugnant election. Two [candidates who have recently rallied to the Republic] . . . and a conservative, vicomte de . . . who married a Jewish woman. . . . I spend all my time persuading the sailors (the only ones I get along with among the Normans) not to vote for any of the three.''[31] While stationed in Normandy, Gyp also tried to influence elections near Mirabeau by urging her local curé, as an influential notable, to promote the nationalist candidate. She confided to Barrès: "I hope it's going to work. . . . Around here I'm told that Laguerre has a chance. I recommended him to my curé, the only influential person there who might have hurt his chances in Pertuis.''[32]

To Gyp's dismay, Laguerre lost his election in Apt (as did Barrès in Nancy). But they were exceptions among nationalists. Although the moderate Republican majority remained stable, a nationalist juggernaut blasted into the Chamber of Deputies, carrying Déroulède, Habert, Boni de Castellane, Drumont (elected on an anti-Semitic platform in Algiers), and others. Furthermore, some prominent Dreyfusards exited the Chamber in disgrace. Joseph Reinach, deputy from the Basses-Alpes for eight years, barely scraped up one thousand votes. Reinach's defeat was particularly satisfying for Gyp and her cronies. Not only was he a particularly vocal advocate of Dreyfus, but he was also the nephew of baron Jacques de Reinach, one of the "villains" of the Panama Scandal and its notable suicide. Anti-Dreyfusard caricaturists deformed the dark, bearded Reinach at every opportunity, often depicting him as a gorilla.

Gyp joined in. The 28 May issue of *Le Rire* features on its cover Bob's caricature, "Monsieur Reinach et ses électeurs." In the drawing, a disconsolate Reinach, his leg weighed down by a chain and ball inscribed with "Affaire Dreyfus," is led away by two priests. In the foreground a worker or artisan snubs his nose at him and scoffs: "He thinks his good pals will restore his virginity, but this time there ain't no way . . . !''[33] With his supporters deserting him, Bob implies, Reinach is doomed. In May 1898 being a Dreyfusard seemed to have its disadvantages. Despite its effective satire, Bob's drawing does not reflect the intensity of Gyp's own hatred of Reinach "the gorilla." She would later admit to having concocted a plan to murder him with her *casse-tête*, a miniature bludgeon always by her side since her 1884 attack with sulfuric acid.[34]

Buoyed by the nationalists' victory, the day after the elections Gyp hurried to Versailles for the scheduled second trial of Zola. In April the High Court of

Appeal had overturned the verdict convicting the author, and a new trial had been set for 23 May. Despite the government's decision to shift the proceeding away from Paris, where serious riots had disrupted the February trial, *La Libre Parole* reported that "Versailles has the look of a besieged city."[35] Police contained with difficulty the crowds of soldiers, journalists, and celebrities trying to catch a glimpse of the accused. Instead the spectators spotted some of the personalities who had given the first trial the air of a gala, among them Anatole France, Arthur Meyer, and Gyp. The day ended anticlimactically. Zola's lawyer, Labori, immediately filed an appeal stating that Zola, as a Paris resident, escaped the Versailles court's jurisdiction. The court rejected the appeal but rescheduled a new trial.

Nothing could stop Gyp from returning to Versailles two months later, on 19 July, to see Zola nailed a second time. The anti-Dreyfusard cause had been energized five days earlier with the arrest and imprisonment of Picquart, who was charged with revealing official documents to his lawyer friend Louis Leblois. Although "100 elegant women"[36] were sighted in the balcony of the sweltering, packed courtroom, few women sat downstairs. Gyp was among them: "Amid the boxes and the uniforms," *La Libre Parole* reported, "Gyp's pale blue dress casts the only light and gay note. Gyp, with a discreetly sardonic air, examines the public that surrounds her."[37] From her privileged vantage point she saw the judges mete out Zola's sentence of a year's imprisonment (he would flee to London, at Clemenceau's urging) and joined the crowd in hissing as the author trudged out. She enjoyed this cruel scenario, yet also resented the fact that for many Zola had become a martyr. Had she been a juror in this trial, she admitted in an interview, she would have voted for acquittal because then "a few Jews would surely have been drowned, and that would have been the beginning of the end."[38]

No sooner had Zola escaped to England than another trial involving him began. The action moved back to Paris, where Zola, in absentia, charged *Le Petit Journal*'s publisher, Judet, with defamation for printing a scandalous "biography" of the author's father largely based on false documents. Gyp could not miss this event, where witnesses and lawyers would undoubtedly trade insults. Judet was her friend and neighbor; she also knew his lawyer, Menard. As the proceedings began, she took her seat in the front row, beside Déroulède and Habert. By the last day, when Judet left the courtroom with a substantial fine to pay, she had finagled her way to the witnesses' bench.

Stationed behind her trademark lorgnette during these trials, Gyp had been gathering impressions about the Affair that were now translated into weekly or biweekly front-page dialogues in *La Libre Parole*. In "Les Dieux d'Israël" ("The Gods of Israel"), for instance, Gyp contrasts a group of workers, who await their hero Judet outside the Palais de Justice, with an idolatrous clan of Jews and "aesthetes" who speak admiringly of their "Gods": Reinach, Dreyfus, Zola.[39] Similarly, in "Le Toast" a Norman beach resort is "invaded" by Protestants, intellectuals, and Jews, who drink a toast to "Bicquart, Sola . . . Lapori and . . . Drarieux!"[40] These cartoonlike dialogues, perfectly adapted to the tastes of *La*

Libre Parole's audience, also reflect Gyp's simplistic conception of the Affair as a cops-and-robbers game for adults.

In the climactic late summer and fall of 1898, a series of spectacular coups de théâtre made Gyp and many other enemies of Dreyfus begin to worry. In late August colonel Hubert Henry of the army's General Staff publicly admitted having fattened with several forgeries the "secret dossier" on the basis of which Dreyfus had been convicted. The fallout from this remarkable confession jolted most of those involved in the scandal. Two generals resigned, followed by three war ministers in succession. Fearing the worst, Henry slit his throat in prison as Esterhazy made off for England. It seemed likely that Henri Brisson's government would collapse. Worse still for the anti-Dreyfusards was Lucie Dreyfus' petition to the government on 3 September for revision of the 1894 verdict, a petition Brisson's cabinet transmitted to the criminal chamber of the Court of Cassation, overriding much opposition. On the twenty-ninth the chamber began to reinvestigate the Dreyfus case. Incredulous at the government's apparent new openness to the possibility of a retrial, Gyp castigated the "old scoundrel"[41] Brisson in a letter to Déroulède.

Despite these ominous events, Gyp knew the army would retaliate. On 21 September she rushed to the Criminal Court in Paris, hoping to see Picquart and Leblois convicted of the espionage charges brought against them by former war minister Godefroy Cavaignac. Again an enormous, "swarming crowd"[42] invaded the courthouse. The courtroom was packed with men, but at the very back, the small faces of Gyp and Séverine were visible. Another *Libre Parole* reporter spotted Gyp, "our so distinguished collaborator . . . in a pearl gray outfit—on her lips the subtle, sardonic smile that she is known for. [She] has the gift of getting on the nerves of kikes whom she grazes in passing."[43] Like Zola's appeal in May, Picquart's September trial was rapidly aborted. The prosecution argued that since his "espionage" crimes came under military jurisdiction, he could not be tried by a court of summary justice. The former staff officer would thus have to face a court-martial in November, which would most likely convict him.

Picquart's opponents could logically rejoice, yet Gyp seemed troubled by the support Picquart had received from the crowd at the trial. "They form a State within a State, Them, the people of the Affair!" she charged in her Sunday *Libre Parole* piece. "They triumph! . . . and their forceful insolence seems to increase every day. . . ." She continued, her hysteria increasing: "It's because They are at Home, *the pigs!* It's Their Picquart. It's **THEIR** court! It's Their affair."[44] To Gyp the Dreyfus Affair pitted against one another two antagonistic yet generic forces: "Us" versus "Them." And since she could not accept otherness in any form, she knew that one side clearly would have to be annihilated.

Gyp could feel heartened by the huge nationalist turnout at a demonstration on 25 October, the day the Chamber of Deputies reconvened. The Radical prime minister Brisson was by now nearly without allies. Enemies of revision detested him as a traitor, while revision's partisans resented his weakness. Georges Clemenceau fumed in *L'Aurore*: "Everyone governs except him, Félix Faure, Zurlinden, Sarrien, Gyp and Drumont. . . ."[45] But Brisson was overwhelmed with problems. Thousands of railway and construction workers preparing Paris for the 1900 World's Fair had recently gone on strike. A more serious danger came from abroad. There was fear in France that the showdown between French and British troops at Fashoda on the Nile might spark a war. The Affair had provoked England's hostility toward France, and Russia had declared herself prepared to mobilize. The government was in a chaotic state due to the colonial crisis (which would be resolved by the French retreat), social unrest was frightening many bourgeois, and the army again seemed to determine the course of the Affair. Would a new Boulanger emerge from this potentially revolutionary situation to sweep away Republican debris and impose military rule?

As in 1887, no coup occurred, but a nasty riot kept police busy all day. As Déroulède and his staff, in Boulanger-like fashion, made their way in carriages from the Madeleine to the place de la Concorde, thousands of nationalist league members cheered them with screams of ''Vive l'Armée! A bas Brisson!'' Groups of Bonapartists, anarchists, and a watchdog committee of socialists became entangled in the melee. Jewish boutiques were pillaged. Members of Guérin's Ligue antisémitique pommeled a police commissioner with their canes, smashing his left cheekbone. That night the balcony of the *Libre Parole* office on the boulevard Montmartre glowed with Bengal lights, while a drunken brawl destroyed the brasserie below, before being quelled by fifty policemen. Brisson's government had indeed fallen that afternoon, following war minister Chanoine's resignation. But Déroulède had not proved to be a new Boulanger. He had dreams but lacked a black horse.

Gyp Versus Trarieux

The apparent vigor of nationalism in October 1898 encouraged Gyp. By November, however, she had other preoccupations. Her second one-woman show at La Bodinière, featuring her pastels and paintings and Bob's drawings and decorated furniture, kept her busy during November, and a production of her one-act play *Miquette* at the Théâtre Pompadour was slated for early December. She was also trying to devote more time to her writing. For, as she admitted to Théophile Gautier fils, to whom she had promised a piece for *La Revue hebdomadaire:* ''This Zola Affair made me lose an enormous amount of time. . . . It excited me so much that, if I hadn't gone to the hearings of the trial, I wouldn't have been able to get anything done at home.'' Switching to a topic that clearly interested her more than her overdue text, she added: ''I don't need to tell you which side I was on. From what I think I guess from you, I believe we were on the same one?. . . .''[46]

But what concerned Gyp most was her upcoming trial, yet another in the rash of libel suits resulting from the Affair. The suit brought against her by Ludovic Trarieux, one of the foremost Dreyfusards and founder of the Ligue des droits de l'homme, was distracting her from all other activities. She apologized to Ferdinand Brunetière, publisher of *La Revue des deux mondes*, for not sending him the final chapters of *La Paix des champs*, explaining that "I have been delayed in my work by . . . a problem—the lawsuit that Monsieur Trarieux has initiated against me. I had to write all over the place to obtain documents that the lawyer asked for, and I lost time."[47]

The suit was precipitated by the August 1898 publication by Flammarion of Gyp's *Journal d'un grinchu*. Dedicated to Barrès, this fictional journal, originally serialized in *La Vie Parisienne*, covers the period from March 1897 to May 1898. The *grinchu*, or "grump," like the *philosophe*, is another of Gyp's male doubles, this time a reactionary and anti-Semitic deputy "born . . . at the same time as the Empire."[48] The journal allows him to comment cynically on the Affair, and also to observe the disintegration of his personal life. His wife takes up with the Jewish count Klebrig, who converts her to Dreyfusism. In the end she divorces her husband and marries Klebrig, just as the *grinchu* loses his seat in the Chamber of Deputies to a socialist.

Many hailed Gyp's latest effort. Rachilde, for one, called it "the realist work par excellence,"[49] while others, including Trarieux, hated it.[50] The former minister of justice was particularly incensed by one passage which contained several false allegations. Gyp, through the *grinchu*, had written that "Monsieur Trarieux is Protestant (yet another one!) but not Protestant by birth. He is—according to the papers—a vulgar renegade. Once a Catholic, he converted with a view to an advantageous marriage."[51] Of course, this was not the first time Trarieux had been slandered. He had already made himself unpopular by denouncing Boulangism first as deputy and then as senator from the Gironde, and by prosecuting the directors of the Union Générale after the Catholic bank's crash in 1882. In return, the rather stern, principled Trarieux was regularly hissed by nationalists at student rallies and taunted in the anti-Dreyfusard press, which seemed fixated on his "dyed" black hair. But these attacks bothered him less than Gyp's suggestions of opportunism. In early November he filed libel charges against her at the Civil Court of the Seine. He requested that Gyp and Flammarion pay fifty thousand francs in damages; that the incriminating passage be deleted from any new edition (otherwise publisher and author would pay a five hundred-franc fine for each unexpurgated copy sold); and that the verdict and sentence be published in fifteen Parisian and twenty-five provincial newspapers at Gyp and Flammarion's expense.[52]

The trial date was set for late December, but the press was already gearing up for this conflict between the roguish Gyp and her solemn adversary. *La Libre Parole* contrasted accused and accuser: "Gyp is mirth, spontaneous mischief, wit embodied in a woman. Trarieux is gloomy coldness, stiff vanity, tediousness in skin and bones."[53] Another journalist to speak up for Gyp before the trial was, ironically, the Dreyfusard and feminist Séverine. Vallès' protégée acknowledged in a *Fronde* article that politically she and "this brawler"[54] Gyp were enemies: "In that affair, we deem one another reciprocally odious and abominable: I damage her henchmen, she mistreats our intellectuals."[55] Séverine's habitual sympathy for the underdog, however, won out over her partisan principles. She begged Trarieux to spare this member of the "weaker sex": "Thus you who have had this privilege, this honor, of having been one of those most outraged for the cause, you would not, among so many bearded adversaries, select this little rag of a woman, this petite blond woman with a mouselike air, to exterminate with the rigor of laws!''[56] As Séverine and everyone else knew, Gyp was hardly ''this little rag of a woman.'' But Séverine would use every available tactic, including sentimentality, to win over Trarieux. In closing, she pointed out to him that clemency toward Gyp would be a further proof of Dreyfusard ''nobility.'' ''She's been very 'vicious,' yes indeed!'' Séverine exclaimed. ''But she's a woman . . . we're all a bit like that! So please, smile, Monsieur senator, display the elegance of an act of forgiveness—and may a 'Dreyfusard,' once again, have the noble role.''[57] Why not kill Gyp with kindness?[58]

Present in the courtroom when her weeklong trial opened on 22 December, Gyp now found herself not a cynical observer but a vulnerable participant in legal proceedings—a far less amusing predicament. Trarieux, a skilled lawyer himself, opened the trial by denouncing this ''most slanderous of lampoons . . . ,''[59] written by ''[one of] my most impassioned adversaries''[60] and first published in ''a newspaper of the demimonde,''[61] *La Vie Parisienne*. It was Gyp's ''inexcusable'' behavior, her cavalier remarks about his private life, that had forced him to file suit: ''[H]er indiscreet and disloyal incursion into my private life, into my marriage, was odious and seemed intolerable to me.''[62] Trarieux denied that he was Protestant and that he had married for money. He offered to read his marriage contract, but Gyp's lawyers declined. Trarieux advanced that ''since I had to defend myself against Madame de Martel, I had to use every available weapon.''[63] What had motivated Gyp to attack him, Trarieux asked? ''Passion, animosity, political hatred.''[64] For Gyp was merely nationalism's spokeswoman, ''the echo of passions and hatreds whose agent she has made herself.'' [65]

Trarieux's eloquent speech preceded an equally convincing plea by his lawyer, Fernand Labori, the zealous defender of Zola and of Lucie Dreyfus. Labori refused to resort to Gyp's ad hominem tactics. He would speak of her, he insisted, ''without even questioning [her] life, [her] ideas, or [her] public role (because she has a public role). . . .''[66] As a woman, Gyp deserved respect, but as a writer, ''she deserves every fear.''[67] Instead of debasing Gyp, Labori proposed to describe Trarieux's ''unassailable life''[68] in order to debunk the myths Gyp had propagated.

After Labori's panegyric, Gyp's lawyer, Chenu, considered one of the most talented attorneys of the Paris bar and a noted anti-Dreyfusard, confronted the court. He had trouble proving the veracity of his client's allegations. He merely noted that Gyp had based them on a prior source, an 1895 article in *La Libre Parole*. As for Trarieux's alleged ''Protestantism,'' didn't his presence at numerous Protestant functions qualify him as a convert of sorts? Realizing the weakness of this argument, Chenu tried another one. Why did Trarieux, who habitually reacted to slander with ''sage indifference,''[69] now choose to chastize one of his attackers? Besides, Chenu told the court, Gyp was the wrong victim. She was not a ''professional slanderer''[70] but rather a respected author whose works reflected her ''complete impartiality.''[71] Furthermore, the large fine Trarieux required would certainly ruin Gyp, an author whose "fortune resides . . . almost entirely in the nib of her pen."[72] Gyp's "innocent" barbs did not merit Trarieux's severe recriminations. Indeed, the contrast between the naughty "child" and the stern "parent" was rather charming. Why not drop the case and leave the public with this picturesque tableau? Chenu's conclusion was a tautological and deterministic plea for the status quo:

> Gyp is Gyp, and Monsieur Trarieux is Monsieur Trarieux. . . . To Monsieur Trarieux, [nature] has given a resonant and solemn voice . . . ; to Gyp, a sharp and mocking whistle. When Monsieur Trarieux strikes, with what force and power, you know it! the other one stings. And when Monsieur Trarieux becomes indignant, gets angry, and thunders forth, Gyp laughs, laughs again, and laughs always, with her incorrigible laugh! They are so different . . . that they complete one another. You must let us keep them both.[73]

Gyp had to wait almost a week for the verdict, which was delivered on 4 January by judge Baudouin. In reaching this decision, the judge explained, the jury was moved by two conflicting considerations: Gyp's popularity and professional reputation—"the fad surrounding the brilliant and artful works of the lady de Martel and the large number of copies that are printed"[74]—and the sanctity of Trarieux's private life. Gyp was indeed guilty of libel but would receive a more lenient sentence than the one Trarieux proposed. She and Flammarion would pay Trarieux five thousand francs instead of fifty thousand, plus ten francs (not five hundred) for every unexpurgated copy sold. They would also have to pay for printing the sentence in ten (and not forty) Parisian and provincial papers of Trarieux's choice. Once again Gyp had been legally and financially squashed by a more powerful opponent. But, of course, she planned an appeal.

Gyp's legal and financial entanglements had distracted her from paying attention to what she considered a most honorable cause: a collection taken up by *La Libre Parole* for the widow and son of colonel Henry, the Affair's notorious forger. Madame Henry needed funds to defray the costs of her upcoming libel trial against Joseph Reinach, who had implied in *Le Siècle* that Henry was Esterhazy's accomplice. The names of donors to the so-called "Monument Henry" were printed in eighteen lists, appearing in the paper between 14 December 1898 and 15 January 1899. By mid-January 131,000 francs from over 25,000 donors had been collected. Not surprisingly, many of the donors were members of the military and the clergy, but workers, artisans, and students also figured prominently on the lists. Messages accompanying some of the donations reflected such prevalent anti-Semitic themes as anticapitalism and the equation of the Jew with corruption, Protestantism, Freemasonry, and intellectuals.[75] Prominent Dreyfusards like Zola and Reinach were also singled out for slander. The sense of insecurity conveyed by many of the inscriptions was matched by a rare level of verbal sadism. An army doctor from Lyons proposed that "vivisection be practiced on Jews rather than on helpless rabbits," while a Lille butcher wished to have "the snouts of all the Jews to make a pâté for his dogs."[76] Finally, the messages of several female contributors revealed a simultaneous rejection of their gender and identification with an authoritarian "masculine" type—desires shared by Gyp. One donor was "[a] young Frenchwoman who would like to wear trousers and march under the orders of Déroulède," another "[a] young lady who deplores the fact that she is not a man. Long live the army!"[77]

Many of Gyp's friends supported the cause. Drumont, the collection's organizer, contributed 100 francs, as did Rochefort. Déroulède offered 50 francs, as did Barrès; Habert and François Coppée donated 20. Not to be outdone, and to convince friends of his anti-Semitic good faith, *Le Gaulois'* Arthur Meyer produced 250. Writers and artists joined in with smaller sums than the politicians and journalists. Willy, Jean Lorrain, and Degas all spared 20 francs. And on the day her trial against Trarieux began, Gyp made her contribution to anti-Semitism's cause célèbre—a modest franc.

X

"Profession: Anti-Semite"

1899–1900

From the Caserne de Reuilly to Rennes

As 1899 began, Gyp found herself involved with a new anti-Dreyfusard move-ment, the Ligue de la patrie française. The group had been created in December 1898 by prominent academics, writers, and artists. Within several months, its membership reached forty thousand. Its goal was to combat, through meetings and propaganda, Dreyfusard "intellectuals," a term once vilified but now vin-dicated by their enemies. Gyp's friends and acquaintances—Barrès, Brunetière, Forain, and others—figured among the league's "patriotic" intellectuals. Their honorary president was the poet and imperialist François Coppée, a man Gyp considered "an exquisite being, full of good humor and wit, who exuded honesty and openness, [but] definitely not a politician."[1] Jules Lemaître presided over the league as president. Gyp applauded her friend and critic for leaving his rarefied literary milieu in order to "travel from meeting to meeting, receive blows during brawls, and subject himself to types of close contact to which he was not accus-tomed."[2]

Gyp's name appeared on the first list of league members. So, too, did those of her husband and son, identified as "Dr. Thierry Martel-Mirabeau." Gyp helped raise funds for the group, as did Madame de Loynes, whose salon became the league's unofficial headquarters. Yet although Gyp approved of the league's pur-pose, she deplored its eclecticism, vague platform, and unwillingness to use vi-olence. She agreed with Déroulède that the timidity of these well-meaning intellectuals only distanced them from the shock troops of nationalism and anti-Semitism. While praising the intentions of "these generous apostles,"[3] the Ligue des patriote's leader criticized their tactics. "Let them talk," Déroulède declared. "We shall act." [4]

While decidedly part of the literary establishment the Ligue de la patrie française represented, Gyp felt more comfortable in the courtroom or the street. The year 1899 would bring her many opportunities for action. She continued to contribute weekly dialogues and editorials to *La Libre Parole*, articles that constituted a detailed anti-Semitic chronicle of the Affair. She inevitably showed up at controversial trials. At the long-awaited confrontation between Madame Henry and Reinach in January, for instance, a *Libre Parole* reporter sighted "the good Gallic woman Gyp, who doesn't miss any of them."[5] And she offered encouragement to notable converts to the anti-Dreyfusard cause, such as Justice Jules Quesnay de Beaurepaire. The former anti-Boulangist, now president of the civil chamber of the Court of Cassation, angrily resigned in January to protest the limitation of Dreyfus' appeal to the criminal chamber of the same court. He claimed the criminal chamber had been "won over" to the Jews, and thus would surely annul the 1894 verdict. He insisted—and his proposition would be accepted—that the appeal be heard before all three of the court's chambers. Gyp hailed Quesnay, now an anti-Dreyfusard hero, for staging this minor victory. "[W]hile I consider Beaurepaire an ambitious scoundrel," Gyp confided to Déroulède, "I would gladly get down on my knees to thank him for what he's done for us, and I sent him Gyp's card."[6]

Quesnay's proposition was being debated in the Senate on 16 February when President Félix Faure, Gyp's acquaintance of thirty years, died suddenly. Two weeks earlier her publisher Paul Calmann-Lévy had died at age forty-seven after an agonizing bout of syphilis that caused severe migraines and reduced him to wearing blue-tinted glasses. As for the president, *La Libre Parole* first mentioned an attack of apoplexy and then spread rumors of a poisoning. But those who had seen Faure's mistress scurry out of his untidy study knew the president had died in medias res. Faure's death worried Gyp and her friends, who knew that the Republic's president had been their secret ally, firmly opposed to a reopening of the 1894 court-martial. According to Barrès, Déroulède had even tried to get Gyp to secure Faure's compliance in the event of a nationalist coup, but Gyp had found Déroulède's plan impractical: "[Faure] was a very good man and I knew he was anti-Dreyfusard, but he was a parlementarian! He never would have carried out a coup d'état."[7]

It was not only Faure's death but also the election to the presidency of his successor that made Dreyfusards nervous. Emile Loubet, president of the Senate, had earned the disdain of nationalists as prime minister during the Panama Scandal. Worse yet, "Panama I" was a sincere supporter of revision. Loubet's election and Faure's upcoming state funeral on 23 February were to serve as pretexts for another coup attempt by Déroulède. This time he felt his plan was flawless. On the day of the funeral the quixotic Déroulède and Habert, his Sancho Panza, intended to lead off général de Pellieux, who was sympathetic to them and had promised to collaborate. Then, followed by an army brigade and a popular mob, Déroulède would storm the Elysée and the Hôtel de Ville. He would declare the Republic of 1875 defunct and announce plans for a plebiscitary regime with a distinctly Caesarean cast.

Déroulède liked fine drama, but the attempted putsch degenerated into farce. On the twenty-third, delegations of nationalist and anti-Semitic leaguers—with some anarchists, Orleanists, and Bonapartists thrown in for good measure—indeed converged, as planned, on the place de la Nation. But Pellieux decided to back out and was replaced at the head of the brigade by another general, Roget. Déroulède, Habert, and Barrès pleaded with Roget to march on the Elysée and even attempted to push his horse in that direction. But the general refused, ordering his troops back to their barracks. At this point Déroulède and his entourage had no choice but to chase Roget's retreating troops, while periodically trying to block or reroute them. Once inside the barracks, the recalcitrant deputies found themselves not leaders of the army but its prisoners. The police soon arrived to escort them to jail. They would be released the next day, pending trial in May before the Assize Court.

Gyp, of course, was back at her observation post when Déroulède and Habert took the witness stand on 29 May, the same day the Court of Cassation finally began deliberating the 1894 verdict convicting Dreyfus. Her celebrity seemed at times to rival even that of Déroulède. *La Libre Parole* reported that she was "rapidly surrounded . . . everyone expresses to her the testimonial of his warm admiration."[8] Déroulède and Habert were acquitted, upon which a huge din filled the courtroom as hundreds of leaguers rushed to congratulate their heroes and to offer them "beautiful and fragrant bouquets."[9] The Dreyfusard publication *Le Siècle* depicted this scene less flatteringly, drawing attention to Gyp—"the impetuous, shameless little woman, always mischievous, that little one!"[10]—who was "yelping" in the back of the courtroom. The next night eight thousand nationalist supporters crashed a victory party attended by Gyp and other members of the nationalist guerilla. Several months later Gyp would nostalgically reflect on "that beautiful evening"[11] when the nationalists appeared invincible.

Indeed, young Dreyfusards like Daniel Halévy felt helpless to check the nationalists' fury, which was often abetted, it seemed, by the government. He would recall his group's predicament: "Madame Gyp was powerful then. She inspired Lemaître and Guérin. Félix Faure died, Loubet was elected; Dupuy, the prime minister, allowed him to be jeered at in Paris. Déroulède attempted his coup, and Dupuy conspired to acquit him. Taking this rebellion seriously, we were fearing the worst."[12] Yet Halévy and his friends were instead ecstatic—and Gyp and her crowd furious—when on 3 June the Court of Cassation voted to annul the 1894 verdict convicting Dreyfus and to send him before a second court-martial in Rennes. Dreyfus' five-year martyrdom on Devil's Island would soon be over, his supporters seemed to feel, and the second court-martial would surely exonerate him.

In the opposing camp, Gyp and other nationalists began to prepare themselves, in the name of the army and of France, for the final offensive. Rules of etiquette no longer applied; new weapons were needed in this fight to the death. This extreme situation called for nothing less than the type of "unheard of indecency" exhibited by Gyp's great-grandfather, Tonneau, during the Revolution. First an appropriate scapegoat was needed; Emile Loubet seemed a likely candidate. The day after the Court of Cassation delivered its verdict, the president was at the Auteuil racetrack, a favorite haunt of elegant aristocrats, many of them sporting on their lapels blue and white chrysanthemums denoting their anti-Semitic and royalist convictions. Suddenly an impeccably dressed reactionary noble, the comte de Christiani, climbed into the box where the president and his wife were seated and, raising his cane, brought down a "terrible blow"[13] on Loubet's head. The president's top hat was completely mangled, but he was otherwise unharmed. He calmly left the track, reassuring the crowd that "it is of no importance. It's a stroke of a cane on a hat. The Republic is more difficult to dishevel!"[14]

But Christiani's hat-bashing was a warning to Loubet. Following the incident at Auteuil, the president received many menacing letters, including one threatening that if he returned to Auteuil "it will not be blows with a cane and rotten eggs that you'll get but a bullet."[15] He was hissed, insulted, and even publicly slapped. To the nickname "Panama I" the press added "Nougat I" (a reference to the specialty of Montélimar, where Loubet, it was said, had illicitly acquired a huge fortune) and "Cornichon ramolli" ("Soggy Pickle," recalling his bashed-in hat). Indeed, a miniature of Loubet's famous hat, contained in a cardboard hatbox, was available from a Paris merchant. And one lucky collector of curios might even purchase Christiani's cane, which *La Libre Parole* announced would soon be sold at auction.[16]

Gyp could not resist getting in her own dig at "the nougatine Machiavelli"[17] in the form of lyrics to a march, "Allons! Petit Pioupiou!" ("March on, Soldier Boy!"), dedicated to Déroulède and printed by the Librairie Antisémite. She exhorted France's brave soldiers to "chase away the nightmare" peopled by Jews and parliamentarians by first evicting "Loubet from Montélimar." A drawing on the sheet music's cover shows the doll-like figures of Dreyfus and Loubet, arm in arm, standing next to two watchful, worried-looking French soldiers.

Gyp considered not only Loubet but all Dreyfusards fair game for slander. In "Le Vrai Grand Complot" ("The True Grand Plot"), a dialogue that appeared in *La Vie Parisienne* on 4 November, she embellished the myth of a plot to acquit Dreyfus. The members of this "syndicate" include Trarieux, Clemenceau, Prime Minister René Waldeck-Rousseau, Chief Rabbi Zadoc-Kahn, and Reinach. The illustrations by Sahib, whose earlier drawings of hunting scenes and Parisian high life had been untinged by right-wing sentiment, show the Dreyfusard leaders conspiring in a smoke-filled room, watched over by a portrait of Dreyfus. And Gyp devoted a dialogue-novel to ridiculing another Dreyfusard protagonist, Picquart. Her 1899 roman à clef, *Les Femmes du colonel (The Colonel's Women)*, depicts the hero of "l'Affaire Judassfrüss" as an idol fawned over by giddy women, effeminate intellectuals, and Jews while he is being manipulated by Trahidieux (Trarieux), Moloc-Raab (Zadoc-Kahn), and other Dreyfusard impresarios. The same year Gyp also published *Les Izolâtres*, her collection of dialogues based on the Zola trials; an anti-Semitic satire, *Les Cayenne de Rio*; three society novels (*Monsieur de Folleuil, Lune de miel,* and *l'Entrevue*); plus dozens of newspaper articles—a productive year for Gyp, yet not atypical.

A member of the elite of nationalism and anti-Semitism, Gyp appeared at many meetings and rallies, which were now more frequent and animated as the Rennes trial approached. On 3 July at Saint-Cloud she joined Barrès, Lemaître, Forain, Coppée, and thousands of others in screeching "Long live Déroulède! Down with the Jews!" Déroulède's earlier attempt to distance himself from anti-Semitism now seemed forgotten. He would accept aid from all who offered it. Gyp's gleeful attitude at these events earned her scorn and ridicule from the Dreyfusard press, which had also become increasingly vehement in tone. As Francis de Pressensé, a founder of the Ligue des droits de l'homme and later its president, cynically reported in *L'Aurore*, she belonged to the "intellectual and moral elite of France . . . who embraced Déroulède in its arms, smothered him with its kisses, let him inhale in his predestined nose the incense of [its] fawning."[18]

A week later the festivities had shifted to another site: Jules Guérin's Grand Occident de France ("Rite antijuif") in the rue de Chabrol. Modeled on Masonic lodges (provincial branches bore the names of illustrious anti-Semites), the G∗O∗F was a paranoiac's version of a secret society. Doors and windows were armored and three metal doors barricaded Guérin's office. A cohort of butchers stood guard outside. This siege mentality was apparent elsewhere in the "fort": a room well-stocked with arms and a skilled trainer were available to prepare members for emergencies. The premises also included offices for medical and legal consultation, rooms for meetings of the Cercle antisémite d'etudes sociales, facilities for printing *L'Antijuif* (the Ligue antisémitique's newspaper), and a billiard room. Guérin's taste for luxury was evident in the marble-and-gold plaque at the entryway announcing the building's function and in the sumptuous suite he kept there. Mercifully for him, this complete anti-Semitic environment was financed by others, notably Orleanists.[19]

Fort Chabrol, as the building came to be called, also housed a vast meeting hall, where on 19 July, under Drumont's patronage, two thousand faithful gathered to commemorate one of anti-Semitism's holy days: the anniversary of the death of Morès. Gyp was spotted sitting on a dais, laughing with her friends,[20] chatting, and giving out autographs with the message "Long live the Emperor! Down with the Jews." The Dreyfusard press remarked that for a professed devout Catholic, Gyp's anti-Jewish crusade in defense of "healthy Catholic morality"[21] seemed hypocritical. But perhaps she was merely perpetuating family tradition, as one journalist suggested. "Daughter of a pontifical Zouave, who enjoyed quite a licentious reputation in the Morbihan, from what I've been told,"[22] Gyp saw no contradiction between private devotion and public extremism. She could thus continue her "journey for God and for No Matter Whom the First"[23] with a clear conscience. Others disapproved.

Drumont wanted to send Gyp to cover the Rennes trial, which was about to begin in early August. She begged off, claiming to be overworked, but revealed the full truth to Barrès: "I have too much work to go there, where I know full well that I would do absolutely nothing but chat and stroll around."[24] The court-martial had just gotten underway when Prime Minister Waldeck-Rousseau unexpectedly complicated affairs for Gyp and her friends. In an effort finally to bring to heel anti-Republican forces, especially during the Rennes trial, Waldeck decided to reinvestigate all the recent demonstrations, from those that disrupted Faure's funeral in February to the June attack on Loubet at Auteuil. Insisting they had been organized in tandem, the prime minister persuaded his government to agree to many arrests for plotting to destroy or change the form of government.[25] The motley crew that was rounded up included anti-Semites (Dubuc, head of the Jeunesse antisémite, known for his bulletproof hats, regarding whom Gyp commented "very nice, I assure you"[26]), Bonapartists, royalists (Lur-Saluces, Buffet, Sabran), and nationalists (among them the ex-Boulangist Barillier, "merchant butcher,"[27] whom Gyp considered "such a good and honest boy"[28]), plus Habert and Déroulède. In November all these accused conspirators would be tried before a special High Court made up of senators. Gyp was outraged by the government's decision, which was proof for her of the triumph of the Dreyfus clan. She fumed to Barrès: "Even wounded, even unsuccessful, these people who tear apart a country I love horrify me. I sense that I hate the Laboris and the Dreyfuses more today than I did yesterday and certainly less than tomorrow."[29]

Guérin, also charged with stockpiling arms and attacking police officers, managed to hustle back to his rue de Chabrol sanctuary before the police could arrest him. On 14 August he began a monthlong holdout in his sentinel-guarded "fort." In fact, the entire incident, a sideshow to the Rennes trial, turned into street theater (albeit a "grotesque comedy"[30] to the Dreyfusard publisher Stock). Gyp prowled around outside. "[V]ery excited by Guérin's gesture, [she] was spending part of her nights in the vicinity of the fort, anxiously awaiting the outcome of the drama."[31] Food, wrapped in linens, reached the "fort" from an adjacent hotel by means of conduits specially attached for the occasion. Mysterious visitors arrived at all hours. The police reported rumors that mail was delivered by hot-air balloons, and that an elaborate system of caves and catacombs facilitated communication with the world outside. There was talk of illness, poisonings, bread shortages.[32] Instead, Guérin and fifteen acolytes calmly exercised in the arms room or listened to a gramophone, hoping a popular revolution might end their boredom. In the street, Parisians out for a Sunday stroll mingled with residents of the suburbs and even foreigners, visiting this "Parisian attraction"[33] on a tour organized by the Cook Travel agency. On 21 September the siege ended undramatically with Guérin's docile submission to the police and transport to the Santé prison, where he joined his fellow conspirators. During his sequestration, he had missed the outcome of the Rennes trial.

Gyp had been so fearful of an acquittal that she had actually prayed to her savior Déroulède for a guilty verdict. She shared her idolatry with Déroulède's sister: "Whatever the decision of the War Council at Rennes, I believe, as you do, that we are nearing the deliverance to which it really seems we are a bit entitled. I . . . have confidence in God . . . and in your brother. I firmly hope they will save us."[34] Gyp's supplications did not go unheeded. On 9 September "the traitor" Dreyfus was again convicted, this time with "extenuating circumstances." Yet this seeming fatal blow to the Dreyfusards was partially alleviated ten days later when an embarrassed Emile Loubet quietly offered Dreyfus a presidential pardon, which he accepted. Thus, the juridical and political phases of the Affair had virtually ended with this Dreyfusard Pyrrhic victory. And once again Gyp found herself on the side of the dispossessed.

"The Anti-Jewish Dowager"

There remained the business of the High Court, now to be part of the epilogue of the Affair. Anxious about the upcoming 1900 World's Fair, Prime Minister Waldeck-Rousseau was trying to get a bill passed in the Chamber of Deputies that would quietly offer amnesty to Déroulède and his cohorts, thus averting (Waldeck hoped) any possibility of civil unrest. But President Loubet insisted the purported conspirators stand trial in November, as planned. In a *Libre Parole* article, Gyp damned "Loulou" for having committed "this ultimate dirty trick"[35] and charged that Déroulède's possible conviction would be the Jews' revenge for that of Dreyfus. Loubet's "repressive measures,"[36] she argued, would be admissible if emanating from a Caesarean power but seemed unacceptable in a parliamentary regime.[37] And she criticized the government for lumping the nationalists and Orleanists together, complaining to Barrès that "they've managed to throw Déroulède into an Orleanist plot."[38]

Gyp became the highly visible sister of mercy to the imprisoned Déroulède and his henchmen. Barred from communicating directly with the prisoners, who were held in the Santé prison and, during the trial, at the Palais du Luxembourg, she made her presence known with gifts: books, roses, pâté for Barillier the butcher, a cake for Sabran ("who doesn't eat *anything* anymore").[39] She wrote Déroulède long letters and was solicitous about his health. Ever the gentleman, Déroulède managed to reciprocate by having his servant, Prudence, deliver to Gyp some "superb" roses and "exquisite" partridges.[40] Those who had survived the hecatomb still gathered at Gyp's on Sundays to reminisce. One week Degas was on hand, as well as Guérin's lawyer, Ménard. "These are peculiar times indeed!"[41] Gyp mused to Déroulède, her absent friend.

The atmosphere at the Palais du Luxembourg was tumultuous on 10 November when the High Court trial, one of nationalism's last stands, began. Hundreds of supporters of the accused encircled the palace singing a menacing anthem, the "Marseillaise antijuive." Inside Rochefort embraced Gyp, amid much applause and picture taking.[42] Around noon friends of the accused—"the good soldiers of nationalism,"[43] including Drumont, Coppée, Lemaître, Barrès, Castellane, among others—began trooping in. Four hundred witnesses jostled each other in the cramped hallways. Amid the pandemonium, Police Prefect Louis Lépine, "bewildered as a rat,"[44] ran through the corridors trying to restore order, unaware that some joker had slapped on his back a flyer proclaiming "Vive Déroulède!"

The first witness Gyp and her friends heard was Hennion, a police commissioner who, at the request of the government, had been gathering evidence proving collusion between nationalists and royalists in the recent demonstrations. Many discounted the report by Hennion, who refused to name his sources. Rochefort, an expert in specious texts himself, mocked the police officer in *L'Intransigeant*, claiming that Hennion's nonsensical report was as valid as the equally preposterous account that "François Coppée, Gyp, Jules Guesde [and] the papal nuncio . . . , at the head of five hundred men, yesterday attacked the powder-magazine at Castelnaudary."[45] Royalists testified next, and at the end of November Barillier, Guérin, and Déroulède took the stand. Gyp was distressed not to be able to attend this session, as she wrote Déroulède: "I'm sorry not to see you before the High Court! And what a High Court! It's really even more despicable than anyone could have imagined."[46] But she soberly thanked her hero for his courage: "Many compliments on your noble, noble attitude."[47] The testimony of Déroulède and his associates lasted several days and covered the 23 February coup attempt, the events at Auteuil, and Guérin's spontaneous sit-in at Fort Chabrol. Gyp found the proceedings "odious."[48] They proved to her, as she let Déroulède know, "what an extraordinary juice you're being made to stew in."[49] The press and audience had been eagerly awaiting Gyp's own 16 December deposition. They knew the uninhibited Gyp would upstage all the other witnesses. And she, a fifty-year-old child, was overjoyed to be in the spotlight. Dressed in her "court session outfit,"[50] a blue, sable-trimmed suit, she advanced to the witness stand, "greeted by the smiles of some elderly gentlemen of the Right."[51] Asked to raise her right hand, she responded by lifting it halfway, fingers splayed: "Like that?"[52] she asked. The next question provoked an even more shocking retort. "Your profession?" "Anti-Semite,"[53] Gyp replied calmly, and the audience laughed.

Gyp's testimony, in contrast to her introductory comments, was relatively matter-of-fact. She acknowledged knowing several of the accused: her cousin, Jean de Sabran; Barillier, whom she described as "extraordinarily gentle,"[54] adding that "he wouldn't have done harm, even to a police officer!";[55] Guérin, to whose Ligue antisémitique she belonged; and Dubuc, who was a friend of her two sons. Yes, she had participated in various nationalist gatherings whose mood "seemed excellent to me because it was mine."[56] She considered these meetings necessary and logical counteroffensives against Dreyfusard gatherings, "which were somehow official and to which we responded as we were able."[57] She then explained how she herself had been falsely accused of involvement in the nationalist "plot" whose result was the High Court trial. According to her account, Melcot, a magistrate in the Court of Cassation, claimed to have learned from a "dame Colomb" that on 22 February 1899 Gyp, généraux Mercier, Cavaignac, and Roget, Quesnay de Beaurepaire, and Barrès had gathered at the lawyer Grosjean's home. There they tried to persuade Roget to march on the Elysée before the end of Faure's funeral. Gyp denounced this story to the court as well as in a letter to Déroulède:-

"This sneak [Melcot] is misinformed. . . . On 22 February there was neither myself nor anyone else at Grosjean's."[58] Gyp's refutation was later substantiated by "the widow Colomb" herself, who retracted her statement, declaring that she was "a southerner and prone to lending a southern exaggeration to the facts."[59]

The rest of Gyp's testimony consisted of a defense of Jean de Sabran. Questioned directly by her royalist cousin, she denied both his purported links to neo-Boulangist circles and his involvement in the events surrounding Faure's funeral and the hat-bashing incident at Auteuil. But given Gyp's close ties to the various anti-Republican movements, as one of the prosecution lawyers noted, wasn't it possible that both she and Sabran had been notified of the upcoming agitation before the fact? No, Gyp answered. She then left the witness stand after first thanking a demure Barillier "for having given me the occasion to say that I have much esteem and friendship for him."[60] Gyp's appearance before the High Court thus ended as "graciously" as it had begun shockingly. She returned to the audience, *L'Eclair* noted, surrounded by "approving smiles" and "general goodwill."[61]

Not surprisingly, Gyp's testimony was a lightning rod for both praise and invective. Barrès lauded it as "a perfect model of French amiableness and spontaneity. . . ."[62] Others, however, were indignant about her cavalier approval of the recent violence at Auteuil and her joyful introduction of herself as a "professional" anti-Semite. Had Gyp been trying, several journalists wondered, to compensate for her declining literary fortunes with an act of notoriety? Was her goal, as *La Paix* suggested, to "restore a bit of luster to twenty or so stale, old-fashioned works, in which the jokes are so painful it makes one want to cry[?]"[63] A journalist for *Le Siècle* agreed, sarcastically remarking that it was preferable for "the anti-Jewish dowager"[64] to state her profession as anti-Semite and not writer, for "her collections of obscenities in dialogue form are outside of literature. What can one say, indeed, about the infantile brat Bob, who shoots off in smutty language to his tutor . . . ? And about Paulette, and Chiffon, and twenty-five other slightly strange young ladies?"[65] And how could "the angelical Gypette"[66] call herself an artist, when all she had produced were "these caricatures that are more silly than lewd . . . [?]"[67] "Furniture maker"[68] might have been a third possibility, but her talent was obviously limited in this domain as well. *Le Siècle*'s correspondent remembered having once seen in a salon "a white laquer standing screen, on which were sprawled some simpletons, burlesquely daubed by the ex-Counselor of Félix-Ubu-Faure. . . ."[69] Evidently, "anti-Semite" was the only "profession" befitting Gyp.

After Gyp's performance, the rest of the trial seemed lackluster. Georges Thiébaud, Boulanger's former campaign manager, testified, as did Habert and, again, Guérin. On 1 January the accused returned to the Santé prison, where workers, women, coachmen, and friends paraded by all day, bringing flowers and encouragement. Gyp was back in the courtroom on 5 January to hear the verdict, which devastated her, as it had during Bazaine's trial. While Sabran, Dubuc, and Barillier were all acquitted, Guérin was sentenced to ten years' detention and Déroulède,

Buffet, and Lur-Saluces to ten years' exile. In a moment of crisis, the Republic, now supported by the socialists, had once again held firm. The beginning of the new century was to mark not only the Republic's apotheosis but nationalism's definitive demise.

"TO TERROR, LET US RESPOND WITH EVEN MORE TERROR"

With Guérin in prison and Déroulède and Habert exiled to San Sebastian, Spain, the revolutionary Right had been temporarily quelled. Nationalists of all stripes were now obliged to regroup under the banner of the Ligue de la patrie française, whose leaders had escaped the recent auto-da-fé staged by the High Court. This more moderate brand of nationalism repudiated street violence, coups d'état, and the extremist anti-Semitic tactics of Guérin's league. It relied instead on meetings (such as a March 1900 "Concert Patriotique," which Gyp attended) and publications (*Les Dimanches politiques et littéraires,* to name one). Gyp, strangely misidentified as a member of the Académie française, was a member of the weekly's "Comité du patronage." The publication, which Barrès directed, would relate political, literary, artistic, and scientific developments. It presented itself as "the voice of the *French* family, and a popular means—which all nationalists will take to heart to encourage—of contributing to the rebuilding and prosperity of our country."[70] This benign journalistic program shared little with the vitriolic efforts of Rochefort and Guérin.

Hard-core anti-Semitism, of course, still had its adepts. A series of fifty-one posters entitled "Le Musée des Horreurs" depicted the lifelike heads of prominent Dreyfusards and Jews attached to the bodies of animals. This terrifying bestiary included Reinach (here identified as "Boule de Juif," an obvious pun on Guy de Maupassant's 1880 short story "Boule de Suif"), Dreyfus as a lizard, and the baron Alphonse de Rothschild as a monkey digging his claws into a chest of gold pieces. A heroic pendant to this series, "Le Musée des Patriotes," featured the lifelike portraits of Gyp, Déroulède, Rochefort, Drumont, Coppée, and Barrès. Gyp, perhaps too optimistically, detected signs that the radical anti-Semitic movement had not lost all its vigor. She reported to Déroulède in mid-1900 that "there is . . . a real dissatisfaction [that] is, above all, taking an *anti-Jewish* form. Anti-Jewish without Guérin, without a flag, without a leader, a very popular and very pronounced anti-Jewishness. And it's the first time that, chatting in the street with people . . . , I hear them shouting about the Jews of their own free will *before I have started!*"[71]

Despite what Gyp interpreted as the basis for a healthy mass movement, however, Déroulède's departure had indeed left nationalism—and Gyp herself—adrift. Again she had been abandoned by a male idol. "Ah, how I'd like to see you," she wrote to Déroulède in exile. "If it were possible to find a boat . . . I would go visit you in September, even if I had to be on the road for a long time."[72] Even absent, Déroulède remained her guide. Using an apt metaphor that, thirty years earlier, had been used to describe her mother, she assured him that

"I'm a very disciplined soldier . . . who follows my leader."[73] She promised to publicize his opinions in *La Libre Parole*.[74] And she also contributed to an art exhibit and album entitled *Hommage des artistes français à Paul Déroulède*, undoubtedly modeled on the 1898–99 Dreyfusard *Hommage des artistes à Picquart*. Gyp offered a seditious song, already popular in Paris. She had written it, as she explained to Déroulède,

> on the beautiful drawing by Job that you'll receive in your album. . . . Devos hired street hawkers who play the fiddle to "launch it," as he says! . . . But I imagine that it won't be launched for long and that the hawker-launchers will be swiftly picked up by the cops. I don't know if you've seen this system of singers. It only began, I believe, after your imprisonment. The hawker climbs up on a bench with his fiddle and sings, and the crowd masses around. When it becomes too congested, they are made to climb down. It has a little touch of "revolution" that is rather pleasant.[75]

Aside from keeping Déroulède's cult alive in Paris, Gyp provided the nationalist leader with news from home. She reported to him on the dazzling opening of the 1900 Exposition Universelle, which would attract forty million international visitors. She was more enthusiastic about this world's fair than she had been about its 1889 predecessor, dwarfed by the "monstrous" Eiffel Tower. "The Fair [is] really *splendid*,"[76] Déroulède learned. Yet Gyp also resented that the fair, which opened in April amid paeans to Republican ideals of progress and humanitarianism, had been adroitly used by the government, in Gyp's view, to dissipate both domestic tensions resulting from Dreyfus' pardon and animosity toward France from foreign nations, which had long believed in Dreyfus' innocence. She made this point publicly in a 15 April *Libre Parole* article entitled "Entrrrrrrez!!!"": "Spain, the Boers, Monsieur Loubet, the Dreyfus Affair, Fashoda, and the World's Fair will be so thoroughly entangled that they will never be separated in the future. It is for It, to avoid the complications that might make It fail, that they abandoned Fashoda, pardoned Dreyfus, ignored the Boers."[77]

Several weeks after the fair opened, municipal elections took place in Paris. The nationalists, now obliged to play by the rules of Republican electoral politics, conducted a vigorous campaign. The results were impressive. Of thirty municipal councilors elected, twenty-five (including Gyp's friend Barillier) were nationalists, one was a Bonapartist, and four were socialists. For the first time in its history, and in contrast to the rest of the country, Paris had tipped to the Right. Yet this seemingly dramatic vote did not reflect a major ideological shift among Parisians. The nationalists had merely succeeded in absorbing votes from the conservative, nonreactionary Right. Nationalism, in effect, had become more moderate.[78]

The nationalists' success on 6 May marked the starting point for one of the most extraordinary incidents in Gyp's life: her kidnapping. She was used to receiving threatening letters from Dreyfusards. And her earlier, infamous encounters with a *vitrioleuse* and a would-be assassin had already identified her as a "professional'' victim. So she had been half-worried, half-delighted when, in early 1898, she got hold of a poster which, fortunately for her, was never distributed:

To the People of Paris
The anti-Semitic bullies, the nationalist bandits wish to terrorize Paris
TO TERROR, LET US RESPOND WITH EVEN MORE TERROR
The Elysée, in cahoots with the *Libre Parole*, wants to make us
Sing the glory of Esterhazy and the General Staff
To this challenge we shall respond with a provocation:
THE COMTESSE DE MARTEL (GYP)
The Pompadour of all manner of anti-Semitic dirty jobs, Queen of France by
　the grace of *Félix* and the complicity of master blackmailer *Drumont*, is in
　our hands.
She is for the moment the sufficient and necessary hostage.
Render us justice and we shall render the lady.
Since innocents go to hard labor, prison, the gallows, let us justly retaliate
　against the guilty.
A group of free men.[79]

Who could be responsible for such a provocation? In Gyp's estimation, it could only have come from one man: Octave Mirbeau. The man with whom Gyp had traded written blows in connection with her 1884 sulfuric acid dousing was now a noted Dreyfusard who contributed regularly to *L'Aurore* and authored the introduction to the *Hommage des artistes à Picquart*. Gyp informed Barrès of Mirbeau's potential for violence: "Mirbeau is . . . capable of everything . . . he's trigger-happy and would shoot you with no qualms. . . . Be careful! Don't give the Dreyfusards the pleasure of letting them beat you up or abduct you."[80]

　Despite her precautions, about a week before her disappearance Gyp received another warning that ''free men'' would no longer stand for the terrorism orchestrated by anti-Semitism's ''queen.'' She described the incident to Déroulède, after thanking him for a gift combining the decorative and the destructive:

> How good of you to think of me in that way and how I thank you for this delightful dagger! . . . I had its *tip* and *blade* sharpened, and I shall always wear it hanging from a hook. . . . In addition to being a beautiful piece of jewelry, this dagger is an excellent weapon. And these days people are after me. There are bizarre people—fake priests, fake alms collectors . . . who come looking for me at odd hours, too—11 o'clock at night for example. I'm constantly receiving letters telling me that I'll probably be done in. Last Saturday someone made a vague attempt. As I was finishing the article for *La Libre Parole*, with the shutters not yet closed, I had the stupid idea to put a lamp on my desk. I was very well lit for people in the street; then someone threw a large, triangular stone . . . that smashed the window pane, passed above the desk, and broke the screen [with drawings from] *Les Gens chics* that is on the other side of the bedroom. The debris from the windowpane was veritable *dust*.[81]

Menacing letters, posters, and smashed windows all foreshadowed the "extraordinary adventure"[82] befalling fifty-year-old Gyp on the eleventh and twelfth of May. Although she claimed to have recounted her story once to a press corps representing about a dozen newspapers, each paper's version was sensationalized in a different way, with Gyp's story either taken seriously or ridiculed. As far as the press (and Gyp) were concerned, this human drama was headline-making news and worth exploiting for profit. "It's about seclusion, kidnapping, masked man, etc.," *Le Siècle* reported, "a whole feuilleton."[83]

Yet all the papers published the same basic narrative. During the evening of 11 May Gyp attended a meeting, organized by the Ligue de la patrie française, where several of the victors in the recent elections were to speak. Leaving her carriage, she approached the entrance to the meeting hall but was stopped by a man claiming to be a friend of Barillier's who wished to escort her to a less crowded entrance. She followed this man, who was soon joined by two others. Suddenly they pushed her into a carriage parked at the curb—"a rather inelegant carriage," Gyp recalled, "something like the coupé of a country doctor"[84]—where a fourth man seated inside threw a cloth over her head and restrained her with his arms. Unruffled, Gyp protested and was assured she would not be harmed. The carriage traveled for about two hours, stopping to pick up a key, before arriving at the gate of a sprawling property. Gyp was taken up to the second floor of a house and into a dark, musty room, identified by her captors as "George's room."[85] The room was empty except for several chairs, a table, and a bed with no linens. When the four men left, she managed to escape through the window, aided by a makeshift rope she fashioned out of the curtains. Jumping several feet to the ground and then climbing over a metal gate, she scraped and bruised herself, tearing her clothes.

She wandered for two hours in the dark, finally found a road, and began walking. On the way she sat down on the grass nearby and, famished, tore out and ate what she thought were carrots. (Several papers would accuse her of fabricating her entire story, insisting that carrots did not grow in May. But she was soon exonerated after a man brought to the police samples of the root Gyp had eaten, which indeed tasted like carrots.) Finally she reached the tollhouse at the porte de Bercy, where, according to some accounts, one of the employees happened to be engrossed in her latest novel. Police officers, journalists, and Gyp herself vied to offer the most gruesome description of her as she entered the tollhouse. She was "bruised, bloodied,"[86] reported former Police Prefect Gustave Macé; "sore, bruised" said *Le Temps*, yet "not at all frightened and constantly laughing."[87] Gyp offered this image of herself: "I was dressed in black. . . . But my dress and hat were in a pitiful state; I had one sleeve in tatters; my booties were covered with mud. Not to mention my face, which looked gory."[88] After explaining her predicament to the tollhouse employees, she was escorted to the nearby home of a friend, nationalist deputy Paulin Méry, where she drank a cordial. Police soon showed up to escort her to Neuilly, where she arrived at 4 A.M.

The investigation following Gyp's abduction featured almost as many astounding twists as the *roman feuilleton* adventures of Rocambole. While *Le Temps* provided readers with almost daily bulletins about the developments, papers traditionally hostile to Gyp, such as *Le Siècle*, remained skeptical of her story and questioned the motives of her captors. Lust? But Gyp "is past the age when women with rather ardent natures usually have themselves kidnapped."[89] Greed? Gyp's purse was intact. Or was this kidnapping perhaps a final settling of accounts, fifteen years after the fact, between Gyp, her former *vitrioleuse*, and her would-be assassin?[90] On the fifteenth Gyp, "not entirely recovered from her emotional ordeal,"[91] according to *Le Temps*, announced that she would not press charges against her aggressors if they were found. The next day a tollhouse employee revealed that the night of the incident he had seen pass by a rundown coupé with white lanterns.[92] Was this the carriage used by Gyp's captors?

Accompanied by her husband, son, and police agents, Gyp spent the following days unsuccessfully trying to locate the château where she had been interned. At one possible site she recreated her leap over a metal gate with a nimbleness that amazed spectators. Meanwhile, some of her nationalist friends staked out a house "[with] a mysterious appearance,"[93] and seemed ready to storm it with "a group of sixty really determined hefty fellows."[94] In fact, the nationalists' search for Gyp's captors seemed like a vigilante counteroffensive, marked by all the paranoia and aggression of the previous two years. A police officer filed the following report: "I heard last night that several members of the Grand Occident de France were on the trail of the individuals who kidnapped Madame Gyp. If they find them, they intend to take justice into their own hands. A great effervescence reigns since this kidnapping in nationalist and anti-Semitic circles."[95]

Two weeks after the kidnapping, the event had already become part of Parisian folklore. The caricaturist Cappiello published a drawing in the 26 May issue of *Le Rire* entitled "Madame de Latude (Gyp) (ou trente-cinq minutes de captivité)," in which the gaunt, snickering figure of Gyp, lorgnette in hand, strolls past some exotic-looking trees; contemporary readers would have understood the ironic reference to the notorious adventurer Jean-Henri de Latude (1725–1805), who, having been accused of plotting against Madame de Pompadour, was imprisoned for thirty-five years; legendary experiences inspired Pixérécourt's melodrama *Latude ou trente-cinq ans de captivité*. Some "incidents of great violence"[96] were provoked by "La fuite en Egypte," a ditty full of allusions to the abduction, when it was sung at the Latin Quarter cabaret Le Grillon by the *chansonnier* Victor Tourtal. Apparently not everyone found the song amusing. About thirty young men seated in the front rows, including Gyp's son Thierry, began throwing glasses and carafes onto the stage, then climbed up and began pommeling the singer. The skirmishes degenerated into a brawl, which was finally broken up by the police.[97]

In early June a few suspects surfaced. Charles Minerot, an eighteen-year-old soldier stationed in Toulon, turned himself in, admitting that a politician who hated Gyp had paid him five hundred francs to kidnap her when he was on leave in Paris. A preliminary investigation revealed that Minerot was a convicted murderer who, with the help of accomplices, had murdered a certain Angèle Delvaux and scattered her *membra disjecta* in the Bois de Boulogne. "It has been hitherto believed," *Le Temps* informed its readers, "that we are dealing with a young soldier who is sick, obsessed by a hallucination."[98] By the next day the police realized Minerot's confession was a sham. A well-known monomaniac, he was notorious for his self-accusations. A doctor called in to examine the soldier promptly declared him "a vicious hysteric."[99] The next suspect was the caricaturist Karl, who swore he had been moved to whisk away Gyp after seeing David's *Enlèvement des Sabines* in the Louvre. Gyp contested Karl's whimsical story; he, in turn, published a letter in *Le Matin* insisting on its veracity,[100] and a police investigation concluded that Karl was indeed the culprit. Thus ended Gyp's real-life feuilleton, which had been reported in all the major Parisian dailies, and even in the international press. A short front-page article in the *New York Times* announced that Gyp's abduction was the work of "a character of the Latin Quarter, and famous for his practical jokes." The hoax had failed, the paper noted, only "owing to the agility of the Comtesse."[101]

The publication of Gyp's saga was felicitous for her, as it diverted the reader's attention from her own literary decline. If she could no longer write best-sellers, she could still live them. Productiveness was never Gyp's problem. In 1900 she published five novels: *La Paix des champs (Peace in the Fields)*, *Martinette*, *Journal d'une qui s'en fiche (The Journal of One Who Doesn't Give a Damn)*, *Balancez vos dames! (Swing Your Ladies!)* and *Trop de chic! (Too Much Chic!)*. This last work was again a source of conflict between Gyp and the book's publisher. Gyp's falling out with Calmann-Lévy had not stopped the firm from continuing publication of some of her innocuous society novels, with the caveat that they be devoid of anti-Semitism. But Gyp could not resist, obliging her publisher to chastize her for using the phrase "horribly Jewish"[102] in the manuscript of her latest novel. "You know how distasteful it is for me to be accused of publishing anti-Semitic books," Georges Calmann-Lévy reminded her in June 1900. "Thus we agreed that you would only give me works that would not belong to that category of ideas."[103] Despite this rebuke, the letter ends on a note that might be interpreted as either apologetic or fiercely ironic: "I hope, dear Madame, that you will excuse my importunity. . . ."[104] That same year three of Gyp's other works were staged: *L'Ange gardien* at the Grand Guignol, *L'Assiette au beurre* at the Théâtre Athénée, and *Une nuit agitée (A Tumultuous Night)* in Grenoble.

The quantity of Gyp's works had remained impressive, whereas their quality, to many readers and critics, had not. "For a while now a slight waning of the literary verve of Madame Gyp has been noticed," André Beaunier noted in his review of *Trop de chic!*, "for which, moreover, she has substituted an intense political activity."[105] Slang-speaking aristocrats no longer seemed to scandalize readers as they had twenty years earlier. And Gyp's unabashed hatreds had alienated many, while poisoning her lively style. The critic Adolphe Brisson commented that "her antipathy is so aggressive that it stops being pleasant. Anger and good humor don't go together at all. When Gyp meddles with writing a pamphlet, her charm disappears beneath invective, her biting words cede to dirty words."[106] Even Rachilde, one of Gyp's staunchest advocates, remarked that both emotionally and stylistically Gyp had matured little: "She will always remain young in spirit, in body, and in conscience, but remaining the same is what makes one age most in France."[107]

If Gyp was a middle-aged gamine, her heroines, like the protagonist of *Le Friquet*, also remained trapped in childhood or adolescence. Serialized in *La Revue hebdomadaire* in 1900 and adapted for the stage in 1904 by Gyp and Willy, *Le Friquet* pushed Gyp's preferred themes of abandonment, oppression, and revenge to a new level of sadism. Gyp's dedication signals the novel's dominant theme: "To Monsieur Degas, who likes and admires strength, I affectionately offer the adventure of a very strong little creature."[108] This "very strong little creature" is Marie, nicknamed "le Friquet" ("the Sparrow"), an adorable blond orphan who has spent her childhood as a horseback rider for the "Great American Circus," which is run by Jacobson, a vile, abusive Jew. She escapes this slavery when the Schlemmers, a rich couple living in Normandy, adopt her, but she soon realizes that she is again trapped, for Nephtali Schlemmer, "a greasy and sweaty fat man,"[109] wishes to seduce her. Meanwhile, she falls in love with a handsome aristocrat, Hubert de Ganges, himself a suitor of Madame Schlemmer. Fleeing Schlemmer, le Friquet returns to the circus and becomes a star. But one night Schlemmer (with Jacobson as his accomplice) appears in her dressing room, where le Friquet stabs him to death. She then begins her performance, but while swinging on the trapeze she spots Hubert with Madame Schlemmer. Distraught, she falls to the ground, dying in the arms of her protector, Mafflu, a sad old clown who had discovered her as an abandoned infant. Le Friquet has indeed proved her/his strength by fleeing Jacobson and murdering Schlemmer. But she cannot enjoy this victory over her oppressors, paid for with her own annihilation.

"The Beautiful Butterfly Crushed . . ."

Gyp's literary stagnation and the increasingly lurid tone of some of her novels perhaps reveal the effects of a personal tragedy: the death in the Sudan on 27 November 1900 of her elder son Aymar. A twenty-seven-year-old cavalry officer, Aymar had been sent to the Sudan in late 1898 as part of a mission searching for the French explorer Paul Flatters. His departure worried his mother, who became even more anxious when, after a year, Aymar decided to prolong his stay. She shared her concern with Déroulède: "I am distressed about Aymar, who insists on staying in the Sudan for another year and for no good reason, I believe. He has two feats of arms. . . . It seems to me that he can come home."[110] But Gyp knew Aymar loved danger, and a letter she received after his death intimated that his most daring exploit had not yet occurred. "I'm going to do something amazing from an athletic point of view," he had written his mother, "but it's possible that I'll die doing it."[111] In October or early November Gyp learned about this reckless marathon. She recounted to Déroulède that "Aymar took off *without orders* into the brush with ten spahis to capture a rebel chief. Encircled by four hundred blacks, they went for 48 hours without drinking, eating, or sleeping, and accomplished prodigious feats of courage and sangfroid. An officer . . . who learned from other blacks that they were lost . . . went to their rescue, *also without orders*, with his detachment. They lost no one (at least on the spot) and they took some horses, but there were 15 wounded."[112] Yet Aymar did not return to France to boast of his exploits. Instead he was sentenced to sixty days in prison for disobedience, where, quite unheroically, he contracted typhus and died.

Souvenir pistols, bows and arrows, and Aymar's bullet-riddled, crimson spahi's jacket accompanied his body back to France. At the funeral Maurice Barrès felt a sense of tragedy: "The priest, garbed in black velvet and gold, was sparkling on the top steps of the luminous altar. A voice rises up that forces us to cry, then suddenly it seems to fall; it is that scarlet spot on the coffin of the poor young man, that beautiful hilt of the saber that alone emerges from the ample spahi's cape. Ah! The beautiful butterfly crushed and that toque, the proud bauble of his youth, and that cross he conquered. . . . The black servants of death dart forth suddenly, bare the coffin."[113] Gyp was distraught, "overwhelmed . . . senseless,"[114] as she described herself to Séverine; "terrified,"[115] another friend learned. She wrote a cousin about her premonition: "I had the absolute conviction that misfortune would befall Aymar in the Sudan and I am terrified by his death, just as much as if I had not anticipated this horrible tragedy for two years."[116] Alone, she mourned her son at a private mass.

Aymar's death, for Gyp, was "certainly the greatest sorrow of her existence."[117] Aymar represented the continuity—and perhaps the realization—of the Mirabeau and Gonneville mystiques. His audaciousness would have made his great-great-grandfather Tonneau proud; he once swam across the Loire River in a suit of armor and a helmet, and in Africa he bathed every evening in the Niger, undaunted by crocodiles.[118] Like his great-grandfather Gonneville, he was a professional soldier, one who, like his grandfather Arundel, had died an accidental death. Aymar was also a third-generation writer whose first work Calmann-Lévy had proposed to publish under the pseudonym "Riquet."[119] Gyp's intended bequest to Aymar of the château Mirabeau and its marquisate would have symbolized the transfer to him of the ancestral legacy, which Gyp had only imperfectly realized. But with Aymar's death, the legacy itself seemed to vanish.

Anatole France *(Reutlinger, Paris)*

Edouard Drumont, the "pope of anti-Semitism"
(Cliché Bruizard, Paris)

"Many women thought of a Bonaparte when seeing him as I painted him at twenty-five. . . ." Portrait of Maurice Barrès in 1890 by Jacques-Emile Blanche (*Bibliothèque Nationale, Paris*)

The "turbulent trio," Nicole, Aymar, and Thierry de Martel *(Sibylle Gaudry collection, Paris)*

Pastel portrait of Thierry and Aymar de Martel in Lion-sur-Mer in 1889 by Louise-Catherine Breslau

The future "man of letters" *(Photo J. Barco, Nancy, Sibylle Gaudry collection, Paris)*

Gyp in 1893 with her trademark lorgnette *(Benque Studios, Sibylle Gaudry collection, Paris)*

Gyp in the 1880s *(Sibylle Gaudry collection, Paris)*

"Madame Gyp." Woodcut of Gyp by Félix Vallotton, which appeared in *La Revue des revues* in January 1898, two weeks before the publication of "J'Accuse"

Portrait of Gyp in 1885 by Albert Aublet *(Musée historique Lorrain, Nancy, Cliché Mignot)*

"There is something unhealthily seductive about that woman. . . ." Pastel portrait of Gyp in 1894 by Giovanni Boldini *(Musée Carnavalet, Paris)*

— Sûr, qu'elle n'est pas à la noce, la France!...

Dessin de GYP.

"Surely, France ain't enjoying herself!" Gyp's drawing for the cover of the 28 December 1895 issue of *Le Rire*

St-puis après ?

Lundi

Monsieur,
je vous donnerai,
quand vous le dési-
-rerez, une photo-
-graphie de Gyp

et des lignes de son écriture.
quant à ce que vous voulez avoir sur
le mouvement mondain, je crois que
je suis absolument incapable de le
faire. Gyp ne le "gobe" pas du tout, le
mouvement mondain, et ne s'en occupe
guère que pour le "blaguer".

Recevez, Monsieur,
mes remerciements
et l'expression de
ma haute considé-
-ration

Mirabeau-Martel

Gyp

Facsimile of Gyp's handwriting

"The enfant terrible of the Dreyfus Affair," postcard

LE SYNDICAT

Place, voici l'armée!... À genoux donc, marauds,
C'est la France qui passe!... Et voici ses hérauts :
Voici Drumont l'apôtre, et Gyp, comtesse garce ;
Voici les vieux marquis, gâteux, à bout de farce ;
Déroulède, à qui Dieu défendit le repos,
Millevoye, Judet, tous trois porte drapeau ;
Voici le bel Arthur, le plus noble des yoctres ;
Voici Blanc, Pellonnais, Humbert, tous les jeanfoutres!
Joignez les mains, priez! — Contemple, ô travailleur :
Voici les Capitans féroces et trembleurs ;
Voici les Condéens marchant à la curée,
Vo ci, coulaonnent, la horde chamarrée,
Boisdeffre, Gavaignac-Dupaty, Pell eux,
Et le spectre d'Henry planant au-dessus d'eux :
Guêtre de blanc voici Félix : voici Méline,
Petit homme à la voix, aux paroles félines ;
Voici les chats-fourrés, les m:asieurs du barreau,
Les préfets, sons-préfets, députés, généraux ;
Voici les noirs corbeaux, voici to.is les jésuites,
Didon, du Lac, Jumont, Cuverville et leurs suites,
Tous ces héros fourbes d'ignorance et d'honneurs
Qui n'ont — pauvres chrétiens ! — que de la haine au cœur ;
Enfin voici la basse, après la haute pègre,
Le bataillon sacré de Guérin, dit « l'Intègre »,
Le bataillon mandit de l'infâme Guérin,
Les hurleurs, les marlous et les rois du surin!...

Et lance au poing, l'œil fauve — avant qu'on ne le pende —
Esterhazy, royal forban, conduit la bande !

Asnières, imprimerie E. NERY, 7, rue du Bois.

"Here is Drumont the apostle, and Gyp, countess bitch. . . ." "Le Syndicat" (ca. 1898), broadside by H. Beronse *(Reproduced by permission of the Houghton Library, Harvard University)*

(facing page) Gyp's preferred writing paper during the Dreyfus Affair

"Madame Latude or thirty-five minutes of captivity." Leonetto Cappiello's 1900 caricature concerning Gyp's kidnapping, first published in *Le Rire* (26 May 1900), here used as an advertisement for *Les Chapons*

Pastel of Thierry de Martel in 1915 by Louise-Catherine Breslau

Gyp in 1919 *(Sibylle Gaudry collection, Paris)*

The "old fossil." Gyp in 1930 *(René Benjamin collection, Savonnières)*

XI

"The Wisdom of Gyp"
1901–1913

I was present at the baptism of nationalism; I am present at
its burial.

Maurice Barrès, *Mes Cahiers*, vol. 3

"The Funeral of Nationalism"

Aymar's death, Philippe Barrès noted, marked "a fracture"[1] in Gyp's thought.
She remained close to the forefront of nationalist politics until World War I and
continued to write at least two novels a year until her death in 1932. Her 1901
dialogue-novel *Jacquette et Zouzou* was a great success with worldly young
countesses at the court of Saxony.[2] Yet she lacked the astounding energy that had
propelled her through Boulangism and the Dreyfus Affair. Health problems
plagued her. She complained frequently of hay fever, pleurisy, laryngitis, pul-
monary congestion, and rheumatism, some of which required shots of morphine.
As early as 1909, she felt her death was imminent. In response to a survey on
death devised by Ferdinand Brunetière, the director of the *Revue des deux mondes*,
Gyp alone answered that she would not regret dying at all.[3] She was constantly
desperate for money as well, expanding her circle of creditors to include not only
her publisher and her editor Brunetière but also her son Thierry. Damning familial
tradition, in 1904 Thierry was absorbed by his internship in surgery. In 1906 he
became head of the surgical clinic at La Salpêtrière hospital in Paris, laying the
foundations for the remarkable career that would follow the war.

Nationalism, too, was on the decline in the years separating the conclusion of
the Dreyfus Affair from World War I. With Dreyfus' definitive acquittal and
reinstatement into the army in 1906, the defensive nationalism of the last two
decades of the nineteenth century had lost its raison d'être. The trauma of the

Affair had, in fact, helped consolidate the Republic, around whose tricolor banner the socialists had tardily rallied. The adherence of the nascent socialist party to republicanism (symbolized by the historic inclusion of a socialist minister in Waldeck-Rousseau's 1899 cabinet) sapped from the nationalist movement much of the working-class support that had fortified it during Boulangism. Waldeck-Rousseau's government of "Republican defense," followed by that of the ferociously anticlerical Emile Combes, set out to uproot the two institutional strongholds of nationalism, the Church and the Army. The dissolution of such fanatic religious orders as the Assumptionist Fathers, as well as purges of anti-Republican cliques in the army, silenced the extremist groups that had helped give nationalism its crusading air. With these extremes eliminated, much of the nationalist Right was absorbed by the traditional, conservative Right, sharing with it a new preoccupation: rallying French enthusiasm for the increasingly plausible prospect of war against Germany.

As Gyp would attest, nationalism was crumbling as much from internal dissensions as from external restraint. The continually shifting and ever-complicated relations among groups claiming allegiance to nationalism—which at times included anti-Semites, monarchists, and even anarchists—were further troubled after 1900 by financial problems and by the absence of Déroulède, whose charismatic leadership had helped compensate for the doctrinal incoherence of the extreme Right. As was the case during the Dreyfus Affair, Gyp participated in the activities of several of the organizations and movements associated with nationalism out of intellectual affinity, friendship for their leaders, or both. She was thus a privileged witness to the decomposition of post–Dreyfus Affair nationalism. And she continued to be a valued and much sought after link among nationalist factions.

Even after the debacles of *la révision* and the High Court, Gyp continued to work for the two organizations most explicitly identified with nationalism, the Ligue des patriotes and the Ligue de la patrie française. Of the two, Déroulède's Ligue des patriotes was still larger, better organized, and more willing to seek recourse to violent and illegal tactics. In the spring of 1899 the league had been the rallying point for all extreme Right groups. A year later, however, it was on especially bad terms with both Drumont and Guérin, who felt that Déroulède had opportunistically used anti-Semitism during the Affair to integrate and control all of nationalism's strands. Gyp corresponded regularly with Déroulède until his return from exile in 1905. She maintained contacts with other members of the Ligue des patriotes' inner circle, too, including Habert and Thiébaud, friends from Boulangist days; Henri Galli, a wealthy lawyer who in Déroulède's absence replaced him as head of the league; and Edmond Archdéacon, a millionaire sportsman who between 1898 and 1904 was the league's principal financial backer, thereby freeing it from monarchist purse strings. It was to Archdéacon that Gyp referred Barrès when he solicited advice about the merits of various Parisian carriage makers. For Archdéacon, Gyp reminded her friend, "has always had nicely harnessed and pretty carriages."[4]

Gyp contributed her talents as propagandist to the Ligue des patriotes' re-vamped newspaper, *Le Drapeau*. Founded in 1883, the undistinguished weekly, which described its political affiliation as "plebiscitary-republican," was a convenient repository for reprinted speeches by Habert and Déroulède. It could never hope to rival in circulation or editorial quality the major dailies with nationalist leanings, such as *L'Intransigeant, Le Gaulois,* or *La Patrie*.[5] In 1901 funds from Archdéacon helped turn *Le Drapeau* into a daily. And the paper's reputation was enhanced when Barrès, whose three-volume *Roman de l'énergie nationale* (1897–1902) was confirming his status as the intellectual center of nationalism, agreed to become editor-in-chief.

In December 1900 Gyp had been approached as a potential contributor to *Le Drapeau* by Galli, who transmitted to her Déroulède's wish that "you be one of us."[6] Gyp accepted immediately, enticed in part by the promise of a hundred francs, but quickly became anxious. Would she have complete freedom to write what she wanted? This question had, of course, prompted her ruptures with *La Fronde*, with her publisher, and, more recently, with *La Libre Parole*, where "[my articles] were cut and censored, under the pretext that *'I specialized in saying things liable to attract lawsuits.'* "[7] Gyp no longer cared if her behavior created legal problems for Drumont, who was furious at her: "I didn't give a damn about having tiffs with *La Libre Parole*."[8] But she would have felt "chagrined" to cause trouble for Déroulède and Barrès, her venerated friends. Still doubting her capacity for self-control, she began to send *Le Drapeau* weekly dialogues by "Bob." Yet she urged Barrès to inform her *"very frankly"*[9] when she was over-stepping the limits of decency.

Gyp was pleased to observe that *Le Drapeau*, the latest vehicle for her slander, was no longer a "sensationalistic rag"[10] but a *"real* newspaper"[11] whose quality was improving. Despite her enthusiastic evaluation and Archdéacon's apparently limitless generosity, however, Barrès informed Gyp not to send him an article the first Sunday in July 1901, nor on the following Sundays. Déroulède's excessive monetary promises, Barrès revealed, had forced him to make cutbacks, and "the best way . . . is for me to eliminate articles from time to time."[12] Whether it was Gyp's indiscretions or Déroulède's exaggerations that caused her exclusion from *Le Drapeau* is unclear. Once again, though, Gyp was being told she was no longer welcome.

The Ligue des patriotes was not only a propaganda machine but an electoral one as well. Gyp followed closely the campaigns of her friends for the 1902 legislative elections. Between February and March she sent a series of nine caricatures, all focused on the upcoming elections, to *La Patrie Illustrée*. In some of these drawings Gyp returned to themes from her work during the Boulangist crisis, such as the call for both a purge of internal enemies and for a savior–leader. The first drawing shows Marianne doing France's "wash," which includes the heads of prominent Jews and Protestants. At the same time she calls out to a figure meant to be Déroulède, who sits astride an oversized red carnation, exactly as did Boulanger in Gyp's 1896 rendering of him in her "Histoire de la Troisième République": "Gotta wash all that! . . . . Come help me!!!!!!"[13] In other drawings

Gyp made appeals for specific candidates, including Jousselin, an anti-Semitic candidate running in the XVIIième arrondissement (where the league was particularly influential), and Barillier, running in La Villette and represented as a menacing butcher with a dagger in his belt.

The intensive, well-coordinated activity of Gyp and other league members before the elections indeed helped influence the success of the twenty-three nationalists from Paris elected in 1902 (the previous Chamber of Deputies had counted fourteen). Gyp's friends Grosjean and Archdéacon were among the victors. Sabran-Pontevès was beaten, however, as was Barillier, despite help from his butcher friends, whom *Le Matin* described as "killers, bleeders, carvers, with broad faces, protruding muscles, enormous shoulders."[14] Yet the success of nationalism in Paris was offset by its debacle in the provinces, where Boni de Castellane, Drumont (running in Algeria), and others all lost their seats. Five months later a demonstration planned by nationalist politicians on the occasion of Zola's state funeral collapsed, dramatically revealing the movement's impotence. In 1904 the nationalists would lose control of the Paris municipal council. And the 1906 legislative and 1908 municipal elections would mark "the swan song of anti-Dreyfusard nationalism."[15]

Gyp's relations with the other group to champion nationalism, the Ligue de la patrie française, were, as ever, more strained than her dealings with Déroulède's organization. In fact, in 1901 she withdrew her membership from the league after it failed to provide electoral backing for Max Régis, a former mayor of Algiers and one of the principal agitators in the Algerian anti-Semitic movement. "I've left that group, which is too patriotic for my taste," Gyp wrote Barrès (who would soon follow her lead), "and which seems to me to put the personal interest of its members far above the interest of the country."[16] Gyp still felt—as she had when the league was first created two years earlier—that she shared little with its respectable bourgeois leadership, which consistently refused to take to the streets, preferring electioneering and speech making. Anti-Semitism, moreover, had never been part of the league's official program. Barrès and the Bonapartist Coppée, Gyp noted, were exceptions. Coppée, unlike the many other members of the Académie française in the league, urged its adherents to storm the Elysée. Yet by 1902 the poet and political militant was tired. Before the elections Gyp found him at home, "in bed and really dreadfully thin and tired."[17] He would die six years later.

Gyp could report at first hand on the headline-making event that marked the definitive demise of the Ligue de la patrie française, namely, the suicide of Gabriel Syveton, one of its founders and its treasurer. Gyp had met Syveton at the home of Coppée. She occasionally entertained his wife and stepdaughter. A provincial lycée teacher of modest origins, Syveton had taken a leave of absence in 1898 to devote himself to nationalist politics. The founding of the Ligue de la patrie française was due largely to his initiative, as well as to that of several other academics. He soon became the league's treasurer and in 1902 was elected deputy in Paris. Yet four years later rumors that Syveton was embezzling league funds began to trouble nationalist circles, leading donors such as Archdéacon to transfer their money away from the now suspect organization. As Gyp observed correctly, "the money—stopped at the Patrie française—flows for the moment to the Action libérale. . . ."[18]

In 1904 allegations of financial improprieties were compounded by legal problems, further discrediting Syveton. On 4 November he rose in the Chamber of Deputies to deliver not a speech but a slap to the cheek of General Louis André, war minister in Combes' cabinet. The source of Syveton's wrath was the infamous Affaire des Fiches, which involved the establishment by the government of a spy network of Freemasons to ferret out information on the political and religious convictions of army officers suspected of antirepublicanism. André was largely responsible for this last bit of post-Dreyfus housecleaning. Gyp lauded Syveton's audacity. "I'm delighted Syveton slapped the war minister," she declared to Barrès. "I would have preferred he slap Jaurès, but we have to be content with what we have. It's already quite nice!"[19]

Yet Syveton's bravado was short-lived. The night of the notorious slap, and while the Chamber was holding a special session to decide Syveton's fate, the hapless deputy sought refuge from the law at Gyp's house. He was frightened by the prospect of both his imminent arrest and a duel with another pro-Republican army officer, de Gail (identified by Gyp as "a scoundrel who is from an excellent family from Alsace")[20]. Even worse for Syveton, new evidence regarding his financial fraud was surfacing (five hundred thousand francs were reported missing from the league's coffers), as were rumors of sexual misconduct (he was accused of molesting his stepdaughter).

Gyp was stunned to find the nationalist desperado, whom she had not seen in a year and a half, at her doorstep ("[W]hen the servant told me he was there, I was flabbergasted!")[21] and to hear of his predicament. After dinner fellow nationalist Boni de Castellane arrived to escort Syveton to an "unassailable domicile."[22] A month later, however, on the eve of his appearance before the Assize Court for premeditated violence, Syveton killed himself. Had he perhaps confirmed de Castellane's evaluation of him as "intelligent and talented, but lacking energy, lacking principles, and violent like all weak people"?[23]

Gyp insisted that despite overwhelming evidence of suicide, Svyeton had been made to drink poisoned coffee and then asphyxiated, probably by Freemasons eager to avenge André's public humiliation. She articulated the plot theory she was publicizing elsewhere in her *Journal d'un casserolé*, another of her semifictionalized chronicles of periods of political turmoil, this one covering the months between January 1903 and December 1904. The Bonapartist army officer who is the "author" of the journal asserts that "Syveton did not not kill himself! . . . Does a guy like that kill himself like a laundress?"[24] "The truth is . . . that he was 'rubbed out' in view of the next day's trial."[25] Like Bazaine, Gyp reasoned, Syveton could not possibly be guilty. It was his allegiance to a vitalized, purified French nation that ensured his own purity. Moreover, she could not permit herself to question a man linked to an order and ethos from which she drew her own sense of identity. Once again the actions of human devils—first revealed to her as a child learning her family's version of the Revolution—provided a convenient explanation.

Syveton's death was one of the last nails in the coffin of nationalism. The anti-Semitic movement was moribund as well after its choice scapegoat, Dreyfus, had been acquitted and one of its leaders, Guérin, condemned by the High Court. There were internal conflicts, too. The older, more intellectual, and Catholic Drumont and the rabble-rousing Guérin hated one another. Gyp, ever the partisan, left *La Libre Parole* to side with the more violent and infinitely more seductive Guérin. In September 1902 she agreed to participate in the last of Guérin's mad ventures by becoming a regular contributor to his new and short-lived paper *La Tribune française*. Guérin's promise of five hundred francs a month plus advertising space for her novels provided Gyp with a sufficient incentive. And a police report indicated that she may also have been blackmailed into working for the former impresario of Fort Chabrol: "[I]t is said that the matter has been imposed on Gyp, who was led to believe that any refusal would be interpreted negatively and that she would be punished through the publication of certain details of her famous kidnapping, formerly recounted in the newspapers."[26]

La Tribune française—to which Gyp began to send weekly installments of *Les Chapons*, a dialogue-novel that attacked Combes' anticlerical policies—billed itself as an "anti-Jewish and nationalist newspaper."[27] Its mission, announced in the first issue, was to "combat all speculators" and to "continue the work of the Grand Occident de France, despite persecutions."[28] It combined slanderous articles about some of nationalism's bêtes noires (Loubet, André, and Trarieux, for instance) with stock accounts of Jewish ritual murder and flagellation. This familiar blend of nationalism and anti-Semitism, dished out by such well-known figures as Gyp, should have assured the paper some measure of success. Instead it foundered when Guérin, living in Brussels, stopped paying his staff three months after the paper's birth. He instead preferred to squander twelve hundred francs a day, much of it supplied by the duc d'Orléans, on two town houses, two carriages, five servants, a loge at the theater, and the "petty expenses"[29] of his mistress. By January 1903 the paper's frustrated typographers stopped working, in March its administrator quit, and by April the staff began to feel, as a police report revealed, that "the comedy has lasted for too long."[30]

Despite fidelity to Guérin, another of her adored absent heroes, Gyp also resigned from the paper in April 1903, five months before its office furniture began to be sold, "but item by item, so that it not be too visible."[31] Staff members who, like Gyp, had left *La Libre Parole* to follow Guérin were "panic-stricken, and didn't know to which saint they should pray."[32] Gyp's attempts to collect the eighteen hundred francs owed her for contributions to *La Tribune française* and also to *L'Antijuif* were rebuffed by an embarrassed and penniless Guérin, whose refusals were apparently accompanied by threats. If Gyp finally abandoned her demands for payment, it was because (as a police report suggested) "she fancies that Louis Guérin [brother of Jules] would be waiting for her in a deserted place to do her in."[33]

The fall of *La Tribune française* was symptomatic of the crumbling of fin-de-siècle anti-Semitism. The movement was unable to replace the issue of Dreyfus' guilt with one of comparable magnitude; opposition to the Republic's anticlerical policies was the best possible substitute. In addition, organized anti-Semitism lacked both leadership (Guérin had died in 1910) and a broad social base. Without these the anti-Semitic press languished, although a greatly modified *Libre Parole* survived until 1923. After 1906 openly anti-Semitic deputies became anachronisms. Anti-Semitism was for the time being forced from the public into the private domain. Although hook-nosed Jews made by now obligatory appearances in Gyp's novels, they were relegated to secondary roles. With the Affair ended, her own anti-Semitic fury had diminished, as had the market for anti-Semitic popular culture. She would thus content herself with seeking out like-minded anti-Semites to whom she could express her views in private—by lending to former anti-Dreyfusard Quesnay de Beaurepaire, for instance, a book entitled *L'Esprit juif*, for which he thanked Gyp effusively, having gleaned from it "some valuable information for my popular conferences."[34]

Gyp's services were thus still being solicited by the dregs of the nationalist and anti-Semitic movements. She was also being courted by the man whose ideas were inspiring the dynamic young group that filled the void created on the extreme Right by the quelling of nationalism. Action française, which by 1908 adhered fully to the theories of Charles Maurras, had been founded in 1899 by dissident members of the Ligue de la patrie française. Although critical of the conservatism of the latter, Action française, like the league it had broken away from, originally situated itself within the republican tradition. At the time this first "Comité d'action française" was formed, Charles Maurras was a thirty-year-old journalist and literary critic covering the Dreyfus Affair for the monarchist paper *La Gazette*. A non-Parisian like Barrès, but with roots in Provence, Maurras had also gravitated to avant-garde literary circles on arriving in the capital, most notably the Ecole romane of the symbolist poet Jean Moréas. The neoclassical aesthetic of order, reason, and logic that was the credo of the Ecole romane also informed the political doctrine Maurras was elaborating in "L'Enquête sur la monarchie" and in other writings that were to convert Action française to monarchism. In these Maurras argued that the Revolutionary ideals of individualism and universalism were abhorrent, and that the republican regime issuing from the Revolution was incompatible with nationalism. Only a monarchy—hereditary, traditional, decentralized, and nonparliamentary—was an appropriate regime for France. Monarchism for Maurras was not merely a pragmatic remedy for nationalism's ills; it was the only logical one. Each of monarchism's "postulates," as Maurras attempted to demonstrate in his writings, corresponded to one of nationalism's and negated one of the Republic's: "[M]onarchy can be demonstrated like a theorem."[35]

During the formative years separating the birth of the republican Comité d'action française in 1899 from that of the monarchist Ligue d'action française in 1905, Maurras tried to win over to his brand of royalism some notable figures from the nationalist Right who had been adrift since the end of the Affair. He considered Gyp, whom he had met in the anti-Dreyfusard ranks several years earlier, an extremely valuable potential recruit, so valuable, in fact, that he deemed her failure to adhere to royalism "more than a problem: it is a scandal."[36] Maurras' interest in Gyp was, of course, in part strategic. Gyp, who was twenty years (and thus a generation) older than Maurras, would be his link to many of the disparate groups of the extreme Right. Yet he also hoped she might help him gain popular support by translating his highly abstract theories into the powerful and violent images associated with novels like *Les Chapons*, which Gyp dedicated to him. The images contained in this novel, which Maurras deemed a "beautiful little book in the form of a dagger,"[37] were mainly of the groups Maurras collectively labeled "anti-France": the "all-powerful" Jews, Protestants, Masons, and *métèques* (mongrels) colonizing France from within and represented in *Les Chapons* by the Ubel de Saint-Sabbas family. Gyp, Maurras asserted, was second only to Drumont in supplying the French imagination with such vivid personifications of the ideas Maurras could only express in dry, nearly mathematical terms.[38] In a highly laudatory review of *Un ménage dernier cri*,[39] which doubled as an exhortation to the recalcitrant imperialist, he hailed Gyp as a vitalizing mentor and declared himself prepared to receive her "good seed."[40] By achieving an equilibrium (as Maurras claimed Gyp had) between "wisdom . . . and skill, . . . reflection . . . and obsession,"[41] Maurras hoped to galvanize and focus the energies of a movement which in the early 1900s was composed of cerebral individuals like himself.

Given Gyp's traditionalism, her antidemocratic leanings, and her hatred of "un-French" elements both within and outside France, her seeming lack of enthusiasm for royalism baffled Maurras. He argued that Gyp had made explicit her doctrinal affinities with Action française in her *Journal d'un casserolé*, a work Maurras hailed as a "breviary of political wisdom."[42] Had she not denounced, through her characterization of the "Suissesse" married to the protagonist, "racial" mixing?[43] Had she not clearly seen the Republic, as Maurras had, as "discussion, criticism, parliamentarism, sterile agitations, elections always temporary and always recommenced?"[44] How, then, could she not "see that the monarchy is the complete opposite, but a radical opposite, a pure opposite?"[45]

Indeed, Gyp could not "see" or understand intellectually the superiority of royalism. Besides, she suspected that the pretender was not sufficiently anti-Semitic for her tastes. "Try as I might," she insisted to Maurras in a 1903 letter thanking him for his flattering review of *Les Chapons*, "I do not believe that the anti-Semitism of the duc d'Orléans is *deep-seated*."[46] Furthermore, Maurras' cold logic and detached personality alienated Gyp, who had always let instinct, sentiment, and élan guide her political choices. Maurras was a theorist, Gyp an agitator. And nostalgia had always led her to champion a man not on a throne but on a horse: the Napoleon whose likeness Gonneville had placed on the wall in her childhood bedroom, Boulanger, Déroulède. As for a choice of regime, Gyp had always expressed a preference for an imperial system or even for a plebiscitary, authoritarian republic similar to the one envisioned by Déroulède. And finally, because of her attachment to the memory and legacy of Mirabeau the Revolutionary, Gonneville the veteran of the Napoleonic wars, and Bacourt the Orleanist, she could not (as did Maurras) consider a complete aberration over a century of French history.

Action française, then, did not receive Gyp's endorsement. Indeed, she would mock the aristocratic pretensions of its members in a series of dialogue-novels, as she did in *Le Grand Coup* (1913), a work that ridiculed the Camelots du Roi, the young shock troops of the league, and also the hawkers of its newspaper. Gyp's "Mégottiers du Roy" ("King's Cigarette Butt Collectors") are portrayed as a gang of silly adolescents for whom the idea of a coup d'état is no more than a prank. They are weaklings compared with the hardened veterans of the "real" combats of Boulangism and the Affair. Although Gyp would remain on polite terms with Maurras himself, the movement he animated would receive only her scorn and occasional stabs from her literary weapons.

In the early years of the century, Gyp felt much more indulgent toward anarchists than toward Action française royalists. Yet these two extremes had much in common.[47] For anarchism was one of many antiparliamentary and extremist movements assaulting the structures of the bourgeois and democratic Third Republic. Indeed, anarchism was popular in many former strongholds of Boulangism, while monarchists funded anarchist meetings; this was the era of ideological crossovers. What Gyp could appreciate in the anarchist doctrine preached by Bakunin and Kropotkin was its appeal to violence and insurrection, to "propaganda by the deed," which had literally exploded between 1892 and 1895 with a series of spectacular bombings in Paris. This spontaneous violence, which Gyp had admired during the Commune (when it was directed against the Republic), was far removed from the lifeless theories of Maurras.

"Propaganda by the deed" was part of a broader anarchist program to blast tyrannical institutions, most notably the state, and to liberate the downtrodden from rules and constraints. Something of this desire is also apparent in Gyp's lifelong tirades against "oppressors," beginning with her mother, and in her literary jibes against bourgeois morality. Although anti-Semitism was lacking at the Ligue de la patrie française, Gyp could find it in certain anarchist circles, where traditional images of Jews as capitalist exploiters of the working classes were often evoked. Finally, anarchism's rejection of modern urban industrial civilization and its nostalgia for an artisanal golden age echoed Gyp's condemnations of electricity, automobiles, and other symbols of what she deemed "the age of fake."[48]

However, as Gyp's tumultuous relationship with Laurent Tailhade illustrates, certain tenets of anarchist "doctrine" (itself full of contradictions) were repugnant to the equally contradictory Gyp. She could never ascribe, for instance, to the anarchists' rabid anticlericalism and antimilitarism. And her penchant for verbally dynamiting the Third Republic never evolved into a call for the stateless society advocated by anarchists. On the contrary, her authoritarian and traditionalist leanings marked her as a woman of the Right. Her anarchism would always be of the "Chat Noir" variety, largely a pose meant to titillate an elite audience.

The ambiguity of Gyp's relationship to anarchism is illustrated by her encounter with Paterne Berrichon, which took place around 1900. Berrichon, né Clément Dufour, was one of many artists and poets active at the fin de siècle who were attracted to anarchism, which he considered a political equivalent of the revolution he and others hoped to bring about in art. When not in trouble with military authorities, Berrichon, a gruff and bitter radical, was busy writing a biography of Rimbaud. After reading several excerpts of his work in *La Revue Blanche*, Gyp sent Berrichon a complimentary note. The writer's response, worthy of Gyp herself, was a plea for money. Always eager to do a little slumming, Gyp complied, making a personal delivery to Berrichon's squalid hotel room. Her fortuitous handout, according to Berrichon, marked the beginning of his metamorphosis. He married Rimbaud's sister, published his biography, and began living respectably, thus ending what Gyp considered a worthwhile yet appropriately short stay in bohemia. "[Gyp's] fraternal gesture," *L'Intransigeant* concluded, "was enough to arouse the upright bourgeois who was slumbering in the heart of the anarchist."[49]

"Upright bourgeois" and "anarchist" also coexisted in the poet and writer Laurent Tailhade, whose extremely turbulent contacts with Gyp spanned several decades. Born into a wealthy family from Tarbes in 1854, Tailhade had first glimpsed Gyp and her mother in the 1860s when they were vacationing in the Pyrénées. A "stuffy little provincial boy,"[50] he had been captivated by the image of the two svelte and elegant young women riding horseback through the rugged mountain landscape. He was even more interested to learn from the "old and devout"[51] townspeople (who revealed this fact in a peculiar tone) that the elder of the two women was the comtesse de Mirabeau, "femme de lettres."

The comtesse de Mirabeau's daughter was already famous when Tailhade arrived in Paris in the early 1880s. He had praised *Petit Bob* and other Gyp novels in various publications and in his correspondence with her. He especially appreciated the author's "hatred of Israel."[52] Known for his dandyish style, his wit, and his insolence (as well as for his addiction to morphine and camphor), Tailhade was soon established in symbolist and Parnassian circles. He wrote several volumes of Parnassian poetry, translated Plautus and Petronius, and penned a cruel satire of bourgeois manners, *Au pays du mufle* (*In the Land of the Boor*). Like many of his friends (especially those from Le Chat Noir), Tailhade flirted with anarchism. Yet this pose did not necessarily reflect a deep sense of conviction but rather his own "outrageous individualism."[53] He wrote for several anarchist publications such as *La Revue Rouge*, fought a duel with Barrès (which left him lame for life), and applauded Auguste Vaillant's bombing of the Chamber of Deputies in December 1893 as a "beautiful gesture." In 1894 Tailhade fell victim to anarchist tactics himself when an explosion in the Restaurant Foyot caused him to lose an eye.

Anarchism had led Tailhade to Dreyfusism, thus temporarily severing his ties with Gyp. He would recall that "I marched under the banners of Zola, my glorious friend and master; Gyp, although so free-thinking, ... turned to the party of Messrs. Saint-Saëns and Frédéric Masson."[54] Tailhade's flattering reviews of Gyp were replaced with invective.[55] As Gyp herself remarked in *L'Age du mufle*: "And then suddenly ... Monsieur Tailhade began to scold me in the Dreyfusard newspapers where he was ... regularly writing, and not attacking my ideas, which were different from his (since only recently), but insulting me personally."[56] Yet through their activities during the Affair, both Gyp and Tailhade were becoming expert at the type of virulent polemics that would help reunite them afterward. Tailhade's *A travers les groins* (*Through the Snouts*) (1899) and *Imbéciles et gredins* (*Imbeciles and Scoundrels*) (1900) matched Gyp's *Libre Parole* pieces in their venomous tone. The anti-Semitism that inspired much of this polemical literature, however, also eased their reconciliation. In a laudatory review of Gyp's 1902 dialogue-novel *Un mariage chic*, Tailhade praised the author as "the foremost woman storyteller"[57] since the death of Judith Gautier. Gyp's insistence on symbolic physical detail, Tailhade wrote, succeeded in conveying the "essence" of the Jews, whom he damned in extremely violent terms as "bedouins transplanted from their original filth"[58] and as "oily yids ... still scarcely washed...."[59] In a telling revelation of his remarkable contradictions, however, Tailhade asserted that Gyp's "charming" collection of Jewish *pupazzi* could not diminish the glory of a Théodore or Salomon Reinach.[60]

Remembering not the factionalism of the Affair but only a shared anti-Semitism and general misanthropy, Gyp wrote compassionately of Tailhade during his 1901 trial. The trial was occasioned by Tailhade's appeal to the spiritual descendants of "the sublime Louvel"[61] (murderer of the duc de Berry) to assassinate the visiting Russian tsar. The polemicist's provocations, which he published in the 15 September issue of the anarchist newspaper *Le Libertaire*, earned him a year in prison, this despite the intervention of Anatole France and other prominent writers. Gyp attended Tailhade's trial and recorded her impressions in her 1902 epistolary novel, *L'Age du mufle* (most likely a reference to Tailhade's 1891 *Au pays du mufle*). The pity and sympathy she felt for Tailhade resulted less from her support for his calls for murder than from her attraction to his "military" air. For Tailhade, Gyp wrote, "with his white hair and his slight paunch, ... looks almost exactly like a retired ... colonel."[62] Tailhade's legendary vanity was touched by Gyp's ambiguous compliment, and he wrote from the Santé prison to thank her. "To be compared to an old Colonel Blimp," one observer noted sarcastically, "had sufficed to delight the 'diehard' antimilitarist."[63]

Two years after the trial, though, Tailhade and Gyp were again sparring. This time the cause of their jibes was Gyp's exceptionally bellicose manifesto in *Gil Blas* entitled "Pour la Guerre! ..." ("For War! ..."). In it Gyp blasted a pacifistic article by Séverine and declared herself, in the name of tradition, race, and nation, "in favor of war with all the force of my instinct."[64] Reflecting on the human costs incurred in war, Gyp concluded that certain lives were expendable: "I even admit ... that I would gladly see a stock of invalids—especially dying ones!—rise up to the sky in a holocaust, if that would make grow, on reconquered soil, a single little boy from Lorraine, quite lively and active."[65] Women might be enlisted for combat, Gyp argued, since the danger they would confront in battle would be no greater than the permanent one they faced in childbirth. War was a useful and grand necessity, then, while peace was "shameful and ridiculous."[66] Gyp urged against disarmament and maintained that a strong army was vital to France's defense.

Gyp's warlike diatribe infuriated the knee-jerk antimilitarist Tailhade, and he responded to her in an equally exalted letter in *L'Action*. Gyp was a hypocrite, Tailhade announced, whose "wanton graces"[67] and pretensions of piety masked her sadism. But her true nature was slowly being revealed, he continued, as her Kate Greenaway bonnet ceded to a winged helmet: "You are transforming yourself into a Walkyrie, into a Velleda, sucker of human blood."[68] Her cruelty, however, was not exceptional but rather typical of her class, which, as Tailhade observed, "for a thousand years has been composed of butchers, brigands, and kept men, which, in order to feed its luxury, its laziness, its vulgar and pompous customs, has had no other resource but armed robbery or else the wages of prostitution, which it has shared with the Church, the nobility, and the bourgeoisie. . . ."[69] Tailhade's vision of class struggle ended with a prophecy. Workers would rise up against these "natural" enemies such as Gyp, who in turn would receive their just punishment: "The hour cannot be far off when the place [reserved for] great military leaders will be in prison and that of 'patriots' in insane asylums."[70]

Two years after publishing this anarchist's call to arms, Tailhade once again did an intellectual about face. Writing in the ultra-*mondain* newspaper *Le Gaulois*, he blasted not the Church and Army but the *opponents* of these institutions as "sinister imbeciles."[71] Perhaps this was merely the latest of the attention-getting stunts of this "pseudorebel."[72] By 1905 Tailhade was indeed worn out from his year in prison and his drug addiction, and was disavowed by his companions. In 1914 he would again meet up with his friend and foe Gyp under the banner of the *union sacrée*.

"The Old Friend"

While Gyp remained a "personality" in the public realm of nationalist politics, she was no longer the brilliant *salonnière* of the 1880s and 1890s. The rifts created by the Dreyfus Affair and Gyp's increasing reclusiveness led to a shrinking of her social circle after 1900. The era of the great fin-de-siècle *salonnières* was also waning. Madame Aubernon died in 1899, Madame de Caillavet in 1910. The death of princesse Mathilde in 1904 particularly saddened the nostalgic imperialist Gyp, who wrote: "The thought that this beautiful woman with soft eyes and chiseled features was the very niece of the Emperor, of the legendary Napoleon, filled me with admiration and respect. . . . With [the death of] princesse Mathilde, it is yet another bit of great history that is disappearing!"[73]

Gyp still entertained from noon until midnight on Sundays, but not as flamboyantly as before Aymar's death in 1900. Guests were largely relatives and neighbors, including Judet, Genest, Barrès and his family. From 1906 or 1907 on, Thierry and his own family lived with Gyp in Neuilly—that is, after it was discovered he had a family. "Thierry has *surprised* us!"[74] Gyp announced to a relative. He had married in England nearly eight years earlier, and had a six-year-old son named Aymar. It is unclear why he kept the marriage a secret for so long; perhaps he feared his family's disapproval of the civil wedding ceremony. This lay service indeed displeased Gyp, but "after having seen the young woman and the little fellow, we decided to accept what had been done (at least, done *half-way*)."[75] Gyp's new daughter-in-law was Yvette Eugénie Saint-Martin, "a Breton woman from the Finistère, from a very honorable yet penniless family."[76] "She is not distinguished-looking," Gyp announced, "but fresh-looking, shapely, with warm blue eyes and a devil of a big mouth that is always laughing."[77] Gyp would grow fond of Yvette, another Breton woman boasting a pedigree but no cash and spunk instead of beauty. Yvette would often be present at her mother-in-law's salon on Sundays, as would Thierry if he could free himself from medical duties; "[He is] so busy at his hospital," Gyp complained, "that we don't see him anymore."[78]

Gyp's daughter, Nicole, was usually present as well, even though she and her mother continued to antagonize one another, as they had during Nicole's adolescence. The latest source of Gyp's dissatisfaction with her daughter was Nicole's indecision about her relationship with Pierre d'Hugues, an administrator in the Ministry of the Interior. "If we didn't know that she is walking around the Madeleine for an hour every day with Monsieur d'Hugues, we would think that she's changed her mind," Barrès learned. "We ended up not knowing whether it is *he* or *she* that doesn't want to? . . . It's a *complicated* generation. . . ."[79] Yet twenty-nine-year-old Nicole's marriage to Pierre d'Hugues in July 1906 was hardly a joyous event for Gyp, whose position as sole provider for the family also entitled her to pay for the wedding. Nicole's draining of her mother's funds resulted in "a terribly difficult end of the year"[80] for Gyp, leading her to turn, as always, to her usually reliable lenders at Calmann-Lévy.

Nicole was not the only woman causing problems for Gyp in the first decade of the century. Her mother, Marie de Mirabeau, who was seventy-three years old in 1900, continued to provoke her daughter's rage, as she had for half a century. Their literary and personal rivalry had not abated, for Marie's last published work, *Coeur d'Or* (*Heart of Gold*), had appeared in 1896. Marie, it seemed, could not forgive the daughter she had tried so hard to dominate for having surpassed her as a literary success. And Gyp took advantage of every opportunity to verbally flay the woman who had stripped her of her name when she was a girl.

It was a book that was at the center of the latest, very public argument between mother and daughter. Novels were, as ever, Gyp's most effective weapons in her prolonged revenge against Marie. The grotesque portrait Gyp had sketched of a former servant of her mother's in her 1908 *Cloclo* had led the man, presumably at Marie's urging, to seek fifty thousand francs in damages before a civil court in Paris. The servant in *Cloclo*, Anatole Malansson, is indeed another of Gyp's purely villainous characters. Breaking all codes of correct behavior for domestics, the physically hideous Malannson terrorizes other servants, smokes and drinks in his room, steals from his pathetic master, the comte d'Erdéval (from whom he tries to finagle an inheritance), and even sits down to eat with the dinner guests he is supposed to serve. Though good, in Gyp's novels, usually triumphs over evil, it is never without a price. The orphan Cloclo, who is the ward of the count and another of Gyp's pert, intelligent, and athletic doubles, reveals Malansson's machinations to local authorities, who arrest him. After this Manichaean struggle, however, Cloclo, physically debilitated and frightened after her confrontation with Anatole (as perhaps Gyp felt when challenging the mother who was once a constant menace to her), refuses a marriage proposal from a man she adores, vowing instead to enter a convent.

No fear is apparent, however, in a remarkably insulting, arrogant, and menacing letter Gyp sent to her mother in 1908. In this poison-pen letter, which was admitted as evidence at the trial and reproduced in the *Grande Revue*, Gyp declared herself unconcerned by her mother's tactics:

> That you spread gossip about me behind my back, I don't care; you've succeeded in getting sold more copies of *Cloclo* than have been sold in the past year. I can only benefit from it. I wrote a novel in which you are, you, treated respectfully, much too much so, given the truth. You want to get angry, go ahead, and to write one against me, about which I don't give a damn in a big way.[81]

Yet Gyp warned her mother not to counterattack with her own novel, in which Marie might choose to sully Gyp's idol, Gonneville. In admonishing her mother, Gyp played not only on Marie's fear of reprisals from her famous daughter but also on her undiminished vanity. Marie was a second-rate writer, her daughter reminded her, and would only compromise her shaky reputation by indulging in slander:

> But listen carefully to what I'm telling you. If in this novel you make the dreadful mistake of having grandfather play any kind of role . . . you'll have to deal with me in such a way that you'll be cooked, I promise you. I wouldn't want to say unpleasant things to you about your talent, but given our respective positions in the press, and the friends that each of us has, I really believe that you won't stand much of a chance against me.[82]

Marie lost her case, leaving Gyp to gloat. But she immediately rebounded by appealing the verdict. Suddenly Gyp was again on the defensive, snared by her mother in this elaborate and relentless cat-and-mouse game that would continue until Marie's death. Tripped up by an unexpected bill from the appeals lawyer for an advance of twenty-five hundred francs, Gyp requested and received the sum from Calmann-Lévy, thus resorting to a pattern of dependence she strove all her life to break.[83]

As usual, Gyp found respite from the vindictiveness she associated with women in the company of men. Her exchanges of gossip and compliments with her new neighbor Robert de Montesquiou was the perfect antidote to her hysterical interactions with her mother. Montesquiou had moved to Neuilly with his secretary and companion, Gabriel de Yturri, in the last years of the century, although Gyp had known him at least since the early 1890s. The Paris suburb was no longer the rural and slightly sinister place Gyp had settled in twenty years earlier but a rapidly changing and increasingly chic magnet for the elite of the faubourg Saint-Germain. Avenues were replacing alleys, elegant new pavilions abounded, and land was being cleared for the newly popular sports of tennis, cycling, and polo.

Neuilly was thus a fitting habitat for Montesquiou, an almost mythical belle époque figure. "Gentilhomme de lettres" (as he identified himself), "king of the witty,"[84] (as others did), aesthete and dandy *extraordinaire*, Montesquiou, a descendant of d'Artagnan, lived as did his literary likenesses des Esseintes and baron Charlus, to uphold Beauty against all forms of mediocrity. Worshiper of France's aristocratic past, Montesquiou was at the same time an influential champion of the new who exalted Japonism, Wagnerism, Whistler, art nouveau, and the Ballets Russes. His weekly fêtes at his Pavillon des Muses in Neuilly were legendary. On these occasions, rabbits, weighed down by collars encrusted with turquoise, slumbered outside the door of the mansion, which was filled with blue hortensias, Montesquiou's favorite flower. At the top of a grand staircase stood the host, perhaps dressed in his signature pearl gray frockcoat (if not in his almond-green suit with a white velvet waistcoat), reciting in his shrill voice a monologue prepared in advance and occasionally stifling one of his laughing fits in his hands in order to hide his bad teeth.[85]

Gyp's relations with Montesquiou, eight years her junior, revolved around their shared and overlapping worlds of literature, art, and society. Gyp viewed the pair's rapport rather cynically, claiming to have seen Montesquiou only sporadically: "[S]ometimes we went six months or even a year without seeing him. Then he would come five or six times in a row, would write every day, usually when he had some sort of trouble."[86] While Montesquiou invited his neighbor to all his "morning parties (really successful)"[87] or for a tête-à-tête with himself and Yturri, the sometimes less than tactful Gyp was never included in his more intimate "little tea parties with the five or six people with whom he was trying to become friends at the moment."[88] One exception to this policy was Montesquiou's luncheon for the Barrès family, the poetess Anna de Noailles (whom he had known since childhood), and the duc and duchesse de Clermont-Tonnerre, whose friendship Montesquiou was trying to cultivate. By inviting Gyp he hoped to rely on his neighbor's flair for detecting hypocrisy, for he wished to discover (according to Gyp's recreation of the conversation), "whether these new friends like me, or whether they are coming over, like the others, to mock me."[89] On other occasions Gyp felt she was "uninteresting"[90] in the world of her fantastic neighbor, presumably because of her infrequent appearances in the inner sanctums of *le monde*. "From a worldly point of view, I didn't exist,"[91] Gyp would write. "I lived like a bear, outside of everything. I was nothing more than the old friend to whom one comes to relate one's little secrets."[92]

Despite Gyp's characteristically understated view of her own importance, Michel Missoffe has asserted that Montesquiou treated her with "admiration and deference,"[93] an attitude born out in correspondence between this descendant of Merovingians and this last of the Mirabeaus, although Montesquiou's exaggerated politeness may well have been a pose. His chaste flirtation with his confidante, who was still delighted by the flattery of younger men, took the form of both gifts (such as a drypoint by the popular belle époque portraitist Paul Helleu, a favorite of Montesquiou's)[94] and tickets to the count's theatrical "lectures" (on Versailles at the Théâtre Fémina in 1907, for example).[95] Montesquiou's homage also included elaborately bound copies of his prose and poetry. Gyp praised *Les Altesses sérénissimes* (*The Most Serene Highnesses*), which was dedicated to Barrès ("with what skill you know how to be terrible and entertaining"),[96] laughed at *Brelan des dames* ("What fun I had! And that's an understatement!"),[97] and found an article on art nouveau glass by Emile Gallé "very beautiful."[98]

Her favorite work, though, was *L'Assemblée des notables*,[99] one of whose chapters, "Monsieur Monde et Madame Mondanité," was dedicated to "la comtesse de Martel." The allegorical figures in this piece, reminiscent of some of Gyp's earlier characters, scorn the arrival of petrol-spouting automobiles on the Champs-Elysées and evoke a more "civilized" age, a time of "discreet intimacy, brilliant conversation, noble assemblies where the sumptuous decor accompanied the artistic spectacle, the feast for the eyes accompanied the one for the mind. All that [is] replaced by Cakewalk and Bridge!"[100] And Gyp agreed wholeheartedly with Montesquiou's aphoristic observation, one of many contained in his letters to her: "To not *discriminate* is the characteristic of our times."[101]

Gyp reciprocated Montesquiou's gifts and invitations with some of her own. The denizen of Le Pavillon des Muses was summoned to eat chocolate cake and inspect Gyp's blue hortensias ("the only pretty thing in my frightful little house")[102] in the company of Anna de Noailles and the Barrès family. Barrès was a mutual friend and neighbor of Montesquiou's, whom he also knew from symbolist circles. He had seconded the count in his well-publicized duel with Henri de Régnier in 1897 (precipitated by Régnier's remark that a muff might be a more appropriate accessory for the count than one of his many canes). In 1911 Barrès dedicated his *Greco* to him. The presence of Barrès or of Dr. Pozzi often convinced Montesquiou to prolong his stay at Gyp's on Sundays, but he would flee at the sight of rival dandy and extravagant party-giver Boni de Castellane holding court in Talleyrand's easy chair, still the seat of choice in Gyp's salon.[103] Social invitations were sometimes accompanied by copies of Gyp's novels, for which he thanked his "dear countess and friend" in flowery notes penned in his stylized art nouveau handwriting. One of these ended with the following accolade, which somehow seems inappropriate for the former Fury of the Dreyfus Affair: "You are like a peacock," Montesquiou exclaimed, "who would strut with its rectangular eyes, always more numerous, which are your scintillating books. . . ."[104]

Moving easily among lyrical, snobby, and businesslike conversations, Gyp and Montesquiou found in each other's company an opportunity to give free reign to their different personae. More important, perhaps, they also shared a certain marginality in relation to their aristocratic milieu: Montesquiou because of his homosexuality and association with avant-garde movements; Gyp due to her status as a woman writer and political militant, and as a notorious public figure. They could thus find silent comfort with one another as well.

"Springtime in Mirabeau"

Gyp's closest friend was still Barrès. The "prince of youth" was now a king whose fame as a novelist, politician, and self-appointed reviver of French energies had earned him election to the Académie française. Hawkers sold seats to his induction ceremony in 1906, which was, according to Jacques-Emile Blanche, "the most sought after in the memory of members of the Academy."[105] Afterward a procession of carriages followed Barrès to Neuilly, where Gyp presided over a lunch she had ordered from the noted Parisian caterers Potel et Chabot, whose most daring culinary feat had been a banquet held in 1900 in the Tuileries for over twenty-two thousand municipal notables.

Gyp was a trusted participant not only in the pomp of Barrès' public life but also in the rituals of his private life. In 1904 she shared responsibility with him for arranging the funeral of his secretary, Calté. Gyp had recommended Calté to Barrès in 1899 as "rather well read (admitted, I believe, to the Ecole Normale), active, hard-working, intelligent (very). . . ."[106] Despite Barrès' dissatisfaction with Calté, a reclusive lawyer who had spent several years in the Foreign Legion due to difficult personal circumstances, he kept him on out of pity and later out of devotion, occasionally lending him to members of Action française or to editors at Fontemoing, the publisher of several of Barrès' works. It was Gyp's servant Jules, bringing the ailing Calté a quiche lorraine, who found him dead. Two hundred francs, supplied by Gyp and Barrès, provided funeral services attended by several mourners at a church in the working-class suburb of Bagneux.[107] Gyp commented on the irony of a public ceremony for the solitary Calté: "It's funny, everyone salutes him when he's dead, no one greeted him when he was living."[108] Walking toward the cemetary on a chilly February afternoon, Barrès, while crossing himself, spied a menacing reminder of earlier days, "a Dreyfusard who was walking on the side and who was shooting dirty looks at us."[109]

In 1907 Gyp simultaneously strengthened her ties to Barrès and detached herself from an important symbol of her ancestral past by selling Barrès the château of Mirabeau. With the death of Aymar, upon whom Gyp had planned to bestow the château and the title of marquis de Mirabeau that accompanied it, the once mighty castle, and the mystique it incarnated, no longer interested its owner. She now wished her body buried in Neuilly, beside Aymar. Her heart, she informed her family, should be removed and placed in an iron coffer in the chapel of Coëtsal, close to the grave of Mirabeau-Tonneau and her Breton roots, which she had always felt were much more firmly embedded in her than those of Provence. The Dreyfus Affair had further strained her always precarious finances, making it nearly impossible to maintain the massive stone building, especially with Gyp in Paris. Thierry could not conceive of leaving his surgical practice in Paris for the near-feudal atmosphere of Mirabeau. And real estate agents had been prowling around the property, eyeing its valuable pine trees. Reluctantly, and violating Lucas de Montigny's vow never to let Mirabeau leave the family, Gyp began to look for a buyer.

Perhaps with ulterior motives, perhaps merely out of sincere friendship, in February 1902 Gyp proposed a stay in Mirabeau to Barrès' wife, Paule:

> It is this month that's the most "thankless" in the French Midi. But it's already pretty. In Mirabeau it is at the end of March that there are lilacs and lilies. No need to tell you, is there, that Mirabeau is always at your disposal, in the event you would like to spend some time there. It's savage—but very healthful. . . . You will notify just a few days in advance Monsieur Arland, blacksmith in *Mirabeau, Vaucluse*, so that he will have the house cleaned.[110]

Two years later Philippe Barrès' sickliness necessitated a stay in the Midi, thus providing an occasion for Barrès and his family to spend a month in Mirabeau. The worshiper of "la terre et les morts" ("the earth and the dead") was also eager to absorb again the "soul" of Provence, which he had visited in 1895 and 1898, and to measure its difference from that of his native Lorraine.[111] Lacking a companion to help him explore his presumed convergence of geography, "race," and morality, he informed Maurras, a Martigues native, of his upcoming stay:

> I am probably going to spend some time, with my wife and without Gyp, at Gyp's in the château of Mirabeau, in the heart of your region, and with automobile. So that if you come there, we shall visit in the most minute detail . . . all these famous towns, villages, and sights. Won't you be able to come? Understand that the château is at my disposal, with freedom to make use of it, and that it is I who invite you. Let me add that Gyp will regret only not to be the complete hostess. That would be admirable. . . .[112]

Upon his arrival in the hamlet in the autumn of 1904, a peasant woman offered Philippe Barrès as a good luck charm a cord that had recently encircled the neck of a man who had hanged himself, thus sending the woman and frightened children screaming through the narrow streets: "It's the hangman's rope! It's the hangman's rope!"[113] Superstitious peasants did not concern Barrès, who preferred carefully mapped out tours of sites with historical or aesthetic interest, some of them recommended by Gyp. "Don't leave without visiting Manosque, Beaumont, and Orgon," she advised her guest. "Orgon is a bit farther, but it's very interesting both because of the passage of the Emperor and because the countryside is wild and rugged."[114] Barrès combined a visit to the museum of Provençal culture in Arles with a call on the Occitan poet (and, in 1904, Nobel Prize winner) Frédéric Mistral, whom both he and Maurras viewed as an eloquent statesman for regionalism and decentralization. Throughout the month, Barrès, in sensual descriptions, noted his impressions of the "wild yet gay solitude"[115] of Provence, with its infertile *garrigue*, or scrubland, covered with olive, cypress, and almond trees, its warm odor of pine and fresh scent of lilac. "Mme de Martel is really a she-goat from this region,"[116] Barrès mused after surveying the severe, majestic countryside, an estimation with which the "Breton" Gyp probably would have disagreed.

The Tharaud brothers insisted that Barrès bought Mirabeau from Gyp in 1907 out of affection and even pity. What other reason, they asked, could compel such a devoted Lorrainer and as modest a man as Barrès to purchase a medieval castle in Provence?[117] Perhaps, as Barrès' portraitist Jacques-Emile Blanche suggested, it was only the existence of an imaginary Mirabeau with which Barrès had become enthralled after his 1904 visit, and which would fade quickly: "[T]he Mirabeau name was transforming a half-ruin into an inanimate castle that he was awakening. The inert countryside, the most untamed, the most austere of our alpine Provence, would be his Campagna Romana."[118] Aside from appreciating the suggestive powers of the property, the deputy and recently elected member of the Académie française perhaps felt that homes in Neuilly, Charmes, and now Mirabeau, with all its aristocratic cachet, befitted his new status. He set out to do with ease what Gyp had accomplished only with enormous difficulty: to become a *grand seigneur* in literature, politics, and society.

The sale of Mirabeau slightly and temporarily strained Gyp's relationship with Barrès. Gyp apprised Montesquiou of the transaction, confessing: "I'm happy that it's to them rather than to others, but I regret Mirabeau."[119] And Barrès revealed his own embarrassment to "Madame and friend" shortly after returning to Mirabeau as its owner: "We have just arrived by automobile in this pleasant [hamlet of] Mirabeau where everything would be perfect if I did not have the feeling that I have deprived you of something pleasurable. But it is true that you take only imaginary pleasure from it, and since you are leaving it as is, it is not a painful thought for you."[120] As Jacques-Emile Blanche noted perceptively, though, it was Barrès, not Gyp, who took only imaginary pleasure from Mirabeau. Barrès' paean to "the divine grace of Provence,"[121] "this setting of eternity,"[122] is contained in his lengthy "Lettre à Gyp sur le printemps à Mirabeau" ("Letter to Gyp about Springtime in Mirabeau"), which was probably written around 1914 and published in 1921 in the *Revue hebdomadaire*. "[I]ntoxicated with sunshine,"[123] Barrès spent his days during yearly trips to Mirabeau marveling at the countryside and almost regretting his northern roots. "Poor man of the north, let us revel in the hour that enchants us,"[124] he advised himself. Throughout his stay Barrès felt himself overwhelmed by the familial mystique pervading the former domain of Gyp's ancestors Cou d'Argent, l'Ami des Hommes, and his brother le Bailli.[125] Barrès even replaced on a pedestal outside the château the bust of the Orator—"the grand Mirabeau, this brigand Mirabeau"[126]—not, he insisted, as the result of a change in his political convictions but rather "in the name of poetry": "[L]et him remain there, like the spirit of the place, with his vices mixed with a type of virtue, amid the ruins that he caused, this powerful spirit. . . ."[127]

Yet even the omnipresence of Mirabeau's tutelary divinities could not shield Barrès from the grim physical realities of life there. Temperatures in the dry and dusty château fluctuated between extreme heat and cold, and gusts of the mistral often blew through the cracks, eventually ruining several rooms.[128] Although he made an obligatory appearance at Mirabeau every year until his death in 1922, entertaining Paul Bourget and others, he soon lost enthusiasm for playing at lord of the manor. The Tharaud brothers easily saw through Barrès' exalted act, noting that "he abhorred the southern life, the cafés, the endless conversations, the sun, the flies, the dust, this soul without shade, and above all he was feeling the discomfort of not being in his place here."[129] Each year, the Tharauds observed, "Barrès used to leave [Mirabeau] without regret."[130]

XII

"The Pig of a Pessimist"
1914–1918

"Gyp wages war."

Abel Hermant, "L'Ennemie du ridicule: Défense
de la langue française," *Le Temps,* 24 Sept. 1918

The Rear

When French troops began mobilizing on 1 August 1914 in response to Germany's entry into the war, Gyp was not stupefied, as she had been in similar circumstances nearly a half-century earlier, but resolved and defiant. The "painful memory"[1] of Prussian soldiers occupying Nancy in 1870 and the ensuing prospect of another war had, in her view, "poisoned" her generation.[2] She now felt prepared for war but regretted not being able to participate in it. "Why can't I fight it, this war, whose threat has weighed on my life . . . ?"[3] This lament by another of her fictional doubles, the "cochon de pessimiste" ("pig of a pessimist") echoes those of her girl–soldier heroines Cricri and Napoléonette. "I'd march with so much joy! How I love destruction, tumult, blows. What a splendid occasion! . . ."[4] The male-centered identification of Gonneville's granddaughter continued to be matched by her idealization of war. For Gyp violence was uplifting, purifying, and essential to her sense of identity.

Unable to do battle, Gyp became, at age sixty-four, an exalted though somewhat pessimistic civilian herald of *la Revanche.* In this she joined others of her generation, like Juliette Adam. "Let me see the so passionately longed for Revenge," the lifelong apostle of a Radical Republican version of *revanchisme* proclaimed to Gyp, "and I shall depart, resurrected in death."[5] Such mystical nuances clashed with Gyp's blunt bellicosity: "I am in favor of war with all the force of my instinct."[6] Her chauvinism fed on her rabid Germanophobia, itself nourished by the racist tirades of the press. After reading an account in *Les Débats* of the German general Stenger's order to his troops to "leave no living Frenchman behind," she characteristically retorted: "[A] magnificent reward should be promised to the one who . . . would capture General Stenger, then wound him, then finish him off later, while taking his time." [7]

A chauvinistic patriot set on revenge, Gyp was also, as ever, a nationalist for whom the internal enemy was as barbaric, and as dangerous, as the one across the Rhine. In 1870 her scapegoat had been Thiers and his Republican government; during the Dreyfus Affair it had been the Jews. In 1914 her new demon was the socialist and syndicalist Left, and then, after the Left's rally to the *union sacrée*, "defeatists" and *embusqués* ("slackers"), men who had managed to avoid front-line combat. She reacted with elation to the assassination on 31 July 1914 of Jean Jaurès, having blamed the pacifism espoused by the socialist leader for France's lack of military preparedness. By the end of the war she could boast to her publisher of having "liquidated the few 'Caillautard' or defeatist relations that I may have had,"[8] just as she had purged her salon, two decades earlier, of Dreyfusards. She viewed the war, like the Affair, as a chance to dispose of any remnants of "anti-France." Even Barrès knelt before Jaurès' tomb at his funeral on 4 August. Yet Gyp had her pessimist sputter: "We're rid of this burdensome windbag for good. . . ."[9]

In 1914, as in 1870, war for Gyp and most other civilians meant material hardship and dislocation. Necessities—heat, shelter, and food—became her luxuries. Such were the vicissitudes of France's wartime economy, shaped by severe inflation, the draining of resources from the rear to the front, and the German seizure of much French heavy industry. Indeed, for the generally prosperous socioprofessional groups Gyp and her family represented, the war was often a disaster. Rarely called back from the front (unlike many industrial workers), and strained by inflated food prices (unlike some peasants, who benefited from them), *rentiers*, members of liberal professions, and others often experienced a descent from comfort into misery.[10] And as her household's female breadwinner, Gyp was ineligible for government benefits for families whose primary income earner was enlisted.

During the winter of 1916, Gyp could afford to heat only her kitchen, and for a mere half hour daily. With virtually all French troops rotating through the killing fields at Verdun, and with French industry focused on equipping a major Franco-British offensive on the Somme, the price of coal was exorbitant for civilians. Yet Gyp refused her mother's offer of a *salamandre*, a slow-combustion heater whose fumes and intense heat she claimed would make her sick.[11] She was scarcely more comfortable the following winter, which was marked by a series of demoralizing Allied defeats. She owed her lingering bronchitis, her publisher learned, to "this horrible cold—without the possibility of heating. . . ."[12] The frigid weather mangled her hands and distorted her handwriting; "I've got the hands of a schoolboy . . . . or a cook . . . . ,"[13] she complained. The war literally threatened to remove the roof over her head when sheets of zinc fell from it during a storm. She bemoaned the absence of "*able-bodied* workers who can climb up on the roofs,"[14] which, along with the quintupling of zinc prices due to the war effort, forced her to make do with a tarpaulin while awaiting a return to prewar costs.

Gyp's chill, leaky home was part of a transformed Neuilly landscape. Her neighbor Robert de Montesquiou, like many wealthy residents of Parisian *beaux quartiers*, had fled, fearing a German siege of the capital, an influx of refugees or, worse perhaps, another Commune. Neuilly was a gloomy place. Zeppelins hovering over Paris made nightly blackouts essential. "There's not *a trace of light at night in Paris, anywhere after 8* P.M.," Gyp informed her mother, who was living in Normandy.[15] "*[I]t's complete, profound darkness* on moonless nights."[16]

The privations and stress of the war affected Gyp physically. Her litany of illnesses continued: bronchitis, cystitis, fever, "excessive weakness," treated with "massive doses . . . of strychnine and other horrors."[17] The "old fossil"[18] was now, in her own words, "the total fossil."[19] The "old bear of boulevard Bineau," she told Montesquiou, had become "a completely white bear."[20] Dressed oddly, as usual, in flowing robes and floppy lace and tulle bonnets, she looked like a nursery-rhyme grandmother, or like the eccentric dowagers she remembered from her childhood in Nancy.

Gyp's illnesses in turn slowed her writing, preventing her from dashing off "the little things—unsigned—that I do here and there to make ends meet."[21] Yet despite her age and self-deprecating image of her infirmity, she produced eight novels during the war, plus weekly dialogues in *L'Excelsior* and pieces for *Le Figaro, Les Lectures,* and *Le Gaulois.* "All that requires a constant exchange of proofs, and errands, and work," she let her mother know, "which is a headache."[22] As always, the normally frenetic pace of her writing was partly a survival strategy. She was supporting a household of eight: the perpetually idle Roger; Thierry's wife, Yvette; possibly Genest; and several servants. Before the war writing had bought Gyp tangible signs of her social status—sumptuous luncheons, a Normandy beach house, elegant clothing—which in turn enhanced her market value as a writer. But the war disrupted the circuit that converted her financial capital into social and literary capital. Now she was writing for her life.

When Gyp's situation became particularly urgent, finding herself "without *anything* in the house" and not knowing "how I shall spend Sunday and Monday morning,"[23] she turned to the men who had been her creditors for thirty years. Her letters to Gaston and Michel Calmann-Lévy were no longer coy or peremptory, no longer accompanied by reminders of her worth. Her requests were uniformly desperate. August 1914: "I don't have a sou left."[24] May 1915: "I am in an infinitely painful situation."[25] December 1917: "I find myself with *nothing* to finish out the year."[26] August 1918: "The rise in the cost of living is such that I am completely overwhelmed. . . . I don't know what shall become of me, myself and those who depend on me."[27] She needed cash fast to pay heat and water bills, but also, noblesse oblige, to purchase New Year's presents and entertain guests from two to seven on Sundays.[28] Whether out of pity, friendship, or self-interest, her publisher agreed to prop Gyp up with regular advances of from one to two thousand francs, which were soon spent. Sixty-eight years old, Gyp mused in an October 1917 letter to her publisher: "There are days when I am really discouraged to have worked so hard, and to think that I shall never, ever rest. . . ."[29]

Gyp's finances were further strained by the sudden death of her mother on 8 March 1916 at the age of eighty-eight. Gyp's raging bitterness toward Marie, as revealed in her rambling letters to her mother in the two years before her death, had not been softened by time, old age, or the trauma of two wars. Framed by a politely affectionate greeting—"dear little Mommy"—and salutation—"I send you a thousand kisses with all my heart. Yours, Gaby"[30]—Gyp's letters represent a final settling of accounts with the woman who always let her daughter know that her existence was simply unfortunate. For Gyp Marie was still, as she herself had admitted to the publisher Hetzel years earlier, a "*very vain* person"[31] who neither understood nor sympathized with her daughter's financial plight. Her suggestion that Gyp leave Neuilly for Normandy outraged her daughter. Gyp rebuked her mother for this three months before Marie's death: "You have *never understood*—having lived with grandfather and grandmother since you had me—and *alone* since then, what it means *to be responsible for* 3 children and a husband. You've only had to look after yourself. . . . You never consider anything except *from your own point of view.*"[32] For Gyp, jeopardizing her livelihood and obliging Marie by trekking to Cossesseville (which Gyp "detested")[33] were unacceptable concessions, the ultimate acknowledgment of her mother's control over her. This was the woman who had alternately foiled and abandoned her, who had perverted her identity by changing her name. Gyp could not forgive her mother even at her death.

Yet the unrelentingly antagonistic relationship between Gyp and Marie owed as much to the similarities between the women as to their differences. Their correspondence betrays their identification with one another. Once again, and for the last time, their struggle concerned names. Two months before her death, Marie signed a letter to the poet Lucie Delarue-Mardrus with her daughter's last name, Mirabeau-Martel. Gyp was astonished: "Are you distracted? . . . I don't understand anything about this business. . . ."[34] But she, in turn, admitted that when addressing envelopes to her mother, she often wrote her own name, comtesse de Martel.[35] By appropriating her daughter's name, Marie perhaps wished to mask herself with the name of the writer whose success clearly outstripped her own— or perhaps again to subdue her perpetually rebellious daughter. Did jealousy, or fear, motivate Marie? And by addressing her mother as herself (hadn't both women attributed the authorship of their early *Vie Parisienne* pieces to the same mythical "officer"?), Gyp unconsciously sealed her bond with another *garçon manqué* turned literary and political reactionary, whose own failed marriage and penchant for scandal foretold those of her daughter. To the end Marie remained Gyp's rival—and her double.

By the very act of dying, Marie outdid her daughter, as Gyp sarcastically acknowledged in a letter to her publisher: "My mother's inheritance—inheritance doesn't always mean money!—is causing me all the worries in the world. She's left nothing but lawsuits, and I inherit nothing but pensions to pay."[36] With profits from the sale of half her mother's furniture, Gyp had a room built in Neuilly to house the other half, items "amid which I was brought up."[37] She sold Cosses-seville in March 1919, but the sale did not cover Marie's debts and other expenses. The complication made Gyp's situation intolerable. As usual, the first to know was her publisher. "This bewildering daily expense terrifies me, and yet we're depriving ourselves of everything," Gyp wrote, thus prefacing a request for funds. "I don't know what I shall become if this continues. . . . I am without money, without fuel, confronted with appalling difficulties."[38]

The Front

Gyp's anxiety during the war arose not only from the discomfort and uncertainties of her daily life but also from concern for two combatants, her son and grandson. Thierry de Martel left for the front in early August 1914. At thirty-eight, he belonged to the eldest third of men mobilized. His own son, Aymar, who had enlisted in 1915, was among the youngest.[39] Tall, gaunt, and impeccably groomed, Thierry slept little and sustained himself on black coffee. In his detached expression those close to him often detected disdain. He inherited his mother's passion for vigorous sports (notably boxing) and right-wing politics. Like his fictional counterpart Ferri in *Le Journal d'un cochon de pessimiste*, Thierry "runs instinctively toward danger. . . ."[40] He was becoming something of a male Gyp, the object of his mother's admiration, but of her jealousy and anger too.

When Thierry left for the front, the so-called 'd'Artagnan of surgery' was already famous. Between the end of his medical studies in 1907 and the outbreak of war, he had laid the foundations for a later, remarkable career in general surgery and especially in neurosurgery. He shunned a series of competitive examinations that would have led to a prestigious and lucrative position as either a surgeon in a Paris hospital or as a professor of medecine, consecrating his status as a medical mandarin. Instead he chose the greater independence of private clinics and established himself as a maverick. In two of his own clinics, as well as in several others around Paris, he performed hysterectomies and abdominal surgery and perfected new techniques for removing brain and bone tumors. He also invented surgical instruments, such as a small power saw for cutting open the skull without damaging the outer layers of the brain. He flew weekly to London, in the early days of airplane travel, to attend operations by Victor Horsely, a pioneering British colleague, and to sharpen his own surgical prowess.

Raised by his mother in the cult of *la Revanche*, and entering combat when troop and civilian morale were relatively high, Thierry was impelled by patriotism. Writing from Alsace after the French recapture of Mulhouse in early August 1914, he assured his mother that "Alsace is well worth the effort we are making for her."[41] The legacy of Cou d'Argent, Tonneau, Gonneville, Arundel, and his brother Aymar—soldiers all—motivated him too. He saw the war as an adventure, both military and surgical. The shrapnel-ridden skulls and damaged brains of war casualties allowed him to practice, in the turmoil of combat, the innovative techniques developed in the quiet of his clinic.

Sent to Clermont-Ferrand as an auxiliary doctor, Thierry immediately asked to be transferred to an active unit at the front. He reached Belgium in late August 1914, just after the French defeat at Charleroi. Calmly operating in a hospital on the front lines, he dazzled a badly injured twenty-one-year-old soldier named Pierre Drieu la Rochelle. Thierry would always remain for Drieu one of his "mythic superegos,"[42] his symbol of the unity of life and death, of heroism and tragedy. From Charleroi Thierry's regiment retreated to the Marne via the Oise, where it began fighting, as Gyp reported to Barrès, "as soon as it got off the train."[43] During the days of combat in early September that ultimately repelled the first German offensive, his regiment was decimated. Piecing together information from postcards that often took weeks to arrive from the front near Paris, Gyp gave Barrès this account: "We know that the 292nd [regiment] was wiped out on September 8th and 9th . . . north of Meaux. On the 8th . . . the colonel fell, twice wounded, and someone saw Thierry pick him up. . . . [S]everal officers shot, 18 wounded, the men in in the same proportion, a skeleton of a regiment!"[44] Her son's reports of mounting casualties, which eluded the military censors' attempts to block such information, made Gyp question her expectation, shared by most French citizens, that the war's end was imminent. "How long it is! My God! This battle!"[45] she exclaimed to Barrès, criticizing the government for not getting it over with more quickly.

Cryptic postcards—one remarked only "It sure is hot, in more ways than one!"[46]—informed Gyp that from the Marne what was left of her son's regiment followed the German retreat north to a village near Soissons on the Aisne. Soldiers and officers camped in the kitchen of a local château whose owners and their servants, though "broken, devastated, having lost this year everything they own," fed and hosted their guests admirably.[47] German troops soon attacked the village. When an ambulance attached to his unit exploded under enemy fire, Thierry seized a gun (disobeying orders which forbade him, as a doctor, from entering combat) and led a charge against advancing troops, at the same time snatching wounded from a burning farmhouse.[48] Hurt himself while working at a first-aid station, he was not arrested for misconduct but decorated by général Nivelle with the Croix de guerre and the Légion d'honneur.[49]

Soon mobilized again, Thierry left for the Dardanelles in September 1915[50] as part of a medical team staffing a hospital-ship. The same year his son, Aymar, enlisted in the spahis and, like his uncle and namesake, left for Algeria.[51] The Allied rationale for creating a second theater of operations in the Balkans was both strategic (to open a supply route to Russia by securing control of the straits) and diplomatic (to gain the support of nonaligned countries such as Italy, Greece, and Roumania by displaying Allied military might in the Balkans). But the campaign was ill-conceived, useless to some, and in the end catastrophic. By the time Thierry arrived, a third of the Franco-British fleet had been liquidated, as would be thousands of Allied troops during the carnage at Gallipoli. The corps Thierry joined in Salonica, Gyp relayed to Barrès, was mired in "distressing conditions, with fresh air . . . and light lacking.''[52] As troops of the Central Powers crushed those of Serbia, Thierry's malaria-ravaged corps looked on helplessly, prompting Clemenceau, who opposed diverting men and materials from the western front, to rail against the "slackers of Salonica."

Publicly—in the press, her novels, and her salon—Gyp too damned as unpatriotic those soldiers who managed to avoid combat. Yet her virulent anti-*embusqué* tone was perhaps the barometer of her embarrassment. For beginning in late 1915, she was utilizing her connections in the War Ministry to expedite Thierry's evacuation from Salonica, ostensibly necessitated by a festering abscess on her son's leg that required surgery. Throughout these negotiations, she insisted on her role as an intermediary who was ceding to pressure from her mother and from her daughter-in-law. She began with War Minister Alexandre Millerand and his wife, whom she knew personally. As she told Barrès in October 1914, she was particularly fond of Jeanne Millerand "because she is very intelligent and not at all feminine.''[53] In January 1916 she apprised Marie that "for the past 8 days since Yvette officially asked me, I've been approaching officials right and left.''[54] Only Thierry, she had learned, could initiate plans for repatriation by requesting a medical leave; once in France, though, *"he will be made to stay."*[55] Yet four days later she dutifully reported to her mother that she had succeeded in procuring "what you wanted, and Yvette too. . . ." She had obtained a War Ministry order for Thierry's return.[56]

Gyp anticipated her son's homecoming with fear and anger. Apprehensive about his possible discovery that she arranged his repatriation, she warned her mother: *"You* will tell Thierry . . . *you* and *Yvette*, that it was *you* who forced me to make him come home . . . *if he finds out and scolds me*. If, by chance, he doesn't find out, I'll be damn lucky.''[57] Yet she was also furious at her son for confusing the family about his plans for returning,[58] and then for insisting he was staying in the Balkans, despite his own secret arrangements for evacuation. "People who lie make me think of Thierry,''[59] Gyp concluded, pronouncing her verdict on her son's character and clearly not recognizing the cycle of filial defiance that her unwanted intervention had set in motion. She fretted as well, although cynically, about the effect on Yvette of her son's renewed dalliances with certain female *collaboratrices*. "On that matter, Yvette hinders him much more than I do," Gyp commented to Marie, "who know—and have known—none of his whores except the Lasseurs.''[60]

Significantly, it was Marie, Gyp's model of abusive parental behavior, who became the privileged interlocutor for Gyp's verbal swipes at her own son. The dutiful daughter, Gyp may have wished to show Marie that she had learned her lesson of cruelty well. The rebellious daughter, Gyp perhaps wanted to retaliate against her mother by acting harshly toward Marie's grandson. Indeed, Gyp's success in making her son an *embusqué* was a highly ambiguous enterprise for her in other ways, too. Her concern for "the poor boy"[61] was mixed with disdain for the liar. She desired Thierry's safety but also his emasculation. Her machinations exposed her unabated need to dominate and manipulate, to prove her power despite her son's attempts to thwart her. "Once again *I look* as if I've been duped,'' Gyp confided to her mother, hinting at her fear of publicly exposing her vulnerability. ''But in the end,'' she added, intent on having the last word, ''I haven't been. . . .''[62]

As grim as Thierry's war experience may have been, he had still known only the ''heroic'' initial phase of the war. He participated in the first ''miracle of the Marne.'' He arrived in the Dardanelles too late to witness the sinking of a third of the Allied fleet and was spared the hell of Verdun. Still, in late February 1916 Gyp found her son, as she described him to Barrès—whose own son, Philippe, was fighting in snow-covered Champagne—thin, nervous, and weakened by ''an abominable attack of malaria, vomiting, chattering teeth.''[63] His return trip to France had been drawn out over a month because a cholera epidemic on board forced the ship to dock three times.[64] Recovered from a leg operation, he was named chief surgeon at the American Hospital and the next year at the Astoria, one of several Paris hotels converted into hospitals to accommodate burgeoning numbers of war casualties.

Gyp's grandson, Aymar de Martel, knew a very different war from that of his father, although the written record of it is sketchy and perhaps intentionally fragmentary. While Thierry lay in a malaria-ridden ship in Salonica in late 1915, Aymar, now a brigadier, returned from Algeria to France. ''You can't understand how amusing it is, you, grandmother, because you haven't done it yet (!). . . . ,''[65] Aymar wrote from the Oise valley, clearly undaunted by laying barbed wire sixty meters from the front lines. As Gyp informed Barrès, Gonneville's reckless namesake wanted to test himself further: ''Unfortunately, this ideal pastime is no longer enough for Aymar, who is taking steps to be transferred—as a sergeant—into the infantry. It's purely idiotic!''[66] This ''infantry fantasy,''[67] Gyp mused, would clearly vex Thierry. Thierry had tried to protect his son—in essence to make him an *embusqué*—by directing him to the cavalry, an elite unit unlikely to see frontline combat (but one in which rapid advance was possible), and also by whisking him to Algeria. In Thierry's absence, Gyp declared her intention to oppose Aymar's plan.[68]

Whether his father and grandmother intervened is unclear, but in February 1916 Aymar was in Morocco and his father was back in France. Thierry's concern for his son's safety, however, matched his desire that Aymar be promoted. Almost immediately after returning from the Balkans, Thierry announced his intention to ''have [Aymar] return to a real cavalry regiment.''[69] Soon after Aymar was again at the front in France.

In late 1916 or early 1917 Aymar was killed, somewhere. His remains were either never found or were too mangled for transport to the family crypt in Neuilly. Thierry's sense of guilt over the death of his son, whom he had pressured to enlist, would resurface twenty-three years later at the time of his own self-inflicted death. Now he became absorbed by both his medical duties and, with Yvette secluding herself in Normandy, by a liaison with Henriette Ballot, a half-sister of Feydeau, who was working during the war as a nurse for the Red Cross.

Despite her efforts, Gyp had been powerless to prevent the deaths of her elder son, Aymar, and of her grandson of the same name. She relived the devastation and paralysis she had felt in 1900. "[S]ince Aymar's death, I haven't written a line that 'hangs together properly,'" her publisher learned in January 1917, as she explained yet another missed deadline. "The death of this poor little boy has crushed me."[70] Yet perhaps she found Aymar's early death a fitting end to a sad life. She had contemplated his fate in a letter to Marie that, written shortly before Aymar's death, reads as a premature elegy:

> That poor Aymar will not have had any luck in life! . . . He will have been *"morally abandoned,"* as they say in the judgments of the police which take children away from parents in order to place them in a foster home. . . . He never had a set mealtime, nor even meals themselves, because when Thierry didn't have to eat lunch or dinner Yvette . . . sometimes ordered nothing, out of forgetfulness. They taught him neither spelling nor manners. The child of poor parents, adopted [by these parents] *against their will*, would not have been less neglected.[71]

A "Sacred Union" of Writers

While the war transformed Gyp's daily routine and family life, it also altered her relationships with friends, notably those who were writers. Talk of the war dominated her correspondence with Barrès, Montesquiou, Willy, and others, and it became the subject of their novels, articles, and poems. For the government encouraged a literary mobilization of intellectuals in support of the war effort, aiming to mold public opinion and lift morale.[72] Gyp thus found herself drawn into a "sacred union" of writers bound not only by common privations (lack of paper, censorship) but also by shared patriotism.

Most of Gyp's chosen fellow combatants were veterans of the anti-Dreyfusard campaigns. Yet this "sacred literary union" included some unusual alliances, as did the *union sacrée* in the general population. Not surprisingly, Pierre Loti, once vehemently anti-Dreyfusard, thanked Gyp effusively for sending him "this precious copy, uncensored and annotated by you!,'"[73] of an anglophobe pamphlet. These routine attacks against France's other "hereditary enemy" (turned ally) by Gyp and Loti, whose grandfather died at Trafalgar and who was "brought up hating those people,'"[74] prolonged the xenophobia they shared during the Affair. Loti himself seemed to acknowledge this: "[I] was quite sure that we were of the same mind, on this point as on so many others, but I thank you a thousand times for having confirmed it for me."[75] More surprising was Gyp's correspondence with a writer who, like most interested foreign oberservers, had believed Dreyfus blameless and his trials a scandal. Edith Wharton was obliged to Gyp for "the beautiful manuscript that you had the great goodness to give me,"[76] which would be sold at a charity auction benefiting tubercular veterans. And no longer in conflict over religion and ideology, but rather drawn together by common roots in Alsace-Lorraine, Gyp and her publisher frequently exchanged news about the war.

For two natives of the "lost provinces," the war inspired a common fervor, with Gyp's polemics and Barrès' lyricism fueling one another. Parliamentarian, head of the Ligue des patriotes (Déroulède had died early in 1914), member of the Académie française, journalist, and fund-raiser for war charities, Barrès, now in his early fifties, resumed with even greater authority and energy than he had mustered two decades earlier his role as leader of a patriotic, *revancharde* crusade. But his frantic activity, including expeditions to the front as well as to Italy and England, sometimes exhausted him. He confided to Gyp—"Madame and friend"—that he spent his days waiting his turn to speak in the Chamber of Deputies "and the rest of the time in bed and sick."[77]

Gyp followed closely her friend's almost daily articles in *L'Echo de Paris*, the influential paper associated with the militarist, Catholic Right. Barrès bemoaned the tight control to which his writing was subject. "[I]f I wrote as I'd like to," he confided to Gyp, referring to his disparaging comments about various ministers, "my article would be censored immediately."[78] As she let Barrès know by mail, Gyp approved of his campaign to focus French élan against enemies both external (German "barbarism") and internal (the "defeatists" Barrès came to verbally thrash in the person of Joseph Caillaux, a former prime minister and early opponent of the war). Yet she remained somewhat skeptical of Barrès' almost fanatical, ridiculous optimism. Her realism was, as ever, a foil to his aestheticism. Barrès's accounts of French youth dying cheerfully and of the merry atmosphere in the trenches indeed earned him the scorn of an emerging pacifist press. In its view Barrès was a "bourreur de crâne" ("brainwasher") and, in Romain Rolland's words, "the Nightingale of carnage."[79] The specter of hundreds of thousands of casualties, however—among them Barrès' twenty-year-old son, Philippe, who was wounded in early 1916—eventually convinced Barrès that moral vigor was a paltry weapon against troops and machines. After 1915 his idealistic tone became more nuanced.

News of their sons and praise or damning of political and military leaders was interspersed in the Gyp–Barrès correspondence with the usual literary business. Gyp asked Barrès to cosponsor the novelist Victor Favet, a candidate for entry into the Société des gens de lettres.[80] And Barrès turned to Gyp when preparing a public introduction of another female novelist, Colette Yver, whose proposed fund for returning soldiers the Ligue des patriotes wished to sponsor. "It was *very, very* good," Gyp replied, communicating her approval of Yver's *Princesses de science*, which Barrès inquired about. "She follows the evolution of women and approves of it without approving. It's complex. . . ."[81]

Far from the front and from his Neuilly neighbors Gyp and Barrès, Robert de Montesquiou had retreated to the château of d'Artagnan in Gascony. Here he railed against the Germans at a safe distance, denouncing the "frightful Kaiser" and Wilhelm, "this monster," in several maudlinly patriotic anthologies.[82] Gyp sent compliments (along with her latest novels), and deemed the count "the only poet for whom the war has inspired beautiful poetry."[83] Montesquiou, in turn, asked for news of Thierry, commented on Barrès' articles in *L'Echo*, and with carefully calibrated solemnity, expressed to Gyp his concern that "nothing too immediate torments you, in this cruel hour."[84]

Willy's son, his editor Albin Michel, and many acquaintances were at the front. Feeling depressed in a depopulated Paris, he sought refuge just across France's border. "Where am I, dear Madame and collaborator? In Geneva, since a little while ago . . . which is starting to seem long to me, although the French-speaking Swiss are good people, Germanophobes. . . ."[85] An invitation from the editor of *La Suisse*, a francophile newspaper, had enticed Gyp's spendthrift "collabo." However, in a May 1917 letter he confessed that "writing articles in *La Suisse*"— despite the paper's serialization of Gyp's *Maman*—"is not the ultimate happiness."[86] On the subject of the war, Willy was purposely reticent; as he told Gyp, his letter would surely be censored. Yet he did confide that having recovered from his "foolishness" of reading and believing German papers, he now had "absolute confidence" in an Allied victory, a curious statement during a month in which both mutinies and massive strikes protesting a rise in the cost of living seriously troubled French morale. Yet Willy was defiant, and the former contributor to the Henry Monument imagined a revenge scenario that must have thrilled Gyp: "[I] wouldn't like to be in the shoes of the Boches, who will be the first to see our army cross the border. Ah! the swine! . . . They'll have to pay!"[87]

A shared desire for Germany's defeat, finally, brought back into Gyp's orbit some political chameleons like Laurent Tailhade. The ex-anarchist, who once damned the bellicose Gyp in print as a Walkyrie and "blood sucker," had lost his fury. A year before his death (in 1919) he was tired and ill, as he admitted to Gyp, "wasted by my stupid abuse of morphine."[88] With the ideological divide of the Dreyfus Affair at least temporarily demolished, Tailhade, living in the Eure-et-Loir not far from Paris, could freely express his long-felt admiration for Gyp the polemicist. He thanked her effusively for sending her novels, which he praised as "charming and cruel,"[89] and promised to review them favorably, although he was dismayed by the prospect of censure.[90] As through all their fallings-out and reconciliations, Gyp and Tailhade continued to enjoy Jew-baiting. Tailhade sent "Jewish jokes" for Gyp's amusement and laced his letters with bigoted remarks (the Reinach family's "frightful ugliness"—by now a rather tired theme—was "an insult to light")[91] But with the Affair over and French energies focused on the enemy across the Rhine, remarks like these, however highly insulting, were politically innocuous. Titillating as anti-Semitism may have been for Gyp and Tailhade, it was now a very private pleasure.

Shortly before the beginning of the major Allied offensive, in the summer of 1918, that repelled the Germans and led to victory, Tailhade felt too weary and disillusioned to share Gyp's confidence that the Allies would prevail. He reminded her nostalgically that there had indeed been a time when ideals, albeit different ones, had inspired both of them: "When you were dreaming about reforming the Third Republic (the Republic without the Jews!), . . . I myself was getting excited about the universal, fraternal Republic and other nonsense."[92] But had it all been worth it? The mishaps of his own life and the horror of this war had convinced him otherwise: "I've done time in prison, earned several duels, many fines; I've lost several attractive positions, all this to end up watching the dismal spectacle of this endless, thankless war, the triumph of the 'brainwashers' and of everything I would hate if I still had the energy to hate anything at all."[93] As a member of the generation of 1870 (he was sixteen during "the terrible year"), and despite his anarchist past, Tailhade might reasonably have longed, as did Juliette Adam and Gyp, for "the so passionately longed for Revenge." But the "destruction of this lovable country,"[94] for which he previously expressed so little affection, dismayed him, and passion ceded to apathy.

"Profiteers" and "Slackers"

Writing for Gyp—as for Barrès, Loti, and others whom either age or gender prevented from enlisting—was a means of *engagement.* "Gyp is mobilized," Abel Hermant aptly declared in a 1918 book review, "Gyp wages war."[95] Between 1916 and 1918 she published five novels about the war: a trio of polemical dialogue-novels ("in the style of the *Vie Parisienne*")[96] published by Fayard and serialized in the newspaper *Excelsior* (*Ceux de "la nuque"* [*Those of "the Rear"*], *Les Flanchards* [*The Quitters*], and *Les Profitards* [*The Profiteers*]); a fourth dialogue-novel, *Ceux qui s'en f . . . ,* [*Those who don't give a D . . .*], published by Flammarion; and *Le Journal d'un cochon de pessimiste,* another of her semifictionalized "diaries," covering events between late July and early October 1914, published by Calmann-Lévy. As in her Dreyfus Affair novels, Gyp used humor to hurt. Not even as solemn a subject as war escaped her mockery. Robert de Montesquiou compared her *"impressions of war"* to "a shell burst, in which there would be a burst of laughter."[97] Abel Hermant ventured that Gyp had developed a new genre: "war ridicule."[98] Aside from the obvious and ever-present financial incentive, writing these novels served a dual purpose for Gyp. It allowed her to respond to the government and army's call to writers to help maintain civilian morale and discipline by blasting enemies—in short, to become propagandists. Moreover, the needs of the wartime government corresponded to Gyp's personal needs. In her war novels she elaborated the familiar conspiracy theories and castigated the malevolent "others" (this time *embusqués*, defeatists and profiteers) who, by opposing what she stood for, paradoxically continued to assure her sense of self-worth. These doppelgängers became for her, to a certain extent, a moral and psychological substitute for the Jews. At the same time, through the creation of fictional doubles she attempted to resolve in print her own nonparticipation in combat. The veteran of Boulangism and the Dreyfus Affair prolonged her public role as polemicist as she continued to battle her personal contradictions.

In 1870 Gyp had cheerily socialized with Prussian officers. During World War I, her novels scarcely mentioned the German "barbarian." She still deemed Austria, unforgiven by her for its role in Napoleon's downfall, the more treacherous enemy. She instead embarked on another crusade to purify France from within.

Rachilde, in a review of *Ceux qui s'en f . . .* , took note of Gyp's "mobilization": "An 'old France' is in the process of standing up . . . against imbeciles, slackers, all internal enemies. . . ."[99] Most odious to Gyp, and to many other French, were the *embusqués*, "these people who *disgust . . . me*."[100] The term, one of many neologisms generated by the war, appeared in the press and political discourse of both Right and Left soon after combat began, when it became clear that some were finding ways to avoid being sent to the front. Gyp's "pig of a pessimist," in "his" journal entry of 7 September 1914, has this to say about the new group: "*The Slackers!* That's the name given to those who escape military service. By that I mean armed service. And despite claims to the contrary, there are a lot of them . . ."[101] Despite the passage of a law, in August 1915, to control the problem (certain key civil servants and other professionals were, of course, exempted from service), the term remained, becoming a more generic, widely used epithet.[102]

Gyp dressed down *embusqués* in her salon. One "swine of a slacker"[103] who, courageously or foolishly, appeared there one day, was warned by Gyp to "stay stuck in his paperwork, and to only run the risk of encountering other slackers like himself."[104] Gyp meted out the same punishment in print. *Ceux de "la nuque"*, "the story . . . of a high-class Slacker,"[105] derides the *embusqués* in the person of the vicomte de Paroly, who fakes a wound to work in a ministerial office. The *embusqués* and their supporters (a Jewish countess, vapid *mondains*), comprising the *nuque,* or rear, of the title, are familiar enemies, for they represent "everything that was formerly Dreyfusard. . . ."[106] In *Les Flanchards* the virtuous Liette Noyelle refuses to marry an *embusqué*, a whiny *nouveau riche* known only as "our son Edgar," preferring instead a brave one-legged lieutenant. In fact, she intends to marry only a mutilated veteran, his wounds serving as a "certificate of his exposure to fire."[107] Gyp's idealization of violent combat—"I admire and I envy those who die a beautiful death, in the apotheosis of a battle"[108]—continued to pervade her novels, remaining at odds with an emerging realist trend in war fiction. The year *Les Flanchards* appeared, the Prix Goncourt was awarded to Henri Barbusse, whose novel *Le Feu* horrifyingly documented life in the trenches and was ultimately considered a pacifist manifesto.

Yet the "*infinite* disgust"[109] Gyp claims to have felt toward the *embusqués* deserves a closer look. She was, of course, performing what was considered a patriotic duty by denouncing these bad patriots, these cowards and weaklings, these members of "anti-France." But the violent intensity of her rage suggests, as it did during the Affair, that her disgust was at least in part self-directed. For was not Gyp, in view of her role in her son's repatriation, an *embuscomane* (in the wartime vernacular), a person who accuses another of being a slacker in order to protect himself? And perhaps she also saw herself as a type of *embusquée* against her own will, someone who yearned to serve but was prevented from doing so, confined to the rear, powerless. "Why can't I fight it, this war . . . ?" Her "horror" of *embusqués*, like a less complex version of her anti-Semitism, was a double-edged sword, a weapon simultaneously pointed at others and at herself.

Gyp also satirized other foes, both collective and individual, in her novels. Profiteers were the object of her displeasure in *Les Profitards*. Franck Wollüstling, a man of uncertain nationality who lusts after sex and money, spreads rumors of peace in well-frequented salons in order to buy out for a pittance a stock of "lamb tablets" used to feed troops, only to resell them at a profit after changing his story and insisting the war will drag on indefinitely. This type of caricature may well have appealed to a public that viewed all war suppliers as profiteers, an impression confirmed by the rapidly acquired and ostentatiously displayed fortunes of some of these suppliers, a measure of the government's exceptional needs in wartime.[110]

Although the term *défaitiste* most commonly designated left-wing activists, Gyp used it against the right-wing Action française, whom she accused of trying to hasten a defeat that would help bring to power the duc d'Orléans.[111] Not surprisingly, she also joined others in execrating Romain Rolland. In a series of articles collectively entitled *Au-dessus de la mêlée (Above the Fray),* printed in a Swiss newspaper shortly after the Marne victory, Rolland advocated pacifism and internationalism, urging France and its allies to exercise "neither vengeance nor reprisals" against Germany. The "complete degenerate" responsible for this "purely disgusting" pamphlet (Gyp's words) soon won the Nobel Prize. But that did not stop Gyp's "pessimist"—who, like his creator, had a decidedly unnuanced view of the war—from blasting Rolland's "stunning cowardice."[112]

Although most of Gyp's wartime views matched her long-held values—love of war, chauvinism, nationalism—she also expressed some surprising sympathies. "A real Frenchman, very distinguished and pedigreed,"[113] was how one of Gyp's spokeswomen described Georges Clemenceau, who took over the premiereship and direction of the war effort in November 1917. Two decades earlier Gyp had despised the ferociously Dreyfusard, zealously anticlerical, and Republican Clemenceau, now a vigorous seventy-six-year-old senator from the Vendée. But with civilian morale at its nadir, she applauded his pitiless campaign against defeatists, his hatred of any type of collectivist movement, be it pacifism or syndicalism, and his committtment to "war, nothing but war." Extremely popular among the French but relatively isolated from the political class, the authoritarian "Tiger" perhaps reminded Gyp of another charismatic "hero" who had emerged during a moment of crisis with a mission to save the nation: général Boulanger.[114]

Gyp's fictional diatribes against the *embusqués, profitards,* and others thus made public the views she was expressing privately in her correspondence and conversations. Yet they also served a more personal function, allowing her to rewrite her life. The portrait of one of her fictional doubles suggests the nostalgia Gyp would increasingly feel until her death: Liette Noyelle in *Les Flanchards,* with her "astonishingly fresh and childlike appearance,"[115] embodies Gyp the *jeune fille* as *garçon manqué,* who remembers playing with soldiers as a child and heeding her grandfather's directive: "no corset, no garters, but dance, fencing, crew."[116] Frustrated at being prevented from serving in the war, Liette dreams of experiencing it vicariously by giving birth to six sons and marrying a wounded veteran. Unlike Gyp's nostalgic double, Liette, Madame de Sermaize (who appears in two novels) is a type of prospective double of Gyp. A lively, elderly widow, she spurns electricity and the telephone; her husband died in the war, not of wounds but—to his wife's regret—of illness. Had Gyp ever really recovered from both the tragedy and the banality of her soldier–father's accidental death, his "frightful and stupid death" at the hands of a negligent comrade?

Gyp's "pessimist," like her "grump" and her "philosopher," is another double, this one male. Although Gyp began taking notes for the *Journal* at the beginning of the war, "the shock caused by Aymar's death"[117] and her health problems delayed its publication for four years. It is simultaneously a chronicle of the war as experienced by civilians (complete with deletions simulating censure); a depiction of Gyp's circle in wartime, with appearances by Chesnay (Genest), Givet (Judet), Sarlèze (Barrès), and a group of publishers, les C . . . ;[118] and Gyp's bittersweet reflection on her life. Antoine de Champreux, the "pessimist" in question, is a painter and illustrator, once well known by the name "Pük." Born a 15 August in Brittany, raised in Lorraine by his grandfather (a former Napoleonic officer), this great-grandson of Mirabeau-Tonneau lives in Neuilly, where he entertains guests on Sundays. Pessimism and regret color his attitude not only toward the war but also his life. Remembering the "terrible year" during which his family quartered Prussian soldiers in the château of "Jarville" (Gyp recreates at great length her stay at Janville), the pessimist muses that the German army, which seemed "unbeatable" in 1870, must now be even more powerful, intent on "new conquests that would allow a final crushing of France . . ."[119] The "miracle of the Marne" convinces the pessimist otherwise, however, as it did for many French citizens. In his last journal entry of 4 October 1914 he asserts that "we shall be the ultimate victors because we have not been immediately beaten . . ."[120]

The pessimist's regret about his own life seems more firmly rooted than his fear about the outcome of the war, again fascinatingly revealing Gyp's own state of mind. First there is regret over the pessimist's lack of personal freedom: "My great mistake is to have an entourage and expenses, when I was born to live free and alone."[121] Then there is regret about the monetary need that forced him/her to work: "Born into a world in which it is customary to do nothing . . . I was obliged, at around the age of thirty, to suddenly improvise a career as a painter . . ."[122] Finally there is the regret—"exasperation," really—about not being able to fight, which makes the pessimist recall a bizarre childhood maiming fantasy: "to have a knife 'that I can really cut m'self with . . .' "[123] These regrets and "lacks" that once emboldened Gyp—"I want to become strong, very strong"—now fatigued her. The self-loathing that impelled her throughout her life was now tempered by frustration and, in the end, resignation. She was truly, in her view, "the old fossil."

"[T]he days in Lorraine and Alsace must have been splendid!"[124] Gyp exclaimed to her publisher in November 1918. She could only imagine the thrill Barrès had felt, nearly two weeks earlier, when he witnessed Philippe Pétain, the "victor of Verdun" and now a marshal, lead victorious Allied troops through a liberated

Metz. Alsace-Lorraine was again, after nearly half a century, part of France; the "so passionately longed for Revenge" was a reality. And with future German aggression seemingly quelled by the terms of the armistice—"Germany will pay," the slogan went—Gyp and many of her compatriots looked forward to an era of peace and well-being.

But at what price? An entire generation? More than a million Frenchmen—Gyp's grandson and several friends and other relatives among them—had been wounded or killed. And she had survived the penury of the war only to confront severe postwar inflation and a steep rise in the cost of living. Her solution to this financial dilemma was, as always, to write a book. The one she proposed to her publisher was a sequel to *Le Journal d'un cochon de pessimiste*, treating the period from the July 1918 Allied offensive in Champagne to the armistice, and alternatively entitled *Le Journal de feu le Cochon de pessimiste* (*The Journal of the Late Pig of a Pessimist*), *On les a!* (*They've Been Had!*), or *De la Marne au Rhin* (*From the Marne to the Rhine*).[125] Her idea for another work, bearing the title *Les Mécontents de la victoire* (*Victory's Malcontents*) or *Les Ronchonneux de la victoire* (*Victory's Grousers*), was based on the pessimistic grumblings—distressing to her—of some members of her circle. Since the armistice, she confided to her publisher, she had "heard so many unpleasant and really *incredible* things after such a beautiful triumph, that I am sickened by it."[126] The postwar period would be one of disillusion for Gyp, but also of illusions. Like many French, but with the added catalyst of old age, she would spend the remaining years of her life glorifying and memorializing the antebellum period, in creating her personal belle époque.

XIII

"The Old Fossil"

1919–1932

~~~━━━━~~~

"I Am Dying . . ."

Gyp's last thirteen years constituted, in her view, a progressive "fossilization." She considered herself antiquated, an inert remnant of a faraway past. And it was to this past that she now began—in her appearance, writings, and reflections—to revert. Her Sunday afternoon gatherings continued, but in "a growing isolation,"[1] due not to disaffection but to death. Relatives and friends from the eras she was memorializing in her writing as "the time of hair and horses" and "the joyous childhood of the Third Republic" were disappearing. In their place their children and grandchildren now came to Neuilly to visit the eccentric, frail yet lively old woman. Her hands were gnarled, the writer René Benjamin remembered. Her grizzled hair hung in long, tightly curled ringlets—like those she had worn as a child—capped by her trademark lace bonnet. She had a bulbous red nose, small, "mischievous" eyes, and an odd, rusty-sounding voice. She reminded Benjamin of the wolf in grandmother's clothing from "Little Red Riding Hood."[2] Gyp was bewildered and offended by her new visitors, this automobile-crazy youth. The progenitor of Petit Bob castigated the mores of the postwar generation, as she had flayed its prewar predecessor, in a novel Calmann-Lévy published just two years before her death, *Les Moins de vingt ans.*

"Dying is difficult, and takes a long time,"[3] Gyp complained to a friend. She wrote to Calmann-Lévy, just after her seventy-fifth birthday and after fighting a serious chest cold, "I thought this was the end, but not at all, it's not it yet. That's a pain! . . . I detest false departures. . . .''[4] Ever her own best publicist, an expert at sensational personal drama—flight from Nancy, acid bath, assassination attempt, kidnapping—she was staging the steps leading to her death. ''I shall not go out again,'' she announced one day. Shortly thereafter, when the strap used to transport her gout-ridden body from bedroom to salon pained her unbearably, she insisted, ''I shall not go downstairs again.'' And a year or two before her death she again reiterated, ''I shall not get up again.''[5]

Still, she outlived most of those closest to her. Robert de Montesquiou died of uremia in December 1921, aged sixty-five. Gyp remembered friendships cemented and broken over literature, art, and politics with the deaths of Degas (1917), Drumont (1917), Loti (1923), France (1924), Forain (1931), and Willy (1931). Participants in Gyp's private life passed away too. In 1919 she informed her publisher of the fatal heart attack of ''our poor friend Genest.''[6] Her discreet yet constant companion exited her life as self-effacingly as he had taken part in it. Following Genest's instructions, Gyp made plans to block any newspaper announcement of his death.[7]

Roger de Martel de Janville, who had been Gyp's husband since before the Franco-Prussian war, did not die as meekly as Genest. In June 1920 he suddenly became extremely ill when an infection caused by an untreated inflammation of the lymph glands spread through his leg. ''Thierry had to perform a very serious emergency operation at the house,''[8] a distracted Gyp told family friend and creditor Michel Calmann-Lévy, explaining both a delayed manuscript and her need for funds. The surgery did not prevent the infection from spreading, however, nor Roger's fever from worsening. In late June Thierry moved his father to his private clinic in the rue Piccini and amputated his leg below the knee. Gyp, who had not left her house for a year and a half, now spent ''frightful days shuttling between rue Piccini and boulevard Bineau.''[9] Roger returned to Neuilly in late July. His infection continued to spread, obliging Thierry to amputate another segment of his father's leg. ''He is considered doomed,''[10] Gyp informed her publisher. Yet feverish and delirious, Roger was nevertheless ''extremely courageous and tough.''[11] No one knew how long he might linger. ''Horribly difficult to care for,''[12] he was also a financial burden to Gyp. She had to hire both a male nurse to lift her husband, who was now very stout, and a female one. Bandages, medication were needed: ''I'm struggling with horrible complications.''[13] Roger received last rites on 28 July, but the next day, ''with extraordinary strength,''[14] he resumed his raving. On 15 August *Le Gaulois* announced his death. The obituary identified the count only as the husband of a famous wife ''whose works, published under the pseudonym Gyp, are so appreciated by all well-read people,''[15] and as the father of ''this young and already famous''[16] surgeon and war hero, Thierry de Martel. During their half-century together, Roger had given Gyp something she needed—the legitimacy conferred on married women—and something she wanted—two sons. She had never counted on him for companionship, nor for love. At best Roger had always been for Gyp an unobtrusive nonentity, at worst a nuisance and an expense.

Three years after Roger, Barrès also died suddenly in Neuilly. He was honored with a national funeral at Notre-Dame. The lengthy, spirited letters he and Gyp traded in the years before his death record the common passions and places that had united the two since their days in Lorraine: writing, nationalist politics, Nancy, Neuilly and Paris, Mirabeau. Gyp's fellow partisan from the days of Boulangism and the Affair, a deputy since 1906, had by the end of his life made peace with the once despised parliamentary Republic. He had a new concern after the war: France's policy in the Rhineland. In *Le Génie du Rhin*—"a truly beautiful book, and infinitely skillful"[17] in Gyp's opinion—Barrès argued for a long-term Allied occupation of the left bank of the Rhine, which he considered a crucial bastion against further German aggression. He was enthusiastic about the proclamation of an ephemeral Rhenish Republic on 1 June 1919, sensing in this expression of the Latin and Germanic "Rhenish genius" the definitive end of the era of Pan-Germanism. With the signing of the Treaty of Versailles, however, it became clear that France's British and American allies opposed any definitive occupation of the Rhineland. They viewed it as contrary to the principle of national self-determination outlined in the Fourteen Points. Barrès, of course, would not live to see the evacuation of the Rhineland in 1930, five years before the scheduled date. And six years later, in 1936, with Hitler's occupation of this region, France would once again find itself—in the ominous phrase formulated by Barrès two decades after France's 1870 defeat by Prussia—"under the eyes of the barbarians."[18]

Informative and chatty as always, the Gyp–Barrès correspondence turned increasingly nostalgic and philosophical before his death. Barrès asked Gyp for news of mutual friends from Nancy, and for descriptions of streets and neighborhoods whose memory was dimming. In another letter he wondered if his friend, when reflecting on her life, felt disillusioned. "I am going to *try* to explain to you . . . what I think," Gyp replied, "if you can call it that, because, when it comes to me, it's rather 'feeling' than thinking."[19] In the next seventeen pages Gyp answered Barrès' question in her typical fashion by telling a story, namely, that of the infamous Liverdun picnic. On that day long ago, frozen in horror and fascination behind a bush while spying on an adulterous couple, she became completely disenchanted. And she had remained that way for the rest of her life. As a girl she came to realize that fidelity, virtue, and respectability were façades, and that women were inherently evil. "No," she affirmed to Barrès,

> there has been no disillusionment. Experience has taught me no more than what I knew in the days of the circus in Nancy. It has only confirmed [what I knew]. I left Nancy at 29, and I saw life as I've seen it since, which didn't prevent me from loving it in an animalistic way, as do those people who are interested in and amused by everything. I wasn't considering things in detail, I wasn't reasoning, I was simply living.[20]

Gyp versus Barrès: the cynic versus the idealist; the militant versus the theorist; frankness versus finesse; "masculine" versus "feminine?" These contrasts explain, in part, their attraction and their friendship. But so does what they shared. They were two refugees from the provinces who had made it in Paris. They were descendants of imperial officers. At moments of national crisis they never doubted to which "axiom, religion, or prince of men"[21] they should turn, nor against whom French "national energy" and their own should be directed. They also complemented each other. The provincial bourgeois and former "prince of youth" was awed by the aristocratic cachet of the "last of the Mirabeau," "countess and friend." Gyp had always been for him "the brilliant young woman"[22] he had first seen at the Nancy circus when he was a boy. Later she became a friend, confidante, and advisor. For Gyp Barrès probably always retained something of the allure he cultivated in his twenties, when—aloof, brilliant, and ambitious—he reminded some of the young Napoleon. Later, the deputy and Academician epitomized the political and literary consecration that might well have been Gyp's had she been a man. Instead, she had to content herself with the ambiguous honor of being nationalism's "feminine" center.

"I Don't Have a *Centime* of Income"

In the last decade of her life Gyp could not disentangle herself from her physical and material difficulties, and from financial problems related to her writing. As she could attest, postwar inflation had dramatically raised the cost of living: "Everything is infinitely more expensive than during the war, and one can no longer say to oneself, as during the war, that, after all, this situation will end at a given moment."[23] Massive strikes were taking place in Paris; Gyp could only complain to her publisher and force herself to write. Yet even writing letters proved problematic. Fine-quality paper had cost her three francs a box before the war. Now she paid seven for paper "that soaks up [ink] like a sponge."[24] Limitations both physical ("I can't take a step")[25] and financial ("taxis are impossibly overpriced for me")[26] prevented her from making the trip to the Calmann-Lévy office in the rue Auber. Her situation confined her to home. But her home for half a century was in serious disrepair. "The house can only be inhabited in certain conditions," she told her publisher, after thanking the latter for emergency funds. "So I shall be obliged to rent it and to go off to someplace in Brittany . . . that seems very hard to me."[27] Yet her house, she claimed, was all she had left. In February 1920 she declared categorically to her publisher: "Life is becoming frightfully difficult for me. I don't have a *centime* of income. I gave my children (especially my daughter) absolutely everything I had. I have nothing but my house. I'm lodged. Period. . . ."[28]

In the past Gyp had always been able to write herself out of financial distress. Now her situation had become much more trying. Usually generous with advances, her publisher flatly declared, first in 1923 and again in 1925, that it was "*absolutely impossible*"[29] to accommodate their author and friend, "despite our desire to oblige you."[30] Was the firm perhaps reluctant, Gyp cynically suggested, to support an author whose death appeared imminent? "I am quite sure you think that I might die from one day to the next? But in that case you would recover . . . the sum rather quickly."[31] Characteristically, her publisher remained guarded on this sensitive point, arguing instead that Gyp's account was in arrears, that her production had slowed, that there were no plans for any new editions of her works,[32] and that publishing costs were also rising. Her publisher did not acknowledge that her novels, like their author, had become anachronistic. The peasants, aristocrats, and priests in *Mon ami Pierrot* (1921), for example, and the novel's evocation of a rural *dolce vita*, seemed firmly rooted in a now unfamiliar antebellum period. One reviewer was not as circumspect as Calmann-Lévy in his treatment of Gyp. He disparaged Flammarion's reedition of *Un raté* as "the umpteenth book by Gyp," asking, "Is this old hag still alive? Or is it an unpublished posthumous work?"[33]

Gyp could no longer retain her habitual pace of one or two novels a year. Nor could she rely on Calmann-Lévy for instant credit; her son assumed this function. Instead, she adopted new literary strategies, squeezing residual benefits from her existing works. She asked Calmann-Lévy to raise the price of some of her novels and cede her the rights to others so she could sell them to firms who wished to publish them.[34] She announced her intention to bring a lawsuit against Fasquelle for refusing to release the rights to *Le Baron Sinaï* and *Le Journal d'un philosophe*.[35] And she was so confident of the success of a dramatic adaptation of *Napoléonette* that a month before it opened she asked her publisher for a large advance to pay interest on a silver service engraved with the Mirabeau arms, now the property of a pawnshop.[36] The five-act comedy by André de Lorde and Jean Marsèle opened on 29 May 1919, at the Théâtre Sarah Bernhardt. The theater's patron found Gyp's enfant terrible, godchild of the emperor, delightful. "I feel I am quite far from your charming talent,"[37] the actress wrote, the "Quand même" ("After all") impressed on her writing paper echoing Gyp's "So what?" Gyp was pleased by the play's critical success. *Le Gaulois'* reviewer praised the "pleasant imagery, brilliant yet light,"[38] of the historical comedy. Yet more important for her, and to her dismay, the production "was a disaster from a financial standpoint because all was against us."[39] A stifling summer heatwave, compounded by a transportation strike, discouraged theatergoers, and eight performances were canceled.[40] Gyp collected nothing from a tour of *Napoléonette*, which took the play to Brussels, Nice, and other Parisian theaters. So her scheme to sustain herself with residuals failed. She now began to rely increasingly on her long-awaited *Souvenirs*, the record of her past, to provide for her present.

"I Would Sign . . . Simply 卅"

By the end of her career Gyp had become a specialist in reeditions and hack writing. But occasionally reasons other than profit motivated her. "I've wanted for a long time to write 'the (abridged!) history of Action française,'" she informed her publisher in January 1926. "I've written so many things that have bored me that I'd like to write one that amuses me before I die."[41] Her public dispute with Maurras dated from before the war. A novel, *Le Grand Coup*, had been her ammunition. She now declared her intent to fire another shot, prolonging the personal tradition of polemic at which she had excelled during the Affair.

It was, in fact, a controversy similar in many ways to *l'Affaire* that incited Gyp in the years before her death. She asserted—wrongly—that the schism created among French Catholics by Action française was much more serious than the divisions provoked by the Affair. The result of this latest "Franco-French war" was the 1926 papal condemnation of Maurras' movement. Its causes were both doctrinal and political. Many clerics had long found Maurras' blend of paganism and positivism offensive. Human nature, in Maurras' view, was determined by a combination of forces: social, biological, environmental, but not moral or spiritual. A professed agnostic, Maurras admired the Church as an instrument of order and propagator of dogma, a crucial pillar of integral nationalism. Yet he saw the Church's role as clearly distinct from that of Action française and restricted to the spiritual realm. To some Catholics this type of neo-Gallicanism—"faith from Rome, politics from home"—smacked of heresy.

The conflict over doctrine masked a power struggle dating back to before the war. At issue was the growing influence of Action française in conservative Catholic circles. From the beginning, the movement's condemnation of social liberalism, democracy, and modernism had attracted many Catholics. And a postwar Catholic revival saw the movement's membership swell in both Paris and *province*.[42] Sympathizers included numerous prominent clergymen and intellectuals, as well as many young people eager to join the league's shock troops, the Camelots du Roi. A 1925 survey of French youth revealed that, among writers of the past quarter century, Maurras was the one whom most respondants considered their "maître."[43] Maurras' movement thus encroached on an area in which the Church also wished to be powerful, namely, shaping public opinion, especially that of Catholic youth.

The gain in popularity of Action française meant growing support for its political program: restoration of the monarchy. Some members of the Church hierarchy denounced Maurras for seemingly using religion for political ends and for identifying religion with a form of government, thus dividing Catholics along political lines. They found the increasingly violent style of the league and its newspaper at odds with Christian values. Specific political questions further estranged Maurras from the Vatican. For example, Pius XI favored the policy of peace and international collaboration pursued after the war by Aristide Briand, whereas Maurras was violently opposed to it.

As early as 1914, seven of Maurras' books and the league's newspaper had been stigmatized by Pius X as "truly very bad and deserving of censure."[44] But the pope, sympathetic to Maurras, never published the decree placing these works on the Index. Rome issued the official condemnation in December 1926. Catholics were forbidden to follow the movement; the 1914 decree outlawing Maurras' books and paper was promulgated. Harsher sanctions which forbade Maurras' faithful from receiving sacraments followed shortly before Easter 1927. The papal decision caused consternation in Action française circles. The movement lost an estimated eighteen hundred members, the paper half its readership. But many flouted the decree and continued to adhere to the movement discreetly or defiantly. In the convulsions resulting from this institutional excommunication, families and salons divided, as they had during the Affair. As a Belgian reporter observed, "Things have come to such a pass that on social occasions one often begins with the stipulation that Action française must not be mentioned. Of course it always is, even in the most elegant and cosmopolitan drawing rooms."[45]

Gyp's salon was no exception. Every Sunday she conspicuously placed on a table a pamphlet, "No, Action française followed neither the Church nor France," "in order to propagandize."[46] Was it habit, conviction, or a profound need to fight the "oppressor" that made her, in her late seventies and now for the last time, join the battle surrounding this latest cause célèbre? Before the war her quarrel with Maurras had been less a matter of doctrine than of temperament. She certainly shared his antidemocratic and antimodernist leanings, but she spurned his intellectualism and the faddishness she associated with the movement. However, the turmoil caused by the papal condemnation, and the movement's brazen snubbing of it, elicited from Gyp a much sharper reaction. She found a sympathetic interlocutor in an army chaplain with whom she exchanged, in 1927 and 1928, long letters condemning the movement. In these private diatribes she damned specific priests who were brandishing the banner of Action française as "the lowest of cretins and cowards,"[47] comparing their agitation to "the wave of hysteria that the Jesuits had formerly let loose on the ladies of Nancy."[48] She dismissed the Camelots du Roi as "ruffians"[49] and mocked "the ignorance, foolishness and stupidity"[50] of the movement's followers.

Gyp inflicted these superficial barbs on *any* foe, whether real or imaginary. But her generic taunts alternated with more substantial concerns. The apologist of national unity castigated Action française for having "ignited and maintained, for more than twenty years, dissension among a youth that only asked to be united."[51] Her imperialism, of course, made her hostile to the movement's proposed regime. Yet, as she suggested in the following ditty, Maurras and Daudet may have been monarchists merely through opportunism:

> The monarchy is my Goddess!
> King Philippe is quite a fellow!
> But, if I must, in my old age
> I will abandon their banner
> I'll turn into a Bonapartist
> Or even, if necessary, a Communist
> Or anything, I don't give a d——[52]

As a Catholic traditionalist, moreover, who described her faith in God and country as "passionate and unshakable," Gyp was outraged by Maurras' affront to the Church. "Can you imagine their impudence?" she fumed. "They are—Maurras especially—convinced they'll get the better of the Church. They don't understand that [the Church] is the greatest force."[53]

Gyp's collision with Action française, finally, marked her clearly as a representative of a fin-de-siècle revolutionary Right whose politics had become more centrist. Once the champion of extremism, the *coup de force*, extraparliamentary tactics, and an appeal to *le peuple*, Gyp now detested these features of Maurras' movement, among others. She stood for the militant nationalism of the Affair, whose master theorist was Barrès, the nationalism of Déroulède and Habert, and, to a lesser extent, of Lemaître and Coppée. Maurras embodied the equally militant youth movement that took its place in the prewar period. And just as the Ligue des patriotes had given way to Action française as the principal agent of revolt against liberal bourgeois democracy, so Action française, in the interwar period and especially after its condemnation, was replaced by more radical groups.

The principal beneficiary of the shake-up in Action française was Georges Valois' Le Faisceau. Anticapitalist, antiparliamentary—indeed, antidemocratic—and corporatist, the movement claimed an eclectic membership: members of the older nationalist generation (Forain), World War I veterans, and angry young men committed to not merely verbal but physical violence as well. The movement also attracted many seceders from Action française, among them Philippe Barrès and Thierry de Martel. The latest in a line of crusaders and dissidents, Gyp's son had been disgusted by the effete, intellectual tone of Action française and by its unwillingness to stage a coup. He confided in a letter to his friend Philippe Barrès that "the stupidity and treason of Action française are evident to everyone, and . . . nothing could be more fortuitous for Le Faisceau—Maurras and [Léon] Daudet are hanging themselves."[54] The same impudent hostility toward Action française bonded mother and son; Gyp's wish was "to see—before sneaking off—the definitive collapse"[55] of the movement. And thirty years apart, each pursued a similar combat against selected internal enemies, Gyp in the anti-Dreyfusard leagues and press, Thierry in what has been called "the first French fascist movement."[56]

Gyp could not be Thierry. Approaching eighty, and a woman, she could not participate in Valois' movement, which embraced a rhetoric of virility and aimed to found "a world in which a morality of warriors and monks prevails."[57] She had, over the years, created other tribunals for herself: her impassioned correspondence, her salon, the press, her novels. She dashed off two of these, and habit led her first to her longtime publisher. In January 1926 she promised Calmann-Lévy that *Le Chambard* (*The Upheaval*) would be written "in a moderate tone."[58] It would gloss over the "swindles and blackmails"[59] of Action française. But the pamphlet might still attract notoriety—or worse, in Gyp's view. That she had written to her publisher at home, for fear her letter would be opened at his office, signaled her paranoia. She also refused to use her pseudonym for the first printing of the book: "I would sign either simply ⊥, or 'a swine of a paying customer.' "[60] And if the firm lacked confidence in the selling power of the injurious brochure, Gyp added, publisher and author might edit it at their own expense. Unsurprisingly, Gyp's generous offer was declined. With the same ambiguous mixture of polite formality and sarcasm that had often been the firm's most effective defense against Gyp's demands, her publisher replied: "I'd like first to thank you for your proposal, but, as you know, we never publish polemical works; this is a principle we have always applied, even during the Dreyfus Affair."[61]

Undaunted, Gyp showed up with another pamphlet two years later. *Le Coup de lapin* also concerned Action française. But the league, she insisted, "will remain in the wings."[62] Under these conditions, wouldn't the firm oblige? The illustrious publisher of literary classics had no reason to allow the elderly author to vent her hostility, and possibly attract a lawsuit, at the firm's expense. And the Affair had left the publisher with a feeling of instinctive vulnerability, as is evident in this reply: "I don't need to tell you how much we always wish to publish everything you write, but you know how timorous our firm is when dealing with a book in which living personalities can be found playing a role, even an unobtrusive one."[63] The publisher's verdict on Gyp's latest muckraking prose echoed that of Michel Calmann, who, when he had evaluated the author's anti-Semitic, anti-Orleanist dialogue-novel *Monsieur le duc* in 1893 declared: "Certainly, I shall not publish it."[64]

Published—and, in Gyp's view, "disgustingly sabotaged"[65]—by Flammarion, *Le Chambard: Roman d'aujourd'hui* (1928) and *Le Coup de lapin* (1929) did not cause a scandal, as Gyp feared, or hoped. Like many of her other novels inspired by political crises, they satirically depict what she knew best: the effects of these convulsions on "the rear"—the salons, the provinces, and elsewhere. The *chambard*, or upheaval, caused by Action française was related, in Gyp's view, to the broader social changes brought about by the war. Women smoking and sporting short dresses, clean-shaven men, and the craze for cars and boxing were, to Gyp, deplorable symptoms of a corrupt society easily seduced by Maurras' movement. In both novels, largely written in dialogue form, Gyp coupled the Action française affiliation of certain characters with a string of by now hackneyed signifiers: Jew, an intellectual (or a stupid person), ugly, effeminate, a snob, lower class (or nouveau riche), fat (or skinny), vulgar, a flashy dresser. This familiar and almost compulsive smearing was combined with glorified fictional evocations of Gyp's role in the Dreyfus Affair. Her tone was odd, at times inappropriate, perhaps befitting the woman who was still chasing devils from her own "belle époque."

Gyp's generic insults, however, were accompanied by forceful arguments against Action française, articulated by a chorus of sympathetic characters who all spoke for Gyp. Action française disserves the monarchy, one character in *Le Chambard* asserts: "The monarchy, for us, was Louis XIV," that of Maurras a blend of monarchist ideas with those of Auguste Comte, served up to "a flock of ignorant people."[66] The movement's cerebral tone and tepid outreach to workers, in another character's opinion, ensured that its promised coup would not succeed. As Gyp herself had learned from the various "failed revolutions" in which she had participated, "a pinch of writers and some bruises doesn't make a revolution nor even a coup. . . . For that, one must have men, and it is necessary also that the goal be popular."[67] Her preferred regime was still an empire, an authoritarian system brought to power through popular revolt, resting on broad popular support, and championing the nation. Unsurprisingly, Gyp was extremely hostile to communism. In the meantime, she would still accept an authoritarian republic. A Clemenceau would do, temporarily. But who, in her view, would be the new Boulanger or Déroulède?

After Gyp's pamphlets appeared, one appreciative reviewer predicted that her "excellent pages of historical chronicle will elicit throughout the country an immense burst of laughter."[68] Yet another, more typical, reviewer stated that "her jokes appear so tainted with bad faith that they don't make anyone laugh."[69] A third paper pronounced Gyp's *Coup de lapin* quite simply "worthless; this *Coup de lapin* is the coup de grâce that this characteristically useless 'novelist' is inflicting on herself."[70] Were meetings held at Action française headquarters, as the press reported, to decide whether to ignore or denounce Gyp's latest volleys?[71] The often violently polemical tone of Maurras' newspaper, in any event, remained relatively mute on this subject. In writing *Le Chambard*, the paper stated, Gyp had revealed only that she was boring, inept, and ignorant, not vicious. "Out of respect for the author," *L'Action française* chose to treat with "extreme sobriety" "this poor novel, which exudes boredom."[72] Apparently Gyp did not even deserve the movement's invective.

Souvenirs . . .

Gyp's public squabbles with Action française in the late 1920s formed a hiatus in her prolonged re-creation, in fact and fiction, of her childhood and young adulthood. Her past and present merged with visits from friends absent from her life for decades. One such guest was Louis Hubert Lyautey. Gyp had last seen the Nancy native turned marshal, war minister, and member of the Académie française when he was twelve and she seventeen. In her memory this architect of France's colonial policy was still, as she let him know, the baby wearing "a little frock with English embroidery and bows on its shoulders."[73] The illustrator Ferdinand Bac, Gyp's cohort from her *Vie Parisienne* days, also visited and sent gifts. In return, the once reluctant writer Bac had first seen darting into a cubicle in Marcelin's office expressed thanks to her "dear collabo" from his "old colleague."[74] Nostalgia often reigned in Gyp's salon, as it did in public talks she gave in the early 1920s on her Second Empire childhood.[75] Tiny, white-haired, and bonneted, she recounted anecdotes, recited poems, and acted out imaginary scenes. Audiences reportedly found her delightful, bizarre, perhaps even exotic, a quaint relic of an era of crinolines and clubmen, carriages and balls.[76]

Gyp's past increasingly inspired her writing, too. Nancy under the Second Empire is the setting for *Souricette* (1922), and Armande d'Ambérieux, one of Gyp's "boyish and devilish little girls, naïve and terrible, frank and audacious,"[77] is its heroine. The novel was among the last of the dozens of fictionalized versions of her childhood she elaborated throughout her long career. Her four volumes of written recollections, by contrast, allowed her to relate her childhood directly for the first time, without pretense of fiction. She had begun writing her *Souvenirs d'une petite fille* (*Recollections of a Little Girl*) as early as 1906, at the suggestion of Barrès, who knew his friend's storytelling talents. She would dedicate the work to his son, Philippe. Calmann-Lévy was impatient to publish Gyp's recollections and René Doumic was eager to serialize them in *La Revue des deux mondes*. But innumerable problems, large and small, delayed their appearance for twenty-one years: the upheaval caused by the war; Gyp's financial turmoil and crippling gout; her squabbles with Calmann-Lévy over the color of the book jacket;[78] and coordination of the book's publication with its serialization in Doumic's widely read *Revue*.[79]

But were these problems also alibis? Gyp's confessions to her publisher and to Barrès suggest that her unusually long delay in finishing the *Souvenirs* was symptomatic of the burden she felt in writing her life. "It's the *beginning* that's devilishly *difficult*,"[80] an exasperated Gyp complained to Barrès four years before her recollections were published. Her compositional problems were linked to those of memory. She had wanted to organize the *Souvenirs* chronologically, based on notes jotted down in the early 1900s. But, as she confided first to her publisher and then to her readers, that proved impossible "because they come back to life in my memory with incredible clarity, but without any order whatsoever."[81] The potential interest of her recollections—the idea that her work "will only seem amusing to a few Lorrainers"[82]—worried her, too. Who would read her "poor little recollections?"[83] During half a century of shamelessly dishing out dialogue-novels to anonymous, credible readers, this question had never concerned her. She had convinced herself she was giving the masses what they wanted. In producing her *Souvenirs*, however, she felt she was no longer plying her familiar trade as a writer ("which I abhor"),[84] no longer inventing, even writing. She was, rather, recording *reality* and, in the process, exposing herself. Indeed, she felt insulted when Barrès told her a draft of her *Souvenirs* seemed unrealistic and contrived. She retorted: "I thought, on the contrary, that truthfulness was my only merit. That I was a type of photographer whose talent (!) resided *solely* in knowing how to focus the lens," adding that "if these poor little things don't even seem real, they stop being the least bit interesting. It's only the narrative of impressions felt by a kid, a jumble of meager banalities."[85]

Gyp's self-deprecating tone belied the nervousness she must have felt in lowering many of her defenses and confronting her readers, her past, even herself. For "this obligation to recount," as she described her task on the opening page of the *Souvenirs*, "troubles and displeases me."[86] Writing her autobiography forced her to give up satire and polemic for confession (never a comfortable mode for her), to trade Gyp for Sibylle and Gabrielle. But this particular instance of "putting black on white" was also an opportunity for her. Relating *her* version of her past allowed her to shape her own story, to triumph, in a sense, over those who had made her obey as a girl—Marie, Gonneville, her teachers at Sacré-Coeur, and others. It enabled her to fulfill her childhood wish of becoming "strong . . . very strong."[87] This possibility, her promise to Barrès to complete the work and, of course, the potential for profit all compelled her to continue.

"Can the recollections of a little girl really hold any interest at all for others than the former little girl, who joyfully remembers the best years of her life? I think not."[88] This first sentence of the *Souvenirs* begins a type of page-long preface, set off from the remaining 250 pages of text. What is most revealing here is the fracturing of Gyp's autobiographical "I" into three personas whose identities separate and merge at various moments in the *Souvenirs*: Gyp the writer, grappling with the problems of writing; the "former little girl," happily remembering and also presumably recording these experiences with detachment; and the little girl who lived this past and gradually emerges as Gyp begins recounting anecdotes from her childhood.[89] Identity confusion, of course, was the essence of the woman (and "man") who was Sibylle, Gabrielle, the comtesse de Martel, and Gyp, among others.

As characteristic of Gyp as her presentation of multiple identities was her attempt to distance herself from her work by attributing it—as she had her earliest *Vie Parisienne* pieces to the "officer" from Nancy—to the "former little girl" who is the primary narrator. Throughout her career Gyp used this distancing strategy to compensate for her social and sexual vulnerability as a writer. At the end of her career, both her denigration of her *Souvenirs* and her sharing of responsibility for their "writing" with "another" also seemed to serve as psychological and emotional buffers against a childhood that was scarcely "joyous" and whose re-creation, for her, was problematic.

In the opening pages of the *Souvenirs*, Gyp blurs not only facets of her identity but also, often through choice of verb tense, related temporal levels. The narrator observes: "It seems to me that the clear simplicity of the impressions of a little girl whom life has not yet corrupted is very close to the clairvoyance of an old woman gradually detached from convention."[90] Gyp's bringing together in her *Souvenirs* of the little girl and the old woman, of her past and present, is again revealing of her personality. Even as an adult Gyp remained somehow childish. Her pranks, role-playing, slangy talk, and preference for child protagonists were essential to her public persona, but they also belie her unwillingness—or inability—to mature. The old woman Gyp was, to a certain extent, emotionally and psychologically still the little girl whose photograph she insisted be included as a frontispiece to the *Souvenirs*. And the closer she approached death, the more persistently Gyp associated herself with her representation of herself as a girl and with this girl's past.

The first volume of Gyp's *Souvenirs* appeared in 1927, both in book form and as a six-part series in *La Revue des deux mondes*. The author's evaluation of her latest work—"better than most Gyps"[91]—was typically understated. But nearly all her critics were laudatory. "Her chef-d'oeuvre,"[92] declared Lucien Corpechot, *Le Gaulois'* reviewer, comparing Gyp's storytelling and comic talents to those of Rabelais. Her lively, dialogue-rich style suited this series of vignettes from her first decade. And true to her prediction, at least one Lorrainer found her evocation of her Nancy childhood wonderful. "Do I need to tell you what delight an old Lorrainer finds in your recollections?"[93] Hubert Lyautey asked. He had read them, he let Gyp know, in an appropriate place, ensconced in his boyhood room in his father's house on the place Carrière, from which he had often observed Gyp's mother on horseback.

Gyp's *Souvenirs* sold well. Their author, after all, was famous—a prolific writer, journalist, playwright, caricaturist, political militant, and *personnalité* at the end of a long and often notorious life and career. And her ties, through birth and profession, to European aristocracy and to the Parisian worlds of letters, the arts, and politics, plus her well-known skill as a raconteur, enticed curious readers. So, too, did her resurrection of the "lost society"[94] of the Second Empire, enjoying twenty years of fragile peace in the face of growing German militarism—an image that may well have intrigued certain interwar readers as both alien and familiar.

In early 1928 Calmann-Lévy published the second, yellow-jacketed volume of Gyp's *Souvenirs d'une petite fille*. Chronologically it overlapped the first, covering the years 1849 to 1864. In the first volume Gyp had sketched her early childhood in Brittany and Lorraine, her memories of Marie and of Gonneville. In the second she recalled her brief contacts with her father—their trip to Frohsdorf, her paternal uncles, her father's death—as well as her childhood visits to Paris, her rebellious school days at Sacré-Coeur. This pendant volume was, according to its publisher, "a very great success" which had both "interested and charmed"[95] readers. The book seemed to reconcile the author with her publisher, who was "very proud"[96] to have helped produce these written recollections of what was in part a shared past. And "the feeling of very respectful friendship that we have had for so many years for you"[97] made her publisher hope that Gyp would soon provide a sequel.

Dedicated to her daughter "Nini, who baptized it,"[98] *Du temps des cheveux et des chevaux: Souvenirs du Second Empire* (*The Time of Hair and Horses: Recollections of the Second Empire*) was published in 1929, followed two years later by *La Joyeuse Enfance de la Troisième République* (*The Joyous Childhood of the Third Republic*).[99] *Les Annales politiques et littéraires* excerpted the first in 1927, and Calmann-Lévy's own *Revue de Paris* published portions of the second in 1931. As their titles indicate, Gyp shifted the focus in these two volumes, which span the years 1865 to 1880, from the intimate world of her childhood to the public—and specifically political—realm, to the "lifetimes" not of people but of regimes. She became just one among a cast of characters both observing and participating in contemporary political upheavals: the Franco-Prussian war and the Commune; the proclamation of the Third Republic; the Bazaine trial. While she also developed her reactions to some important events in her private life, such as Gonneville's death, she glossed over others completely. She barely mentioned her marriage to Roger, her reasons for leaving Nancy for Neuilly, or her decision to become a writer. Not surprisingly, these moments were for her either uncomfortable or unmemorable. This type of suppression, plus her merging of her story with the larger "story" of French history, again provided much-needed distance from the difficulties of her past. Nevertheless, readers and critics proved unanimously enthusiastic. Shortly after *La Joyeuse Enfance* appeared, Gérard d'Houville, in a front page article in *Le Figaro*, pronounced it "a resounding success."[100]

In late 1929 Gyp began work on a fifth volume of recollections to which she assigned the tentative title *Marianne s'amuse* (*Marianne Has a Good Time*).[101]

It was to cover the period from 1885 to the outbreak of World War I. Doumic had indicated interest in serializing it in *La Revue des deux mondes*. But Gyp refused to comply with his single directive that there be no mention of Boulangism or the Dreyfus Affair. Was it strategy, faltering memory, or her characteristic historical "amnesia" that made her minimize the importance of these national crises as "belonging to anecdotal history"?[102] As she asserted to her own publisher while trying to defend herself against Doumic, "[I]t's already far enough in the past for people to talk about it without passion and to consider only the picturesque side of things."[103] Had three decades erased Gyp's image of herself as a professional anti-Semite, intent on chasing all Jews from France in an effort to purify her nation? Despite Doumic's—and undoubtedly her publisher's—apprehension, she continued working on her revisionist history of the Third Republic, even hinting at undertaking a sixth volume, about World War I and its aftermath, "if I don't die before that."[104]

XIV

"Et Puis Après?..."

In late December 1930, eighty-one-year-old Gyp wrote to her publishers, as she had every year for the past half century, to wish them a happy new year. "It was a hundred years ago that the revolution of 1830 took place," she mused. "And I remember that when I was little, people around me talked about the July Days as one talks about the Armistice today. . . ."[1] A century earlier Gonneville had traveled by coach from Normandy to Poitiers, peering out at a boisterous crowd that was cheering the overthrow of one king and the ascension of another. In December 1930 it was not a king who had fallen but a cabinet. André Tardieu's government had survived neither the beginning of the international financial–economic crisis nor a domestic banking scandal that implicated at least one cabinet member. That same year French troops completed their evacuation of the Rhineland, as the government voted to authorize construction of a line of fortifications in northeastern France. Although the country was celebrating the centenary of the taking of Algeria, that same year in Indochina a military revolt by Annamite soldiers marked the beginning of an anticolonialist movement that signaled the eventual end of the French empire. Clearly, as Gyp may have reflected, the Third Republic's "joyous childhood" had ceded to its somber old age.

But at Gyp's home in Neuilly, from 1930 until her death two years later, there seemed an atmosphere of timelessness—charming to some, to others reeking of "*provincial boredom.*"[2] The fresh greenness of the lawn (under which a dozen dogs lay buried) contrasted with the house's faded yet sun-filled interior, with its bibelots, its "pretty yellow armchairs . . . numerous paintings . . . chandeliers.

Everything in colors that are a bit faded."[3] Cats and children roamed everywhere. Gyp herself was vividly captured in notes by one of her visitors, René Benjamin, a writer with close ties to Action française. He found Gyp in her salon one Sunday awaiting guests, a tiny, bonneted figure nestled in a large armchair, her knees covered by an imposing animal skin and sporting on her index finger a moonstone ring—"a bit like the actress," Benjamin observed, "who waits to see the effect she's made."[4] On another of his visits Gyp chatted animatedly for two hours to whoever would listen. Benjamin was among those intrigued by this "fairy-tale grandmother": "She is truly very amusing. Immobile with a brain constantly in motion. . . . She amuses others and herself. She's playful and droll. . . . *She's remained young*—and rejuvenates the others. *The hours pass* without notice. . . . An impression of *great charm*."[5] On his third visit a year later, however, Gyp felt too ill to leave her room. Visitors congregated in the salon for tea and cake, receiving bulletins from upstairs: Gyp refused to sit up in bed; she refused to eat; she was subsisting only on orange juice. In the absence of the salon's star, guests found little else to talk about: "[T]he talk revolves around Gyp, about how she is delightful and intolerable, impatient, impossible to care for. . . ."[6] With "a saddened amusement"[7] guests wandered through the house and into the garden, discussing the fact that "she might well die and we would never again see any of this."[8]

Gyp's children Nicole and Thierry were often to be found in Neuilly. Nicole, fifty-three years old in 1930, was her mother's main caretaker and her secretary. Gyp's once rebellious daughter, whose 1906 marriage Gyp scornfully claimed nearly bankrupted her, had become obedient—even submissive—exhibiting none of the fury Gyp had shown her own mother before her death. "[Nicole] cares for me admirably,"[9] Gyp declared in a letter her daughter dutifully transcribed. René Benjamin described Nicole far less glowingly: "Gyp's daughter, with her head-band, her dishwater-green dresses, doesn't seem very pleasant, doesn't look very nice."[10]

Benjamin found Thierry de Martel even more dislikable, even repellent. The man Benjamin saw arriving at Gyp's house one day in June 1931, accompanied by three Pekingese dogs and his new wife ("a bitch, covered with two silver foxes"),[11] was at that time consolidating his international reputation as France's premier neurosurgeon. Head surgeon of the American Hospital in Paris, he also traveled constantly to receive honors, attend international conferences, and watch colleagues operate at the Mayo Clinic and at Boston's Brigham Hospital. At the same time, he made notable advances in the use of local anesthesia in brain surgery. But these accomplishments did not impress Benjamin, whose attention was drawn to Thierry's face and mien—"with [his] bizarre cheekbones, [his] shifty expression"[12]—which frightened him. Equally alarming to Benjamin, as a practicing Catholic, was Thierry's apparently dispassionate directive (perhaps not surprising for a surgeon)—"pronounced . . . in a tone of perfect boredom, with no apparent trace of feeling,"[13]—to let his mother die in the interest of relieving her suffering.

Conscious of her declining health—but still "a bit like the actress who waits to see the effect she's made"—Gyp began to make her final exit. "I am not buried, but I am already dead or almost, and I have come to bid you adieu,"[14] she informed the anti–Action française priest who had been her correspondent in the late 1920s. And to her publisher that same year she wrote, in addition to the news that she had started work on a new book (*1930*): "Yesterday I was very ill. It was only a false departure. But I really believe it's the bell that announces the train."[15] A vicar from her church in Neuilly had been bringing her communion every month. Sometime in early 1932 she received last rites. A few days before Gyp's death, Nicole let another priest know that "my mother has fallen, this time for good, on 23 June,"[16] and that Nicole and Thierry had been with her since the twenty-fifth. Strangely, her doctors could find absolutely nothing wrong with her. She seemed to suffer, rather, from "a type of discouragement and depression."[17] She spent the days leading up to 28 June in bed, sipping orange juice and, according to Nicole, "calling for death with all her soul."[18]

Gyp's funeral, on 2 July, bore little resemblance to the modest event she had prescribed in her 1898 will. The large crowd that gathered at the Eglise Saint-Pierre-de-Neuilly was a microcosm of the different, overlapping worlds to which she belonged. There were relatives whose names indicated both their class and, in some cases, their profession: comte and comtesse de Montfort, général comte and comtesse de Viry, comte and comtesse de Casamajor, colonel comte de Froidefond, lieutenant de Bonneville. There were writers: André Maurois, Paul Morand, Fernand Gregh, the Tharaud brothers, André de Lorde, Paul Valéry. There were politicians of diverse allegiances: Alexandre Millerand and Gabriel Hanotaux represented the parliamentary politics of the Third Republic; Philippe Barrès, Jeanne Déroulède, and the duchesse d'Uzès stood for nationalist politics of the fin de siècle. Marshal Lyautey was present, as was the society portraitist Félix Gandéra, several prominent doctors, and members of both the Académie française and the Parisian *grand monde*. Gaston Calmann-Lévy also attended the funeral. Calmann's youngest son now headed the firm that fifty years earlier helped launch "Gyp" with *Petit Bob*. The former perpetrator of Gyp's "Semitic troubles" sent a bouquet of roses and received this reply: "From the bottom of our hearts, thank you on behalf of your old friend who so loved flowers and especially roses. Thank you infinitely, Thierry and Nicole."[19] The Mirabeau burial site Gyp had envisioned for herself now belonged to the Barrès family. She was buried instead under a simple gray granite cross in Neuilly, together with her husband, Roger, and her elder son Aymar "de Martel-Mirabeau," as his headstone reads.

"Gyp is dead." "Gyp is no longer." "A *grande dame* of letters . . . is dead."[20] Nearly all the Parisian dailies ran front-page articles on Gyp in the days following her death. And many reviews featured reminiscences by some of her numerous friends and acquaintances.[21] One of the most succinct yet perceptive and wry reflections was provided by Janet Flanner, an American journalist who covered interwar French society, politics, and culture for *The New Yorker* and wrote, like

Gyp, under an androgynous nom de plume: Genêt. Describing for her American readers the Parisian "event" that was Gyp's death, Flanner wrote:

> "Gyp" . . . is dead. Descendant of Mirabeau, pugnacious aristocrat, transplanted Bretonne, anti-Semite whose wicked wit helped skin Dreyfus alive, romancière old enough to have twice come back as a best seller in her life (once in '90 and again before the war) . . . "Gyp" saw and made history, detailing the fall of the polite Third Empire [*sic*] and the rise of the impolite modern generation with its uncorseted *jeunes filles* and its divorcing duchesses. . . . She was a trenchant conversationalist, no prude, despised the tepid mind, hated fakes, fatuousness, and, on the whole, the Third Republic, under which she died.[22]

All the obituaries touched on parts of Flanner's vivid sketch. Yet their tones ranged from laudatory to spiteful: Gyp, even after death, continued to polarize. Most remembered her as a prolific, successful writer. The writer whose works were for Octave Mirbeau a dung heap and for Ezra Pound "unreadable . . . a sort of ladylike slither about sex,"[23] was praised post mortem by the British critic George Saintsbury as "worthy of the best times of French literature for gaiety, satire, acuteness and style. . . ."[24] Others remembered Gyp the writer as a dialogue-novelist who fused novel and drama, creating, as Gérard d'Houville put it, "a novel on the stage."[25] These were chatty novels, quickly produced, quickly read: "No popular French writer," Flanner observed, "ever covered so much time or took so little trouble about it. . . ."[26] Gyp was the progenitor of enfants terribles male and female: of Petit Bob, the fin-de-siècle aristocratic Gavroche, blasé child–hero of novels for grownups; and of Paulette, Loulou, Chiffon, Bijou, Friquet, Napoléonette, and dozens of other young aristocratic heroines (and unwitting models), both independent and submissive, rebellious and reactionary, like Gyp herself. She was also remembered as a "psychological novelist" who exposed the souls, in Gérard d'Houville's words, of "young women in love, deceived, passionate, miserable";[27] a practitioner of what Louis-Ferdinand Céline, another right-wing anarchist from Gyp's stock, would mockingly refer to as "high psychological literature, 'know what I mean!'"[28] Finally, she was viewed as a chronicler and satirist, a malicious observer of her own milieu and her times: "In the period 1882–1910," the *New York Times* obituary stated, " 'Gyp' was a favorite with American readers of French novels. Her very Parisian characters . . . were types of a gay, witty, unpuritanical society, all created by her in a sparkling dialogue and with piquant satire."[29] Again, Flanner assessed Gyp's value as a chronicler more tersely—and correctly: "Much of what she wrote will be immediately discarded. Some of it will be permanent, a calender of customs to be consulted in the future. . . ."[30]

And yet, despite this public acknowledgement of her importance as a writer, Gyp had asserted the following in 1908:"What I insist on making explicitly clear for posterity is that I took no pleasure in writing."[31]

Many considered Gyp's writing, and indeed Gyp herself, an emblem of the early Third Republic. "Society under the Third Republic, such might be the general title of Gyp's oeuvre,''[32] one journalist declared. For the literary critic Albert Thibaudet, in a not entirely complimentary reflection on ''the good countess'' in *La Nouvelle Revue française*, ''Third Republic'' described not only the content of Gyp's writing but also its style, ''with all its passing and passé brilliance. . . .''[33] For a journalist from *Le Journal des débats* ''Gyp remains [fixed] in history around the time of the 1889 World's Fair and Boulangism.''[34] To another journalist Gyp was terribly ''1900'': ''People awaited her latest novel [as they awaited] Willy's latest pun, Boni de Castellane's latest frock coat. . . . Her ideas, like her writing, wear the color of a bygone era—there is, in them, Art Nouveau arabesques, outdated Lalique . . . an odor of ylang-ylang . . . a glimmer of furs, of mutton-chop sleeves, of phaetons driven by coachmen with mutton-chop whiskers.''[35] In Céline's view the prewar period was quite simply ''the era of Gyp.''[36]

And yet to a journalist from *La Volonté* ''no one in the world lived more outside her time [than she did].''[37]

For many of Gyp's necrologists her fame as a *''grande dame* of letters''—as well as an illustrator, dramatist, journalist, *salonnière*, society figure, memorialist, storyteller, great-grand-niece of Mirabeau, and mother of an eminent surgeon— was obscured by her political militancy. She was still, in the memory of many, the ''grotesque shrew''[38] of Boulangism and the Dreyfus Affair. She had ''perfected'' a new genre: the anti-Semitic novel. And she was unrepentant. When the *Carnets de Schwartzkoppen*, which seemed definitively to incriminate Esterhazy and exonerate Dreyfus, were published in 1930, several former anti-Dreyfusards, including Gyp, were asked to admit their error. Gyp refused. ''And yet,'' one journalist ironically reminded his readers, ''[she] was a good Christian.''[39]

Gyp's case exemplifies the new nationalist formula of the late nineteenth century—authoritarian, populist, anti-Semitic, drawing strength from both Right and Left—which resurfaced, in modified form, between the two world wars. It was Gyp's class and eclectic political background that partly conditioned her reaction against the grounding of a liberal and democratic bourgeois republic, led to her defense of traditional institutions as bulwarks against social decay, and explained her attraction to a certain type of ambiguous populism—all features of this revolutionary Right. And it was her complex relation to her gender that channeled itself, to a certain extent, into both a call for a strong, male authority and, at the same time, a vindication of the rights of the oppressed *against* such authority— again features of this Right. Hadn't she, when questioned in a survey, listed her favorite heroes as ''the strong''?[40] But wasn't she also, according to Gérard d'Houville and others, the champion of the powerless, of children, youth, and women?[41] Was she a precursor or an atavist?

The same question can be asked about Gyp as a woman. At the time of her death, some continued to laud her as a feminist. ''[W]hat she wanted for women,'' Gérard d'Houville asserted, ''was sincerity, physical and moral activity, intellectual health, the abolition of outdated conventions and prejudices. . . .''[42] But if she did indeed denounce such ''conventions and prejudices''—the corset, arranged marriages—she also denounced womanhood. Indeed, as early as 1883 at least one astute reviewer had already begun to brand some of her literary depictions as "the cruelest indictment ever leveled against women."[43] Gyp's reluctant "feminism," her antifeminist feminism, resembled her anti-Semitism, anti-Republicanism, and other creative hatreds that guided her life and work. All these credos rested on an esthetic of rejection—a gigantic "so what?"—born of Gyp's own self-loathing.

After his mother's death, Thierry de Martel continued to pursue extremist politics in the circles of *Gringoire* and *Candide*, the two mass-circulation dailies of the radical Right. In a July 1940 article *Candide* referred to him as "our faithful collaborator."[44] Antiparliamentary, antisocialist, anticommunist, violently anti-Semitic, *Candide* soon welcomed marshal Pétain as a savior. These papers asserted that France's real enemies lay not across the Rhine but within its own borders. "Better Hitler than Blum," they argued, echoing a similar cry—"Better Bismarck than Blanqui"—that had marked the Third Republic's beginnings.

With the declarations of war in September 1939, Thierry's professional duties intensified. As in World War I, most of his cases were skull and brain injuries, and attempted suicides. Until late May 1940 he was optimistic that a German attack would be beaten back, writing to a colleague that "we must bear this with dignity and detachment, and I am still convinced that victory will belong to the spiritual forces."[45] To André Maurois, who had just witnessed the panicked retreat of French troops from Belgium in May 1940, he retorted: "We'll stop them at the Seine, and it will be even more beautiful than the Marne."[46] Despite his almost mystical faith in the *furia francese*, however, he bitterly criticized the government's seeming inability to lead France out of crisis.

But with the apocalyptic events of late May and early June 1940, Thierry's belief that French élan would overcome German military might evaporated. As German troops marched toward Paris, he assigned his staff to other hospitals farther south and sent his wife to Bordeaux as part of a mass exodus from the capital. When he learned that Paris would not be defended, he asked American Ambassador William Bullitt for permission to leave his post at the American Hospital. Bullitt refused.

The day before the German invasion of the capital, Thierry left several suicide notes. To William Bullitt he wrote: "I promised you not to leave Paris. I didn't tell you whether I would remain here dead or alive. If I stayed here alive, I would be giving a blank check to my enemy. If I stay here dead, it's a canceled check I give him. Adieu."[47] He was found at home on 14 June, one of about fifteen Parisians, including the mayor of Clichy, known to have killed themselves in the panic of the invasion.

The few newspapers that succeeded in reporting Thierry's death hailed it as an act of patriotism, a type of hara-kiri, motivated by "a certain idea of France." Yet one cannot help but wonder to which geographic and symbolic location this "certain idea of France" would have led him had he lived: London or Vichy? To many who had known him, he had been a Resistant before the fact—the passive hero of the Resistance, to the writer Jean Paulhan, and de Gaulle the active one.[48] A colleague declared flatly that had Thierry not committed suicide, "he would have done everything possible to reach London and to be among the first faithful to rally to de Gaulle."[49] In that event, Thierry would have joined others who had veered from the monarchist Right to organized resistance: Emmanuel d'Astier de la Vigerie, Philippe Barrès, and Thierry's political mentor, Georges Valois, whose Resistance activities led to his internment and death in Bergen-Belsen.

But might not Thierry, on the other hand, have joined his admirer Drieu la Rochelle and others he had known in the circles of Le Faisceau and *Candide* in doing the Nazis' bidding? Thierry loathed the "idiot Jacobins"[50] of the Third Republic. In his view they had emasculated France. And he was not immune to anti-Semitic rhetoric. It was part of his mother's legacy.

Notes

Introduction

1. "Le jour même où Paris fut occupé, le Docteur de Martel, gloire chirurgicale française, s'est tué d'une piqûre de strychnine," *Paris-Soir*, 17 July 1940, 1.

2. Thierry de Martel, letter to Dr. Charles Lucas, 7 Feb. 1940, Dr. Charles Lucas collection, Paris.

3. "La Fin antique de Thierry de Martel," n.p., n.d.

4. "la brillante femme de lettres célèbre sous le nom de Gyp." Georges Menegaux, "Thierry de Martel, 1875–1940," Académie de Chirurgie, Paris, 21 Jan. 1953 (Paris: Masson, n.d.), 3. All translations are mine unless otherwise indicated.

5. "La Fin antique de Thierry de Martel."

6. "une âme partisane, sans justice et sans charité." Menegaux, 7.

7. "une ordure." Octave Mirbeau, "La Littérature en justice," *La France*, 24 Dec. 1884, 2.

8. Ezra Pound, "Pastiche: The Regional," *The New Age*, 7 Aug. 1919, 252.

9. Henry James, "Preface," *The Awkward Age* (New York: Scribner's, 1908), xii.

10. Charles Maurras, "Les Images puissantes: *Un ménage dernier cri,*" *La Gazette de France*, 9 Aug. 1903, 1–2.

11. "le centre féminin du nationalisme." Philippe Barrès, "Gyp, ou la féerie," *Les Nouvelles littéraires*, 9 July 1932, 2.

12. A pamphlet circulating during the Revolution bore the title "Indécence inouïe du vicomte de Mirabeau et de l'abbé Maury envers la nation."

13. See India, "Esquisses féminines: Gyp," *La Libre Parole Illustrée*, 24 Feb. 1894, 3.

14. "Walkyrie buveuse du sang humain." Laurent Tailhade, "Lettre casquée—Sermo Galeatus—à Gyp—comtesse de Mirabeau-Martel—Gyp," *L'Action*, 10 Dec. 1903, 1–2.

15. "Elle griffe, elle mord . . . [Elle] fait la guerre." Abel Hermant, "L'Ennemie du ridicule: Défense de la langue française," *Le Temps*, 24 Sept. 1918, 00.

16. The concept of a "revolutionary Right" is developed by Zeev Sternhell in *La Droite révolutionnaire, 1885–1914: Les Origines françaises du fascisme* (Paris: Seuil, 1978).

17. "Mesdames les féministes, les sportives, les écrivains, vous devez beaucoup à Gyp." Gérard d'Houville, "Gyp, théâtre vivant," *Le Figaro*, 11 July 1932, 5.

18. Barbara Tuchman, "Biography as a Prism of History," *Telling Lives: The Biographer's Art*, ed. Marc Pachter (Philadelphia: U of Pennsylvania P, 1981), 133–47.

19. "Cette femme . . . a quelque chose de malsainement tentateur." Edmond and Jules de Goncourt, *Journal: Mémoires de la vie littéraire*, vol. 3 (1887–1896), ed. Robert Ricatte (Paris: Laffont, 1989), 1204.

Chapter I

1. "l'an Mil huit Cent quarante neuf, le dix sept août à neuf heures du Matin . . . est comparu arroudel joseph Requitie Comt de Mirabeau, propretair âgé de vingt-huit ans, demeurant au Chathaux de Coëtsal en cette commune, Lequel nous a présenté un enfant du sexe féminin née hier à onze heures du Matin au dit Chathaux de Coëtsal, de lui déclarant, et de Marie Le Harivel de Gonneville, son épouse, . . . âgée de vingt-deux ans, et auquel il a déclaré vouloir donner les prénoms de Sibille émée marie antoinette. . . . " Birth certificate, Sibille de Mirabeau, 17 Aug. 1849, ADMorbihan.

2. "le nom de Gabrielle oublié soit ajouté, que l'on écrive Arundel au lieu d'Arroudel, Riquetti au lieu de Requitie, Comte au lieu de Comt, Aimée au lieu d'émée." "Jugement de rectification de l'acte de naissance de la demoiselle de Mirabeau," 26 May 1853, ADMorbihan.

3. It is impossible to know in which order these first names were given. While the rectified birth certificate names the infant Sibille Aimée Marie Antoinette Gabrielle, one finds later references to Gabrielle-Sibylle-Aimée-Marie-Antoinette and to Sybille-Gabrielle-Aimée-Marie-Antoinette. The spelling of these names is also elusive. The "Sibille" of the birth certificate has become "Sibylle" in the *Souvenirs*, yet mentions of "Sybille" are also common. I have adopted Sibylle's own spelling of her name in the *Souvenirs*, which is the one most commonly employed in secondary sources about her.

4. This date corresponds to the one mentioned on his marriage certificate, although according to Sibylle Arundel was born on 21 December 1820, in the château of Coëtsal. Marriage certificate of Arundel de Mirabeau and Marie Le Harivel de Gonneville, 30 Oct. 1848, ADMeurthe-et-Moselle.

5. Legitimism is the term used after 1830 to distinguish those partisans of the "legitimate" (i.e. Bourbon) monarchy from those supporting the younger Orléans branch. The Legitimists' ideological lineage can be traced back to counterrevolutionaries such as Tonneau, who were fanatic partisans of the absolute monarchy, and precursors of the Restoration ultraroyalists. The latter refused to accept the Restoration Charter, which they considered an unacceptable compromise between Revolution and Restoration (in its establishment of religious freedom, for example). Intransigence characterized the counterrevolutionaries, *ultras*, and Legitimists. See René Rémond, *Les Droites en France* (Paris: Aubier Montaigne, 1982), esp. 46–83.

6. "une charmante figure, des yeux clairs, des cheveux châtains et de jolies moustaches blondes et légères." Gyp, *Souvenirs d'une petite fille* (Paris: Calmann-Lévy, 1928), vol. 2, 4.

7. Ibid., 24.

8. "[Ils] avaient poussé à la diable . . . sans surveillance et sans éducation." Ibid., 3.

9. "la lande désolée et charmante, et la mer verte du Morbihan, qui sont restées plus que tout présentes à mes yeux." Gyp, *Souvenirs*, vol. 1, 2.

10. See Gyp, letter to Maurice Barrès, 28 [?] 1921, #125, MB.

11. Quoted in Marvin L. Brown, *The Comte de Chambord: The Third Republic's Uncompromising King* (Durham, NC: Duke UP, 1967), 77.

12. "le 30 septembre 1860, à six heures et demie du matin, les tirailleurs de Mirabeau et de Bessey se trouvaient ensemble de garde à l'Artillerie, et voulant vérifier leurs armes (ces deux militaires étant tous deux armés de Pistolets dits revolvers) l'arme de de Bessey fit feu par inadvertance, et le coup blessa mortellement de Mirabeau, qui mourut à l'instant, ayant été frappé par la balle à la tête." Death certificate of Arundel de Mirabeau, 15 Nov. 1860, ADMeurthe-et-Moselle.

13. Gyp, *Souvenirs*, vol. 2, 79.

14. "[E]tre tué à la guerre me semblait normal et prévu, et c'était, à mes yeux, la plus belle de toutes les morts." Ibid., 78.

15. "de beaux cheveux châtain clair, épais et soyeux, qu'elle porte en bandeaux; les épaules larges, la taille exagérément fine. Ses mains sont grandes, mais superbes, de vraies mains de statue. Son physique est plutôt commun, mais son air est distingué." Gyp, *Souvenirs*, vol. 1, 15.

16. "Pour cette fois-ci, y a rien à faire, mais plus tard, quand on voudra me faire des choses comme ça, je me défendrai . . . Je veux devenir forte . . . très forte . . . " Ibid., 86. Ellipses in original.

17. "Mon grand-père a tenu dans ma vie la première et la meilleure place. Il est ce que j'ai le plus complètement et le mieux aimé. Son influence sur moi a été profonde. Je lui dois ce que j'ai eu de bon. Son souvenir est lumineux et pur sans une tache." Will of Gabrielle de Mirabeau-Martel, 2 March 1898, Sibylle Gaudry collection, Paris.

18. "C'est entre ce Napoléon et ces batailles que j'ai vécu jusqu'à seize ans." Gyp, *Souvenirs*, vol. 1, 5.

19. Quoted in General Baron Ambert, "Portrait militaire: le colonel de Gonneville," preface to Aymard Le Harivel de Gonneville, *Souvenirs militaires du colonel de Gonneville*, ed. Marie de Mirabeau (Paris: Perrin, 1895), vii.

20. Gonneville's military career can be pieced together from military archives and his *Souvenirs militaires*, which provide detailed accounts of the Napoleonic campaigns. He speaks little of his reactions to the events in which he is participating, nor does he refer to his private life. He does not mention that in 1810, between campaigns, he married his first cousin, Agathe le Pailleur de Langle. Her death in 1816 preceded those of his infant son (1819), father (1821), daughter (1822), and mother (1823). Despite such tragedy, on 10 August 1825, in accordance with military protocol, Gonneville presented his request to marry to the minister of war. A week later, forty-one-year-old Gonneville wed Antoinette Françoise Sophie Fourrier de Bacourt, fifteen years his junior, in Nancy.

21. "un de nos meilleurs officiers de cavalerie . . . un officier de la première distinction." "Etat des services, campagnes et blessures de M. Le Harivel de Gonneville," [?] June 1816, Dossier Aymard Le Harivel de Gonneville, AA.

22. Gonneville, *Souvenirs militaires*, 319.

23. "Rapport fait au Ministre [de la Guerre]," 9 [July?] 1815, Dossier Aymard Le Harivel de Gonneville, AA.

24. Ibid., 30 July 1816.

25. Gonneville, *Souvenirs militaires*, 376.

26. "Rien ne m'a jamais paru aussi hideux qu'une émeute populaire." Ibid., 374.

27. "la dame qui a fait les livres à dos rouges qui sont dans la bibliothèque de Petite mère." Gyp, *Souvenirs*, vol. 1, 59.

28. General Ambert, preface to Gonneville, *Souvenirs militaires*, v.

29. Gyp, *Souvenirs*, vol. 1, 7.

30. "les jolies mains, c'est Grand'mère; les grosses moustaches, c'est Grand-père . . . C'est d'ailleurs lui que je connaissais déjà le mieux." Ibid. Ellipses in original.

31. "Grand-père me semble tout bonnement magnifique. Je ne vois que sa très haute taille, sa tournure élégante, ses yeux bleus, et sa distinction extrême. Je ne remarque pas que ses lèvres trop grosses déparent sa belle figure. Je le trouve admirable, je le dévore des yeux, et c'est lui qui, dès cet instant, domine et dominera toute ma vie." Ibid., 16–17.

32. "J'ai adoré sauvagement et tendrement mon grand-père, et c'était pourtant le seul de mes parents que je craignais." Gyp, "Pour la guerre! . . . ," *Gil Blas*, 4 Dec. 1903, 1.

33. "Je connais peu de gens dont l'esprit puisse être comparé à celui de M. de Bacourt, et je n'en ai *jamais* rencontré de plus honnête." Quoted in Alfred Dumaine, "Adolphe de Bacourt, un diplomate de la Monarchie de Juillet," *La Revue d'histoire diplomatique*, April–June and July–Sept. 1928, 11.

34. See André Billy, "Du cachet de Stendhal et des débuts de Gyp," *Le Figaro littéraire*, 18 June 1955, 2.

35. Gyp, *Souvenirs*, vol. 1, 193-94.

36. Ibid., 42.

37. Louis-Philippe's father, "Philippe Egalité," committed to Revolutionary principles, had been among those Convention deputies voting in favor of his cousin Louis XVI's death in 1792.

38. Eugen Weber, "France," in *The European Right: A Historical Profile*, ed. Hans Rogger and Eugen Weber (Berkeley: U of California P, 1966), 92.

39. Rémond, 76.

40. See the introduction, note 12, in this book.

41. "[I]l monte à la tribune en même temps que lui [Mirabeau] et l'écrase de sa corpulence. Ce n'est qu'après une longue discussion qu'il cède la place à Mirabeau." F.-A. Aulard, "Un humoriste à l'Assemblée Constituante: Mirabeau-Tonneau," *La Nouvelle Revue* 6 (1880): 797.

42. "Puisque le roi renonce à son royaume, un gentilhomme n'a plus besoin d'épée pour le défendre." Quoted in Aulard, 798.

43. The marquis de Toustain, an émigré who joined Tonneau's legion, provides another description of Mirabeau-Tonneau in his *Mémoires du marquis de Toustain, 1790–1823* (Paris: Plon, 1933), 15–16.

44. "un mauvais garçon adorable et plein d'esprit." Quoted in P.L., "Souvenirs d'une visite chez Gyp dans sa maison de Neuilly," *La Gazette de France*, n.d.

45. "un scélérat achevé, et qu'il fallait soustraire au souvenir des humains." Quoted in Guy Chaussinand-Nogaret, *Mirabeau* (Paris: Seuil, 1982), 23.

46. "ta fille . . . me fait si peu l'effet d'être une fille . . ." Gyp, *Souvenirs*, vol. 2, 25. Ellipses in original.

47. "Cette petite a tous les goûts d'un garçon! . . . Elle ne joue qu'avec des soldats, n'aime que les choses violentes . . ." Ibid., vol. 1, 48. Ellipses in original.

48. "Je compris que, en route, Grand-père et lui avaient parlé de ce que j'étais pas un garçon! . . . C'est un reproche qu'on me fait souvent, de n'être pas un garçon! . . . Et personne, bien sûr, ne le regrette autant que moi! . . . " Ibid., 113. Ellipses in original.

Chapter II

1. This was the population in 1869. See René Taveneaux, *Histoire de Nancy* (Toulouse: Privat, 1978), 343–70.

2. In a letter to Maurice Barrès, Sibylle would recall Nancy's Jewish ghetto: "[E]verything situated between the marketplace, the cavalry district, and the prison was more or less *Jewish*. The rue de l'Equitation, the only one that had chains (unfastened) in my day, was *exclusively* Jewish. Christians didn't live there. . . . " "[C]e qui était compris entre le marché, le quartier de cavalerie, et la prison, était *Juif* plus ou moins. La rue de l'Equitation, la seule qui avait des chaînes (non fermées) de mon temps, était *seulement* Juive. Des chrétiens n'y habitaient pas. . . . " Gyp, letter to Maurice Barrès, 25 May [1917?], MB.

3. Gyp, *Du temps des cheveux et des chevaux: Souvenirs du Second Empire* (Paris: Calmann-Lévy, 1929), 11.

4. Ibid., 26.

5. "[sa] monomanie des têtes couronnées." Gyp, *Souvenirs d'une petite fille* (Paris: Calmann-Lévy, 1928), vol. 2, 14.

6. "[était] brouillée avec la moitié de la ville. . . ." Ibid., 184.

7. "femmes un peu peintes." Gyp, *Du temps des cheveux et des chevaux*, 98.

8. Badinguet was the name of the mason whose clothes Louis-Napoleon reputedly borrowed to disguise himself during his 1846 escape from the fortress of Ham, six years after his attempted coup d'état in Boulogne. Political enemies of Napoleon III adopted the sobriquet when deriding the former conspirator turned emperor.

9. "Elle a poussé comme un champignon étrange et baroque dans une famille dévouée uniquement aux Bourbons . . . " Gyp, *Souvenirs*, vol. 2, 71. Ellipses in original.

10. "un petit tas amorphe." Ibid., 244.

11. "cocasse . . . et cauchemardante à la fois." Ibid., 53.

12. "le plus brave garçon qui soit." Ibid., 52.

13. Ibid., 4.

14. "quinteux, injuste, bourru et très bon." Ibid., 220.

15. "[t]out petit, mais solide, bâti en force, avec des petits yeux foncés et brillants, un nez immense et une bouche moqueuse." Ibid., 215.

16. Ibid., 4.

17. "très bon, très charmant et infiniment séduisant." Gyp, "La Société sous le Second Empire: Ceux que j'ai connus," Paris, 27 Nov. 1923, in *Conférencia* 3, 15 Jan. 1924, 118.

18. Ibid., 116.

19. "fourmillante cité, cité pleine de rêves" Charles Baudelaire, *The Flowers of Evil,* trans. Roy Campbell, ed. Mathiel and Jackson Mathews (New York: New Directions, 1963), 111.

20. "du plaisir à perdre haleine." Jacques Offenbach, *La Vie parisienne.*

21. "[c]e défilé était ravissant. Les voitures [étaient] bien attelées, les toilettes [étaient] un peu cachées en hiver par des cascades de fourrures qui couvraient les genoux et s'étalaient en grosses vagues dans les victorias et les calèches. . . En été, les robes débordaient légères comme des nuages." Gyp, *Du temps des cheveux et des chevaux*, 107–8.

22. "ce qu'il y avait de plus joli et de plus complètement chic." Gyp, *Souvenirs*, vol. 2, 265.

23. "Inconsciemment, j'ai aimé un gouvernement qui faisait la vie facile et gaie, et qui a donné pendant vingt ans à la France pas mal de gloire et beaucoup de bonheur." Gyp, "La société sous le Second Empire: Ceux que j'ai connus," 114.

24. "Instruction religieuse: Bien; Ecriture: Malpropre, pas soignée; Arithmétique: Ne la comprend pas; Grammaire française: Ne l'apprend pas; Style: Négligé; Géographie: Ne la sait jamais."Gyp, *Souvenirs*, vol. 2, 149.

25. "J'étais religieuse sans être pieuse. . . . Mais j'avais une inébranlable foi, la conviction absolue que ma religion était la meilleure, et la résolution formelle de ne jamais la fronder. J'étais catholique comme j'étais Française, passionnément et immuablement." Ibid., 337.

26. Octave Feuillet, *Histoire de Sibylle* (Paris: M. Lévy frères, 1863).

27. "Il faut lui ôter définitivement son nom de Sibylle . . . Elle devient trop laide pour s'appeler comme ça . . . !" Ibid., 309. Ellipses in original.

28. Jean-Jacques Rousseau, *Julie ou la nouvelle Héloïse*, ed. Michel Launay (Paris: Garnier-Flammarion, 1967), 4.

29. "Pascal et moi nous sommes tout à fait d'accord . . ." Gyp, *Souvenirs d'une petite fille* (Paris: Calmann-Lévy, 1928), vol. 1, 251. Ellipses in original.

30. In her Société des gens de lettres dossier, the comtesse de Mirabeau is listed as a *pensionnaire* who presumably received a small pension as an officer's widow.

31. "le goût et l'habitude du travail." Comtesse de Mirabeau, letter to Monsignor Dupanloup, 29 April 1869, Naf 24699, #152–53, BN.

32. See James F. McMillan, *Housewife or Harlot? The Place of Women in French Society, 1870–1914* (New York: St. Martin's Press, 1981), especially chapter 1.

33. According to a study of 616 writers active between 1865 and 1905, only 2 percent were women, and most of these specialized in children's literature or autobiography. It is possible, however, that many writers presumed men were actually women writing under male pseudonyms. See Rémy Ponton, "Le Champ littéraire en France de 1865 à 1905," Ph.D. diss., Ecole de Hautes Etudes en Sciences Sociales, Paris, 1977.

34. Quoted in Béatrice Slama, "Femmes écrivains," in *Misérable et glorieuse: La Femme du XIXe siècle*, ed., Jean-Paul Aron (Brussels: Editions Complexe, 1984), 222.

35. See Anne-Marie Thiesse, *Le Roman du quotidien: Lecteurs et lectures populaires à la Belle Epoque* (Paris: Chemin Vert, 1984), 196.

36. *Histoire des deux héritières* (Paris: Michel Lévy frères, 1864); *Veillées normandes* (Paris: Putois-Cretté, 1867; in the "Lectures morales et littéraires" collection); *Hélène de Gardannes (Un caprice)*, published successively by E. Maillet and Pierre-Paul Didier in 1868 and 1877; and *Le Baron d'Aché*, again published by Maillet and then by Didier in 1869 and 1877, respectively.

37. *Les Jeunes Filles pauvres*; *Le Passé et l'avenir*; *Le Revenant de Mériadec*; *Marguerite d'Erigny*, published in Paris, first by Dupray de la Mahérie in 1863, then by E. Dentu in 1866.

38. Comtesse de Mirabeau, letter to père Lagrange, 30 March 1869, Naf 13337, #281–82, BN.

39. "[S]i Monseigneur d'Orléans ne me trouve pas indigne d'écrire pour la Sainte Cause, ma plume y sera consacrée. Veuillez dire à sa Grandeur que je suis la nièce . . . de Monsieur de Bacourt auquel il accordait son amitié. J'invoque ce cher souvenir dans l'espérance que Monseigneur accueillera ma supplique avec plus d'indulgence." Ibid.

40. "sa Sainte Bénédiction qui portera bonheur à ma fille." Comtesse de Mirabeau, letter to père Lagrange, 24 April 1869, Naf 13337, #285–86, BN.

41. Comtesse de Mirabeau, letter to père Lagrange, 29 April 1869, Naf 24699, #152–53, BN.

42. "[qui] a protégé mon oeuvre comme lui-même m'a protégée. . . . " Ibid.

43. "Madame de Mirabeau écrit facilement, avec élégance même, et . . . elle pourra

se faire une place favorable dans le monde des lettres le jour où elle aura acquis un peu plus d'expérience." Alfred des Essarts, letter to the Société des gens de lettres, SGL dossier 454AP288, AN.

44. "à peu près les seuls jeunes gens chics de Nancy." Gabrielle Mirabeau-Martel, letter to Maurice Barrès, [?] June 1923, #132, MB.

45. "[L]es enfants élevés seuls au milieu des grandes personnes ont généralement l'oeil pointu. Je ne crois pas avoir été une exception. Les enfants voient des tas de choses desquelles ils ne parlent jamais, et ils réfléchissent—inconsciemment—beaucoup." Ibid.

46. "fourrée dans le taillis aussi avant que j'avais pu." Ibid.

47. "J'étais tellement bouleversée que j'avais les jambes en coton." Ibid.

48. "[J]'étais effroyablement révoltée, et dégoûtée, et presque malade. Moi, qui avais un appétit terrifiant d'ordinaire, je n'ai pas pu déjeuner. . . ." Ibid. Ellipses in original.

49. "*l'amour*, dont mes grandes cousines et leurs amies parlaient devant moi en levant leurs yeux au ciel et avec des airs penchés et prétentieux faisait faire de biens vilaines choses." Ibid.

50. "c'est presque toujours l'histoire de Liverdun qui s'est immuablement répétée." Ibid.

51. "regrettant le mal qu'il fait—quand il en fait—et se faisant des cheveux quand il est trompé, parce qu'il en a tout bêtement du chagrin et, dans tous les cas, cherchant à faire valoir, à grandir et à auréoler aux yeux des autres, la femme qu'il aime." Ibid.

52. "retenue, calculatrice, adroite, habile toujours . . . et se faisant, quand elle est trompée, une bile terrible, non par chagrin, mais *par vanité*." Ibid.

53. "la première rosserie féminine." Ibid.

54. "[Ç]a m'a été *horrible*. Je ne soupçonnais pas le cynisme, ni l'effronterie, ni rien de ce qui m'est apparu ce jour-là, en me laissant une impression d'amertume et du dégoût." Ibid.

55. "Quand, du matin au soir, on répète à une fille de seize ans, qui n'est nullement disposée à se gober, qu'elle est laide, disgracieuse, maladroite et agaçante à voir, il est impossible qu'elle n'admette pas que c'est presque la vérité." Gyp, *Du temps des cheveux et des chevaux*, 12.

56. "Agile, strong, supple, astonishingly well built, I would have 'made it' in a circus much better than in a salon." ("Agile, forte, souple, étonnamment découplée, j'aurais 'réussi' dans un cirque beaucoup mieux que dans un salon.") Ibid.

57. "aux traits heurtés et hommasses, aux yeux pétillants de malice, qui se coiffe comme une concierge et s'habille on ne sait comment et d'on ne sait quoi. . . ." Gyp, *Souvenirs*, vol. 1, 207.

58. "vêtements, linge, . . . bijoux, et autres objets." Marriage contract, Monsieur le comte et Madame la comtesse de Martel de Janville, 30 Nov. 1869, Notarial Archives, AN.

59. "Du jour au lendemain je passai au rang de vedette." Gyp, *Du temps des cheveux et des chevaux*, 10.

60. Ibid., 7–8.

61. "La pensée qu'un monsieur aurait le droit d'entrer chez moi à toute heure, de tournailler comme chez lui, de me parler, et qu'il me faudrait le tolérer, lui répondre et paraître enchantée de le voir là, me donnait le frisson." Ibid., 8–9.

62. Ibid., 48.

63. "superbe. [T]rès grand, bâti en force, avec de magnifiques yeux et des cils énormes. Il avait l'air distingué et bon. C'était, dans toute sa pureté, le beau type du Français de l'Ouest." Ibid., 49.

64. Official records describe the Martel de Janville family as "very distinguished and rightfully well esteemed in its region, where it owns much property" ("très distinguée et justement considérée dans son pays, où elle possède beaucoup de biens"). Etat nominatif pour les grades de Lieutenant et Sous-Lieutenant, 5ᵉ Bataillon de la Garde nationale mobile de la Seine-Inférieure, Dossier Roger de Martel de Janville, AA.

65. Gyp, *Du temps des cheveux et des chevaux*, 54.

66. "une espèce de sauvage, élevée en garçon . . . " Ibid., 53. Ellipses in original.

67. Ibid., 78.

68. "Le désir que j'ai d'être utile à mon pays, et l'honorabilité de ma famille, me font espérer que vous accueillerez favorablement ma demande." Letter from Marie François Roger de Martel de Janville, 12 March 1869, Dossier Roger de Martel de Janville, AA.

Chapter III

1. Gyp, *Du temps des cheveux et des chevaux: Souvenirs du Second Empire* (Paris: Calmann-Lévy, 1929), 130.

2. The Prussian victory at Sedan on 2 September 1870 confirmed Germany's political unity. With the proclamation of the German empire at Versailles on 18 January 1871, Bismarck had achieved his dream of unifying under Prussian hegemony all German states.

3. "C'est en Normandie que ton mari sera mobilisé et restera probablement . . . Donc, c'est en Normandie que tu dois aller . . ." Gyp, *Du temps des cheveux et des chevaux*, 133. Ellipses in original.

4. Ibid., 194.

5. On the psychological effects of the defeat, see Claude Digeon, *La Crise allemande de la pensée française* (Paris: Presses Universitaires de France, 1959), 1.

6. Gyp, *Du temps des cheveux et des chevaux*, 182.

7. "J'étais stupéfaite. Je n'avais pas pensé à ça! . . . Pas un instant l'idée ne m'était venue que parce que l'Empereur était battu on allait le chasser." Gyp, *Du temps des cheveux et des chevaux*, 143. Ellipses in original.

8. Ibid., 153.

9. Gyp, *La Joyeuse Enfance de la Troisième République* (Paris: Calmann-Lévy, 1931), 37.

10. "Tout concourait pour assurer un retour de cette royauté boiteuse à laquelle je préférais beaucoup la République." Ibid.

11. "On avait été battu par les Prussiens, c'est vrai, mais cette armée donnait une impression intense de puissance et de vie, et le pays vaincu respirait la vigueur, la richesse, l'élégance et la joie." Ibid., 67.

12. "cet ami de toutes les heures pour lequel j'avais un culte." Ibid., 106.

13. Ibid., 100.

14. Ibid.

15. "C'était ma jeunesse heureuse qui s'envolait. Lui seul avait eu de l'influence sur moi et j'avais, avec lui, une confiance et un abandon absolus que je savais bien ne retrouver jamais avec personne." Ibid.

16. "Bazaine . . . fût malheureux et non coupable!" Aymar de Flagy [comtesse de Mirabeau], *Maréchale Bazaine* (Paris: Lachaud et Burdin, 1874), 18. Excerpts from this pamphlet also appeared on the front page of *Le Figaro* on 23 December 1873.

17. "Le Maréchal n'était pas un incapable; il n'était pas 'à la hauteur,' voilà tout.

Superbement brave, il manqua de clairvoyance et de tact." Gyp, *La Joyeuse Enfance*, 127.

18. "une honte bien plus grande que l'invasion des étrangers." Aymar de Flagy, *Maréchale Bazaine*, 18.

19. "une déclaration qui anéantira, sans aucun doute, les injustes accusations portées contre le Maréchal." Prince Frederick-Charles, letter to comtesse de Mirabeau, 26 Sept. 1873, quoted in Michel Missoffe, *Gyp et ses amis* (Paris: Flammarion, 1932), 50.

20. "sa conduite . . . est . . . celle d'un patriote et d'un chevalier." Field Marshal von Manteuffel, letter to comtesse de Mirabeau, 10 Jan. 1874, 320AP3, AN. See also Missoffe, *Gyp et ses amis*, 52–56.

21. "ma haute estime pour le Maréchal Bazaine." Prince Frederick-Charles, letter to comtesse de Mirabeau, 20 Dec. 1874, quoted in Missoffe, *Gyp et ses amis*, 51.

22. "Tout ce que vous me dites du Maréchal Bazaine m'a intéressé, et je voudrais bien savoir combien de duels Madame la comtesse aurait eus, avec sa noble franchise, si elle était en vérité un Lieutenant. Le fait est amusant et caractéristique." Field Marshal von Manteuffel, letter to comtesse de Mirabeau, 10 Oct. 1874, 320AP3, AN.

23. Gyp, *La Joyeuse Enfance*, 122.

24. "ce type parfait du gentilhomme d'autrefois." Comtesse de Mirabeau, *Henri de l'Espée* (Nancy: Crespin-Leblond, 1871), 5.

25. "la haine personnelle que le peuple voue presque toujours à celui qui les gouverne." Ibid., 2.

26. "[qui] n'avait d'autre culte sur terre que celui de la famille royale." Comtesse de Mirabeau, *Le Baron d'Aché* (Paris: Didier, 1877), 15.

27. "L'auteur fait des pieds et des mains pour le porter au théâtre." Francisque Sarcey, "Chronique Théâtrale: *Châteaufort* par la comtesse de Mirabeau," *Le Temps*, 17 July 1876, 1–2.

28. "[C]ette femme est une débutante [qui] a innocemment, naïvement porté sur la scène ce qu'elle avait vu dans le monde." Ibid.

29. Ibid.

30. "La pièce de Madame la comtesse de Mirabeau est donc tombée le premier soir; et il n'y a pas apparence qu'elle se relève jamais de cette déplorable chute." Ibid.

31. "le genre *un peu échevelé*." Comtesse de Mirabeau, letter to Pierre-Jules Hetzel, [15 or 19] Jan. 1878, Naf 16958, #63–65, BN. The Bibliothèque Nationale mistakenly attributes to Gabrielle the two letters from the comtesse de Mirabeau to Hetzel.

32. "mon temps [est] tellement *pris* que je suis désolée quand je fais une course inutile." Comtesse de Mirabeau, letter to Pierre-Jules Hetzel, 13 Jan. 1878, Naf 16958, #62, BN.

33. "Je n'ose pas vous dire que mes articles ont du succès; j'aurais l'air d'une personne *très vaniteuse*." Comtesse de Mirabeau, letter to Pierre-Jules Hetzel, [l5 or l9] Jan. 1878, Naf 16958, #63–65, BN.

34. "On les attribue à un officier, et *on cherche l'officier*." Ibid.

35. "Je vous prie de me garder *le secret*. . . . Les articles que j'écris sont *très peu féminins*, et, si j'étais connue, cela paralyserait ma plume." Ibid.

36. Calmann-Lévy would publish the following works by the comtesse de Mirabeau, writing under various pseudonyms: *Chut!!!* (1880); *Péchés mignons* by "Chut!!" (1881); *L'Impératrice Wanda* by "***" (1884); *Hors du monde* by "Jack Frank" (1885); and *Fredaines* by "Chut" (1890).

37. Conflicting accounts situate Gabrielle's first article between 1880 and 1882, but

it more likely dates from 1879. See Missoffe, *Gyp et ses amis*, 59–62; Francis de Croisset, "La Société et la vie sous la Troisième République: L'Univers de Gyp," *Conférencia* 20, 1 Oct. 1934, 388; André Billy, "Propos du samedi: Du cachet de Stendhal et des débuts de Gyp," *Le Figaro littéraire*, 18 June 1955.

38. Quoted in Marie-Aline Raynal, "Gyp," *La Revue bleue*, 14 Oct. 1928, 427. Ellipses in original.

39. "Pendant l'Inauguration," dated 6 September 1879 and most probably written by Gabrielle, is signed "Scamp." The piece is an epistolary exchange, set in Paris, Deauville, and Nancy, between an aspiring subprefect (Bonapartist under the Republic, opponent of the Jesuits and Thiers), his male confidant, and the married marquise he tries to seduce.

40. Croisset, "La Société et la vie sous la Troisième République," 388.

41. "la personne qui signe Gyp . . . de passer à nos bureaux." Quoted in Raynal, "Gyp," 427.

42. "l'Officier à la grosse écriture qui envoyait de Nancy des dialogues, à faire toucher son compte aux bureaux du Journal." Quoted in Missoffe, *Gyp et ses amis*, 60–61.

43. "Je ne pouvais faire que ça [la littérature] ou le cirque." Ibid., 61.

44. "La littérature m'assomme." Ibid., 69.

45. "je n'étais pas très femme? . . . Au sens 'féminin' du mot, c'est possible. Au sens 'animal,' je l'étais. La preuve, c'est que, ayant instinctivement l'horreur d'une vie forcée à deux, je me suis mariée parce que je voulais absolument des enfants." Gyp, letter to Maurice Barrès, [?] June 1923, #132, MB. Ellipses in original.

46. "Je préférerais, pour ma part, élever six garçons plutôt qu'une seule fille." Gyp, "Morale et philosophie: Les Enfants terribles," *Les Annales politiques et littéraires* [1912], 515.

47. "Roger me trompait déjà tant qu'il pouvait et assez tapageusement." Gyp, letter to Maurice Barrès, [?] June 1923, MB.

48. "Ca m'était égal." Ibid.

49. "je me considérais comme parfaitement autorisée à disposer de ma personne." Ibid.

50. See Armand Lanoux, *Maupassant le Bel-Ami* (Paris: Grasset, 1979), 492–93, 512–13; on d'Estoc, see Roger L. Williams, *The Horror of Life* (Chicago, IL: U of Chicago P, 1980).

51. "La province n'est pas tendre aux gens de lettres! Elle ne voit que la singularité qui l'offusque. Le mieux qu'ils en puissent espérer c'est l'indifférence, qui les sauve de la persécution." Gyz-El, "De l'inconvénient d'être noix sur le chemin des corneilles," *Noir sur blanc: Récits lorrains* (Nancy: Voirin, 1887), 71–72.

52. "cette jeune femme . . . dût fuir devant l'acharnement d'une ville entière la poursuivant de ses sarcasmes, de ses lazzis cruels, de sa curiosité impitoyable. Sous ses allures excentriques qu'on flétrissait, nul ne sut découvrir la profonde originalité d'un talent qui germait et qui se manifesta bientôt sur une scène plus vaste. En attendant, on avait traité cette femme d'intelligence supérieure comme la dernière venue." Ibid.

53. "une province peu hospitalière, où plusieurs sociétés formaient de petits groupes hostiles les uns aux autres, et où les réceptions avaient toujours un caractère d'apparat." Gyp, *Souvenirs d'une petite fille* (Paris: Calmann-Lévy, 1928), vol. 2, 192–93.

54. "Pour les nouveaux venus originaux ou excentriques, la province est . . . féroce. Elle ne pardonne pas à ceux qui attirent ou cherchent à attirer l'attention. . . ." Gyp, *Un raté* (Paris: Flammarion, 1925), 11. Calmann-Lévy published the original edition in 1891.

55. "Là on potine, on épluche, on juge, on médit, et surtout, surtout on calomnie!" Ibid., 8.

Chapter IV

1. See Roger Wahl, *Essai d'une histoire illustrée de Neuilly-sur-Seine* (Neuilly-sur-Seine: n.p., 1935).

2. "Je suis en *province* à Neuilly." Gyp, letter to Georges Montorgueil, n.d., 428AP2, AN. Montorgueil was the literary critic for the newspaper *L'Eclair*.

3. For analyses of the relation between Parisian social geography and the fin-de-siècle literary field, see Anne-Marie Thiesse, *Le Roman du quotidien: Lecteurs et lectures populaires à la Belle Epoque* (Paris: Chemin Vert, 1984), 228–29; and Christophe Charle, *La Crise littéraire à l'époque du naturalisme* (Paris: Presses de l'Ecole Normale Supérieure, 1979), 182.

4. For other descriptions of Gyp's house, see Paul Acker, "Comment ils travaillent," *Je Sais Tout*, 15 Feb. 1905, 17–25; Gaston Bonnefont, *Les Parisiennes chez elles: Nos grandes dames—Madame la comtesse de Martel (Gyp)* (Paris: Flammarion, [1895]), 3–15; Lucien Corpechot, "Souvenirs d'un journaliste: Gyp," *La Revue universelle*, 15 May 1936; Maurice Guillemot, "Gyp," *Fémina*, 15 Nov. 1902, 343–45.

5. The "droit à l'aisance," or "right to leisure or laziness," was an idea initially given credence by Paul Lafargue in a tract published in 1883, the year his father-in-law, Karl Marx, died, and then popularized by the Russian anarchist Kropotkin, whose work was translated into French in 1892. Although "the right to laziness" became the anarchist Left's rallying cry against the bourgeois work ethic, it also alludes to the development of a leisure industry during the Belle Epoque. See Charles Rearick, *Pleasures of the Belle Epoque: Entertainment and Festivity in Turn-of-the-Century France* (New Haven, CT: Yale UP, 1985), 27–52.

6. "une petite dame élégante, portant visage avenant, pâle et mince, ombragé d'une de ces capotes pointues à brides qui prolongeaient mal les grâces du Second Empire." Ferdinand Bac, "Madame Gyp: Un souvenir de cinquante ans," *Les Débats*, 24 July 1932.

7. "avec le désir visible de ne pas attirer l'attention." Ferdinand Bac, *Intimités de la Troisième République* (Paris: Hachette, 1935), 221.

8. To Bac's assertion that it was Gabrielle who brought him to the public's attention, she responded: "No, I certainly did not, as you say, 'invent' Bac! I simply pointed him out to Marcelin, who did not know him, and whom I sent . . . to see a watercolor that he bought immediately, and that depicted a small woman in a Japanese dress." ("Non, certes, je n'ai pas, comme vous le dites, 'inventé' Bac! Je l'ai tout bonnement signalé à Marcelin qui l'ignorait, et que j'envoyai . . . voir une aquarelle qu'il acheta tout de suite, et qui représentait une petite femme en robe japonaise.") Gyp, letter to Ferdinand Bac, [?] March 1896, MS 14168, #98, AR.

9. On the disadvantages for women of the dotal system, see Anne-Martin Fugier, *La Bourgeoise: Femme au temps de Paul Bourget* (Paris: Grasset, 1983), 45–49; and Theodore Zeldin, *France, 1848–1945: Ambition and Love* (Oxford: Oxford UP, 1979), 287–91.

10. *La Vie Parisienne*: 15 May 1881; 24 Sept. 1881; 8 April 1882; 24 Sept. 1881.

11. Quoted in Michel Missoffe, *Gyp et ses amis* (Paris: Flammarion, 1932), 62.

12. "une femme du meilleur monde." Henri de Bornier, "Revue du théâtre," *La Nouvelle Revue* 15 Dec. 1883, 195.

13. " 'La Vie Parisienne' a fait en province un grand mal et de considérables dégâts. Elle a 'défraîchi' quelques jeunes filles. Elle a fait croire à trop de jeunes femmes que le dévergondage, lorsqu'il est élégant et raffiné, est parfaitement acceptable; qu'il faut—pour

être chic—admettre certaines libertés, certaines façons de se tenir, de parler et de s'habiller." Quoted in Missoffe, *Gyp et ses amis*, 62.

14. "Tout le côté 'Faubourg' de la famille me sécha. . . . Je comprenais parfaitement leur réprobation, qui me paraissait très normale. *Je ne m'étais pas sympathique.*" Ibid.

15. Gyp, "Notre enquête sur les pseudonyms," *La Revue Lorraine*, 1898.

16. See Guillemot, "Gyp," 344.

17. See Janet Flanner [Genêt], *Paris Was Yesterday*, ed. Irving Drutman (New York: Penguin Books, 1981), 85; and Noël Sabord, "Gyp et Toto," *Paris-Midi*, 17 May 1926, 2.

18. On the choice of a male pseudonym by certain nineteenth-century women writers, see Sandra M. Gilbert and Susan Gubar, *The Madwoman in the Attic: The Woman Writer and the Nineteenth-Century Literary Imagination* (New Haven, CT: Yale UP, 1979), 65–71.

19. See Jean-Yves Mollier, *Michel et Calmann Lévy ou la naissance de l'édition moderne, 1836–1891* (Paris: Calmann-Lévy, 1984), 413; and Jean-Yves Mollier, "Postface," in *Histoire de l'édition française*, ed. Roger Chartier and Henri-Jean Martin. Vol. 3: *Le Temps des éditeurs: Du romantisme à la Belle Epoque* (Paris: Fayard, 1990), 569–93.

20. "en pleine démocratie, une aristocratie du commerce." Quoted in Mollier, *Michel et Calmann Lévy*, 447.

21. "[L]orsqu'une famille . . . peut prendre, sans fléchir, 40% sur tous les livres d'un temps . . . et créer, en plein XIXᵉ siècle, cette tradition féodale et shakespearienne (voyez Shylock), j'estime . . . que cette famille a des droits indiscutables à la noblesse." Ibid., 448.

22. Comtesse de Mirabeau and vicomte de Grenville, *Histoire des deux héritières* (1864); *Chut!!* by the author of *Shocking!!* (1880); ****, *L'Impératrice Wanda* (1881); Chut!!, *Péchés mignons* (1881); Jack Frank, *Hors du monde* (1885); Chut!!, *Fredaines* (1890); preface to *Lettres de Talleyrand et la maison d'Orléans* (1890).

23. "Monsieur Calmann-Lévy était un type curieux et amusant. Court, solide, vivant, autoritaire et spirituel, il avait des boutades et des drôleries imprévues . . . qui faisaient ma joie." Gyp, *La Joyeuse Enfance de la Troisième République* (Paris: Calmann-Lévy, 1931), 201.

24. Chut, "Réserviste," *La Vie Parisienne,* 27 Sept. 1879, 564–65.

25. "Rien ne pousse à la fainéantise comme le métier de fainéant que je mène." Paul Calmann-Lévy, letter to the vicomte Spoelberch de Lovenjoul, 4 Oct. 1879, Fonds Spoelberch de Lovenjoul, IF.

26. "Il n'est pas un de mes officiers auxquels elle n'ait pas écrit quand elle n'allait pas elle-même les voir pour leur demander pour moi des permissions." Ibid.

27. Contract between the comtesse de Martel and Calmann-Lévy, 13 May 1884, CL.

28. "pas de nature à convenir à sa clientèle." Ibid.

29. As for the first edition of each work—size: in-18; cost: three francs, fifty centimes; quantity: at least 1,500 copies. Royalty: fifty centimes per copy sold, roughly 15 percent of the sale price. For new editions: a 10 percent royalty, the sum to decrease with each subsequent printing. Calmann-Lévy gave Gyp twelve free copies of each first edition and ensured that the book earned proper attention from the press through reviews and advertising. In exchange, Gyp allowed Calmann-Lévy to negotiate both translations of her works and reprints of them in newspapers, with author and publisher splitting the remuneration. In the event of a stage adaptation of any of her books (as had just been the case with *Autour du mariage*), Calmann-Lévy had priority in publishing the script. Finally, Calmann-Lévy claimed the rights to the four Gyp books the firm published before 1884 and therefore

not yet covered by the terms of the contract: *Petit Bob* (1882), *La Vertu de la baronne* (1882), *Autour du mariage* (both the collection of dialogues and the dramatic adaptation), and *Ce que femme veut . . . ?* (1883).

30. ''Aux Champs-Elysées, dans une très élégante salle à manger. MONSIEUR JOHN O'STER, noble Irlandais; cinquante-huit ans, cheveux blancs, teint cramoisi, taille plus large que haute, abatis majestueux, intelligence épaisse.'' Gyp, *Sans voiles!* (Paris: Calmann-Lévy, 1885), 1.

31. ''[T]oute leur psychologie consiste dans le noeud de leur cravate et dans la nuance de leur gilet.'' Georges Pellissier, ''La Littérature dialoguée en France: Gyp, Lavedan, Donnay, Provins,'' *La Revue des revues*, 24, 1 Jan. 1898, 31; see also Georges Pellissier, ''La Littérature dialoguée,'' in Georges Pellissier, *Etudes de littérature contemporaine*, 1st ser. (Paris: Perrin, 1898), 251–71.

32. For a fuller comparison between dialogue-novel and theater, see Vivienne Mylne, ''Théâtre et roman: indications scéniques,'' *Le Dialogue dans le roman français: De Sorel à Sarraute* (Paris: Universitas, in press).

33. Albert Thibaudet, *Histoire de la littérature française: De Chateaubriand à Valéry* (Paris: Stock, 1936), 512–15.

34. Henry James, Preface to *The Awkward Age* (New York: Scribner's, 1908), xii and xxi.

35. J. Ernest-Charles, ''La Fin d'un genre: Les dialogues,'' *Les Samedis littéraires*, 2nd ser. (Paris: Perrin, 1904), 313.

36. According to Maurice Barrès, ''Madame de Martel once told me that her style was the offspring of Henri Monnier's dialogues.'' (''Madame de Martel m'a dit un jour que sa manière était fille des dialogues de Henri Monnier.'') Maurice Barrès, *Mes cahiers*, vol. 3 (Paris: Plon, 1931), 151.

37. ''se composent de chapitres détachés et qui, chacun pris à part, ont tout aussi peu d'unité que nos recueils de dialogues.'' Pellissier, ''La Littérature dialoguée en France,'' 25.

38. Ibid., 33.

39. ''ces corsages-blouses, dont la soie molle indique aux yeux un libre dessin et laisse à l'imagination une agréable liberté.'' Gaston Deschamps, *La Vie et les livres*, 3rd ser. (Paris: Armand-Colin, 1896), 103.

40. ''Parce que c'est d'une facilité révoltante, alors que le récit demande un semblant d'application. Je suis sans illusions sur la valeur intellectuelle d'une succession de tableaux bâclés et galopés comme tout ce que je fais.'' Quoted in Missoffe, *Gyp et ses amis*, 64.

41. ''Cela ne demande ni invention, puisque le dialogue n'a vraiment pas de 'sujet,' ni composition, puisque les personnages y parlent à bâtons rompus, ni style, puisque le langage de 'la haute' est, paraît-il, un affreux charabia.'' Pellissier, ''La Littérature dialoguée en France,'' 31–32.

42. ''Dans mon pays, notaire, médecin, magistrats se réunissaient pour s'enchanter à la lecture du *Petit Bob*. . . . '' Corpechot, ''Souvenirs d'un journaliste: Gyp,'' 420. Another critic insists that Gyp's readership was not limited to members of the bourgeoisie: ''[S]he maintained, especially in the provinces, a faithful readership, and especially in these milieus she knew so well: country squires, regional aristocracy, upper-class land-owning bourgeoisie. They read her books regularly, as soon as they came out. (''[E]lle conservait, surtout en province, des lecteurs fidèles, et en particulier dans ces milieux qu'elle connaissait si bien: hobereaux, aristocratie régionale, grande bourgeoisie fermière. On y lisait régulièrement ses livres dès qu'ils apparaissaient.'') Edmond Jaloux, ''Gyp et le Petit Bob,'' *Le Temps,* 8 July 1932, 3.

43. "entre deux stations de chemin de fer, au bain, au lit, à bicyclette." Pellissier, "La Littérature dialoguée en France," 31.

44. Ibid.

45. Charles Rearick notes that interruptions programmed into the Folies-Bergères or the circus allowed viewers to stroll, chat, daydream, or read the papers during breaks. Such a discontinuous time frame may have provided viewers with welcome relief from work rhythms that were becoming increasingly mechanistic, or "Taylorized." Rearick, *Pleasures of the Belle Epoque*, 153–54.

46. "une précoce déliquescence." Pellissier, "La Littérature dialoguée en France," 30.

47. "Je n'ai ni amour-propre ni grande considération pour les lecteurs puisque je vois ce qui leur plaît." Quoted in Missoffe, *Gyp et ses amis*, 64.

48. On the related developments of children's literature and the comic strip in late nineteenth-century France, see M. Mozet, "La Presse enfantine et la bande dessinée," in *Manuel d'histoire littéraire de la France*, vol. 5, ed. Claude Duchet (Paris: Editions Sociales, 1977), 601–7.

49. See Marius-Ary Leblond, "L'Enfant d'après le roman français contemporain," *La Revue des revues,* 1 July 1901, 44–63; Henry Bordeaux, "Les Livres et les moeurs: L'Ame des enfants," *La Revue hebdomadaire*, Nov. 1898, 269–78. See also Rosemary Lloyd, *The Land of Lost Content: Children and Childhood in Nineteenth-Century French Literature* (New York: Oxford UP, 1992).

50. "le gamin avec n'importe quelle personnalité empesée." Barrès, *Mes cahiers*, 142.

51. "Bob s'étend comme un veau sur le tapis, en pleurant presque de satisfaction." Gyp, *Petit Bob* (Paris: Calmann-Lévy, 1882), 149.

52. Jaloux, "Gyp et le Petit Bob."

53. "j'ai mis . . . beaucoup de l'enfant que j'étais jadis." Gyp, "Les Contemporains: Petit Bob et Miquette," *Les Annales politiques et littéraires*, 1 Nov. 1912, 573.

54. "Môme sinistre." Tabarant, "La Vie," n. pl., n.d.

55. Hippolyte Durand, *Le Règne de l'enfant* (Paris: Lecène-Oudin, 1889), 357–58.

56. *Little Bob*, trans. A. Hallard (The Pioneer Series, 1900). The novel was also published in a Spanish translation.

57. "Gyp," *New York Times*, 24 July 1898, sec. 4, 11.

58. Marius-Ary Leblond, *La Société française sous la Troisième République d'après les romanciers contemporains* (Paris: Alcan, 1905), 17.

59. "Gavroche 'du meilleur monde.' " Louis Périé, "La Littérature 'Vie Parisienne': Gyp," *Le Courrier du Centre*, 4 July 1932.

60. Jaloux, "Gyp et le Petit Bob."

61. Maxime Gaucher, "Notes et impressions," *La Revue politique et littéraire*, 29 July 1882, 155.

62. "Je n'ai pas voulu faire un petit mufle, mais un petit garçon . . . instinctif, taquin, indiscipliné, curieux, un peu fruste, mais très bon, et, surtout, très naïf. On a voulu voir en Bob un type de gosse méchant et vicieux. Ce n'est pas ça du tout." Gyp, "Les Contemporains," 573. See also Missoffe, *Gyp et ses amis*, 63.

63. Abel Hermant, "L'Ennemie du ridicule: Défense de la langue française," *Le Temps*, 24 Sept. 1918.

64. Gyp, *Elles et lui* (Paris: Calmann-Lévy, 1885), 22. Ellipses in original.

65. "le plaisir sans gêne." Ibid., 249.

66. "J'ai toujours eu envie d'voir des gens s'battre . . . " *Petit Bob*, 100. Ellipses in original.

67. "pourrie par vingt années de corruption." Gyp, *La Vertu de la baronne* (Paris: Calmann-Lévy, 1882), 30.

68. "nez brutalement retroussé, aux lèvres roulées d'un rouge intense . . . [aux] cheveux noirs et ondulés . . . [aux] yeux fauves . . . épais sourcils . . . physionomie sauvage . . . oreilles grandes et mal ourlées, les doigts des pieds et des mains spatulés et les attaches lourdes." Ibid., 39–40.

69. "drôle de petit produit moderne! . . . " Gyp, *Autour du divorce* (Paris: Calmann-Lévy, 1886), 169.

70. See Anne-Marie and Charles Lalo, "La Faillite de la beauté," *Le Mercure de France*, 1 Aug. 1913, 493–523.

71. "le type féminin le plus moderne, celui qui appartient peut-être le plus en propre à ces dix dernières années, celui d'un être quelque peu androgyne, très féminin par le caprice, la nervosité et l'illogisme, mais masculin par l'allure, par le dédain du sentiment, et un peu aussi par le costume. Contraste piquant, ou l'élément garçonnier fait ressortir l'autre, rend la femme plus tentante et plus savoureuse." Jules Lemaître, "Gyp et la vie parisienne," *Impressions de théâtre*, 1st ser. (Paris: Lecène-Oudin, 1888), 302.

72. "des femmes du dernier tiers de ce siècle ont été, sont, seront des Paulette. . . . " Lucien Muhlfeld, *Le Monde où l'on imprime: Regards sur quelques lettrés et divers illettrés contemporains* (Paris: Perrin, 1897), 231.

73. "[V]ers 1883 . . . je me suis aperçue avec ahurissement, que Paulette, qui n'était à mes yeux qu' 'une jolie petite poison,' était gobée, admirée et prise pour modèle par les jeunes femmes de ce temps-là." Quoted in Missoffe, *Gyp et ses amis*, 63.

74. "[Ce] petit être indépendant et étrange . . . travaille, pioche, passe ses examens, son baccalauréat, parle plusieurs langues. . . ." Gyp, "La Femme de 1885," rpt. in *Le Figaro*, 16 July 1932, 5.

75. "Elle a le tort d'être trop *bon garçon* et de manquer totalement de tenue. . . . " Ibid.

76. "Je suis de toutes forces contre le corset; ça '*banalise*' les tailles; . . . ça abîme celles qui sont jolies, sans embellir celles qui sont laides." Gyp, letter to [?], MD.

77. "Ces pages écrites par une femme sont le plus cruel acte d'accusation que l'on ait jamais dressé contre les femmes et ce qui résulte de l'ouvrage, c'est que la femme est la grande coupable, le principal agent de la désorganisation sociale." Bornier, "Revue du théâtre," 195–96.

78. "une révolutionnaire . . . presque une nihiliste." Lemaître, *Impressions de théâtre*, 303.

79. "la petite sauvage et . . . la fille du meilleur monde." Marguerite Bourcet, "Gyp: Docteur ès éducation," *Le Noël*, 5 Oct. 1933, 419.

80. Francisque Sarcey, "La Vie littéraire," *Le Temps*, 22 Oct. 1883, 2.

81. "très froid . . . glacial." Ibid. The fiasco of *Autour du mariage* so upset Deslandes, director of the Théâtre du Vaudeville, that on 12 November he wrote to Zola's friend Henri Céard to renege on his promise to stage Céard's *Renée Mauperin*, pending revisions. Deslandes apparently refused to stage another play in which so little action took place. See Emile Zola, *Correspondance*, ed. B. H. Bakker (Montreal: Bibliothèque Nationale du Québec, 1983), vol. 4, 412–13.

82. "un journal où le respect de toutes les convenances [est] de tradition. . . . " "[E]n publiant de Madame de Martel, auteur dramatique et journaliste, un portrait aussi soigné que possible, nous n'avions pas cru ni dépasser notre droit, ni surtout causer à cet écrivain le moindre préjudice. . . . Espérons que Madame de Martel s'y rangera et qu'elle ne gardera pas à *La Vie Moderne* plus de rancune que nous lui en gardons nous-mêmes." "Le Procès

de *La Vie Moderne*," *La Vie Moderne*, 10 Nov. 1883, 714. See also Jean Desplanches, "Théâtres: *Autour du Mariage*," *La Vie Moderne*, 27 Oct. 1883, 692.

83. "Donc, cher monsieur, voulez-vous lire *Le suis-je?* et me dire tout simplement si c'est mauvais? Si, au contraire, vous trouvez que c'est *jouable*, vous seriez mille fois bon de me l'écrire *'d'un air convaincu'*; je leur montrerais *votre avis*, et ça leverait toutes les difficultés." Gyp, letter to Ludovic Halévy, 27 Feb. 1886, MS 4485, #398, LH.

84. Gyp, letter to Ludovic Halévy, 3 March 1886, MS 4485, #392, LH.

85. "la bonne qui devient cocotte. . . . " Gyp, letter to Ludovic Halévy, 1887, MS 4485, #394, LH.

86. "J'ai bien vu qu'ils *vont vous consulter* pour savoir si ça convient à Milly. Je vous en prie, dites-leur que c'est *charmant*!!! (Même si vous n'en pensez pas un mot.)" Ibid.

Chapter V

1. "un des coins les plus amusants de Paris." Gyp, *La Joyeuse Enfance de la Troisième République* (Paris: Calmann-Lévy, 1931), 199. On the Librairie Nouvelle, see Jean-Yves Mollier, *Michel et Calmann Lévy ou la naissance de l'édition moderne, 1836–1891* (Paris: Calmann-Lévy, 1984), 412, 433–34.

2. "Borgne, intelligent, vivant, ayant tout vu, tout lu et tout retenu, il n'était jamais en défaut. On pouvait lui poser les questions les plus imprévues; lui demander des dates, des chiffres d'éditions, tout ce qu'on voulait; il renseignait à l'instant et sans la moindre hésitation les acheteurs." Gyp, *La Joyeuse Enfance*, 199.

3. "très pâle, avec de magnifiques yeux bruns, veloutés et profonds d'une douceur et d'une intelligence infinies." Ibid., 204–5.

4. "[E]lle ne mérite vraiment pas l'honneur que vous lui faites." Gyp, letter to Ludovic Halévy, [1882], MS 4485, #385, LH.

5. "Je ne puis vous dire à quel point Gyp est stupéfait et flatté de voir que vous ayez *lu* 'Ce que femme veut . . . ?' " Gyp, letter to Ludovic Halévy, [1883], MS 4485, #387, LH. "Gyp" is male here, as in all Gabrielle's correspondence. While her letters to Halévy are signed "Mirabeau-Martel" or "MM," Gabrielle refers only to "Gyp" (in the third person) when discussing her work.

6. Gyp, letters to Ludovic Halévy, [1883], MS 4485, #388 and #389, LH.

7. "Votre *Princesse* est charmante et *vraie*; on croirait que vous avez été *jeune fille!*" Gyp, letter to Ludovic Halévy, 16 Nov. 1886, MS 4485, #393, LH.

8. Gyp, letter to Ludovic Halévy, [1887], MS 4485, #397, LH.

9. Gyp, letter to Alexandre Dumas fils, 26 [Nov. 1884], Naf 14666, #46, ADF.

10. "C'est *superbe*, et j'aurais voulu vous dire toute mon admiration, mais on ne vous trouve jamais avenue de Villiers, n'est-ce pas?" Gyp, letter to Alexandre Dumas fils, [?] Jan. [1885], Naf 14666, #48, ADF.

11. Gyp, letter to Alexandre Dumas fils, [1887?], Naf 24638, #487, ADF.

12. "puisque vous voulez bien me considérer comme un confrère." Gyp, letter to Ludovic Halévy, [1883], MS 4485, #387, LH.

13. "au fin fond du Morbihan." Gyp, letter to Ludovic Halévy, 12 May 1888, MS 4485, #398, LH.

14. Roger de Martel de Janville, letter to the Société des gens de lettres, 3 May 1888, 454AP273 (Gyp), AN.

15. Gyp, letter to the Société des gens de lettres, 15 May 1888, 454AP273, AN.

16. "dont le grand talent ne peut qu'honorer notre société." Ludovic Halévy and Alexandre Dumas fils, letters to the Société des gens de lettres, 454AP273, AN.

17. "souvenirs très affectueux de votre filleul, Gyp." Gyp, letter to Ludovic Halévy, 14 May 1888, MS 4485, #399, LH.

18. For Gyp's description of her first visit to the Chat Noir, see Gyp, "Les Contemporains: Souvenirs de jeunesse," lecture, 2 Feb. 1923, published in *Annales politiques et littéraires*, [1923], 458.

19. The phrase is taken from Jerrold Seigel, *Bohemian Paris: Culture, Politics, and the Boundaries of Bourgeois Life, 1830–1930* (New York: Penguin, 1987), 239.

20. See Yves-Gérard Le Dantec, "Mes souvenirs de Gyp," in *Livre d'or de l'Académie de Neuilly: Arts–Lettres–Sciences* (Paris: Académie de Neuilly, 1958), 27.

21. "un monsieur d'une trentaine d'années, très distingué, aux yeux très doux, à la barbe frisée et qui me présentait un flacon de sels en m'éventant de l'autre main." Quoted in Le Dantec, "Mes souvenirs de Gyp," 29.

22. Ibid., 28–29.

23. "parfaitement ignoré, sauf de quelques lettrés. . . . Sa gaucherie, sa timidité, son ignorance absolue des usages mondains, tout le prédestinait à demeurer *à côté*, quel que fût d'ailleurs son talent." Gyp, letter to Madame Gaston de Caillavet, n.d., reprinted in Jeanne-Maurice Pouquet, *Le Salon de Madame Arman de Caillavet* (Paris: Hachette, 1926), 39–40. Gyp recorded another first impression of France as "indecisive and elusive, unreliable and nonchalant, offhanded and casual" ("flottant et insaisissable, incertain et nonchalant, flâneur et désinvolte"). Gyp, *La Joyeuse Enfance*, 201.

24. "[elle] l'a éduqué de pied en cap." Gyp, letter to Madame Gaston de Caillavet, quoted in Pouquet, *Le Salon de Madame Arman de Caillavet*, 40.

25. In 1885 approximately eighty thousand Jews resided in France, with fifty thousand in Paris. On French Jewish demography at the fin de siècle, see Michael Marrus, *The Politics of Assimilation: A Study of the French Jewish Community at the Time of the Dreyfus Affair* (New York: Oxford UP, 1971), 30–31.

26. Michel Winock, *Edouard Drumont et Cie: Antisémitisme et fascisme en France* (Paris: Seuil, 1982), 38.

27. "Tout vient du Juif; tout revient au Juif." Quoted in *Le Nationalisme Français: Anthologie, 1871–1914*, ed. Raoul Girardet (Paris: Seuil, 1983), 143.

28. "un illuminé." Quoted in François Bournand, *Les Juifs et nos contemporains: L'Antisémitisme et la question juive* (Paris, Pierret, [1898]), 135.

29. Léon Blum has identified the successes of a handful of bourgeois Jews—"the indiscreet intrusion of nouveau-riche Jews or the penetration of industrious Jews, which was deemed too rapid" ("l'intrusion indiscrète de Juifs enrichis ou la pénétration, jugée trop rapide, de Juifs studieux")—as one of the primary causes of fin-de-siècle anti-Semitism. *Souvenirs sur l'Affaire* (Paris: Gallimard, 1981), 68.

30. "la France de jadis, la jolie France mousse-de-champagne, toujours légère et toujours victorieuse." Rachilde, review of Gyp's *Israël*, *Le Mercure de France*, 26, April–June 1898, 231.

31. Edouard Drumont *La Fin d'un monde: Etude psychologique et sociale* (Paris: Savine, 1889).

32. "je me sois laissée éblouir par la question d'argent." Gyp, letter to [?] Calmann-Lévy, 28 July 1909, CL.

33. "Je veux devenir forte . . . très forte . . . " Gyp, *Souvenirs d'une petite fille* (Paris: Calmann-Lévy, 1928) vol. 1, 86. Ellipses in original.

34. Stephen Wilson, *Ideology and Experience: Anti-Semitism in France at the Time of the Dreyfus Affair* (East Brunswick, NJ: Associated University Presses, 1982), 597.

35. "une image inquiétante qui est la sienne. . . ." Jean-Paul Sartre, *Réflexions sur la question juive* (Paris: Flammarion, 1954), 23–24.

36. "Ils sont le chef-d'oeuvre du Créateur; au dessous d'eux, il y a le genre humain tout entier; au dessus d'eux, personne!" Gyp, *La Vertu de la baronne* (Paris: Calmann-Lévy, 1882), 118.

37. "[qui] sait à peine lire, mais [qui] compte merveilleusement et donne des fêtes splendides auxquelles il n'a pu encore obtenir la présence du gratin." Gyp, *Autour du divorce* (Paris: Calmann-Lévy, 1886), 343.

38. "Pour faire oublier cela, il faudrait une grande guerre." Quoted in Léon Daudet, *Souvenirs politiques*, ed. René Wittmann (Paris: Albatros, 1974), 22. Meyer is also satirized in Gyp's 1887 work *Dans l'train*.

39. "directeur du journal *Le Panache du High Life* (critique de la mondanité), l'homme du monde par excellence (en dépit de sa couleur)." Gyp, *Une gauche célèbre* (Paris: Monnier, 1886), 1–2.

40. "un vieux [juif], tout sale, qu'est v'nu une fois acheter des vieux bouquins à m'sieu l'abbé . . . "Gyp, *Petit Bob* (Paris: Calmann-Lévy, 1882), 139. Ellipses in original.

41. Paul Valéry, letter to Gustave Fourment, [1887], reprinted in Paul Valéry and Gustave Fourment, *Correspondance générale, 1887–1933* (Paris: Gallimard, 1957), vol. 7, 50–51. Valéry hastened to add that those French authors enjoying the most brisk sales in Italy certainly did not represent "the best part of our literature."

42. "une jeune femme, portant un vieux nom, et connue en littérature par quelques livres à scandale." "Hier et demain: Une vendetta parisienne." n. pl., 1884.

43. "une femme correctement vêtue, d'une taille moyenne, la figure voilée d'une gaze épaisse roulée autour d'une toque à aigrette." Gustave Macé, *La Police parisienne: Femmes criminelles* (Paris: Fasquelle, 1904), 35.

44. "un liquide *brûlant et glacé.*" Ibid.

45. "Hier et demain."

46. "sur lesquelles planaient de vagues soupçons." Macé, *La Police parisienne*, 35.

47. Gyp, letter to [police prefect], 13 Nov. 1884, EA 30, APP.

48. "c'est *décidément* à la sortie de chez Monsieur Marcelin qu'on m'attend." Gyp, letter to [police prefect], 22 Nov. 1884, EA 30, APP.

49. Notes, EA 30, APP.

50. On the significance of "l'affaire Gyp" for Octave Mirbeau, see Pierre Michel, "Mirbeau et l'affaire Gyp," *Littératures* 26 (Spring 1992): 201–19; and Pierre Michel and Jean-François Nivet, *Octave Mirbeau: L'Imprécateur à coeur fidèle* (Paris: Séguier, 1990), 221–23, 238–41, 361–67.

51. "[elle] avait, pour lui Mirbeau, un goût qu'il se refusait péremptoirement à satisfaire." J.-H. Rosny aîné, *Mémoires de la vie littéraire* (Paris: Crès, 1927), 21.

52. "Je comprends qu'elle mette en rut les impuissantes obscénités des vieux juges. Mais je ne l'engage pas à jouer les Phryné avec eux, car j'ai remarqué hier, comme elle se penchait, qu'elle a le cou fort abîmé d'écrouelles. Je crois que voilà une bonne nouvelle à répandre, *Les Ecrouelles de Gyp*, roman judiciaire." Octave Mirbeau, letter to Robert de Bonnières, 7 or 8 April 1886 (collection of Madame de Saint-Germain), in Octave Mirbeau, *Correspondance générale*, ed. Jean-François Nivet (Lausanne: L'Age d'Homme, forthcoming).

53. "Quand sur une route, je rencontre une ordure étalée, je l'évite; quand je vois

certains noms en tête de certains livres, je passe rapidement en me bouchant le nez. . . . Je ne sais rien de bête, comme ces aventures écrites avec l'eau sale des bidets. . . . '' Octave Mirbeau, ''La Littérature en justice,'' *La France*, 24 Dec. 1884, 2.

54. ''sauf pour quelques initiés.'' Macé, *La Police parisienne*, 35.

55. Ibid.; ''Faits divers,'' *Le Temps*, 1 Aug. 1885 and 21 Jan. 1886; *Entracte*, 21 Jan. 1886.

56. ''La vérité est que nous sommes enveloppés de mystère, que nous vivons dans le mystère.'' Edouard Drumont, *La Dernière Bataille* (1890), quoted in Winock, *Edouard Drumont et Cie*, 52.

57. In a chapter on political myths of conspiracy, Raoul Girardet notes that ''tout complot, toute entreprise de manipulation clandestine tend à assurer sa légitimité en se présentant comme un contre-complot, une contre-entreprise de manipulation clandestine.'' *Mythes et mythologies politiques* (Paris: Seuil, 1986), 59.

58. On the connection between anti-Semitism and occultism, see Winock, *Edouard Drumont et Cie*, 48–52; Willa Z. Silverman, ''Anti-Semitism and Occultism in *fin-de-siècle* France: Three 'Initiates,' '' in *Modernity and Revolution in Late Nineteenth-Century France,* ed. Mary Donaldson-Evans and Barbara C. Cooper (Wilmington: U of Delaware P, 1992), 155–63; Philippe Muray, *Le Dix-Neuvième Siècle à travers les âges* (Paris: Denoël, 1984). Muray asserts that ''tout l'imaginaire 19e [est] hanté par la figure archi-occultiste et bien entendu antisémite du 'juif errant' '' (p. 195).

59. ''Si, au lieu de s'acharner, comme on le fait, à cacher les hontes, on les dévoilait d'une façon retentissante, j'imagine que tout n'en irait que mieux.'' Gyp, *Le Druide, roman parisien* (Paris: Harvard, 1885), 1.

60. Ibid., 141.

61. ''sous le patronage inexpliqué d'un financier.'' Ibid., 142. In a chapter of *La France juive* entitled ''Paris Juif et la société française'' that is partly devoted to an attack on Arthur Meyer, Drumont recommends *Le Druide* to his readers. *La France juive: essai d'histoire contemporaine* (Paris: Marpon et Flammarion, 1886), vol. 2, 190.

62. ''qui ne travaille 'ouvertement' que dans certains coins où tu ne vas pas.'' Gyp, *Le Druide*, 159.

63. ''La peau . . . épaisse, l'oreille canaille, les hanches lourdes, les attaches engor-gées . . . '' Ibid., 128.

64. ''épouvantable coquine.'' Octave Mirbeau, letter to a journalist, July 1885, Col-lection Pierre Michel.

65. ''Je ne sais ce qui s'est passé dans sa vie, ça doit être bien extraordinaire car il se trouve comme inculpé dans une vilaine affaire à la requête de cette Madame de Martel qui signe Gyp et qui a fait sur lui le livre qui s'appelle *Le Druide*. Je le crois à la veille de grands ennuis.'' Claude Monet, letter to Alice Hoschedé, 30 April 1888, cited in Octave Mirbeau, *Correspondance avec Claude Monet*, ed. Pierre Michel and Jean-François Nivet (Paris: Lérot, 1990), 71.

66. ''très disposée à croire au merveilleux.'' ''Enquête sur le merveilleux,'' *L'Echo du merveilleux*, 15 Dec. 1898.

67. ''Nature physique et morale,'' 12 Jan. 1882, Sibylle Gaudry collection, Paris.

68. Ibid.

69. Ibid.

70. Ibid.

71. Ibid.

72. Ibid.

73. Ibid.

74. "Ne redouterait même pas de donner ou de recevoir des coups. Grande confiance dans sa force physique qui est réelle et peu commune chez une femme. . . ." Ibid.

75. "je vois un autre rayonnement qui cette fois ne viendra pas de vous directement mais plutôt d'un enfant." Ibid.

76. "je serais bien surpris si *vous-même* ne deveniez pas célèbre un jour." Ibid.

Chapter VI

1. "C'était un peu du Second Empire que l'on mettait en terre, avec sa frivolité élégante et sa délicieuse imprévoyance." Ferdinand Bac, *Intimités de la Troisième République* (Paris: Hachette, 1935), 29.

2. "invraisemblable crise d'exaltation sur un képi, une barbe de pékin et un cheval noir." Jacques-Emile Blanche, *La Pêche aux souvenirs* (Paris: Flammarion, 1949), 210.

3. Michel Winock, *La Fièvre hexagonale: Les Grandes Crises politiques de 1871 à 1968* (Paris: Calmann-Lévy, 1986), 89.

4. "s'annonça comme César, vécut comme Catilina . . . succomba comme Roméo!" Quoted in Adrien Dansette, *Le Boulangisme* (Paris: Fayard, 1946).

5. "Ce coup de revolver dans le cimetière d'Ixelles est un nouveau triomphe pour la République." L'abbé Mugnier, *Journal, 1879–1939,* ed. Marcel Billot (Paris: Mercure de France, 1985), 63.

6. Léon Blum, *Souvenirs sur l'Affaire* (Paris: Gallimard, 1981), 70.

7. René Rémond, *Les Droites en France* (Paris: Aubier Montaigne, 1982), 150.

8. "Gyp se lança éperdument." Michel Missoffe, *Gyp et ses amis* (Paris: Flammarion, 1932), 129.

9. "Quand la voiture est sortie de la rue de Rivoli, qu'on avait dû barrer pour assurer le passage des voitures, l'énorme foule compacte de la place a poussé un hurlement qui était vraiment effarant. Ça c'était un mouvement populaire pour tout de bon." Quoted in Missoffe, *Gyp et ses amis,* 131–32.

10. "Le véritable tout à l'égout," *La Libre Parole Illustrée,* 2 Feb. 1894.

11. For an analysis of Boulanger and Napoleon as prototypes in the context of political myths of "the savior," see Raoul Girardet, *Mythes et mythologies politiques* (Paris: Seuil, 1986), 63–95.

12. See Rémond, *Les Droites en France,* 153. Zeev Sternhell and other historians have focused on the nationalist ideology, violence, propaganda, and antiliberal stance of Boulangism, identifying this mass movement as an embryonic form of fascism. See Zeev Sternhell, *La Droite révolutionnaire, 1885–1914: Les Origines françaises du fascisme* (Paris: Seuil, 1978). For a synthesis of different interpretations of Boulangism, see Winock, *La Fièvre hexagonale,* 130–34.

13. "Elle lui prêta généreusement les qualités des conquérants qui, malheureusement, lui manquaient: l'audace, la fermeté, la bravoure, l'intelligence, le cran enfin, cette vertu magique qu'elle estimait par-dessus tout." Madeleine Zillhardt, *Louise-Catherine Breslau et ses amis* (Paris: Editions des Portiques, 1932), 205.

14. "Gyp résolut d'employer les loisirs de sa villégiature en faveur du candidat révisionniste. Jamais agent électoral ne mit au service d'une cause plus de verve humoristique ni plus d'ardeur infatigable. Il fallait entendre Gyp . . . célébrant Monsieur Boulanger, haranguant les paysans et les pêcheurs, bourrant leurs enfants de bonbons et de caresses,— trottant du matin au soir par les routes boueuses avec son grand manteau feuille morte,

les brides vertes de son chapeau-capote flottant au vent.'' ''Gyp boulangiste et agent électoral,'' *Le Temps,* 12 Jan. 1890, 3.

15. ''On tira vingt et un coups de canon, on pavoisa, on illumina, le champagne coula à flots.'' Ibid.

16. ''une belle dame très chic' qui arrachait les affiches officielles quand on en collait sur sa maison . . . elle avait l'truc pour ça comme personne . . .'' Ellipses in original. Gyp, *Une élection à Tigre-sur-Mer, racontée par Bob* (Paris: Editions du Gaulois, 1896). Gyp dedicated this work to ''vicomte Henry de Blagny, en souvenir des élections du 22 septembre 1889.''

17. ''Ca, c'était un'dame qui s'promenait avec ses chiens . . . en distribuant des p'tites brochures et des suppléments du *Gaulois* . . . la nuit, elle en semait partout . . . qu'les gens trouvaient l'matin en allant au marché . . .'' Ellipses in original.

18. ''Et puis l'portrait du général! . . . c'était l'empereur qu'on avait r'peint . . . on lui avait fait un'barbe blonde au lieu d'un' moustache noire, un ch'val noir au lieu d'un ch'val blond . . . mais c'tait beau tout d'même . . .'' Ellipses in original.

19. Un'manifestation de haine
   Fait'au lend'main des élections
   Du mois d'septembre; v'la c'qui amène
   Les demandeurs en cassation.
   Ils ont messieurs, c'est trist'à dire,
   Offert un vrai charivari,
   A un homm'que chacun admire,
   Qui est adoré dans l'pays!
   Ils ont promené des lanternes,
   Poussé des cris séditieux,
   Et qualifié de badernes
   Ceux qui ne faisaient pas comm'eux!

Gyp, *C'est nous qui sont l'histoire!!!* (Paris: Calmann-Lévy, 1891), 237.

20. Ibid., 240.

21. ''ces révolutionnaires / Ces aristos, qui veulent le combat.'' Ibid., 242.

22. ''une cocodette de l'Empire,'' ''une dame qui était très jolie en 1841.'' Gyp, ''Feu Longchamps,'' ms., n.d., Special Collections Department, Northwestern University Library, Evanston, IL, 1–3.

23. Ibid., 2.

24. Ibid., 31–33.

25. ''c'que j'trouv'ça idiot, la Tour Eiffel!'' Gyp, *Bob à l'Exposition* (Paris: Calmann-Lévy, 1889), 2.

26. ''même leur nom . . . m'dégoûte!'' Gyp, ''Ce qu'en dit Bob,'' *Le Triboulet,* 13 Oct. 1889, 4.

27. ''Il était superbe, dans sa jolie victoria toute simple, avec un beau cheval.'' *Bob à l'Exposition,* 5.

28. ''un gouvernement qui ne monte pas à ch'val, c'est pas un gouvernement! . . .'' Ibid. Ellipses in original.

29. ''T,'' ''Billets du Matin: A Monsieur Bob, à propos du dernier livre de Gyp: *Bob à l'Exposition,''* *Le Temps,* 10 Oct. 1889, 2.

30. ''un 'honnête homme' qui ne vous paraît pas suffisamment 'décoratif.' '' Ibid.

31. ''Or, si vous aimez tant les 'zigs' et les hommes de 'crâne allure,' comment vous arrangez-vous, mon cher monsieur Bob, pour admirer à ce point l'homme . . . de la fuite à Londres. . . . Le cheval noir suffit-il à compenser tant de traits fâcheux?'' Ibid.

32. "cette soirée . . . la plus originale de la saison." Jules Lemaître, "Gyp au théâtre des marionettes," *Impressions de théâtre*, 4th ser. (Paris: Lecène-Oudin, 1891), 333. See also Robert Desarthis, "Les Disparus: N'oublions pas que Gyp fut revuiste," *Comoedia*, 15–16 July 1932, 2.

33. "exquise, très élégamment incohérente." Lemaître, "Gyp au théâtre des marionettes," 335.

34. On Gyp's mockery of Stendhal, see Jean Mélia, *Stendhal et ses commentateurs* (Paris: Mercure de France, 1911), 364–66; see also Gyp, *Ohé! . . . les psychologues!*, published by Calmann-Lévy in 1889, the same year as Stendhal's *Journal*.

35. Pour les banquiers, c'est fini!

La Bourse par terre

Tapez d'ssus, allez-y!

Agioteurs! la guerre!

Livrons aux flammes, au fer,

Leurs temples d'enfer!

Ah! tapez-les, tapez-les, tapez-les!

Piff, paff, pouff, tapez-les!

Qu'ils casquent,

Qu'ils casquent,

Mais grâce jamais, non jamais!

Gyp, *Tout à l'égout!* (Paris: Calmann-Lévy, 1889), 18–19.

36. "On s'amusait beaucoup." Lemaître, "Gyp au théâtre des marionettes," 334.

37. "Aux égouts! . . . Allons aux égouts! Puisque c'est là que l'Histoire se passe! . . ." Gyp, *Tout à l'égout!*, 36. Ellipses in original.

38. "Vous n'êtes plus qu'un cadavre . . . et le fossoyeur attend. . . ." Ibid., 45. Ellipses in original.

39. On the Ligue des Patriotes, see Peter M. Rutkoff, *Revanche and Revision: The Ligue des Patriotes and the Origins of the Radical Right in France* (Athens, OH: Ohio UP, 1981); and Sternhell, *La Droite révolutionnaire,* 77–145.

40. "ses yeux enfoncés et incertains, son beau masque . . . portant des traces de la petite vérole, sa crinière noire, faite de flammes crépelées, flammes de révolté et d'exaltation." Bac, *Intimités de la Troisième République,* 98.

41. See Eric Vatré, *Henri Rochefort ou la comédie politique au XIXᵉ siècle* (Paris: Lattès, 1984); and Henri Rochefort, *Les Aventures de ma vie,* ed. Jean Guichard-Meili (Paris: Ramsay, 1980).

42. "[a]ristocrate [souffrait] de nausées au contact du peuple." Dansette, *Le Boulangisme,* 150.

43. "était destructeur au-delà de tout." Boni de Castellane, *Mémoires, 1867–1932,* ed. Emmanuel de Waresquiel (Paris: Perrin, 1986), 163.

44. "Les coups qu'il portait, commençaient par faire des bleus, puis des égratignures, puis des brûlures, puis des blessures graves." Léon Daudet, *Souvenirs politiques,* ed. René Wittmann (Paris: Albatros, 1974), 11.

45. "en état permanent d'insurrection." Quoted in Francis de Croisset, "La Société et la vie sous la Troisième République: L'Univers de Gyp: Bob et Miquette," *Conférencia* 20, 1 Oct. 1934, 390–91.

46. "Quand donc le gouvernement sautera-t-il, avec ou sans bombe?" Gyp, letter to Henri Rochefort, [1894], Naf 16802, #120–25, BN.

47. "quand elle était une brillante jeune femme et lui encore un gamin, aux représentations du cirque, dans la loge centrale où la saluaient les écuyères qui savaient son amour

des chevaux.'' Philippe Barrès, ''Gyp, ou la féerie,'' *Les Nouvelles littéraires,* 9 July 1932, 1.

48. ''Bien des femmes pensaient à un Bonaparte en le voyant tel que je le peignais à vingt-cinq ans, les cheveux pauvres et plats, la peau olivâtre, maigre, en veste grise, un oeillet jaune à la boutonnière, les bras croisés sur la poitrine.'' Jacques-Emile Blanche, *Mes modèles: Souvenirs littéraires* (Paris: Stock, 1984), 11.

49. Barrès attracted a devoted following of Latin Quarter students. To consecrate his popularity, during a facetious ceremony at the Café Vachette Paul Adam presented Barrès with a coin bearing the head of Alexander Severius and the title ''Principi Juventutis.''

50. Mugnier, *Journal,* 482.

51. Dansette, *Le Boulangisme,* 329.

52. ''par qui naissent les grandes espérances.'' Maurice Barrès, ''Monsieur le général Boulanger et la nouvelle génération,'' *La Revue indépendante* 8, April 1888.

Chapter VII

1. ''Vous êtes prié de faire à Bob et à Gyp, l'honneur de venir regarder leurs images et pastels exposés dans les galeries de la Bodinière.'' See Stéphane Mallarmé, *Correspondance,* vol. 5 (1892), ed. Henri Mondor and Lloyd James Austin (Paris: Gallimard, 1981), 51.

2. Francisque Sarcey, rev. of *Sauvetage, Le Temps,* 28 April 1890. On ''La Bodinière,'' see *The Graphic Arts and French Society, 1871–1914,* ed. Phillip Dennis Cate (New Brunswick, NJ: Rutgers UP, 1988), 38.

3. A. de Lostalot, ''Poil et Plume,'' *L'Illustration,* 18 April 1891, 338–39.

4. ''suite de portraits surprenants de vie et de sincérité.'' Firmin Javel, ''Les Petits Salons: Gyp et Bob,'' *Gil Blas,* 4 March 1892, 3. See also ''Gyp et Bob,'' *Le Temps,* 4 March 1892, 3; and ''Bob et Gyp à la Bodinière,'' *L'Univers illustré,* 12 March 1892, 124–25.

5. Gyp, letter to [?], [1892], 87AP3, AN.

6. An article in the *Neuilly-Journal* on ''Les Peintres de Neuilly'' at the Salon du Champ de Mars, praised the portraits by the ''brilliant author Gyp, who honors Neuilly with her subtle and biting talent as a writer as well as with her spirit and skill as an artist'' (''le brillant écrivain Gyp, qui honore Neuilly de son talent fin et mordant de littérateur comme de son brio et de sa science d'artiste''). *Neuilly-Journal,* 5 May 1894.

7. Gyp, ''A l'exposition d'Aublet,'' *La Revue illustrée,* 8, June–Dec. 1889, 345–48.

8. Gyp, ''Billet du matin,'' *Le Temps,* 11 April 1893, 2.

9. ''faire retirer *tout de suite* les photographies qui sont dans les différentes boutiques où vous les avez fait placer.'' Gyp, letter to [Paul] Nadar, [n.d.], Naf 24272, XIII, #488, BN.

10. ''très simplement mise . . . se glissait discrètement dans la foule où elle n'était reconnue que de quelques amis. Sous sa capote vert mousse, ornée d'une souris de velours, ses yeux malicieux, derrière sa face-à-main, passaient en revue les tableaux et les gens dont aucun ridicule ne lui échappait.'' Madeleine Zillhardt, *Louise-Catherine Breslau et ses amis* (Paris: Editions des Portiques, 1932), 90.

11. ''purement hideux et ridicule aussi, et d'une prétention fantastique.'' Gyp, letter to Robert de Montesquiou, [1887–90], Naf 15166, CLI-CLV, #87–90, BN.

12. Zillhardt, *Louise-Catherine Breslau et ses amis,* 74.

13. ''dans le magnifique regard de Forain vivait une haine terrible.'' Ferdinand Bac, *Intimités de la Troisème République* (Paris: Hachette, 1935), 501.

14. ''Madame Gavroche en robe de bal.'' See Arsène Alexandre, ''Madame de Martel,'' *La Lecture illustrée,* [1894], 65.

15. ''Ce soir, est venue pour la première fois chez Daudet Mme Martel ou plutôt Gyp. Un grand nez, une blondeur un peu fanée, mais une élégance brisée de corps dans une toilette blanche d'un goût tout à fait distingué, et voluptueuse, excitante. Elle parle avec amour des bêtes, de son cheval, qui lui écrase les pieds et auquel elle ne peut s'empêcher de porter tous les jours des morceaux de sucre, des chats qu'elle adore, des chiens dont son hôtel est une maison de refuge; et comme on cause nourriture, elle dit qu'elle n'aime que les côtelettes et les oeufs à la coque et qu'il lui arrive quelquefois de dîner et de déjeuner uniquement avec cela.'' Edmond and Jules de Goncourt, *Journal: Mémoires de la vie littéraire*, vol. 3 (1887–1896), ed. Robert Ricatte (Paris: Laffont, 1989), 930–31.

16. ''Gyp . . . serrait à pleins bras une gerbe de fleurs de son jardin de Neuilly. Elle portait une robe . . . blanche . . . dont je ne saurais rien expliquer de la forme, sinon qu'elle était longue, étroite et ne ressemblait à aucune de celles que nous étions alors accoutumés de voir. Pénétrer dans une réunion d'une trentaine d'hommes de lettres, les plus célèbres de leur temps . . . pénétrer dans ce cabinet de travail, où se trouvaient peut-être, ce soir-là, Loti et Jules Lemaître, les familiers du 'Grenier Goncourt,' avec ces fleurs, cette robe blanche (alors, les jeunes filles ou les très jeunes femmes seules se seraient permis cette *hardiesse*), témoignait d'une façon d'être, d'une éducation, d'acquisitions et d'une simplicité, sûres et particulières.

Les cheveux étaient d'un châtain blond, séparés au milieu de la tête, le regard et les dents avaient leur clarté. Et la nouvelle venue offrit ses fleurs avec une grâce exquise à cet homme âgé . . . qui lui tendait les mains.'' Albert Flament, ''Tableaux de Paris,'' *La Revue de Paris*, 1 Aug. 1932, 706–7.

17. For a sociological analysis of the salons, see Christophe Charle, *La Crise littéraire à l'époque du naturalisme: Essai d'histoire sociale des groupes et des genres littéraires* (Paris: Presses de l'Ecole Normale Supérieure, 1979), 182.

18. ''Jamais je n'ai vu l'intimité avec l'histoire poussée à ce degré de naturel. . . .'' Philippe Barrès, ''Gyp, ou la féerie,'' *Les Nouvelles littéraires,* 9 July 1932, 2.

19. ''un majestueux et profond fauteuil.'' Tout-Paris, ''Bloc-Notes Parisien: Gyp,'' *Le Gaulois,* 1 March 1895, 1.

20. ''peu ménagé, mangé par le soleil et par le temps.'' Philippe Barrès, ''Gyp, ou la féerie,'' 2.

21. ''La chère était délicieuse et choisie . . . d'exquises pâtisseries confectionnées selon de précieuses recettes.'' Lucien Corpechot, ''Souvenirs d'un journaliste: Gyp,'' *La Revue universelle*, 15 May 1936, 428.

22. See Zillhardt, *Louise-Catherine Breslau et ses amis,* 105.

23. Corpechot, ''Souvenirs d'un journaliste: Gyp,'' 428.

24. Ibid.

25. Véga, ''Gyp telle que je l'ai connue,'' *La Revue des deux mondes,* 15 Sept. 1932, 451.

26. ''les yeux pétillants de malice.'' Corpechot, ''Souvenirs d'un journaliste: Gyp,'' 423.

27. ''un petit rire cristallin et nerveux.'' Tout-Paris, ''Bloc-Notes Parisien: Gyp.''

28. ''[E]lle cause, cette Gyp, de tout et de tous; de la littérature qu'elle sait à fond, d'Edouard Drumont . . . à qui elle dédie son livre nouveau, de ses promenades à cheval,

de la peinture qu'elle adore; c'est vraiment une personnelle, une originale.'' Julia Daudet, *Souvenirs autour d'un groupe littéraire* (Paris: Charpentier, 1910), 185–86.

29. ''ses yeux clairs, vifs et railleurs, tout pétillants d'esprit où se reflétaient les plus fugitives impressions de vie; ils s'animaient au feu de la conversation d'une telle intensité que l'on en oubliait la forme et la couleur.'' Zillhardt, *Louise-Catherine Breslau et ses amis,* 105.

30. ''Tous les potins de Paris aboutissent à son salon, d'où ils se déversent dans ses livres.'' Adolphe Brisson, ''Gyp,'' *Portraits intimes,* 2nd ser. (Paris: Armand-Colin, 1904), 26. For additional descriptions of Gyp's salon, see Robert Evreux, ''Il y a quatre-vingt-dix ans naissait Gyp,'' *L'Ordre,* 19 Aug. 1939, 2; Maurice Guillemot, ''Gyp,'' *Fémina,* 15 Nov. 1902, 344; India, ''Esquisses féminines: Gyp,'' *La Libre Parole illustrée,* [1894], 3; Yves-Gérard Le Dantec, ''Mes souvenirs de Gyp,'' *Livre d'or de l'Académie de Neuilly,* 26–30; Andrée Viollis, ''Chez Gyp,'' *Le Petit Parisien,* 1 March 1929, 1–2.

31. ''[J']y voyais autant de monde, *sinon plus,* qu'à Paris.'' Gyp, letter to the comtesse de Mirabeau, [25 Dec. 1915], Sibylle Gaudry collection, Paris.

32. ''plus trapu que son frère . . . une bonne figure gaie . . . mal fichu . . . facilité et paresse . . . signe particulier: extraordinairement fort.'' Gyp, *Un trio turbulent* (Paris: Hachette, 1929), 6. The book bears the dedication: ''A Thierry et à Nini, Hommage de leur victime principale, Gyp.''

33. ''un fils de sa race.'' Zillhardt, *Louise-Catherine Breslau et ses amis,* 102.

34. ''Long, mince, nerveux, distingué, l'air narquois, très bien tenu.'' Gyp, *Un trio turbulent,* 5.

35. ''toute blonde et rose . . . le nez en l'air, les yeux malins . . . menue et solide à la fois.'' Ibid., 7.

36. ''yeux vifs . . . reparties . . . cheveux blonds ébouriffés par le vent de mer.'' Roger Martin du Gard, letter to Madame Félix Le Dantec, 30 Nov. 1917, in Roger Martin du Gard, *Correspondance générale,* vol. 2 (1914–1918), ed. Pierre Bordel (Paris: Gallimard, 1980), 207.

37. ''le respectueux hommage de son compagnon de jeux marins, lui-même le père d'une fillette de dix ans.'' Ibid.

38. ''Hier, je l'ai rencontrée dans la rue du village, tenant par la main deux petits mendiants à qui elle allait acheter des culottes. Elle nourrit tous les chiens perdus. C'est une excellente créature.'' Anatole France, letter to Léontine Arman de Caillavet, n.d., quoted in Jeanne-Maurice Pouquet, *Le Salon de Madame Arman de Caillavet* (Paris: Hachette, 1926), 158.

39. See Dino Gambini, ''Le Châlet Vernet à Lion-sur-Mer: Quatre années d'amitié entre Gyp et Anatole France,'' *Ouest-France,* 20 Sept. 1979, 9.

40. Gyp, letter to Jeanne-Maurice Pouquet, n.d., in Pouquet, *Le Salon de Madame Arman de Caillavet,* 123–24.

41. ''Quel superbe éventail que vous m'avez envoyé!'' Gyp, letter to Anatole France, n.d., Naf 13121, #71–72, AF. Gyp's letters to France are frequently undated. From references in the correspondence, one may assume they were written between 1890 and 1894.

42. ''Que je vous remercie de l'eau de cologne!'' Gyp, letter to Anatole France, n.d, Naf 13121, #98–99, AF.

43. ''Voici votre installation: Suzon au *Châlet Vernet,* dans la chambre de Nicole, une grande chambre à deux lits qui, jusqu'à cette année, était la chambre d'Aymar et de Thierry. Vous, à *la Farandole*(!) en face; vous y serez *seul* tant que vous voudrez. . . . Vous aurez une chambre au premier, et le salon avec bureau . . . pour travailler à vous *tout seul;* . . . salon et salle à manger de *réunion* sont au Châlet Vernet. . . . On déjeune à midi.

On dine à 7 heures ½. Chacun déjeune (le premier déjeuner) à l'heure qui lui plaît, et voilà la vie! la oilà! . . . pas très drôle, mais très, très *indépendante*.'' Gyp, letter to Anatole France, n.d., Naf 13121, #114–117, AF.

44. "Madame de Martel est une excellente créature. Je la vois qu'aux repas, et le reste du temps elle ne se montre que par des soins et des prévenances.'' Anatole France, letter to Léontine Arman de Caillavet, n.d., quoted in Pouquet, *Le Salon de Madame Arman de Caillavet,* 158.

45. "des petits hobereaux normands qui m'ennuient.'' Anatole France, leter to Léontine Arman de Caillavet, n.d. Ibid., 157.

46. "France était délicieux, toujours content de tout, de bonne humeur, égal et gentil.'' Gyp, letter to Jeanne-Maurice Pouquet, n.d. Ibid., 154.

47. "Souvent vers six heures, il allait se promener. Les enfants le suivaient, récoltant d'autres enfants, qui se mettaient aussi à suivre. . . . Nous dînions à huit heures, mais presque tous les autres baigneurs dînaient à sept heures et demie ou même à sept heures. A huit heures et demie France n'était pas rentré et les parents affolés mobilisaient tous leurs domestiques pour les lancer sur la maison. Vers neuf heures, France arrivait, souriant et satisfait, suivi de son troupeau.'' Ibid.

48. "Les derniers Bergeret sont exquis!'' Gyp, letter to Anatole France, [1893], Naf 13121, #77–78, AF.

49. "J'ai lu hier soir la suite du *Philosophe.* C'est très bien et cela m'intéresse beaucoup. Et puis c'est une façon de vous retrouver un peu.'' Anatole France, letter to Gyp, 30 Aug. 1893, Naf 15422, #18–19, AF.

50. "J'apprends que vous buvez jusqu'à la lie les délices de la vie inimitable, où votre mari vous a entraînée.'' Anatole France, letter to Léontine Arman de Caillavet, [July 1893], Naf 15422, AF.

51. "Ma chambre est très bien, mais elle ne vaut pas le cabinet de travail de l'avenue Hoche.'' Anatole France, letter to Léontine Arman de Caillavet, n.d., quoted in Pouquet, *Le Salon de Madame Arman de Caillavet,* 153.

52. "Je deviens stupide loin de vous.'' Ibid.

53. "J'espère que vous ne croyez pas que c'est moi qui suis négligente et malhonnête et qui ne fais pas passer la copie quand on me la remet. Mais je n'ai *rien* reçu de France(!)'' Gyp, letter to Maurice Barrès, 1892, private collection.

54. "mince, fragile . . . des yeux magnifiques et une masse de cheveux d'un blond chaud. L'air très intelligent.'' Gyp, *Un trio turbulent,* 57.

55. "Elle ne cesse de me parler de vous avec l'accent d'un respectueux attachement. Vous lui avez donné, Madame, de longues heures d'or, dont le souvenir la charmera encore.'' Anatole France, letter to Gyp, [1892], Naf 15421, #160–61, AF.

56. "a été vue fumant . . . et cela m'a fait *des potins*. Elle sait parfaitement que je lui défends de fumer *même à la maison*. Je ne peux pas du tout avoir confiance en elle pour les choses de tact ou de mesure. Elle en manque complètement et a besoin d'une surveillance *directe*. Elle n'est pas du tout comme Suzon qui a un tact infini.'' Gyp, letter to Anatole France, [22 Nov. 1895?], Naf 13121, #45– 48, AF.

57. "dont je soupçonnais *vaguement* la nature.'' Gyp, letter to the comtesse de Mirabeau, 25 Oct. [1915], Sibylle Gaudry collection, Paris.

58. "Je réponds tout de suite à ce que tu me dis au sujet: ''*des 2 ou trois mois passés à la mer, et qui, heureusement, ne nuisaient pas à mes gains*''(!!!!) que, d'abord, . . . toi . . . tu ne t'étonnais pas que j'aie pu élever les trois enfants, soigner leurs dents, leurs vêtements, leur éducation, leurs santés, les conduire à la mer—car c'est *à cause de Thierry* qu'on y est allé *depuis 1885 jusqu'en 1896*—avoir—à cause du même Thierry, qui ne

travaillait pas au lycée—un précepteur, avec les 9,000 francs de revenus que j'avais, et où la maison—c'est à dire le logement—comptait pour 5,000!!!. . . . J'avais *pris* la maison, il a fallu *la payer*. . . . Donc, *en 1895*, pour pouvoir payer la maison de Lion, . . . je suis restée *seule à Neuilly* (ce qui te prouve que *je trouvais que le séjour à la mer "nuisait à mes gains!!'")* Ibid.

59. "When your dear father refused [to publish] *Dans l'train*, he told me: 'I don't wan't to because there are things in it that might vex Arthur Meyer.' Arthur Meyer having sent me flowers 'for these things that might vex him,' I recounted this to Monsieur Calmann, who explained to me: 'It wasn't only for Arthur Meyer but for the Jews. When the work contains anything offensive to the Jews, don't bother offering it to me.' " ("Quand Monsieur votre père m'a refusé *Dans l'train*, il m'a dit: 'Je ne veux pas, parce qu'il y a des choses désagréables pour Arthur Meyer.' Arthur Meyer m'ayant envoyé des fleurs 'pour ces choses désagréables,' je l'ai raconté à M. Calmann qui m'a expliqué, 'ce n'était pas seulement pour Arthur Meyer, mais pour les Juifs. Quand il y aura quelque chose contre les Juifs, il est inutile de m'offrir le livre.' " Gyp, letter to [?] Calmann-Lévy, 16 Aug. 1897, CL.

60. "les plus grands égorgeurs, les plus féroces usuriers de la littérature." Edmond et Jules de Goncourt, *Journal*, vol. 3, 665.

61. See Michael Marrus, *The Politics of Assimilation: A Study of the French Jewish Community at the Time of the Dreyfus Affair* (New York: Oxford UP, 1971), esp. chaps. 3 and 4.

62. "pas de nature à convenir à sa clientèle." Contract between Gyp and Calmann-Lévy dated 13 May 1884, CL. The 18 March 1889 contract contains the same wording.

63. "où Drumont poursuivait Moïse . . . où il y avait des *couplets* et des *pages entières sur eux deux*, où Moïse était beaucoup plus déplaisant que mon Baron Sinaï. . . ." Gyp, letter to [?] Calmann-Lévy, 4 Aug. 1892, CL.

64. "Je vous promets aussi dans *Madame la Duchesse* d'ôter ce qui pourrait vous choquer." Ibid.

65. "foule de choses désagréables." [Paul?] Calmann-Lévy, notes on the *Journal d'un philosophe*, [1893], CL.

66. Gyp, letter to [?] Calmann-Lévy, 4 Aug. 1892, CL.

67. Ibid.

68. Gyp, letter to [Paul] Calmann-Lévy, [July-Aug?] 1892, CL.

69. "des embêtements sémitiques." Gyp, letter to Anatole France, [1892], Fonds Ricci, #114, AF.

70. Paul Calmann-Lévy, telegram to Gyp, [4 Aug. 1892], CL.

71. For more on the professionalization and commercialization of the book trade in late nineteenth-century France, see Jean-Yves Mollier, "L'Edition française s'est-elle convertie au capitalisme?" *L'Histoire* 133 (May 1990): 74–75; and Jean-Yves Mollier, *L'Argent et les lettres: Histoire du capitalisme d'édition, 1880–1920* (Paris: Fayard, 1988), 374–79.

72. "notre situation comme administrateurs . . . est des plus difficiles, et va même en s'aggravant. . . . Dans ces conditions, vous devez comprendre quelle extrême réserve nous est imposée." Paul Calmann-Lévy, letter to Gyp, 17 Oct. 1892, CL.

73. "il y a des choses *du même genre*." Gyp, letter to [?] Calmann-Lévy, 1 June 1893, CL.

74. "le plus grand nombre possible de volumes de Gyp." Paul Calmann-Lévy, letter to Gyp, 11 May 1888, CL.

75. "Comment . . . nous résignerions-nous à voir un livre de vous édité par un de nos

confrères avec notre consentement? . . . Le *Petit bleu* publié ailleurs, c'est toujours le nom de Gyp sur un autre catalogue; vous cessez ainsi . . . d'appartenir à notre maison, et voilà ce que nous tenons absolument à éviter. Pour vous comme pour nous, chère Madame, il est préférable et plus avantageux à tout égard . . . de vous défendre de cet éparpillement de vos oeuvres, de cette dispersion de votre nom. . . . Le mieux est . . . que nous missions complètement . . . nos bonnes volontés en vue de nos intérêts communs.'' Paul Calmann-Lévy, letter to Gyp, 11 May 1888, CL.

76. On the world of late nineteenth-century French publishers and their authors, see James Smith Allen, *In the Public Eye: A History of Reading in Modern France, 1800–1940* (Princeton, NJ: Princeton UP, 1991); Christophe Charle, ''Le Champ de la production littéraire,'' in *Histoire de l'édition française*, ed. Roger Chartier and Henri-Jean Martin. Vol. 3: *Le Temps des éditeurs: Du romantisme à la Belle Epoque* (Paris: Fayard, 1990), 137–75; Odile and Henri-Jean Martin, ''Le Monde des éditeurs,'' in Chartier and Martin, eds., *Histoire de l'édition française,* 176–244.

77. ''Je ne fais pas de la littérature seulement pour mon plaisir.'' Gyp, letter to [?] Calmann-Lévy, 16 Aug. 1897, CL.

78. ''il ne lui restait *rien*, pas 5f de revenus.'' Gyp, letter to the comtesse de Mirabeau, 25 Oct. [1915], Sibylle Gaudry collection, Paris.

79. ''Les fermiers paient de moins en moins, les appartements se louent mal et, de plus, les *très beaux* cadeaux que me faisait ma grand-mère sont supprimés depuis qu'elle n'a plus la disposition de ses revenus.'' Gyp, letter to Paul Calmann-Lévy, 1887, CL.

80. ''parce que j'ai absolument besoin de cette somme.'' Gyp, letter to [?] Calmann-Lévy, 17 June 1894, CL.

81. ''par *raisonnement* plus rapace que je ne le serais par *tempérament*.'' Gyp, letter to [?] Calmann-Lévy, 16 Aug. 1897, CL.

82. ''[C]hez vous ça marche tellement mieux qu'ailleurs.'' Gyp, letter to [?] Calmann-Lévy, 28 July 1909, CL.

83. See chapter 5, note 32, in this book.

84. ''Je ne pouvais pas *diminuer* (pour *l'oeil,* au moins) le *train* et *l'entretien* de Neuilly, attendu que, si on avait vu une maison délabrée, des domestiques sales, ou pas de domestiques du tout, on m'aurait *immédiatement* offert 3 sous la ligne qu'on me payait 10.'' Gyp, letter to the comtesse de Mirabeau, 25 Oct. [1915], Sibylle Gaudry collection, Paris.

85. ''l'accroc du Baron Sinaï.'' Gyp, letter to [?] Calmann-Lévy, July 1893, CL.

86. ''un admirateur de sa crânerie et de son talent—Gyp.'' Gyp, *Le Journal d'un philosophe* (Paris: Charpentier et Fasquelle, 1894).

87. ''[E]lle regrette—j'en suis sûr—de ne pas être l'homme.''

88. Maurice Barrès, ''L'Esprit de révolte en littérature,'' *Scènes et doctrines du nationalisme*, vol. 1 (Paris: Plon, 1925), 239–43.

89. ''trop étroite mais si intéressante, des écrivains qui, par tempérament, sont peu disposés à se satisfaire des hommes et des choses uniquement parce que celles-ci sont légales, et que ceux-là sont puissants.'' Ibid., 239.

90. ''J'ai un fichu caractère qui m'empêche de me taire quand j'ai envie de crier, et je ne peux pas voir des gens malpropres entourés de considération sans avoir, au suprême degré, cette envie! Et voilà pourquoi le Philosophe.'' Gyp, letter to Alexandre Dumas fils, [1894], Naf 14666, #54, AD.

91. ''J'ai bien réfléchi. Non seulement il m'est impossible de défigurer un personnage qui sera le *héros* d'un *livre*, mais encore je ne peux pas faire de changements sans qu'ils

soient interprétés d'une façon qui me blesserait infiniment.'' Gyp, letter to Georges Calmann-Lévy, [26 Oct. 1893], CL.

92. ''[S]i l'on supprime l'attrait des personnalités et la puissance fascinante des *clefs*, il ne reste que peu de choses comme intérêt. . . . Certes, je ne publierai pas—quoi que aimant beaucoup le talent de Madame de Martel, lorsqu'elle s'exerce spontanément.'' Notes of [?] Calmann-Lévy on Gyp's *Journal d'un philosophe*, [1893], CL.

93. On Gyp's relations with her publisher, see Willa Z. Silverman, '' 'Semitic Troubles': Author-Publisher Relations in *fin-de-siècle* France: The Case of Gyp and Calmann-Lévy,'' *Historical Reflections/Réflexions Historiques*, 19, no. 3, Nov. 1993, 309–34.

94. ''Voulez-vous avoir la bonté, quand on fera des annonces comme celles du *Gaulois* ou de *L'Echo*, de faire parler de Gyp au *masculin*, 'le plus joli *qu'il* ait publié' au lieu de '*qu'elle* ait publié?' '' Gyp, letter to [?] Calmann-Lévy, [5 Sept. 1894?], CL.

95. ''en parlant de *lui*, on dise 'Gyp' *tout court*, pas Madame.'' Gyp, letter to [Georges Montorgueil], n.d., 428AP2, AN.

96. See ''Il y a 50 ans: De Mirabeau au 'Petit Bob,' '' n.pl., 26 Oct. 1938.

97. See ''Choses du jour,'' *Petit journal pour rire*, 142, [Oct. 1888], 6.

98. ''toujours fleuri de gardénias, couvert de bagues et puant de parfumerie, avec des ongles peints.'' L'abbé Mugnier, *Journal, 1879–1939*, ed. Marcel Billot (Paris: Mercure de France, 1985), 94.

99. Jean Lorrain, ''Dans les salons: Une petite-fille de Mirabeau,'' *L'Evénement*, 23 Nov. 1889; reprinted in Jean Lorrain, *Femmes de 1900* (Paris: Editions de la Madeleine, 1932), 145.

100. Ibid., 147.

101. Ibid., 150.

102. ''les noms tragiques et pompeux des chers grands hommes dont nous gardons jalousement la mémoire. . . .'' Ibid., 148.

103. Ibid., 150.

104. ''Il est trop périlleux de vouloir toucher à certaines gloires.'' Ibid.

105. ''étant donné le talent spirituellement pervers de Madame de Martel, ses boutades de Loulou et son 'bobisme' exagéré, son joli profil à l'évent, et ses coiffures de chien fou sur ses grandes capotes de velours *Kate Greenaway*, j'aimerais autant *Mirabelle*: ce serait plus savoureux, plus elle-même, plus trouvé.'' Ibid.

106. Act of 10 June 1895, mentioned in Etude XLVI–1318, Notarial Archives, AN.

107. ''Cahier de charges pour parvenir à la vente d'une maison à Paris rue de la Barouillière—requête de Monsieur le comte de Martel de Janville,'' 16 Nov. 1895, XLVI–1320, Notarial Archives, AN.

108. ''Procuration par Mme la comtesse de Martel de Janville,'' 16 Dec. 1895, XLVI–1318, Notarial Archives, AN.

Chapter VIII

1. ''Dieu sait que je n'ambitionnais pas cette magistrature et que je n'ai rien fait pour l'obtenir. Je veux faire mon devoir et j'ai besoin du concours de mes amis—vous êtes, Madame, des meilleurs—ainsi, je [veux] de vous la constance de cette sympathie que vous me témoignez depuis si longtemps.'' Félix Faure, letter to Gyp, [Jan.] 1895, private collection, Paris.

2. Maurice Barrès, *Mes cahiers*, vol. 9 (Paris: Plon, 1935), 275.

3. "Je continue à adorer les Faure—qui le méritent, je vous assure—tout comme s'ils n'étaient pas Présidents, mais ça ne me fait pas aimer le gouvernement, oh! non! . . . seulement, Bob n'y peut plus toucher, ça l'embête, et moi aussi. . . . Je n'ai pas beaucoup de manières pour l'Elysée! . . . et je ne sais guère me gêner." Gyp, letter to Ludovic Halévy, 22 Jan. 1895, MS4485, #413, LH.

4. "la tête serrée dans sa petite capote légendaire et riant derrière son face-à-main." Jean Drault, *Drumont, "La France juive" et "La Libre Parole"* (Paris: Hérisson, 1935), 91.

5. Ibid., 162.

6. "nous faisait une patricienne spirituelle et caustique et une révolutionnaire de l'école de Vallès. Ce contraste achevait de souligner la note d'un journal déjà lu 'par des curés et des communards.' " Ibid.

7. Maurice Barrès, *Scènes et doctrines du nationalisme* (Paris: Editions du Trident, 1987), 27–34.

8. Gyp, "Sûr, qu'elle n'est pas à la noce, la France! . . ." ("France ain't having fun, that's for sure!") *Le Rire,* 28 Dec. 1895, 1.

9. "avec l'indépendance d'un féodal, le courage d'un demi-solde et la gouaille d'un gavroche." Michel Missoffe, *Gyp et ses amis* (Paris: Flammarion, 1932), 117.

10. Stephen Wilson remarks that "the Jews were sometimes identified with femininity, and hostility to Jews may have been an expression of women's rejection of their gender and its disabilities." Stephen Wilson, *Ideology and Experience: Antisemitism in France at the Time of the Dreyfus Affair* (East Brunswick, NJ: Associated UP, 1982), 597.

11. "ses petits rats chéris, qu'elle adore." Gyp, "Histoire de la Troisième République," *Le Rire,* 14 Nov. 1896, 13.

12. "est devenue puissante. Elle ne tremble que devant l'ami auquel elle ne sait rien refuser." Ibid., 16.

13. "Bonne Galette de France—Article d'Exportation." Ibid.

14. For this interpretation, see Jean-Paul Sartre, *Réflexions sur la question juive* (Paris: Gallimard, 1954), 54.

15. Stephen Wilson discusses "sexual anti-Semitism"—which, according to the author, seemed particularly virulent during the Affair—as an "externalization and projection of a sexuality that is for some reason repressed." Wilson, *Ideology and Experience,* 585. See also Pierre Birnbaum's chapter on "Hermaphrodisme et perversions sexuelles" in his book *Un mythe politique: La "République juive" de Léon Blum à Mendès France* (Paris: Fayard, 1988), 196–236.

16. "voluptueuse, excitante." "Cette femme a quelque chose de malsainement tentateur." Edmond and Jules de Goncourt, *Journal: Mémoires de la vie littéraire,* vol. 3 (1887–1896), ed. Robert Ricatte (Paris: Laffont, 1989), 930 and 1204.

17. Dombasle, "Jules Lemaître et Gyp," *Le Siècle,* 14 May 1900, 2.

18. Str., "Echos du jour: La Femme du jour—Gyp," *Le Siècle,* 19 Dec. 1899, 1.

19. The phrase is taken from George Mosse, *Nationalism and Sexuality: Respectability and Abnormal Sexuality in Modern Europe* (New York: Howard Fertig, 1985), 10.

20. See Mosse, "Introduction," 1–22.

21. "beau et brave, comme un lion." Barrès, *Scènes et doctrines du nationalisme,* 233.

22. "un reître botté et casqué échappé de l'obscurantisme du Moyen Age." Quoted in Drault, *Drumont, "La France juive" et "La Libre Parole,"* 122.

23. "un viveur à outrance." Police report, n.d., BA1193, APP.

24. "un aventurier dont les qualités d'action et d'initiative sont très réelles." Ibid.

25. "cette espèce de sollicitude pour le peuple, affichée par des messieurs bien mis, chaussés de bottes vernies, gantés de frais. . . ." Police report, 13 Oct. 1892, BA1193, APP.

26. "Il n'aime faire sonner les titres de noblesse aux oreilles de prolétaires que pour mieux les emballer." Police report, 4 April 1892, BA1193, APP.

27. "braves gens d'un antisémitisme à faire frémir." Drault, *Drumont, "La France juive" et "La Libre Parole,"* 172.

28. "Hallali du juif." Ibid.

29. "de véritable massues fort bien travaillées du reste. . . ." Police report, 13 June 1892, BA1193, APP.

30. "la France archaïque et la France moderne [s'unissant] dans une même âme." Barrès, *Scènes et docrines du nationalisme,* 235. On Morès, see also Donald W. Dresden, *The Marquis de Morès: Emperor of the Badlands* (Norman, OK: U of Oklahoma P, 1970); and Zeev Sternhell, *La Droite révolutionnaire en France, 1885–1914: Les Origines françaises du fascisme* (Paris: Seuil, 1978), 215–44.

31. "solide petit bataillon des femmes modernes"; "[c]e gracieux essaim de femmes un peu trop blondes, un peu trop mièvres, un peu trop délicates, un peu trop idéales peut-être. . . ." Gyp, "Les Femmes," n. pl., Jan. 1893, 20.

32. "Les femmes qui écrivent sont antipathiques à presque tous, et je voudrais faire oublier le plus possible que Gyp est une femme." Gyp, letter to Ludovic Halévy, 10 March 1895, MS4485, #414, LH.

33. See Anne-Marie and Charles Lalo, "La Faillite de la beauté," *Le Mercure de France,* 1 Aug. 1913, 493–523.

34. "visage . . . inachevé et bizarrement chiffonné, la taille gracile, les mouvements gauches." Gyp, *Tante Joujou* (Paris: Calmann-Lévy, 1893), 24.

35. "Je sais très bien que je suis, non pas jolie, mais gentille . . . que je plais . . . que je suis . . . attirante. . . ." Gyp, *Une passionnette* (Paris: Calmann-Lévy, 1891); quoted in Lalo and Lalo, "La Faillite de la beauté," 504. Ellipses in original.

36. "je n'ai rien d'une femme . . . je suis un sauvage . . ." Gyp, *Le Mariage de Chiffon* (Paris: Calmann-Lévy, 1940), 101. Ellipses in original. The first edition was published in 1894.

37. "c'est pas une femme, c'est un joujou! . . ." Gyp, *Tante Joujou,* 24. Ellipses in original.

38. "garçon en diable." Hippolyte Durand, *Le Règne de l'enfant* (Paris: Lecène-Oudin, 1889), 350. See also Anatole France, "Loulou," *La Vie littéraire,* 2nd ser. (Paris: Calmann-Lévy, 1890), 245–51.

39. "un grand gars breton . . . insouciant et léger." Gyp, *Une passionnette,* 22.

40. "un effarement terrible, une douloureuse révolte. Elle appuya comme un bébé ses petits poings fermés sur ses yeux et s'enfuit ne voulant plus voir." Gyp, *Tante Joujou,* 70.

41. "Il avait tout de même des 'principes,' le Joujou! . . . c'est pour ça qu'il est cassé! . . ." Ibid., 193. Ellipses in original.

42. Edmond de Goncourt was annoyed that Gyp's novel seemed so closely modeled on one of his own, as his journal entry of 27 June 1894 makes plain: "The literature of the moment really relies on the characters I've created! *Le Mariage de Chiffon* is almost a reedition of *Renée Mauperin.* . . ." ("Vraiment, la littérature du moment vit joliment sur mes types! *Le Mariage de Chiffon,* c'est presque une réédition de *Renée Mauperin.* . . .") Edmond and Jules de Goncourt, *Journal: Mémoires de la vie littéraire,* vol. 3, 982.

43. Gyp, *Le Mariage de Chiffon,* 11.

44. "Très vulgaire d'allure et d'aspect." Ibid., 13.

45. "nulle finesse de sentiments ni de sensations. . . ." Ibid.

46. "les gens qui se massent pour tomber les isolés . . ." Ibid., 94. Ellipses in original.

47. "une merveilleuse petite créature." Gyp, *Bijou* (Paris: Collection Nelson, 1914), 12. First published by Calmann-Lévy in 1896, *Bijou* was also serialized in *La Revue de Paris* in March and April 1896.

48. Ibid.

49. "ce petit monstre à l'air de candeur, qui porte autour d'elle la catastrophe et le suicide . . . avec des mines de petite-fille. . . ." Marguerite Bourcet, "Gyp: Docteur ès Education," *Le Noël*, 12 Oct. 1933, 457.

50. "C'est l'égoïste la plus renforcée qui ait jamais existé sur la terre. Elle n'aime absolument qu'elle." Emile Faguet, rev. of *Bijou*, *Cosmopolis*, 6 Oct. 1896, 170.

51. "Dominer, dominer sans cesse, dominer toujours, dominer sans que personne échappe à son empire. . . ." Ibid.

52. "Bijou, c'est un peu Bel-Ami en femme; . . . l'exploiteur de femmes, le comédien froid et féroce de l'amour, soyez sûr qu'il a commencé par aimer les femmes." Ibid., 172.

53. "Bijou finira par être méchante." Ibid.

54. "Il y a déjà quelques traces de cela dans l'histoire de sa jeunesse telle que Gyp nous l'a contée, et qui sont . . . chez l'auteur l'intuition de ce que son personnage deviendra plus tard. . . ." Ibid.

55. On women in Gyp's novels, see Georges Pellissier, "La Femme mariée et l'adultère dans le roman français moderne," *La Revue des revues,* 15 Feb. 1899, 353–68; Théodore Joran, "Le Portrait de la jeune fille dans les romans de Gyp (1)," *La Femme contemporaine,* Feb. 1910, 142–55.

56. "approbations . . . critiques . . . [et] justes revendications." " 'La Fronde,' " *Le Temps,* 7 Dec. 1897, 1.

57. "Bob pourra-t-il toucher à *tout*? Quelle sera la couleur du journal?" Gyp, letter to Marguerite Durand, [1897], 091, MD.

58. "Vous êtes mille fois aimable d'insister pour avoir Bob, mais il ne se sentirait *pas assez libre*. . . . Décidément, nous sommes, Bob et moi, des êtres trop indépendants pour faire du journalisme et qu'il nous faut nous en tenir à nos petits bouquins où nous caricaturons en pleine liberté tout ce qui nous 'chante.' Je suis très touchée de votre si gracieuse insistance, je vous en remercie. . . ." Gyp, letter to Marguerite Durand, [1897], 091, MD.

59. "Je n'aurais jamais eu la pensée de toucher à la religion. Etant moi-même très croyante, je respecte les croyances des autres quelles qu'elles soient. Quant à ne pas être antisémite, c'est impossible à Bob. . . . La question juive . . . est absolument *impossible* à laisser de côté dans la caricature *d'actualité*. . . . Et puis, Madame, si vous avez regardé les Bob, vous avez dû voir que les profils Hébreux jouent un rôle que je ne saurais pas supprimer." Ibid.

60. "Je regrette beaucoup de ne pouvoir pas collaborer à *La Fronde*—dont le titre est charmant. . . ." Ibid.

61. "Gyp nous avait promis, pour chaque semaine, un dessin de Bob, qui aurait été notre 'Forain,' mais elle aurait voulu pouvoir faire de l'antisémitisme. Sur mon refus, elle s'est retirée. Notre journal, en effet, sera le journal de toutes les femmes françaises." " 'La Fronde,' " *Le Temps,* 7 Dec. 1897. One critic remained convinced that Gyp continued to write for *La Fronde* under a pseudonym. See Han Ryner, *Le Massacre des amazones: Etudes critiques sur deux cents bas-bleus contemporains* (Paris: Chamuel, 1899), 201.

62. "Si Gyp n'est point des nôtres, ce n'est pas que 'nous n'en voulûmes point,' car

une place lui fut offerte, et nous regrettons son absence. . . . Elle déclina l'invitation, ne voyant à quel propos, hors la Synagogue et l'Elysée, excercer parmi nous son brio, sa verve, son incisif et délicieux talent.'' Séverine, ''Notes d'une frondeuse: Réponse à Ponchon,'' *La Fronde,* 21 Dec. 1897, 1.

63. See Jacques des Gachons, rev. of *Mademoiselle Eve, L'Ermitage,* April 1895, 240; Jacques du Tillet, rev. of *Mademoiselle Eve, La Revue politique et littéraire,* 23 March 1895, 379–80; and Albin Valabrègue, rev. of *Mademoiselle Eve, L'Illustration,* 9 March 1895, 195.

64. See Gyp, letter to Alexandre Dumas fils, [May 1892?], #94, AD; Gyp, letter to Ludovic Halévy, [May 1892?], MS4485, #409, LH. See also Francisque Sarcey, ''Le Premier Sentiment de Loulou,'' *Le Temps,* 16 May 1892, 2.

65. ''la comtesse de Martel [représentait] à ce moment-là pour nos Escholiers l'esprit parisien dans ce qu'il a d'aigu et de satirique . . . mais à cette époque j'étais troublé par autre chose que par le parisianisme. Qu'y pouvais-je?—Gyp était . . . 'étincelante' et Ibsen ne l'était fichtre pas!'' Aurélien Lugné-Poe, *La Parade.* Vol. 1: *Le Sot du tremplin* (Paris: Gallimard, 1930), 219.

66. ''du Gyp, de second cru, et même troisième.'' Francisque Sarcey, ''Chronique théâtrale,'' *Le Temps,* 7 Oct. 1895, 2.

67. ''il faudrait se référer aux documents littéraires et artistiques de l'époque, aux romans de Gyp. . . .'' Léon Blum, *Souvenirs sur l'Affaire* (Paris: Gallimard, 1981), 68.

68. ''l'écrivain qui a déterminé dans l'esprit des Français les images d'antisémitisme les plus puissantes.'' Charles Maurras, ''Les Images puissantes: *Un ménage dernier cri,''* *La Gazette de France,* 9 Aug. 1903, 1–2.

69. Marc Angenot, *Ce que l'on dit des Juifs en 1889: Antisémitisme et discours social* (Saint-Denis: Presses Universitaires de Vincennes, 1989), 132.

70. ''[C]e sont des choses comiques, de [la] littérature légère.'' Letter to Félix Pissarro in *Correspondance de Camille Pissarro,* vol. 4 (1895–1898), ed. Janine Bailly-Herzberg (Paris: Valhermeil, 1989), 381.

71. These works include: *Les Gens chics* (1895), *Ohé! les dirigeants* (1896), *En Balade* (1897), *Le Baron Sinaï* (1897), *Le Journal d'un grinchu* (1898), *Israël* (1898), *Les Cayenne de Rio* (1899), *Les Izolâtres*(1899), *Les Femmes du colonel* (1899).

72. On the Jewish character and anti-Semitism in French literature, see Robert Byrnes, *Antisemitism in Modern France* (New Brunswick, NJ: Rutgers UP, 1950), vol. 1, 104–10; Moses Debré, *The Image of the Jew in French Literature from 1800 to 1908,* trans. Gertrude Hirschler (New York: Ktav, 1970); Charles C. Lehrmann, *The Jewish Element in French Literature* (Rutherford, NJ: Fairleigh Dickinson UP, 1971); Béatrice Philippe, *Etre juif dans la société française* (Paris: Montalba, 1979), 206–17; Léon Poliakov, *Histoire de l'antisémitisme,* (Paris: Calmann-Lévy, 1977) Vol. 4, 45–83; Earle Stanley Randall, *The Jewish Character in the French Novel, 1870–1914* (Menasha, WI: Banta, 1941); Wilson, *Ideology and Experience.*

73. On this genre, see Susan Rubin Suleiman, *Authoritarian Fictions: The Ideological Novel as a Literary Genre* (New York: Columbia UP, 1983).

74. ''devant le profil du bouc, ténébreusement émissaire d'une nouvelle société, elle a tiré simplement la langue.'' Rachilde, rev. of *Israël, Le Mercure de France* 26, April–June 1898, 232.

75. ''*Israël* est une satire mordante de la sale *youtrerie* prétentieuse et parvenue . . . [qui] jou[e] un triste rôle dans notre vieille société moderne, et [qu']il est bon de . . . dénoncer.'' Albert Keim, rev. of *Israël, La Cité d'Art* 3, March 1898, 106.

76. ''Gyp promène avec jouissance le fer rouge de son ironie sanglante sur les plaies

vives qui sont l'humiliation de notre société." Georges Sénéchal, rev. of *Israël, La Nouvelle Revue* no. 3, March–April 1898, 753.

77. Ibid.

78. "ostensiblement volé dans tous les pays et dans toutes les affaires . . ." Gyp, *Israël* (Paris: Flammarion, 1898), 22–23.

79. "quand la République parlementaire fera place à une dictature, ou à un empire, ou à un boulangisme quelconque, la liquidation . . . sera plutôt pénible . . ." Ibid., 281–82. Ellipses in original.

80. The phrase is borrowed from Frederic Jameson, *Fables of Aggression: Wyndham Lewis, The Modernist as Fascist* (Berkeley, CA: U of California P, 1979), 27. On the use of metonymy and other forms of polemical rhetoric during the Dreyfus Affair, see Richard Griffiths, *The Use of Abuse: The Polemics of the Dreyfus Affair and Its Aftermath* (New York: Berg, 1991).

81. "très gras, d'une graisse jaune et flasque. Les yeux bouffis, le nez épaté, les lèvres molles. Les cheveux noirs." Gyp, *Israël*, 30.

82. Albert Sonnenfeld, "The Poetics of Antisemitism," *Romanic Review* 76, no. 1, Jan. 1985, 77.

83. The words of Moses in *En Balade* exemplify Gyp's deformation of language: "Baris c'est la derre bromisse . . . ch'ai enfie té m'y vixer bur y fivre." Gyp, *En Balade* (Paris: Mongrédien, 1897), 183. Ellipses in original.

84. "[Elle] parle de la façon la plus étrange, en faisant pour articuler un effort violent." Gyp, *Israël,* 162.

85. Sonnenfeld, "The Poetics of Antisemitism," 79. Drumont dwells at some length on the Jews' perversion of language. For a discussion, see Sonnenfeld, p. 80, and Wilson, *Ideology and Experience,* 607, 614.

86. "les quartiers d'où une prévoyante police les invitait à ne pas sortir . . . il y avait d'ailleurs des chaînes pour fermer . . . à la bonne heure! . . . parlez-moi de la police de ce temps-là! . . ." Gyp, *Les Gens chics* (Paris: Charpentier et Fasquelle, 1895), 74. Ellipses in original.

87. "Alors, c'est ça, les gens chics! . . . ce que je les renverrais chez eux . . . ou ailleurs . . . quel nettoyage, Seigneur! . . ." Ibid, 50. Ellipses in original.

88. "je les mettrais . . . dans un mortier et je [les] pilerais au petit bonheur . . ." Ibid., 25.

89. Drumont harps on the theme of aristocratic decadence in *La France juive*, often drawing parallels between Jews and aristocrats, as when he writes that "the aristocrat's brain is ordinarily structured in a very feeble manner" ("le cerveau de l'aristocrate est d'ordinaire très faiblement organisé"). Edouard Drumont, *La France juive: Essai d'histoire contemporaine,* (Paris: Marpon et Flammarion, 1886), vol. 2, 77.

90. "j'ai ceux de ma race en horreur! . . ." Gyp, *Israël*, 203. Ellipses in original.

91. "C'est l'espoir de la France." Gyp, *En Balade,* 84–85.

92. It was Drumont who offered the classic guidelines for how to recognize a "Jew": "The main signs by which one can recognize the Jew are these: the famous hooked nose, the blinking eyes, the clenched teeth, the projecting ears, the fingernails square instead of being almond-shaped, the torso too long, the flat feet, the round knees, the extraordinarily prominent ankles, the soft and slimy hands of the hypocrite and the traitor. They also often have one arm shorter than the other." Drumont, *La France juive*, vol. 1, 34, quoted and translated in Wilson, *Ideology and Experience,* 477.

93. For more on Gyp as an anti-Semitic caricaturist, see Jacques Lethève, *La Caricature sous la IIIᵉ République* (Paris: Armand Colin, 1986), 86–90; and Phillip Dennis

Cate, "The Paris Cry: Graphic Arts and the Dreyfus Affair," in *The Dreyfus Affair: Art, Truth, and Justice,* ed. Norman Kleeblatt (Berkeley, CA: U of California P, 1987), 62–95.

94. "la question importante du papier à lettres." Baronne Staffe, "Carnet mondain," *La Nouvelle Revue* 3, March–April 1898, 575.

95. "Cette enragée frondeuse, qui se pique de ne ménager aucun pouvoir. . . ." Abraham Dreyfus, "Le Cas de Gyp," *L'Aurore,* 26 Dec. 1897, 1.

96. " ' ça se portera encore beaucoup cet hiver.' " Ibid.

97. "Moi bon nègre juif, moi pas méchant, moi aimer toujours Gyp, malgré boulangisme et antisémitisme. Moi, bien fâché de lui voir perdre peu à peu verve et gaieté que goût tant autrefois. . . . Bien bruyante aujourd'hui, bonne Gyp! mais plus beaucoup d'esprit. . . . Oh! non, presque plus du tout. . . ."

98. "Petit village de la Provence montagnarde, à l'air sarrasin, avec ses maisons entassées et brûlées, ses rues étroites, sa place, sa fontaine et son cours ombragé de platanes." Maurice Barrès, "Lettre à Gyp sur le printemps à Mirabeau," *La Revue hebdomadaire* 7, April 1921, 374.

99. "château ancien, entièrement restauré." Bill of sale, 9 Aug. 1897, Hypothèques d'Apt, vol. 690, #60, AD Vaucluse.

100. "[I]l ne me paraît pas possible que j'aie Mirabeau, et que vous ne veniez pas l'inaugurer—si vilain qu'il soit?" Gyp, letter to Anatole France, [Aug. 1897], Naf 15386, #61, AF.

101. "une rude maison forte, flanquée de quatre tours à toits plats, aux tuiles brûlées par le soleil. . . ." Jérôme et Jean Tharaud, *Mes années chez Barrès* (Paris: Plon, 1928), 238.

102. "[O]n m'a raconté ce que fut votre arrivée: aux premières maisons, une petite fille vous attendait avec un bouquet, et dans la cour du château, l'orphéon du village, trois musiciens menés par le vieux Camille . . . vous régalèrent d'une aubade." Barrès, "Lettre à Gyp," 373.

103. "je suis, je crois, après France, celui de vos auteurs qui . . . se vend le plus. J'ai dû faire gagner de grosses sommes à votre maison." Gyp, letter to [?] Calmann-Lévy, 16 Aug. 1897, CL.

104. "Contrariée et gênée." Gyp, letter to [?] Calmann-Lévy, 9 Aug. 1897, CL.

105. "[L]es bergers se souviennent encore de sa lumière qui brillait toute la nuit à sa fenêtre ouverte, . . . tandis qu'elle achevait *Totote,* dans ce grand bureau du rez-de-chaussée. . . ." Philippe Barrès, "Gyp, ou la féerie," *Les Nouvelles littéraires,* 9 July 1932, 1.

106. See Chapter 5, note 32, in this book.

107. "For some time now, especially when you stopped giving me advances, it has become impossible for me to get by only with what I publish with you." ("Depuis quelques temps surtout, où vous ne me faites plus d'avances, il m'est impossible de m'en tirer seulement à ce qui paraît chez vous.") Gyp, letter to [?] Calmann-Lévy, [?] Aug. 1897, CL.

108. Gyp purchased the chapel from the municipality for five hundred francs. Bill of sale, chapel of Sainte-Madeleine, Hypothèques d'Apt, vol. 715, #40, AD Vaucluse. Gyp thanked Paul Mariéton, one of the promoters of the Félibrige, a movement to revive Occitan poetry, for a "small drawing, naïve and lifelike" ("ce petit dessin naïf et ressemblant") of this chapel. "It is ravishing, I adore it, and it is there that I shall be buried." ("Elle est ravissante, je l'adore, et c'est là que je serai enterrée.") Gyp, letter to Paul Mariéton, [1899], MS4658, #21–22, Bibliothèque Municipale, Avignon.

109. Gyp, Will, 2 March 1898, Sibylle Gaudry collection, Paris.

110. "Si je fais cette demande excentrique, c'est pour éviter l'embaumement plus long et plus sale." Ibid.

111. Ibid.

112. "afin d'éviter tout ennui avec l'église." Ibid.

113. "un être admirable et exquis." Ibid.

114. "je ne veux pas qu'il me quitte." Ibid.

115. "On fera un service d'avant-dernière classe. Celle immédiatemment avant celle des pauvres." Ibid.

Chapter IX

1. "Elle était insatiable et très convaincue, très solidement sincère." Eugénie Buffet, *Ma vie, mes amours, mes aventures* (Paris: Figuière, 1930), 48.

2. Quoted in François Bournand, *Les Juifs et nos contemporains: L'Antisémitisme et la question juive* (Paris: Pierret, [1898]), 134.

3. "Ce que je voudrais . . . *les voir partir, qu'on leur fasse donc peur!* Je ne demande pas personnellement qu'on les tue. . . . Mais qu'on les chasse, qu'on ne fasse pas comme les Russes qui les gardent et les parquent. Qu'on les chasse!" Quoted in Bournand, *Les Juifs et nos contemporains,* 136.

4. "comtesse garce." H. Beronse, "Le Syndicat," [1898], The Houghton Library, Harvard University. The title is an ironic allusion to the anti-Dreyfusard assertion of the existence of a Jewish/Dreyfusard "syndicate," or plot.

5. "comme un obus chargé de gaz asphyxiant, [empoisonnant] et [détruisant] les meilleures et les plus fidèles amitiés." Madeleine Zillhardt, *Louise-Catherine Breslau et ses amis* (Paris: Editions des Portiques, 1932), 119.

6. Paul Morand, *1900* (Paris: Flammarion, 1931), 25.

7. "Je flanque à la porte mon garde de Mirabeau qui est Dreyfusard." Gyp, letter to Paul Déroulède, [May 1900?], 401AP9, #7544, PD.

8. "étant américaine, il est normal qu'elle nous exècre inconsciemment et se tourne d'instinct vers qui veut nous tomber." Gyp, letter to Paul Déroulède, [Aug.–Sept. 1899?], 401AP9, #39849, PD.

9. "Sauf elle, je ne reçois plus personne de ce camp-là." Ibid.

10. Gyp, letters to Maurice Barrès, [? 1898] and [Jan.–May 1898], MB.

11. See Pierre Chanlaine, "Il y a cent ans naissait Gyp: romancière de la Belle Epoque," *L'Opéra,* 17 Aug. 1949; Michel Missoffe, *Gyp et ses amis* (Paris: Flammarion, 1932), 86–87; "Au temps de l'Affaire," *Sur la Riviera,* 27 Nov. 1921; Gyp, letter to the editor of *Sur la Riviera,* [1921], Naf 15443, #136–40, AF.

12. "le trait d'union entre ces politiciens qui, avec des arrière-pensées diverses, visent à la destruction de la République. "Gyp et Déroulède," *Le Siècle,* 7 Aug. 1899.

13. "Non, certes, je n'aime ni la République, ni les Parlements, et je suis d'instinct avec tous ceux qui sont contre ces gens-là! Je suis impérialiste, césarienne, pour mieux dire. Mon rêve, c'est un chef à qui l'on puisse couper le cou, s'il trahit le pays . . . un homme . . . responsable personnellement et directement. . . . [C]omme je suis à la fois autoritaire et démocrate, je me trouve tout près de Déroulède, qui est un républicain plé-biscitaire, et voilà tout." Quoted in Serge Basset, "Chez Gyp: Les Opinions politiques d'une 'bien parisienne,' " *Le Matin,* 6 Aug. 1899.

14. Gyp, letter to Paul Déroulède, [Sept. 1898?], 401AP9, #41243, PD.

15. "on les dévore en parlant de vous." Gyp, letter to Paul Déroulède, [18 Dec. 1899?], 401AP9, #39679, PD.

16. "un garçon extraordinairement brave et intelligent." "Gyp et Déroulède."

17. Jules Guérin, letter to Paul Déroulède, 2 Oct. 1898, in BA1105, APP.

18. On Guérin and the Ligue antisémitique, see Stephen Wilson, *Ideology and Experience: Antisemitism in France at the Time of the Dreyfus Affair* (East Brunswick, NJ: Associated UP, 1982), 179–96; and Zeev Sternhell, *La Droite révolutionnaire, 1885–1914: Les Origines françaises du fascisme* (Paris: Seuil, 1978), 215–44.

19. "Pour l'honneur et le salut de la France, n'achetez rien aux Juifs. Vive le Roy!" Interior minister's report, 4 April 1899, BA1262, APP.

20. Gyp, "Un chic type! . . . . . ," *La Libre Parole*, 3 Dec. 1899.

21. "Une si gentille nature, un être exquis." Quoted in Basset, "Chez Gyp."

22. "il y a trop de juifs autour du duc d'Orléans." Ibid.

23. "Gyp est tout simplement R.é.p.u.b.l.i.c.a.i.n.e.. La peau de Marianne lui dit!" P.L., "La 'peau' . . . et Gyp," *La Gazette de France*, 22–23 May 1899, 2.

24. Morand, *1900*, 25.

25. "Les Izolâtres," *La Libre Parole*, 3 March 1898, 1.

26. "épouvantables à voir." Ibid.

27. "la jolie Juive blonde." Ibid.

28. "On les trouvait . . . à l'intérieur des barricades de planches qui longeaient le bout de la rue Réaumur alors en construction. Les 'quarante sous' marchaient pour nous ou pour les dreyfusards. Chaque fois que l'on m'a confié le soin . . . d'aller [les] engager . . . pour une sortie d'audience qu'on prévoyait houleuse, j'ai toujours choisi ceux qui m'ont semblé être les pires, les plus 'apaches.' Et j'ai toujours reçu des compliments sur mes 'quarante sous.' C'étaient les meilleurs, les plus crânes." Quoted in Missoffe, *Gyp et ses amis*, 148–49.

29. "Est-ce que vos petits nationalistes ne feraient pas bien *à la sortie* de ça? . . . Ils ont souvent troublé chez nous et on ne trouble jamais chez eux . . . et puis, on pourrait mieux que troubler." Gyp, letter to Maurice Barrès, [1899–1900?], #64, MB.

30. "cris furieux et discours très insanes." Anatole France, *Monsieur Bergeret à Paris* (Paris: Calmann-Lévy, [1974]), 64.

31. "Nous avons ici Dimanche une élection répugnante. Deux ralliés d'hier . . . et un conservateur, le vicomte de . . . qui a épousé une Juive. . . . Je passe tout mon temps à persuader aux marins, (les seuls avec qui je m'entends parmi les Normands,) de ne voter pour aucun des trois." Gyp, letter to Paul Déroulède, [April–May 1898], 401AP9, #17934, PD.

32. "J'espère que ça va marcher. . . . De chez moi, on me dit que Laguerre a des chances. Je l'ai recommandé à mon curé, le seul influent là-bas et qui aurait pu lui nuire à Pertuis." Gyp, letter to Maurice Barrès, [April–May 1898], #50, MB.

33. "-y croit que ses bons amis lui r'front core un'virginité . . . mais la fois-ci y a pas mèche . . . !" *Le Rire*, 28 May 1898.

34. Francis de Croisset, "La Société et la vie sous la Troisième République: L'Univers de Gyp: Bob et Miquette," *Conférencia* 20, 1 Oct. 1934, 391.

35. "Versailles fait ville assiégée." *La Libre Parole*, 24 May 1898.

36. *La Libre Parole*, 19 July 1898.

37. "Parmi les loges et les uniformes, le costume bleu pâle de Gyp jette seul une note claire et gaie. Gyp, d'un air discrètement narquois, examine le public qui l'environne." Ibid.

38. ''on aurait sûrement jeté quelques juifs à l'eau et cela aurait été le commencement de la fin.'' Quoted in Bournand, *Les Juifs et nos contemporains,* 136.

39. "Les dieux d'Israël," *La Libre Parole,* 7 Aug. 1898, 1.

40. "Le Toast," *La Libre Parole,* 17 Aug. 1898, 1.

41. ''vieille canaille.'' Gyp, letter to Paul Déroulède, [Sept. 1898?], 401 AP9, #38833, PD.

42. *La Libre Parole,* 22 Sept. 1898.

43. ''notre si distinguée collaboratrice . . . en toilette gris perle—sur les lèvres le fin sourire narquois qu'on lui connaît. [Elle] a le don de porter sur les nerfs des Youtres qu'elle frôle au passage.'' Raphaël Viau, "Avant et autour de l'audience," *La Libre Parole,* 22 Sept. 1898.

44. ''Ils sont un Etat dans l'Etat, Eux, les gens de l'Affaire! Ils triomphent! . . . et leur force d'insolence semble grandir chaque jour. . . . C'est qu'Ils sont chez Eux les *groins*! C'est Leur Picquart. C'est LEUR Palais! C'est Leur affaire. . . .'' "Les Triomphants," *La Libre Parole,* 25 Sept. 1898, 1.

45. ''Tout le monde gouverne hors lui, Félix Faure, Zurlinden, Sarrien, Gyp et Drumont. . . .'' Georges Clemenceau, "Grandes Manœuvres," *L'Aurore,* 26 Oct. 1898.

46. ''Cette affaire Zola m'a fait perdre un temps énorme. . . . Elle me passionnait tellement que, si je n'étais pas allée aux audiences, je n'aurais rien pu faire chez moi. Je n'ai pas besoin de vous dire de quel côté j'étais. D'après ce que je crois deviner de vous, je crois que nous étions du même? . . .'' Gyp, letter to Théophile Gautier fils, [1898?], MS Thiers 678, Fondation Thiers, Paris.

47. ''j'ai été arrêtée dans mon travail par . . . un ennui—le procès que me fait Monsieur Trarieux. J'ai dû écrire de tous les côtés pour avoir des documents demandés par l'avocat, et j'ai perdu mon temps.'' Gyp, letter to Ferdinand Brunetière, [Nov.–Dec. 1898], Naf 25039, #623–24, BN.

48. ''né . . . en même temps que l'Empire.'' Gyp, *Journal d'un grinchu* (Paris: Flammarion, 1898), 7.

49. ''l'oeuvre réaliste par excellence.'' Rachilde, rev. of *Journal d'un grinchu, Le Mercure de France* 27, July–Sept. 1898, 815. See also the review by Georges Sénéchal, *La Nouvelle Revue* 114, 15 Oct. [1898], 753–54.

50. For a highly critical review, see ''Quatre femmes de lettres,'' *La Revue des revues,* 1 Nov. 1898, 280–87.

51. ''Monsieur Trarieux est protestant (Encore un!) mais non protestant de naissance. C'est—dit la chronique—un vulgaire rénégat. Autrefois catholique, il se convertit en vue d'un mariage avantageux.'' Gyp, *Journal d'un grinchu,* 243.

52. The text of Trarieux' suit appeared in several newspapers, including *Le Siècle* ("M. Trarieux contre Gyp," *Le Siècle,* 5 Nov. 1898).

53. ''Gyp, c'est la gaîeté, c'est la malice primesautière, c'est l'esprit fait femme. Trarieux, c'est la froideur morne, c'est la vanité guindée, c'est l'ennui en chair et en os.'' Gaston Méry, "Au jour le jour: Trarieux contre Gyp," *La Libre Parole* 4 Nov. 1898.

54. ''cette batailleuse.'' Séverine, "Notes d'une frondeuse: Requête à Monsieur Trarieux," *La Fronde,* 7 Nov. 1898.

55. ''Dans cette affaire-là, nous nous jugeons réciproquement odieuses et abominables: je lui abîme ses prétoriens, elle malmène nos intellectuels.'' Ibid.

56. ''Ainsi, vous qui avez eu ce privilège, cette gloire, d'être un des plus outragés pour la cause, vous n'iriez pas, entre tant d'adversaires barbus, choisir ce petit chiffon de

femme, cette blonde menue aux airs de souris, pour l'exterminer sous la rigueur des lois!'' Ibid.

57. ''Elle a été très 'rosse,' oh! ça oui! Mais c'est une femme . . . on l'est toutes un peu! Allons, souriez, Monsieur le sénateur, ayez l'élégance du geste d'absolution—et qu'un 'dreyfusard,' encore cette fois, ait le beau rôle.'' Ibid.

58. In the next day's issue of *La Fronde*, Séverine responded to another journalist who had accused Séverine of actively intervening on Gyp's behalf. This was not her intention, she asserted: ''[Gyp] has teeth and nails to defend herself; she has proven it, alas. . . .'' (''[Gyp] a bec et ongles pour se défendre; elle l'a prouvé, hélas. . . .''). What motivated Séverine, she affirmed, was her desire not to see sullied the Dreyfusard ideal— ''The Idea, for which we have fought, [which] seems to me so noble and so beautiful'' (''L'Idée, pour laquelle nous avons combattu, [qui] m'apparaît si haute et si belle'')—by what might be deemed a tasteless attack by Trarieux on a member of the ''weaker sex.'' Séverine, ''Notes d'une frondeuse: Réponse aux 'Droits de l'Homme,' '' *La Fronde*, 8 Nov. 1898.

59. ''un pamphlet des plus diffamatoires. . . .'' ''M. Trarieux et le *Journal d'un grinchu*,'' *La Revue des grands procès contemporains* 27, 1899, 297.

60. ''[un de] mes adversaires les plus passionnés.'' Ibid., 296.

61. Ibid., 306.

62. ''[S]on incursion indiscrète et déloyale dans ma vie privée, dans ma vie de ménage m'a été odieuse et m'a semblé intolérable.'' Ibid., 300.

63. ''puisque j'avais à me défendre de Madame de Martel, il me fallait user de toutes mes armes.'' Ibid.

64. Ibid., 304.

65. ''l'écho des passions et des haines dont elle s'est fait l'instrument.'' Ibid., 305.

66. ''Sans même mettre en cause ni [sa] vie, ni [ses] idées, ni [son] rôle public (car elle a un rôle public). . . .'' Ibid., 308.

67. Ibid.

68. Ibid.

69. Ibid., 333.

70. Ibid., 335.

71. ''si parfait désintéressement.'' Ibid., 336.

72. ''Sa fortune tient . . . presque tout entière dans le bec de sa plume.'' Ibid., 333.

73. ''Gyp est Gyp, et Monsieur Trarieux est Monsieur Trarieux. . . . A Monsieur Trarieux, [la nature] a donné la voix sonore et grave . . . ; à Gyp, un sifflet aigu et moqueur. Quand Monsieur Trarieux frappe, avec quelle force et quelle puissance, vous le savez! l'autre pique. Et quand Monsieur Trarieux s'indigne, se fâche et tonne, Gyp rit, rit encore et rit toujours, de son incorrigible rire! Ils sont si différents . . . qu'ils se complètent; il faut nous les laisser l'un et l'autre.'' Ibid., 350.

74. ''la vogue qui s'attache aux oeuvres brillantes et fines de la dame de Martel et du nombre important des tirages qui en sont faits.'' Ibid., 352.

75. See Stephen Wilson, ''Le Monument Henry: La Structure de l'antisémitisme en France, 1898–1899,'' *Annales ESC*, March–April 1977, 265–91.

76. ''on pratiquait la vivisection sur les Juifs plutôt que sur d'inoffensifs lapins''; ''le groin de tous les juifs pour en faire un pâté pour ses chiens.'' Quoted in Pierre Quillard, *Le Monument Henry: Liste des souscripteurs classés méthodiquement et selon l'ordre alphabétique* (Paris: Stock, 1899).

77. Quoted and translated in Wilson, *Ideology and Experience*, 154.

Chapter X

1. "un être exquis, plein de belle humeur et d'esprit, qui respirait l'honnêteté et la franchise, [mais] pas politicien pour deux sous. . . ." Quoted in Michel Missoffe, *Gyp et ses amis* (Paris: Flammarion, 1932), 164.

2. "courir les réunions, recevoir des horions dans les bagarres et subir des promiscuités auxquelles il n'était pas accoutumé." Ibid., 165.

3. Quoted in M.V., "Les Deux Ligues," *Le Radical,* 10 Jan. 1899.

4. "Qu'ils parlent. On agira." Ibid. For more on the league's problematic relations with the other anti-Dreyfusard leagues, see Zeev Sternhell, *La Droite révolutionnaire, 1885–1914: Les Origines françaises du fascisme* (Paris: Seuil, 1978), 131–42.

5. "la bonne Gauloise Gyp, qui n'en manque pas une." *La Libre Parole,* 28 Jan. 1899.

6. "[T]out en considérant Beaurepaire comme une ambitieuse fripouille, je le remercierais volontiers à genoux de ce qu'il a fait pour nous et je lui ai envoyé la carte de Gyp." Gyp, letter to Paul Déroulède, [Jan. 1899?], 401AP9, #41164, PD.

7. "[Faure] était un très brave homme et je savais qu'il était antidreyfusard, mais c'était un parlementaire! Il n'aurait jamais fait de coup d'état." Quoted in "L'Affaire: Madame Gyp," [*Le Journal*?], 6 July 1899. See also Maurice Barrès, *Mes cahiers* (Paris: Plon, 1935), vol. 9, 275–76.

8. "vivement entourée . . . chacun lui apporte le témoignage de sa sympathique admiration." *La Libre Parole,* 31 May 1899.

9. "de beaux et odorants bouquets." "Autour de l'audience: La Conciergerie envahie," *Le Gaulois,* 3 May 1899.

10. "la fougueuse petite effrontée, toujours espiègle, cette petite!" "Gyp glapit dans le fond de la salle." René Dubreuil, "Le Procès Déroulède-Habert," *Le Siècle,* 1 June 1899, 2.

11. Gyp, letter to Paul Déroulède, [Aug.–Dec. 1899], 401AP9, #7543, PD.

12. "Madame Gyp était puissante alors. Elle inspirait Lemaître et Guérin. Félix Faure mourait, Loubet était élu; Dupuy, Premier ministre, le laissait huer dans Paris. Déroulède essayait son coup de force, et Dupuy conspirait à son acquittement. Prenant cette Fronde au sérieux, nous redoutions le pire." Daniel Halévy, "Apologie pour notre passé," *Cahiers de la quinzaine,* 10, ser. 11, Oct. 1907–Jan. 1910.

13. "Le Guet-Apens d'Auteuil: Attentat contre M. Loubet," *Le Radical,* 6 June 1899, 2.

14. "c'est sans importance. C'est un coup de canne sur un chapeau. La République est plus difficile à décoiffer!" Ibid.

15. "ce ne sera pas coups de canne et oeufs pourris que tu recevras mais une balle dans la peau." Anonymous letter to Emile Loubet, June 1899, BA 53, APP.

16. *La Libre Parole,* 23 July 1899.

17. "le Machiavel nougateux." Henri Rochefort, "Le Truc de Loubet," *L'Intransigeant,* 9 Nov. 1899.

18. "l'élite intellectuelle et morale de la France, avec Gyp et Guérin venus à la rescousse, l'enlaçaient [Déroulède] de leurs bras, l'étouffaient de leurs baisers, faisaient respirer à son nez prédestiné l'encens de leurs flagorneries." Francis de Pressensé, "Trop tard, M. Déroulède!," *L'Aurore,* 4 July 1899.

19. See BA 1198, APP.

20. "Chez les antisémites: Commémoration et inauguration," *Le Matin,* 20 July 1899.

21. Gausy, "'Ma chère Gyp,'" *Les Droits de l'homme,* 27 June 1899, 1.

22. "Fille d'un zouave pontifical qui jouissait dans le Morbihan d'une réputation fort gaillarde, à ce qu'on m'a dit. . . ." Ibid.

23. "voyage pour Dieu et pour N'importe Qui Ier. . . ." Ibid. See also Bradamante, "Chrétiens! A vos canons!," *L'Aurore,* 11 June 1899.

24. "[J']ai trop à travailler pour aller là-bas, où je sais très bien que je ne ferais rien du tout que causer et flâner." Gyp, letter to Maurice Barrès, [July–Aug. 1899], MB.

25. Other charges included: "Incitements to citizens or inhabitants to arm themselves against the constitutional authority—Bombings—Acts of execution and attempted acts— Rebellion—Attempted, premeditated homicide—Provoking military personnel, with the goal of diverting them from their duties and from the obedience they owe their leaders." ("Excitations aux citoyens ou habitants à s'armer contre l'autorité constitutionnelle— Attentat—Actes d'exécution et tentatives—Rébellion—Tentative d'homicide avec pré-méditation—Provocations à des militaires, dans le but de les détourner de leurs devoirs et de l'obéissance qu'ils doivent à leurs chefs.") See *La Revue des grands procès contemporains,* 1901, 769–70.

26. "Gyp et Déroulède," *Le Siècle,* 7 Aug. 1899.

27. Ibid.

28. "un si bon et si brave garçon." Ibid.

29. "Même blessés, même malheureux, ces gens qui écartèlent un pays que j'aime me font horreur. Je sens que je haïs les Labori et les Dreyfus plus aujourd'hui qu'hier et certainement moins que demain." Gyp, letter to Maurice Barrès, [Aug. 1899], MB.

30. P.-V. Stock, *Mémorandum d'un éditeur: L'Affaire Dreyfus anecdotique* (Paris: Stock, 1938), 133.

31. "[T]rès emballée par le geste de Guérin, [elle] passait une partie de ses nuits aux environs du fort, attendant, anxieuse, l'issue du drame." Jean Drault, *Drumont, "la France Juive" et "La Libre Parole"* (Paris: Hérisson, 1935), 267.

32. BA1198, APP.

33. Drault, *Drumont,* 25.

34. "Quelle que soit la décision du Conseil de Guerre de Rennes, je crois comme vous que nous approchons de la délivrance à laquelle il semble vraiment que nous avons un peu droit. J'ai . . . confiance en Dieu . . . et en votre frère. J'espère fermement qu'ils nous sauveront." Gyp, letter to Jeanne Déroulède, [Sept. 1899], 401AP9, #39127, PD.

35. "cette malpropreté suprême." Gyp, "Quel coup pour Emile!," *La Libre Parole,* 5 Nov. 1899, 1.

36. Ibid.

37. Ibid. See also Gyp, "Conspuez Loulou! . . . ," *La Libre Parole,* 10 Dec. 1899, 1.

38. "ils sont arrivés à fourrer Déroulède dans un complot orléaniste." Gyp, letter to Maurice Barrès, [7 Aug. 1899], MB.

39. Gyp, letter to Paul Déroulède, [Oct.–Nov. 1899], 401AP9, #18041, PD.

40. Gyp, letter to Paul Déroulède, [Oct.–Nov. 1899], 401AP9, #18042, PD.

41. "C'est tout de même un singulier temps que celui-ci!" Gyp, letter to Paul Déroulède, [Oct.–Nov. 1899], 401AP9, #7546, PD.

42. H.L., "Chez les témoins," *La Libre Parole,* 11 Nov. 1899.

43. "les bons soldats du nationalisme." Maurice Barrès, *Scènes et doctrines du nationalisme* (Paris: Editions du Trident, 1987), 179.

44. "affolé comme un rat." Ibid.

45. "François Coppée, Gyp, Jules Guesde [et] le nonce du pape . . . ont, hier, à la tête de cinq cent hommes, attaqué la poudrière de Castelnaudary." Henri Rochefort, "Hommage à la Haute Cour," *L'Intransigeant,* 9 Dec. 1899.

46. "Je suis désolée de ne pas vous voir devant la Haute Cour! Quelle Haute Cour! C'est vraiment plus ignoble encore qu'on ne s'y attendait." Gyp, letter to Paul Déroulède, [Nov. 1899], 401AP9, #18339, PD.

47. "Beaucoup de compliments de votre belle, belle attitude." Ibid.

48. Gyp, letter to Paul Déroulède, [Nov. 1899], 401AP9, #18041, PD.

49. "à quelle extraordinaire sauce on vous mange." Ibid.

50. "sa toilette d'audience." "La Haute Cour," *L'Aurore,* 16 Dec. 1899.

51. "accueillie par les sourires des vieux messieurs de la droite." M. Delphin, "La Haute Cour," *Le Siècle,* 16 Dec. 1899, 2.

52. For a transcript of Gyp's deposition, see "La Haute Cour," *L'Eclair,* 17 Dec. 1899.

53. Ibid.

54. Ibid.

55. "il n'aurait pas fait de mal, même à un agent de police!" Ibid.

56. "m'a paru excellent parce que c'était le mien." Ibid.

57. "qui étaient en quelques sorte officielles et auxquelles on répondait comme on pouvait." Ibid.

58. "Ce mouchard [Melcot] est . . . mal renseigné. Le 22 février, il n'y avait ni moi, ni personne, chez Grosjean." Gyp, letter to Paul Déroulède, [Oct.–Dec. 1899], 401AP9, #39845, PD.

59. "méridionale et portée à méridionaliser les faits." Quoted in Barrès, *Scènes et doctrines,* 179, note.

60. "de m'avoir fourni l'occasion de dire que j'ai beaucoup d'estime et d'amitié pour lui." "La Haute Cour," *L'Eclair.*

61. "sourires approbatifs . . . de la sympathie générale." Ibid.

62. "un modèle parfait d'amabilité et de spontanéité françaises. . . ." Barrès, *Scènes et doctrines,* 181, note.

63. "rendre un peu de lustre à une vingtaine d'ouvrages fanés, vieillots, et où la blague est si pénible qu'elle donne envie de pleurer[?]" Edouard Beaufils, "Episodes: Le Coup de fer," *La Paix,* 17 Dec. 1899.

64. Str., "Gyp," *Le Siècle,* 19 Dec. 1899.

65. "ses recueils d'obscénités dialoguées sont en dehors de la littérature. Que dire, en effet, de l'enfantelet voyou, Bob, qui décoche en langue verte à son précepteur . . . ? Et de Paulette, et de Chiffon, et de vingt-cinq autres jeunes filles un peu étranges?" Ibid.

66. Ibid.

67. "ces caricatures plus niaises qu'ordurières. . . ." Ibid.

68. "fabricante de meubles." Ibid.

69. "un paravant laqué blanc, où s'étalent des bonshommes burlesquement peintur-lurés par l'ex-Egérie de Félix-Ubu-Faure. . . ." Ibid. Gyp had tried to increase her profits from the publications of *Les Gens chics* (1895) and *En Balade* (1897) by exhibiting their illustrations, displayed as panels of a folding screen and in a bookcase, at the 1896 and 1897 Salons du Champ de Mars. See G.M., "Le Salon du Champ de Mars," *La Libre Parole,* 24 April 1896; and G.M., "Le Salon du Champ de Mars," *La Libre Parole,* 23 April 1897.

70. "l'organe de la famille *française,* et un moyen populaire, que tous les nationalistes auront à coeur d'encourager, pour collaborer au relèvement et à la prospérité de notre pays." *Les dimanches politiques et littéraires,* flyer, 1900.

71. "il y a . . . un mécontentement réel [qui] se dessine surtout dans le sens *antijuif.* Antijuif sans Guérin, sans drapeau, sans chef, antijuif très populaire et très accentué. Et

c'est la première fois que, causant dans la rue avec des gens . . . , je les entends crier d'eux-mêmes sur les Juifs *avant que j'aie commencé!*'' Gyp, letter to Paul Déroulède, [April–May 1900?], 401AP9, #7545, PD.

72. ''Ah! que je voudrais vous voir. Si c'était possible de trouver un bateau . . . j'irais vous voir en septembre, même si je devais être longtemps en route.'' Gyp, letter to Paul Déroulède, [April–May 1900?], 401AP9, #7547, PD.

73. ''Je suis un soldat très discipliné . . . qui suit mon chef.'' Gyp, letter to Paul Déroulède, [Aug. 1900?], 401AP9, #7548, PD.

74. Ibid.

75. ''sur le beau dessin de Job que vous recevrez dans votre album. . . . Devos a loué des camelots joueurs de crincrin pour 'la lancer' comme il dit! . . . Mais je m'imagine qu'on ne la lancera pas longtemps et que les camelots lanceurs seront cueillis avec prestesse par les sergots. Je ne sais pas si vous avez vu ce système de chanteurs. Ça n'a commencé, je crois, qu'après votre emprisonnement. Le camelot monte sur un banc avec son crincrin et chante, et la foule se masse autour. Quand ça encombre trop, on les fait descendre. Ca a un petit air 'révolution' assez gentil.'' Gyp, letter to Paul Déroulède, [May 1900?], 401AP9, #7544, PD.

76. ''L'Exposition [est] vraiment *splendide*.'' Gyp, letter to Paul Déroulède, [April–May 1900?], 401AP9, #7547, PD.

77. ''L'Espagne, les Boers, Monsieur Loubet, l'affaire Dreyfus, Fachoda, et l'Exposition seront echevêtrés si bien qu'on ne les séparera plus jamais dans l'avenir. C'est pour Elle, pour éviter les complications qui pouvaient La faire rater, qu'on a lâché Fachoda, gracié Dreyfus, passé outre aux Boers.'' ''Entrrrrrrez!!!,'' *La Libre Parole,* 15 April 1900, 1. See also R. D. Mandell, ''The Affair and the Fair: Some Observations on the Closing Stages of the Dreyfus Case,'' *Journal of Modern History* 39, no. 3 (1967), 253–65.

78. See David Shapiro, ''The Nationalist Movement in Paris, 1900–1906,'' in *The Right in France, 1890–1918,* ed. David Shapiro (Carbondale: Southern Illinois UP, 1962), 49–84.

79. **Au peuple de Paris**

Les bravaches antisémites, les bandits nationalistes veulent terroriser Paris
A TERREUR, TERREUR ET DEMIE
L'Elysée, de mèche avec la *Libre Parole*, veut nous faire
chanter la gloire d'Esterhazy et de l'état major
A ce défi nous répondrons par une provocation:
LA COMTESSE DE MARTEL (GYP)
la Pompadour à tout faire des besognes antisémites, reine de France par la grâce de *Félix* et la complicité du maître chanteur *Drumont*, est entre nos mains.
C'est pour le moment l'ôtage suffisant et nécessaire.
Qu'on nous rende justice et nous rendrons la dame.
Puisqu'aux innocents le bagne, la prison, l'échafaud, contre les coupables les justes représailles.
Un groupe d'hommes libres

Poster, [Feb.–March 1898], private collection, Paris.

80. ''Mirbeau est . . . capable de tout . . . il a le pistolet léger et il vous tirerait dessus sans douleur. . . . Prenez garde à vous! Ne faites pas aux Dreyfusards le plaisir de vous laisser démolir ou enlever par eux.'' Gyp, letter to Maurice Barrès, [1900], MB.

81. ''Que vous êtes bon de penser ainsi à moi et que je vous remercie de ce ravissant stylet! . . . Je lui ai fait rendre sa *pointe* et son *fil*, et je vais le porter toujours suspendu à

un crochet. . . . En même temps qu'un bijou ravissant, ce stylet est une arme excellente. Et dans ce moment-ci on m'en veut. Il y a des gens bizarres—faux prêtres, fausses quêteuses . . . qui viennent me demander à des heures bizarres aussi, 11 heures du soir, par exemple. Je reçois tout le temps des lettres où l'on me dit qu'on me fera probablement mon affaire. Samedi dernier on a vaguement essayé. A l'instant où je finissais l'article de *La Libre Parole*, les volets n'étaient pas encore fermés, j'ai eu l'imbécilité de mettre une lampe sur mon bureau. J'étais très bien éclairée pour les gens de la rue; alors, on a lancé une grosse pierre triangulaire . . . qui a traversé le carreau, passé au dessus du bureau et été casser le paravent des *Gens chics* qui est à l'autre bout de la chambre. Les débris du carreau étaient de la véritable *poudre*.'' Gyp, letter to Paul Déroulède, [May 1899], 401AP9, #7545, PD.

82. ''l'abracadabrante aventure.'' Pangloss, ''Le Feuilleton de Gyp,'' *Le Siècle,* 13 May 1900, 1.

83. ''Il s'agit de séquestration, d'enlèvement, d'homme masqué, etc., tout un feuilleton.'' Ibid. Similarly yet in a tone much more sympathetic to Gyp, Gaston Méry reported on the ''odious ambush'' (''un guet-apens odieux'') in an article that occupied the front page of *La Libre Parole*, in which he asked readers: ''[H]aven't we been living in a gigantic *roman feuilleton* for the past two years?'' (''[N]e vivons-nous pas dans un gigantesque roman-feuilleton depuis deux ans?'') Gaston Méry, ''Un guet-apens: Gyp séquestrée par les Dreyfusards,'' *La Libre Parole,* 13 May 1900, 1. For Gyp's own account of her adventure, see Gyp, ''Récit d'un témoin,'' *La Libre Parole,* 20 May 1900, 1.

84. ''une voiture assez peu élégante, quelque chose comme un coupé de médecin de campagne.'' ''Affaire Mystérieuse,'' n.pl., 14 May 1900, 1.

85. Ibid.

86. ''meurtrie, sanglante.'' Gustave Macé, *La Police parisienne: Femmes criminelles* (Paris: Fasquelle, 1904), 37.

87. ''courbaturée, meurtrie . . . nullement effrayée d'ailleurs et toujours rieuse.'' ''L'Enlèvement de Gyp,'' *Le Temps,* 12 May 1900.

88. ''J'étais habillée de noir. . . . Mais, robe et chapeau étaient dans un état lamentable; j'avais une manche en loques; mes bottines étaient couvertes de boue. Je ne parle pas de la figure qui était comme ensanglantée.'' Quoted in ''Affaire Mystérieuse.''

89. ''a passé l'âge où les femmes de tempérament un peu chaud se font enlever d'ordinaire.'' Dombasle, ''Jules Lemaître et Gyp,'' *Le Siècle,* 14 May 1900, 2.

90. Ibid. See also ''Les Aventures de Gyp,'' *Le Siècle,* 17 May 1900, 2.

91. ''imparfaitement remise de ses émotions.'' ''L'Enlèvement de Gyp,'' *Le Temps,* 15 May 1900.

92. ''L'Enlèvement de Gyp,'' *Le Temps,* 16 May 1900.

93. Police report, 23 Aug. 1900, F7 2882–83, APP.

94. ''une soixantaine de gaillards bien déterminés.'' Ibid.

95. ''J'ai entendu dire hier soir que plusieurs membres du Grand Occident de France étaient sur les traces des individus qui ont enlevé Madame Gyp. S'ils les retrouvent, ils ont l'intention de faire eux-mêmes justice. Une grande effervescence règne depuis cet enlèvement dans les milieux nationalistes et antisémites.'' Police report, [14 or 16] May 1900, BA 1193, APP.

96. ''A propos de l'enlèvement de Gyp,'' *Le Temps,* 24 May 1900.

97. See Michel Herbert, *La Chanson à Montmartre* (Paris: La Table Ronde, 1967), 378.

98. ''On croit, jusqu'ici, que l'on est en présence d'un jeune soldat malade, obsédé par une hallucination.'' ''L'Enlèvement de Madame de Martel,'' *Le Temps,* 6 June 1900.

99. Ibid.

100. "L'Enlèvement de Madame de Martel," *Le Temps,* 17, 18, and 20 June 1900.

101. "Gyp's Story Was True," *New York Times,* 16 June 1900, 1.

102. [Georges] Calmann-Lévy, letter to Gyp, 29 June 1900, CL.

103. "Vous savez combien il m'est désagréable d'être accusé d'éditer des livres antisémites. Aussi il a été convenu entre nous que vous ne me donneriez plus que vos ouvrages qui ne rentreraient pas dans cet ordre d'idées." Ibid.

104. J'espère, chère Madame, que vous excuserez mon importunité. . . ." Ibid.

105. "On a remarqué depuis quelques temps un léger affaiblissement de la verve littéraire de Madame Gyp. A quoi, d'ailleurs, elle suppléa par une intense activité politique." André Beaunier, rev. of *Trop de chic!, La Revue bleue,* 26 June 1900, 699–700.

106. "son antipathie est si aggressive qu'elle cesse d'être plaisante. La colère et la bonne humeur ne vont point ensemble. Lorsque Gyp se mêle d'écrire un pamphlet, sa grâce disparaît sous l'invective, ses mots piquants cèdent le pas au gros mots." Adolphe Brisson, *Portraits intimes,* 2nd ser. (Paris: Armand Colin, 1904), 30.

107. "Elle demeurera toujours jeune d'esprit, de corps et de conscience, mais demeurer le même est certainement ce qui vieillit le plus en France." Rachilde, rev. of *Le Friquet, Le Mercure de France,* April 1901, 191.

108. "A Monsieur Degas, qui aime et admire la force, j'offre affectueusement l'aventure d'un petit être très fort." Gyp, *Le Friquet* (Paris: Flammarion, 1901).

109. "poussah graisseux et suintant." Ibid., 131.

110. "Je suis tourmentée d'Aymar qui s'entête à rester au Soudan une année de plus et bien inutilement, je crois. Il a deux beaux faits de guerre. . . . Il me semble qu'il peut revenir." Gyp, letter to Paul Déroulède, [Nov.–Dec. 1899?], 401AP9, #7548, PD.

111. "Je vais faire quelque chose d'épatant au point de vue sportif, mais il est possible que j'y reste." Quoted in Maurice Barrès, *Mes cahiers* (Paris: Plon, 1931), vol. 3, 236.

112. "Aymar est parti *sans ordre* dans la brousse avec dix spahis, pour prendre un chef rebelle. Cernés par quatre cents noirs, il sont restés 48 heures sans boire, manger, ni dormir, et ont fait des prodiges de courage et de sang froid. Un officier . . . qui a su par d'autres noirs qu'ils étaient perdus . . . est allé à leurs secours *sans ordre aussi* avec son détachement. Ils n'ont perdu personne (du moins sur place) et ils ont pris des chevaux, mais il y a eu 15 blessés." Gyp, letter to Paul Déroulède, [Oct.–Nov. 1900], 401AP9, #7547, PD. See also Barrès' description of Aymar's struggle against Toureg tribesmen in *Mes cahiers,* vol. 3, 236–37; and Jérôme and Jean Tharaud, *Mes années chez Barrès* (Paris: Plon, 1928), 237.

113. "Le prêtre vêtu de velours noir et d'argent étincelait sur les hautes marches de l'autel lumineux. Une voix s'élève qui nous force à pleurer, puis soudain il semble qu'elle tombe, c'est cette tache écarlate sur le cercueil du pauvre jeune homme, cette belle poignée de sabre qui seul émerge du large manteau de spahi. Ah! le beau papillon écrasé et cette toque, le fier hochet de sa jeunesse, et cette croix qu'il conquit. . . . Les noirs serviteurs de la mort soudain s'élancent, dépouillent le cercueil." Maurice Barrès, *Mes cahiers,* (Paris: Plon, 1931), vol. 4, 29.

114. "bouleversée . . . stupide." Gyp, letter to Séverine, [Nov.–Dec. 1900], MD.

115. Gyp, letter to Arvède Barine, [Nov.–Dec. 1900], Naf 18346, #43–47, BN.

116. "J'avais la conviction absolue qu'il arriverait malheur à Aymar au Soudan et je suis terrifiée de sa mort autant que si je n'avais pas attendu pendant deux ans cet horrible malheur." Gyp, letter to Madame de Vielcastel, [Nov.–Dec. 1900], private collection, Paris.

117. "certainement le plus grand chagrin de son existence." Madeleine Zillhardt, *Louise-Catherine Breslau et ses amis* (Paris: Editions des Portiques, 1932), 206.

118. Barrès, *Mes cahiers*, vol. 3, 236.

119. In August 1897 Gyp and Calmann-Lévy were collaborating on the publication of Aymar's first work, with Gyp correcting the proofs and Calmann-Lévy attending to publicity. "What shall we do to publicize Aymar . . . ? Calmann-Lévy wrote Gyp. "I would like to launch his first work carefully in order to create a readership for him immediately." ("Que ferons-nous pour le service de publicité d'Aymar . . . ? Je voudrais lancer son premier ouvrage avec soin, afin de lui créer tout de suite des lecteurs en librairie.") [Georges?] Calmann-Lévy, letter to Gyp, Aug. 1897, CL.

Chapter XI

1. Philippe Barrès, "Gyp, ou la féerie," *Les Nouvelles littéraires*, 9 July 1932.

2. See Guy de Balignac, *Quatre ans à la cour de Saxe* (Paris: Perrin, 1913), 186–89.

3. See Jacques Bainville, "Chronique: Une enquête délicate," *La Gazette de France*, 8 Nov. 1902.

4. "a toujours eu des voitures bien attelés et jolies." Gyp, letter to Maurice Barrès, 1901, MB.

5. See Zeev Sternhell, *La Droite révolutionnaire, 1885–1914: Les Origines françaises du fascisme* (Paris: Seuil, 1978), 116.

6. "vous serez des nôtres." Gyp, letter to Maurice Barrès, [Jan.–May] 1901, MB.

7. "on coupait et on supprimait, sous prétexte que *'j'avais la spécialité de dire des choses capables d'attirer des procès.'* " Ibid.

8. "[j]e me fichais d'avoir des piques avec *La Libre Parole*." Ibid.

9. Gyp, letter to Maurice Barrès, 1901, MB.

10. "une feuille de choc." Gyp, letter to Maurice Barrès, [Jan.–May 1901], MB.

11. Ibid.

12. "le meilleur moyen . . . c'est que je supprime de temps à autre des articles." Maurice Barrès, letter to Gyp, 8 July 1901, Harry Ransom Humanities Research Center, The University of Texas at Austin.

13. "Faut lessiver tout ça! . . . . viens m'aider!!!!!!" Bob, *La Patrie Illustrée*, 22 Feb. 1902.

14. "des tueurs, des saigneurs, des découpeurs de viande, aux figures larges, aux muscles saillants, aux épaules énormes." Paul Lefranc, "Silhouettes électorales: Monsieur Barillier," *Le Matin*, 20 April 1902.

15. Sternhell, *La Droite révolutionnaire*, 143.

16. "J'ai quitté ce groupement trop patriotique à mon gré, et qui me semble mettre l'intérêt personnel de ses membres très au-dessus de l'intérêt du pays." Gyp, letter to Maurice Barrès, 1901, MB.

17. "couché et vraiment effrayant de maigreur et de fatigue." Gyp, letter to Maurice Barrès, [Jan.–April 1902], MB.

18. "l'argent—arrêté à la Patrie Française—afflue pour l'instant à l'Action Libérale. . . ." Gyp, letter to Paule Barrès, [Jan.–March 1902], MB.

19. "Je suis enchantée que Syveton ait giflé le ministre de la guerre. J'aurais préféré qu'il giflât Jaurès, mais il faut se contenter de ce qu'il est. C'est déjà bien gentil!" Gyp, letter to Maurice Barrès, [November 1904], MB.

20. "une canaille qui est d'une excellente famille d'Alsace." Ibid.

21. "quand le domestique m'a dit qu'il était là, je suis restée baba!" Ibid.

22. Ibid.

23. "intelligent avec du talent, mais sans énergie, sans principes, et violent comme tous les faibles." Boni de Castellane, *Mémoires, 1867–1932*, ed. Emmanuel de Waresquiel (Paris: Perrin, 1986), 152.

24. "Syveton ne s'est pas tué! . . . [E]st-ce qu'un type comme ça se tue comme une blanchisseuse?" Gyp, *Journal d'un casserolé* (Paris: Juven, 1905), 334.

25. "La vérité est . . . qu'il a été 'supprimé' en vue du procès de demain." Ibid., 330.

26. "[I]l paraît que la chose a été imposée à Gyp à qui on a [laissé entendre] que tout refus serait pris en mauvaise part et qu'on la punirait en publiant certains détails sur son fameux enlèvement raconté jadis par les journaux." Police report, 17 Aug. 1902, BA 1198, APP.

27. "un journal antijuif et nationaliste." *La Tribune française*, 1 Sept. 1902, 1.

28. "combattre tous les spéculateurs"; "continuer le travail du Grand Occident de France, malgré persécutions." Ibid.

29. Police report, 6 Sept. 1902, BA 1105, APP.

30. "la comédie dure depuis trop longtemps." Police report, 4 April 1903, BA 1198, APP.

31. "mais pièce par pièce, pour que cela ne soit pas trop visible." Police report, 10 Sept. 1903, BA 1198, APP.

32. "affolés, et ne savent à quel saint se vouer." Police report, 27 Sept. 1903, BA 1198, APP.

33. "elle se figure que Louis Guérin l'attendrait dans un endroit désert pour lui donner un mauvais coup." Police report, 19 March 1904, APP.

34. "de précieuses indications pour mes conférences populaires." Jules Quesnay de Beaurepaire, letter to Gyp, 5 April 1901, private collection, Paris.

35. "[L]a monarchie se démontre comme un théorème." Charles Maurras, quoted in *Le Nationalisme français: Anthologie, 1871–1914*, ed. Raoul Girardet (Paris: Seuil, 1983), 198.

36. "plus qu'un problème: c'est un scandale." Charles Maurras, "L'Esprit politique de Gyp," *L'Action Française*, 1 Aug. 1905, 222.

37. "beau petit livre en forme de poignard." Charles Maurras, "Notes de critique: *Les Chapons* de Gyp," *La Gazette de France*, 26 March 1903, 1.

38. See Charles Maurras, "Les Images puissantes: *Un ménage dernier cri*," *La Gazette de France*, 9 Aug. 1903, 1–2.

39. Maurras was equally impressed by several other works by Gyp (notably *Le Friquet* and *La Fée*), which he praised in both the press and letters to the author. Gyp, letter to Charles Maurras, 1901, private collection, Paris; Charles Maurras, "Notes de critique: Petites lettres," *La Gazette de France*, 13 Nov. 1902.

40. "la bonne semence de Gyp." Maurras, "Les Images puissantes," 2.

41. "sagesse . . . et science, . . . réflexion . . . et obsession." Ibid., 1.

42. "un bréviaire de sagesse politique." Charles Maurras, "L'Esprit politique de Gyp," 216.

43. Ibid., 214–16.

44. "discussion, critique, parlementarisme, agitation stérile, élection toujours provisoire et toujours recommencée?" Ibid., 222.

45. "voir que la royauté est tout le contraire, mais un contraire radical, un contraire pur?" Ibid.

46. "J'ai beau faire, je ne crois pas que l'antisémitisme du duc d'Orléans soit *bon teint*." Gyp, letter to Charles Maurras, [March 1903], private collection, Paris.

47. See Richard Sonn, ''The Context of Extremist Politics: 'Les Extrêmes se Touchent,' '' in his *Anarchism and Cultural Politics in Fin de Siècle France* (Lincoln: U of Nebraska P, 1989), 31–48.

48. Gyp, *L'Age du toc* (Paris: Flammarion, 1908).

49. ''[Le] geste fraternel [de Gyp] avait suffi à réveiller l'honnête bourgeois qui sommeillait dans le coeur de l'anarchiste.'' Un Parisien, ''Comment Gyp sauva Paterne Berrichon de l'anarchie,'' *L'Intransigeant*, 10 July 1932, 2.

50. ''[p]etit provincial fort engoncé.'' Laurent Tailhade, *La Médaille qui s'efface* (Paris: Crès, 1924), 98. This description is drawn from Tailhade's review of *Un mariage chic*, which appeared in *La Vérité* on 27 May 1918.

51. Tailhade, *La Médaille qui s'efface*, 98.

52. Ibid., 99.

53. Sonn, *Anarchism and Cultural Politics*, 257.

54. ''Je marchai sous les étendards de Zola, mon glorieux ami et mon maître; Gyp, si libre cependant, . . . se tourna vers le parti de MM. Saint-Saëns et Frédéric Masson.'' Tailhade, *La Médaille qui s'efface*, 99.

55. See Francis Jourdain, *Sans remords ni rancunes* (Paris: Corréa, 1953).

56. ''Et puis, tout à coup, . . . monsieur Tailhade se mit à m'attraper dans les journaux dreyfusards où il écrivait . . . régulièrement, et non pas en attaquant mes idées différentes des siennes, (depuis peu de temps) mais en m'injuriant personnellement.'' Gyp, *L'Age du mufle* (Paris: Juven, 1902), 251.

57. ''la première des conteurs femmes.'' Tailhade, *La Médaille qui s'efface*, 106.

58. ''bédouins transplantés de leur crasse originelle.'' Ibid., 107

59. ''ioutres oléagineux . . . mal débarbouillés encore.'' Ibid., 100.

60. Ibid.

61. *Le Libertaire*, 15 Sept. 1901.

62. ''avec sa tête blanche et son bedonnement léger . . . a assez exactement l'aspect d'un colonel . . . en retraite.'' Gyp, *L'Age du mufle*, 252.

63. ''Etre comparé à une vieille culotte de peau avait suffi à remplir d'aise l'antimilitariste 'convaincu.' '' Jourdain, *Sans remords ni rancunes*, 89.

64. ''Je suis pour la guerre de toutes les forces de mon instinct.'' Gyp, ''Pour la Guerre! . . .'' *Gil Blas*, 4 Dec. 1903, 1.

65. ''J'avoue même . . . que je verrais sans douleur monter au ciel en holocauste un stock de valétudinaires—agonisants, surtout!—si ça devait faire pousser, sur une terre reconquise, un seul petit Lorrain bien vivace et grouillant.'' Ibid.

66. Ibid.

67. Laurent Tailhade, ''Lettre casquée—Sermo Galeatus—à Gyp—Comtesse de Mirabeau-Martel—Gyp,'' *L'Action*, 10 Dec. 1903, 1.

68. ''Vous vous transformez en Walkyrie, en Velléda buveuse du sang humain.'' Ibid.

69. ''pendant mille ans, se compose de bouchers, de larrons et d'hommes entretenus, qui, pour alimenter son luxe, sa fainéantise, ses moeurs grossières et pompeuses, n'eut d'autre ressource que le vol à main armée ou bien encore le salaire de la prostitution qu'elle partageait avec l'Eglise, la noblesse et la bourgeoisie. . . .'' Ibid.

70. ''L'heure ne peut tarder où la place des grands capitaines sera au bagne et celle des 'patriotes' dans les maisons de fous.'' Ibid.

71. Ibid.

72. Jourdain, *Sans remords ni rancunes*, 89.

73. ''La pensée que cette belle femme aux doux yeux et aux traits de marbre était la

propre nièce de l'Empereur, du Napoléon de la légende, me remplissait d'admiration et de respect. . . . Avec la princesse Mathilde, c'est encore un peu de la grande histoire qui s'en va!'' Gyp, letter to [?], 3 Jan. 1904, reprinted in Michel Missoffe, *Gyp et ses amis* (Paris: Flammarion, 1932), 109–10.

74. ''Thierry nous a fait une *surprise!*'' Gyp, letter to Albert [?], [1906–7?], private collection.

75. ''Après avoir vu la jeune femme et le petit bonhomme, nous nous sommes décidés à accepter ce qui était fait (du moins fait *à moitié*).'' Ibid.

76. ''une bretonne du Finistère, d'une famille très honorable et sans aucune fortune.'' Ibid.

77. ''Elle n'est pas distinguée, mais fraîche, bien tournée, avec de bons yeux bleus et une grande diablesse de bouche qui rit toujours.'' Ibid.

78. ''[Il est] tellement pris à son hôpital que nous ne le voyons plus.'' Gyp, letter to [?], [1902], private collection, Paris.

79. ''Si nous ne savions pas qu'elle tourne chaque jour pendant une heure autour de la Madeleine avec Monsieur d'Hugues, nous croirions qu'elle a changé d'avis. Nous en arrivions à ne plus savoir si c'est *lui* ou *elle* qui ne veut pas? . . . C'est une génération *compliquée*. . . .'' Gyp, letter to Maurice Barrès, Jan. 1902, #9, MB.

80. ''une fin d'année terriblement difficile.'' Gyp, letter to [?] Calmann-Lévy, 13 Dec. 1906, CL.

81. ''Que tu clabaudes sur moi, peu importe; tu es arrivée à faire vendre plus de *Cloclo* qu'il ne s'en est vendu en un an. J'y ai tout intérêt. J'ai fait un roman où tu es, toi, traitée respectueusement, beaucoup trop, étant donné la vérité. Il te plaît de te fâcher, ça m'est égal, et d'en faire un contre moi, ce dont je me contrefiche dans les grands prix.'' Quoted in ''Au Palais,'' *La Grande Revue*, 25 Feb. 1908, 831.

82. ''Mais écoute bien ce que je te dis. Si dans ce roman tu as le malheur de faire jouer un rôle quelconque à grand-père . . . tu auras affaire à moi de façon qu'il t'en cuira, je te le promets. Je ne voudrais pas te dire des choses désagréables sur ton talent, mais étant donné nos situations respectives dans la presse et les amis que nous y avons toutes les deux, je crois bien que tu ne mèneras pas large en face de moi.'' Ibid.

83. Gyp, letter to [?] Calmann-Lévy, 25 June 1908, CL. On the trial, see also *La Gazette des Tribunaux*, 1 Feb. 1908, 101, and 29 Feb. 1908.

84. ''roi des beaux esprits.'' Paul Morand, *1900* (Paris: Flammarion, 1931), 200.

85. On Montesquiou, see Philippe Jullian, *Robert de Montesquiou: Un Prince 1900* (Paris: Perrin, 1987).

86. ''[Q]uelquefois on était six mois ou même un an sans le voir. Puis il venait cinq ou six fois de suite, écrivait tous les jours. Cela, généralement, quand il avait un embêtement quelconque.'' Gyp, letter to Michel Missoffe, 14 Oct. 1929, in Missoffe, *Gyp et ses amis*, 104.

87. ''grandes matinées (vraiment réussies).'' Ibid., 106.

88. ''petits goûters des cinq ou six personnes avec lesquelles il essayait de se lier pour l'instant.'' Ibid.

89. ''si ces nouveaux amis m'aiment bien ou s'ils viennent comme les autres pour se f—— de moi.'' Ibid.

90. Ibid., 107.

91. ''Au point de vue mondain, je n'existais pas.'' Ibid., 105.

92. ''Je vivais comme un ours, en dehors de tout. J'étais, sans plus, la vieille amie à laquelle on vient raconter ses petites affaires.'' Ibid., 107.

93. Missoffe, *Gyp et ses amis*, 103.

94. Gyp, letter to Robert de Montesquiou, [30 Oct. 1913?], Naf 15168, #152–156, RM.

95. Gyp, letter to Robert de Montesquiou, [Oct. 1907], Naf 15071, #88–92, RM.

96. ''avec quel art vous savez être terrible et divertissant.'' Gyp, letter to Robert de Montesquiou, [1907], Naf 15144, #114–20, RM.

97. ''Ce que je viens de m'amuser, c'est rien de le dire!'' Gyp, letter to Robert de Montesquiou, [1912], Naf 15161, #65–70, RM.

98. Gyp, letter to Robert de Montesquiou, n.d., Naf 15166, #84–85, RM.

99. Gyp, letter to Robert de Montesquiou, [1907], Naf 15154, #180–81, RM.

100. ''l'intimité discrète, la conversation brillante, les nobles assemblées, où le décor somptueux s'alliait au spectacle d'art, la fête des yeux, à celle de l'esprit. Tout cela [est] remplacé par le Cake-Walk et le Bridge!'' Robert de Montesquiou, *L'Assemblée des notables*. ''Monsieur Monde et Madame Mondanité'' was originally published in *La Vie Parisienne* on 10 Aug. 1907. Gyp had solicited Montesquiou's contribution on behalf of Saglio, the new director of *La Vie Parisienne*, who was an admirer of the count's. See Gyp, letter to Robert de Montesquiou, [1907], Naf 15154, #180–207, and Naf 15072, #573, RM.

101. ''Ne pas *distinguer* est le propre de notre temps.'' Robert de Montesquiou, letter to Gyp, 9 Nov. 1910, private collection, Paris.

102. ''la seule chose jolie de mon affreuse petite maison.'' Gyp, letter to Robert de Montesquiou, [1910–11], Naf 15159, RM.

103. See Jullian, *Robert de Montesquiou*, 216.

104. ''Vous êtes comme un paon qui ferait la roue avec des yeux rectangulaires, toujours plus nombreux, lesquels sont vos livres chatoyants. . . .'' Robert de Montesquiou, letter to Gyp, 1913, private collection, Paris.

105. ''la plus courue de mémoire d'académicien.'' Jacques-Emile Blanche, *La Pêche aux souvenirs* (Paris: Flammarion, 1949), 269.

106. ''assez lettré (entré, je crois, à l'Ecole Normale), actif, travailleur, intelligent (très). . . .'' Gyp, letter to Maurice Barrès, [1899], #60, MB.

107. See Gyp, letter to Maurice Barrès, 26 Feb. 1904, MB.

108. ''C'est drôle, tout le monde le salue quand il est mort, personne ne le saluait quand il était vivant.'' Quoted in Maurice Barrès, *Mes Cahiers* (Paris: Plon, 1931), vol. 3, 198.

109. ''un Dreyfusard qui marchait sur le côté et nous lançait des regards noirs.'' Ibid.

110. ''C'est ce mois-ci qui est le plus 'ingrat' dans le Midi français. Mais c'est déjà joli. A Mirabeau, c'est à la fin de mars qu'il y a des lilas et des lys. Inutile de vous dire, n'est-ce pas, que Mirabeau est toujours à votre disposition, au cas où il vous plairait d'y passer du temps. C'est sauvage—mais très sain. . . . Vous préviendriez seulement quelques jours d'avance Monsieur Arland, forgeron à *Mirabeau, Vaucluse*, pour qu'il fasse nettoyer la maison.'' Gyp, letter to Paule Barrès, [Feb. 1902], #11, MB.

111. ''One must know the soul of a region,'' Barrès wrote during his 1904 stay in Provence. ''One must find its soul, that which shaped it.'' (''Il faut connaître l'âme d'un pays, il faut trouver son âme, ce qui l'a façonné.'') Maurice Barrès, *Mes Cahiers*, vol. 3, 295.

112. ''Je vais sans doute faire un séjour, avec ma femme et sans Gyp, chez Gyp au château de Mirabeau, au coeur de votre région, et avec l'automobile. De sorte que si vous y venez, nous visiterons dans le plus minutieux détail . . . toutes ces villes, villages et aspects fameux. Ne pourrez-vous y venir? Comprenez: le château est mis à ma disposition, avec liberté d'en user, et c'est moi qui vous invite. J'ajoute que Gyp regrettera seulement

de n'être pas l'hôtesse complète. Ce serait admirable. . . ." Maurice Barrès, letter to Charles Maurras, 7 Oct. 1904, reprinted in Maurice Barrès and Charles Maurras, *La République ou le Roi: Correspondance inédite, 1883–1923*, ed. Hélène and Nicole Maurras (Paris: Plon, 1970), 427–28.

113. "C'est la corde du pendu! C'est la corde du pendu!" Ibid., 386–87.

114. "Ne partez pas sans voir Manosque, Beaumont et Orgon. Orgon est un peu loin, mais c'est très intéressant et à cause du passage de l'Empereur et parce que le pays est sauvage et rude." Gyp, letter to Maurice Barrès, 12 Nov. 1904, #4, MB.

115. "Solitude sauvage et gaie pourtant. . . ." Barrès, *Mes Cahiers*, vol. 3, 290.

116. "Mme de Martel est bien une chèvre d'ici." Ibid.

117. Jérome et Jean Tharaud, *Mes années chez Barrès* (Paris: Plon, 1928), 234.

118. "[L]e nom de Mirabeau transformait une demi-ruine en un castel inanimé qu'il réveillerait. Le paysage inanimé, le plus sauvage, le plus âpre de notre Provence alpestre, serait sa Campagna Romana." Blanche, *La Pêche aux souvenirs*, 270.

119. "Je suis heureuse que ça soit à eux plutôt qu'à d'autres, mais je regrette Mirabeau." Gyp, letter to Robert de Montesquiou, [1907], Naf 15144, #114–20, RM.

120. "Nous venons d'arriver en automobile dans cet aimable Mirabeau où tout serait parfait si je n'avais la sensation de vous avoir enlevé un plaisir. Mais c'est vrai que vous n'en jouissez qu'en imagination, et comme vous le laissez tel quel, ce n'est pas une pensée pénible qu'il doit vous donner." Maurice Barrès, letter to Gyp, [1907], MB.

121. Maurice Barrès, "Lettre à Gyp sur le printemps à Mirabeau," *La Revue hebdomadaire* 7, April 1921, 376.

122. "ce cadre d'éternité." Ibid., 380.

123. "ivre de soleil." Maurice Barrès, *Mes Cahiers* (Paris: Plon, 1932), vol. 5, 284.

124. "Pauvre homme du Nord, jouissons de l'heure qui nous enchante." Maurice Barrès, "Lettre à Gyp," 381.

125. "The mark of these exceptional leaders remains everywhere on the hill. . . . The hill is their relic, that is, their thought made concrete. One breathes it there, one feels there the sensitivity of these dead." ("L'empreinte de ces chefs exceptionnels demeure partout sur la colline. . . . La colline est leur relique, c'est à dire leur pensée rendue concrète. On y respire, on y touche la sensibilité de ces morts.") Ibid., 382.

126. "le grand Mirabeau, ce brigand de Mirabeau." Ibid., 394.

127. "au nom de la poésie"; "[q]u'il demeure, comme le génie du lieu, avec ses vices mêlés d'une espèce de vertu, au milieu des ruines qu'il a causées, ce puissant esprit. . . ." Ibid.

128. Ibid., 387.

129. "Il avait en horreur la vie méridionale, les cafés, les palabres, le soleil, les mouches, la poussière, cet esprit sans ombre, et par-dessus tout il éprouvait la gêne de ne pas être ici à sa place." Jérôme et Jean Tharaud, *Mes années chez Barrès*, 274.

130. "Barrès quittait [Mirabeau] sans regret." Ibid., 275.

Chapter XII

1. Gyp, *Le Journal d'un cochon de pessimiste* (Paris: Calmann-Lévy, 1918), 5.

2. "The existence of my generation has been poisoned by this shadowy menace that exasperates me! . . . ." ("L'existence de ma génération a été empoisonnée par cette vaine menace qui m'exaspère! . . . ."). Ibid., 24. Ellipses in original.

3. "Pourquoi ne puis-je pas la faire, cette guerre dont la menace a pesé sur ma vie . . . ?" Ibid., 48.

4. "Je marcherais avec tant de joie! J'aime tant la casse, le tumulte, les coups. Quelle belle occasion! . . ." Ibid. Ellipses in original.

5. "Que je vois la si passionnée Revanche, et je m'en irai resuscitée dans la mort." Juliette Adam, letter to Gyp, 1 Aug. 1915, private collection, Paris.

6. See chapter 11, note 64, in this book.

7. "[O]n devrait promettre une récompense magnifique à celui . . . qui prendrait le général Stenger, le blesserait ensuite, et l'acheverait plus tard, en prenant son temps." Gyp, letter to Maurice Barrès, [1914?], MB.

8. "j'ai liquidé les quelques relations caillautardes ou défaitistes que je pouvais avoir." Gyp, letter to [?] Calmann-Lévy, 15 Dec. 1918, CL. Joseph Caillaux (1864–1944), a politician known for his his support of a pro-German foreign policy, and then for his opposition to the war, was violently attacked by those in favor of the war.

9. "On est débarrassé pour toujours de ce boursouflé encombrant. . . ." Gyp, *Le Journal d'un cochon de pessimiste*, 46. A 1923 letter to Barrès confirmed her feeling: "I had heard him chatting at length with [Anatole] France on several occasions . . . during the Zola Affair, and I found him mediocre and erudite, which makes, to my mind, a foul combination. . . ." ("Je l'avais entendu causer longuement avec [Anatole] France, à plusieurs reprises . . . pendant l'affaire Zola, et je le trouvais médiocre et érudit, ce qui fait, à mon sens, un mélange nauséabond. . . .") Gyp, letter to Maurice Barrès, 7 [?] 1923, #130, MB.

10. See Philippe Bernard, *La Fin d'un monde, 1914–1929* (Paris: Seuil, 1975), 58–59.

11. Gyp, letter to Marie de Mirabeau, 4 Jan. [1916], Sibylle Gaudry collection, Paris.

12. "ce froid horrible—sans chauffage possible. . . ." Gyp, letter to [?] Calmann-Lévy, 26 Jan. 1917, CL.

13. "C'est des mains de collégien . . . . ou de cuisinière. . . ." Gyp, letter to [?] Calmann-Lévy, 21 Feb. 1917, CL. Ellipses in original.

14. "d'ouvriers *valides* qui puissent monter sur les toits." Gyp, letter to Marie de Mirabeau, 30 [1916–1917?], Sibylle Gaudry collection, Paris.

15. In October 1878 Marie purchased the château of Cossesseville, which had been built around 1870 near the site of a manor house that once belonged to the Le Harivel de Gonneville family. In 1912 she rented the château and adjoining farm and moved to the nearby town of Mondeville.

16. "Il n'y a pas *un soupçon d'éclairage la nuit à Paris, nulle part à partir de 8 heures du soir. . . . [C]'est l'obscurité complète et profonde*, les nuits sans lune." Gyp, letter to Marie de Mirabeau, 25 Dec. [1915], Sibylle Gaudry collection, Paris.

17. "une excessive faiblesse"; "de doses massives . . . de la strychnine et d'autres horreurs." Gyp, letter to Robert de Montesquiou, 1917, Naf 15192, #48–53, RM.

18. Ibid.

19. "le fossile intégral." Gyp, *Le Journal d'un cochon de pessimiste*, 6.

20. "le vieil ours du boulevard Bineau, qui est maintenant un ours tout blanc." Gyp, letter to Robert de Montesquiou, [1917], Naf 15192, #48–53, RM.

21. "les petites choses—non signées—que je fais de côté et d'autre, pour me tirer d'affaire." Gyp, letter to [?] Calmann-Lévy, 26 May 1915, CL.

22. "Tout ça nécessite un va et vient d'épreuves, et de courses, et de travail qui est un casse-tête." Gyp, letter to Marie de Mirabeau, 18 [Feb. 1916], Sibylle Gaudry collection, Paris.

23. "sans *rien* à la maison"; "comment je passerai la journée de Dimanche et la matinée de Lundi." Gyp, letter to [?] Calmann-Lévy, 29 April 1915, CL.

24. "[J]e n'ai plus un sou." Gyp, letter to [?] Calmann-Lévy, 13 Aug. 1914, CL.

25. "[J]e suis dans une situation infiniment pénible." Gyp, letter to [?] Calmann-Lévy, 29 April 1915, CL.

26. "Je me trouve sans *rien* pour finir l'année. . . ." Gyp, letter to [?] Calmann-Lévy, 17 Dec. 1917, CL.

27. "L'augmentation de la vie est telle que je suis totalement débordée. . . . [J]e ne sais pas ce que je vais devenir, moi et ceux qui me dépendent." Gyp, letter to [?] Calmann-Lévy, 28 Aug. 1918, CL.

28. "[I have] *enormous* New Year's gifts to give. . . ." ("[J]'ai] des étrennes *énormes* à donner. . . .") Gyp, letter to [?] Calmann-Lévy, 17 Dec. 1917, CL.

29. "Il y a des jours où je suis vraiment découragée d'avoir tant travaillé, et de penser que je ne me reposerai jamais, jamais. . . ." Gyp, letter to [?] Calmann-Lévy, 19 Oct. 1917, CL.

30. "Chère petite mère"; "Je t'embrasse mille fois de tout coeur. A toi, Gaby."

31. See chapter 3, note 33, in this book.

32. "Tu n'as *jamais compris*—ayant vécu chez grand-père et grand-mère depuis que tu m'avais—et *seule* depuis, ce que c'est que d'avoir 3 enfants et un mari *à sa charge*. Tu n'as eu à t'occuper que de toi. . . . Tu ne juges jamais que *de ton point de vue à toi*." Gyp, letter to Marie de Mirabeau, 25 Oct. [1915], Sibylle Gaudry collection, Paris.

33. Ibid.

34. Est-ce que tu as une distraction? . . . Je ne comprends rien à cette histoire. . . ." Gyp, letter to Marie de Mirabeau, [Jan. 1916], Sibylle Gaudry collection, Paris.

35. Gyp, letter to Marie de Mirabeau, 29 [Jan. 1916?], Sibylle Gaudry collection, Paris.

36. "La succession de ma mère—succession ne veut pas toujours dire argent!—me cause tous les tracas du monde. Elle n'a laissé que des procès, et je n'hérite que des pensions à payer." Gyp, letter to [?] Calmann-Lévy, 26 Jan. 1917, CL.

37. "au milieu duquel j'ai été élevée." Gyp, letter to [?] Calmann-Lévy, [1916–17?], CL.

38. "Cette dépense effarante de chaque jour m'affole, et pourtant nous nous privons de tout. . . . Je ne sais pas, si cela dure, ce que je vais devenir. . . . Je suis sans argent, sans feu, dans des difficultés affolantes." Gyp, letter to [?] Calmann-Lévy, 31 [? 1919?], CL.

39. For a statistical breakdown of combatants by age group, see Antoine Prost, *Les Aciens Combattants et la société française, 1914–39* (Paris: Presses de la Fondation Nationale des Sciences Politiques, 1977), vol. 2, 5.

40. "il court d'instinct vers le danger. . . ." Gyp, *Le Journal d'un cochon de pessimiste*, 288.

41. "L'Alsace vaut bien la peine que nous nous donnons pour elle." Quoted in Gyp's letter to Maurice Barrès, 19 [Oct. 1914], #100, MB.

42. Dominique Desanti, *Drieu la Rochelle: Le Séducteur mystifié* (Paris: Flammarion, 1978), 354.

43. "en descendant du train." Gyp, letter to Maurice Barrès, 19 [Oct. 1914], #100, MB.

44. "Nous savons que le 292ᵉ avait été écrasé le 8 et le 9 septembre à [? kil] au nord de Meaux. Le 8 . . . le colonel était tombé, blessé deux fois, on avait vu Thierry le ramasser. . . . [P]lusieurs officiers tirés, 18 blessés, les hommes en proportion, un régiment squeletté!" Ibid.

45. "Que c'est long! Mon Dieu! Cette bataille!" Gyp, letter to Maurice Barrès, [Sept.–Oct. 1914], #101, MB.

46. "Ce qu'il fait chaud de toutes les façons!" Quoted in Gyp, letter to Maurice Barrès, 23 Sept. [1914], #104, MB.

47. "abîmés, dévastés, ayant perdu cette année tout ce qu'ils ont." Gyp, letter to Maurice Barrès, 30 [Sept. 1914], #106, MB.

48. See Philippe Barrès, " 'Je ne veux pas les voir,' dit Thierry de Martel . . . et il se tue," *Paris-Presse*, 13 June 1945.

49. The citation accompanying his promotion to Chevalier de la Légion d'honneur (he would be promoted to officier in 1919) reads: "[Thierry de Martel] showed in numerous circumstances remarkable courage and energy by proceeding to search for wounded under very intense fire. On 21 September, as wounded soldiers were in danger in a burning farmhouse, he gathered his medics, led them to the farmhouse under extremely intense fire, and succeeded in rescuing the wounded." ("[Thierry de Martel] a montré en de nombreuses ciconstances un courage et une énergie remarquables en procédant sous un feu très violent à la recherche des blessés. Le 21 septembre, des blessés étant en danger dans une ferme incendiée, il a entraîné ses infirmiers sous un feu extrêmement violent, les a conduit à la ferme et a réussi à sauver ces blessés.")

50. "I believe Thierry must be sent to the Dardenelles. But only in September, and by then Constantinople will perhaps be ours." ("Je crois que Thierry doit être envoyé aux Dardanelles. Mais en septembre seulement, et d'ici là, Constantinople sera peut-être à nous.") Gyp, letter to Maurice Barrès, 28 [Jan.–Aug. 1915], #99, MB.

51. Gyp, letter to Maurice Barrès, [1915?], #95, MB.

52. "des conditions pénibles de manque d'air . . . et de manque de lumière." Gyp, letter to Maurice Barrès, [Jan. 1916], #96, MB.

53. "parce qu'elle est très intelligente et pas pour deux sous féminine." Gyp, letter to Maurice Barrès, 3 [Oct. 1915?], #102, MB.

54. "De tous les côtés, je fais des démarches depuis 8 jours qu'Yvette me l'a formellement demandé." Gyp, letter to Marie de Mirabeau, 12 [Jan. 1916], Sibylle Gaudry collection, Paris.

55. "*on le fera rester.*" Ibid.

56. "ce que tu as voulu, et Yvette aussi. . . ." Gyp, letter to Marie de Mirabeau, 16 [Jan. 1916], Sibylle Gaudry collection, Paris.

57. "*Vous* direz bien à Thierry . . . *toi* et *Yvette*, que c'est *vous* qui m'avez forcé la main pour le faire rentrer . . . *s'il apprend et m'attrape*. Si, par hasard, il ne l'apprend pas, j'aurai une sacrée veine!" Gyp, letter to Marie de Mirabeau, 28 [Jan. 1916], Sibylle Gaudry collection, Paris.

58. "*Naturally*, Thierry did not tell me he was returning . . . . . *since it's the truth.*" ("Thierry ne m'a *naturellement* pas dit qu'il revenait . . . . . *puisque c'est la vérité.*") Gyp, letter to Marie de Mirabeau, 18 [Feb. 1916], Sibylle Gaudry collection, Paris. Ellipses in original.

59. "Les gens qui mentent me font penser à Thierry. . . ." Gyp, letter to Marie de Mirabeau, 26 [Jan. 1916], Sibylle Gaudry collection, Paris.

60. "Pour ça Yvette le gêne beaucoup plus que moi, qui ne connais—et n'ai connu—de ses grues que les *seules* Lasseur." Gyp, letter to Marie de Mirabeau, 18 [Feb. 1916], Sibylle Gaudry collection, Paris. Similarly, Gyp revealed her concern that Yvette, while visiting Thierry in the hospital on his return, "will disrupt the visits of the Lasseur women, and other Denyses of all types, who are going to rush to his bedside." ("troublera les

visites des Lasseur, et des autres Denyses, de tous les genres, qui vont se précipiter à son chevet.'') Ibid.

61. Gyp, letter to Marie de Mirabeau, [1916], Sibylle Gaudry collection, Paris.

62. ''Une fois de plus, *j'ai l'air* d'avoir été roulée. . . . Mais, au fond, je ne le suis pas. . . .'' Gyp, letter to Marie de Mirabeau, 26 [Jan. 1916], Sibylle Gaudry collection, Paris. Ellipses in original.

63. ''un abominable accès de fièvre paludéenne, vomissements, claquements de dents.'' Gyp, letter to Maurice Barrès, 25 [Feb. 1916], #97, MB.

64. Ibid.

65. ''Vous ne pouvez pas comprendre à quel point c'est amusant, vous, grand-mère, parce que vous ne l'avez pas encore (!) fait. . . .'' Quoted in Gyp's letter to Maurice Barrès, 6 [Dec. 1915 or Jan. 1916], #96, MB.

66. ''Malheureusement, ce passe temps idéal ne suffit plus à Aymar, qui fait des démarches pour passer—comme sergent—dans l'infanterie. C'est purement idiot!'' Ibid.

67. ''cette fantaisie d'infanterie.'' Ibid.

68. Ibid.

69. ''faire revenir [Aymar] dans un régiment de vraie cavalerie.'' Gyp, letter to Marie de Mirabeau, [Feb. 1916], Sibylle Gaudry collection, Paris. Ironically, in her letter Gyp mistakenly refers to Aymar as Thierry: ''Thierry has decided to make Thierry come back. . . .'' (''Thierry se décide à faire revenir Thierry. . . .'')

70. ''[D]epuis la mort d'Aymar, je n'ai pas écrit une ligne qui 'se tienne convenablement.' La mort de ce pauvre petit m'a atterrée.'' Gyp, letter to [?] Calmann-Lévy, 26 Jan. 1917, CL.

71. ''C'est le pauvre Aymar qui n'aura pas eu de veine dans la vie! . . . Il aura été *'moralement abandonné'* comme disent les jugements de police qui enlèvent les enfants aux parents pour les placer dans un asîle. . . . Il n'a jamais eu d'heure pour manger, ni même souvent de repas, car quand Thierry ne devait pas déjeuner ou dîner, Yvette . . . ne commandait quelquefois rien, par oubli. Ils ne lui ont appris ni l'orthographe, ni la politesse. L'enfant de parents pauvres, recueilli *à contre coeur*, n'aurait pas été moins négligé.'' Gyp, letter to Marie de Mirabeau, 18 [Feb. 1916], Sibylle Gaudry collection, Paris.

72. See Geneviève Colin, ''Writers and the War,'' in Jean-Jacques Becker, *The Great War and the French People*, trans. Arnold Pomerans (Warwickshire, Eng.: Berg, 1985), 161–77.

73. ''ce précieux exemplaire non censuré et annoté de votre main!'' Pierre Loti, letter to Gyp, [1914–18], private collection, Paris.

74. ''j'ai été élevé dans la haine de ces gens-là.'' Ibid.

75. ''[J']étais bien sûr que nous étions du même avis, sur ce point comme sur tant d'autres, mais je vous remercie mille fois de me l'avoir confirmé.'' Ibid.

76. ''le beau manuscrit que vous avez eu la grande bonté de me donner.'' Edith Wharton, letter to Gyp, 6 Nov. [1917–1918], private collection, Paris.

77. ''et le reste du temps couché et malade.'' Maurice Barrès, letter to Gyp, [1916?], private collection, Paris. Gyp confirmed to Montesquiou that ''Barrès has been ill from overexertion. . . . He was feeling better, but *L'Echo* having announced the resumption of his contributions that morning, people were already ringing his doorbell again all the time, and he just decided on the spot to leave for the Midi, without telling anyone where he would go. . . .'' (''Barrès a été malade à force de surmenage. . . . Il allait mieux, mais *L'Echo* ayant annoncé la reprise de sa collaboration ce matin-là, on recommençait déjà à

se pendre à sa sonnette, et il venait de se décider à l'instant à partir pour le midi, sans dire où il irait. . . .'') Gyp, letter to Robert de Montesquiou, [1916], N.a.f. 15192, #48–53, RM.

78. "[S]i j'écrivais comme je voudrais, mon article serait immédiatement supprimé." Maurice Barrès, letter to Gyp, [1914?], private collection, Paris.

79. "le Rossignol du carnage."

80. Gyp, letter to Maurice Barrès, [1915], #95, MB.

81. "C'était *très, très* bien. Elle suit l'évolution de la femme et l'approuve sans l'approuver. C'est complexe. . . .'' Maurice Barrès, letter to Gyp, 20 Feb. 1917, private collection, Paris; and Gyp, letter to Maurice Barrès, 20 [Feb.] 1917, #113, MB.

82. "le Kaiser affreux"; "Ce monstre." See Philippe Jullian, *Robert de Montesquiou: Un prince 1900* (Paris: Perrin, 1987), 280.

83. "le seul poète auquel la guerre eut inspirée de beaux vers." Gyp, letter to Robert de Montesquiou, [1916], N.a.f. 15192, #48–53, RM.

84. "rien de trop immédiat ne vous tourmente, à cette heure cruelle." Robert de Montesquiou, letter to Gyp, 12 Feb. 1915, private collection, Paris.

85. "Où je suis, Madame et chère collaboratrice? A Genève, depuis un bout de temps . . . qui commence à me sembler long, quoique les suisses romands soient de braves gens, germanophobes. . . .'' Willy, letter to Gyp, 21 May 1917, private collection, Paris.

86. "Ecrire des articles dans *La Suisse* n'est pas le bonheur suprême." Ibid.

87. "je ne voudrais pas être à la place des boches, qui verront les premiers notre armée franchir la frontière. Ah! les cochons! . . . Faudra payer!'' Ibid.

88. "désolé par le stupide abus que j'ai fait de la morphine." Laurent Tailhade, letter to Gyp, 10 July 1918, private collection, Paris.

89. Laurent Tailhade, letter to Gyp, 1 June 1918, private collection, Paris.

90. "Do I need to tell you how heartbroken I am by the mutilations my poor article has suffered?" ("Ai-je besoin de vous dire à quel point je suis navré des mutilations que mon pauvre article a subies?") Laurent Tailhade, letter to Gyp, 27 May 1918, private collection, Paris.

91. "la laideur effroyable de ces gens-là est une insulte à la lumière." Laurent Tailhade, letter to Gyp, 10 July 1918, private collection, Paris.

92. "Quand vous rêviez d'amender de la Troisième République (la République sans les juifs!), . . . je m'emballais, moi, sur la République universelle, fraternelle et autres billevesées." Laurent Tailhade, letter to Gyp, 29 May 1918, private collection, Paris.

93. "J'ai fait de la prison, récolté plusieurs duels, une quantité d'amendes; j'ai perdu quelques belles situations, le tout pour assister au lugubre spectacle de cette guerre sans fin ni merci, au triomphe des "bourreurs de crâne" et de tout ce que je haïrais si j'avais la force encore de haïr quoi que ce soit." Ibid.

94. "la destruction de cet aimable pays." Laurent Tailhade, letter to Gyp, 1 June 1918, private collection, Paris.

95. "Gyp est mobilisée. Gyp fait la guerre." Abel Hermant, "L'Ennemie du ridicule: Défense de la langue française," *Le Temps*, 24 Sept. 1918.

96. Gyp, letter to Marie de Mirabeau, 28 [Jan. 1916], Sibylle Gaudry collection, Paris.

97. "Vos *impressions de guerre* . . . survivront sous leur titre comique et violent, comme un éclat d'obus, dans lequel il y aurait un éclat de rire." Robert de Montesquiou, letter to Gyp, 17 March 1919, reprinted in Michel Missoffe, *Gyp et ses amis* (Paris: Flammarion, 1932), 112.

98. Abel Hermant, "L'Ennemie du ridicule: Défense de la langue française."

99. "une 'vieille France' est en train de se poser . . . , face aux imbéciles, aux emb-

usqués, à tous les ennemis de l'intérieur. . . .'' Rachilde, review of Gyp, *Ceux qui s'en f . . .* , *Le Mercure de France*, 16 Feb. 1918, 675.

100. "ces gens *qui me font . . . horreur.*" Gyp, letter to Marie de Mirabeau, 28 [Jan. 1916], Sibylle Gaudry collection, Paris.

101. *"Les Embusqués!* C'est le nom que l'on donne à ceux qui coupent au service militaire. J'entends au service armé. Et quoiqu'on veuille affirmer le contraire, il y en a beaucoup . . .'' Gyp, *Le Journal d'un cochon de pessimiste*, 226. Ellipses in original.

102. See Catherine Slater, *Defeatists and Their Enemies: Political Invective in France, 1914–1918* (Oxford, Eng.: Oxford UP, 1981), 18–24.

103. un ''cochon d'embusqué.'' Gyp, letter to Marie de Mirabeau, [Jan. 1916], Sibylle Gaudry collection, Paris.

104. "rester dans ses paperasses, et de ne s'exposer à rencontrer que d'autres Embusqués comme lui.'' Ibid.

105. "l'histoire . . . d'un Embusqué de marque.'' Gyp, letter to Marie de Mirabeau, 28 [Jan. 1916], Sibylle Gaudry collection, Paris.

106. "tout ce qui fut jadis Dreyfusard. . . .'' Gyp, *Ceux de "la nuque"* (Paris: Fayard, 1916).

107. "un certificat de présence au feu.'' Gyp, *Les Flanchards* (Paris: Fayard, 1917), 97.

108. "J'admire et j'envie ceux qui meurent en beauté, dans l'apothéose d'une bataille. . . .'' Gyp, *Le Journal d'un cochon de pessimiste*, 358.

109. "L'embusqué me dégoûte *infiniment.* . . .'' Gyp, letter to Marie de Mirabeau, [Jan. 1916], Sibylle Gaudry collection, Paris.

110. See Bernard, *La Fin d'un monde*, 36–38.

111. "I don't believe that [Action française] would have been very disappointed by a total disarray of the country . . . disarray from which the duc d'Orléans would have emerged like the Savior . . . in an apotheosis. . . .'' ("[J]e ne crois pas que [l'Action française] eût été très navrée d'un désarroi total du pays . . . désarroi duquel le duc d'Orléans fût sorti comme le Sauveur . . . dans une apothéose. . . .'') Gyp, *Le Journal d'un cochon de pessimiste*, 282. Ellipses in original. In 1915 the league did renew its political activities, stepping up a campaign to distribute royalist propaganda to the troops. See Becker, *The Great War and the French People*, 64–65.

112. "le dégénéré intégral''; ''purement dégoûtant''; ''une effarante couardise.'' Gyp, *Le Journal d'un cochon de pessimiste*, 340–42.

113. "Un vrai français, bien racé et de bonne race.'' Gyp, *Les Profitards* (Paris: Fayard, 1918) 125. See also *Le Journal d'un cochon de pessimiste*, 161–62.

114. The comparison between Clemenceau and Boulanger is suggested by Bernard, *La Fin d'un monde*, 84.

115. "son aspect étonnamment frais et enfantin.'' Gyp, *Les Flanchards*, 90.

116. "pas de corset, pas de jarretières, de la danse, de l'escrime, et de l'aviron.'' Ibid., 91–92.

117. "la secousse causée par la mort d'Aymar.'' Gyp, letter to [?] Calmann-Lévy, 7 [? 1918?], CL.

118. The *clefs* reflect Calmann-Lévy's worry about a possible accusation of libel. "[A]llow me to draw your attention to the danger that might result from designating by their real names . . . politicians, artists, etc., who appear in your work, especially if you are giving them a role . . . that would be of a nature to offend them. Beware of accusations of slander, both for yourself and for us, whom the law renders responsible for what we publish.'' (''[L]aissez-moi appeler votre attention sur le danger qu'il pourrait y avoir à

désigner sous leurs vrais noms ... les personnages politiques, artistes, etc. qui figurent dans votre ouvrage, surtout si vous leur prêtez un rôle ... qui serait de nature à leur porter ombrage. Gare aux poursuites en diffamation pour vous et pour nous-mêmes que la loi rend responsables de ce que nous publions.'') [?] Calmann-Lévy, letter to Gyp, 23 Oct. 1917, CL.

119. "[des] conquêtes nouvelles qui permettraient un écrasement définitif de la France ..." Gyp, *Le Journal d'un cochon de pessimiste*, 196. Ellipses in original.

120. "nous serons définitivement vainqueurs puisque nous n'avons pas tout de suite été battus ..." Ibid., 357. Ellipses in original.

121. "Mon grand tort est d'avoir un entourage et des charges, alors que j'étais fait pour vivre libre et seul." Ibid., 2.

122. "Né dans un monde où l'on a coutume de ne rien faire ... il m'a fallu, par nécessité, vers trente ans, m'improviser subitement peintre ..." Ibid. Ellipses in original.

123. "d'avoir un couteau 'avec quoi que j'puisse vraiment m'couper ...'" Ibid., 151. Ellipses in original.

124. "[L]es journées de Lorraine et d'Alsace ont dû être splendides!" Gyp, letter to [?] Calmann-Lévy, 15 Dec. 1918, CL.

125. Gyp, letter to [?] Calmann-Lévy, 31 Oct. 1918, CL.

126. "jai entendu tellement de choses antipathiques et *incroyables* vraiment après un si beau triomphe, que j'en suis écoeurée." Gyp, letter to [?] CL, 15 Dec. 1918, CL.

Chapter XIII

1. Philippe Barrès, "Gyp, ou la féerie," *Les Nouvelles littéraires*, 9 July 1932, 2.

2. René Benjamin, notes from a visit to Gyp, 6 April 1930, François Benjamin collection, Savonnières, France.

3. "C'est long et difficile de mourir." Quoted in Liane de Pougy, *Mes cahiers bleus* (Paris: Plon, 1977), 272.

4. "Je pensais que c'était la fin, mais pas du tout, ça n'est pas encore pour cette fois-ci. C'est embêtant! ... Je déteste les faux départs. . . ." Gyp, letter to [?] Calmann-Lévy, 29 [?] 1924, CL.

5. "Je ne sortirai plus"; "Je ne descendrai plus"; "Je ne me lèverai plus." See Philippe Barrès, "Gyp, ou la féerie"; and Gyp, letter to Louis Lyautey, 23 [? 1927], 475AP295, AN.

6. Gyp, letter to [?] Calmann-Lévy, 19 June 1919, CL.

7. Gyp, letter to Maurice Barrès, 20 June 1919, #115, MB.

8. "Thierry a dû faire une opération très grave, d'urgence, à la maison." Gyp, letter to Michel Calmann-Lévy, 16 June 1920, CL.

9. "des journées affreuses à faire la navette entre la rue Piccini et le boulevard Bineau." Gyp, letters to Michel Calmann-Lévy, 22 June and 5 July 1920, CL.

10. "On le considère comme perdu." Gyp, letter to [Michel?] Calmann-Lévy, 22 July 1920, CL.

11. Ibid.

12. Gyp, letter to [Michel?] Calmann-Lévy, 29 July 1920, CL.

13. "Je me débats dans des complications horribles ..." Gyp, letter to [Michel?] Calman-Lévy, 22 July 1920, CL.

14. Gyp, letter to [Michel?] Calmann-Lévy, 29 July 1920, CL.

15. "dont les oeuvres publiées sous le pseudonyme de Gyp sont si appréciées de tous les lettrés." *Le Gaulois*, 15 Aug. 1920.

16. Ibid.

17. "un vrai beau livre, et infiniment adroit." Gyp, letter to Maurice Barrès, 4 [?] 1921, #123, MB.

18. Maurice Barrès, *Sous l'oeil des barbares* (Nantes: Le Temps Singulier, 1980).

19. "Je vais *essayer* de vous expliquer . . . ce que je pense, si ça peut s'appeler comme ça, car, quand il s'agit de moi, c'est plutôt 'sentir' que penser." Gyp, letter to Maurice Barrès, June 1923, #132, MB.

20. "Non, il n'y a pas eu de désenchantements. L'expérience ne m'a rien appris de plus que je ne savais au temps du cirque de Nancy. Elle n'a fait que confirmer seulement. J'ai quitté Nancy à 29 ans, et je voyais la vie telle que je l'ai vue ensuite, ce qui ne m'empêchait pas de l'aimer animalement, comme ceux que tout intéresse et qui s'amusent de tout. Je ne détaillais pas, je ne raisonnais pas, je vivais." Ibid.

21. "axiome, religion ou prince des hommes." Barres, *Sous l'oeil des barbares*, 168.

22. Philippe Barrès, "Gyp, ou la féerie."

23. "Tout est infiniment plus cher que pendant la guerre, et on ne peut plus se dire, comme pendant la guerre, que, tout de même, cela prendra fin à un moment donné." Gyp, letter to [?] Calmann-Lévy, 21 Sept. 1920, CL.

24. "qui boit comme une éponge." Gyp, letter to [?] Calmann-Lévy, 26 June 1919, CL.

25. "Je ne peux pas faire un pas." Gyp, letter to [?] Calmann-Lévy, 28 April 1920, CL.

26. "les taxis sont à des prix impossibles pour moi." Ibid.

27. "La maison ne peut être habitée que dans certaines conditions. Alors, je serai obligée de la louer et de m'en aller quelque part en Bretagne . . . ça me paraît très dur." Gyp, letter to [?] Calmann-Lévy, 11 Aug. 1924, CL.

28. "La vie me devient affreusement difficile. Je n'ai pas un *centime* de revenu. J'ai donné à mes enfants (à ma fille surtout) absolument tout ce que j'avais. Je n'ai que ma maison. Je suis logée. Un point c'est tout . . ." Gyp, letter to [?] Calmann-Lévy, 21 Feb. 1920, CL.

29. [?] Calmann-Lévy, letter to Gyp, 12 Dec. 1925, CL.

30. "malgré notre désir de vous être agréable." [?] Calmann-Lévy, letter to Gyp, 8 Nov. 1923, CL.

31. "Je pense bien que vous pensez que je peux mourir d'un jour à l'autre? Mais, dans ce cas, vous rattraperiez . . . la somme assez vite." Gyp, letter to [?] Calmann-Lévy, 11 June 1923, CL.

32. After the war, Calmann-Lévy published Gyp's *Mon ami Pierrot, conte bleu* (1921), *Souricette* (1922), and *Les Moins de vingt ans* (1930), as well as four volumes of recollections.

33. "le nième livre de Gyp"; "Cette bonne femme vit donc encore? Ou s'agit-il d'un ouvrage posthume inédit?" Georges Barbarin, rev. of *Un raté* by Gyp, *La Revue des lettres*, March 1925.

34. In the case of *Un raté, Aller et retour, Le Monde à côté,* and several others, Calmann-Lévy obliged.

35. Gyp, letter to [?] Calmann-Lévy, 17 June 1922, CL.

36. Gyp, letter to [?] Calmann-Lévy, 5 May 1919, CL.

37. "Je me sens bien loin de votre adorable talent." Sarah Bernhardt, letter to Gyp, [1920], private collection.

38. "imagerie agréable, brillante, mais légère. . . ." Louis Schneider, "Les Premières," *Le Gaulois*, 30 May 1919, 3.

39. "a été un désastre au point de vue argent parce que tout a été contre nous." Gyp, letter to [?] Calmann-Lévy, 20 Oct. 1919, CL.

40. Gyp, letters to [?] Calmann-Lévy, 23 June and 20 Oct. 1919, CL.

41. "Je veux, depuis longtemps, écrire l'histoire (abrégée!) de l'Action Française. . . . J'ai écrit tant de choses qui m'ont embêtée, que je voudrais en écrire une qui m'amuse avant de mourir." Gyp, letter to [?] Calmann-Lévy, 28 Jan. 1926, CL.

42. Gyp complained about "[the] decent provincial folk who are throwing themselves into the arms [of Action Française]" ("[les] braves provinciaux qui se précipitent dans [les] bras [de l'Action Française]"), but added that they were "to be blamed more than pitied. Folly is not attractive." ("plus à blâmer qu'à plaindre. La bêtise n'est pas intéressante.") Gyp, letter to [Roserot de Melin?], 11 March 1927, MS2977, #1022, Bibliothèque de Troyes.

43. See Adrien Dansette, *Histoire religieuse de la France contemporaine* (Paris: Flammarion, 1965), 769–70. Barrès was in third place, after Paul Bourget.

44. Quoted in Eugen Weber, *Action Française: Royalism and Reaction in Twentieth-Century France* (Stanford, CA: Stanford UP, 1962), 222.

45. Dumont-Wilden in *La Nation belge*, quoted in *L'Action Française*, 19 Feb. 1927, in turn quoted in Weber, *Action Française*, 234.

46. Gyp, letter to [Roserot de Melin?], 14 July 1927, MS2977, #1025, Bibliothèque de Troyes.

47. "les derniers des crétins et des pleutres." Gyp, letter to [Roserot de Melin?], 11 March 1927, MS2977, #1022, Bibliothèque de Troyes.

48. "le vent de folie que les Jésuites avaient jadis déchaîné sur les dames de Nancy." Ibid.

49. "vilains." Gyp, letter to [Roserot de Melin?], 14 July 1927, MS2977, #1025, Bibliothèque de Troyes.

50. "l'ignorance, la sottise et la stupidité." Gyp, letter to [Roserot de Melin?], 2 Aug. 1927, MS2977, #1027, Bibliothèque de Troyes.

51. "allumé et entretenu, depuis plus de vingt ans, la discorde dans une jeunesse qui ne demandait qu'à s'unir." Gyp, letter to [Roserot de Melin?], 7 March 1927, MS2977, #1021, Bibliothèque de Troyes.

52. "La Royauté, c'est ma Déesse! / Le Roi Philippe est un gaillard! / Mais, s'il le faut dans ma vieillesse, / Je lâcherai leur étendard. / Je me ferai Bonapartiste / Ou même au besoin communiste / Ou n'importe quoi, je m'en f . . ." Gyp, letter to [Roserot de Melin?], 26 March 1927, MS2977, #1023, Bibliothèque de Troyes.

53. "Vous n'imaginez pas leur outrecuidance? Ils sont—Maurras surtout—convaincus qu'ils auront raison de l'Eglise. Ils ne comprennent pas que c'est la plus grande force." Gyp, letter to [Roserot de Melin?], 7 March 1927, MS2977, #1021, Bibliothèque de Troyes.

54. "la stupidité et la trahison de l'Action Française sont évidentes pour tous et . . . rien ne pouvait être plus heureux pour le Faisceau—Maurras et Daudet se pendent eux-mêmes." Thierry de Martel, letter to Philippe Barrès, 1926, private collection.

55. "voir—avant de filer—l'effondrement définitif. . . ." Gyp, letter to [Roserot de Melin?], 11 March 1927, MS2977, #1022, Bibliothèque de Troyes.

56. Zeev Sternhell, *Ni droite, ni gauche: L'Idéologie fasciste en France* (Paris: Seuil, 1983), 120. On the reaction of the older right-wing movements to a nascent interwar protofascism, see pp. 113–21.

57. "un monde où prévaut une morale de guerriers et de moines." Sternhell, *Ni droite, ni gauche*, 26. Sternhell refers here to the aims of the Cercle Proudhon, which Valois wished to pursue in Le Faisceau.

58. Gyp, letter to [?] Calmann-Lévy, 28 Jan. 1926, CL.

59. "escroqueries et chantages." Ibid.

60. "Je signerais soit simplement ⟨symbol⟩, soit 'un cochon de payant.'" Ibid.

61. "Je tiens d'abord à vous remercier de votre proposition, mais, vous le savez, nous n'éditons jamais d'ouvrages de polémique; c'est un principe que nous avons toujours appliqué, même pendant l'affaire Dreyfus." [?] Calmann-Lévy, letter to Gyp, 30 Jan. 1926, CL.

62. "Elle restera dans la coulisse." Gyp, letter to [?] Calmann-Lévy, 8 Feb. 1928, CL.

63. "Je n'ai pas besoin de vous dire combien nous sommes toujours désireux de publier tout ce que vous écrivez, mais vous savez combien notre maison est timorée quand il s'agit d'un livre où des personnalités vivantes se trouvent jouer un rôle, même un peu effacé." [?] Calmann-Lévy, letter to Gyp, 9 Feb. 1928, CL.

64. See chapter 7, note 92, in this book.

65. "dégoûtamment saboté." Gyp, letter to [?] Calmann-Lévy, 25 July 1928, CL.

66. "La royauté pour nous c'était Louis XIV . . .'"; "servi . . . à un troupeau d'ignorants." Gyp, *Le Chambard: Roman d'aujourd'hui* (Paris: Flammarion, 1928), 40.

67. "Une pincée de littérateurs et de bosses ne fait pas une révolution ni même un coup. . . . Pour cela, il faut des hommes, et il faut aussi que l'objectif soit populaire. . . ." Ibid., 43.

68. "Ce roman qui contient d'excellentes pages de chronique historique soulèvera à travers le pays un immense éclat de rire." "Courage féminin," *La Voix*, 12 Jan. 1930.

69. "ses plaisanteries se révèlent si entachées de mauvaise foi qu'elles ne font pas rire." Jean Charpentier, rev. of *Le Coup de lapin*, *Le Mercure de France*, 15 May 1930, 151–52.

70. "nulle; ce coup de lapin est le coup de grâce que se donne cette 'romancière' typiquement inutile." "La Chose littéraire," *D'Artagnan*, 16 Jan. 1930.

71. "Courage féminin" *La Voix*.

72. "Par respect pour l'auteur, *L'Action Française* n'a parlé qu'avec une extrême sobriété du dernier roman de Gyp"; "ce pauvre roman qui sue l'ennui." "Une vilenie," *L'Action Française*, 15 April 1928.

73. "une petite robe de broderie anglaise et des noeuds sur les épaules." Marshal Hubert Lyautey, letter to Gyp, 5 April 1927, 475AP295, AN; see also Gyp, letter to Maurice Barrès, 6 [?] 1923, #130, MB.

74. Gyp, letter to Ferdinand Bac, 22 [?] 1923, 14177, #128, Bibliothèque de l'Arsenal.

75. "Souvenirs de jeunesse," 2 Feb. 1923; and "La Société sous le Second Empire: Ceux que j'ai connus," 27 Nov. 1923 and 3 Dec. 1923, at the Théâtre du Colisée in Paris.

76. See, for example, Pierre Plessis, "Gyp, le Second Empire, et la bête à bon dieu," *Le Gaulois*, 4 Dec. 1923.

77. "ces fillettes garçonnières et diaboliques, naïves et terribles, franches et hardies. . . ." Rev. of *Souricette*, *Le Figaro*, 12 Dec. 1922.

78. Gyp, letter to [?] Calmann-Lévy, 9 July 1923, CL.

79. Gyp, letter to [?] Calmann-Lévy, 6 Jan. 1923, CL.

80. "C'est le *commencement* qui est *difficile* en diable. . . ." Gyp, letter to Maurice Barrès, 6 [?] 1923, #127, MB.

81. "parce qu'ils revivent dans ma mémoire avec une incroyable netteté, mais sans

ordre aucun.'' Gyp, *Souvenirs d'une petite fille* (Paris: Calmann-Lévy, 1927), vol. 1, 2; see also Gyp, letter to [?] Calmann-Lévy, 24 March 1924, CL.

82. ''ne paraîtra amusant qu'à quelques Lorrains. . . .'' Gyp, letter to Maurice Barrès, 6 [?] 1923, #127, MB.

83. Gyp, *Souvenirs*, vol. 1, 1–2.

84. Gyp, letter to Maurice Barrès, 19 June 1923, #131, MB.

85. ''Je croyais, au contraire, que la vérité était mon seul mérite. Que j'étais une sorte de photographe dont le talent (!) consistait *uniquement* à savoir mettre l'appareil au point. Si ces pauvres petites choses ne paraissent même pas vraies, elles cessent d'avoir le moindre intérêt. C'est uniquement le récit d'impressions ressenties par un gosse, et de petits faits bêtas; un chaos de grêles banalités.'' Ibid.

86. ''cette obligation de se raconter soi-même . . . me trouble et me déplaît.'' Gyp, *Souvenirs*, vol. 1, 1.

87. See chapter 1, note 16, in this book.

88. ''Est-ce que, vraiment, les souvenirs d'une petite fille peuvent avoir un quelconque intérêt pour d'autres que l'ancienne petite fille, qui se rappelle joyeusement les meilleures années de sa vie? Il me semble que non. . . .'' Ibid.

89. See Amy Millstone, ''Gyp and the Reconstruction of (Self-)Consciousness, *Biography* 10, no. 3. (Summer 1987), 189–207.

90. ''Il me semble que la simplicité claire des impressions d'une petite fille que n'a pas encore déformée la vie, est très proche de la clairvoyance d'une vieille femme peu à peu détachée des conventions.'' Gyp, *Souvenirs*, vol. 1, 2.

91. ''mieux que la plupart des Gyp.'' Gyp, letter to [?] Calmann-Lévy, 6 Jan. 1923, CL.

92. Lucien Corpechot, ''Entretiens littéraires: *Souvenirs d'une petite fille*,'' *Le Gaulois*, 13 Aug. 1927: 3.

93. ''Est-il besoin de vous dire quelles délectations un vieux Lorrain trouve à vos souvenirs?'' Hubert Lyautey, letter to Gyp, 10 March 1927, 475AP295, AN.

94. Maurice Talmeyr, ''Les Souvenirs de Gyp: Un grand monde vu par un enfant,'' *La Croix*, 13–14 Jan. 1929.

95. [?] Calmann-Lévy, letter to Gyp, 26 Sept. 1929, CL.

96. [?] Calmann-Lévy, letter to Gyp, 28 Jan. 1928, CL.

97. ''la très respectueuse amitié que nous avons depuis de si nombreuses années pour vous.'' Ibid.

98. ''A Nini, qui l'a baptisé.'' Gyp, *Du temps des cheveux et des chevaux: Souvenirs du Second Empire* (Paris: Calmann-Lévy, 1929).

99. Gyp had begun working on this volume in 1927 and had tentatively titled it *La Joyeuse Enfance de Marianne: La République du maréchal*. Gyp, letter to [?] Calmann-Lévy, 19 July 1927, CL.

100. ''un retentissant succès.'' Gérard d'Houville, ''L'Heure qui passe: Gyp raconte,'' *Le Figaro*, 14 Aug. 1931, 1.

101. Other possible titles included: *La Belle Jeunesse de Marianne* (*Marianne's Beautiful Youth*), *Le Chahut* (*The Rumpus*) and *Marianne chahute* (*Marianne Makes a Rumpus*). Gyp, letter to [?] Calmann-Lévy, 5 Oct. 1931, CL.

102. ''de la petite histoire.'' Gyp, letter to [?] Calmann-Lévy, 11 Dec. 1929, CL.

103. ''c'est déjà assez lointain pour qu'on en parle sans passion et en prenant seulement le côté pittoresque des choses.'' Ibid.

104. ''si je ne suis pas morte avant.'' Gyp, letter to [?] Calmann-Lévy, 5 Oct. 1931, CL.

Chapter XIV

1. "Il y a cent ans que la Révolution de 1830 a eu lieu. Et je me souviens que quand j'étais petite, on parlait autour de moi des journées de juillet comme on parle aujourd'hui de l'armistice. . . ." Gyp, letter to [?] Calmann-Lévy, 23 Dec. 1930, CL.

2. René Benjamin, notes, 31 Feb. 1931, François Benjamin collection, Savonnières, France.

3. "jolis fauteuils jaunes . . . tableaux en quantité . . . lustres. Tout cela de couleurs un peu passées. . . ." Ibid., 6 April 1930.

4. "un peu de l'actrice qui attend son effet." Ibid., 31 Feb. 1931.

5. "Elle est vraiment très amusante. Immobile avec une cervelle sans cesse en mouvement. . . . Elle amuse et s'amuse. Elle est enjouée et cocasse. . . . *Elle est restée jeune—* et rajeunit les autres. *Les heures passent*, sans qu'on y songe. . . . Une impression de *grand charme.*" Ibid., 6 April 1930.

6. "[O]n parle de Gyp, de ce qu'elle est délicieuse et intolérable, impatiente, impossible à soigner. . . ." Ibid., June 1931.

7. Ibid.

8. "il se pourrait bien qu'elle meure et que nous ne revoyions jamais rien de tout cela." Ibid.

9. "[Nicole] me soigne admirablement." Gyp, letter to [a priest], 2 Aug. 1931, MS2977, #1042, Bibliothèque de Troyes.

10. "La fille de Gyp, avec son serre-tête, ses robes vert d'eau, n'a pas un côté bien plaisant, une tête bien sympathique." René Benjamin, notes, 31 Feb. 1931, François Benjamin collection, Savonnières, France.

11. "un chameau, couvert de deux renards argentés." Ibid., June 1931. Thierry and Yvette Saint Martin divorced in November 1930. In May 1931 Thierry married Marie Louise Henriette Fouquier in a civil ceremony. On Henriette Fouquier, see Jeanne Blancheney, *Visages de mon temps* ([Switzerland]: n.p., n.d.), 168–73.

12. "aux pommettes bizarres, au regard qui échappe." René Benjamin, notes, June 1931, François Benjamin collection, Savonnières, France.

13. "dite . . . sur un ton de parfait ennui, sans trace apparente de sensibilité." Ibid.

14. "Je ne suis pas ensevelie, mais je suis déjà morte ou presque, et je viens vous dire adieu." Gyp, letter to [Roserot de Melin?], 2 Aug. 1931, MS2977, #1042, Bibliothèque de Troyes.

15. "Hier, j'ai été très malade. Ca n'été qu'un faux départ. Mais je crois bien que c'est la cloche qui annonce le train." Gyp, letter to [?] Calmann-Lévy, 4 [? 1931?], CL.

16. "ma mère est tombée, pour de bon, le 23 juin." Nicole d'Hugues, letter to [a priest], [June 1932], MS 2977, #1042, Bibliothèque de Troyes.

17. "une sorte de découragement et de dépression." Ibid.

18. "appelant la mort de toute son âme." Ibid.

19. "De tout coeur, merci pour votre vieille amie qui aimait tant les fleurs et surtout les roses. Infiniment merci, Thierry et Nicole." Thierry de Martel and Nicole d'Hugues, note to Gaston Calmann-Lévy, [July 1932], CL. On Gyp's funeral, see "Obsèques de la comtesse de Martel," *Les Débats*, 3 July 1932.

20. G.L.C., "Gyp est morte," *Le Journal*, 30 June 1932, 1; "Gyp n'est plus," Agence France Presse, 1 July 1932; Pierre Lagarde, "Une grande dame de lettres: Gyp est morte," *Comoedia*, 30 June 1932, 1.

21. See, for example, Rachilde, "Souvenir sur Gyp," *Corymbe*, July–Aug. 1932; Véga, "Gyp telle que je l'ai connue," *La Revue des deux mondes*, 15 Sept. 1932, 451–

57. Michel Missoffe's *Gyp et ses amis* was also published by Flammarion the year of her death.

22. Janet Flanner [Genêt], *Paris Was Yesterday, 1925–1939*, ed. Irving Drutman (San Diego, CA: Harcourt Brace Jovanovich/Harvest, 1988), 84–85.

23. Ezra Pound, "Pastiche: The Regional," *The New Age*, 7 Aug. 1919, 252.

24. George Saintsbury, *French Literature and Its Masters from the Beginnings to 1900* (New York: Knopf, 1938), 300.

25. "un roman à la scène." Gérard d'Houville, "Gyp, théâtre vivant," *Le Figaro*, 11 July 1932, 5.

26. Flanner, *Paris Was Yesterday*, 85.

27. "[de] jeunes amoureuses déçues, passionnées, misérables." d'Houville, "Gyp, théâtre vivant."

28. "[de] la haute littérature psychologique, quoi!" *Cahiers Céline I: Céline et l'actualité littéraire, 1932–1957*, ed. Jean-Pierre Dauphin and Henri Godard (Paris: Gallimard, 1976), 169.

29. "Countess de Janville, Novelist Gyp, Dead," *New York Times*, 30 June 1932, 25.

30. Flanner, *Paris Was Yesterday*, 85. Another journalist echoed Flanner's statement: "People will consult [Gyp's novels] in the future as they consult Restif de la Bretonne or Saint-Simon. The visage of an era will be rediscovered there, with its blemishes, its warts, and its wrinkles, highlighted by a pitiless and mischievous magnifying glass." ("On les consultera plus tard comme on consulte Restif de la Bretonne ou Saint-Simon. On y retrouvera le visage d'une époque, avec ses tares, ses verrues et ses rides, mises en valeur par une loupe impitoyable et malicieuse.") Pierre Lagarde, "Une grande dame de lettres: Gyp est morte."

31. "Ce que je tiens expressément à fixer pour la postérité, c'est que je n'ai eu aucun bonheur à écrire." "Création d'un nouveau mode d'interview: L'Interview nécrologique: Le plus sincère," *Le Matin* 26 April 1908.

32. "La société sous la Troisième République, tel pourrait être le titre général de l'oeuvre de Gyp." Roger Giron, "Les Lettres et les arts: Gyp," *L'Ami du peuple*, 30 June 1932.

33. "avec tout son brillant passager et passé. . . ." Albert Thibaudet, "Réflexions sur la littérature," *La Nouvelle Revue française*, April 1920, 570.

34. "Gyp reste dans l'histoire aux environs de l'Exposition de 1889 et du boulangisme." Henry Bidou, "Gyp," *Le Journal des débats politiques et littéraires*, 30 June 1932, 1.

35. "On attendait son dernier roman comme le dernier calembour de Willy, la dernière redingote de Boni de Castellane. . . . Ses idées comme son écriture ont la couleur d'une époque disparue—il y a, en elles, des arabesques modern'style, du Lalique démodé . . . une odeur d'ylang-ylang . . . un reflet de fourrures, de manches à gigot, de phaétons conduits par des cochers à côtelettes." Maurice Bourdet, "Gyp, reflet d'une époque et d'une société," *Miroir du monde*, 9 July 1932, 41–42.

36. "Le 'voyage' au cinéma" (Céline's imaginary cinematographic adaptation of the beginning and end of his *Voyage au bout de la nuit*), *Cahiers de l'Herne: Louis-Ferdinand Céline*, ed. Dominique de Roux (Paris: L'Herne, 1963), vol. 1, 191.

37. "Nul être au monde n'a plus vécu en dehors de son temps." Gustave Rodrigues, "Message: Une philosophie de fossile," *La Volonté*, 5 July 1932.

38. "la mégère grotesque." "Gyp n'est plus," Agence France Presse, 1 July 1932.

39. "Et cependant, [elle] était une bonne chrétienne. . . ." Armand Charpentier, "Message: Gyp," *La Volonté*, 4 July 1932.

40. See Rodrigues, "Message: Une philosophie de fossile." Gyp's comment caused the author of this article to remark: "Simplistic as well and bizarrely outdated, this idea of a world of masters who command and slaves who obey is from another time." ("Simpliste aussi et singulièrement dépassée, cette idée d'un monde de maîtres qui commandent et d'esclaves qui obéissent est d'un autre temps.")

41. d'Houville, "Gyp, théâtre vivant."

42. "[C]e qu'elle voulait pour les femmes, c'était la sincérité, l'activité physique et morale, la santé de l'intelligence, l'abolition des conventions et des préjugés surannés. . . ." Ibid.

43. See chapter 4, note 77, in this book.

44. "Thierry de Martel," *Candide*, 24 July 1940, 2.

45. "il faudra supporter cela avec hauteur et détachement et je reste convaincu que la victoire restera aux forces spirituelles." Thierry de Martel, letter to Dr. Charles Lucas, Feb. 1940, private collection, Paris.

46. "On les arrêtera sur la Seine, et ce sera plus beau que la Marne." Quoted in André Maurois, "Les destins exemplaires: Thierry de Martel," [*Nouvelles*?], 2 Aug. 1948, 6.

47. "Je vous ai fait la promesse de ne pas quitter Paris, je ne vous ai pas dit si je resterai à Paris mort ou vivant. En y restant vivant, c'est un chèque barré que je remets à mon adversaire. Si j'y reste mort, c'est un chèque sans provisions. Adieu." Thierry de Martel, letter to William Bullitt, 13 June 1940, quoted in Isabelle Mahéo–de la Tocnaye, "Thierry de Martel, fils de la romancière Gyp, pionnier de la neurochirurgie française, 1875–1940" (Ph.D. diss., Univ. of Rennes I, 1979), 148.

48. See Dominique Desanti, *Drieu la Rochelle: Le Séducteur mystifié* (Paris: Flammarion, 1978), 371.

49. "il aurait tout fait pour gagner Londres et figurer aux côtés du Général de Gaulle parmi les premiers fidèles." Jacques Hepp, "Un grand chirurgien du début de ce siècle," *La Semaine des hôpitaux de Paris* 57, nos. 21–24 (1981), 1054.

50. See the introduction, note 2, in this book.

Selected Works

Abbreviations

AA	Archives de l'Armée, Service Historique, Vincennes
AD	Archives Départementales
ADF	Alexandre Dumas fils papers, Bibliothèque Nationale
AF	Anatole France papers, Bibliothèque Nationale
AN	Archives Nationales, Paris
APP	Archives de la Préfecture de Police, Paris
AR	Bibliothèque de l'Arsenal, Paris
BHVP	Bibliothèque Historique de la Ville de Paris, Paris
BN	Bibliothèque Nationale, Paris
CL	Calmann-Lévy Archives, Paris
IF	Institut de France, Paris
LH	Ludovic Halévy papers, Institut de France
MB	Maurice Barrès papers, Bibliothèque Nationale
MD	Bibliothèque Marguerite Durand, Paris
Naf	Nouvelles Acquisitions Françaises
PD	Paul Déroulède papers, Archives Nationales
RM	Robert de Montesquiou papers, Bibliothèque Nationale
SGL	Société des gens de lettres

Primary Sources

Archives and Libraries

Archives Nationales, Paris
Notarial archives: Etude XLVI
Private archives: 46AP3 (Ducos); 87AP3 (J. Simon); 114AP3 (Duruy and Glachant); 278AP10 (comte de Calonne); 320AP3 (Letter to the comtesse de Mirabeau regarding the Bazaine trial, 1873–74); 333AP5 (Lamy); 428AP2 (Montorgueil); 401AP9 (Déroulède); 400AP200 (Napoleon); 475AP295 (Lyautey)

Police archives (F7): 12452–53 and 12875 (Haute Cour), 12463 and 2882–83 (Anti-Semitism), 12922–23
Société des gens de lettres dossiers: 454AP273 (Gyp), 454AP288 (comtesse de Mirabeau)

Archives de la Préfecture de Police, Paris
Series B/A: 52–53 (Loubet), 71–72, 188–94 (Panama), 947 (Barillier), 1032–34 (Déroulède), 1105, 1193–94 (Morès), 1198 (Guérin), 1262 (Sabran-Pontevès), 1276 (Syveton),
1287 (Trarieux), 1533 (Dreyfus Affair)
Series E/A: 30 (Gyp), 128 (Dreyfus Affair)

Archives de l'Armée, Service Historique, Vincennes
Dossiers Aymar Le Harivel de Gonneville, Roger de Martel de Janville, Thierry de Martel
de Janville

Bibliothèque de l'Arsenal, Paris
Dossier on Gyp prepared by l'abbé Béthléem
Press clippings and miscellaneous documents: Rf 61770, 61773, 61777, 61781, 61811,
61822, Fol. W379
MS 13515, 13594, 14168, 14177, 14212 (Ferdinand Bac), 14365, 15060

Bibliothèque Historique de la Ville de Paris, Paris
Fonds Bouglé: Carton 4247
Photographs of Gyp

Bibliothèque Nationale, Paris
Private archives: Fonds Barrès (uncatalogued); Alexandre Dumas fils: Naf 14666, 24638,
24669; Anatole France: Naf 10800, 13121, 15159, 15386, 15421, 15422, 15428, 15434,
15443; Robert de Montesquiou: Naf 15029, 15071–73, 15082, 15087, 15120, 15136–
37, 15140, 15144, 15148–49, 15154, 15159, 15161, 15166, 15168–69, 15187, 15190,
15192, 15216, 15226, 15239, 15245, 15251, 15293, 15300, 15302, 15308, 15339,
15434; Félix and Paul Nadar: Naf 14695, 24272
Additional private archives: Naf 13337 (Lagrange); 16802 (Rochefort); 16804; 16810
(Herpin); 16958 (Hetzel); 17388; 17590; 18346 (Arvède Barine); 18474; 22469 (Goncourt); 24290 (Mortier and Aurel); 24412 (du Bled); 24699 (Dupanloup); 25039 (Brunetière)

Calmann-Lévy Archives, Paris
Letters exchanged between Gyp and her publisher (1880–1932); miscellaneous correspondence; contracts; records of payment and other financial records; notes

Departmental Archives and Libraries
Archives Départementales du Calvados, Caen
Archives Départementales de Meurthe-et-Moselle, Nancy
Archives Départementales du Morbihan, Vannes
Archives Départementales du Vaucluse, Avignon
Bibliothèque Municipale d'Avignon
Bibliothèque de Bordeaux
Bibliothèque Municipale de Grenoble
Bibliothèque Municipale de Nancy

Bibliothèque Municipale de Troyes
Bibliothèque Municipale de Versailles

Institut de France, Paris
Private archives: MS4485 (Ludovic Halévy); MS7228 (Anna de Noailles); MS1147–48,
Fonds Lovenjoul (Buloz)

Fondation Thiers, Paris
MS 678 (Théophile Gautier fils)

Bibliothèque Marguerite Durand, Paris
Dossier 091 (Gyp)

Additional Archives and Library Collections Consulted
W. T. Bandy Center for Baudelaire Studies, Vanderbilt University
Beinecke Rare Book and Manuscript Library, Yale University
Biblioteca Nacional, Madrid
Bibliothèque Jacques Doucet, Paris
British Library, Department of Manuscripts
Charavay Archives, Paris
Harry Ransom Humanities Research Center, University of Texas, Austin
The Houghton Library, Harvard University
Mairie de Cossesseville (Calvados)
Mairie de Douvres-la-Délivrande (Calvados)
Mairie de Plumergat (Morbihan)
Musée de l'Armée, Paris
Musée de Bretagne, Rennes
Musée Carnavalet, Paris
Musée Historique Lorrain, Nancy
Musée National de la Légion d'Honneur, Paris
Northwestern University Library, Special Collections Department
Ordre des Avocats de la Cour de Paris, Paris
Service Culturel, Neuilly-sur-Seine
Société des Auteurs et Compositeurs Dramatiques, Paris
Société des gens de lettres, Paris

Private Collections

Numerous private collections were consulted for this biography. These contained correspondence, legal documents, photographs, drawings, and personal objects. To safeguard
anonymity, several names have been omitted.

M. and Mme. Paul Bazin; M. François Benjamin; M. Thierry Bodin; M. Hervé de Boisguilbert; Mme. Jean Chagnaud-Forain; M. d'Isoard de Chenerilles; M. Michel Dixmier;
Mme. Sibylle Gaudry; General Jean Le Harivel de Gonneville; Dr. Charles Lucas; M.
Jacques Maurras; Mme. de Maigret; M. Patrick de Montfort; M. Gilles Picq; M. Henri
de Sancy de Rolland; M. Jean-Claude Wartelle

Selected Works by Gyp

A relatively complete bibliography of works by Gyp is found in H. Talvert and G. Place, *Bibliographie des auteurs modernes de langue française* (Paris: Editions de la chronique des lettres françaises, 1928), vol. 7, 416–28. I have listed below only the works (and editions) actually cited.

Books

L'Age du mufle. Paris: Juven, 1902.
Autour du divorce. Paris: Calmann-Lévy, 1886.
Bijou. Paris: Collection Nelson, 1914.
Bob à l'Exposition. Paris: Calmann-Lévy, 1889.
C'est nous qui sont l'histoire!!!. Paris: Calmann-Lévy, 1891.
Ceux de "la nuque". Paris: Fayard, 1916.
Le Chambard: Roman d'aujourd'hui. Paris: Flammarion, 1928.
Du temps des cheveux et des chevaux: Souvenirs du Second Empire. Paris: Calmann-Lévy, 1929.
Le Druide, roman parisien. Paris: Havard, 1885.
Elles et lui. Paris: Calmann-Lévy, 1885.
En Balade. Paris: Mongrédien, 1897.
Les Flanchards. Paris: Fayard, 1917.
La Friquet. Paris: Flammarion, 1901.
Les Gens chics. Paris: Charpentier et Fasquelle, 1895.
Israël. Paris: Flammarion, 1898.
Journal d'un casserolé. Paris: Juven, 1905.
Le Journal d'un cochon de pessimiste. Paris: Calmann-Lévy, 1918.
Le Journal d'un philosophe. Paris: Charpentier et Fasquelle, 1894.
Journal d'un grinchu. Paris: Flammarion, 1898.
La Joyeuse Enfance de la Troisième République. Paris: Calmann-Lévy, 1931.
Le Mariage de Chiffon. Paris: Calmann-Lévy, 1940.
Petit Bob. Paris: Calmann-Lévy, 1882.
Les Profitards. Paris: Fayard, 1918.
Sans voiles! Paris: Calmann-Lévy, 1885.
Souvenirs d'une petite fille. 2 vols. Paris: Calmann-Lévy, 1927–28.
Tante Joujou. Paris: Calmann-Lévy, 1893.
Totote. Paris: Per Lamm, 1897.
Tout à l'égout! Paris: Calmann-Lévy, 1889.
Un raté. Paris: Flammarion, 1925.
Un trio turbulent. Paris: Hachette, 1929.
Une élection à Tigre-sur-Mer, racontée par Bob. Paris: Editions du Gaulois, 1896.
Une gauche célèbre. Paris: Monnier, 1886.
Une Passionnette. Paris: Calmann-Lévy, 1891.
La Vertu de la baronne. Paris: Calmann-Lévy, 1882.

Articles and Lectures

"Les Contemporains: Petit Bob et Miquette." Paris, 6 May 1912, published in *Les Annales politiques et littéraires*, 1 Nov. 1912, 573–83.
"Les Contemporains: Souvenirs de jeunesse." Paris, 2 Feb. 1923, published in *Conférencia: Journal de l'Université des Annales*, 1 May 1923, 451–63.

"La Femme de 1885." *Le Figaro*, 16 July 1932, 5.

"Morale et philosophie: Les Enfants terribles." *Journal de l'Université des Annales*, 15 April 1912, 514–31.

"Pour la guerre! . . ." *Gil Blas*, 4 Dec. 1903, 1.

"La Société sous le Second Empire: Ceux que j'ai connus." Paris, 27 Nov. 1923, published in *Conférencia* 3, 15 Jan. 1924, 114–31.

Selected Articles and Dialogues in La Libre Parole

The following articles and dialogues all appeared on the front page of *La Libre Parole*:
"Les Izolâtres," 3 March 1898; "Les Dieux d'Israël," 7 Aug. 1898; "Le Toast," 17 Aug. 1898; "Boycottons-les! . . . ," 25 Aug. 1898; "La Loi de Moïse," 4 Sept. 1898; "Les Triomphants," 25 Sept. 1898; "Les Sarrieux et les Trarien," 6 Oct. 1898; "L'Affaire chez les morts," 26 Feb. 1899; "Le Jour du sacre," 10 March 1899; "Dans la foule," 19 March 1899; "A la sortie du Pré-aux-Clercs," 26 March 1899; "A la foire au pain d'épice," 4 April 1899; "Conciliabule," 16 April 1899; "A la sortie du Pré-aux-Clercs," 26 April 1899; "Vive la Ligue," 7 May 1899; "Pronostics," 14 May 1899; "Aux Mille Colonnes," 28 May 1899; "A bas les juifs! . . . ," 6 June 1899; "Fife Loupet! . . . ," 11 June 1899; "L'Oeillet fantôme," 18 June 1899; "Youtrecuidance," 25 June 1899; "Leurs ames!," 2 July 1899; "Le Dernier Cri de la muflerie," 9 July 1899; "Le Mot de la fin," 16 July 1899; "Un rude lapin," 23 July 1899; "Vive l'Armée," 1 Aug. 1899; "Aux armes, citoyens," 20 Aug. 1899; "La Peur des coups," 27 Aug. 1899; "Quel coup pour Emile!," 5 Nov. 1899; "Un chic type! . . . ," 3 Dec. 1899; "Conspuez Loulou! . . . ," 10 Dec. 1899; "Un geignard," 1 April 1900; "Enfin! En voilà un! . . . ," 11 April 1900; "On demande un veau!," 29 April 1900; "Fife Falteck tictadeur!" 22 April 1900; "Entrrrrrrez!!!," 15 April 1900; "Le Coupable!," 6 May 1900; "L'homme!," 27 May 1900; "V . . . (??? . . .)," 5 June 1900; "Vive Loubet! . . . Vive la Sociale! . . . ," 18 June 1900; "L'Est bouché," 24 June 1900; "Monsieur Trarieux! (Qui n'est pas Protestant)," 19 Aug. 1900.

Other Publications Containing Material by Gyp

L'Antijuif, *Cosmopolis*; *Le Drapeau*; *Le Gaulois*; *Gil Blas*; *L'Illustration*; *Le Journal*; *Lectures pour tous*; *La Libre Parole illustrée*; *La Patrie illustrée*; *La Revue bleue*; *La Revue d'art dramatique*; *La Revue de l'art*; *La Revue de Paris*; *La Revue des deux mondes*; *La Revue du Palais*; *La Revue hebdomadaire*; *La Revue illustrée*; *Le Rire*; *Le Temps*; *Le Triboulet*; *La Tribune française*; *La Vie Parisienne*; *Le Voleur*

Selected Reviews of Gyp's Works

Anon. Rev. of *Israël*. *La Libre Parole*, 15 Feb. 1898.

Arnaud, Charles. Rev. of *Joies d'amour*. *Polybiblion*, 80, [1897], 26–27.

Athis, Alfred. "Les Premières—Gymnase—*Le Friquet*." *L'Humanité*, 1 Oct. 1904, 2.

Badin, Ad. Rev. of *Monsieur de Folleuil*. *La Nouvelle Revue*, 118, 1 June 1899, 379.

Barbarin, Georges. Rev. of *Un raté*. *La Revue des lettres*, March 1925.

Beaunier, André. Rev. of *Trop de chic!* *La Revue bleue*, 26 June 1900, 699–700.

Bidou, Henry. Rev. of *Le Monde à côté*. *Les Annales*, 26 Sept. 1920.

Bornier, Henri de. Rev. of *Autour du mariage*. *La Nouvelle Revue*, 15 Dec. 1883, 194–201.

Charpentier, Jean. Rev. of *Le Coup de lapin*. *Le Mercure de France*, 15 May 1930, 151–52.

Corpechot, Lucien. "Entretiens littéraires: *Souvenirs d'une petite fille.*" *Le Gaulois*, 13 Aug. 1927, 3.

Drault, Jean. Rev. of *Le Monde à côté. La Libre Parole*, 2 Sept. 1920.

Faguet, Emile. Rev. of *Bijou. Cosmopolis*, 6 Oct. 1896, 166–73.

Filon, Auguste. Rev. of *Petit bleu. La Revue bleue*, 2 March 1889, 282–83.

———. Rev. of *Un raté. La Revue bleue*, 18 April 1891, 508–9.

Franc-Nohain. Rev. of *Un raté. L'Echo*, 10 Aug. 1922.

France, Anatole. "La Sagesse de Gyp" (rev. of *Les Séducteurs*). *La Vie littéraire.* 2nd ser. Paris: Calmann-Lévy, 1890, 237–44.

———. Rev. of *Une passionnette. Le Temps*, 17 May 1891.

G.M. Rev. of *Les Gens chics. La Libre Parole*, 24 June 1895.

Gachons, Jacques des. Rev. of *Mademoiselle Eve. L'Ermitage*, April 1895, 240.

Gilbert, Eugène. Rev. of *Miquette. En marge de quelques pages: Impressions de lecture.* Paris: Plon, 1900, 231–36.

Keim, Albert. Rev. of *Israël. La Cité d'art* 3, March 1898, 106.

Mathiex, Paul. "A propos d'un vieux roman: Le Héros d'une tragédie romantique" (rev. of *Un raté*). *La Patrie*, 12 Aug. 1922.

Maurras, Charles. "Les Images puissantes: *Un ménage dernier cri.*" *La Gazette de France*, 9 Aug. 1903, 1–2.

———. "Notes de critique: *Les Chapons* de Gyp." *La Gazette de France*, 26 March 1903, 1–2.

———. "Notes de critique: Petites lettres." *La Gazette de France*, 13 Nov. 1902, 1–2.

Mendès, Catulle. "Premières représentations: *Le Friquet.*" *Le Journal*, 1 Oct. 1904.

Rachilde. Rev. of *L'Age du mufle. Le Mercure de France*, May 1902, 456.

———. Rev. of *Les Cayenne de Rio. Le Mercure de France*, June 1899, 764–65.

———. Rev. of *Ceux qui s'en f . . . . Le Mercure de France*, 16 Feb. 1918, 674–75.

———. Rev. of *La Dame de Saint-Leu. Le Mercure de France*, 16 April 1914, 811.

———. Rev. of *Les Flanchards. Le Mercure de France*, 1 June 1917, 507.

———. Rev. of *Le Friquet. Le Mercure de France*, April 1901, 191.

———. Rev. of *Israël. Le Mercure de France*, April–June 1898, 231–36.

———. Rev. of *Journal d'un grinchu. Le Mercure de France*, July–Sept. 1898, 815–16.

———. Rev. of *Mademoiselle Loulou. Le Mercure de France*, 15 March 1924, 751.

———. Rev. of *Mon ami Pierrot. Le Mercure de France*, 15 Dec. 1921, 715.

———. Rev. of *Les Profitards. Le Mercure de France*, 16 Sept. 1918, 312–13.

———. Rev. of *Totote. Le Mercure de France*, Jan.–March 1898, 227.

Rumigny, Th. de. Rev. of *La Dame de Saint-Leu. L'Excelsior*, 20 March 1914.

Sarcey, Francisque. Rev. of *Autour du mariage. Le Temps*, 22 Oct. 1883, 2.

———. Rev. of *Mademoiselle Eve. Le Temps*, 7 Oct. 1895, 2.

———. Rev. of *Le Premier Sentiment de Loulou. Le Temps*, 16 May 1892, 2.

———. Rev. of *Rencontre. Le Temps*, 7 Oct. 1895, 2.

———. Rev. of *Sauvetage. Le Temps*, 28 April 1890.

Sénéchal, Georges. Rev. of *Les Cayenne de Rio. La Nouvelle Revue* 118, 15 June 1899, 755.

———. Rev. of *Israël. La Nouvelle Revue* 111, March–April 1898, 753–54.

———. Rev. of *Journal d'un grinchu. La Nouvelle Revue* 114, Oct. 1898: 753–54.

———. Rev. of *Lune de Miel. La Nouvelle Revue* 118, 1 May 1899, 174.

Tillet, Jacques du. Rev. of *Mademoiselle Eve. La Revue politique et littéraire*, 23 March 1895, 379–80.

Valabrègue, Albin. Rev. of *Mademoiselle Eve. L'Illustration*, 9 March 1895, 195.

Works by Marie de Mirabeau and Reviews

Mirabeau, comtesse de. *Le Baron d'Aché*. Paris: Didier, 1877.

Mirabeau, comtesse de, and vicomte de Grenville. *Hélène de Gardannes*. Paris: Didier, 1877.

Mirabeau, comtesse de. *Henri de l'Espée*. Nancy: Crespin-Leblond, 1871.

***[comtesse de Mirabeau]. *L'Impératrice Wanda*. Paris: Calmann-Lévy, 1884.

Mirabeau, comtesse de. *Madame Lauffray*. Paris: P. Mouillot, 1884.

Flagy, Aymar de [comtesse de Mirabeau]. *Maréchale Bazaine*. Paris: Lachaud et Burdin, 1874.

Sarcey, Francisque. Rev. of *Châteaufort*. *Le Temps*, 17 July 1876, 1–2.

Other Primary Sources

I have considered as primary sources books and articles published during Gyp's lifetime or shortly thereafter.

Books

Armory. *Cinquante ans de vie parisienne: Souvenirs et figures*. Paris: Jean-Renard, 1943.

Bac, Ferdinand. *Intimités de la Troisième République*. Paris: Hachette, 1935.

Bailly-Herzberg, Janine, ed. *Correspondance de Camille Pissarro*. Vol. 4 (1895–1898). Paris: Valhermeil, 1989.

Balignac, Guy. *Quatre ans à la cour de Saxe*. Paris: Perrin, 1913.

Barrès, Maurice. *Mes cahiers*. 14 vols. Paris: Plon, 1929–38, 1949–57.

———. *Scènes et doctrines du nationalisme*. Paris: Editions du Trident, 1987.

———. *Scènes et doctrines du nationalisme*. Vol. 1. Paris, Plon, 1925.

———, and Charles Maurras. *La République ou le Roi: Correspondance inédite, 1883–1923*. Ed. Hélène and Nicole Maurras. Paris: Plon, 1970.

Bernanos, Georges. *Lettres retrouvées*. Ed. Jean-Loup Bernanos. Paris: Plon, 1983.

Blanche, Jacques-Emile. *Mes modèles: Souvenirs littéraires*. Paris: Stock, 1984.

———. *La Pêche aux souvenirs*. Paris: Flammarion, 1949.

Blanchenay, Jeanne. *Visages de mon temps*. N.pl. [Switzerland]: n.p., n.d.

Blum, Léon. *Souvenirs sur l'Affaire*. Paris: Gallimard, 1981.

Bonnefon, Jean de. *La Corbeille des roses ou les dames de lettres*. Paris: De Bouville, 1909.

Bonnefont, Gaston. *Les Parisiennes chez elles: Nos grandes dames—Madame la comtesse de Martel (Gyp)*. Paris: Flammarion, [1895].

Bournand, François. *Les Juifs et nos contemporains: L'Antisémitisme et la question juive*. Paris: Pierret, [1898].

Bouvard et Pécuchet. *Un côté de l'Affaire Dreyfus: Coups de gueule, coups de trique*. Paris: Pierret, [1899].

Brisson, Adolphe. *Portraits intimes*. 2nd ser. Paris: Armand Colin, 1904.

Brun, Charles. *Le Roman social en France au XIXe siècle*. Paris: V. Giard et E. Brière, 1910.

Buffet, Eugénie. *Ma vie, mes amours, mes aventures*. Paris: Figuière, 1930.

Calvet, J. *L'Enfant dans la littérature française de 1870 à nos jours*. Paris: Lanore, 1930.

Castellane, Boni de. *Mémoires, 1867–1932*. Ed. Emmanuel de Waresquiel. Paris: Perrin, 1986.

Charasson, Henriette. *Vingt-cinq ans de littérature française.* Vol. 3: *La Littérature féminine.* Paris: Librairie de France, 1925.

Colette. *Lettres à ses pairs.* Ed. Claude Pichois and Roberte Forbin. Paris: Flammarion, 1973.

Corpechot, Lucien. *Souvenirs d'un journaliste.* 4 vols. Paris: Plon, 1936–42.

Curinier, C. E. *Dictionnaire national des contemporains.* 5 vols. N.pl.: Office Général d'Edition, 1899–1906.

Dagan, Henri. *Enquête sur l'antisémitisme.* Paris: Stock, 1899.

Daudet, Julia. *Souvenirs autour d'un groupe littéraire.* Paris: Charpentier, 1910.

Daudet, Léon. *Souvenirs politiques.* Ed. René Wittmann. Paris: Albatros, 1974.

———. *Au temps de Judas.* Paris: Grasset, 1933.

Deschamps, Gaston. *La Vie et les livres.* 3rd ser. Paris: Armand Colin, 1896.

Donnay, Maurice. *J'ai vécu 1900.* Paris: Fayard, 1950.

Drault, Jean. *Drumont, "La France juive" et "La Libre Parole".* Paris: Hérisson, 1935.

Drumont, Edouard. *La France juive: Essai d'histoire contemporaine.* 2 vols. Paris: Marpon et Flammarion, 1886.

Durand, Hippolyte. *Le Règne de l'enfant.* Paris: Lecène-Oudin, 1889.

Ernest-Charles, J. *Les Samedis littéraires.* 2nd ser. Paris: Perrin, 1904.

Gide, André. *Journal, 1889–1939.* Paris: Gallimard, 1951.

Gilbert, Eugène. *En marge de quelques pages: Impressions de lecture.* Paris: Plon, 1900.

———. *Le Roman en France pendant le XIXe siècle.* Paris: Plon, 1896.

Gille, Philippe. *La Bataille littéraire.* 3rd ser. (1883–86). Paris: Havard, 1890.

———. *Les Mercredis d'un critique.* Paris: Calmann-Lévy, 1894.

Ginisty, Paul. *L'Année littéraire.* Paris: Giraud, 1886 (1st ser.); Paris: Charpentier, 1887–89 (2nd–5th ser.); Paris: Fasquelle, 1892 (7th ser.).

Glaser, Philippe-Emmanuel. *Le Mouvement littéraire.* Paris: Ollendorff, 1905–12.

Goncourt, Edmond and Jules de. *Journal: Mémoires de la vie littéraire.* Vol. 3 (1887–1896). Ed. Robert Ricatte. Paris: Laffont, 1989.

Gonneville, Aymard Le Harivel de. *Souvenirs militaires du colonel de Gonneville.* Ed. Marie de Mirabeau. Paris: Perrin, 1895.

Guiches, Gustave. *Le Banquet.* Paris: Spès, 1927.

Gyz-El. *Noir sur blanc: Récits lorrains.* Nancy: Voirin, 1887.

James, Henry. *The Awkward Age.* New York: Scribner's, 1908.

Keim, Albert. *Le Demi-siècle: Souvenirs de la vie littéraire, 1876–1946.* Paris: Albin-Michel, 1950.

Larnac, Jean. *Histoire de la littérature féminine en France.* Paris: Kra, 1929.

Léautaud, Paul. *Journal littéraire.* Vol. 1 (1893–1906). Paris: Mercure de France, 1954.

Leblond, Marius-Ary. *La Société française sous la Troisième République d'après les romanciers contemporains.* Paris: Alcan, 1905.

Leclercq, Julien. *La Physiomonie, visage et caractères: Quatre-vingt-cinq portraits contemporains d'après les principes d'Eugène Ledos.* Paris: Larousse, [1896].

Le Goffic, Charles. *Les Romanciers aujourd'hui.* Paris: Vanier, 1890.

Lemaître, Jules. *Les Contemporains: Etudes et portraits littéraires.* 3rd ser. Paris: Lecène-Oudin, 1887.

———. *Impressions de théâtre.* 1st and 4th ser. Paris: Lecène-Oudin, 1888–91.

Levrault, Léon. *Le Roman des origines à nos jours.* Paris: Mellottée, 1932.

Lorrain, Jean. *Femmes de 1900.* Paris: Editions de la Madeleine, 1932.

Lugné-Poe, Aurélien. *La Parade.* 3 vols. Paris: Gallimard, 1930.

Macé, Gustave. *La Police parisienne: Femmes criminelles.* Paris: Fasquelle, 1904.

Mallarmé, Stéphane. *Correspondance.* 11 vols. Ed. Henri Mondor and Lloyd James Austin. Paris: Gallimard, [1959]–85.

Martin du Gard, Roger. *Correspondance générale.* Ed. Pierre Bordel. Vol. 2 (1914–18), Paris: Gallimard, 1980; vol. 3 (1919–25), Paris: Gallimard, 1986.

Massis, Henri. *Evocations: Souvenirs.* Vol. 1 (1904–11). Paris: Plon, 1931.

Mélia, Jean. *Stendhal et ses commentateurs.* Paris: Mercure de France, 1911.

Mirbeau, Octave. *Correspondance avec Claude Monet.* Ed. Pierre Michel and Jean-François Nivet. Paris: Lérot, 1990.

Missoffe, Michel. *Gyp et ses amis.* Paris: Flammarion, 1932.

Montégut, Emile. *Dramaturges et romanciers.* Paris: Hachette, 1890.

Morand, Paul. *1900.* Paris: Flammarion, 1931.

Mouttet, A. *Une arrière-petite-nièce de Mirabeau.* Aix-en-Provence: Achille Macaire, 1889.

Mugnier, l'abbé. *Journal, 1879–1939.* Ed. Marcel Billot. Paris: Mercure de France, 1985.

Muhlfeld, Lucien. *Le monde où l'on imprime: Regards sur quelques lettrés et divers illettrés contemporains.* Paris: Perrin, 1897.

Pellissier, Georges. *Etudes de littérature contemporaine.* 1st ser. Paris: Perrin, 1898.

Polaire. *Polaire par elle-même.* Paris: Figuière, 1933.

Pougy, Liane de. *Mes cahiers bleus.* Paris: Plon, 1977.

Pouquet, Jeanne-Maurice. *Le Salon de Madame Arman de Caillavet.* Paris: Hachette, 1926.

Proust, Marcel, and Jacques Rivière. *Correspondance, 1914–22.* Ed. Philip Kolb. Paris: Plon, 1976.

Le Provincial. *Franchises.* Paris: Editions de la Connaissance, 1928.

Quillard, Pierre. *Le Monument Henry: Liste des souscripteurs classés méthodiquement et selon l'ordre alphabétique.* Paris: Stock, 1899.

Rosny aîné, J.-H. *Mémoires de la vie littéraire.* Paris: Crès, 1927.

Ryner, Han. *Le Massacre des amazones: Etudes critiques sur deux cents bas-bleus contemporains.* Paris: Chamuel, 1899.

Schwob, Marcel. *Chroniques.* Ed. John Alden Green. Geneva: Droz, 1981.

Stock, P.-V. *Mémorandum d'un éditeur: L'Affaire Dreyfus anecdotique.* Paris: Stock, 1938.

Tailhade, Laurent. *La Médaille qui s'efface.* Paris: Crès, 1924.

Talmeyr, Maurice. *Souvenirs d'avant le déluge, 1870–1914.* Paris: Perrin, 1927.

Tharaud, Jérôme, and Jean Tharaud. *Mes années chez Barrès.* Paris: Plon, 1928.

Toustain, marquis de. *Mémoires du marquis de Toustain, 1790–1823.* Paris: Plon, 1933.

Willy. *Souvenirs littéraires . . . et autres.* Paris: Editions Montaigne, 1925.

Zillhardt, Madeleine. *Louise-Catherine Breslau et ses amis.* Paris: Editions des Portiques, 1932.

Zola, Emile. *Correspondance.* Vol. 4 (June 1880–Dec. 1883). Ed. B. H. Bakker. Montreal: Bibliothèque Nationale du Québec, 1983.

Articles

"A travers: Visages de Gyp." [*Européens*?], 30 Sept. 1932.

A.C. "Gyp." *L'Illustration*, 9 July 1932, 351.

Acker, Paul. "Comment ils travaillent." *Je sais tout*, 15 Feb. 1905, 17–25.

Alexandre, Arsène. "Madame de Martel." *La Lecture illustrée*, [1894], 62–67.

"Au temps de l'Affaire." *Sur la Riviera*, 27 Nov. 1921.

Aulard, F.-A. "Un humoriste à l'Assemblée Constituante: Mirabeau-Tonneau." *La Nouvelle Revue* 6 (1880), 788–815.

''Autour de l'audience: La Conciergerie envahie.'' *Le Gaulois*, 3 May 1899.

''Les Aventures de Gyp.'' *Le Siècle*, 17 May 1900, 2.

Bac, Ferdinand. ''Madame Gyp: Un souvenir de cinquante ans.'' *Les Débats*, 24 July 1932.

Bainville, Jacques. ''Chronique: Une enquête délicate.'' *La Gazette de France*, 8 Nov. 1902.

Barrès, Maurice. ''Lettre à Gyp sur le printemps à Mirabeau.'' *La Revue hebdomadaire* 7, April 1921, 365–404.

Barrès, Philippe. ''Gyp, ou la féerie.'' *Les Nouvelles littéraires*, 9 July 1932, 1–2.

———. '' 'Je ne veux pas les voir,' dit Thierry de Martel, . . . et il se tue.'' *Paris-Presse*, 13 June 1945.

Basset, Serge. ''Chez Gyp: Les Opinions politiques d'une 'bien parisienne.' '' *Le Matin*, 6 Aug. 1899.

Beaufils, Edouard. ''Episodes: Le coup de fer.'' *La Paix*, 17 Dec. 1899.

Bidou, Henry. ''Gyp.'' *Le Journal des débats politiques et littéraires*, 30 June 1932, 1.

''Billets parisiens: Gyp.'' *La Libre Belgique*, 2 July 1932.

Billy, André. ''Du cachet de Stendhal et des débuts de Gyp.'' *Le Figaro littéraire*, 18 June 1955, 2.

———. ''Gyp et ses amis.'' *Gringoire*, 16 Sept. 1932, 4.

''Bob et Gyp à la Bodinière.'' *L'Univers illustré*, 12 March 1892, 124–25.

Boiseguin. ''Gyp.'' *La République française*, 7 Feb. 1895, 1.

Bordeaux, Henry. ''Les Livres et les moeurs: L'Ame des enfants.'' *La Revue hebdomadaire*, Nov. 1898, 269–78.

Bourcet, Marguerite. ''Gyp: Docteur ès Education.'' *Le Noël*, 5 Oct. 1933, 418–21 (pt 1) and 12 Oct. 1933, 455–58 (pt 2).

Bourdet, Maurice. ''Gyp, reflet d'une époque et d'une société.'' *Miroir du monde*, 9 July 1932, 41–42.

Bradamante. ''Chrétiens! A vos canons!'' *L'Aurore*, 11 June 1899.

———. ''Sa profession.'' *L'Aurore*, 18 Dec. 1899.

Bussy, Charles de. ''Profils de femmes: Gyp.'' *Femmes de France*, 4 March 1928, 24.

Canivet, Charles. ''Gyp-Bob-Chiffon.'' *Le Soleil*, 22 Feb. 1895.

Chanlaine, Pierre. ''Il y a cent ans naissait Gyp: Romancière de la Belle Epoque.'' *L'Opéra*, 17 Aug. 1949, 1–2.

Charpentier, Armand. ''Message: Gyp.'' *La Volonté*, 4 July 1932.

''Chez les antisémites: Commémoration et inauguration.'' *Le Matin*, 20 July 1899.

''Choses du jour.'' *Le Petit Journal pour rire* 142, [Oct. 1888], 6.

Clemenceau, Georges. ''Grandes manœuvres.'' *L'Aurore*, 26 Oct. 1898.

Corpechot, Lucien. ''Souvenirs d'un journaliste: Gyp.'' *La Revue universelle*, 15 May 1936, 419–36.

''Le Costume féminin: Enquête universelle.'' *Le Gaulois*, 27 Aug. 1895, 2.

Coutant, Henry. ''La Bicyclette et les écrivains.'' *Les Nouvelles littéraires*, 21 July 1934, 1.

Croisset, Francis de. ''La Société et la vie sous la Troisième République: L'Univers de Gyp: Bob et Miquette.'' *Conférencia* 20, 1 Oct. 1934, 387–400.

Daumazy, Me. ''L'Ex-avocat Trarieux contre Gyp.'' *La Libre Parole*, 22 Dec. 1898.

Desarthis, Robert. ''Les Disparus: N'oublions pas que Gyp fut revuiste.'' *Comoedia*, 15–16 July 1932, 2.

Deschamps, Gaston. ''Trois moralistes: Gyp, Lavedan, Donnay.'' *Le Temps*, 24 Feb. 1895.

Dombasle. "Jules Lemaître et Gyp." *Le Siècle*, 14 May 1900, 2.

Dreyfus, Abraham. "Le Cas de Gyp." *L'Aurore*, 26 Dec. 1897, 1.

Dubreuil, René. "Le Procès Déroulède-Habert." *Le Siècle*, 1 June 1899.

Dumaine, Alfred. "Adolphe de Bacourt: Un diplomate de la Monarchie de Juillet." *La Revue d'histoire diplomatique*, April–June and July–Sept. 1928, 1–56.

Dy, P. "Gyp et le Grand Guignol." *Le Mercure de France*, [8 Jan.?] 1932.

E.F. "L'Enlèvement de Gyp." *L'Illustration*, 19 May 1900, 317.

"En souvenir de Gyp." *Pays lorrain* 26, 1934, 288–94.

"L'Enlèvement de Gyp." *Le Temps* 12, 15–18 and 20 May 1900.

Evreux, Robert. "Il y a quatre-vingt-dix ans naissait Gyp." *L'Ordre*, 19 Aug. 1939, 2.

Flament, Albert. "Tableaux de Paris." *La Revue de Paris*, 1 Aug. 1932, 706–9.

"La Fronde." *Le Temps*, 7 Dec. 1897, 1–2.

G.M. "Le Salon du Champ de Mars." *La Libre Parole*, 24 April 1896.

———. "Le Salon du Champ de Mars." *La Libre Parole*, 23 April 1897.

Gambini, Dino. "Le Châlet Vernet à Lion-sur-Mer: Quatre années d'amitié entre Gyp et Anatole France." *Ouest-France*, 20 Sept. 1979, 9.

Gaucher, Maxime. "Notes et impressions." *La Revue politique et littéraire*, 29 July 1882, 155.

Gausy. "Ma chère Gyp." *Les Droits de l'homme*, 27 June 1899, 1.

Giron, Roger. "Les lettres et les arts: Gyp." *L'Ami du peuple*, 30 June 1932.

Gohier, Urbain. "Ceux de Coblentz." *L'Aurore*, 9 Jan. 1899, 1.

Guermantes. "Le centenaire de Gyp." *Le Figaro*, 23 Aug. 1949.

Guillemot, Maurice. "Gyp." *Fémina*, 15 Nov. 1902, 343–45.

Guy, Michel. "Gyp." *A la page*, 7 July 1932.

"Gyp." *New York Times*, 24 July 1898, sec. 4, 11.

"Gyp." *Aux écoutes*, 2 July 1932.

"Gyp boulangiste et agent électoral." *Le Temps*, 12 Jan. 1890, 3.

"Gyp et Bob." *Le Temps*, 4 March 1892, 3.

"Gyp et Déroulède." *Le Siècle*, 7 Aug. 1899.

"Gyp's story was true." *New York Times,* 16 June 1900, 1.

Halévy, Daniel. "Apologie pour notre passé." *Cahiers de la quinzaine* 10 (11th ser.), Oct. 1907–Jan. 1910.

"La Haute Cour." *L'Aurore*, 16 Dec. 1899.

Hermant, Abel. "L'Ennemie du ridicule: Défense de la langue française." *Le Temps*, 24 Sept. 1918.

Houville, Gérard d'. "L'Heure qui passe: Gyp raconte." *Le Figaro*, 14 Aug. 1931, 1.

———. "Gyp, théâtre vivant." *Le Figaro*, 11 July 1932, 5.

India. "Esquisses féminines: Gyp." *La Libre Parole illustrée*, 24 Feb. 1894, 3.

Jaloux, Edmond. "Gyp et le Petit Bob." *Le Temps*, 8 July 1932, 3.

———. "La Mère du Petit Bob." *Le Gaulois*, 1 Aug. 1912, 1.

Javel, Firmin. "Les Petits Salons: Gyp et Bob." *Gil Blas*, 4 March 1892, 3.

Jean-Bernard. "Feuillets d'hier et d'aujourd'hui: Quand Gyp avait dix ans—Le comte de Chambord à Frohsdorf." *L'Avenir*, 21 Aug. 1927, 1–2.

Joran, Théodore. "Le Portrait de la jeune fille dans les romans de Gyp (1)." *La Femme contemporaine*, Feb. 1910, 142–55.

Kemp, Robert. "Gyp est morte ce matin." *La Liberté*, 30 June 1932.

Kimon, D. "Les Grands Judaïsants: Trarieux." *L'Antijuif*, 1 Dec. 1898.

Lagarde, Paul. "Une grande dame de lettres: Gyp est morte." *Comoedia*, 30 June 1932, 1.

Lalo, Anne-Marie, and Charles Lalo. "La Faillite de la beauté." *Le Mercure de France*, 1 Aug. 1913, 493–523.

Leblond, Marius-Ary. "L'Enfant d'après le roman français contemporain." *La Revue*, 1 July 1901, 44–63.

Le Dantec, Yves-Gérard, "Mes souvenirs de Gyp." *Livre d'or de l'Académie de Neuilly-Arts–Lettres–Sciences*. Paris: Académie de Neuilly, 1958.

Levaillant, Maurice. "Questions de littérature et d'histoire: Talleyrand, trafiquant d'archives." *Le Figaro*, 23 Dec. 1933.

Lostalot, A. de. "Poil et plume." *L'Illustration*, 18 April 1891, 338–39.

"M. Trarieux contre Gyp." *Le Siècle*, 5 Nov. 1898.

"M. Trarieux et le *Journal d'un grinchu*." *La Revue des grands procès contemporains* 17, 1899, 295–352.

Mangeot, Albert. "Les Années d'enfance de Gyp à Nancy." *L'Est illustré*, 10 and 24 July 1932, 5–6.

Marmande, R. de. "Autour de Gyp." *L'Ere nouvelle*, 6 July 1932, 1.

Mathiex, Paul. "A propos d'un vieux roman: Le Héros d'une tragédie romantique." *La Patrie*, 8 Dec. 1922.

Mauclair, Camille. "Les Salons littéraires à Paris." *La Revue des revues* 18, 1899.

Maurras, Charles. "L'Esprit politique de Gyp." *L'Action française*, 1 Aug. 1905, 212–22.

Méry, Gaston. "Au jour le jour: Trarieux contre Gyp." *La Libre Parole*, 4 Nov. 1898.

———. "Un guet-apens: Gyp séquestrée par les Dreyfusards." *La Libre Parole*, 13 May 1900.

Michel, Guy. "Gyp." *A la page*, 7 July 1932.

Mirbeau, Octave. "La Littérature en justice." *La France*, 24 Dec. 1884.

Néron, Marie-Louise. "Pour nos fils." *La Revue des revues* 30, 15 July 1899, 131–43.

P.L. "La 'peau' . . . et Gyp." *La Gazette de France*, 22–23 May 1899, 1–2.

———. "Souvenirs d'une visite chez Gyp dans sa maison de Neuilly." *La Gazette de France*, n.d.

Pangloss. "Le Feuilleton de Gyp." *Le Siècle*, 13 May 1900, 1.

Pellissier, Georges. "La Femme mariée et l'adultère dans le roman français moderne." *La Revue des revues*, 15 Feb. 1899, 353–68.

———. "La Littérature dialoguée en France: Gyp, Lavedan, Donnay, Provins." *La Revue des revues* 24, 1 Jan. 1898, 23–33.

Périé, Louis. "La Littérature 'Vie Parisienne': Gyp." *Le Courrier du Centre*, 4 July 1932.

Pound, Ezra. "Pastiche: The Regional." *The New Age*, 7 Aug. 1919, 252.

Pressensé, Francis de. "Trop tard, M. Déroulède!" *L'Aurore*, 4 July 1899.

"Quand Rachilde interviewait Gyp." *Comoedia*, 14 Sept. 1932, 2.

Rachilde. "Souvenir sur Gyp." *Corymbe*, July–Aug. 1932.

Raynal, Marie-Aline. "Gyp." *La Revue bleue*, 14 Oct. 1928.

"Récit d'un témoin." *La Libre Parole*, 20 May 1900, 1.

Rochefort, Henri. "Hommage à la Haute Cour." *L'Intransigeant*, 9 Dec. 1899.

Rodrigues, Gustave. "Message: Une philosophie de fossile." *La Volonté*, 5 July 1932.

Rousseaux, André. "Gyp." *Le Figaro*, 30 June 1932, 1.

Sabord, Noël. "Gyp et Toto." *Paris-Midi*, 17 May 1926, 2.

Scaferlati. " 'L'Homme' du jour: Gyp." *L'Ordre*, 29 Aug. 1939.

Séverine. "Notes d'une frondeuse: Réponse aux 'Droits de l'Homme.' " *La Fronde*, 8 Nov. 1898.

———. "Notes d'une frondeuse: Réponse à Ponchon." *La Fronde*, 21 Dec. 1897.

———. ''Notes d'une frondeuse: Requête à Monsieur Trarieux.'' *La Fronde*, 7 Nov. 1898.

Souday, Paul. ''Gyp.'' *L'Eclair*, 29 July 1909.

Staffe, baronne. ''Carnet mondain.'' *La Nouvelle Revue* 3, March–April 1898, 575.

Str. ''Echos du jour: La Femme du jour—Gyp.'' *Le Siècle*, 19 Dec. 1899, 1.

''T.'' ''Billets du Matin: A Monsieur Bob, à propos du dernier livre de Gyp: *Bob à l'Exposition.*'' *Le Temps*, 10 Oct. 1889, 2.

Tailhade, Laurent. ''Lettre casquée—Sermo Galeatus—à Gyp—comtesse de Mirabeau-Martel—Gyp.'' *L'Action*, 10 Dec. 1903, 1–2.

Tharaud, Jérôme, and Jean Tharaud. ''Gyp: Arrière-petite-nièce de Mirabeau.'' *Paris-Midi*, 7 July 1932.

Thibaudet, Albert. ''Réflexions sur la littérature.'' *La Nouvelle Revue française*, April 1920, 570.

''Thierry de Martel.'' *Candide*, 24 July 1940, 2.

Toussaint, Maurice. ''Chez Gyp.'' *L'Intransigeant*, 17 March 1911, 1.

Tout-Paris. ''Bloc-Notes Parisien: Gyp.'' *Le Gaulois*, 1 March 1895.

Un Parisien. ''Comment Gyp sauva Paterne Berrichon de l'anarchie.'' *L'Intransigeant*, 10 July 1932, 2.

Valmont. ''Pendant qu'on a conduit la maman de 'Bob' à sa dernière demeure.'' *Paris-Midi*, 3 July 1932.

Vautel, Clément. ''Mon film.'' *Le Journal*, 1 July 1932, 1.

Véga. ''Gyp telle que je l'ai connue.'' *La Revue des deux mondes*, 15 Sept. 1932, 451–57.

Viau, Raphael. ''Avant et autour de l'audience.'' *La Libre Parole*, 22 Sept. 1898.

Viollis, Andrée. ''Chez Gyp.'' *Le Petit Parisien*, 1 March 1929, 1–2.

Weindel, Henri de. ''L'Extraordinaire Aventure de Mme la comtesse de Martel (Gyp).'' *La Vie illustrée*, 18 May 1900, 100–101.

II. Secondary Sources

Books

Allen, James Smith. *In the Public Eye: A History of Reading in Modern France, 1800–1940*. Princeton, NJ: Princeton UP, 1991.

Angenot, Marc. *Ce que l'on dit des Juifs en 1889: Antisémitisme et discours social*. Vincennes: Presses Universitaires de Vincennes, 1989.

Arnaud, Noël. *Alfred Jarry: d'Ubu Roi au Docteur Faustroll*. Paris: La Table Ronde, 1974.

Aron, Jean-Paul, ed. *Misérable et glorieuse: La Femme du XIXe siècle*. Brussels: Editions Complexe, 1984.

Bancquart, Marie-Claire. *Anatole France: Un sceptique passionné*. Paris: Calmann-Lévy, 1984.

Becker, Jean-Jacques. *The Great War and the French People*, trans. Arnold Pomerans. Warwickshire, Eng.: Berg, 1985.

Bernard, Philippe. *La Fin d'un monde, 1914–1929*. Paris: Seuil, 1975.

Billy, André. *L'Epoque 1900*. Paris: Tallandier, 1951.

———. *La Vie littéraire à Paris pendant la deuxième moitié du XIXe siècle*. Paris: Flammarion, 1954.

Birnbaum, Pierre. *Un mythe politique: La ''république juive'' de Léon Blum à Mendès France*. Paris: Fayard, 1988.

Blum, Léon. *Souvenirs sur l'Affaire*. Paris: Gallimard, 1981.

Bredin, Jean-Denis. *L'Affaire*. Paris: Julliard, 1983.

Busi, Frederick. *The Pope of Antisemitism: The Career and Legacy of Edouard-Adolphe Drumont*. Lanham, MD: UP of America, 1986.

Byrnes, Robert. *Antisemitism in Modern France*. Vol. 1. New Brunswick, NJ: Rutgers UP, 1950.

Caradec, François. *Feu Willy: Avec et sans Colette*. Paris: Carrère, 1984.

Carassus, Emilien. *Le Snobisme et les lettres françaises de Paul Bourget à Marcel Proust, 1884–1914*. Paris: Armand Colin, 1966.

Charle, Christophe. *La Crise littéraire à l'époque du naturalisme: Essai d'histoire sociale des groupes et des genres littéraires*. Paris: Presses de l'Ecole Normale Supérieure, 1979.

Chartier, Roger, and Henri-Jean Martin, eds. *Histoire de l'édition française*. Vol. 3: *Le Temps des éditeurs: Du romantisme à la Belle Epoque*. Paris: Fayard, 1990.

Chaussinand-Nogaret, Guy. *Mirabeau*. Paris: Seuil, 1982.

Chiron, Yves. *Maurice Barrès: Le Prince de la jeunesse*. Paris: Perrin, 1986.

Crosland, Margaret. *Women of Iron and Velvet: French Women Writers after Georges Sand*. New York: Taplinger, 1976.

Dansette, Adrien. *Le Boulangisme*. Paris: Fayard, 1946.

———. *Histoire religieuse de la France contemporaine*. Paris: Flammarion, 1965.

Dauphiné, Claude. *Rachilde: Femme de lettres 1900*. Périgueux: Pierre Fanlac, 1985.

Debré, Moses. *The Image of the Jew in French Literature from 1800 to 1908*. Trans. Gertrude Hirschler. New York: Ktav, 1970.

Delhorbe, Cécile. *L'Affaire Dreyfus et les écrivains français*. Paris: Attinger, 1932.

Digeon, Claude. *La Crise allemande de la pensée française*. Paris: Presses Universitaires de France, 1959.

Dominique Desanti, *Drieu la Rochelle: Le Séducteur mystifié*. Paris: Flammarion, 1978.

Ducatel, Paul. *Histoire de la Troisième République à travers l'imagerie populaire et la presse satirique*. Vol. 3: *La Belle Epoque*. Paris: Grassin, 1976.

Duchet, Claude, ed. *Manuel d'histoire littéraire de la France*. Vol. 5. Paris: Editions sociales, 1977.

Flanner, Janet [Genêt]. *Paris Was Yesterday, 1925–1929*. Ed. Irving Drutman. San Diego, CA: Harcourt Brace Jovanovich/Harvest, 1988.

Fouquières, André de. *Cinquante ans de panache*. Paris: Pierre Horay-Flore, 1951.

Fugier, Anne-Martin. *La Bourgeoise: Femme au temps de Paul Bourget*. Paris: Grasset, 1983.

Gilbert, Sandra M., and Susan Gubar. *The Madwoman in the Attic: The Woman Writer and the Nineteenth-Century Literary Imagination*. New Haven, CT: Yale UP, 1979.

Girardet, Raoul. *Mythes et mythologies politiques*. Paris: Seuil, 1986.

———, ed. *Le Nationalisme français: Anthologie, 1871–1914*. Paris: Seuil, 1983.

Griffiths, Richard. *The Use of Abuse: The Polemics of the Dreyfus Affair and Its Aftermath*. New York: Berg, 1991.

Heilbrun, Carolyn G. *Writing a Woman's Life*. New York: Ballantine, 1988.

Jourdain, Francis. *Sans remords ni rancunes*. Paris: Corréa, 1953.

Jullian, Philippe. *Jean Lorrain ou le Satyricon 1900*. Paris: Fayard, 1974.

———. *Robert de Montesquiou: Un prince 1900*. Paris: Perrin, 1987.

Kleeblatt, Norman, ed. *The Dreyfus Affair: Art, Truth, and Justice*. Berkeley, CA: U of California P, 1987.

Lanoux, Armand. *Maupassant, le Bel-Ami*. Paris: Grasset, 1979.

Lehrmann, Charles C. *The Jewish Element in French Literature*, trans. George Klin. Rutherford, NJ: Fairleigh Dickinson UP, 1971.

Leroy, Géraldi, ed. *Les Écrivains et l'Affaire Dreyfus*. Paris: Presses Universitaires de France, 1983.

Lethève, Jacques. *La Caricature sous la IIIe République*. Paris: Armand Colin, 1986.

Lloyd, Rosemary. *The Land of Lost Content: Children and Childhood in Nineteenth-Century French Literature*. Oxford: Oxford UP, 1992.

McClelland, J.S., ed. *The French Right from de Maistre to Maurras*. New York: Harper and Row, 1970.

McMillan, James F. *Housewife or Harlot? The Place of Women in French Society, 1870–1914*. New York: St. Martin's Press, 1981.

Mahéo–de la Tocnaye, Isabelle. ''Thierry de Martel, fils de la romancière Gyp, pionnier de la neurochirurgie française, 1875–1940.'' Ph.D. diss., University of Rennes I, 1979.

Marrus, Michael. *The Politics of Assimilation: A Study of the French Jewish Community at the Time of the Dreyfus Affair*. New York: Oxford UP, 1971.

Mayeur, Jean-Marie. *Les Débuts de la IIIe République, 1871–1898*. Paris: Seuil, 1973.

Michel, Pierre, and Jean-François Nivet. *Octave Mirbeau: L'Imprécateur à coeur fidèle*. Paris: Séguier, 1990.

Mignot-Ogliastri, Claude. *Anna de Noailles: Une amie de la Princesse Edmond de Polignac*. Condé-sur-L'Escaut: Méridiens Klincksieck, 1986.

Mollier, Jean-Yves. *Michel et Calmann Lévy ou la naissance de l'édition moderne, 1836–91*. Paris: Calmann-Lévy, 1984.

Mosse, George. *Nationalism and Sexuality: Respectability and Abnormal Sexuality in Modern Europe*. New York: Howard Fertig, 1985.

Muray, Philippe. *Le Dix-Neuvième Siècle à travers les âges*. Paris: Denoël, 1984.

Nye, Robert. *Crime, Madness, and Politics in Modern France: The Medical Concept of National Decline*. Princeton, NJ: Princeton UP, 1984.

Osterwalder, Marcus, ed. *Dictionnaire des illustrateurs français, 1800–1914*. Paris: Hubschmidt and Bouret, 1983.

Pachter, Marc, ed. *Telling Lives: The Biographer's Art*. Philadelphia: U of Pennsylvania P, 1981.

Pierrard, Pierre. *Juifs et catholiques français, 1886–1945*. Paris: Fayard, 1970.

Plessis, Alain. *De la fête impériale au mur des fédérés, 1852–1871*. Paris: Seuil, 1979.

Poliakov, Léon. *Histoire de l'antisémitisme*. Vols. 3–4. Paris: Calmann-Lévy, 1968–77.

Randall, Earle Stanley. *The Jewish Character in the French Novel, 1870–1914*. Menasha, WI: Banta Publishing Co., 1941.

Rearick, Charles. *Pleasures of the Belle Epoque: Entertainment and Festivity in Turn-of-the-Century France*. New Haven, CT: Yale UP, 1985.

Rebérioux, Madeleine. *La République radicale?: 1898–1914*. Paris: Seuil, 1975.

Rémond, René. *Les Droites en France*. Paris: Aubier Montaigne, 1982.

Rioux, Jean-Pierre. *Nationalisme et conservatisme: La Ligue de la Patrie Française, 1899–1904*. Paris: Beauchesne, 1977.

Rogger, Hans, and Eugen Weber, eds. *The European Right: A Historical Profile*. Berkeley: U of California P, 1966.

Rutkoff, Peter M. *Revanche and Revision: The Ligue des Patriotes and the Origins of the Radical Right in France*. Athens: Ohio UP, 1981.

Saintsbury, George. *French Literature and Its Masters from the Beginnings to 1900*. New York: Knopf, 1938.

Sartre, Jean-Paul. *Réflexions sur la question juive*. Paris: Gallimard, 1954.

Selected Works

Serman, William. *Les Officiers français dans la nation*. Paris: Aubier Montaigne, 1982.

Seigel, Jerrold. *Bohemian Paris: Culture, Politics, and the Boundaries of Bourgeois Life, 1830–1930*. New York: Penguin Books, 1987.

Shapiro, David, ed. *The Right in France, 1890–1918*. Carbondale: Southern Illinois UP, 1962.

Slater, Catherine. *Defeatists and Their Enemies: Political Invective in France, 1914–1918*. Oxford: Oxford UP, 1981.

Smith, Bonnie. *Ladies of the Leisure Class: The Bourgeoises of Northern France in the Nineteenth Century*. Princeton, NJ: Princeton UP, 1981.

Sonn, Richard. *Anarchism and Cultural Politics in Fin de Siècle France*. Lincoln: U of Nebraska P, 1989.

Sorlin, Pierre. *"La Croix" et les Juifs, 1880–1899*. Paris: Grasset, 1967.

Sternhell, Zeev. *La Droite révolutionnaire, 1885–1914: Les Origines françaises du fascisme*. Paris: Seuil, 1978.

———. *Maurice Barrès et le nationalisme français*. Brussels: Editions Complexe, 1985.

———. *Ni droite, ni gauche: L'Idéologie fasciste en France*. Paris: Seuil, 1983.

Suleiman, Susan Rubin. *Authoritarian Fictions: The Ideological Novel as a Literary Genre*. New York: Columbia UP, 1983.

Taveneaux, René. *Histoire de Nancy*. Toulouse: Privat, 1978.

Thiesse, Anne-Marie. *Le Roman du quotidien: Lecteurs et lectures populaires à la Belle Epoque*. Paris: Chemin Vert, 1984.

Weber, Eugen. *Action Française: Royalism and Reaction in Twentieth-Century France*. Stanford, CA: Stanford UP, 1962.

———. *France, Fin de Siècle*. Cambridge, MA: Harvard UP, 1986.

Wilson, Stephen. *Ideology and Experience: Antisemitism in France at the Time of the Dreyfus Affair*. East Brunswick, NJ: Associated University Presses, 1982.

Winock, Michel. *Edouard Drumont et Cie: Antisémitisme et fascisme en France*. Paris: Seuil, 1982.

———. *La Fièvre hexagonale: Les Grandes Crises politiques de 1871 à 1968*. Paris: Calmann-Lévy, 1986.

Zeldin, Theodore. *France, 1848–1945: Ambition and Love*. Oxford: Oxford UP, 1979.

Articles and Essays

Czyba, Lucette. "La Fronde de Gyp." *Romantisme* 77, no. 3 (1992), 67–76.

Ferlin, Patricia. "Gyp: Une aristocrate à la Belle Epoque." *Historia* 522 (June 1990), 99–106.

Joly, Bertrand. "Les Antidreyfusards avant Dreyfus." *La Revue d'histoire moderne et contemporaine* 39, no. 2 (April–June 1992), 198–221.

Mandell, R.D. "The Affair and the Fair: Some Observations on the Closing Stages of the Dreyfus Case." *Journal of Modern History* 39, no. 3 (1967), 253–65.

Michel, Pierre. "Mirbeau et l'Affaire Gyp." *Littératures* 26 (Spring 1992), 201–19.

Millstone, Amy. "Gyp and the Reconstruction of (Self-)Consciousness." *Biography* 10, no. 3 (Summer 1987), 189–207.

———. "Out of the Mouths of Babes: Children as Right-Wing Propagandists in the Novels of Gyp, 1881–1901." *Historical Reflections/Réflexions Historiques* 17, no. 3 (Fall 1991), 205–231.

Rostand, Jean. "Hommage à Thierry de Martel." *Les Nouvelles littéraires*, 20 June 1946, 6.

Silverman, Willa. "Anti-Semitism and Occultism in *fin-de-siècle* France: Three

'Initiates.'" In *Tradition and Modernity in Late Nineteenth-Century France*, ed. Barbara T. Cooper and Mary Donaldson-Evans (Newark, NJ: Associated University Presses, 1992), 155–63.

———. "Gyp et l'Affaire Dreyfus." *Modern and Contemporary France* 43 (Oct. 1990), 5–16.

———. "Mythic Representations of Napoleon in the Life and Works of Gyp." In *Correspondances: Studies in Literature, History, and the Arts in Nineteenth-Century France*, ed. Keith Busby (Amsterdam: Rodopi, 1992), 203–12.

———. "'Semitic Troubles': Author–Publisher Relations in *fin-de-siècle* France—The Case of Gyp and Calmann-Lévy." *Historical Reflections/Réflexions Historiques* 19, no. 3 (Nov. 1993), 309–34.

Simon, Joel. "Une descendante de Mirabeau contre la République." *Miroir de l'Histoire*, April–May 1978, 14–19.

Sonnenfeld, Albert. "The Poetics of Antisemitism." *Romanic Review* 76, no. 1 (Jan. 1985), 76–93.

Thiesse, Anne-Marie. "Les Infortunes littéraires: Carrières de romancières populaires à la Belle Epoque." *Actes de la recherche en science sociale*, Nov. 1985, 32–46.

Wartelle, Jean-Claude. "Gyp: Une 'réactionnaire' émancipée sous la IIIe République." *L'Histoire* 25 (July–Aug. 1980), 88–90.

Wilson, Stephen. "Le Monument Henry: La Structure de l'antisémitisme en France, 1898-1899." *Annales ESC*, March–April 1977, 265–91.

Zillhardt, Madeleine. "Gyp." *Neuilly Solidarité* 8, nos. 2–3 (1950), 6, 8.

Index